Accounting theo...

Accounting theory & development

M R Mathews
M H B Perera

third edition

Nelson

An International Thomson Publishing Company

Melbourne • Bonn • Boston • London • Madrid • Mexico City • New York • Paris • Singapore
Tokyo • Toronto • Albany NY • Belmont CA • Cincinnati OH • Detroit MI

Thomas Nelson Australia
102 Dodds Street
South Melbourne 3205

I(T)P Thomas Nelson Australia is an International Thomson Publishing
company

First published in Australia in 1996

10 9 8 7 6 5 4 3 2 1
99 98 97 96

National Library of Australia
Cataloguing-in-Publication data

Mathews, M. R. (Martin Reginald), 1940– .
    Accounting theory and development.
    3rd ed.
    Includes index.
    ISBN 0 17 009102 3.
    1. Accounting. I. Perera, M. H. B. II. Title.

Cover designed by Tony Palmer
Text designed by Tony Palmer
Typeset by Post Typesetters
Printed in Australia by McPherson's Printing Group

Nelson Australia Pty Limited ACN 004 603 454 (incorporated in Victoria)
trading as Thomas Nelson Australia.

The I(T)P trademark is used under licence.

Within the publishing process Thomas Nelson Australia uses resources,
technology and suppliers that are as environmentally friendly as possible.

Contents

List of abbreviations

Accounting Education Change Commission	AECC
Accounting Principles Board	APB
Accounting Research Advisory Board	ARAB
Accounting Research Committee	ARC
Accounting Research and Standards Board	ARSB
Accounting Series Release	ASR
Accounting Standards Authority of Canada	ASAC
Accounting Standards Board	ASB
Accounting Standards Committee	ASC
Accounting Standards Review Board	ASRB
Accounting Standards Steering Committee	ASSC
African Accounting Council	AAC
American Accounting Association	AAA
American Association of Public Accountants	AAPA
American Institute of Accountants	AIA
American Institute of Certified Public Accountants	AICPA
Asean Federation of Accountants	AFA
Association of Accountancy Bodies in West Africa	AABWA
Association of Certified Accountants	ACA
Association of Southeast Asian Nations	ASEAN
A Statement of Basic Accounting Theory	ASOBAT
Auditing Standards Committee	ASC
Australian Accounting Research Foundation	AARF
Australian Accounting Standard	AAS
Australian Accounting Standards Board	AASB
Australian Ethical Pronouncements	AEP
Australian Ethical Rulings	AER
Australian Securities Commission	ASC
Australian Society of Certified Practising Accountants	ASCPA
Business Accounting Deliberations Council	BADC
Canadian Institute of Chartered Accountants	CICA
Capital asset pricing model	CAPM
Certified Public Accountant	CPA
Chartered Institute of Public Finance and Accountancy	CIPFA
Chief Financial Officer	CFO
Closer Economic Relations	CER
Committee on Accounting Procedures	CAP
Confederation of Asian and Pacific Accountants	CAPA
Consultative Committee of Accountancy Bodies	CCAB
Continuously contemporary accounting	CoCoA
Current cost accounting	CCA
Current purchasing power accounting	CPP
Efficient market hypothesis	EMH
Enterprise accounting standard	EAS
European Union	EU
Exposure draft	ED

Fédération des Experts Comptables Européenes	FEE
Final qualifying examination	FQE
Financial Accounting Foundation	FAF
Financial Accounting Standard	FAS
Financial Accounting Standards Board	FASB
Financial Reporting Council	FRC
Financial Reporting Standard	FRS
Financial Reporting Standards Board	FRSB
first-in-first-out	FIFO
General purchasing power accounting	GPP
Generally accepted accounting principles	GAAP
Gulf Cooperation Council	GCC
Historical cost accounting	HCA
Human resource accounting	HRA
Institute of Chartered Accountants in Australia	ICAA
Institute of Chartered Accountants in England and Wales	ICAEW
Institute of Chartered Accountants of Ireland	ICAI
Institute of Chartered Accountants of Scotland	ICAS
Institute of Cost Management Accountants	ICMA
Institute of Internal Auditors	IIA
Institute of Management Accountants	IMA
Inter-American Accounting Association	IAA
International Accounting Standard	IAS
International Accounting Standards Committee	IASC
International Organisation of Securities Commission	IOSC
International Standards of Accounting and Reporting	ISAR
Japanese Institute of Certified Public Accountants	JICPA
last-in-first-out	LIFO
line-of-business	LOB
London Business School	LBS
multinational corporation	MNC
National Companies and Securities Commission	NCSC
New Zealand Society of Accountants	NZSA
Nordic Federation of Accountants	NFA
North American Free Trade Association	NAFTA
Organisation for Economic Cooperation and Development	OECD
Positive accounting theory	PAT
Present value accounting	PVA
Professional Practices Board	PPB
Provisional Statement of Standard Accounting Practice	PSSAP
Public Sector Accounting Standards Board	PSASB
Replacement price accounting	RPA
Securities Exchange Commission	SEC
Social indicators accounting	SIA
Social responsibility accounting	SRA
Societal accounting	SA
Socio-economic accounting	SEA
South Asian Federation of Accountants	SAFA

Statement of Accounting Concept	SAC
Statement of Accounting Practice	SAP
Statement of Accounting Theory and Theory Acceptance	SATTA
Statement of Standard Accounting Practice	SSAP
Statement of Financial Accounting Standard	SFAS
Statement of Financial Accounting Concept	SFAC
Total impact accounting	TIA
Union of European Accountants	UEC
United Nations	UN
Value for money	VFM
Work Institute in America	WIA
World Trade Organisation	WTO

Preface to the third edition

The curricula and pedagogy of accounting theory has undergone major changes over the past few years. The third edition of *Accounting Theory and Development* has been extensively revised to reflect these changes.

Revised content entails the further development of international conceptual frameworks and accounting standards, including the trend towards legal backing for the latter. Recent developments in the areas of environmental accounting, human resource accounting and accounting for the value of brands have also been incorporated into this edition. Chapter 17, Comparative accounting, now includes new sections on Eastern Europe, the Peoples' Republic of China, the harmonisation of accounting between Australia and New Zealand and the history of International Accounting Standards.

In terms of pedagogy, we have responded to suggestions made by students and their instructors from many institutions, and have included a more detailed analysis of positive accounting theory and used a more user-friendly approach throughout.

Although refinements to content and presentation were necessary, the basic structure of the book and its philosophical underpinnings remain unchanged: to present the discipline of accounting as socially constructed and reflecting the needs of society for information about the important institutions in our midst. One accounting theory course which uses this text was selected by the International Accounting Section of the American Accounting Association as an example of an internationalised accounting programme, and the course outline was made available to about 500 colleges and universities around the world.

We would like to acknowledge all those whose works have contributed to the success of this book. Our thanks to the staff of Thomas Nelson Australia for their support and our best wishes to those who use this edition.

M. R. Mathews
M. H. B. Perera
Massey University
Palmerston North
New Zealand
June 1995

Chapter 1
Introduction

This chapter introduces the field covered by the entire book and comments briefly on the relationship between the various sections and chapters. The overall theme of the book is explored in this chapter in order to provide the reader with a clear view of its content and purpose.

Section 1, entitled Accounting from past to present, introduces the reader to a brief study of accounting history. The purpose of this coverage is to ensure that all readers have assimilated some background material before studying the present position of the accounting discipline. It cannot be stressed too strongly, however, that the purpose is background or preparatory study and not the study of accounting history *per se*.

Chapter 2 deals with the history of accounting to 1900 and is made up of three parts: a review of ancient accounting systems, a discussion of the emergence of double entry bookkeeping and a consideration of nineteenth century developments. The history of accounting is considered to be important for the development of an understanding of the present and an appreciation of what may be the future of the discipline. The historical development of accounting is addressed here as a means of facilitating the understanding and appreciation already referred to.

It is considered important for the reader to understand the ancient origins of measurement and recording activities which always appear to accompany social organisation and activity. Chapter 2 reviews briefly features of the ancient accounting systems of Mesopotamia, Greece, Rome, China and the British manorial system.

The modern accounting systems of most countries are based upon double entry bookkeeping. Consequently, students of modern Anglo-American accounting should be aware of the origins of this technique so far as they are known. The section covers familiar ground to enable the reader to appreciate the nature of early double entry systems.

The nineteenth century was a period of dramatic change which extended to the development of accounting. Industrial, commercial, legal and political changes all acted upon accounting and these developments are explored because of their effects on more recent accounting practices. The assumption of professional status by accountants also dates from this period.

Chapter 3 deals with twentieth century Anglo-American accounting developments. These include the search for accounting principles, the development of an institutional structure for accounting, a number of approaches to the search for accounting principles and a discussion of accounting as a social phenomenon. The development of the accounting discipline during the twentieth century has not been a simple continuation of the work of the previous period. In this chapter both individual and collective efforts to determine the principles of accounting are considered. This search occupied a number of people over a lengthy period and both the activity and the outcomes are considered to be important. The institutional structure of accounting and its development are also important to an understanding of where the discipline is now and an appreciation of where it may travel in the future. The institutional structure refers not only to the profession, but also the standard setting and regulatory bodies which have become such an important part of the life of the modern accountant.

The final section of Chapter 3 considers accounting as a social phenomenon which is socially constructed but which is also socially constructing.

Section 2 of the book is entitled Accounting theory and consists of two chapters. The first (Chapter 4) examines the philosophy of science and research methodology. This chapter is divisible into two parts dealing, in turn, with the philosophy of science and research methodology and then the application of scientific method and naturalistic research methods to accounting research.

The examination of the philosophy of science covers the contributions made by induction and deduction, falsificationism, Lakatosian Research Programmes, Kuhnian paradigms and disciplinary matrices and, finally, Feyerabend's view of research and scientific endeavour. After considering the philosophical bases, the application of these ideas to accounting is examined through selected contributions to the literature.

The second main part of this chapter is concerned with accounting research, through the application of scientific method and, in some cases, by the use of what have been termed naturalistic research methods. The contributions of different approaches to both the academic and practising parts of the accounting discipline are considered.

The second chapter in this section (Chapter 5) deals with accounting theory formulation. In this chapter the nature of accounting theory and the issues of accounting theory construction, verification and validation are discussed. It has long been asserted that accounting, being a practical activity, is conditioned by the demands of practical circumstance. However, such conditioning has left a legacy of unordered and conflicting rules. On the other hand, one could also argue that it would be unrealistic to assert that the rules chosen lacked a theoretical base, because every one of the vast range of alternative practices implies a particular theory or a way of looking at the circumstances which stimulated its invention. The actual state of accounting is not that it has no theories, but that it has a large number of implicit, partial and contradictory theories. What is lacking is a coherent theory by reference to which established practices and newly proposed practices may be appraised. A definite link exists between accounting theory and

accounting practice. Accounting theory construction stems from the need to provide a rationale for what accountants do or expect to be doing.

Section 3 is entitled Accounting frameworks. In this section two chapters consider, firstly, conceptual frameworks for financial accounting and reporting and, secondly, standard setting in a political environment.

Over the past twenty or so years the accounting profession, through collective efforts by groups of practitioners and academics, has addressed the issue of whether a conceptual framework can be developed. The attempts undertaken in the USA, Canada, the UK, Australia and New Zealand are examined in a reasonably detailed manner and their similarities and differences are noted. In particular, the qualitative characteristics of accounting information are considered. Finally, the strengths and weaknesses, advantages and disadvantages and likely future developments in this field are discussed.

In Chapter 7 the political nature of accounting standard setting and the available options are considered. Discussion begins with the situation of 'responsibility without power' which faces the accounting profession at the present time. The accounting profession has been given responsibility for ensuring that the financial statements of publicly held companies present a 'true and fair view' but without any legal powers to enforce its decisions. In this position there are two alternatives available to the accounting profession, namely, decrease its responsibility or increase its power. However, it is highly unlikely that the accounting profession will succeed in doing the first because society expects a greater commitment on the part of the accounting profession to the principle of more 'true and fair' disclosure rather than less. The only way to achieve the second appears to be for standard setting to be placed in the public sector, but this may not be what most accountants want.

The chapter demonstrates how accounting standard setting has been pushed into the political arena. It is now recognised that accounting information has an important economic impact on society and, therefore, accounting issues must be addressed in a manner which ensures that the public interest is protected. The conflict of interests which often exists in the information market and the desire of different groups to foster accounting standards beneficial to themselves are also discussed. If successful this would mean that, if a proposed standard has a possible adverse impact on them, some groups could be expected to work to prevent the establishment of that standard. The chapter concludes by considering the different approaches which could be taken in accounting standard setting under these circumstances, for example the incremental political approach which views the process of standard setting as a political one, and the scientific–theoretical approach which concentrates on theoretical and empirical evidence rather than political power to support accounting standards. The current debate on government intervention in standard setting is examined in the concluding section.

Section 4 is one of the largest sections in the book, containing six chapters. Entitled Issues in conventional financial accounting and reporting, this section covers the measurement of assets (Chapter 8) and liabilities (Chapter 9), accounting and income determination (Chapter 10), price variation accounting (Chapter 11), incremental financial disclosures (Chapter 12) and human resource accounting (Chapter 13).

The treatment of assets in accounting involves three distinct problems: of definition, recognition and measurement. Definition is important because it is necessary to know to what real world objects these terms refer; recognition is important because it is necessary to identify particular assets by using a set of rules; measurement is important because measurements impart

greater information and users of financial information want this information.

Chapter 8 discusses the issues involved in the measurement of assets. The main issues here are concerned with (a) the property or the attribute to be measured and (b) the unit of measurement to be used. There are at least four properties that can be measured in respect of an asset: historical cost, replacement cost, exit price and the present value of expected future economic benefits. Similarly, the measurement can be done by using either the units of money or the units of general purchasing power. The discussion in Chapter 8 includes identification of the features of each of the above elements of the properties and units of measurement together with an examination of the types of information that they are likely to generate. The issues of asset classification and income determination in relation to asset measurement are also addressed.

Despite the importance of liabilities in managing business affairs and in reporting the position of the business to outside parties, the theory of liability identification, measurement and disclosure is not well defined. Chapter 9 examines currently used definitions of liabilities, systems for measuring the value of liabilities and finally the means by which they may be disclosed. In the course of this examination it is argued that a sound theory of liabilities is not applied at the present time, leading to a number of controversial areas. These include leases and executory contracts, pension commitments and the inclusion of contingent liabilities and contra assets as liabilities. It is concluded that the theory of liabilities is in need of re-examination in the light of the points raised in this chapter.

Chapter 10 deals with accounting and income determination, including the concept of accounting income, revenues and expenses, the allocation of costs, realisation and the matching principle.

In Chapter 11 the extent of the accounting problems caused by price variations is discussed together with an examination of the various methods adopted or suggested as solutions in different countries, particularly the UK, Canada, Australia and New Zealand. This includes a survey of approaches aimed at a partial solution to the problem as well as those aimed at a comprehensive solution. The chapter concludes with a consideration of the future of price variation accounting.

In any given period of time, two types of price variation are likely to occur: variations in the general level of prices (inflation or deflation) and variations in the structure of prices or shifts in specific prices. The former affects the financial position of everybody in the community by decreasing or increasing the value of money (that is a change in the purchasing power of the monetary unit), whereas the latter affects the financial positions of the owners of specific assets differently. Therefore, both these price variations are important accounting inputs. The two types of price variation take place concurrently and are interdependent. However, although a rise in the general level of prices, for example, reflects the combined effect of the changes in all prices, it is not necessarily indicative of the rate or even the direction of change of any particular price, for that is determined by the demand and supply conditions of the product concerned. In a period of inflation the price of a specific asset may increase at a lower or higher rate than that of the general price level, or it may remain unchanged, or it may even change in the opposite direction. Alternatively, there may be a change in the price structure without any change in the general level of prices if the rises and falls in prices offset each other. Therefore, although the two types of price variation are interdependent, they are capable of affecting the financial position of an individual or business independently.

Price variations have created many problems for accounting. Because the conventional style of accounting is not capable of

incorporating their effects into the accounting system, the information provided through that system has been identified as defective and misleading. Therefore, various attempts have been made to overcome this problem.

Section 4 continues with a discussion of some developments of current importance under the heading of Incremental financial disclosures. One of the stated objectives of this book was to enable the reader to understand the present and to appreciate likely future developments of the discipline. In order to achieve this objective, Chapter 12 reviews a number of incremental financial disclosures, that is additions to, rather than improvements of, widely established practices. The coverage afforded to each topic is necessarily brief and there is no suggestion that all topics are of equal importance or degree of acceptance.

It is quite likely that there are some important developments which will have been overlooked or not included by the authors. Topics covered include segmental reporting, value added statements, leases and executory contracts, debt defeasance, corporate financial forecasts and accounting for brands. In each case the treatment is the same. We attempt to identify the origin of the development, provide a description or definition and make an exploration of the technique where appropriate. References are supplied to enable readers to follow up selected topics for themselves.

Chapter 13 discusses human resource accounting, examines its applications and presents a possible procedure for the development and implementation of a human resource accounting system.

Section 5 examines a number of emerging issues in financial accounting and reporting. These include creative accounting (Chapter 14), insider trading (Chapter 15), professional ethics (Chapter 16), an introduction to comparative accounting (Chapter 17), culture and accounting (Chapter 18) and social accounting

(Chapter 19). Together these chapters make up a challenging introduction to areas of accounting which should be addressed by senior students and qualifying accountants.

The newly emphasised issue of creative accounting is the modern equivalent of the distortions of reported information which have been previously identified, for example income smoothing, selection of information and the application of corporate pressure to discourage the development of standards in sensitive areas. Chapter 14 attempts to define creative accounting, examines legal and ethical–professional attitudes towards creative accounting and outlines moves which have been, or are likely to be, taken against creative accounting. The problem of creative accounting is viewed in the light of other aspects of the accounting problematic including the development of a conceptual framework and the politicisation of standard setting.

Chapter 15 defines insider trading, outlines legal moves to restrict or outlaw insider trading and attempts to predict the effect which insider trading may have on the market for securities. The problem of insider trading cannot be ignored by accountants. Insider trading may have existed for some time but attention has recently been drawn to what is seen by many observers as a particularly pernicious problem. The market for securities and the need for safeguards for investors provides the accounting profession with much of its livelihood. Consequently, any actions which may seriously affect the regulation and operation of capital markets must be of concern to accountants.

Chapter 16 provides an introduction to the subject of professional ethics by considering what makes a particular employment grouping into a profession, how professional ethics develop, particularly in the area of accounting and professional ethics, and the New Zealand Society of Accountants (NZSA). Change in the way the public responds to the accounting

profession is of obvious importance since it is vital for the wellbeing of individual accountants. This topic is included among the emerging issues because of the changing nature of professional relationships between groups of accountants and the public. The older characteristics of professional standing are giving way to a new dimension.

The existence of a worldwide diversity of accounting requirements and practices has been established by various research studies carried out over the last two decades. Attempts to explain this diversity have resulted in an enhanced awareness of the importance of the environment in which accounting operates. This in turn has led to further efforts at identifying the relevant environmental factors. Chapter 17 considers attempts to explain the worldwide diversity of accounting requirements and practices in terms of a variety of environmental factors. It also includes a discussion of how countries have been classified into different groups on the basis of their accounting practices and the identified characteristics of such groups. Various issues of international accounting are then examined. The concept of international harmonisation of accounting standards and various efforts aimed at achieving accounting harmonisation at global and regional levels are considered in the final section.

Culture is often identified as one of the important environmental factors which are likely to impact on accounting. In Chapter 18 an exploration of the link between culture and accounting is provided. The discussion is based on the management literature which is characterised by frequent references to the influence of culture on various aspects of management. The chapter presents a framework designed to demonstrate the mechanism by which culture is likely to influence accounting. The discussion includes the identification of: (a) a set of work-related societal value dimensions which are considered to reflect the cultural orientation of a country; (b) a set of accounting values which are likely to be directly influenced by the identified work-related societal value dimensions; and (c) some aspects of accounting practice which may be directly influenced by accounting values. The implications of the associations between culture and accounting for a number of international accounting issues, such as harmonisation of accounting standards and the transfer of accounting technology between countries, are also discussed.

Chapter 19 introduces social accounting — a new development of the accounting discipline which could have widespread implications. It is divided into two parts. The first part deals with arguments in support of non-traditional disclosures and the expenditure of additional resources on this form of reporting. The arguments considered are those based on market support, the social contract between business and society and organisational legitimacy. The second part attempts to define social accounting by illustrating the form it is currently taking. To facilitate the illustration a structure is provided which incorporates both private and public sector, short- and long-term, and financial and non-financial dimensions. The categories of social accounting which are developed assist in clarifying the different forms which may be employed in practice or discussed in the literature. Not all of the categories discussed are of equal importance at any one time. Since 1990 the emphasis has changed to reporting the effects of organisations on the environment.

The overall position taken by the authors is comprehensive with regard to the future of accounting. By identifying future directions, sometimes in non-traditional areas, the expectation is that the discipline is capable of greater involvement in modern society and that appropriate evolution will take place. At the same time there will be changes to, but not an abandonment of, the traditional roles of the discipline.

Section 1

Accounting from past to present

Chapter 2
The history of accounting to 1900

Learning objectives

After studying this chapter the reader will be able to:

- identify similarities and differences between ancient and modern accounting systems
- present arguments relevant to the position of accounting as both a socially constructed and socially constructing activity.

Introduction

This chapter provides a brief examination of the development of record keeping and accounting from earliest times to 1900. An appreciation of the history of accounting is considered to be important for the development of an understanding of the present position and an appreciation of what may be the future directions of the discipline. The historical development of accounting is addressed here, not as a subject area in itself, but as a means of facilitating the understanding and appreciation already referred to. It is considered important for the reader to know of the ancient origins of the measurement and recording activities which always seem to accompany social organisation and human activity. In this chapter features of the ancient recording systems of Mesopotamia, Greece, Rome, China and the British manorial system are briefly reviewed.

The next section is concerned with events of the period 1400–1600 AD, particularly the evolution of double entry bookkeeping. The modern accounting systems of most countries are based upon double entry bookkeeping. Consequently, students of modern Anglo-American accounting should be aware of the origins of this technique so far as they are known.

The nineteenth century was a period of domestic change in the UK which extended to the development of accounting. Industrial, commercial, legal and political changes all acted upon accounting and these developments are explored because of their influences on more recent accounting practices. The assumption of professional status by accountants also dates from this period.

There are two main objectives involved in the study of past accounting systems. First, to enable the reader to identify such similarities and differences as may exist between earlier recording systems and those of modern Anglo-American approaches to accounting and, second, to demonstrate that accounting is socially constructed, that is, there is a relationship between social needs and the form of accounting in use at any particular time.

Ancient accounting systems reviewed

Mesopotamia

Mesopotamia was the home of a number of flourishing civilisations between 4500 and 500 BC (Keister, 1965, p.18). Here could be found a society sufficiently complex that a record-keeping system was needed to account for the ownership of property and transactions between parties.

Keister describes the use of clay tablets impressed with the markings of the cuneiform script by the scribe, a forerunner of the present day accountant. Although the system was relatively simple by modern standards, Keister has argued that 'the Mesopotamian economy did not require a more advanced system' (1965, p.23). Goldberg (1949) refers to the recording of quite complex transactions in grain, involving several individuals, on a tablet only a few square centimetres in area.

The relationship between the needs of the Mesopotamian society of the period and the provision of services by the record-keeping (accounting) system was obviously close. It may be argued that accounting has been socially constructed from the time of the Mesopotamians. However, the view that accounting also has an effect on society cannot be ignored and is discussed in a later chapter.

Greece and Rome

The Greeks invented coinage in about 630 BC and, although this development could be expected to change recording methods, it has been noted that the spread of coinage was slow and its impact on accounting only gradual.

Chatfield (1977) refers to the extensive systems of estate records used in parts of the Athenian Empire, in particular the system of responsibility accounting employed by Zenon. The collection of records known as the Zenon Papyri demonstrates the existence of an elaborate and, at one level, meticulous system to detect fraud and inefficiency.

Unfortunately, there was little concern for decision making, efficiency or profitability and perhaps this feature might be said to invalidate a lot of the work that went into operating the system. The system used by Zenon was developed in Greece from the fifth century BC and later modified by the Romans.

As noted by Chatfield (1977, p.11):

> Zenon kept records not so that he could report to outsiders, or calculate taxes due, or help maximise or even determine income, but simply to expose losses due to theft, fraud, or inefficiency . . . The principles of stewardship were reflected in such accounts but never the doctrine of materiality.

Goldberg (1949, p.6) describes the use in ancient Rome of the memorandum book (*adversaria*) and the transfer, at least monthly, of entries to the ledger (*codex tabulae*) which had legal standing. He notes that it is quite likely that the ledger in the double entry system was derived from the codex of Roman times.

Accounting in ancient Greece and Rome was concerned with recording and not decision making, with asset protection rather than financial management. In pursuing this course of action it is most likely that the accounting of the period was fulfilling societal needs and expectations.

China

The Mesopotamian, Greek and Roman accounting systems were concerned with the records of merchants, temples and estates. Although governments were involved, the extent of this involvement was apparently limited. An example of extensive government involvement has been described by Fu (1971) in his translation of writings about the record keeping of the Chou dynasty (1122–1256 BC). The Chou Government was feudal and expansionist, leading to a particular type of accounting system. The system which was developed had to allow for large physical distances, several layers or hierarchies of officials and the need to collect taxes in the form of goods for use by the Imperial government. In other words, the surplus product of the economy was collected for transport and use elsewhere.

There was a system of funds — a general reserve fund, a special reserve fund and a reserve fund — the details of which are given by Fu (1971). Not only were the funds named but the source of the goods, the purposes for which they were used, the frequency of taxes being levied and the ceilings of each tax were also supplied. However, it is one thing to set up a system in detail and another to administer it through several levels of officials and over large distances. Control was achieved by having detailed audit reports at intervals of ten days, thirty days and one year, and by appointing audit officials at a higher level in the Imperial service than those who were being audited. Presumably there were appropriate penalties for non-compliance or defalcation. The important point to note about the Chou system is that the form of accounting was adapted to the social and political system of the period. Unfortunately, there are no extant records of this system, which survives only in the descriptions of Chinese society of the period.

Summary of ancient accounting

There are a number of characteristics common to ancient and modern accounting systems, including notions of stewardship, the recording of both physical and monetary resource movements and the need for a separate, independent audit of recorded data. It should also be noted that there was an absence of income measurement or potential for evaluating alternative decisions and courses of action in ancient accounting systems.

The medieval manorial system

The system of record keeping used in England during the Middle Ages had many features of ancient accounting systems and yet remained in use until the nineteenth century. Known as the charge and discharge, the manorial or estate accounting system was of major importance at a time when the feudal estate or manor was the major economic and social unit within the country.

The structure of a feudal society places individuals as members of groups with duties and responsibilities appropriate to their position in the hierarchy. The same relationship applied to property which was held by individuals within the hierarchy so that manors were parts of larger estates which, at the top of the hierarchy, were held by the Crown. Manors were frequently administered by stewards and, therefore, manorial accounting

was the system used by the steward to report on his management of the manor or economic unit. Other officials used a similar system to report to the Crown.

The feudal socio-economic system required that a surplus be generated and overall was not a subsistence economy; the number of great houses and cathedrals built would not indicate subsistence levels for the total economy. However, there does not appear to have been any perceived need to measure the efficiency by which the surplus was generated and no notion of income and/or return on capital employed. The manorial system was primarily an interlocking check on the honesty of different levels of officials in a stratified and regulated society.

The charge and discharge system of accounting followed a similar outline to that given below (James, 1955, p.26).

Arrears
Rents and farms
Other receipts   Total (the charge)
Expenses
Money delivered Total (the discharge)
                           The balance (remainder)

The accounts frequently included both monetary and non-monetary receipts and disposals, the latter being recorded in terms of quantities not values. The charge and discharge accounting system was audited initially by 'hearing the accounts', from which the term audit is derived.

The system was surprisingly durable, lasting from the twelfth to the nineteenth centuries. However, bookkeeping for merchants was often in single entry form, rather than by charge and discharge, prior to the arrival in England of bookkeeping by the Italian method.

The emergence of double entry bookkeeping
The antecedents of bookkeeping

In a well-known article, Littleton (1933) refers to the conditions which, in his view, had to be present before double entry book-keeping could develop. He also suggests the features of contemporary life which could have caused the actual emergence of the technique in the Italian city states.

The conditions identified by Littleton are:

1

A Material (something which needs to be reworked)
a   Private property (power to change ownership)
b   Capital (wealth productively employed)
c   Commerce (interchange of goods)
d   Credit (present use of future goods)

2

A Language (a medium for expressing the material)
a   Writing (a means of making a perma-nent record)
b   Money (medium of exchange 'common denominator')
c   Arithmetic (a means of computation)

These elements, when energised by favourable economic and social circum-stances, produce:

3

A Methodology (a plan for systematically ren-dering the material into the language)

Littleton notes that each of the seven antecedents had been present in different places and times but never together at the one time. Furthermore, they were present when the social upheaval of the Crusades led to a considerable movement of people through the city states of northern Italy (which was not then a unified country) which acted as a trading point between Europe and the Near East.

He concludes:

> It is evident from all this that the condi-tions surrounding commerce, capital and credit in the Middle Ages were very dif-ferent from those which accompanied the same elements in the period of

ancient history. And it becomes increasingly apparent that these atten-dant circumstances so changed the size and extent of commerce and the pur-poses for which capital and credit were employed, that the latter elements could now become the vitalised antecedents of bookkeeping, whereas before they were without issue. They now led directly to the development of double entry. (Littleton, 1933, pp.28–29)

The age of stagnation

After the initial development of double entry bookkeeping in the Italian city states there were relatively few changes to the for-mat of accounts over a long period. Indeed, so long was the period of relative inactivity, when double entry techniques were spread-ing through Europe by word of mouth and plagiarised texts (copies of the work by Pacioli), that it has been referred to as the age of stagnation. Changes in social, political and economic conditions were not rapid and consequently there were few pressures for changes in accounting. The changes that did take place were the result of altered social and commercial conditions including the decline of the agrarian economy, the increased size of commercial activities and the tendency for entrepreneurs to view their activities in the longer term compared with the older trading ventures. Major changes were also the result of changes in philosophy or value systems by major groups as a result of the Reformation, the Calvinist doctrine and the decline of the influence of the Catholic Church.

At the end of this relatively dormant period, before the start of the Industrial Revolution (approximately 1750), there were several accounting systems in use in Britain. In many cases the agricultural sec-tor, the traditional estates and older institu-tions were still using charge and discharge accounting which remained from the defunct manorial system. Merchants were using single entry and double entry book-keeping, often without regular closing entries and income determination capabilities. Neither of these approaches was satisfactory when large scale industrial activity began in the nineteenth century, nor could these systems cope with the introduction of capital raising and the separation of ownership and control.

Merchant accounting and charge and discharge systems do not function efficiently when faced with large scale manufacturing and commercial activities which utilise capital assets for large scale production. A theory of depreciation is needed, together with the separation of capital and revenue items. Depreciation was one of the major conceptual problems of nineteenth century accounting because for the first time in history equipment was becoming obsolete through technological change.

Sombart's thesis

Although the conventional view is that accounting is socially constructed as a result of social, economic and political events, there are alternative approaches which suggest that accounting may be socially constructing. One such theory was that put forward by Sombart (1924) who suggested that double entry bookkeeping was such a powerful tool that it led to the development of a new social and economic system which we call capitalism. This view should be contrasted with the conventional approach that the new system of production, distribution and exchange demanded improvements in accounting and hence double entry bookkeeping was developed.

To really appreciate the detail of the arguments, readers are referred to the works of Yamey (1964) and Winjum (1971) and to the surviving records of early traders. Much of the argument hinges on whether early double entry bookkeeping provided owners and managers with information to aid their wealth maximising

decisions, or whether the accounts in use were deficient in guiding these decision-making activities. The weight of evidence does appear to be in favour of Yamey's position and against that of Winjum (and Sombart), suggesting that double entry bookkeeping was the product of economic and social change. Nevertheless, this is an interesting aspect of the development of accounting and one which has been developed by radical theorists in the accounting literature during the past decade (Tinker, 1985).

The Industrial Revolution and its aftermath, 1750–1900

This section deals with the period 1750–1900 and the resulting changes in accounting, in particular the Industrial Revolution, the legal changes of the nineteenth century and the development of professional bodies of accountants. The changes to accounting which date from this period have a direct relevance to our own time. For example, the importance of the statutory audit to present day accountants is traceable to the legal requirements of the nineteenth century.

The Industrial Revolution

The social and economic changes of this period were far reaching, hence the use of the term revolution. Within the space of not much more than a lifetime, England moved from 'a green and pleasant land' to one of 'dark satanic mills' with the invention of powered machinery, the building of factories and towns, the separation of ownership and control (capitalism) and the emergence of large-scale industrial and commercial activities. The effects of these changes on accounting were profound, in particular the development of recording, measuring and disclosure systems to deal with factories, railways, aggregations of labour and capital equipment, new concepts of production, ownership and control and depreciation. We shall consider these in the remainder of this section.

The transition from craft production to factory production was via an intermediate step of 'putting out work' or cottage industries where workers were employed in their own homes using small scale production methods (craft techniques), with the employer often supplying the materials. Accounting systems would have been needed to ensure that the number of garments produced approached the number that were theoretically possible (that is that the worker had not retained any of the employer's goods). This phase appears not to have lasted very long and the accumulation of workers and machinery in factories was soon widespread. The supply of labour and the newly developed techniques of powered propulsion, first by the use of water power and then steam power, enabled factory production systems to produce enormous quantities of relatively standardised goods, easily undercutting the prices of hand-crafted goods.

The factory system resulted in new information needs which the existing accounting (manorial charge and discharge and merchant accounting) could not meet. The aggregation of capital equipment in one place in a changing technological environment resulted in problems of calculating depreciation for inclusion in product costs, the valuation of inventories and the determination of income.

The newly developed railways were affected by the lack of a theory of depreciation, which enabled promoters to produce very high income figures during the initial years of operation and consequently to sell additional stock (shares), which would earn much less than the original investment as the equipment ultimately deteriorated. Prior to this period accounting systems did not have to contend with large capital items which changed in value over time, that is the issue of depreciation on a systematic basis (Chatfield, 1977, p.94).

It should be noted that where depreciation was not charged, costs were understated, profits overstated and dividends were paid out of capital. However, at the time there were no company taxation provisions for depreciation or accounting standards, or accepted theories of depreciation. Early theories of depreciation included replacement accounting which argued that there was no need for depreciation if the assets were maintained in good condition. Clearly, this was a theory which would produce as many problems as it was meant to solve.

There was a tendency to provide for depreciation when the income figure could support the added charges, a form of income smoothing (Chatfield, 1977, p.97) which was justified since: 'Most corporate officials took the view that so long as they acted in good faith, it was up to them what disclosure to provide in financial statements' (Chatfield, 1977, p.99).

In addition to the development of the railways, the Industrial Revolution is famous for the rapid manner in which aggregated capital was used to build factories in which workers were employed in repetitive tasks using powered equipment for the first time in recorded history. Alternatives to existing accounting practices were needed to accommodate these developments.

The concentration of equipment brought problems of depreciation, as we have seen, but in addition the proportion of fixed costs (compared with variable costs such as labour and materials) would also have risen. In short, the problem of the absorption or allocation of overhead charges would eventually have to be dealt with. One strategy to minimise the impact of overhead charges is to increase output (to spread depreciation and fixed charges over a greater number of units of production). However, this strategy brings with it a further range of problems since increased output almost certainly means producing the final product ahead of sales. Consequently, storage and other inventory charges will be incurred and require records and accounting systems to cope with the new approach to the organisation of the firm.

The massing of labour in factories led to the need for systems to pay wages, overtime, bonuses and piece work payments as well as managing the large number of employees who were necessary for the new industries. At one time cost accounting texts devoted considerable space to developing systems to ensure that wages and other payments were kept under control. These systems were under the control of the accounting function and were, of course, non-existent in the years before the Industrial Revolution.

The aggregation of capital and labour required new concepts of production, ownership and control, frequently through joint stock companies. The joint stock form of organisation resulted in owners who were less familiar with the day-to-day running of the corporation and the employment of paid managers who needed to report to the owners on a periodic basis. In some ways profit determination became more important because it was necessary to pay a dividend to owners. In turn, managers needed more information to exercise their decision-making and control functions on behalf of absent owners.

In time the separation of ownership and control resulted in divergent accounting systems, published accounts for bankers, creditors and shareholders, and management and cost accounting systems to assist managers in making decisions.

Economic and legal changes

Some of the economic changes resulting from the Industrial Revolution are obvious from the previous sections, particularly the aggregation of both capital and labour in new locations and the mass production of standardised products for large markets. The capital required for these developments

came initially from small numbers of wealthy individuals; however, it soon became necessary to harness the savings of those individuals of lesser means. In turn, there followed the pressure for legal changes which have influenced Anglo-American accounting systems ever since. As noted by Goldberg (1949, p.22) the economic changes were reflected in legislative enactments; those having particular importance for accounting practice were those relating to companies and bankruptcy.

The history of companies legislation in the UK is often dated to the 'Bubble' Act 1719 which declared unincorporated companies (those which were not formed by Royal charter or by an Act of Parliament) to be common nuisances. This Act was repealed in 1825, having proved ineffectual in checking the growth of joint stock companies. These organisations were unincorporated and consisted of a large body of (possibly changing) individuals. Consequently, a person contracting with them did not know with whom the contract was being made or whom to sue in the event of a dispute. A partial attempt to control this situation was made in 1834 by empowering the Crown to grant to companies the ability to sue and be sued by a public officer even though they remained unincorporated.

The modern history of companies legislation began with the first companies act, the *Joint Stock Companies Registration Act* 1844. This Act provided that the majority of companies could be incorporated without the use of a Royal charter or special Act of Parliament. In return it also provided for the proper keeping of accounts, the balancing of the books, the preparation and audit of a balance sheet, the production of an auditor's report and the circulation of a printed copy of the balance sheet and the auditor's report to shareholders before the annual meeting and its filing with the registrar of joint stock companies (Goldberg, 1949, p.24). This Act provided for the legal existence of joint stock companies. The principle of limited liability which has been of such importance was added by means of the Act of 1855.

The two principles of joint stock companies and limited liability were consolidated in an Act of 1862 which prohibited business associations of more than twenty people unless registered as a company. However, the 1862 Act omitted all reference to the presentation and audit of accounts which had been covered in the 1844 Act, excepting as a schedule to the Act which set out a model set of articles of association for companies which did not prepare their own rules of association. A further refinement was an 1879 Act that provided for the audit of the accounts of banking companies and the certification of balance sheets as being true and correct.

The next major act was the *Companies Act 1900* which restored the provisions of the 1844 Act in respect of the audit of company accounts. Every company was to have at least one auditor and the mode of appointment was prescribed in the Act. The directors were required to send an audited report to shareholders at least seven days before the statutory meeting. The audit was to apply to details of shares allotted and receipts and payments of capital.

There are sufficient similarities between the forms of organisation described and modern commercial organisations for the connections between the two to be quite clear. The provision of the statutory audit has been an important feature of the accounting profession since the nineteenth century.

The second most important field of legislative activity affecting accounting practice related to bankruptcy (Goldberg, 1949, p.22). Changes were made over a lengthy period of time from a system which allowed for the imprisonment (permanent in some cases) of debtors for small sums to one which provided for the discharge of bankrupts by legal process.

A major change resulted from the placing of insolvents under the jurisdiction of a court through which they could seek their discharge. This took place in 1813 and Goldberg records that in the following thirteen years over 50 000 debtors were released from prison (Goldberg, 1949, p.26). A large number of Acts followed, of which the most important are perhaps those of 1825, 1832, 1838, 1861 and 1869.

The 1825 Act consolidated the procedure for providing bankruptcy relief to traders and also provided for a debtor to start bankruptcy proceedings. The *Bankruptcy Court Act* 1832 set up the court and a system of official assignees who were to work with the creditors' assignees in disposing of a bankrupt estate. The *Insolvency Act* 1838 allowed debtors to remain free from imprisonment by giving up all their goods and the filing of an insolvency petition enabled the matter to be dealt with under the bankruptcy laws.

The *Bankruptcy Act* 1861 finally merged the two matters of insolvency and bankruptcy; all debtors, whether private or traders, were covered by the same provisions. The *Bankruptcy Act* 1869 repealed all previous legislation and codified the law into the form which largely exists today. Goldberg notes the likelihood that the accountancy profession has benefited from this legislation in a variety of ways, including the roles of trustee and assignee in bankruptcy.

The assumption of professional status by accountants

Goldberg (1949, pp.18–22) provides a brief history of the profession of accountancy to the end of the nineteenth century. The modern accounting profession began in Edinburgh in 1853 with the Society of Accountants in Edinburgh (chartered in October 1854) followed shortly after by a similar organisation in Glasgow (the Institute of Accountants and Actuaries in Glasgow, chartered in March 1855).

Although there were many accountants operating in England it was not until 1870 that a society was formed in Liverpool and then the Institute of Accountants in London in the same year. In 1871 the Manchester Institute of Accountants was formed. In 1880 the existing societies and institutes were incorporated into the Institute of Chartered Accountants in England and Wales (ICAEW) by Royal charter. Conditions were set for admission including general education examinations, five years of articles served with a member of the institute, and intermediate and final examinations in a range of subjects.

In the USA, the American Association of Public Accountants (AAPA) was incorporated under New York State law in 1887 (Goldberg, 1949, p.21). This was strengthened by the passage of a state law in 1896 which regulated the profession of public accountant and the use of the title of Certified Public Accountant (CPA). In due course other states followed this lead.

There can be no doubt that the legal, commercial and industrial changes of the nineteenth century resulted in the development of bodies of accountants with legitimate aspirations to professional status. It is arguable that these aspirations were not fulfilled until the twentieth century.

Chapter summary

This chapter has sketched very briefly the development of accounting to the end of the nineteenth century. Initially, accounting existed in terms of relatively primitive recording and control devices which were used to satisfy the needs of unsophisticated traders and estate owners who were more concerned with keeping tallies of what was owned and owed than with measuring income or potential income. Indeed, without considerable modification, the ancient systems would not have been capable of use in decision making.

The same comment could be made about the earliest published versions of double entry bookkeeping, which many writers suggest marks the real start of modern accounting. Although potentially of great significance, the early forms were incomplete and often not fully utilised in that closing entries were not always made and final accounts frequently dispensed with. Nevertheless, when social and economic conditions were appropriate for the development of a system of accounting which provided not only for totals of what was owned and owed but also for calculating income and potential income, it was developed out of merchants' double entry bookkeeping.

The changed economic and social conditions engendered by the Industrial Revolution after 1750 led to a rapid dissatisfaction with some aspects of merchant double entry bookkeeping and the almost total disappearance of other systems. These changed conditions included the aggregation of capital and labour in factories where steam and other power sources were applied in producing standardised goods on a large scale. The aggregation of capital resulted in problems associated with depreciation, fixed costs and the allocation of overheads, producing goods for general sale and, consequently, the inventory costing issue and pricing problems. The aggregation of labour resulted in control problems as well as issues of wage, overtime, bonus and piece work payments. It is important to recognise that many of these accounting problems were new and had not existed in the days of craft industries and owner managers.

The need for large amounts of capital resulted in pressures for the development of joint stock companies and limited liability for shareholders, both of which were achieved around the middle of the nineteenth century. This change in the legal framework resulted in the rapid development of the corporate form of organisation and the accounting and auditing functions which went with it. The separation of ownership and control necessitated the eventual provision of external reports, which were attested as true and correct for the new shareholding class. Further work for accountants was generated by changes in the legislation relating to debtors and insolvent traders which eventually resulted in the modern system of bankruptcy law. Accountants found business as assignees in bankruptcy and in representing the interests of creditors.

The development of more modern accounting systems together with the greater opportunities for accountants in many different fields led eventually to aspirations to professional status. Considerable advances had been made in both the UK and the USA towards achieving this status by the end of the nineteenth century.

Essay and examination questions

2.1   To what extent does the development of accounting to 1900 support the argument that accounting is socially constructed?

2.2   Briefly outline the arguments used by Yamey and Winjum to comment on Sombart's thesis that double entry bookkeeping led to the rise of capitalism.

2.3   Comment on the suggestion that although accountants had legitimate professional aspirations by the end of the nineteenth century these had not yet been satisfied.

2.4   Consider the effect which nineteenth century legislative changes had (and continue to have) on the accounting profession. Can the effect be over-estimated?

2.5   Generally accepted accounting principles did not really exist before the start of the Industrial Revolution. To what extent can it be said that a body of generally accepted principles existed by 1900?

2.6   Discuss the problems of accounting theory (or a lack of it) which were demonstrated during the railway era.

2.7   Consider the manufacturing industry of the late nineteenth century. What problems were likely to be incapable of solution by merchants' double entry bookkeeping?

2.8   Chatfield (1977, p.91) has noted that: 'The accounting profession lacked influence. Unless fraud was involved, courts generally — and philosophically — chose not to interfere in questions of accounting doctrine. Nor were companies encouraged to narrow areas of reporting difference by the implied threat of government regulation'. To what extent does this situation still persist?

2.9   Henderson and Peirson (1983) have referred to the period 1800 to 1955 as the General Scientific Theory period. So far as the first part of the period is concerned, indicate areas to which their label might be applied.

2.10 Critically examine the arguments put forward by Littleton as an explanation for the beginning of double entry bookkeeping in his paper on the antecedents of bookkeeping.

2.11 To what extent would you agree with the statement that modern accounting began with the publication of the first book on double entry bookkeeping in 1494?

2.12   The accounting profession would not exist without the legal developments of the mid-nineteenth century. Explain.

2.13   Explain the notion that accounting is not only socially constructed but also socially constructing. Give examples.

2.14   How useful is the study of accounting history in understanding the development of the discipline as a whole? Argue in whichever direction you think appropriate.

2.15   Accounting, in one form or another, appears to be essential to the development of society as we know it. Discuss.

References and additional reading

Chatfield, M. (1977). *A History of Accounting Thought*. New York: Kreiger.

Fu, P. (1971). Governmental accounting in China during the Chou dynasty (1122BC–256BC). *Journal of Accounting Research*, 40–51.

Goldberg, L. (1949). The development of accounting in Gibson, C.T., Meredith, G.G. and Peterson, R. (Eds) (1971). *Accounting Concepts Readings*. Melbourne: Cassell.

Henderson, S. and Peirson, G. (1983). *Financial Accounting Theory: Its Nature and Development*. Melbourne: Longman Cheshire.

Henderson, S. and Peirson, G. (1988). *Issues in Financial Accounting* (4th edn). Melbourne: Longman Cheshire.

James, M.E. (1955) (Ed.). *Estate Accounts of the Earls of Northumberland 1562–1637*. Durham and London: Surtees Society.

Keister, O.R. (February 1965). The mechanics of Mesopotamian record-keeping. *The National Association of Accountants Bulletin*, 18–24.

Littleton, A.C. (1933 reprinted 1966). The antecedents of double-entry bookkeeping. *Accounting Evolution to 1900*. New York: Russell and Russell. 13–21.

Sombart, W. (1924). *Der Moderne Kapitalismus* (Sixth edition). Munich: Dunker and Humblot.

Tinker, A.M. (1985). *Paper Prophets*. New York: Praeger.

Winjum, J.O. (1970). Accounting in its age of stagnation. *The Accounting Review*, 743–761.

Winjum, J.O. (1971) Accounting and the rise of capitalism: an accountant's view. *Journal of Accounting Research*, 333–350.

Yamey, B.S. (1940). The functional development of double-entry bookkeeping. *The Accountant*, 333–342.

Yamey, B.S. (1947). Notes on the origin of double-entry bookkeeping. *The Accounting Review*, 263–272.

Yamey, B.S. (1949). Scientific bookkeeping and the rise of capitalism. *The Economic History Review*, 99–113.

Yamey, B.S. (1964). Accounting and the rise of capitalism: further notes on a theme by Sombart. *Journal of Accounting Research*, 117–136.

Chapter 3
Twentieth century Anglo-American accounting developments

Learning objectives

After studying this chapter the reader will be able to:

- outline the search for accounting principles by individuals and organisations
- relate the sequence of events in the structural development of accounting practice through a number of periods
- enumerate the varied pressures and influences which have shaped twentieth century accounting practices
- identify the difference between accounting as a socially constructed and a socially constructing discipline.

Introduction

The nineteenth century was a period of great change in industry, commerce and social life. The twentieth century has perhaps been even more dramatic, witnessing two world wars, a major economic depression and the creation of massive and competing economic and political blocs. These developments have all impacted on Anglo-American social structures, including accounting, and consequently the development of the discipline during this century has not been a simple continuation of the work of the previous period.

The main features of twentieth century Anglo-American accounting developments which will be discussed here are the search for accounting principles (including the stress placed upon establishing accounting as a scientific activity); the development of the institutional structure for accounting (including standard setting and regulatory bodies) and a consideration of accounting as a social phenomenon.

This period of accounting development has been characterised by: the involvement of the USA through commercial and political influence; the development of the academic branch of the discipline through the involvement of universities as well as professional bodies; the search for accounting principles or a general theory of accounting, beginning in the 1920s and 1930s;

attempts to apply scientific method and supporting methodologies to accounting; and the movement towards regulation, specification and standardisation, initially on a voluntary basis, but increasingly through internal (professional) regulations.   .

The search for accounting principles

There appears to be relatively little evidence of any search for accounting principles prior to the 1920s. The general approaches of the period were to account in the way management desired or the way that the accountant had been brought up to account. Theory of a sort existed, but the practices in use varied widely.

The first attempts at deriving accounting principles were carried out by individual researchers; later on there were several organised or collective attempts designed to achieve the same ends. These attempts have been described as part of the General Scientific Theory period (Henderson and Peirson, 1983), general because they were not directed at any specific accounting activity but covered the whole field, and scientific because empirical investigation was practised. In other words, the researchers were observing actual practices (empirical) and not simply stating what ought to be done (normative). Unfortunately, this approach produced undesirable side effects since the results of the studies were taught as 'what constitutes accounting'. This led to a practice–theory– practice cycle and tended to retard the progress of accounting, because there was no value judgement exercised in respect of the practices which were observed. In other words, there was no opportunity to examine critically what was being practised before the next generation of accountants were prepared in the same manner.

Individual efforts

There are a number of well-known individual studies including those of Paton (1922), Sanders, Hatfield and Moore (1938), Gilman (1939), Paton and Littleton (1940) and Grady (1965). Their findings were as follows.

Paton (1922) identified eleven accounting postulates. These were concerned with: the distinct business entity; going concern and continuity; total assets must equal total equities; the balance sheet is a complete representation of the financial condition of the enterprise; money is a constant measuring unit; cost gives value for initial statement; cost expended attaches value to production; accrual principles need to be followed; losses are first to be deducted from accumulated profits; payments to shareholders should come from earnings; and first-in-first-out (FIFO) cost movements were assumed.

The work of Sanders, Hatfield and Moore (1938) was developed by interviewing preparers and users of financial statements, studying the existing literature and considering current legal conditions. Their statement of accounting principles was divided into general principles, income statement principles, balance sheet principles, consolidated statements and comments and notes. The most important principles were:
- accounting should provide information relating to financial condition and income earning aspects of the business

- there must be a proper separation of capital and revenue items
- the accounts should provide historical record which is capable of analysis
- capital must be apportioned over long periods where appropriate
- consistent treatment should be given to the same items
- a generally conservative approach should be taken
- income statement should show all relevant details
- unrealised income should not be included
- non-operating income should be shown separately
- provision must be made for losses on current items
- if corrections must be made for previous errors they should be made to the income statement
- the balance sheet should be based on cost less depreciation for fixed assets and lowest of cost or market for current assets
- care must be given to reporting deferred charges
- contingent liabilities should be included if material.

Gilman (1939) discussed the doctrines and conventions of accounting. The doctrines included conservatism, consistency, disclosure and materiality. The accounting conventions included entity, valuation and accounting period.

Paton and Littleton (1940) produced a number of basic concepts or assumptions of accounting. These included: the business entity; continuity; measured consideration involving exchange activities (cost, expense, revenue, income); costs attached to production and services; effort and accomplishment (matching, periodicity); and verifiable objective evidence.

Grady (1965) was mainly a reiteration of the conventions previously identified. He identified these conventions which probably still hold: the entity convention; the going concern convention; the monetary convention; the consistency convention; the diversity convention; the convention of conservatism; the objectivity convention; the materiality convention; and the accounting period convention. The study made by Grady was commissioned by the American Institute of Certified Public Accountants (AICPA) but has been included under this section because it was the research work of an individual rather than that of a large group or committee.

This section has described briefly the work of a number of individuals who chose the codification of existing practice as a means of developing accounting theories. This approach to theory construction often leads to a practice–theory–practice cycle through which doubtful or outdated practices are perpetuated. The same method was employed in the example of a collective approach to developing accounting principles which is discussed in the next section.

Collective efforts

The most important example of a collective attempt to research and document existing practice was the 1936 American Accounting Association (AAA) publication *Tentative Statement of Accounting Principles*. This was an important venture because it marked the first attempt at collective research of a type which has become important in the development of accounting. As discussed in the sections on institutional structures and conceptual frameworks, organised committee activities have played an important part in more recent developments.

The 1936 *Tentative Statement* was significant because the AAA was an important body of both academic and professional accountants. The statement shows an early (and a continuing) interest in establishing accounting principles and was the first in a long line of deliberations by the AAA. These include revisions of the *Tentative Statement, A Statement of Basic Accounting Theory*

(ASOBAT) AAA, 1966 and the *Statement on Accounting Theory and Theory Acceptance* (SATTA) in AAA, 1977. There have also been many AAA sponsored committee reports on topical issues from time to time.

The *Tentative Statement* was criticised by both academics and professional accountants, thereby increasing the volume of literature on the subject (Scott, 1937; Rorem, 1937). It was also modified and reported by Paton and Littleton (1940).

The historical cost basis of accounting received considerable emphasis through the *Tentative Statement*. There were also references at this time to accounting as a science. Rorem (1937) in a commentary on the *Tentative Statement* uses phrases such as 'scientific method' and 'scientifically defensible facts', which may be seen as the forerunners of the postwar scientific accounting debate.

The contents of the *Tentative Statement* may be summarised as twenty propositions divided into three groups dealing with the determination of costs and values, the measurement of income and differentiation of capital and surplus. The statement was limited to the special problems of the financial statements of private corporations.

The *Tentative Statement* generated comments from some of the important accountants of the day. Rorem (1937) comments from a practitioner's viewpoint while Scott (1937) puts the view of an academic.

Rorem (1937) commented on the seven propositions dealing with costs and values which included: cost gives value for purposes of initial statement; the need to allocate original costs between periods; cost is measured by cash outlay or the fair market value of property acquired by exchange; cost is determined at the time of a substantial change in beneficial ownership; an estimation of expired costs is needed to provide for depreciation and similar charges; expired value of inventories necessitates their being written down; and there was some evidence of a general rule of conservatism.

The section concerned with the measurement of income contained six propositions, which were more classification than measurement. The propositions included: a weak definition of accruals; the need for a proper separation of recurrent and non-recurrent items and operating and extraordinary items; the latter must not be charged directly to surplus nor be merged with ordinary income and expenses; the measurement system must not be used to smooth income.

The last section was concerned with capital and surplus and consisted of seven propositions mainly concerned with the distinction between paid-in capital and earned surplus. The income account must be used for disclosure and no losses charged directly to earned surplus.

Rorem (1937, p.138) was generally supportive of the *Tentative Statement*, regarding it as a step in the progress of accounting as a science. He notes the emphasis on the need for clarity and directness in accounting reports and states: 'In the final analysis the accountants' obligation is to use scientific method and to present scientifically defensible facts'. This is an important indication of the thinking of the period and leads into the discussion of the philosophy of science and related matters in Chapter 4. It is clear that the use of terms such as scientifically defensible facts was rather imprecise and probably not as we would use them today. Rorem (1937, p.138) was right when he observed that: 'The task of the American Accounting Association has only just begun. The *Tentative Statement* covers only a few aspects of accounting theory'.

Scott (1937) was more critical of the *Tentative Statement*, which he thought would tend to produce rigidity in practice and a tendency to ignore changing economic and social events.

The section on costs and values was a reflection of the dominance of the record function of accounts and of historical cost; the use of costs which arose from a substantial change of ownership.

The section dealing with the measurement of income was criticised because income is not defined except by inference. It consisted of two parts: incomes and expenses of operations, and a catchall for all other items. Furthermore, much of the section deals with the rewriting of income statements from previous years, a practice which Scott thought should only be done on very serious grounds. The currency of balance sheet figures was of concern to Scott (1937, p.301):

> There appears to run through the *Tentative Statement* of principles a tacit assumption that the balance sheet should be as nearly as possible an automatically derived summary of the results of past transactions. The idea that the balance sheet should be an accurate presentation of the present financial position of the enterprise is subordinated to such a tacit assumption.

Clearly, the historical cost principle (without revaluations) was already entrenched at this time. Scott concluded with a much more critical evaluation of the *Tentative Statement* than Rorem (1937):

> With its narrow conception of accounting and its generally conservative interpretation of theory and practice, the Tentative Statement of principles would, if consistently adopted, tend to retard the development of accounting. In fact the statement envisages no constructive development of accounting theory and, in the opinion of the writer, that is the point upon which major emphasis should be placed. (Scott, 1937, p.303)

The *Tentative Statement* appears to have satisfied those who were seeking a straightforward codification of current practices but not those seeking to change those practices. As we shall find out, these are fairly common reactions to reports by accounting bodies, including the later conceptual frameworks.

Development of the institutional structure of accounting

At the beginning of the twentieth century the condition of accounting was very different from that of the present time, particularly in terms of what we will term the institutional structure of accounting. Although professional bodies of accountants existed in both the UK and the USA, they were not of great numerical or political strength. Furthermore, in the UK, case law tended to support a view of external reporting which gave management considerable latitude in determining what to put into the shareholders' accounts. UK company law had only restored the annual statutory audit in 1900 and the next major change was the requirement for a profit and loss account contained in the 1929 *Companies Act*.

Consequently, so far as the UK was concerned, the institutional structure consisted of a relatively young profession working within the context of limited company law, which provided for the issuance of a set of audited accounts including a balance sheet. There was a body of case law which did not lay great store by regulated uniform accounting reports and a set of accounting principles which were not codified and, if they had been, would have reflected the varied practices in use at the time. There were no academic accounting specialists in the UK at that time and accounting was not a subject studied at university. The route to membership of a UK professional body consisted of a long period of articles with a member of the accounting profession and the passing of professional examinations. There is strong support for stating that the educational process in use retarded the development of accounting in the UK for a number of years.

The major contribution to the development of the institutional structure of accounting for the first thirty or forty years

of this century came from the USA. There are a number of reasons for this position, including the growing economic strength of the country, the nature of accounting education which frequently involved university study and a body of academics who wished to conduct research in the area of accounting. The accounting profession was very young and small in number, but growing rapidly to cope with the demands of industry and commerce and of additional taxes on both corporations and individuals. World War I programmes also required the assistance of accountants.

The individual and collective searches for accounting principles stimulated debate and assisted in fostering the view that standardisation of some aspects of accounting reports might be appropriate under certain circumstances.

A knowledge of the institutional structure of accounting is important to an understanding of modern accounting and an appreciation of future directions which the discipline might take. The institutional structure refers not only to professional bodies but equally to the standard-setting and regulatory bodies which have become such an important part of the life of the modern accountant. For ease of exposition the remainder of this section will be discussed in three separate parts: the formative years 1920–1952; the postwar period 1953–1969; and the modern period 1970 to the present. The first period will include mainly US developments, the second both US and UK and the third will refer to features of US, UK and Australasian accounting structures.

The formative years, 1920–1952

This section will describe developments in the US and UK professions, pressures towards the standardisation of accounting reports and moves towards the regulation of disclosures. The categorisation is not always clear and, like the time periods employed, it must be seen as an attempt to guide the reader through a period of accounting development which is important for a general understanding of the present, but the detail of which is of lesser importance.

Goldberg (1949) notes that the importance of the USA in accounting development began very early in the century. The American accounting profession was in its infancy, since the title CPA was first recognised in 1899 with forty-five members of the AAPA. Their activities were at first restricted to the State of New York but spread to a number of other states early in the period under review. These additional states granted legal recognition to accountants. Practitioners formed state societies which united in 1902 as the Federation of Societies of Public Accountants in the United States of America. This body sponsored the first International Congress of Accountants in 1904 and in 1905 the Federation and the AAPA merged. The united body began to publish the *Journal of Accountancy* in the same year (Goldberg, 1949, p.29).

By 1910 the membership of the Association was approximately 1000. In 1916 the AAPA was superseded by the Institute of Accountants in the USA with 1150 members. In 1917 another name change produced the American Institute of Accountants (AIA) which lasted until 1957 when the AICPA was formed.

The AAA was formed in 1916 as an organisation for those accountants who taught in universities. The teaching of accounting within the university system marks an important difference between UK and US accounting development. The UK taught accountants mainly on a part time correspondence study basis, which often involved more rote learning and training than education. Certainly, there was much less accounting research carried out in the UK at that time because research is an important aspect of university work. The US accountants were involved with univer-

sity based study from an early stage and US academic accountants were involved in research as reported in an earlier section. Those US accountants mainly concerned with cost and management accounting were served by the National Association of Cost Accountants (now the National Association of Accountants).

In the UK the profession developed during this period by setting up additional bodies. In other words expansion was achieved not only by increasing the size of the existing bodies but also by the addition of new organisations, some of which did not obtain Royal charters but remained as incorporated societies. Many of these organisations had specialist territories within the overall field of accounting, together with varying experience and examination requirements for membership. This fragmentation of the UK profession still exists despite the dominance of the English Institute, and discussions about amalgamations are a feature of professional accounting life in the UK. The divided nature of the profession has had ramifications for standard setting and the regulation of external reporting, for example in the need for an Accounting Standards Committee (ASC) with the membership divided between the various professional bodies.

In addition to the effects which the search for accounting principles may have had upon practising accountants during this period, other pressures were applied in order to encourage the standardisation of accounting reports. Moonitz (1970) refers to three sources of accounting principles developed prior to 1930. These may be regarded as encouraging standardisation because of the authoritative sources behind them.

The first was a 1917 project for uniform accounting by the American Association of Public Accountants, which was prepared at the request of the Federal Trade Commission and after approval transmitted to the Federal Reserve Board. A revised version was issued in 1929. The Federal Reserve Board acts on behalf of the banking community in the USA and it may be said that these early uniform accounts had the weight of the bankers behind them. The requirements of the uniform accounts covered inventory valuation (lower of cost or market), factory overhead, extraordinary items, the use of net sales and the treatment of discounts, and materiality.

Moonitz (1970, p.147) notes that although the 1917 and 1929 publications were prepared by the Institute they were disseminated by commercial bankers, who had control over bank loans, and consequently the principles, rules and procedures were taken seriously by businessmen and their accountants.

The second source referred to by Moonitz (1970) was the series of detailed articles published in the students' section of the *Journal of Accountancy*. The purpose of these articles was to advise both students and practitioners of what was considered good practice. The series ran from 1914 until the 1940s.

The third influence named by Moonitz was a series of thirty-three bulletins issued by the American Institute of Accountants between 1920 and 1929. These were issued by the librarian in response to specific questions received from members. The bulletins provided answers which were obtained in the form of opinions from accountants of good standing. Moonitz notes that they were advisory and not intended to be dictatorial. It would appear that the time was not then right for the regulation of disclosures, a process which began in the form of recommendations and led eventually to accounting standards.

Kohler (1953) provides a description of three separate series of actions by different organisations which all have the common result of moving towards the regulation of disclosures. He appears to be describing moves towards the establishment of accounting standards, while using the more accepted term principles in the title of his paper:

The publications of these three societies — the American Accounting Association, the American Institute of Accountants, and the Institute of Chartered Accountants in England and Wales — have had a somewhat different genesis, aim and form, but the general effect has been much the same. Standards and uniformity have been suggested where at least some laxity and uncertainty had been noted, and uniformity has been developed out of alternative procedures. As a result, improvements in both the content and readability of financial statements have been widely observed. (Kohler, 1953, p.30)

The AAA publication to which Kohler refers is the 1936 *Tentative Statement* which was introduced as an example of collective development of accounting principles. In due course it was recast and reissued in 1941 and 1948. During 1951 and 1952 the 1948 statement was provided with four supplements by the Committee on Concepts and Standards of the AAA. There is no need to pursue the AAA approach any further since this body does not regulate professional actions, but it does have an educational and persuasive role in the development of accounting.

In 1939 the Committee on Accounting Procedure of the AIA started to publish a series of bulletins to generate greater uniformity in accounting and auditing. A total of forty-two bulletins was issued covering a wide range of topics. Kohler (1953, p.34) notes:

It anticipated that its pronouncements would be accepted in many quarters as authoritative . . . the 'burden of proof' would attach to any accountant who failed to follow the 'rules' it proposed issuing from time to time.

The topics covered by the series of bulletins are given below.
1 Seven rules dealing with profit, paid in capital, earned surplus, treasury shares

and dividends, receivables, stock and reacquisition of stock (1939)

2 Unamortised discount upon refunding (1939)
3 Quasi-reorganisations (1939)
4 Foreign gains and losses (1939)
5 Depreciation or appreciation (1940)
6 Comparative statements (1940)
7 Definitions (1940)
8 Combined statement of income and earned surplus (1941)
9 Definitions (1941)
10 Real and personal property taxes (1941)
11 Stock dividends (1941)
12 Definitions (1941)
13 Postwar reserves (1942)
14 Treasury notes (1942)
15 Re-negotiation liability (1942)
16 Depreciation (1942)
17 Excess-profits-tax refund (1942)
18 Income-tax saving (1942)
19 CPFF contracts (1942)
20 Depreciation (1943)
21 Re-negotiation liability (1943)
22 Definitions (1944)
23 Allocation of income taxes (1944)
24 Amortisation of intangibles (1944)
25 Contract termination (1945)
26 Postwar reserves (1946)
27 Emergency facilities (1946)
28 Contingency reserves (1947)
29 Inventory pricing (1947)
30 Current assets and liabilities (1947)
31 Inventory reserves (1947)
32 Surplus charges (1947)
33 Depreciation basis (1947)
34 Use of the word reserve (1948)
35 Exclusions from net income (1948)
36 Annuity costs (1948)
37 Stock options (1948)
38 Long term lease disclosures (1949)
39 Surplus (1949)
40 Business combinations (1950)
41 Net income (1951)
42 Amortisation of emergency facilities (1952)

Although a number were concerned with specific wartime conditions, the number and

nature of the bulletin topics indicate a pre-occupation with a level of detail which many critics would argue is still true of the Financial Accounting Standards Board (FASB) approach to the production of standards.

The ICAEW issued a number of broader, less specific recommendations to members. This process began in 1942 and was intended to advise on 'best practice' on the following topics.

1 Tax Reserve Certificates (1942)
2 *War Damage Act* transactions (1942)
3 Recognition of income tax liability (1943)
4 Income tax on dividends and interest (1943)
5 Profit appropriations (1943)
6 Reserves and provisions (1943)
7 Consolidated statements (1944)
8 Statement forms (1944)
9 Depreciation (1945)
10 Inventory valuation (1945)
11 Excess profits tax refunds (1946)
12 Price level increases (1949)
13 Fixed assets in prospectuses (1949)
14 Statements of deceased persons and certain trusts (1949)
15 Changing purchasing power (1952)

A number of these recommendations were clearly designed to assist with the abnormal conditions of wartime and the immediate postwar period. Others, such as depreciation and price level matters, were of a much more general nature.

Kohler (1953, p.50) notes that, although the various publications discussed in his paper may not be regarded as standards, the important point is that 'a substantial framework of rules has been devised for the accounting profession to which the stamp of authority has been affixed'. The progression from the recording of elementary principles, to providing detailed recommendations, to the setting up of standard-setting bodies is clearly a long term activity. The development of standards is discussed in the next section.

The period 1953–1969

The period 1953–1969 was one of consolidation for Anglo-American accounting, with a strengthening of the pressures leading towards regulation and standardisation of accounting reports. These pressures occurred as the result of both external events (legislation) and internal developments consistent with the self-regulation of the profession.

The AICPA Committee on Accounting Procedure continued to produce bulletins until it was replaced in 1959 by the Accounting Principles Board (APB). That body continued in existence until replaced by the FASB in 1974. In place of the bulletins, the APB issued Opinions, which were binding upon members of the AICPA when reporting as auditors on the published accounts of client corporations.

The APB commissioned a study by Moonitz into the fundamentals of the discipline. This inquiry was reported as Accounting Research Study No. 1, *The Basic Postulates of Accounting,* published in 1961. Sprouse and Moonitz co-authored Accounting Research Study No. 3, entitled *A Tentative Set of Broad Accounting Principles for Business Enterprises*, in 1962. Neither study was totally successful in meeting the needs of the accounting profession or of academia. There were many other studies during this period, which has been described by Henderson and Peirson (1983) as the General Normative Theory period from 1955 to 1970. The establishment of the APB was intended to strengthen the structural framework within which USA accountants operated. This pressure has continued to develop since the formation of the FASB.

In the UK, the ICAEW continued to produce the series of recommendations which were referred to in the previous section. It was not until the Accounting Standards Steering Committee was set up in 1970 that British based accountants had to contend with professionally determined mandatory standards. However, the UK companies acts are updated regularly with major changes at intervals of about twenty years. In particular, the Acts of 1948 and 1967 provided detailed structures through the appropriate schedules. British accountants were thus subjected to pressures towards uniformity through legislation rather than accounting standards during this period.

The modern period, 1970 to the present

The period since 1970 has been referred to by Henderson and Peirson (1983) as the Specific Scientific Theory period which succeeded the General Normative Theory period (1955–1970). The latter produced a great deal of theorising, in particular about various methods of changing accounting disclosures to allow for varying price levels, but ultimately there were very few changes to actual accounting practices. The reasons for this outcome are many and perhaps need not be dealt with here, except to note that the age of normative theorising gave way to one of renewed empiricism of a very different type to that of the 1920s to 1940s. The new empiricism is highly specific in addressing particular problems to be analysed in depth using advanced mathematical and statistical techniques and utilising computer assistance where appropriate.

The discontinuity which occurred around 1970 was as big a change as that which had occurred previously, when research turned in the direction of normative theorising, from a study of what was done in practice in order to codify current events. However, the institutional pressures which affect the profession have not always been in tune with the changing fashions of academia and accounting research. Standard setting and the regulation of disclosures are not governed by either normative or empirical research but by the interplay of complex forces which are discussed in a later chapter. The external pressures have resulted in changes within the various professional bodies, and it is to these changes that we shall now turn.

The APB was set up in 1959 to replace the AICPA Committee on Accounting Procedure which operated as a codifier of existing practice. The objective of the change was to bring a greater degree of institutional structure to the regulation of accounting disclosures by the issuing of Opinions. The APB Opinions were binding on members when acting as auditors of published accounts. The Opinions were given the status of generally accepted accounting principles (GAAP) and were produced frequently, in some cases by using the previously issued AICPA bulletins as a base.

The APB came under increasing criticism for not approaching its regulatory task in a more independent manner and for producing Opinions which did not have an adequate conceptual basis. Eventually, the criticism led to the formation of a committee by the AICPA (the Wheat Committee) which recommended the replacement of the APB by a new private sector standard-setting body, the FASB. The FASB began operating in 1974.

The FASB appears to be set for a long-term role and has produced over 100 standards, as well as other lower status forms of determination such as standard operating procedures (SOPs). The FASB is a small full-time group, which is intended to be independent of the accounting profession and backed by increased funding and research assistance. We shall pay more attention to the actions of the FASB in the chapters dealing with conceptual frameworks and standard setting (Chapters 6 and 7).

The other strong institutional pressure which affects the US profession is the Securities Exchange Commission (SEC) which is charged with governing the external disclosures of corporations. In practice, the SEC will accept as GAAP those standards which are produced by the FASB, although the SEC could always change this policy if it wanted to. Because the SEC is a government body, the USA has government monitored accounting standards operated under delegated authority.

The institutional structure of accounting in the UK has continued to be influenced by the large number of professional bodies and consequent efforts to coordinate at least some of their activities, especially in the area of accounting standards.

The development of accounting standards in the UK dates from 1970 when the ICAEW formed the Accounting Standards Steering Committee (ASSC), now known as the ASC. Other members of the committee were the Institute of Chartered Accountants of Scotland (ICAS) and the Institute of Chartered Accountants of Ireland (ICAI; 1970), the Association of Certified Accountants (ACA), the Institute of Cost and Management Accountants (ICMA; 1971) and the Chartered Institute of Public Finance and Accountancy (CIPFA; 1976).

The terms of reference for the ASC were:

Bearing in mind the intention of the governing bodies to advance accounting standards and to narrow the areas of difference and variety in accounting practice by publishing authoritative statements on best accounting practice which will wherever possible be definitive —

a To keep under review standards of financial accounting and reporting.
b To publish consultative documents with the object of maintaining and advancing accounting standards.
c To propose to the Councils of the governing bodies statements of standard accounting practice.
d To consult as appropriate with representatives of finance, commerce, industry and government and other persons concerned with financial reporting.

In 1976 the ASC was reconstituted as a joint committee of the six member bodies, with twenty-three members. The ICAEW had a majority of twelve members.

To accompany this standard-setting activity the ASC set up a consultative group covering a wide range of parties interested in external reporting. They also developed procedures by which accounting standards are developed. The working arrangements included the following sequence: research, drafting subcommittee, internal exposure, publication for general comment, the evaluation of comments and finally the production of a Statement of Standard Accounting Practice (SSAP).

In addition to the development of SSAPs by the ASC, the regulatory mechanism in the UK includes the *Companies Act* and the legislation produced by the European Economic Community (EEC), now named the European Union (EU).

The *Companies Act* of 1980 was a relatively minor set of adjustments to existing disclosures. However, the 1981 *Companies Act* was a major change which reflected the influence of the EU on UK legislation. The 1981 Act is prescriptive to a degree previously unknown in the Anglo-American accounting tradition, since it states exactly how certain matters are to be disclosed, with no latitude for professional judgement in matters of layout. It might be argued that many aspects of Continental accounting traditions are now impinging on the 'true and fair' approach of British accounting.

This impression is strengthened by recent events, in particular the Dearing Report (1988) which advocated, *inter alia*, the abolition of the ASC and the use of some form of government agency to set accounting standards. Subsequent developments include the setting up of the Accounting Standards Board (ASB) and the adoption of the International Accounting Standards Committee (IASC) conceptual framework. Clearly, accountants in Commonwealth countries and those with an Anglo-American accounting tradition will want to keep a close watch on these changes.

The institutional structure of the accounting profession in Australia may be briefly described as follows. The professional accounting body is divided between two bodies, the Australian Society of Certified Practising Accountants (ASCPA) with a membership of about 75 000 (the third largest in the world) and the Institute of Chartered Accountants in Australia (ICAA) with a much smaller membership of about 15 000. The ICAA dates from the nineteenth century, while the ASCPA is the result of a series of amalgamations of other bodies, the last of which took place in 1965. The ASCPA has a wide following in terms of different branches of the profession, but the membership of the ICAA is far more specific and limited mostly to those accountants in public practice. There has always been rivalry between the two bodies and integration proposals have failed on two occasions.

However, the Councils of the two bodies have cooperated to fund the Australian Accounting Research Foundation, which carries out research to support accounting standards which are in turn issued jointly by the two bodies. This condition persists with the exception that all proposals for accounting standards are now vetted by the Accounting Standards Review Board (ASRB), a government organisation which reviews draft standards and, if they are acceptable to the ASRB, the standard becomes legally binding upon directors of public companies. The profession has yielded some of its autonomy in return for the legal backing given to the accounting standards.

In 1989 the Australian Accounting Research Foundation (AARF) and the ASRB were brought much closer together in order to facilitate better communication between research and implementation. In 1991 the ASRB was replaced by the Australian

Accounting Standards Board (AASB). Statements of Accounting Concepts and Australian Accounting Standards (AASs) are developed by the AASB, either alone or in conjunction with the Public Sector Accounting Standards Board.

The accounting profession in New Zealand is in the hands of the NZSA which has been created as the result of a series of amalgamations of other bodies dating from 1894. The NZSA draws members from all branches of the profession. In 1994 the NZSA undertook a review of structure and educational requirements for entry and announced a name change to the Institute of Chartered Accountants of New Zealand. However, this must await approval by Act of Parliament.

From 1 July 1994 standard setting in New Zealand is to be undertaken by the NZSA through the Financial Reporting Standards Board (FRSB) of the NZSA and approval is to be given by the ASRB. All previously approved standards are deemed to be authoritative, but will be reviewed by the ASRB over a period of time. New standards termed Financial Reporting Standards (FRSs) have been in force since 1 July 1994 and will eventually be the only approved form of standard once the older SSAPs have been replaced.

The *New Zealand Companies Act* 1955 was replaced in 1993 by the new *Companies Act* and a *Financial Reporting Act*, both to become fully effective from 1 July 1994. The *Companies Act* provides for an increase to the structure within which corporate management must work, and the *Financial Reporting Act* gives legal backing to approved accounting standards. Together these two Acts mark an important and long overdue tightening up of reporting requirements.

The history of twentieth century Anglo-American accounting developments is expressed in Figures 3.1 and 3.2. Figure 3.1 shows in an idealised manner the way in which alternative forms of disclosure have been gradually removed during the past 100 years. At the beginning of the century accountants and managers had a considerable latitude within which to present information to their limited readership. This latitude has been gradually but consistently eroded, first through the recognition of GAAP, and later through the development of statute laws related to corporations and the formulation of accounting standards. The result is a more highly proscribed profession, although there is still more freedom for professional judgement than exists outside of Anglo-American accounting.

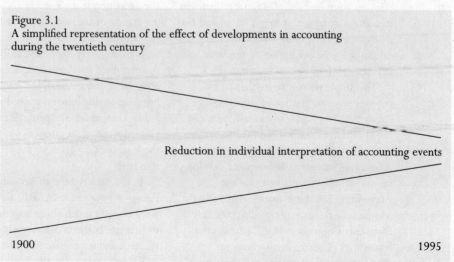

Figure 3.1
A simplified representation of the effect of developments in accounting during the twentieth century

Reduction in individual interpretation of accounting events

1900   1995

The various pressures which impact on modern accounting in finding solutions to new and existing disclosure problems are shown in Figure 3.2. Not only must the accountants acknowledge the influences of GAAP and accounting standards (often with legal backing), but they must also acknowledge the influence of culture, history, the legal system, overseas developments and other factors.

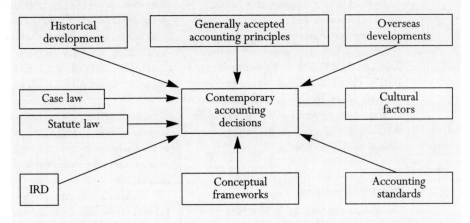

Figure 3.2
Some of the pressures which are exerted on contemporary accounting decisions

Accounting as a social phenomenon

The traditional view

Accounting is a socially constructed activity, as distinct from a discipline such as physics, which sets out to discover information about what actually exists in the world around us. The composition of the discipline changes with the demands of society at any time; thus the record systems used in ancient civilisations were concerned with recording physical flows (assets and liabilities measured in grain for example) and preventing theft, rather than acting to assist in any form of measurement of surpluses or deficiencies. This approach continued until the medieval period when manorial accounting was employed on landed estates which were the main economic forces at that time. Basic double entry bookkeeping was used by merchants, along with various forms of single entry bookkeeping, mainly to record and process entries rather than to determine income or to assist with decision making, because the systems were often used in an incomplete form.

The Industrial Revolution produced conditions which rendered both charge and discharge and merchants' bookkeeping inadequate. The new system had to provide for the depreciation of capital equipment, the use of powered machinery, the concept of overheads and large inventories and mass work forces. Decision making, the pricing of goods and the determination of income and financial position for external owners were now important functions of the accounting system.

The many social changes of the twentieth century have produced conditions necessitating alterations to accounting systems and external reporting. Management accounting has become more advanced to cope with the information needs of management and the making of decisions involves a greater number of variables, including information about the social consequences of the decisions to be made. External reporting has become more complex, reflecting the perceived needs of investors and regulatory agencies to be able to monitor and, if necessary, control the activities of organisational management in the light of changed circumstances.

In all of these examples, changes in social organisation and processes are seen as preceding developments in accounting and reporting, which are consequent on those developments. This is the conventional view and does not make any allowance for the opposite effect, namely that of changes to society which result from developments in the discipline of accounting. The opposite view is now considered.

An alternative view

The theory put forward by Sombart (1924), that the development of double entry bookkeeping was so important that it led to the rise of capitalism, has already been referred to. Sombart's work has been both criticised and supported in the literature, but because the source material is fragmented and incomplete and refers to periods several hundred years ago, the issues are not particularly relevant to present day conditions.

During the past few years a group of radical theorists have challenged accepted views in many areas of accounting using perspectives which are often Marxist, Critical Theorist and Deconstructionist. Examples include the history of accounting (Loft, 1986), the development of the accounting profession (Willmott, 1986), professional ethics (Lehman, 1987), conceptual frameworks and ideology (Tinker, Merino and Neimark, 1982), accounting policy, standards and general aspects of reporting (Merino and Neimark, 1982; Cooper and Sherer, 1984), research methodology (Laughlin, Lowe and Puxty, 1986; Chua,

1986), public interest accounting (Tinker, 1984; 1985) and recent financial events (Puxty, Sikka and Willmott, 1994).

Although the radical perspective has not prevailed in terms of changing the views of management or the accounting profession, which still believes that the traditional relationship prevails, academic thought has been more sympathetic to some degree. It is, therefore, appropriate to note that the basis of the arguments put forward by the radical theorists is in disagreement with the current organisation of Western society. The radicals oppose the capitalist system with its reliance upon the market place which uses marginalist value systems to ensure the profitability of business ventures. They point out that large numbers of people cannot participate in the exchange process through markets because they have neither wealth nor income. The resulting welfare economics of recent capitalism creates hierarchies and status societies which are maintained by those with high status at the expense of low status citizens. The radical perspective maintains that accounting and accountants assist in maintaining the hierarchy because professional groups have vested interests in maintaining inequalities. Their case is interesting and provocative, but most accountants would not accept it as a true picture of the relationship of the discipline with society.

Chapter summary

Twentieth century Anglo-American accounting developments are obviously an important basis for our present and future accounting systems. This chapter has considered these developments under two headings: firstly, the search for accounting principles which occupied much of the first half of the century, and secondly, the development of a more complex institutional framework within which accounting works. A brief reference was made to accounting as a social phenomenon.

The search for accounting principles was

carried out by individuals and accounting organisations (professional and academic). The basic idea was to find out 'what accountants did in practice' and to codify this as accounting theory.

The institutional framework within which accounting is carried out was examined in three periods, 1920–1952, 1953–1969 and 1970 to the present. All three periods have been characterised by a greater degree of structure by the profession, the legislature and standard-setting organisations.

Increased legislation and the requirements of accounting standards have resulted in a much more controlled environment for modern accountants with fewer alternatives available to deal with an increasing number of issues. The involvement of government in standard setting must place increasing pressures on the accounting professions in many countries which have hitherto been able to rely upon internal rule setting and monitoring activities.

The nature of accounting as a social phenomenon is a topical issue at the present time. The conventional view, that accounting is the result of social organisation and associated pressures, is being challenged by critical theorists. They argue that accounting practices can and do affect the society in which we live, in particular by supporting existing hierarchies and power systems. Clearly, this is an issue which will be debated for many years.

Essay and examination questions

3.1   To what extent is accounting moulded by societal developments? Give appropriate examples.

3.2   Discuss the arguments which have been advanced to change the direction of causation between societal development and accounting change.

3.3   Outline the search for accounting principles carried out between 1920 and 1940 in the USA.

3.4   To what extent is the development of modern accounting the history of standard setting? Explain.

3.5   There are similarities between some aspects of accounting as practised in the UK, USA, Australia and New Zealand. Summarise these in respect of professional structure, legislative basis and standard-setting activities.

3.6   Standard setting is too important to be left to accountants! Discuss.

3.7   Compare and contrast the General Scientific Theory period with that of the General Normative Theory period (Henderson and Peirson, 1983).

3.8   Compare and contrast the General Normative Theory period with that of the Specific Scientific Theory period (Henderson and Peirson, 1983).

3.9   To what extent was the 1936 *Tentative Statement of Accounting Principles* a milestone in the history of accounting development? Explain.

3.10   Consider the development of Anglo-American accounting in the twentieth century. To what extent may we project the past and present into the future to predict what the accounting of the future may look like? Give suitable examples.

3.11   Describe some of the pressures which are now brought to bear on contemporary accounting practitioners when they confront an accounting problem for the first time.

3.12   Modern accountants are less professional than were previous generations of accountants. Discuss.

3.13 The current concern with the reduction of choice by accountants is a direct result of social pressure. Discuss.

3.14 Argue the case for (and against) the provision of legal backing for accounting standards.

3.15 The easiest way to solve problems caused by variations in accounting treatment is to legislate for all possible outcomes. Prepare a statement supporting or repudiating this statement.

References and additional reading

American Accounting Association (1936). *Tentative Statement of Accounting Principles*. New York: AAA.

American Accounting Association (1966). *A Statement of Basic Accounting Theory*. Sarasota: AAA.

American Accounting Association (1977). *Statement of Accounting Theory and Theory Acceptance*. Sarasota: AAA.

Chua, W.F. (1986). Theoretical considerations of and by the real. *Accounting, Organizations and Society*, **11**(6), 583–598.

Consultative Committee of Accountancy Bodies (1988). *The Making of Accounting Standards*. Milton Keynes: Chartac.

Cooper, D.J. and Sherer, M.J. (1984). The value of corporate accounting reports: arguments for a political economy of accounting. *Accounting, Organizations and Society*, **9**(3/4), 207–232.

Dearing, R. (1988). *The Making of Accounting Standards*. Milton Keynes: Chartac.

Gilman, S. (1939). *Accounting Concepts of Profit*. New York: Ronald Press.

Goldberg, L. (1949). The development of accounting, in C.T. Gibson, C.G. Meredith and R. Peterson (Eds) (1971). *Accounting Concepts Readings*. Melbourne: Cassell.

Grady, P. (1965). *An Inventory of Generally Accepted Accounting Principles for Business Enterprises*. Accounting Research Study No. 7. New York: AICPA.

Henderson, H.S. and Peirson, C.G. (1983). *Financial Accounting Theory: Its Nature and Development*. Melbourne: Longman Cheshire.

Kohler, E.L. (1953). Recent developments in the formulation of accounting principles. *Accounting Research*, 30–35.

Laughlin, R.C., Lowe, F. A. and Puxty, A.G. (1986). Designing and operating a course in accounting methodology: philosophy, experience and some preliminary empirical tests. *British Accounting Review*, **18**(1), 17–42.

Lehman, C.R. (1987). Accounting ethics: surviving survival of the fittest. *Advances in Public Interest Accounting*.

Loft, A. (1986). Towards a critical understanding of accounting: the case of cost accounting in the UK 1914–1925. *Accounting, Organizations and Society*, **11**(2), 137–169.

Merino, B.D. and Neimark, M.D. (1982). Disclosure regulation and public policy: a sociohistorical appraisal. *Journal of Accounting and Public Policy*, **1**, 33–57.

Moonitz, M. (1961). *The Basic Postulates of Accounting*. Accounting Research Study No. 1. New York: AICPA.

Moonitz, M. (1970). Three contributions to the development of accounting principles prior to 1930. *Journal of Accounting Research*, 145–155.

Paton, W.A. (1922). *Accounting Theory*. Reprinted 1973, Lawrence, Kansas:
   Scholars Book Co.

Paton, W.A. and Littleton, A.C. (1940). *An Introduction to Corporate Accounting
   Standards*. AAA.

Puxty, A., Sikka, P. and Willmott, H. (1994). (Re)forming the circle: education,
   ethics and accountancy practices. *Accounting Education*, **3**(1), 77–92.

Rorem, C.R. (1937). Accounting theory: a critique of the Tentative Statement of
   accounting principles. *The Accounting Review*, 133–138.

Sanders, T.H., Hatfield, H.R. and Moore, U. (1938). *A Statement of Accounting
   Principles*. American Institute of Accountants, reprinted AAA, 1959.

Scott, DR (1937). The Tentative Statement of principles. *The Accounting Review*,
   386–401.

Sombart, W. (1924). *Der Moderne Kapitalismus* (Sixth edition). Munich: Dunker
   and Humblot.

Sprouse, R.T. and Moonitz, M. (1962). *A Tentative Set of Broad Accounting Principles
   for Business Enterprises*. Accounting Research Study No. 3. New York: AICPA.

Tinker, A.M. (Ed.) (1984). *Social Accounting for Corporations*. New York: Marcus
   Weiner.

Tinker, A.M. (1985). *Paper Prophets: A Social Critique of Accounting*. New York:
   Praeger.

Tinker, A.M., Merino, B.D. and Neimark, M.D. (1982). The normative origins of
   positive theories: ideology and accounting thought. *Accounting, Organizations
   and Society*, **7**(2), 167–200.

Willmott, H.C. (1986). Organising the profession: a theoretical and historical
   examination of the development of the major accountancy bodies in the
   UK. *Accounting, Organizations and Society*, **11**(6), 555–580.

Section 2

Accounting theory

Learning objectives

After studying this chapter the reader will be able to:
* define philosophy of science
* explain the various theories of the philosophy of science
* discuss the relevance of the philosophy of science to accounting
* apply the theories of the philosophy of science to accounting
* examine the issues associated with the choice of accounting research methods from a philosophy of science perspective.

Introduction

This chapter contains two main sections. The first deals with the philosophy of science and research methodology. The second covers the application of scientific method and naturalistic research methods to accounting research.

The examination of the philosophy of science covers the main approaches: induction and deduction, falsification, Lakatosian research programmes, Kuhnian paradigms and disciplinary matrices and, finally, Feyerabend's view of research and scientific endeavour. After considering the philosophical bases, the application of these ideas to accounting is examined through selected contributions to the literature.

The second part of the chapter is concerned with accounting research, through the application of scientific method and, in some cases, by the use of what have been termed naturalistic research methods.

Questions about the nature of the workings of our environment, both physical and social, have been answered in radically different ways at different periods in history. Reference to custom and tradition, the classical reference works of past periods, or to the normative statements of 'authorities' were at one time the recognised approaches to finding out the 'what, when, how, why and by whom' of specific situations. This is no longer necessarily the case and, although the literature and accumulated theory about

particular circumstances are obviously an important and necessary part of research, there is also another most important dimension, that of examining the real world. This is known as empirical research. In order that we should understand empirical and other research methods and their application to the accounting discipline, it is necessary that we consider a number of philosophical bases which underlie the scientific research method.

The basic objectives addressed in this chapter are: to understand the basic concepts and arguments involved in a study of the philosophy of science; to understand what is meant by 'scientific method'; and to develop some knowledge of attempts which have been made to apply the philosophy of science and scientific methods to accounting.

Inductivism and falsificationism

Inductivism

Scientific method is based upon some variant of induction. The most simplified form of the inductivist philosophy is that based on naive inductivism (Chalmers, 1982, p.2) which bases all scientific reasoning upon observation. Observation, it is argued, enables the observer to produce singular statements which, by a process of generalisation, lead to the production of universal statements, which may be elevated to theories and laws after a large number of similar observations. There are a number of conditions which must be applied to the observations. These are that the number of observations must be large, repeated under a wide variety of conditions and that no observation is made which conflicts with any law derived from previous observations of the same phenomena. Thus, science is based upon the principle of induction which states that: 'If a large number of A's have been observed under a wide variety of conditions, and if all those observed A's without exception possessed the property B, then all A's have the property B' (Chalmers, 1982, p.5).

The naive inductivist bases the development of science upon the aggregation of observed data into laws and theories. However, the more sophisticated inductivist recognises the need to offer theories which go further than combining the results of observations; theories need to be able to predict or explain features of the environment. The discipline of logic is required to progress from observation based theories to the prediction or explanation of phenomena. Logical deduction is based upon the if . . . then progressive from premises to logical deduction. Figure 4.1 provides a simple representation.

Figure 4.1
The route from observation to explanation

The validity of the conclusion depends upon the premises, since it is possible to derive logically sound conclusions which are false because the premise is incorrect. The truth of the deduction is, therefore, separate from its validity because of the if . . . then relationship: 'Deductive logic alone . . . does not act as a source of true statements about the world. Deduction is concerned with the derivation of statements from other given statements' (Chalmers, 1982, p.7).

Naive inductivism claims to be the basis of science because observation and inductive reasoning are objective and the result will be objective laws and theories.

There are a number of difficulties associated with the employment of observation as the basis of scientific method and the development of scientific knowledge. To begin with, how can the principle of induction be justified? Chalmers suggests that this can

only be done by an appeal to logic or to experience.

The appeal to logic is based on the inductive–deductive principle that a secure foundation can be built by multiple and varied observations leading from singular observations to universal statements. Unfortunately, this is not always valid since only one contrary observation is needed to destroy the theories which have been established by prior observations. It is quite possible to have an inductive inference with true premises which leads to a false conclusion.

If an individual researcher (who was a naive inductivist) wanted to determine on which side of the road New Zealanders drive, a large number of observations might be made on all types of road throughout the length and breadth of the land, and finally it might be concluded that in New Zealand everybody drives on the left. However, if we encountered a US visitor on a country road, who had not seen another vehicle for twenty miles and had suffered a lapse of concentration, we might be painfully reminded of the breakdown in our logic of moving from the specific to the general!

A further attempt to justify inductivism can be made by an appeal to experience. In other words, the principle of induction worked in attempts 1, 2, 3 and therefore we may conclude that the principle of induction always works. This is, of course, using the principle of induction to justify itself, and is therefore invalid because of the circular reasoning it contains: 'A universal statement asserting the validity of the principle is here inferred from a number of singular statements recording past successful applications of the principle' (Chalmers, 1982, p.15).

There are also problems in determining the number of observations and the circumstances under which they take place. In other words, how does the researcher decide how many observations are to be made and what are the relevant variables? These questions are answered by referring to some theoretical basis or knowledge about the situation. Theory is, therefore, playing a role prior to observation and this is a criticism of naive inductivism, which attempts to use only observation.

More sophisticated inductivists seek to avoid some of the above criticism by using concepts of probability in discussing the induction–deduction process. The probability of being able to predict or explain phenomena on the basis of observation will be increased by increasing the number of observations, as well as the variety of conditions under which they are made.

The modified principle of induction leads to the following position in respect of universal statements: 'on the basis of a finite number of successes . . . all applications of the principle will lead to general conclusions that are probably true' (Chalmers, 1982, p.17).

Any universal statements which are based upon a finite number of observations must tend towards a zero probability of success, regardless of the number of observations. The response to this problem has been to avoid generalised predictions and to concentrate instead on the probability of individual predictions being correct. This tends to lead to fragmentation of the field and a reduction in the production of generalised knowledge. Furthermore, the observation is associated with the development of theories of a specific and not a generalised nature.

One of the main objections to induction as a basis of science is the theory dependent nature of observation. Observation statements presuppose some level of theory, even if it is at quite a low level. Furthermore, although two observers may have the same visual images, they do not have the same perceptual experiences.

Induction argues that science starts with observation and that observation yields a secure basis from which knowledge can be derived. In practice, however, we need some form of theoretical basis in order to know what to observe and thus to derive an appropriate mechanism for carrying out observation. This problem has been expressed by Chalmers (1982) as follows:

> In everyday language, it is often the case that an apparently unproblematic 'observation statement' is found to be false when an expectation is disappointed, due to the falsity of some theory presupposed in the assertion of the observation statement. (p.31)

The other way in which observation is theory dependent is related to the manner in which the observer interprets what is 'seen' or observed by his or her faculties. There are many factors which intervene in the process of 'seeing' something. These can be physical, such as colour blindness or an inability to hear certain frequencies, which will clearly affect observers' reactions to the stimuli of sound and colour. There are also non-physical factors such as culture, prior experience, education and training which will affect the interpretation placed upon some physical stimuli. An annual report will be physically the same whether examined by a qualified accountant or a relatively naive shareholder and yet the amount of information and knowledge gained from reading it will be quite different. To this must be added the human failings of attempting to justify preconceived notions or previously stated positions; conditions which are often found in practice.

The inductivist position cannot be supported, because science does not begin with observation statements since theory precedes them. Furthermore, observation statements do not always provide a firm basis for scientific knowledge because they are fallible. Attempts to rectify this situation have produced what is called falsificationism.

Falsificationism

Falsificationism is based upon a different view of the process of theory derivation from that of the naive inductivist. To begin with, observation is guided by the presupposed theory. Second, falsificationists make no claim that the theories that they develop are true or probably true because theories are constructed to deal with deficiencies in previous theories or to account for aspects of the behaviour of the world or universe. Speculative theories have to be thoroughly tested by observation and if they fail the process will be repeated, leading to the production of new theories. Science progresses by trial and error and only a few theories will survive; even these will be regarded by falsificationists as not true, but better than those which they have replaced.

There is logical support for the falsificationist position because, while we have seen that there are problems in trying to move from observation statements to universal laws, the falsity of universal statements can be deduced from suitable singular statements.

The quality of falsifiability is central to the philosophy of the falsificationist. Science is the development of hypotheses to describe or account for behaviour. These must be falsifiable if they are to contribute to knowledge by becoming theories or laws. The quality of falsifiability is essential because it is only by eliminating sets of logically possible observation statements that better laws and theories may be constructed in their turn. Clearly, the more falsifiable the hypothesis the better (given that this is an important quality) and what are termed bold precise hypotheses are more useful because, if they cannot be falsified, considerable advances are possible and precise hypotheses are more easily falsified than those that are imprecise.

In the falsificationist view of science we start with a problem, to which a falsifiable hypothesis is presented as offering a possible solution. The hypothesis is criticised and tested and attempts are made to eliminate it by falsification. If the hypothesis cannot be falsified immediately, further attempts will be made using more stringent tests. If the hypothesis continues to resist falsification it may be regarded more highly and the results incorporated into laws and theories, but these are never regarded as true, only as not untrue up to that point.

Theories which have not been falsified are said to be confirmed. Significant advances come from the confirmation of bold conjectures and the falsification of cautious conjectures and much less is learnt from the falsification of a bold conjecture or the confirmation of a cautious conjecture. The boldness or otherwise of the conjecture must be seen against the background of the general knowledge in the specific area under investigation.

Although many would argue that the falsificationist view of science is superior to that of the inductivists, there are limitations to falsificationism. In particular, falsificationism may be criticised for relying on observation which leads to the theory dependence of observation and the fallibility of falsifications of hypotheses. The theory dependence of observation is the basis of falsification since: 'If true observation statements are given, *then* it is possible to logically deduce from them the falsity of some universal statements, whereas it is not possible to deduce . . . the truth of any universal statement' (Chalmers, 1982, p.60).

Note the importance of the observation statements which were shown to be problematic in relation to inductivism. It is possible that faulty observation statements may lead to premature falsification of a theory: 'However securely based on observation a statement may seem to be, the possibility that new theoretical advances will reveal inadequacies in that statement cannot be ruled out. Consequently, straightforward, conclusive falsifications of theories are not achievable' (Chalmers, 1982, p.61).

Other difficulties in making falsificationism operational arise from the complexity of realistic test situations and the problems which may result from premature rejection of theories. Many modern test situations are complex, involving interconnected premises. If the prediction of events under a particular theory was inaccurate, it is difficult to tell whether the fault lay with the theory or with some other part of a complex test situation. Chalmers (1982, pp.66–75) challenges falsificationism on historical grounds and shows that in some instances the falsification of theories (had this been accepted) would have been detrimental to the progress of science.

Research programmes and paradigms

The work of Lakatos (1974) and Kuhn (1970) has been directed at the explication of theories as structured wholes. This is necessary because inductivist and falsificationist ideas do not take into account the complexity of real life research. Chalmers (1982, p.79) suggests that there are three

reasons why theories must be seen as structured wholes: first, historical study shows this to be the case; second, concepts need a coherently structured theory to give them a precise meaning; and, finally, there is a need for science to grow. Science must have signposts to follow and open ended structures to provide for research programmes.

Research programmes

This view has been propagated by Lakatos who suggests that a research programme is made up of three components: the negative heuristic, the protective belt and the positive heuristic.

The negative heuristic is made up of a hard core of basic assumptions which underlie the programme. These provide the defining characteristics and cannot be rejected or modified by workers within the area. If an individual researcher could no longer accept the negative heuristic he or she would have to leave that particular research programme.

The protective belt is made up of auxiliary hypotheses which may be tested, rejected and replaced without damaging the negative heuristics of the programme. This concept has also been referred to as a maze of assumptions.

The positive heuristic provides rough guidelines on how the programme might be developed and the direction which that development might take. Research programmes are either progressive or degenerating, leading or failing to lead somewhere. Degenerating programmes cannot be changed by modifying the hard core since that would be to opt out of that research programme. If a researcher accepts the hard core, he or she is deciding to work within a particular research programme, regardless of how progressive or degenerative the programme may be. The research programme is directed by the positive heuristic in order to supplement the hard core and aid in the explanation and prediction of real phenomena by the theory.

The Lakatosian research programme aims at the confirmation and not the falsification of theories. To be recognised as meritorious, a research programme must have coherence and lead to the discovery of novel phenomena from time to time. Modifications to theories are acceptable, provided that they are independently testable; those additions and modifications which are not independently testable or which are not compatible with the hard core (negative heuristic) are not acceptable.

The theory dependence and cultural effects of observation which cause problems for the inductivist and falsificationist approaches are dealt with as follows: 'The bearing of observation on an hypothesis under test is relatively unproblematic within a research programme because the hard core and the positive heuristic serve to define a fairly stable observation language' (Chalmers, 1982, p.85).

Paradigms

In contrast to Lakatos, whose research programmes may coexist within particular disciplines, the paradigmatic approach offered by Kuhn requires all practising researchers to subscribe to one theoretical structure at a time.

The Kuhnian view has been introduced into many fields including accounting, and this feature is discussed in a later section. Like Lakatos, Kuhn developed his theory after a study of the history of science. His theory is characterised by its revolutionary nature through which one theoretical structure is replaced in its entirety by another, and by its acknowledgement of the sociological nature of scientific communities.

According to Kuhn (1970), science progresses by a series of revolutions as illustrated by Figure 4.2.

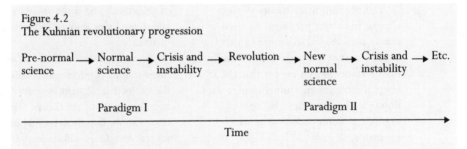

Figure 4.2
The Kuhnian revolutionary progression

Pre-normal science → Normal science → Crisis and instability → Revolution → New normal science → Crisis and instability → Etc.

Paradigm I   Paradigm II

Time

The progression is thus through pre-science, normal science, crisis, revolution and then new normal science. The paradigm is adhered to by the scientific community, which accepts the general theoretical assumptions, laws and techniques which constitute 'normal' science. In a mature science there is a single paradigm which directs research and separates science from non-science. Normal science requires explicitly stated laws, theoretical assumptions, standard ways of applying the fundamental laws, very general metaphysical principles and very general methodological principles.

The normal scientist is uncritical of the paradigm, just as researchers in a particular research programme accept the negative heuristic. The minor changes which are necessary to deal with anomalies as they are discovered are not seen as a rejection or falsification of the paradigm because: 'normal science involves detailed attempts to articulate a paradigm with the aim of improving the match between it and nature. A paradigm will always be sufficiently imprecise and open ended to leave plenty of that kind of work to be done' (Chalmers, 1982, p.91).

The discovery of anomalies, where the extant theory fails to explain or predict specific conditions in the environment, need not produce a crisis. However, crises and later revolution and paradigm shift will be more likely to occur if: an anomaly strikes at the fundamentals of the paradigm, is resistant to eradication as the result of further research, is serious in the context of social needs, is accompanied by other anomalies or where one or more anomalies exist for an extended period. When anomalies have these characteristics a period of 'pronounced professional insecurity' may follow. If this condition continues for long the paradigm may be replaced by a new paradigm which is accepted by the entire scientific community and a new normal science is born. The normal science concept, it is argued, provides the conditions under which scientists can work on the details of a theory undisturbed by major conflict.

The revolutionary nature of the change from one paradigm to another is partly sociological in nature in that the change cannot be explained rationally. Furthermore, Kuhn argues that the whole scientific community must change paradigms at the same time because paradigms are incompatible or mutually exclusive.

In a later work Kuhn drops 'paradigm' in favour of the concept of a 'disciplinary matrix' which contains four elements. These are: symbolic generalisations common to the discipline; shared commitments which help in determining the acceptance or otherwise of research results; shared values between researchers, and exemplars of how to seek solutions to problems. The basic idea of the Kuhnian revolutionary progression of science is not dependent on the use of paradigm or disciplinary matrix, although the latter is referred to in the literature which attempts to apply the Kuhnian position to accounting.

Anarchic theory of knowledge: Feyerabend

Feyerabend (1975) claims that none of the methodologies discussed above have been successful. The basis of his position appears to be that methodologies which produce rules for the guidance of scientists, in terms of their choices and decisions, are incorrect or inappropriate. The research programme concept put forward by Lakatos is acceptable to Feyerabend because it does not provide rules for the choice of programme by individual researchers, although they are still subject to societal pressures and influences. However, the Kuhnian paradigmatic or disciplinary matrix model does require all participants to subscribe to the normal science if they wish to research at all. Chalmers (1982, p.136) notes that: 'Feyerabend successfully argues against method insofar as he has shown that it is not advisable for the choices and decisions of scientists to be constrained by the rules laid down by or implicit in methodologies of science'.

Feyerabend uses a device called incommensurability to demonstrate his view of the subjective element in science, particularly in respect of the theory dependence of observation. Two theories may have fundamental principles which are so incompatible that they cannot be compared or related to each other, excepting through their compatibility as observed in specific situations. These theories are incommensurable and their existence demonstrates the existence of a subjective element in scientific research, which is projected as being an objective discipline.

Feyerabend goes further in his criticism of scientific methodology by arguing that scientific knowledge is not superior to other forms of knowledge. Furthermore, he argues that the institutionalisation of scientific research in our society is incompatible with a humanitarian attitude and the freedom of the individual.

The last point is strongly contested by Chalmers (1982) in the following manner:

> Feyerabend's subsequent talk of freedom of the individual fails to give adequate attention to the constraints operating in society. Just as a scientist hoping to make a contribution to science is faced with an objective situation, so an individual hoping to improve society is faced with an objective social situation. (p.144)

There seems to be no doubt that researchers are subject to subtle pressures to conform to prevailing fashions in subject choice and the research method to be employed. The Kuhnian revolutionary theory became extremely popular as an explanation for many phenomena, including accounting, as discussed in the next section.

The application of the philosophy of science to accounting

The Kuhnian view

Wells (1976) and the AAA *Statement of Accounting Theory and Theory Acceptance* (SATTA; AAA, 1977) have both adopted, in part or in whole, the Kuhnian view of the progression of science and attempted to apply this to accounting. Their approach has been criticised and some of the literature (Peasnell, 1978; Laughlin, 1981) is reviewed in this section.

Wells (1976) explains the period of normative theorising in accounting research as a part of the Kuhnian crisis pattern which could be followed by a change in normal science (a paradigm shift). In particular he was referring to the debate about accounting during periods of price changes. He accepts the modified Kuhnian view (1970) using the disciplinary matrix which consists of four parts: symbolic generalisations; shared commitments; values; and exemplars, which are explained in the following way. The symbolic generalisations include

accepted notions such as double entry, concepts of income, ratios and classifications. Shared commitments include the realisation and matching principles, going concern and the basis of asset valuation. Shared values include conservatism, consistency, materiality and other similar positions. Exemplars include textbooks and expositions in current use.

Wells (1976) uses the problems of modern accounting to illustrate a possible crisis position and the various *ad hoc* solutions being applied at that time. The article highlights continuing problems and argues that a new paradigm or disciplinary matrix is needed. He concludes that a number of schools of thought had developed (such as CPP, CCA, CoCoA) and that given sufficient time one of these would emerge as the new normal science.

The AAA (1977) also takes a Kuhnian perspective in the discussion of accounting theory. The committee subscribes to the view that the accounting discipline was passing through a period in which different paradigms or schools of thought were engaging in paradigm wars. The AAA (1977) notes three approaches to accounting theory — classical, decision usefulness and information economics. The report discusses the testing of competing paradigms and the judgemental process involved in selecting a new paradigm and notes that:

> defenders of a particular paradigm are forced to rely on persuasion rather than logic and empirics in attempting to defend a proposal. While consensus may eventually develop, the transformation that occurs is primarily a psychological matter rather than a dispassionately intellectual phenomenon. (AAA, 1977, p.48)

This condition, they argue, has implications for policy in that until there is a consensus the degree of acceptance shown towards policies and standards will always be partial.

Peasnell (1978) examines both Wells (1976) and AAA (1977) and concludes that both are too readily influenced by Kuhn (1970). His main arguments are that the existence of a variety of theoretical approaches does not mean that there is a multiplicity of competing paradigms that in turn implies a Kuhnian condition of professional insecurity and impending crisis or revolution.

Furthermore, Peasnell does not believe that Kuhn's ideas can necessarily be applied to accounting. Kuhn was basing his theory on physics and perhaps the other natural sciences. There is no evidence to show that Kuhn argued for any widespread extension to the social sciences. In particular, psychology might (or might not) be included; therefore, asks Peasnell:

> Is the committee seriously suggesting that accounting has developed to the point where it is . . . a science when there remains doubt . . . that some other social science disciplines . . . have yet reached this stage of development? (Peasnell, 1978, p.219)

Peasnell concludes that SATTA and Wells have adopted a fashionable Kuhnian approach and attempted to fit developments in accounting theory to the crisis or revolution stage of the Kuhnian framework. Neither work has established that accounting is a science or, if it is, that it has passed the pre-science stage of confusion. Peasnell also argues that in developing the report the SATTA authors had manipulated the schools of accounting to provide categories which fitted the arguments being employed.

Laughlin (1981) notes that both the committee on theory acceptance (AAA, 1977) and Wells (1976) use a Kuhnian framework. His paper argues that the Kuhnian paradigmatic/disciplinary matrix normal science model does not fit the discipline of accounting, and that a different methodology is needed. The Kuhnian model includes the acceptance of a para-

digm, working within the paradigm conducting normal science, becoming dissatisfied with the paradigm and searching for a new one. The AAA (1977) and Wells (1976) imply that the third and fourth stages have been reached, but Laughlin (1981) argues that the first stage may not have been reached if a tighter definition is employed.

The existence of multiple paradigms, as argued by Wells (1976) and the AAA (1977), means either a state of pre-science or revolution within the Kuhnian theory. If a state of revolution exists then we should be able to observe a period of normal science as having existed for some time. Laughlin argues that this has not been the case. The lack of a normal science condition in presenting accounting is further illustrated by the absence of some of the conditions of normal science. Normal science takes the practice of the field and uses it to make good predictions. However, present practice in accounting is more concerned with 'accountability' and 'accurate reporting of facts' than it is with predictions. The use of accounting ratios to predict corporate failure might be an appropriate use of normal science within the paradigm. However, the ratios produced do not actually predict failure; this is done by the individual analyst and this process is outside the paradigm and normal science. Consequently, accounting does not exhibit the characteristics of normal science. Laughlin suggests that the authors of articles and reports which used a Kuhnian model did so because it was easier to fit historical developments to this, than to the work of Lakatos or Popper.

Using Feyerabend

Laughlin (1981) does not favour the use of the Kuhnian approach for the reasons outlined. In addition, Laughlin favours a more flexible and less compulsory approach to research. He quotes Feyerabend on attempts to turn disciplines into sciences:

The recipe according to these people is to restrict criticism, to reduce the comprehensive theories to one and to create a normal science that has only one theory as its paradigm. (Feyerabend, 1970 quoted by Laughlin, 1981, p.338)

Laughlin goes on to argue that social science models may be more appropriate than the natural sciences. Three points are made, after Feyerabend, that science is anything which tries to discover knowledge, the aims of the discipline need to be clearly defined and the methodology employed should be geared to a purpose. Accounting does not have to follow a stereotype of natural science:

Feyerabend's ideas allow the discipline of accounting to be entirely liberated from the methodological stereotypes from the natural or social sciences — it is free to design its own or borrow appropriate methodology depending on what the discipline is trying to achieve. (Laughlin, 1981, p.340)

Scientific method and the naturalistic research method

Scientific method

This chapter has outlined various philosophical approaches to science such as: induction, deduction, and falsification; and theories about the way in which research progresses, including those put forward by Lakatos, Kuhn and Feyerabend, who challenge the need for prescriptive approaches. These philosophies and theories underlie the accepted approach to empirical research which is often called the scientific method. Accounting researchers since about 1970 have rejected normative theorising and descriptive studies and in large measure have practised empirical research of the following type.

1
Theories are formulated in terms of the relationships between categories and based on a review of the existing academic literature.

2
The theory is used to establish a research problem.

3
The problem is resolved into hypotheses and the dependent and independent variables are identified.

4
Precise and highly structured predetermined procedures for data collection are established. The data collected are usually in quantitative form.

5
The data are subjected to mathematical or statistical analysis leading to an almost exclusively quantitative evaluation of the hypotheses being tested. (Adapted from Tomkins and Groves, 1983, p.361.)

There is no doubt that in many instances empirical research, performed under strict conditions of scientific method, can be productive and make useful additions to our knowledge about accounting and its effect on the environment. However, there are a number of assumptions which appear to be present when this type of research is being undertaken. These are, first, that the social world, like the physical world, can be frozen into a structured immobility such that an objective form of measurement can be carried out. Second, that, if necessary in the interests of the research, human beings can be subjected to deterministic and controllable external forces. Third, by examining lawful relations between the elements abstracted from their context, social scientists can reveal the nature of the world. This approach ignores uniqueness, instability, sensitivity, lack of realism and epistemological differences (Ng, 1984).

A final assumption that underlies the application of scientific method to some accounting problems is that by so doing the researcher becomes a scientist and the discipline is recognised as a science!

Naturalistic research method

Tomkins and Groves (1983) have noted the current overwhelming preference for empirical research using scientific method. They argue that some use could be made of naturalistic research methods such as are used in the social sciences, particularly in psychology, sociology and education.

In order to demonstrate the range of possible research areas, some of which could be accessed by naturalistic research methods, they have employed a six-part ontological framework which is outlined below together with their brief suggestions of where these ideas fit into accounting research.

1
Reality as a concrete structure; this is the basis for the scientific method.

2
Reality as a concrete process; the first stage in moving away from the strict application of scientific method; open systems theory. The effect of accounting reports on different parts of the organisation might be a suitable research topic within the naturalistic approach.

3
Reality as a contextual field of information process; cybernetics, the relationship between the behaviour of parts of the organisation and external stimuli might be an appropriate area for naturalistic research.

4
Reality as a symbolic discourse; symbolic interactionism, an example of naturalistic research applied to accounting in this area might be the perceptions of individuals at different levels within the organisation towards the financial control system.

5
Reality as social construction; existential phenomenology and ethnomethodology. This area is concerned with attempts to explain the behaviour of individuals.

6
Reality as a projection of human imagination; existentialism; transcendental phenomenology.

Accounting researchers have not responded to the availability of naturalistic research methods. The major outlets for research work, university departments and refereed journals, have not shown much interest in alternative approaches to the now established scientific method in the accounting field. Nevertheless, some of the ideas suggested by Tomkins and Groves (1983) are of interest and deserve to be pursued.

Chapter summary

This chapter was concerned with a review of the philosophy of science and a brief introduction to scientific method and naturalistic research methods.

The philosophy of science was examined by considering inductivism and falsificationism, two approaches which have provided the impetus towards our present scientific methods but which, in their elementary forms, have significant logical and practical problems. In particular, the problem of obtaining value free observations appears to be very significant.

The structured approach to science as exemplified by the work of Kuhn and Lakatos was next considered. The Kuhnian theory in particular has attracted some attention in the accounting literature and this was examined and criticised as being perhaps opportunistic.

The radical views of Feyerabend were briefly mentioned. The accounting literature contains some attempts to apply this approach to accounting but on the whole this has not been successful.

In the last part of the chapter the scientific method was clearly stated together with the alternative naturalistic research method put forward by Tomkins and Groves (1983). Some of the assumptions underlying the scientific method were stated and these should always be borne in mind when conducting or considering accounting research which has been carried out in this way.

Essay and examination questions

4.1   Discuss the arguments which may be used in favour of empirical research in accounting.

4.2   Argue the case for retaining a strong normative tradition in accounting research.

4.3   Explain the logical problems which Chalmers suggests are fatal to inductivism as a basis for science.

4.4   Explain the basic assumptions and tenets of falsification.

4.5   Compare and contrast the theories of scientific development put forward by Lakatos and Kuhn.

4.6   For several years the Kuhnian theory of scientific revolutions was applied to accounting. Review the arguments employed both for and against this position.

4.7   Why is Feyerabend concerned about the way in which science progresses and the structures employed to aid progression?

4.8   What is meant by 'scientific method'? Give a number of accounting examples from different areas.

4.9   What do Tomkins and Groves (1983) mean by naturalistic research methods? To what extent can their ideas be applied to accounting research?

4.10 Accounting is (or is not) a science. Discuss with reference to the literature on the philosophy of science, scientific method and accounting.

4.11 Why should accounting students (and accounting practitioners) be concerned with research into accounting problems?

4.12 If accounting is socially constructed (or socially constructing) the resources devoted to research into accounting problems are misapplied. Discuss.

4.13 Accounting processes are more an art form than a scientific activity. Discuss.

4.14 The development of an institutional structure to control the practice of accounting (see Chapter 3) makes the application of research methods in accounting superfluous. Discuss.

4.15 Argue the case for accounting research taking a Lakatosian rather than a Kuhnian form.

References and additional reading

American Accounting Association (1977). *Statement of Accounting Theory and Theory Acceptance*. Sarasota: AAA.

Chalmers, A.F. (1982). *What is This Thing called Science?* Brisbane: University of Queensland Press.

Chua, F.C. (1988). *Lakatos' Methodology of Research Programmes and Its Applicability to Accounting*. Discussion Paper No. 76. Palmerston North: Massey University, Department of Accountancy.

Feyerabend, P. (1975). *Against Method: Outline of An Anarchic Theory of Knowledge*. London: New Left Books.

Henderson, S. and Peirson, C.G. (1983). *Financial Accounting Theory: Its Nature and Development*. Melbourne: Longman Cheshire.

Kelly, M. (1988). *Tomkins and Groves Revisited*. Discussion Paper No. 75. Palmerston North: Massey University, Department of Accountancy.

Kuhn, T. (1970). *The Structure of Scientific Revolutions*. Chicago: Chicago University Press.

Lakatos, I. (1974). Falsification and the methodology of scientific research programmes, in I. Lakatos and A. Musgrove (Eds). *Criticism and the Growth of Knowledge*. Cambridge: Cambridge University Press.

Laughlin, R.C. (1981). On the nature of accounting methodology. *Journal of Business Finance and Accounting*, **8**(3), 329–351.

Ng, L.W. (1984). *The 'Interpretive Humanistic' Approach to Social Science and Accounting Research*. Discussion Paper No. 28. Palmerston North: Massey University, Department of Accounting and Finance.

Peasnell, K.V. (1978). Statement of accounting theory and theory acceptance: A review article. *Accounting and Business Research*, **31**, 217–225.

Popper, K.R. (1968). *The Logic of Scientific Discovery*. London: Hutchinson.

Selvaratnam, A.M. (1985). *A Critical Evaluation of Feyerabend's Anarchic Theory of Knowledge and Its Applicability to Accounting Theory and Research*. Discussion Paper No. 39. Palmerston North: Massey University, Department of Accounting and Finance.

Tilley, I. (1972). Accounting as a scientific endeavour: Some questions the American theorists tend to leave unanswered. *Accounting and Business Research*, **1–2**, 287–297.

Tomkins, C. and Groves, R.E.V. (1983). The everyday accountant and researching his reality. *Accounting, Organizations and Society*, **8**(4), 361–374.

Van der Linden, Y.P. (1986). A *Consideration of the Applicability of the Kuhnian Philosophy of Science to the Development of Accounting Thought*. Discussion Paper No. 46. Palmerston North: Massey University, Department of Accounting and Finance.

Wells, M.C. (1976). A revolution in accounting thought. *The Accounting Review*, **51**, 471–482.

Young, C.B. (1985). *Rationalism and Relativism in Accounting Research*. Discussion Paper No. 38. Palmerston North: Massey University, Department of Accounting and Finance.

Learning objectives

After studying this chapter the reader will be able to:
- explain the main characteristics of a theory
- discuss the nature of accounting theories
- examine the different approaches to the construction of an accounting theory
- consider the issues of theory verification in accounting
- describe the relationship between accounting theory and practice
- comment on the underlying assumptions of normative and positive accounting theories.

Introduction

It has long been asserted that accounting, being practice-oriented, is conditioned by the demands of practical circumstances. While this is true to a certain extent, such conditioning has left a legacy of conflicting rules. One could argue that it would be unrealistic to assert that the rules chosen lacked a theoretical base, because every one of the wide range of alternative accounting practices implies a particular theory or a way of looking at the circumstances which stimulated its invention. The actual state of accounting, therefore, is not that it has no theories, but that it has a vast number of implicit or partial theories which are not necessarily consistent with each other. As a result, accounting lacks a coherent theory by reference to which established, new and proposed practices may be appraised.

In this chapter the nature of accounting theory, and the processes of accounting theory construction and verification, will be discussed.

Accounting theory and practice

There is a definite link between accounting theory and accounting practice, in the sense that accounting theory construction stems from the need to provide a rationale for what accountants do or expect to be doing. In other words, changes in the principles

occur mainly as a result of the various attempts to provide solutions to emerging accounting problems and to formulate a theoretical framework for the discipline (Belkaoui, 1993, p.9). The application of theory can have very real practical implications. For example, a decision to use a particular accounting method of recognising revenue, made on theoretical grounds, may affect the lives of certain interested parties. The relationship between accounting theory and accounting practice is clearly explained thus:

> Theory is about practice. If we are informed about our subject, we can hardly be content with its frequent deficiencies, its incapacity to stand up to the canons of scientific method. If we are applying a method which lacks obvious inconsistencies, our practice will be the more confident, our conclusions more informed, our services to our management or to our clients more valuable. (Chambers, 1950, p.351)

Theory construction

A theory is defined as 'a set of interrelated constructs (concepts), definitions and propositions that present a systematic view of phenomena by specifying relations among variables with the purpose of explaining and predicting the phenomena' (Kerlinger, 1964, p.11). According to

Chambers (1972), 'a theory is a well-ordered set of statements about classes of things and classes of events which are in some way connected in our experience of them' (p.138). The function of accounting theory is explained thus:

> The function of a theory is to explain how things and events are connected . . . Every theory of a method of accounting should be an explanation of the way in which certain symbols, which singly or together correspond with some actual events and results, can be used by managers and others to draw conclusions about the past or make calculations and estimates about the future courses of action they can take. The loose discussion of separate ideas does not constitute 'theory', to describe what 'cost', 'revenue', 'going concern', and other terms mean is not theory, it is simply definition. But definition is useless unless what each term means corresponds with some event or circumstance in the domain of events. (p.150)

Hendriksen and Van Breda (1992) define accounting theory as 'a coherent set of hypothetical, conceptual, and pragmatic principles forming a general frame of reference for inquiring into the nature of accounting'. The main objective of accounting theory, given this definition, is to provide a coherent set of logically derived principles that serve as a frame of reference for evaluating and developing accounting practice.

Accounting theory is also defined as those substantive propositions that relate accounting measurements to decision models and decision making (Sterling, 1970b). Based on this view, two broad areas having operational and confirmable significance for accounting researchers may be identified: (a) the predictive power of accounting measurements; and (b) the behavioural implications of accounting measurements. In general, the main function of an accounting theory is to provide a framework for the development of new ideas and to help the process of accounting choice.

The following have been identified as the main characteristics of a theory:
- composed of a body of knowledge
- internally consistent
- explains and/or predicts phenomena
- represents the ideal
- ideal reference to guide practice
- addresses problems and provides solutions.

The process of theory construction and verification has, for many years, been the subject of examination by researchers interested in the philosophy of science. Only recently has it become a topic for research and discussion in accounting. This interest has manifested itself in various forms, ranging from statements seeking to identify the relationship between accounting theory and accounting practice to more abstract statements concerning metaphysical and philosophical issues.

A fundamental requirement of theory construction is that it must come to terms with the conditions of knowledge. The study of knowledge is the domain of epistemology, which is concerned with the nature and derivation of knowledge, the scope of knowledge and the reliability of claims to knowledge. In other words, epistemology purports to address the questions such as, 'How do we know what we know?', 'How do we distinguish knowledge from opinion or faith?', 'How do we recognise truth from falsehood?' and so on. There are two main epistemological theories: empiricism and rationalism. While empiricists claim that all our ideas are derived from experience, rationalists argue that we do have knowledge which is independent of experience, such as the principles of logic or truths of mathematics.

A theory is a set of coherent propositions or statements. A proposition is an indicative sentence which has a truth value (true, false, probably true and so on).

Depending on the nature of the evidence required to establish their truth value, propositions can be categorised into two groups: *a priori* and *a posteriori*. *A priori* propositions are statements whose truth value can be known by pure reason or by analysing the meaning of the words used, for example, '2 + 2 = 4' or 'a triangle has three sides'. These are also known as analytic propositions and are used as the basis for constructing theories in analytical sciences such as mathematics and logic (Carnap, 1966, p.266). *A posteriori* propositions are statements whose truth value can be determined only after facts or by virtue of the way the world is, for example, 'a red light indicates "stop"' or 'John is a bachelor'. The truth value of these statements cannot be established on the basis of the meaning given to the words used and needs further checking with the facts. These are also known as synthetic or empirical propositions and are used as the basis in constructing theories in empirical sciences such as physics and accounting.

Theories as language systems

A theory is expressed in words and signs. The study of signs is known as semiology in the philosophy of science literature. Semiology is divided into three parts: syntactics, semantics and pragmatics. Syntactics is the study of grammar or the relationship of signs to signs. The main question of interest here is 'Are the words and signs used logically consistent?' Semantics is the study of meaning or relationship of signs to objects and events. The main question of interest here is 'What does each of the words and signs mean?' Pragmatics is the study of the actual purpose and effects of statements or applications of the actual use. The main question of interest here is 'What will be the effect of these words and signs on readers?' (Hendriksen, 1982, p.14). It is important to note that by themselves propositions in the syntactical part have no empirical content.

It is possible, of course, to define a particular sign by showing how it relates to other signs, but it is impossible to define all signs in this way. The definition of a sign by reference to other signs is an internal definition and it lacks empirical meaning. Caws (1965) explains this as follows:

> Definitions of terms by reference to other terms belonging to the same language system (for example, the language of physics) are internal definitions, and one might, by using this kind of definition . . . build a whole ingrown language whose terms referred to each other but to nothing else. Definitions which go outside the language system to something else — perception, for instance, are external definitions, and they are required if the whole system is to mean anything. (p.46)

As stated above, for a language system to have an empirical meaning, the terms used must be defined by reference to objects and events outside the system.

Given the semantic rules for linking signs to objects or events and the syntactical rules for linking signs to signs, propositions with empirical content can be formed. In contrast to the analytic propositions discussed above, these empirical propositions are intended to say something about the real world and therefore their truth value is contingent upon observation.

The above discussion suggests that sciences may be classified as empirical or non-empirical. Examples of the latter are logic and mathematics. These sciences are composed exclusively of analytic propositions and, therefore, do not depend upon empirical findings for their truth value. The empirical sciences have for their purpose the explanation and prediction of occurrences in the real world. The propositions of empirical science, therefore, are said to be true only if they correctly explain or predict some real world phenomena.

Despite the empirical test for the assignment of truth value, the theories of empirical science are not composed entirely of propositions which can be verified by observations. Instead, a theory in empirical science is composed of a combination of analytic and empirical propositions. The syntactical or logical part of a theory can be abstracted and studied in isolation from the empirical part of that theory. This process is usually called the axiomatisation or formalisation of a theory and the result is called an axiomatic or formal system. It is clear from the above discussion that (a) the formal system *per se* is not an empirical theory, and (b) in order for the formal system to function as a theory of empirical science the semantic rules must be added.

In summary, a theory of empirical science may be divided into two parts:
* a formal system which is composed of abstract symbols and a set of syntactical rules for manipulating those symbols and
* an interpretation of the formal system

Figure 5.1
Propositions and their truth value

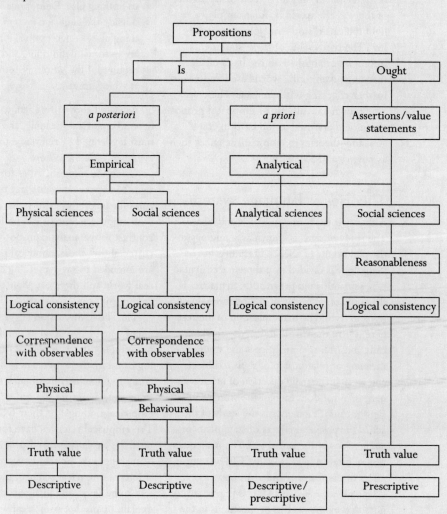

which connects certain symbols to observations via semantic rules.

The process of ascertaining the truth of *a priori* (analytic) and *a posteriori* (synthetic) propositions is illustrated in Figure 5.1.

Accounting can be viewed as an empirical science in the sense described, and accounting theory construction can be discussed in terms of the features of theory construction in the empirical sciences in general. The scientific method of inquiry, as the name suggests, was developed for the natural and physical sciences and not specifically for social sciences such as accounting. There are some clear limitations on the application of this research methodology to accounting; for example, the influence of people and the economic environment makes it impossible to hold the variables constant. Nevertheless, the method can indicate how research should be conducted. The researcher and the user of the findings should keep the limitations in mind so that no one places an improper reliance on the results.

In the syntactic area, accounting has an entire history of attempts to develop 'concepts' or 'principles'. The purpose of stating such concepts and principles is to allow one to deduce the appropriate procedure in a specific case, forming a deductive system (for example Sprouse and Moonitz, 1962; Mattesich, 1964). There have also been attempts to describe the extant system formally, forming an inductive system (for instance Ijiri, 1967; Sterling, 1970a). Both types of attempts can be described as axiomatisation. The pragmatic area includes the whole of 'behavioural' research in accounting. Accounting reports are signs which affect the behaviour of people, and a number of attempts have been made to test this effect. Lists of such studies are given in Williams and Griffin (1969) and Perera and Mathews (1990). Less research effort has been directed towards the semantic area. However, there have been attempts to test the feasibility and objectivity of various accounting measures.

Classification of accounting theories

Theories can be classified on the basis of the method of reasoning used and the objectives.

Classification based on the method of reasoning used

The following have been described in the literature (for example Schroeder, McCullers and Clark, 1987, pp.20–23; Hendriksen and Van Breda, 1992, Chapter 1; Belkaoui, 1993) as being the approaches or methodologies adopted in accounting theory construction:
- the deductive approach
- the inductive approach
- the pragmatic approach
- the ethical approach
- the behavioural approach and
- the communication theory approach.

Deductive approach

Deductive reasoning entails a valid argument in which it is impossible to assert the premises and to deny the conclusion without contradicting oneself.

The deductive approach to accounting theory construction begins with establishing the objectives of accounting. Once the objectives have been identified, certain key definitions and assumptions must be stated. The researcher must then develop a logical structure for accomplishing the objectives, based upon the definitions and assumptions. This methodology is often described as 'going from the general to the specific', because the researcher is developing a structure that includes the objectives of accounting, the environment in which accounting is operating, the definitions and assumptions of the system and the procedures and practices, all of which must follow a logical pattern.

The validity of any theory developed through this process is highly dependent upon the ability of the researcher to correctly identify and relate the various components of the accounting process in a logical manner. To the extent that the researcher is in error about the objectives, the environment or the ability of the procedures to accomplish the objectives, the conclusions reached will also be in error.

The deductive approach includes:
• specifying the objectives of financial statements
• selecting the 'postulates' of accounting
• deriving the 'principles' of accounting and
• developing the 'techniques' of accounting (Belkaoui, 1993, p.60).

It is clear from the above description that the theoretical structure of accounting defined by the sequence of objectives, postulates, principles and techniques rests on a proper formulation of the objectives of accounting (see also Chapter 4.).

Inductive approach

Induction is a method of reasoning by which a general law or principle is inferred from observed particular instances. This approach emphasises making observations and drawing conclusions from observations. Thus, this method is described as 'going from the specific to the general', because the researcher generalises about the universe on the basis of limited observations of specific situations. Applied to accounting, the inductive approach begins with observations about the financial information of business enterprises and proceeds to construct generalisations and principles of accounting from those observations on the basis of recurring relationships.

The inductive approach includes:
• recording all observations
• analysis and classification of those observations to detect recurring relationships ('likes' and 'similarities')
• inductive derivation of generalisations and principles of accounting from obser-

vations that depict recurring relationships and
• testing the generalisations (Belkaoui, 1993, p.61).

The underlying objective of an inductivist is to draw theoretical and abstract conclusions from rationalisations of accounting practice. Therefore, in induction, the truth of the propositions depends on the observation of sufficient instances of recurring relationships. In an attempt to defend the inductive approach, Ijiri (1975) says:

> This type of inductive reasoning to derive goals implicit in the behaviour of an existing system is not intended to be pro-establishment to promote the maintenance of the status quo. The purpose of such exercise is to highlight where changes are most needed and where they are feasible. Changes suggested as a result of such a study have a much better chance of being actually implemented. Goal assumptions in normative models or goals advocated in policy discussions are often stated purely on the basis of one's conviction and preference, rather than on the basis of inductive study of the existing system. This may perhaps be the most crucial reason why so many normative models or policy proposals are not implemented in the real world. (p.28)

Accounting propositions that result from inductive inference imply special accounting techniques with more or less high probability, whereas the accounting propositions that result from deductive inference lead to specific accounting techniques with certainty.

Inductive and deductive approaches are not mutually exclusive. Although the deductive approach starts with general propositions, the formulation of the propositions is often accomplished by inductive reasoning, conditioned by the author's knowledge of and experience with accounting practice. In other words, the general propositions are formulated through an inductive process, but the principles and techniques are derived by a deductive process. As Yu (1976, p.20) suggests, inductive logic may presuppose deductive logic. Far from being either/or competitive approaches, deduction and induction are complementary in nature and are often used together (Carnap, 1951, pp.199–202; Rudner, 1966, p.66). Hakansson (1969, p.37), for example, suggests that the inductive method can be used to assess the appropriateness of the set of originally selected premises in a primarily deductive system. Obviously, changing the premises can change the logically derived conclusions. The research process itself does not always follow a precisely laid out pattern. Researchers often work backwards from the conclusions of other studies by developing new hypotheses that appear to fit the data. They then attempt to test the new hypotheses (see also Chapter 4).

Pragmatic approach

As Schroeder, McCullers and Clark (1987, pp.21–22) explain, present generally accepted accounting principles are primarily the result of the pragmatic approach. The objective here may be to find a 'workable' solution to a problem, not necessarily an optimum solution. The solutions have been adopted as 'generally accepted accounting principles', rather than as an expedient resolution to a problem in accounting practice. In other words, those procedures found to have ' utility' have become generally accepted, irrespective of whether they were tested for any relevance to a particular hypothesis.

On the question of whether generally accepted accounting practices make a theory of accounting, Chambers (1966) makes the following point:

What is generally understood by the study of accounting is the study of accounting methods and rules. That a knowledge of methods and rules is useful is obvious. But statements of methods and rules are not statements about accounting. They are part of accounting as it is practiced or as it is recommended to be practiced. As such, they give no understanding of the nature and function of accounting. (p.2)

The point made here is that observation of the total environment is necessary if a theory of accounting is to be developed using rigorous methods.

The explanation of an object or event requires many ideas not given in the original description of that object or event. Those ideas have meaning in the context of the theories in which they occur. For example, when sugar is added to hot water it sinks to the bottom and some is dissolved. If the water is stirred, all the sugar will dissolve quickly. Why does this happen? The explanation lies in the physical properties of sugar. They are not things we observe directly, but theoretical constructs devised to explain things we observe (Chambers, 1972, p.138). Similarly, in accounting it is not possible to understand completely the nature of accounting simply by observing accounting practice.

Other approaches

Various writers have at times discussed the ethical, behavioural and communication theory approaches to accounting theory construction. There is no doubt about their significance to accounting researchers as guides to action. But, for the purpose of the present discussion, they are regarded as only supportive considerations which influence the attitude of the researcher in constructing a theory. In other words, those considerations cannot by themselves lead to tightly reasoned conditions or scientific inquiry. The scientific method of inquiry is essentially a combination of deductive and inductive reasoning.

Ethical approach

The ethical approach places emphasis upon the concepts of truth, justice and fairness. Ethical considerations are becoming increasingly important at the present time. Some of the questions involved here include: fair to whom, for what purpose and under what circumstances? Because of questions such as these, this approach is operationally limited when applied to accounting theory (Schroeder, McCullers and Clark, 1987, p.23).

Behavioural approach

This approach emphasises the way individuals and groups perceive and react to accounting information. This is important in view of the fact that the purpose of accounting is often said to be the provision of information for decision making (Schroeder, McCullers and Clark, 1987, p.23).

Communication theory approach

This approach, like the behavioural approach, emphasises the information providing function of accounting. As Schroeder, McCullers and Clark, (1987, p.23) state:

> When applied to accounting, this method strives to determine whether the user of accounting information perceives the same message from the data as the preparer or the accountant intends. Again, this approach, though important, cannot be the total research methodology.

Classification based on the objective used

In addition to theories being classified as deductive or inductive, they may also be categorised as normative (prescriptive) or positive (descriptive). A normative theory attempts to justify what ought to be, rather than what is. For example, a premise stating that accounting reports should be based on a particular method of asset measurement would indicate a normative system. Among the normative theories in accounting are those contained in Edwards and Bell (1961), AAA (1966) and Chambers (1966). By contrast, descriptive theories attempt to find relationships that actually exist. The descriptive theories of accounting include those of Grady (1965), Ijiri (1967) and Watts and Zimmerman (1986). A detailed account of the descriptive and normative methodologies and of the resulting theories is provided in AAA (1977).

While there are exceptions, it is usually the case that deductive systems are normative and inductive systems attempt to be descriptive. This categorisation derives from the nature of the deductive and inductive methods. The deductive method is basically a closed, non-empirical system. Its conclusions are based strictly on its premises. Conversely, the inductive method, because it tries to find and explain real world relationships, is in the descriptive realm (Wolk, Francis and Tearney, 1992, pp.29–32).

Theory verification

Theory verification or validation is an integral part of theory construction. Machlup (1955) describes this process as follows:

> Verification in research and analysis may refer to many things, including the correctness of mathematical and logical arguments, the applicability of formulas and equations, the trustworthiness of reports, the authenticity of documents, the genuineness of artifacts or relics, the adequacy of reproductions, translations, and paraphrases, the accuracy of historical and statistical accounts, the corroboration of reported events, the completeness in the enumeration of circumstances in a concrete situation, the reproducibility of experiments, the explanatory or predictive value of generalizations. (p.1)

This statement refers to a variety of measures that can be taken in verifying a theory. As described in Figure 5.1, the particular measure to be taken will depend on the types of propositions used in constructing the theory. For example, theories in analytical sciences such as mathematics can be verified by testing their logical consistency, whereas theories in empirical sciences need both logical and empirical testing, because they normally have both analytical and empirical propositions. Again, within the empirical sciences, the empirical content can be either physical (as in physics) or people related (as in psychology) or both physical and people related (as in accounting). Therefore, in verifying an accounting theory, in addition to the analytical and physical testing, consideration should also be given to the behavioural aspects of the theory.

According to Popper (1959), the testing of deductive theories could be carried out along four lines:

> First, there is the logical comparison of the conclusions among themselves, by which the internal consistency of the system is tested. Secondly, there is the investigation of the logical form of the theory with the object of determining whether it has the character of an empirical or scientific theory, or whether it is, for example, tautological. Thirdly, there is the comparison with other theories, chiefly with the aim of determining whether the theory would constitute a scientific advance should it survive our various tests, and finally, there is the testing of the theory by way of empirical applications of the conclusions which can be derived from. (p.33)

The last step is necessary to determine how the theory stands up to the demand of practice. If its predictions are acceptable, then the theory is said to be *verified* or *corroborated* for the time being. If the predictions are not acceptable, then the theory is said to be *falsified*.

The question of theory verification or validation has received less attention in accounting than has theory construction. Indeed, very few attempts have been made to identify that which constitutes verification. Following Kuhn, the Committee on Accounting Theory Construction and Verification of the AAA (AAA, 1971) states:

> Scientific theories provide certain 'expectations' or 'predictions' about phenomena and, when these expectations occur, they are said to 'confirm' the theory. When unexpected results occur, they are considered to be anomalies which eventually require a modification of the theory or the construction of a new theory. The purpose of the new theory or the modified theory is to make the unexpected expected, to convert the anomalous occurrence into an expected and explained occurrence. (p.53)

Until the early 1970s, accounting theory largely consisted of a set of competing *a priori* arguments about the relative merits of alternative accounting measurements. As Ijiri and Jaedicke (1966, p.474) pointed out, accounting was plagued by the existence of alternative measurement methods. For many years, accountants had been searching for criteria which could be used to choose the best measurement alternative. Currently, there is a growing body of research that is attempting to establish an empirical tradition in accounting verification. On the question of the verification of empirical theories, Hempel (1966) says:

> The verification of the output is indispensable if the theory is intended to be empirical. It is not required that every proposition in an empirical theory be verifiable; there are many terms which operate within the formal system that are not subject to observation. (These are often called 'Theoretical terms' in

contrast to 'Observational terms'.)
However, an empirical theory must have
some propositions that are verifiable.
The verification of these individual
propositions is taken as a test of the
theory. If the propositions are found to
be true, then the theory is said to be
'validated' or 'confirmed'. (p. 30)

Predictive ability

The growing interest in empiricism in
accounting has placed emphasis on the use
of predictive ability, that is the ability to
predict events of interest to decision makers, as a criterion in evaluating alternative
accounting measurements. Accordingly, the
measures with the greatest predictive
power with respect to a given event are
considered to be the best for that particular
purpose. This criterion is well established in
the social and natural sciences as a method
for choosing among competing hypotheses
(Devine, 1960).

Beaver, Kennelly and Voss (1968) provide
a detailed discussion of the predictive ability
criterion as applied in accounting. What follows is largely based on that discussion. The
following features have been identified as
being common to competing hypotheses and
alternative accounting measures. First, because there are many ways to abstract from
reality, an unlimited number of mutually
exclusive alternatives can be generated.
Hence there is a need for a set of criteria for
choosing among them. Second, tests of logical propriety provide one basis for evaluation. Conformity to these tests is a
necessary but insufficient condition for
selecting the 'best'. Two or more alternatives may pass the test, and in that event it is
futile to argue which is 'more logical'.
Ultimately, the choice must be made on the
basis of which abstraction better captures
the relevant aspects of reality. There is a
need for an additional criterion that evaluates the alternatives in terms of the purpose
for which they are being generated.

Third, a primary purpose is the prediction of events and hence the comparison
of alternatives according to their relative
predictive power is a meaningful basis for
evaluation. Predictive power is defined as the
ability to generate operational implications
(that is prediction) and to have those predictions subsequently verified by empirical evidence. More precisely, a prediction is a
statement about the probability distribution
of the dependent variable (the event being
predicted) conditional upon the value of the
independent variable (the predictor). It must
be verified by investigating the empirical correspondence between what the prediction
asserts and what is in fact observed. Thus,
the determination of predictive ability is inherently an empirical question. Fourth, the
use of the predictive ability criterion presup-
poses that the alternatives under consideration have met the tests of logic and that each
has a theory supporting it.

A key issue in accepting the predictive
ability approach is the contention that it is a
purposive criterion. No decision can be
made without, at least implicitly, making a
prediction, although a prediction can be
made without making a decision. Thus the
use of a predictive ability criterion in empirical research can be justified on a utilitarian basis that presumes the better the
prediction, the better the decision.

However, in spite of the obvious appeal
of the idea that accounting data ought to be
useful, the utilitarian approach has lacked
operationality. Chambers (1963) identified
this:

> For, if accounting is utilitarian there
> must have been some concept or some
> theory of the tests which must be ap-
> plied in distinguishing utilitarian from
> nonutilitarian procedures . . . It is
> largely because the tests of 'utilitarian-
> ness' . . . have not been made explicit
> that the body of accounting practices
> now employed contains many divergent
> and inconsistent rules. (p. 3)

One reason for the inability to specify tests of usefulness is the manner in which usefulness is interpreted. Almost without exception, the literature has related usefulness to the facilitation of decision making. For example, an AAA Committee (AAA, 1966) stresses the primacy of decision making when it says:

> The Committee defines accounting as the process of identifying, measuring and communicating economic information to permit informed judgements and decisions by users of the information. (p.1)

However, the use of the decision-making criterion faces two problems. First, it requires the definition of the decision models (or processes) of potential users of accounting data; and, second, even after the decision model is specified, it is not sufficient for determining which accounting measure produces the better decision. Many, if not all, of the decision variables are capable of being measured in more than one way.

The crucial feature to note about decision models is that they, like hypotheses, are abstractions of a much more complex process. A complete specification would require:

• the optimisation rule, decision criteria or goals of the decision maker
• all feasible acts available to the decision maker
• all possible events or states that may occur over the decision horizon
• probability distributions relating to the set of possible events (note such distribution must be generated for each possible act as well) and
• a set of payoffs, conditional upon the state and act.

Abstractions of the complete process may take place at any of the five levels cited above. Because these models are abstractions, there is an unlimited number of ways of abstracting and hence an unlimited number of decision models that may occur to the human mind.

In view of the extremely complex nature of the process, one wonders whether a complete specification will ever be attainable. This causes a major concern about the whole issue and that is, until the decision processes are completely specified, the evaluation of alternative accounting measurements through the use of the predictive ability criterion cannot be completely achieved. Chambers (1972) identified this and suggested a less extensive test. He said:

> Of one thing we are certain. There is no prospect of establishing the validity of any theory of accounting by reference to the actual outcomes of decisions based on any specified class of asset magnitudes. Decision-making is too complex a process to be analysed in such a way that precise weights may be assigned to financial information, expectations and selected goals. For a theory of accounting, we must settle for the less extensive tests of whether a given class of financial magnitude, if used in financial statements, would be more useful — usable in a wider range of problem contexts — than any other class of information. And that is a sufficient test, for, after all, that is the test of all information providing systems. (p.18)

Having discussed various aspects of accounting theory construction and verification, we can now summarise some of the key elements of that discussion. Table 5.1 incorporates those elements (see also Gaffikin, 1988, p.26).

Table 5.1
Aspects of theories, their construction and verification

Distinguishing features	Analytic (a priori) propositions	Synthetic (a posteriori) propositions
Source	Assumptions	Specific observations
Epistemological basis	Rationalism	Empiricism
Reasoning	Deductive	Inductive
Type of science	Analytical	Empirical
Language system	Syntactic	Syntactic, semantic, (pragmatic)
Theory type	Prescriptive	Descriptive
Verification	Logical	Logical, empirical

Normative (prescriptive) and positive (descriptive) theories

A theory is a set of propositions. Deductive systems are based on *a priori* (analytical) propositions, whereas inductive systems are based on *a posteriori* (syntactic/empirical) propositions. The distinction between *a priori* and *a posteriori* propositions signifies the traditional philosophical disputes over the nature and conditions of knowledge (e.g. rationalism versus empiricism). However, both types of propositions are needed when formulating theories in any discipline, except for purely analytical disciplines such as mathematics and logic (Yu, 1976, pp.84–85). As shown in Figure 5.1, this also means that no theory can be entirely free of *a priori* propositions.

Normative and positive theories have different objectives, however, the distinction between them is not always clear. Schreuder (1984) suggests that 'the terms of "positive" and "normative" have been used in so many different contexts that they have lost all clarity of meaning' (p.215). Butterworth, Gibbins and King (1984) hold a similar view. They state:

> [T]he distinction between normative and positive theory is sometimes subtle, and it is not at all unusual to see the same

theoretical constraints interpreted as either normative or positive depending on the researcher's specific needs. In other words, a theory is not inherently normative nor positive but can be either depending on the way in which the theory is used. For example, if asked to classify the neo classical theory of the firm as normative or positive, many respond 'normative', having in mind the kind of statement it generates (e.g. 'to maximize profits, set marginal cost equal to marginal revenue'). But Friedman (1953) treats it as a positive theory, whose value (to him) depends on its ability to predict the response of a firm in the marketplace to alternative demand/supply schedules. (p.229)

Chambers (1993, p.9) points out that scientific knowledge is simultaneously positive and normative. As an example, he states that if it is true that gases and liquids expand on the application of heat or the reduction of pressure, it is true that one, anyone and everyone, must apply heat or reduce pressure to bring about an expansion of gases and liquids. The former is positive and the latter is normative. They are logically and practically equivalent. This means that what is descriptive may be made prescriptive, and vice versa, by simply changing the way in which they are expressed.

In fact, there are some similarities between positive and normative theories. For example, as Butterworth, Gibbins and King (1984, p.229) point out, both types of theory involve the use of deductive logic from *a priori* assumptions. Gaffikin (1988) also argues that the philosophical foundations are similar in research carried out in the general prescriptive and specific descriptive periods. He says:

> a priorists are said to be normative because they start from certain assumptions which they claim the theory should explain or justify. The uncritical empiricist, nowadays referred to as a positive researcher, is not really proceeding any differently. The selection of his or her problem and the possible solution to it are equally normative. (p.30)

The distinction lies in the fact that positive statements are empirically verifiable, whereas normative statements are not. Furthermore, the positive theories are concerned with the prediction of observable phenomena, while normative theories are concerned with means–end statements such as, 'if the relevant attributes of your problem can be represented by model X, and you wish to achieve B, then do A'. The fundamental problem here is that there is no way a normative statement can be falsified. For example, if we do A and C (instead of B) occurs, this does not absolutely falsify the prescription, because we cannot know whether X was an adequate descriptor in the circumstances (Butterworth, Gibbins and King, 1984, p.228).

Normative accounting and positive accounting

From an historical point of view theoretical investigation in accounting has undergone significant changes in terms of the issues addressed and the methods adopted in addressing those issues. Henderson, Peirson and Brown (1993, p.53) use different labels to identify different periods, for example the General Prescriptive Theory Period (1955–1970) and the Specific Descriptive Theory Period (post 1970). In recent years positive accounting has attracted the attention of many accounting researchers. It is generally held that positive accounting represents the dominant paradigm in current accounting research. This section provides an overview of normative and positive investigations in accounting with a particular emphasis on the issues related to positive accounting research.

Normative accounting theories

The general prescriptive or normative theory period, particularly the 1960s, has been described as the Golden Age in the history of *a priori* research in accounting (Nelson, 1973, p.4). This period was characterised by significant contributions to the methodological debates in accounting research, for example Edwards and Bell (1961), Mattesich (1964), Bedford (1965), AAA (1966), Chambers (1966), Ijiri (1967) and Sterling (1970a). Chambers (1955) called for methodological rigour in accounting research and argued that the methodology applied by scientists are applicable to all theoretical investigation. The theories developed by Chambers, Sterling and Mattesich also exhibit their knowledge of the philosophy of science literature. (For a brief discussion on the contributions of the leading accounting researchers during this period, see Gaffikin, 1988.)

The major normative accounting theories of the 1960s were continuously contemporary accounting (CoCoA; Chambers, 1966) and replacement price accounting (RPA; Edwards and Bell, 1961). Others include price-level adjusted historical cost accounting or current purchasing power accounting (CPP), deprival value accounting (based on the concept of value

to the business) and present value accounting (PVA). Current cost accounting (CCA),
which became popular in the 1970s and
early 1980s, was a variation of RPA and was
based on the concept of value to the business. The two major theories have a number
of similarities. First, they are market based
theories which use some other method than
the historical cost method. Second, they
have their own concepts of true income and
financial position. Third, they assume that
profit maximisation is the primary goal of
management. Fourth, they have been constructed on the basis of deductive reasoning
and conceptual rigour. Fifth, they take a
decision-usefulness approach in that the
provision of information for decision making is regarded as the main function of
financial statements. Chambers (1955) was
one of the first to highlight the importance
of (a) logical consistency among the ideas
used in a theory and (b) decision usefulness
function of accounting information. He
said:

> A formal information providing system
> would conform with two general propo-
> sitions. The first is a condition of all logi-
> cal discourse. The system should be
> logically consistent; no rule or process
> can be permitted that is contrary to any
> other rule or process . . . The second
> proposition arises from the use of
> accounting statements as a basis for mak-
> ing decisions of practical consequence.
> The information yielded by any such sys-
> tem should be relevant to the kinds of
> decision the making of which it is
> expected to facilitate. (pp. 21–22)

However, CoCoA and RPA differ in
terms of the underlying assumptions with
regard to the behaviour of business firms in
a market economy. For example, CoCoA
assumes that the main objective of a business firm is to adapt to changing circumstances in order to be able to take advantage of the opportunities presented to
it, whereas RPA assumes that continual

operation is the main objective. Based on
their assumptions, CoCoA and RPA arrive
at different conclusions regarding the type
of information that needs to be provided
through financial statements. According to
CoCoA, financial statement information
should be based on the net realisable value
(market selling price) of assets, whereas
according to RPA, it should be based on
replacement prices (buying prices) of assets
(see also Chapter 11).

The research outputs of this period were
subsequently criticised as being unscientific,
unproductive and of doubtful value, mainly
because they were normative, not positive
(see Dopuch and Revsine, 1973, p. 32;
Nelson, 1973, p. 15). On the other hand,
researchers such as Wells (1976) argued
that those who criticise *a priori* research do
not seem to understand its value:

> those criticisms are based on a misun-
> derstanding of the role of so-called *a
> priori research* in the overthrow of out-
> dated ideas and practices. Far from being
> unproductive, the works referred to
> were a necessary step in the revolution
> currently underway in accounting
> thought. Far from being of doubtful
> value, those works have helped to place
> us in a significantly different position
> from that of 1960. (p. 471)

A normative theory is constructed, in a
logically consistent manner, upon the foundation of the stated objective of the proposed
theory. The major criticism of normative
theories is that they are based on value
judgements. Accordingly, since the stated
objective represents the value judgement of
the author, the theory based on value judgements cannot be regarded as scientific. The
failure to produce a generally acceptable
accounting theory was another cause for dissatisfaction with the normative theories.
Different theories based on different objectives advocated different accounting methods. As a result, those who expected theories
to guide practice were disappointed.

Normative accounting research has been criticised for the absence of a welfare framework or methodology for conducting such research. In attempting to address this issue, Mozes (1992) suggests that the conceptual framework for financial reporting (see Chapter 6) provides accounting researchers with a framework and methodology for structuring normative research, and that such research can be undertaken in accordance with the scientific method. For this purpose, using the methodology stated in SFAC 2 and SFAC 6 (FASB, 1980; 1985) for evaluating rules, Mozes (1992) organises normative accounting research into six categories as follows:

1

research on an accounting rule's *consistency* with other accounting rules

2

research on an accounting rule's *understandability*

3

research on an accounting rule's *relevance*

4

research on an accounting rule's *neutrality*

5

research on whether an accounting rule results in reporting or disclosure that is *representationally faithful* to the underlying economic events being reported and

6

investigation of an accounting rule's costs and benefits.

Mozes explains how research can be undertaken in each of these categories. For example, an objective of consistency research would be to provide evidence to support the argument that users' perception of the integrity of financial statements will be harmed by inconsistent standards. An objective of understandability research would be to test a representative group of users to determine how they interpret financial accounting information.

A shift towards empiricism

During the 1970s there was a major shift towards empiricism in accounting research. Gaffikin (1988) explains the circumstances that led to this shift.

> Generally speaking, empirical research has been *prescribed* as *the* only acceptable form of research. This prescription has been the result of strong influences exerted on researchers, directly or indirectly, from many quarters, including the predilections of *some* journal editors; research training (degree requirements); research technology; 'official' research 'manuals' (e.g., Abdel-khalik and Ajinkya, 1979); research fashion-leaders (e.g. prizes to members of the Rochester School); and influential economic theories. (p.29)

Feltham (1984) suggests that the shift towards empiricism was a natural extension of the research activities of the 1960s. Accordingly, in the 1960s the emphasis placed on the need for accounting reports to be more relevant to decision makers has resulted in the development of empirical, experimental and analytical research in accounting. The empirical research influenced by research in finance explored the impact of accounting reports on investor decisions, as reflected in changes in stock market prices, using publicly available data about past events. The experimental research influenced by research in psychology explored the impact of information on individual decisions. The analytical research influenced by research in information economics examined the impact of alternative information systems on hypothetical, rational decision makers in hypothetical decision contexts.

Jensen (1976; 1983) argues that positive research is necessary in finding solutions to normative issues in accounting such as: 'should accountants adjust asset values to reflect price-level changes?' Positive research attempts to explain the reasons why firms adopt particular techniques, why standard-setting bodies adopt particular standards and the effects of alternative accounting valuation rules on the value of the firm and manager's wealth.

Positive accounting theory

Positive accounting theory (PAT) is descriptive rather than prescriptive. It sets out to explain and predict what the consequences will be if managers pursue given options. Unlike the normative theories which are based on the premise that managers should maximise the profitability or the utility provided from their firms, positive theory is based on the premise that people always act from totally self-seeking motives and attempt to maximise their own personal returns. Positive accounting theory is explained fully in Watts and Zimmerman (1986). They argue that the profit maximisation premise has not been proven and is often at odds with the empirical evidence. Their main criticism against existing normative accounting theories is that they are based on value judgements. They emphasise that accounting theory construction should be free of the value judgements of the theorist, and that there is a need for a new approach. They make their position in this matter clear in the following statements: 'The objective of accounting theory is to explain and predict accounting practice' (p.2), and '. . . theory, as we describe it, yields no prescription for accounting practice. It is concerned with explaining accounting practice' (p.7).

Watts and Zimmerman (1977; 1978) provide the beginnings of PAT, although early development of the ideas incorporated in PAT can be found in Watts (1974; 1977). There have also been earlier attempts in the 1960s to promote the idea of a PAT (e.g. Gordon, 1964). Watts and Zimmerman (1986) state that their ultimate aim is to develop a positive theory of the

determination of accounting standards. They focus on the question of why firms would expend resources in an attempt to influence the determination of accounting standards. Based on the assertions that (a) management plays a central role in the determination of accounting standards and (b) firms will engage in lobbying standard-setting bodies as financial accounting standards have potential effects on the firm's future cash flows, Watts and Zimmerman explore those factors influencing management's attitudes on accounting standards which are likely to affect corporate lobbying on accounting standards, that is to support or oppose a particular standard. They identify taxes, regulation, management compensation plans, bookkeeping costs and political costs as factors that provide incentives for managers to engage in such lobbying. These factors are combined into a model which predicts that large firms experiencing reduced earnings due to changed accounting standards favour the change.

Positive accounting theory has been described as an exclusively economics-based accounting theory (Watts and Zimmerman, 1986, p.1). Boland and Gordon (1992) identify methodological individualism and the neoclassical maximisation hypothesis as the two main features of an economics-based theory (p.144). Methodological individualism is the commitment to explain every social phenomenon as being a consequence of individual decision making. For example, when a standard-setting committee makes a decision, it is explained as a decision made by each member of the committee (Watts and Zimmerman, 1978, p.113). The neoclassical maximisation hypothesis claims that every individual makes decisions, subject to given constraints exclusively to maximise his or her personal utility. For example, Watts and Zimmerman (1986) state that: 'we assume that all these various parties in selecting or recommending accounting and auditing procedures act so as to maximize their own welfare' (p. 3). Accordingly, the individual is presumed to choose action A only if the net utility gained is greater than would be obtained by choosing action B. This highlights the importance of the concept of self-interest in PAT.

Watts and Zimmerman (1979) consider accounting theories as economic goods, produced in response to the demand for theories. They examine the nature of the demand for theories in both unregulated and regulated economic environments. They argue that government regulation affects the demand for accounting theories, because government regulation creates incentives for individuals to lobby for or against proposed accounting procedures, and that accounting theories are useful in justifying a particular view in the lobbying process. Therefore, there will be a demand for a variety of accounting theories to justify different positions taken by different groups participating in the political process. Watts and Zimmerman argue that the motivation for researchers to produce normative accounting theories lies in the fact that such theories are used as excuses for political action. Politicians and bureaucrats demand public interest testimony for use in justifying their actions to the media and their constituents. Influenced by contemporary economics literature, Watts and Zimmerman challenge the underlying public interest assumption in normative accounting theories and propose as an alternative assumption that individuals involved in the political process act in their own interest. They conclude that given the existing economic and political institutions and the incentives of voters, politicians, managers and investors to become involved in the process by which accounting standards are determined, the only accounting theory that will provide a set of predictions that are consistent with observed phenomena is one based on self-interest. Henderson, Peirson and Brown (1993) explain the importance of the concept of self-interest to PAT:

Positive accounting theory extends the assumption of self-interest to all those individuals whose wealth can be affected by accounting techniques or methods. This includes shareholders, debtholders, managers, employees, regulators, professional accounting bodies, politicians and public servants. Naturally, the self-interested objectives of these individuals can at times conflict. How that conflict is resolved plays a large part in determining the accounting methods and practices that are observed. (p. 327)

The hard core of the positive accounting theory has been identified by Mouck (1990) to include the following propositions:

1
decision makers have correct knowledge of their economic situation

2
decision makers prefer the best available alternative given their knowledge of the situation and of the means at their disposal

3
given (1) and (2), situations generate their internal 'logic' and decision makers act appropriately to the logic of their situation

4
economic units and structures display stable, coordinated behaviour

5
the wants and preferences of individuals are autonomous with respect to the market system

6
all decision makers are motivated by their narrowly defined self-interest and not by public interest

7
the firm is considered to be a nexus of (explicit or implicit) contracts among self-interested parties.

Information economics

As an economics-based theory, PAT is heavily influenced by contemporary economics, particularly information economics and literature. The use of the concept of 'rational decision maker' in constructing PAT is a direct result of that influence. The term 'information economics' represents the subject matter that analyses the economic impact of and demand for alternative information systems. The economic consequences of accounting information have attracted the attention of many accounting researchers in recent years (e.g. Gerboth, 1973; Zeff, 1978; Solomons, 1978; Holthausen and Leftwich, 1983; Blake, 1992). Information economics is an extension of statistical decision theory. It also draws on insights from the 'theory of teams' developed by Marschak and Radner (1972) and on the economic theory of choice (Belkaoui, 1993, p.512). In statistical decision theory, an individual is assumed to make a choice according to the rank ordering of expected values. Information economics extends this model, for example in formulating each expected value as conditioned on the receipt of information. Feltham (1984) provides a comprehensive survey of various developments in information economics and its significance for financial accounting research. He focuses on the implications of information economics for understanding the impact of and demand for alternative external financial reporting systems. (For a survey of information economics research that has implications for management accounting, see Baiman, 1982).

Information economics studies are characterised by two key elements: the assumptions made and the analysis performed. In constructing models, assumptions are made about the nature of the decision makers, the decision contexts they face and the systems that provide them with information. The models are then analysed to derive conclusions regarding the decision maker's demand for information and the impact of alternative information systems. For example, if an individual is uncertain about the consequences of a set of alternative actions, he or she is likely to value information that reduces his or her uncertainty about the consequences, creating a demand for such information. To formally explore the nature of the demand for information, a model of choice when confronted with uncertainty is constructed. During the 1970s the focus of information economics research shifted from single-person models to multi-person models. In both cases the traditional economic concept of 'rational decision maker' is central to the analysis (Feltham, 1984).

Agency theory

The explanation and prediction under PAT is based on a contracting process or agency relationship between managers and other groups, such as shareholders and lending institutions. The basic premises of agency theory include a theory of the firm that takes into account the motivational behaviour of managers, the management costs and, under certain circumstances, the ownership structure of the capital employed in the firm. It is concerned with a search for the most preferred feasible contract between principal and agent. Agency theory has had a strong impact on the construction of PAT.

Agency theory is an extension of information economics. Jensen and Meckling (1976) define an agency relationship as a 'contract under which one or more persons (the principal(s)) engage another person (the agent) to perform some service on their behalf which involves delegating some decision-making authority to the agent' (p.308). 'Principal' in this case means owner, shareholder or superior and 'agent' means management, department head or subordinate. The service to be performed by the agent on behalf of the principal involves managing an entity (firm, department, workplace or other risk situation expected to yield a return or outcome). The agent is compensated with a share of the outcome for providing this service. The agent's share of the outcome may range from a fixed remuneration to a percentage of the total outcome. This is specified in terms of the agency contract between the principal and the agent, which also includes penalties for failing to fulfil the contract. The agency contract, depending on the terms included, delegates to the agent the responsibility to manage an entity and thereby transfers a certain amount of enterprise risk to the agent.

The principal, however, may not always be able to obtain the most desirable outcome through the agent's action. In other words, the agent's optimisation behaviour may not result in maximising the principal's objective function. This can happen due to a number of factors. First, there may be a conflict of interests between the agent and the principal in that the agent's objective (or utility function) may be different from that of the principal. In this situation, the agent may tend to maximise his or her own utility at the expense of the principal's utility. Second, the agent's action itself, or the ensuing outcome, may not be observable, for example the agent's attitude towards risk taking may be different from that of the principal, that is, one is risk averse whereas the other is risk neutral. This is likely to jeopardise the contractual relationship between the principal and the agent. The basic agency problem, therefore, is inducing an agent to behave as if she or he were maximising the principal's welfare. In this situation, an information system is required to inform the principal and the agent about the outcome. Both the principal and the agent are interested in the particular information available to them, because both parties are aware that their ultimate share or wealth might be dependent on it as well as on the total outcome. The information

about the action of the agent becomes an important tool for the principal's decision making. Such information will provide a basis for maintaining the contractual relationship.

The agent's actions involve decisions regarding accounting choice. The extent to which accounting choice affects the contracting parties' wealth, that is, the agent's compensation and the principal's share of the total outcome depends on the relative magnitude of the various contracting costs.

Firms engage in many types of contracts. PAT has focused on two types of contracts: management contracts and debt contracts. Both of these are agency contracts. Agency costs arise because, as mentioned earlier, the agent's interests do not necessarily coincide with those of the principal. Agency costs include monitoring expenditures, bonding expenditures and residual loss (Jensen and Meckling, 1976, p. 308). Monitoring is an activity undertaken by or on behalf of the principal (e.g. employing an auditor). The objective is to reduce the loss of the principal's share of wealth due to the divergence of interests between the agent and the principal. The costs involved are incurred by the principal. Bonding is a guarantee given by the agent (e.g. preparing periodic financial statements or some other guarantee that the agent will or will not undertake certain activities). The assumption here is that it is of benefit to the agent to incur expenditure in bonding himself or herself to act in line with the interests of the principal. The bonding costs are incurred by the agent. However, monitoring and bonding expenditures will not eliminate the divergence of interests between the agent and the principal completely, and some divergence will remain. Residual loss represents the resulting reduction in firm value.

Researchers have been concerned about the impact of political costs incurred by firms on accounting choice. Political costs arise as a result of the political visibility of a

firm rather than as a result of any
agent–principal relationship. Large firms
attract the attention of the media, politicians and the public in general, compared
with small firms, particularly if their profits
appear to be high. They are likely targets for
costly regulation. This can lead to increased
taxes and compliance costs. Using the concept of self-interested behaviour, it is
argued that large firms have an incentive to
use accounting methods which reduce
accounting profit.

The agency costs associated with debt
and management compensation contracts
together with the costs associated with the
political process provided three hypotheses:
the bonus plan hypothesis, the debt–equity
hypothesis and the political cost hypothesis.
The early PAT research almost entirely
involves the testing of these hypotheses. The
bonus plan hypothesis is that:

> managers of firms with bonus plans are
> more likely to use accounting methods
> that increase current period reported
> income. Such selection will presumably
> increase the present value of bonuses if
> the compensation committee of the
> board of directors does not adjust for
> the method chosen. (Watts and
> Zimmerman, 1990, p.138)

The debt–equity hypothesis is that:

> the higher the firm's debt–equity ratio,
> the more likely managers use accounting
> methods that increase income. The
> higher the debt–equity ratio, the closer
> (i.e. 'tighter') the firm is to the con-
> straints in the debt covenants (Kalay
> 1982). The higher the covenant con
> straint, the greater the probability of a
> covenant violation and of incurring costs
> from technical default. Managers exer-
> cising discretion by choosing income
> increasing accounting methods relax
> debt constraints, and reduce the costs
> of technical default. (Watts and
> Zimmerman, 1990, p.139)

The political cost hypothesis is that:

> large firms rather than small firms are
> more likely to use accounting choice
> that reduce reported profits. Size is a
> proxy variable for political attention.
> Underlying this hypothesis is the
> assumption that it is costly for individu-
> als to become informed about whether
> accounting profits really represent
> monopoly profits and to 'contract' with
> others in the political process to enact
> laws and regulations that enhance their
> welfare. Thus, rational individuals are
> less than fully informed. The political
> process is no different from the market
> process in that respect. Given the cost of
> information and monitoring, managers
> have incentive to exercise discretion
> over accounting profits, and the parties
> in the political process settle for a ratio-
> nal amount of ex post opportunism.
> (Watts and Zimmerman, 1990, p.139)

However, the more general approach
suggested agency and other costs associated
with other contracts (e.g. sales contracts)
could also affect accounting choice. As a
result, researchers started to use 'contracting costs' instead of 'agency costs'. In addition to agency costs, other contracting costs
include:

* transaction costs (brokerage fees and
  cost of issuing debt)
* information costs (the costs of becoming
  informed)
* renegotiation costs (the cost of rewriting
  existing contracts because the circumstances have changed) and
* bankruptcy costs (the legal costs of
  bankruptcy).

Positive accounting theory emphasises
the contractual role of accounting information. For example, Watts and Zimmerman
(1978; 1979) state that accounting procedures are devices used to reduce the agency
costs of contracts. As a legal entity, the
company enjoys many of the legal rights of

a real person, such as the right to enter into contracts with others. Since the company itself is an artificial person, such contracts must be agreed to by its officers who are empowered to act on its behalf. These officers act as agents of the stakeholders. The contracts cover a wide range of activities, involving, for example, the acquisition of goods and services from external parties, the sale of products, workforce, management compensation and creditors. Since almost all of these contracts involve the exchange of monetary considerations, information about market transactions is a natural component of the firm's information system.

According to Butterworth, Gibbins and King (1984), in any economic situation involving a business enterprise, there are several distinct, but not mutually exclusive, uses of information. They are as follows:

1

Reduction of management uncertainty with respect to future market demands and operating costs.

2

Reduction of investor uncertainty with respect to future economic events, e.g. future market prices of securities and commodities.

3

The provision of a contractual basis for the efficient sharing of risk among economic agents, e.g. among the managers, creditors and owners.

4

The provision of a contractual basis for the efficient sharing of beliefs with respect to the relative likelihood of future economic events.

5

The provision of a contractual basis for incentives designed to encourage efficient execution of contracts between the man-

agers of a corporation and their subordinates (management control information).

6

The provision of a contractual basis for incentives designed to encourage efficient execution of contracts between the investors and managers of a corporation (managerial performance evaluation information).

7

Retrospective understanding, i.e. making sense of past actions and events.

Financial economics

Positive accounting theory is also strongly influenced by the ideas developed in contemporary financial economics literature, particularly that which is related to the portfolio selection problem and efficiency of capital markets. The ideas related to the former are included in the capital asset pricing model (CAPM), whereas those related to the latter are included in the efficient market hypothesis (EMH). Watts and Zimmerman (1986, Chapter 2) emphasise the importance of EMH and the CAPM to accounting research. As Hendriksen and Van Breda (1992) explain, market efficiency is determined by certain conditions: (a) there are no transaction costs in the trading of securities; (b) all available information is equally available to all traders without cost; and (c) all traders have homogeneous expectations regarding the implications of available information (p.169). Three forms of the EMH have been identified based on the type of information presented. They are: weak form of market efficiency, semistrong form of market efficiency and strong form of market efficiency. The weak form of market efficiency assumes that the current price of a security reflects information implied by the historical sequence of prices, that is, information that can be derived from simply observing security prices. The semi-strong form of market efficiency assumes that the current price of a security reflects all publicly available information, that is, past prices, annual reports and economic data as soon as it becomes available. The strong form of market efficiency assumes that the price of a security reflects all information, including prices, publicly available information and 'insider' information (Watts and Zimmerman, 1986, p.19). Normally, a semi-strong form of market efficiency is assumed under EMH. The use of capital markets for testing the relevance of accounting information under PAT is justified by this assumption.

The EMH explains the effect of relevant information on security prices. The CAPM aims to test for market efficiency or for relevancy of information by explaining the factors that determine security prices in equilibrium. It is assumed that risk and return are the determining factors. The CAPM is a model of equilibrium prices used for securities trading in an efficient market (Hendriksen and Van Breda, 1992, p.184). The CAPM is based on the assumptions that there are perfect markets, rational, risk-adverse, maximising inventors, costless access by all to information and homogeneous expectations (Watts and Zimmerman, 1986, p.23).

Positive accounting theory is heavily influenced by the ideas developed in information economics, agency theory and financial economics literature. Mouck (1990) describes the various elements of PAT (the efficient market hypothesis, the capital asset pricing model, the theory of rational expectations, contracting and agency theory, the theory of the political process, various empirical testable hypotheses) and various assumptions necessary to implement empirical testing as its protective belt from a Lakatosian research programme point of view (p.216).

Contribution

Watts and Zimmerman (1990) provide an overview of the progress of PAT since its introduction a decade ago. It includes a summary of review articles on Watts and Zimmerman (1978; 1979) and their response to some of the issues raised by various critiques. Watts and Zimmerman (1990) claim that evidence is consistent with all the three hypotheses tested (bonus plan hypothesis, debt–equity hypothesis and political cost hypothesis). According to them, the PAT literature has contributed to accounting by:

- discovering systematic patterns in accounting choice . . . and providing specific explanations for the patterns
- providing an intuitively plausible framework for understanding accounting
- highlighting the central role of contracting costs in accounting theory
- explaining why accounting is used and providing a framework for predicting accounting choices
- encouraging research that is relevant to accounting through its emphasis on predicting and explaining accounting phenomena (Watts and Zimmerman, 1990, pp.150–151).

Some concerns

Watts and Zimmerman (1990, pp.140–149) attempt to respond to criticisms against PAT. They classify the criticisms against positive accounting research into two mutually exclusive sets: those concerning research methods (including the inferences drawn) and those concerning methodology (including the philosophy of science). They do, however, fail to address certain important issues, for example those raised by Demski (1988). Sterling (1990) and Chambers (1993) also examine various elements of positive accounting research, for example the foundation of PAT, the accounting phenomena studied, its assumptions, claims of support from economics and science and so on. The remainder of this section includes a discussion of some of these issues.

The use of neoclassical economics

Positive accounting theory uses neoclassical economics with its maximisation hypothesis as the primary basis for understanding accounting theory. The use of maximisation as a method of analysis requires the existence of states of equilibrium (Jensen, 1976, p.15–16). In an equilibrium state, the prevailing price is expected to clear the market, that is, demand is equal to supply. A necessary condition for deliberate maximisation is that the decision maker must be able to calculate the benefits and costs based on the correct prices which are, in fact, equilibrium prices. However, if any market is not cleared, that means demand is not equal to supply at the going price and, therefore, the going price is not an equilibrium price. This also means not everyone is maximising. Neoclassical economics is designed to explain equilibrium states, not disequilibrium states. Therefore, there is no basis under neoclassical economics to determine which of the demanders or suppliers are not maximising (Boland and Gordon, 1992, p.154). Since the presumption of universal maximisation which requires equilibrium prices is central to the methodology adopted in PAT, it is not possible to consider market failures or any other disequilibrium situations within its framework.

Demski (1988, p.626) questions the adequacy of neoclassical economics as the basis for accounting research. He says that neoclassical economics is inadequate on questions of dynamics. His main concern with PAT is the applicability of its implicit assumption of perfect markets. In a perfect market, it is assumed that each individual maximiser has sufficient knowledge of the correct prices, the objective constraints other than prices, and his or her utility function, to make a successful decision prior to realisation. Demski (1988) expresses the view that the recognition of contracting and political costs under PAT is an important acknowledgement that markets are not perfect (pp.625–626).

As Boland and Gordon (1992, p.148) point out, some economists have claimed that the assumed process of maximisation is not logically possible since it requires knowledge beyond what is logically possible (see Shackle, 1972). Others claim that although maximisation may be logically possible, it is still not practical (see Simon, 1959). Furthermore, under neoclassical economics, it is assumed that what is good for the individual decision maker is also good for society as a whole. This is true only if public interest is thought to be the sum of all individuals' private interests (i.e. their personal utilities).

The proponents of agency theory argue that regulation is inefficient and that private contracting is more cost effective. However, it has been pointed out (Ronen, 1979) that the issue of regulation (whether regulation is necessary) is much more complex than what agency theory assumes. For example, it requires a consideration of net social benefits. Agency theory is not adequate to address such issues because one of its underlying assumptions is that public interest is equivalent to the sum of individual interests. Ronen (1979) concludes that indirect regulation through standards will be required to reduce audit costs and direct government regulation will be required to monitor the auditors. On the issue of the cost effectiveness of private contracting costs, Whittington (1987, p.334) argues that the proponents of agency theory have failed to consider the true cost of private contracting.

Watts and Zimmerman (1979) criticise existing accounting theories as ventures in the production of excuses. However, they seem to have produced an excuse to outdo all other excuses. For example, Chambers (1993) states:

> The self-interest hypothesis entails that every device that any person or firm chooses to employ is justified, excused. It follows that all the logical and

practical flaws that have occupied the attention of practitioners, academics, lawyers, administrators and others are excusable, and objections to them otiose; 'no one is fooled by accounting' is the slogan forever. (p.22)

The aversion to prescription

Watts and Zimmerman (1979) attempt to draw a normative–positive distinction. The discussion in Watts and Zimmerman (1986, pp 7–8) under the heading 'Positive and Normative Propositions' also indicates that the authors are of the view that all propositions (and all theories) can be easily divided into those two categories. But this is not always possible. Further, Watts and Zimmerman seem to use the positive–normative distinction to undermine normative theories and to highlight the superiority of positivism. However, as Chambers (1993, p.10) points out, the object of the positive–normative distinction has not been to distinguish the 'good' from the 'bad', but to distinguish the testable from the untestable (Bronowski, 1964, p.61). Positive accounting theory is based on the mistaken assumption that only empirically testable propositions lead to advancement of knowledge. Sterling (1990) states:

> It is often said in science that we cannot know what all these new empirical results mean until after some armchair theorist has figured it out. The import of that remark is that conceptual work is also needed to conclude the empirical research. In fact, empirics and reasoning iterate at all stages of inquiry and thus both are needed — neither can replace the other — so the claims that imply that they are mutually exclusive are mistaken. (p.106, footnote 10)

Chambers (1993) suggests that the aversion to prescription in PAT may have stemmed from a misunderstanding of constraints in the natural and physical sciences. He says:

In those fields (natural and physical sciences) it is of no consequence, and therefore improper, to describe any phenomenon as good or bad, preferable or not preferable. A phenomenon is simply what it is. But in human and social affairs that embargo does not hold. A chair, a rule, a theory may be good or bad, and therefore preferred or not, according as it performs well its intended function. (p.10)

It appears that Watts and Zimmerman have taken a normative position with regard to the objective of accounting theory without realising that they are doing so. They say 'the objective of accounting theory is to explain and predict accounting practice' (1986, p.2). Obviously there are other views about the objectives of accounting theory. The history of accounting is full of examples of theoretical investigations attempting to improve accounting practice, addressing the fundamental question: 'What should accounting practices be?' Therefore, the view put forward by Watts and Zimmerman should be regarded as *their own view* on the issue of the objective of accounting theory. What they are really saying is that 'the objective of accounting theory should be to explain and predict accounting practice'. Ironically, although PAT claims to be descriptive, it seems to endorse conventional accounting which is quite clearly prescriptive.

Sterling (1990) questions PAT's claim that it is descriptive, and not prescriptive:

> (Watts & Zimmerman) are normative about being positive when teaching. They *prescribe* that textbook authors and teachers *describe* practices. They are also normative about being positive when researching and theorizing. They *prescribe* that theorists and researchers *prescribe* practices . . . A parallel is grandparents who are convinced that permissive child rearing is good (and directive is bad) but who direct their children to raise the grandchildren permissively, thereby contradicting their own conviction . . .

Why do they feel the need to become normative about being positive? (p.120)

As Butterworth, Gibbins and King (1984) point out, ideally what is needed is a theory that will enable us not only to predict the economic consequences of accounting rules, but also to order preferences among them. If it is accepted that the function of accounting theory includes provision of guidance to accounting standard setters, such theory must take a normative form. The choices made by standard setters will necessarily benefit some individuals at the expense of others. Positive theories can help standard setters understand the consequences of alternative accounting choices, but such theories which are merely catalogues of the games people play (Chambers, 1993, p.24), or filing cabinets for data, cannot in any sense indicate which consequences are most desirable because desirability is a normative issue which requires making a choice. In other words, standard setting involves deciding what is desirable accounting practice.

The claim to be value free

The main claims of PAT to legitimacy include that it is free of value judgements and that it is scientific. However, both these claims have been rebutted in the literature (see Ronen, 1979; Tinker, Merino and Neimark, 1982; Christensen, 1983; Whittington, 1987; Hines, 1988; Sterling, 1990). For example, Christensen (1983) argues that PAT fails to pass Popper's (1959) test of a scientific theory:

> Contrary to the empirical method subjecting theories to severe attempts to falsify them, the Rochester School introduces *ad hoc* arguments to excuse the failures of their theories. This tactic is a violation of the norms which, according to Popper . . . must be followed if a system of propositions is to be considered 'scientific'. (p.20)

Whittington (1987) strongly rejects the claim that PAT is free of value judgements or prescriptive implications. Commenting on Watts and Zimmerman (1986), he states:

> The principal deficiency of their book is that, in their enthusiasm for their own preferred type of work they denigrate the work of earlier accounting theorists and other contemporary researchers who adopt a different approach. This is unfortunate because it is unnecessary and tends to divert attention from the central issue, that *all* approaches to accounting theory are, at the present time, in a fairly rudimentary stage of evolution and desperately need further constructive development. Moreover, in their enthusiasm, they tend to ignore or forget the restrictive assumptions and relatively narrow focus of their own work. This creates the danger that they may never explore the full potential of studies of choice of accounting method. (p.335)

Watts and Zimmerman (1986) state: 'Throughout this book, we use science's concept of theory (positive theory). Under that concept, the objective of accounting theory is to explain and predict accounting practice (broadly defined)' (p.338). However, Sterling (1990, p.108) points out that none of the sciences use what Watts and Zimmerman allege is 'science's concept of theory'. On this issue Chambers (1993) also makes an interesting point when he says:

> The greater part of the scientific enterprise is directed, not to the tolerance or preservation of inherited knowledge and devices, but to the improvement or supersession of both . . . But PAT champions conventional accounting against its critics, the so-called normatives. (p.9)

There seems to be some confusion about the application of the so-called 'science's, concept of theory' in PAT. Watts and Zimmerman (1986) emphasise that the objective of accounting theory is to explain and predict accounting practice. However, they also say that given the training in finance of the forerunners of PAT, 'it was natural for them to concentrate on explaining and predicting security price behaviour and not on explaining and predicting accounting practice' (p.16).

On the issue of explaining and predicting security price behaviour, Chambers (1993) points out that most of the important indicators of a firm's performance and prospects which determine security price behaviour, such as solvency, the riskiness of assets, debt–equity relationships and the rate of return, are completely ignored by PAT (pp.7–8). Furthermore, considering the rapid changes in the social, economic, political and business environment which tend to create new accounting problems for a diverse range of firms within an economy, PAT focuses on a small proportion of firms which have their shares listed on the stock exchange.

Watts and Zimmerman (1990) state that they adopted the label 'positive' from economics. It appears that there is no commonly agreed upon meaning to the label 'positive' in the economics literature. For example, Boland and Gordon (1992, p.158) identify four different versions of positive economics: Harvard positivism, MIT positivism (Massachusetts Institute of Technology), Chicago positivism and LSE (London School of Economics) positivism. The methodology of PAT seems to be that of the Chicago School economists Stigler and Becker (1977; Watts and Zimmerman, 1986, p.176). This indicates their preference for one version of positive economics in comparison with other versions, that is, a value judgement.

Chapter summary

A theory is constructed on the basis of a set of propositions. These propositions can be classified into two categories, that is, 'is' and 'ought', depending on how they are expressed. 'Is' propositions are sub-divided into *a priori* and *a posteriori*, depending on

how the truth value is ascertained. The nature of the propositions used in constructing a theory is determined by the subject matter and the intended objective of the theory. A theory in an analytical science (mathematics or logic) is entirely based on *a priori* propositions. A theory in an empirical (natural) science (physics) is largely based on *a posteriori* propositions. A theory in an empirical (social) science (accounting) can be based largely on either *a priori* or *a posteriori* propositions, depending on the objective of the theory. For example, if the objective is to be descriptive, emphasis will be placed on *a posteriori* propositions, whereas if the objective is to be prescriptive, emphasis will be placed on *a priori* propositions. *A priori* propositions can also take the form of 'ought' propositions or value statements, depending on how they are expressed. In other words, an *a priori* proposition can be stated either as an 'is' statement or as an 'ought' statement. For example, the proposition 'a triangle has three sides' represents a self-evident truth (an 'is' statement), whereas the proposition 'a triangle should have three sides' represents a value position (an 'ought' statement). No theory is completely free from *a priori* propositions.

In accounting, theory construction and theory validation cannot be value free. The form and content of all theories, prescriptive or descriptive, are based to a considerable extent on value judgements. To validate an accounting theory is to provide proof that an application of the theory has worthwhile consequences. It is not possible to avoid making value judgements in determining the nature of these consequences.

Whatever the objective or the procedures followed, no theory can be perfect. In accounting there are weaknesses in both positive and normative theories. However, it is also important to point out that competing theories with differing viewpoints have the potential to provide important insights into the various issues raised within the accounting discipline.

Essay and examination questions

5.1   What is meant by accounting theory construction?

5.2   Define and evaluate the deductive and inductive approaches to the construction of an accounting theory.

5.3   Inductive logic may presuppose deductive logic. Comment on the applicability of this statement to accounting theory construction.

5.4   Elaborate on the differences between a descriptive and a prescriptive accounting theory.

5.5   Discuss the pragmatic, ethical, behavioural and communication theory approaches to accounting theory construction.

5.6   What is meant by accounting theory verification or validation?

5.7   Evaluate the criteria used in theory verification or validation in accounting.

5.8   Critically examine the underlying assumptions of PAT.

5.9   Identify the main features of *a priori* and *a posteriori* propositions.

5.10 Explain the different methods used in classifying accounting theories.

References and additional reading

Abdel-khalik, A.R. and Ajinkya, B.B. (1979). *Empirical Research in Accounting: A Methodological Viewpoint*. Sarasota: AAA.

American Accounting Association (1966). *Statement of Basic Accounting Theory*. Chicago: AAA.

American Accounting Association (1971). Report of the 'Committee on Accounting Theory Construction and Verification'. *The Accounting Review*, Supplement to Vol. XLVI, 53–79.

American Accounting Association (1977). *Statement of Accounting and Theory and Theory Acceptance*. Sarasota: AAA.

Baiman, S. (1982). Agency research in managerial accounting: A survey. *The Journal of Accounting Literature*, **1**, 154–213.

Beaver, W.H., Kennelly, J.W. and Voss, W.M. (1968). Predictive ability as a criterion for the evaluation of accounting data. *The Accounting Review*, October, 675–683.

Bedford, N. (1965). *Income Determination Theory: An Accounting Framework*. Addison-Wesley.

Belkaoui, A.B. (1993). *Accounting Theory* (Third edition). New York: HBJ.

Blake, J. (1992). A classification system for economic consequences issues in accounting regulation. *Accounting and Business Research*, **22**(88), 305–321.

Boland, L.A. and Gordon, I.M. (1992). Criticizing positive accounting theory. *Contemporary Accounting Research*, **9**(1), 147–170.

Bronowski, J. (1964). *Science and Human Values,* London: Penguin.

Butterworth, J.E., Gibbins, M. and King, R.D. (1984). The Structure of Accounting Theory: Some Basic Conceptual and Methodological Issues, in Mattesich, R. (Ed.). *Modern Accounting Research: History, Survey and Guide*. Research Monograph 7. Vancouver: The Canadian Certified General Accountants' Research Foundation, 209–250.

Carnap, R. (1951). *The Nature and Application of Inductive Logic*. Chicago: University of Chicago Press.

Carnap, R. (1966). *Philosophical Foundations of Physics.* New York: Basic Books.

Caws, P. (1965). *The Philosophy of Science.* New York: Reinhold Van Nostrand.

Chambers, R.J. (1950). The relationship between accounting and financial management. *The Australian Accountant,* **20**, 333–355.

Chambers, R.J. (1955). Blue print for a theory of accounting. *Accounting Research* (UK) **6** (1), 17–25.

Chambers, R.J. (1963). Why bother with postulates? *Journal of Accounting Research,* Spring, 3–15.

Chambers, R.J. (1966). *Accounting, Evaluation and Economic Behavior.* Englewood Cliffs, New Jersey: Prentice Hall.

Chambers, R.J. (1972). Accounting theory construction. Paper presented at the Third International Conference on Accounting Education, Sydney. Reproduced in R.J. Chambers and G.W. Dean, (Eds) (1986). *Chambers on Accounting.* Vol. III, 138–151. New York: Garland Publishing Inc.

Chambers, R.J. (1973). The validation of an accounting theory. *Waseda Business and Economics Studies,* **7**, 13–18.

Chambers, R.J. (1993). Positive Accounting Theory and the PA Cult. *Abacus* **29**(1), 1–26.

Christensen, C. (1983). The methodology of positive accounting. *The Accounting Review,* January, 1–22.

Demski, J. (1988). Positive accounting theory: A review. *Accounting, Organizations and Society,* **13** (6), 623–629.

Devine, C.T. (1960). Research methodology and accounting theory formation. *The Accounting Review,* July, 387–399.

Dopuch, N. and Revsine, L. (Eds) (1973). *Accounting Research 1960–1970: A Critical Evaluation.* Illinois: Centre for International Education and Research in Accounting.

Edwards, E.O. and Bell, P.W. (1961). *The Theory and Measurement of Business Income.* Los Angeles: University of California Press.

Feltham, G. (1984). Financial Accounting Research: Contributions of Information Economics & Agency Theory, in Mattesich, R. (Ed.). Modern Accounting Research: History, Survey Guide. Research Monograph 7. Vancouver: The Canadian Certified General Accountants' Research Foundation, 179–207.

Financial Accounting Standards Board. (1980). *Qualitative Characteristics of Accounting Information,* SFAC 2, Stamford: FASB.

Financial Accounting Standards Board. (1985). *Elements of Financial Statements* (a replacement of SFAC 3 incorporating an amendment of SFAC 2), SFAC 6, Stamford: FASB.

Friedman, M. (1953). The Methodology of Positive Economics, in *Essays in Positive Economics.* Chicago: University of Chicago Press.

Gaffikin, M.J.R. (1988). Legacy of the golden age: Recent developments in the methodology of accounting. *Abacus,* **24**, No. 1.

Gerboth, D.L. (1973). Research, intuition and politics in accounting inquiry. *The Accounting Review,* **58**(3), 476–482.

Gordon, M. (1964). Postulates, principles and research in accounting. *The Accounting Review,* **39**(2), 251–263.

Grady, P. (1965). *Inventory of Generally Accepted Accounting Principles for Business Enterprises,* Accounting Research Study — 7. AICPA.

Hakansson, N. (1969). Normative accounting theory and theory of decision. *International Journal of Accounting Education and Research,* Spring, 33–48.

Hempel, C. (1966). *Philosophy of Natural Sciences.* Englewood Cliffs, NJ: Prentice Hall.

Henderson, S., Peirson, G. and Brown, R. (1993). *Financial Accounting Theory: Its Nature and Development.* Melbourne: Longman Cheshire.

Hendriksen, E.S. (1982). *Accounting Theory,* 4th edn. Homewood, IL: Irwin.

Hendriksen, E.S. and Van Breda, M.F. (1992). *Accounting Theory* (Fifth edn). Homewood, Illinois: Irwin.

Hines, R.D. (1988). Popper's methodology of falsificationism and accounting research. *The Accounting Review,* **63** (4), 657–662.

Holthausen, R.W. and Leftwich, R.W. (1983). The economic consequences of accounting choice: Implications of costly contracting and monitoring. *Journal of Accounting and Economics.* **5**, 77–117.

Ijiri, Y. (1967). *Foundations of Accounting Measurement.* Englewood Cliffs, New Jersey: Prentice Hall.

Ijiri, Y. (1975). Theory of accounting measurement. *Studies in Accounting Research,* No. 10. Evanston, Illinois: AAA.

Ijiri, Y. and Jaedicke, R.K. (1966). Reliability and objectivity of accounting measurements. *The Accounting Review,* July.

Jensen, M.C. (1976). Reflections on the State of Accounting Research and the Regulation of Accounting, *Stanford Lectures in Accounting.* Stanford University.

Jensen, M. C. (1983). Organization theory, accounting and methodology. *Accounting Review,* **58**(2), 319–339.

Jensen, M.C. and Meckling, W.H. (1976). Theory of the firm: Managerial behavior, agency costs and ownership structure. *Journal of Financial Economics,* **3**, 305–360.

Kerlinger, F.N. (1964). *Foundations of Behavioural Research.* New York: Holt, Rinehart and Winston.

Kuhn, T.S. (1962). *The Structure of Scientific Revolutions.* Uni. of Chicago Press.

Machlup, F. (1955). The problem of verification in economics. *The Southern Economic Journal,* July.

Marschak, J. and Radner, R. (1972). *Economic Theory of Teams.* Yale Uni. Press.

Mattesich, R. (1964). *Accounting and Analytical Methods.* Homewood, IL: Irwin.

Moonitz, M. (1961). *The Basic Postulates of Accounting.* Accounting Research Study — 1. AICPA.

Mouck, T. (1990). Positive accounting theory as a Lakatosian research programme. *Accounting and Business Research,* **20**(79), 231–239.

Mozes, H. (1992). A framework for normative accounting research, *Journal of Accounting Literature,* **11**, 93–120.

Nelson, C. (1973). A Priori Research in Accounting, in Dopuch, N. and Revsine, L. (Eds.). *Accounting Research 1960–1970: A Critical Evaluation.* Illinois: Centre for International Education and Research in Accounting.

Perera, M.H.B. and Mathews, M.R. (1990). The cultural relativity of accounting and international patterns of social accounting. *Advances in International Accounting,* Vol. 3, 215–51.

Popper, K.R. (1959). *The Logic of Scientific Discovery.* London: Hutchinson.

Ronen, J. (1979). The Dual Role of Accounting: A Financial Economic Perspective, in Bicksler (Ed). *Handbook of Financial Economics,* North Holland. Chapter 20, 415–454.

Rudner, R. (1966). *Philosophy of Social Science*. Englewood Cliffs, NJ: Prentice Hall.

Schreuder, H. (1984). Positively Normative (Accounting) Theories, in Hopwood, A. and Schreuder, H. (Eds). *European Contributions to Accounting Research*. Amsterdam: Free University Press, 213–231.

Schroeder, R.G., McCullers, L.D. and Clark, M. (1987). *Accounting Theory*. New York: John Wiley.

Scott, DR (1941). The basis for accounting principles. *The Accounting Review,* December, 341–349.

Shackle, G. (1972). *Epistemics and Economics*. Cambridge University Press.

Simon, H. (1959). Theories of decision making economics. *American Economic Review,* June, 223–283.

Solomons, D. (1978). The policization of accounting. *Journal of Accountancy.* **146**(5), 65–72.

Sprouse, R.T. and Moonitz, M. (1962). *A Tentative Set of Broad Accounting Principles for Business Enterprises*. Accounting Research Study — 3. AICPA.

Sterling, R. (1970a). *Theory of the Measurement of Enterprise Income*. Lawrence: University of Kansas Press.

Sterling, R. (1970b). On theory construction and verification. *The Accounting Review,* July, 449–454.

Sterling, R. (1990). Positive accounting: An assessment, *Abacus,* **26**(2), 97–135.

Stigler, G. and Becker, G. (1977). De gustibus non est disputandum, *American Economic Review*, March, 76–90.

Tinker, A.M., Merino, B.D. and Neimark, M.D. (1982). The normative origins of positive theories: Ideology and accounting thought. *Accounting, Organizations and Society,* **7**(2), 167–200.

Watts, R. (1974). Accounting Objectives, *Working Paper Series No. 7408*. Graduate School of Management, University of Rochester, April.

Watts, R.L. (1977). Corporate financial statements: A product of the market and political processes, *Australian Journal of Management,* April, 52–75.

Watts, R.L. and Zimmerman, J.L. (1978). Toward a positive theory of the determination of accounting standards. *The Accounting Review,* **53**(1), 112–134.

Watts, R.L. and Zimmerman, J.L. (1979). The demand for and supply of accounting theories: The market for excuses. *The Accounting Review,* **54**(2), 273–305.

Watts, R.L. and Zimmerman, J.L. (1986). *Positive Accounting Theory*. Englewood Cliffs, New Jersey: Prentice Hall.

Watts, R.L. and Zimmerman, J.L. (1990). Positive accounting theory: A ten year perspective. *The Accounting Review,* **65**(1), 131–156.

Wells, M.C. (1976). A revolution in accounting thought. *The Accounting Review,* July, 471–482.

Whittington, G. (1987) Positive accounting: A review article. *Journal of Accounting and Business Research.* **17**(68), 327–336.

Williams, T.H. and Griffin, C.M. (1969). On the nature of empirical verification in accounting. *Abacus,* **5**, 143–178.

Wolk, H.I., Francis, J.R. and Tearney, M.G. (1992). *Accounting Theory — A conceptual and Institutional Approach,* third edition. Cincinnati, Ohio: South-Western Publishing Co.

Yu, S.C. (1976). *The Structure of Accounting Theory*. University of Florida.

Zeff, S.A. (1978). The rise of 'economic consequences'. *Journal of Accountancy,* **146**(6), 56–63.

Section 3

Accounting frameworks

Learning objectives

After studying this chapter the reader will be able to:
- list the various attempts at producing conceptual frameworks
- identify the conceptual frameworks which have a US origin and those which have a UK origin
- explain the basic differences between the different frameworks, including underlying philosophies
- identify and evaluate the basic arguments to be found in the literature concerning the utility of conceptual frameworks as a foundation for setting accounting standards
- formulate and express a considered opinion on the overall issue of conceptual frameworks in accounting.

Introduction

Over the past fifteen to twenty years the accounting discipline, through the collective efforts of groups of professionals and academics, has addressed the issue of a conceptual framework. In this chapter the attempts undertaken in the USA, Canada, the UK, Australia and New Zealand are examined and their similarities and differences are noted.

The qualitative characteristics of accounting information are considered, in particular those of relevance, comparability and reliability.

Finally, the whole issue of conceptual frameworks is reconsidered including their strengths and weaknesses, advantages and disadvantages and the likely future developments in this field.

Conflict of interest in the provision of information

The provision of information about the performance and status of an economic entity in the private sector is regulated by law (companies acts, income tax acts), the stock exchange, professional accounting bodies (statements of standard accounting practice) and by custom and usage (generally accepted accounting principles). In the case of public sector organisations there are requirements policed by various organisations such as the Audit Office. To a considerable extent there is still a debate about who the users of this information are and it is appropriate to briefly consider the range of possible users.

The traditional position or conventional wisdom argues that it is the ordinary shareholders who have a stake in the business, but, unlike institutional shareholders, they are unable to exert pressure on the organisation to get access to information and consequently they are in need of protection. It has not been demonstrated by research that the ordinary shareholders always use the information provided, but the fact that it has to be made available in an audited and reasonably usable form is held to provide a safeguard for all actual and potential shareholders.

Employees have a stake in the employing organisation, and although there may not be generally established 'rights to know', in some cases disclosures are made directly to trade union negotiators as part of the bargaining process. Consequently, it may be argued that rank and file employees should also receive information about aspects of organisation performance such as expansion and contraction, job security and representation, which directly affect them.

Government departments might claim some stake in information about the organisation, particularly in times of managed economies and fiscal and monetary intervention in the market place. Of course, government departments can obtain information more directly than through the statutory annual reports; this is a costless (to them) and relatively simply obtained source of information.

It may be argued that the general public are entitled to information about the performance and condition of organisations which exist within a political and economic system which derives its ultimate legitimation from the citizenry. This point of view is put forward in the Corporate Report (ASSC, 1975). The general public incorporates shareholders, employees, contributors to pension schemes which purchase company stock, customers, creditors, suppliers and taxpayers. It may be seen from this list that many individuals may have several stakes in the content of the information which is provided, through membership in more than one group.

Other parties with an interest in the published reports of corporations include financial analysts, journalists and commentators, competitors and suppliers of funds, goods and services.

There is a conflict between the wishes of various parties for more information and the reluctance of the supplier to incur the cost or inconvenience of supplying the information. Consequently, the range of information supplied varies from the minimum required by law to considerably beyond this point; from the simple quantitative financial material to the complex qualitative and quantitative material found in some reports, which appear to mix accounting and public relations presentations.

The conceptual frameworks reviewed in this chapter support many of the approaches set out above, which serves to render the study of the theoretical basis of accounting both interesting and complex.

The objectives of financial statements

Strictly speaking, financial statements cannot have objectives; only those individuals who cause the statements to be produced and who use them can have objectives. What are often referred to as the objectives of financial statements are really the functions of financial statements. These functions include the demonstration of stewardship, the provision of information to aid decision making (the decision-usefulness notion) and the means of demonstrating the accountability of one group to another.

Demonstrating stewardship

This is the oldest of the functions of financial accounts and actually predates the modern period. Stewardship accounting has been practised since ancient times and was particularly important at the time of the manorial accounting period when stewards had to establish the credibility of their tenure to the often absent landlord. Since the middle of the nineteenth century the concept of stewardship in accounting has referred to the separation of ownership and control which resulted from the use of the joint stock company structure. Thus, modern stewardship refers to the relationship between the managers and the owners (shareholders). The function of the financial statement then becomes that of demonstrating that the resources entrusted to management have been used in a proper manner.

The emphasis of stewardship for external reporting is on showing that investments have been made in productive assets, in an attempt to make profits within the objectives of the specific organisation, as set down in the memorandum of association. This requires a balance sheet and profit and loss account, from which the owners can trace aggregate financial movements during the period concerned.

Providing information to aid decision making

The stewardship function of the financial statement has been referred to as the classical approach to distinguish it from a more recent view, that of decision usefulness. This view is that the function of accounting statements is to aid various parties in making decisions (AAA, 1977). In particular, the parties making the decisions are shareholders and creditors, both actual and potential. Actual and potential shareholders require information to make decisions about holding, buying or selling company shares. Creditors and potential creditors must make decisions about lending or advancing funds to the company or withdrawing those which have already been lent.

It has been argued that accounting information would have a greater degree of decision usefulness if it was expressed in current values for assets and liabilities and by the provision of information from which future cash flows could be predicted. This aspect of accounting information is covered in detail in Chapter 11.

It has been suggested that decision usefulness can be extended to include the needs of those parties who seek to exercise an oversight or monitoring role over the social performance of the corporation (Henderson and Peirson, 1988, p.14). However, most of the literature on decision usefulness relates only to the needs of shareholders and creditors. The function of financial and other statements with respect to wider user groups is discussed under the heading of accountability in the following section.

Demonstrating accountability

The original means of demonstrating accountability was by the stewardship concept. This section has been deliberately separated from stewardship and placed under a different heading in order to demonstrate that a much wider concept is involved.

Over time the stakeholders affected by financial statements have been enlarged to incorporate not only shareholders and creditors, but also employees, suppliers, customers, government agencies and society at large (ASSC, 1975). In other words, a much wider group may expect the company to be accountable for actions taken in various market places for products, services, employment and care of the environment.

The socially constructed nature of accounting will mean that as a wider accountability is sought by various groups, so will accounting statements alter to accommodate the various pressures involved. However, it must be admitted that the pressures for wider accountability have varied over time, with a consequent blunting of the edge contained in the Corporate Report (ASSC, 1975). Nevertheless, much of the literature relating to conceptual frameworks is affected by the enlarged view of accountability, rather than the narrow view of decision usefulness.

Towards a conceptual framework

Thus far we have noted that conflicts of interest exist in the provision of accounting information and, furthermore, that the objectives of financial reporting (which are really functions) include stewardship, decision usefulness and accountability. The conceptual frameworks developed by accountants in a number of countries (USA, Canada, UK, Australia and New Zealand) reflect these functions, as well as the various conflicts of interest between the different parties.

A conceptual framework, according to the FASB, is: 'a coherent system of interrelated objectives and fundamentals that can lead to consistent standards and that prescribes the nature, function, and limits of financial accounting and financial statements' (FASB, 1976, p.2).

American conceptual frameworks

As noted previously, in the USA collective attempts to determine accounting matters began as long ago as the 1936 AAA *Tentative Statement of Accounting Principles*. More recently, the AICPA commissioned Accounting Research Study No. 1 (Moonitz, 1961) and Accounting Research Study No. 3 (Sprouse and Moonitz, 1962), the Accounting Principles Board Statement No. 4 on the *Basic Concepts and Principles Underlying Financial Statements of Business Enterprises* in 1970 and the Trueblood Report (AICPA, 1973). The AAA published *A Statement of Basic Accounting Theory* (ASOBAT) (AAA, 1966) and a *Statement of Accounting Theory and Theory Acceptance* (SATTA) (AAA, 1977).

The APB was replaced by the FASB in 1974. The FASB initiated an ambitious conceptual framework project for the production of Statements of Financial Accounting Concepts (SFACs). The first statement was devoted to the *Objectives of Financial Reporting by Business Enterprises* and published in 1978.

For clarity of exposition and in order to reduce the amount of repetition and overlap, this section will consider only two of the contributions listed above: the Trueblood Report (AICPA, 1973) and SFAC 1 (FASB, 1978). The basic positions will be described in order that the reader may compare and contrast these two frameworks and be able to trace their influence through other conceptual frameworks.

The study group set up by the AICPA to report on the objectives of financial statements was chaired by Robert Trueblood and is known as the Trueblood Report. Their findings were published in 1973 and reflect a traditional approach to the accounting function as reporting to shareholders and creditors, in financial terms, on the periodic income and financial position of companies. There are strong decision-usefulness additions in the call for information from which decision makers could predict future cash flows. The various objectives are set out below with some brief comments on each.

> The basic objective of financial statements is to provide information useful for making economic decisions.

The report states that this objective should apply to both the private and public sectors and, by ensuring a more efficient allocation of resources, accounting reports contribute to the attainment of broad social goals. This view will be challenged by those who want accounting to allow for non-market relations such as externalities and who believe that the objectives of organisations in the public and private sectors are, or should be, fundamentally different.

The financial statements are produced for users without special sources of information or the bargaining power to obtain additional data, hence:

> An objective of financial statements is to serve primarily those users who have limited authority, ability, or resources to obtain information and who rely on financial statements as their principal source of information about an enterprise's economic activity.

A number of objectives deal with the decision-usefulness goal of being able to predict enterprise cash flows and earning power. Therefore:

> An objective of financial statements is to provide information useful to investors and creditors for predicting, comparing and evaluating potential cash flows to them in terms of amount, timing, and related uncertainty.

and:

> An objective of financial statements is to provide users with information for predicting, comparing and evaluating enterprise earning power.

The need to monitor the attainment of overall corporate objectives through financial statements is covered by:

> An objective of financial statements is to supply information useful in judging management's ability to utilize enterprise resources effectively in achieving the primary enterprise goals.

The disclosure of underlying assumptions, as detailed in the following objective, is clearly a necessary part of any conceptual framework:

> Basic underlying assumptions with respect to matters subject to interpretation, evaluation, prediction or estimation should be disclosed.

When considering the content of the financial statements required to achieve the objectives listed above, the report concluded with a very traditional recommendation, namely, a statement of financial activities, thus:

> An objective is to provide a statement of financial position useful for predicting, comparing and evaluating enterprise earning power. This statement should provide information concerning enterprise transactions and other events that are part of incomplete earnings cycles. Current values should also be reported when they differ significantly from historical cost. Assets and liabilities should be grouped or segregated by the relative uncertainty of the amount and timing of prospective realization or liquidation. An objective is to provide a statement of periodic earnings useful for predicting, comparing and evaluating enterprise earning power. The net result of completed earnings cycles and enterprise activities resulting in successive statements of financial position should also be reported, but separately, since they differ in terms of their certainty of realization.

The report recommends that financial statements should be structured in such a way that the preparer does not have to make judgements about the data or interpret the contents on behalf of the reader or user:

> An objective is to provide a statement of financial activities useful for predicting, comparing and evaluating enterprise earning power. This statement should report mainly on factual aspects of enterprise transactions having or expected to have significant cash consequences. This statement should report data that require minimal judgement and interpretation by the preparer.

If management forecasts are to be employed to aid the users of financial statements in making decisions, then these forecasts should be designed to enhance the reliability of users' predictions and not simply the accuracy of the forecasts themselves. Thus:

> An objective of financial statements is to provide information useful for the predictive process. Financial forecasts should be provided when they will enhance the reliability of users' predictions.

Finally, the Trueblood Report contains two objectives which do not appear to fit completely with those previously considered. These are concerned with accounting for not-for-profit organisations and the role of the enterprise within the social environment. When preparing financial statements for governmental and not-for-profit organisations it is recommended that the objectives of the particular organisation be considered:

> An objective of financial statements for governmental and not-for-profit organizations is to provide information useful for evaluating the effectiveness of the management of resources in achieving the organization's goals. Performance

measures should be quantified in terms of identified goals.

However, these performance measures have not been identified within traditional accounting practices except in the usual financial accounting manner by means of ratios obtained from financial statements. The whole area of performance measurement for government and not-for-profit organisations has developed separately from, and outside of, the conceptual framework projects.

The last objective given by the Trueblood Report attempts to relate accounting for both private and social goals. There is an underlying assumption that financial statements which benefit private users will also lead to an increase in aggregate social welfare. There is no automatic mechanism which will ensure that financial statements will lead to an overall betterment of social conditions for the whole of society despite the assertion that:

> An objective of financial statements is to report on those activities of the enterprise affecting society which can be determined and described or measured and which are important to the role of the enterprise in its social environment.

Many of the ideas expressed in the Trueblood Report were carried through into the FASB project to produce SFACs. Six statements were produced in a series which began as a fairly conservative position on financial reports and became increasingly a statement of existing conventions and definitions. We shall consider mainly the first statement (SFAC 1) which deals with the objectives of financial reporting by business enterprises, although SFAC 2, which deals with qualitative characteristics, will be briefly referred to.

Several important factors underlie the conclusions made in the statement. These are:

- information is not costless and, therefore, the benefits of usage should exceed the costs of production
- accounting reports are by no means the only source of information about enterprises available to investors
- accrual accounting is extremely useful for assessing and predicting earning power and cash flows of an enterprise
- although the information provided should be useful, users make from it their own predictions and assessments.

The objectives given in SFAC 1 may be summarised as follows.

1

Financial reporting is intended to be decision useful in orientation.

2

Objectives of financial reporting will change over time as a result of changes in the economic, legal, political and social environment.

3

Financial reporting information is limited by the nature of the information provided in that it relates to micro-business units, results from the use of approximate measures, is historical in orientation, is only one source of information available to users and is not costless.

4

SFAC 1 is only concerned with general purpose external reporting by business enterprises, in particular for external users who lack the authority to obtain information other than that provided to them. Furthermore, the objectives are broad and directed towards estimating cash flows.

5

SFAC 1 refers to financial reporting in general and not simply to financial statements.

6

Financial reporting should provide information which will enable present and potential investors, creditors and other users to make rational investment decisions provided that the users have a reasonable understanding of business and are prepared to study the information provided.

7
Financial reporting should enable users to assess the amount, timing and uncertainty of prospective cash flows.

8
Financial reporting should provide information about economic resources and claims on economic resources (which would allow the computation of owners' equity).

9
Expectations of future performance must be based, at least in part, on past performance.

10
Financial reporting is mainly concerned about earnings rather than financial position.

11
Financial reporting should be based on accrual accounting, because generally this approach provides a better prediction of cash flows than information about past cash flows.

12
Financial reporting will provide not only information about periodic financial performance but also enable users to see how well management has discharged its stewardship role.

13
Financial reporting provides only an indirect valuation of the business.

14
Users of information contained in financial reports predict cash flows and estimates. No matter how useful the information may be, it is the user who is responsible for the employment of the data.

15
Management can assist users by providing details of events and circumstances of particular importance to the enterprise.

The SFAC 2 deals with the qualitative characteristics of accounting information. The particular quality which is sought for the overall financial reporting system is that of decision usefulness, which is affected by relevance and reliability. Relevance exists where the information provided is capable of making a difference to a decision. It is affected by predictive value, feedback value and timeliness. Reliability of information means that users can depend on it to represent economic conditions or events. Reliability is dependent on the qualities of verifiability, representational faithfulness and neutrality.

It is clear that the Trueblood Report and SFAC 1 have very much in common. Although there are minor points of disagreement, such as the expertise which may be expected from users, there are many more areas of agreement. The view of accounting contained in this conceptual framework is centred on decision usefulness, with users firmly categorised as market participants who use the information to predict cash flow. Historical cost is the basis for preparing statements of financial position which, however, take second place to information about income of the period. General purpose accounting reports are thought appropriate for users who are unable to obtain information other than that which is provided by management. There is no reference to the social consequences of enterprise performance other than one objective in the Trueblood Report which suggests that accounting aids social welfare by assisting with a more rational resource distribution. There is no consideration of the information needs of employees or the general public.

UK: the Corporate Report and the Government Green Paper
The approach taken by UK accounting bodies to the objectives of the accounting

process was quite different from that of their US counterparts. The Corporate Report, prepared by a committee chaired by Derek Boothman on behalf of the ASSC, is a radical document which was not accepted by the accounting profession but which has nevertheless had some effect on accounting practice throughout the Commonwealth. The Corporate Report was also part of the foundation of a UK Government Green Paper which did not become law, but which has also influenced accounting practices.

The underlying premise of the Corporate Report is that of a social contract between business and society. In other words, society permits business to exist through legislation and by allowing the market place to function, and in return business owes certain duties to society. These duties include reporting on activities, not only to shareholders and creditors, but also to employees and other interested parties and ultimately the general public. Consequently, the Corporate Report is not about providing general purpose financial statements to shareholders and creditors but about providing a wide range of information, including financial data, to a full range of user groups. This information could make use of a range of statements, both those traditionally used and a number to be developed.

The Corporate Report begins with a number of philosophical statements which may be summarised as follows: corporate reports should satisfy the needs of users; every significant economic entity, regardless of legal constitution, has the responsibility to report publicly; the public accountability of significant entities is separate from any formal legal requirements to disclose because stewardship is much wider than the traditional relationship with shareholders; general purpose reports should be prepared for general purpose users; and users of reports are those who have reasonable rights to the information about the report-

ing entity. The list of users provided includes equity investors, loan creditors, employees, analysts, advisors, business contacts, government and the public.

In their summary, the committee reiterated the main points of the discussion, which marks the Corporate Report as a distinctive contribution to the debate about the objectives (functions) of accounting reports. The main points are set out below. Corporate reports should:

1

satisfy the needs of users for information about economically significant entities. The fundamental objective is expressed as follows: 'In our view the fundamental objective of corporate reports is to communicate economic measurement of and information about the resources and performance of the reporting entity useful to those having reasonable rights to such information

2

attempt to satisfy the needs of users with a reasonable right to information; a comprehensive list is provided

3

enable users to evaluate the performance and standing of the enterprise in a wide variety of activities including the achievement of stated objectives; stewardship; employment, investment and profit distribution plans; economic stability, liquidity and capital requirements; future prospects; intergroup performance; economic performance in relation to society and social costs and benefits; compliance with legal requirements, business and products; comparisons over time; users' present and prospective interests and ownership and control

4

be 'relevant, understandable, reliable, complete, objective, timely and comparable' (para. 8.4)

5

satisfy the fundamental objectives, so far as is possible, while recognising that particular cases will be limited by practical considerations of cost and confidentiality

6

provide information about the performance of entities which recognises the importance of new user groups, including employees and the public; distributable profit is no longer regarded as the sole or premier indicator of performance in corporate reports

7

be timely, frequent and regular, but probably not more frequent than annually

8

be sent to all shareholders as well as being freely available to anybody on request

9

provide additional statements (beyond the traditional income statement, balance sheet and statement of funds flow), including a statement of value added, an employment report, a statement of money exchanges with government, a statement of transactions in foreign currency, a statement of future prospects and a statement of corporate objectives

10

contain disaggregated data in respect of turnover, value added, profits or losses before tax, capital employed and number of employees

11

include descriptive and interpretive statements by chief officers, appropriate summaries of income and expenditure, financial position and flow of funds statements for at least the previous five years

12

be expressed in terms of a standard unit of measurement

13

include inflation adjusted financial statements on an equal basis with historical cost data.

The Government Green Paper (a discussion document intended to obtain feedback prior to the preparation of a White Paper which contains proposed legislation) was published in July 1977. It acknowledges the Corporate Report as an important source of ideas. The contents of the Government Green Paper were aimed mainly at companies with more than 500 employees or a turnover (in 1977) of £5 million or more.

A number of additional forms of disclosure were advocated including: a statement of value added, an employment statement, a statement of sources and applications of funds, information about short term borrowings, details of leases and similar revenue commitments, disclosure of pension commitments, details of transactions in foreign currencies, details of research and development expenditures, disaggregated reports, information about foreign trade, a statement of future prospects, developments in social accounting and a statement of energy usage.

In conclusion, the Government Green Paper states:

> In putting forward these proposals the Government believes that it is taking an important step towards ensuring that company reports give a broader and more balanced view of company operations while, at the same time, improving the quality of the financial accounts. Reports and accounts in the form proposed will be more valuable to all those concerned with a company, whether shareholders, employees, creditors, customers or the Government. (para. 59)

It is clear that the approaches by US and UK bodies during the 1970s were quite different. The value positions taken in respect of accounting varied between market based wealth maximisation and a social contract approach. The attempts at developing conceptual frameworks for accounting in Canada, Australia, New Zealand and the IASC may be examined in the light of the influences and directions contained in the US and UK material reviewed in these two sections.

A somewhat different approach from that of the 1970s was pursued in 1991 and the ASB adopted the Internal Standard Committee's 'Framework for the Preparation and Presentation of Financial Statements' (ASB, 1991). The ASB has thus embraced decision usefulness as a basis for the preparation and presentation of financial statements, in contrast to an accountability and stewardship approach.

Page (1992, p.77) notes that although the adoption of this framework would appear to avoid duplication of effort, there are difficulties in adopting a decision-usefulness approach:

> However, it is worth questioning the central assumption of the project, namely:
> The objective of financial statements is to provide information about the financial adaptability of an enterprise that is useful to a wide range of users in making economic decisions.

Page (1992) correctly stated that a number of questions may be asked of the decision-usefulness approach: Has it assisted financial reporting to date? Does it explain existing practice? What changes in reporting practice would it imply? Are its assumptions reasonable? Is it consistent with other desirable objectives of financial reporting? He concludes that:

> The statement of principles is wasted opportunity to affirm the importance of stewardship reporting and the place of financial reporting in enriching the set of feasible economic relationships which firms can enter into. (p.84)

Canada: CICA (1980) and ASAC (1987)

There have been two attempts at producing a Canadian conceptual framework for accounting. The first, by the Canadian

Institute of Chartered Accountants (CICA) in 1980 was entitled *Corporate Reporting: Its Future Evolution*. It was heavily influenced by the Corporate Report and not received with enthusiasm by CICA members. Consequently, the report appears not to have made a deep impression upon accounting in Canada. A more recent attempt was made by the Accounting Standards Authority of Canada (ASAC), a body supported by the Certified General Accountants in Canada. The ASAC document was heavily influenced by the SFAC project.

The CICA report provides guidelines for standard setters, suggests user groups, indicates the purposes of reports and statements, and makes reference to the possible content of such documents. The overall approach seeks to expand the notion of accountability and to add further disclosures to existing annual reports.

Although the ASAC document entitled *Conceptual Framework for Annual Reporting* is based on the SFAC material, it is argued that there are three major reasons for the development of a Canadian conceptual framework. First, the Canadian environment requires a framework which is oriented towards a broad user group because the user group towards which the SFACs are directed is too narrow. Second, the establishment of a uniquely Canadian accounting entity is a desirable accomplishment in its own right. The position must be seen as part of the long established objective of maintaining a separate Canadian identity wherever possible. Finally, to foster the development of accounting it is argued that a framework must provide conceptual positions on fundamental issues such as the asset–liability view (compared to a revenue–expense view) and measurement issues regarding the attributes and scales to be used in reporting. This is not done by the SFAC project.

The development of a Canadian conceptual framework may be justified if the commercial and industrial environment is sufficiently different from that of the UK or the USA to require an alternative view of the reporting world. Furthermore, having a different conceptual framework will assist in developing or generating an individual Canadian accounting model. It is equally an opportunity to correct a number of perceived defects in the SFAC project, including the inherent conservatism and limited view of reporting requirements.

One of the major weaknesses of the ASAC document is that it does not clearly state what the perceived deficiencies of the SFACs are and how they are to be corrected. Nevertheless, there are going to be changes to the conceptual framework in Canada because the CICA will almost certainly produce a response to the ASAC in an attempt to maintain their position as the body responsible for setting standards in that country.

Australia: AARF Statements of Accounting Concepts

At the end of 1987 the AARF and the Public Sector Accounting Standards Board (PSASB) combined to initiate a very ambitious project for the development of an *Australian Conceptual Framework for Regulated Financial Reporting*. The planned outline of the project contains nineteen building blocks of which only a limited number have been made available so far. We shall consider the first four Statements of Accounting Concepts (SAC 1–4), pointing out particular strengths, weaknesses and differences so that an overall evaluation may be made. The definition of a conceptual framework is set out as follows:

> The conceptual framework is a set of inter-related concepts which will define the nature, subject, purpose and broad content of financial reporting. It will be an explicit rendition of the thinking which is governing the decision-making of the [standards setters] when they set

down requirements, including accounting standards. It is not expected that the framework will ever be fully completed, in the sense that the Boards expect it to evolve on a continuing basis as the demands on financial reporting, and capabilities open to such reporting, change. (AARF, 1987)

The completed parts of the framework are designated SAC 1–4. We shall consider each of these in turn.

SAC 1: definition of the reporting entity
This SAC is concerned with the concept of a reporting entity and the quality of reporting appropriate to such an entity. In paragraph 6 a number of definitions are set down and are reproduced here:

a. Control . . . capacity of an entity to dominate decision-making, directly or indirectly, in relation to the financial and operating policies of another entity, so as to enable that other entity to operate with it in achieving the objectives of the controlling entity.
b. Economic Entity . . . a group of entities comprising a controlling entity, and one or more controlled entities operating together to achieve objectives consistent with those of the controlling entity.
c. Entity . . . any legal, administrative, or fiduciary arrangement, organisational structure or other party (including a person) having the capacity to deploy scarce resources in order to achieve objectives.
d. General purpose financial report . . . a financial report intended to meet the information needs common to a range of users who are unable to command the preparation of reports tailored so as to satisfy, specifically, all of the information needs of those users.

Paragraphs 7–9 cover financial reporting and reiterate the previously stated position that financial reports are prepared 'to provide users with information about the reporting entity which is useful in making and evaluating decisions about the allocation of scarce resources'.

These reports will also be the means by which the managers and governing bodies discharge their accountability to users. Entities that need to report should do so, but others should not be placed under any similar obligation. This provision may be compared with the requirement which the Corporate Report places on significant economic entities. General purpose financial reports are to be used where the range of users' needs have common elements.

The reporting entity concept is dealt with in paragraphs 16–18. The existing bases for reporting are the legal entity concept in the private sector and the accountability of elected representatives and appointed officials in the public sector. These existing bases are rejected in favour of: 'a concept of the reporting entity which is tied to the information needs of users and the nature of general purpose financial reports'.

The individual reporting entities should be identified through the users of general purpose financial reports for making and evaluating resource allocation decisions. In other words, if an entity has such users then it becomes a reporting entity and must produce the appropriate reports. The discussion then turns to the criteria for identifying a reporting entity (paras 19–22). These include the separation of management from the economic interest, the economic or political importance or influence and financial characteristics including size. The implications of applying the reporting entity concept are worked through in paragraphs 23–37. Included would be most government departments and statutory authorities, the government as a whole at both central and local levels

and, in the private sector, as a result of the separation of ownership or membership and management, reporting should be undertaken by public companies, listed investment trusts, entities raising debt funds and those of particular size and economic significance.

The SAC 1 rejects any suggestion that size of entity or ownership criteria alone might eliminate the need to produce general purpose financial reports. The criterion for non-production is that where users who are dependent on the information for the purposes of making and evaluating resource allocation decisions do not exist, no report is required. Consequently, sole traders, partnerships, privately-owned companies and trusts where the public is not involved will probably not have to report. The SAC 1 concludes with the following:

> Para. 40 —
> Reporting entities are all entities (including economic entities) in respect of which it is reasonable to expect the existence of users dependent on general purpose financial reports for information which will be useful to them for making and evaluating decisions about the allocation of scarce resources.

> Para. 41 —
> Reporting entities shall prepare general purpose financial reports. Such reports shall be prepared in accordance with Statements of Accounting Concepts and Accounting Standards.

SAC 2: objective of general purpose financial reporting

The overall focus of this SAC is given as general purpose external financial reporting by entities in both the private and public sectors. Users of this information are covered in paragraphs 16–25. The users include resource providers who may be compensated directly or indirectly for the resources provided, including employees, lenders, creditors, suppliers, investors and contributors. In the case of public sector organisations, users include parliament, tax payers and rate payers. A second group of users includes the recipients of goods and services such as customers and beneficiaries. A third group includes those performing a review or oversight function.

The objective of general purpose financial reports is given in paragraphs 26–27 as: 'To provide information to users that is useful for making and evaluating decisions about the allocation of scarce resources'.

Paragraphs 28–38 discuss the types of information to be disclosed and include references to revenues, expenses, assets, liabilities, equity, cost of goods and services, changing control over resources and the capacity to generate cash. In addition, the subject of non-financial and semi-financial information will be the subject of a separate SAC.

The concluding paragraphs set down the SAC including the definitions incorporated in the discussion part of the document:

> Para. 43 —
> General purpose financial reports shall provide information useful to users for making and evaluating decisions about the allocation of scarce resources.

> Para. 44 —
> Managements and governing bodies shall present general purpose financial reports in a manner which assists in discharging their accountability.

> Para. 45 —
> General purpose financial reports shall disclose information relevant to the assessment of performance, financial position, and financing and investing, including information about compliance.

SAC 3: qualitative characteristics of financial information

The qualitative characteristics referred to in SAC 3 include comparability, materiality, relevance, reliability and understanding. In addition to providing definitions of these qualitative characteristics, the statement discusses two constraints on relevant and reliable information, namely timeliness and cost/benefit considerations.

The SAC on qualitative characteristics concludes as follows:

> Para. 48 —
> General purpose financial reports shall include all financial information which satisfies the concepts of relevance and reliability, and which passes the materiality test.

> Para. 49 —
> General purpose financial reports shall be presented on a timely basis and in a manner which satisfies the concepts of comparability and understandability.

SAC 4: definition and recognition of the elements of financial statements

This particular SAC is divided into five parts dealing with assets, liabilities, equity, revenues and expenses, followed by an extensive appendix which covers areas such as the issue of equally unperformed (executory) contracts and the specific application of the contents of the SAC.

Definition and recognition of assets

The definition of an asset is given in paragraph 12: 'Assets are service potential or future economic benefits controlled by the reporting entity as a result of past transactions or other past events'.

The SAC discusses essential and other characteristics of assets before arriving at criteria for the recognition of assets. The essential characteristics include service potential or future economic benefits, control over the service potential or future economic benefits, and a transaction or other event which has already occurred. Other characteristics include acquisition at a cost, tangibility, exchangeability, and legal enforceability.

The criteria for the recognition of assets are given in paragraph 36:

> An asset shall be recognised in the statement of financial position when and only when:
> (a) it is probable that the service potential or future economic benefits embodied in the asset will eventuate; and
> (b) the asset possesses a cost or other value that can be measured reliably.

Where these criteria are not met, the matter in question may be appropriately indicated by means of notes to the accounts.

Definition and recognition of liabilities

Liabilities are defined in paragraph 46:

> 'Liabilities' are the future sacrifices of service potential or future economic benefits that the entity is presently obliged to make to other entities as a result of past transactions or other past events.

The SAC 4 goes on to discuss the essential characteristics of liabilities including the existence of a present obligation and the necessary sacrifice of service potential or future economic benefits. Criteria for the recognition of liabilities are given in paragraph 60:

> A liability shall be recognised in the statement of financial position when and only when:
> (a) it is probable that the future sacrifice of service potential or future economic benefits will be required; and
> (b) the amount of the liability can be measured reliably.

The discussion which follows refers to the issues of probability and reliability: probability requires that the chance of sacrifice is greater than that of no sacrifice, and reliability requires some form of verifiable evidence about which a judgement can be made.

Where the recognition criteria cannot be met, there may still be a need for disclosure by means of notes to the accounts.

Definition and recognition of equity

Equity is defined in paragraph 67: 'Equity is the residual interest in the assets of the entity after deduction of its liabilities'. The term equity was chosen to avoid the partiality attendant upon alternate terms such as shareholders' funds. Equity cannot be defined independently of the other aspects of financial position, which must follow the definitions of both assets and liabilities. Equity is also affected by decisions about capital inflows and outflows (contributions by owners and distributions to owners). Paragraph 128 defines contributions by owners as:

> Contributions by owners means service potential or future economic benefits that have been contributed to the entity by parties external to the entity, other than those which result in liabilities of the entity, that establish a financial interest in the new assets of the entity which:
> (a) conveys entitlement both to distributions of service potential or future economic benefits by the entity during its life, such distributions being at the discretion of the ownership group or its representatives, and to distributions of any excess of assets over liabilities in the event of the entity being wound up; and/or
> (b) can be sold, transferred or redeemed; and 'distributions to owners' means service potential or future economic benefits distributed by the entity to all or part of its ownership group, either as a return on investment or as a return of investment.

Definition and recognition of expenses

The SAC 4 puts revenues and expenses together under the general heading of performance. Revenues are defined in paragraph 95 as:

'Revenues' are inflows or other enhancements, or savings in outflows, of service potential or future economic benefits in the form of increases in assets or reductions in liabilities of the entity, other than those relating to contributions by owners, that result in an increase in equity during the reporting period.

The characteristics of revenues are discussed in paragraphs 96–98, including what constitutes revenue and the circumstances surrounding the recognition of revenue. A separate section examines the situation where revenue results from the saving of outflows. Criteria for the recognition of revenue are given in paragraph 109:

A revenue shall be recognised in the operating statement, in the determination of the result for the reporting period, when and only when:
(a) it is probable that the inflow or other enhancement or saving in outflows of service potential or future economic benefits has occurred; and
(b) the inflow or other enhancement or saving in outflows of service potential or future economic benefits can be measured reliably.

The definition of expenses is given in paragraph 101:

Expenses are consumptions or losses of service potential or future economic benefits in the form of reductions in assets or increases in liabilities of the entity, other than those relating to distributions to owners, that result in a decrease in equity during the reporting period.

The discussion of the characteristics of expenses which follows does not enter any new territory, neither do the criteria for recognition of expenses which are given in paragraph 116:

An expense shall be recognised in the operating statement, in the determination of the result for the reporting period, when and only when:
(a) it is probable that the consumption or loss of service potential or future economic benefits resulting in a reduction in assets and/or an increase in liabilities has occurred; and
(b) the consumption or loss of service potential or future economic benefits can be measured reliably.

The same notions of probability and reliability of measurement apply to expenses as were applied to liabilities; the probability of the event taking place must exceed the probability that it will not take place and some minimum level of measurement reliability must exist for professional judgement to be satisfied, particularly where estimates are involved.

Other aspects of performance

Other aspects of performance discussed by SAC 4 include recognition techniques, the display of revenues and expenses, contributions by owners and distributions to owners and capital maintenance adjustments.

The section on recognition techniques includes familiar material on the matching of revenues and expenses, including a clear statement (para. 123) that systematic allocation of service potential over several periods may be necessary, particularly for buildings, plant and equipment, goodwill, patents and trademarks.

The SAC 4 does not specify any particular form of presentation of revenues and expenses, and there is no extensive discussion of such topics as extraordinary items compared to operating items. The SAC 4 notes in paragraph 125 that:

it may be useful to distinguish revenues and expenses resulting from the entity's major or central operations and those resulting from other operations. These are matters of display which, although important to assessments of performance, are beyond the scope of this statement.

Contributions by owners and distributions to owners are defined in paragraph 128.

The SAC 4 briefly discusses the notion of capital maintenance adjustments which are defined as: 'Capital maintenance adjustments are adjustments made under certain accounting models to the entity's capital to take account of the effects of price changes on the entity's assets and liabilities' (para. 132).

Paragraph 136 notes that SAC 4 is not premised on the adoption of any particular measurement model, and indicates that a future SAC will address the fundamental issue of alternative measurement models.

Transitional provisions

The provisions of SAC 4 apply to each reporting entity for the first reporting period ending on or after 1 January 1994 (para. 3). All entities producing general purpose financial reports, whether or not they meet the definitions of reporting entities, are required to follow these provisions.

There is one exception to this general requirement which is set down in paragraphs 138 and 139. The effect of the transitional provision in paragraph 138 is to allow a one-year delay in applying SAC 4 to some or all agreements which are equally proportionately unperformed. This area of discussion was a major feature in several exposure drafts (ED 42C, ED 42D, ED 46B in particular) but in the final SAC it is dealt with as part of an appendix (paras 3–14) and implementation is subject to the transitional arrangements.

Where the transitional arrangements are employed, paragraph 139 provides for a catch-up adjustment:

Where assets and liabilities which arise from agreements equally proportionately unperformed are first recognised in the statement of financial position during the transitional period specified in paragraph 138 or during the first reporting period that ends on or after 1 January 1995, the net amount of those adjustments shall be adjusted against retained profits (surplus) or accumulated losses (deficiency) in the reporting periods in which the assets and liabilities are first recognised.

The appendix provides a discussion of the issues involved in evaluating agreements which are equally proportionately unperformed. Examples include purchase orders for materials or equipment, leases, forward exchange contracts, commodity futures contracts and certain types of employment agreements (para. 3). The critical considerations are said to be:

whether the entity has control over the service potential or future economic benefits and whether the entity has a present obligation to sacrifice service potential or future economic benefits in completing its acts of performance under the agreements. (para. 4)

These notions have been incorporated into criteria for the recognition of assets and liabilities under the specific circumstances:

Assets and liabilities that arise from agreements equally proportionately unperformed would need to be recognised where:
(a) it is probable that:
    (i) in respect of the assets, the service potential or future economic benefits arising from the agreement will eventuate; and
    (ii) in respect of the liabilities, the future sacrifice of service potential or future economic benefits under the agreement will be required; and

(b) the amounts of those assets and liabilities can be measured reliably. (para. 5)

Further attention is given to the evidence of likely benefits and sacrifices which would be required, together with reliable measurements of those benefits and sacrifices, before recognition could be given in practice to the asset and liability.

Leases, whether operating or finance, are likely to be covered by the provisions of SAC 4, giving rise to both assets and liabilities. The critical issue is the non-cancellable nature of the contract, together with the imposition of a penalty clause (paras 10–11).

Although purchase commitments have not been generally reported in the past, the application of the provisions of SAC 4 would be likely to require their disclosure, where the agreement is enforceable and therefore non-cancellable. The practice of providing for an expected loss on a purchase commitment does not constitute the proper recognition of a liability, which should reveal the total liability and corresponding asset, with the asset being written down to an appropriate carrying amount (paras 12–13).

Paragraph 14 considers employment agreements which may, under rare circumstances, give rise to assets and liabilities. However, the appendix to SAC 4 notes that: 'Most employment agreements merely serve to evidence the intentions of the employer and the employee, and in substance are avoidable by either party'. The extension of recognition of assets and liabilities in the manner described in the appendix is a good example of the advances which may be possible using a modern conceptual framework.

Controversies surrounding the implementation of SAC 4

The impact which SAC 4 could be expected to have on financial reporting has been debated for some time. The controversy has extended to other SACs, the AASB and the ASB, and at one time threatened to destroy the whole conceptual framework project (*Financial Forum,* May 1993). This was averted by removing the mandatory status of SAC 4 (*Financial Forum*, June 1993) despite the strong opposition of the ASB (*Financial Forum*, August and September 1993). The whole issue of the content of SAC 4 is to be addressed in a redraft due out in late 1994, although no decision has been reached on the mandatory nature of any revised concept. (At the time of going to press the redraft had not been published.)

The difficulties connected with the content and mandatory status of SAC 4 have revealed underlying problems with the development of new accounting standards, and the corporate sector has requested that greater influence be exerted over their preparation. In particular, any attempt to produce accounting concepts or standards which are considered to be in advance of the international position, contain measurement systems involving other than modified historical costs, and take what is described as an academic rather than a practical approach, results in strong criticism. Criticism has come not only from industry and commerce, but also from representatives of the accounting profession, which appears to be attempting to regain lost influence over the standard-setting activity. The response of the AASB has been to set up a consultative body to improve communications, especially on emerging issues. However, the problems are continuing over specific standards.

The problems outlined above are inevitable in concept and standard development and where socially constructed activity is being reconstructed or modified. The difference from most previous debates is that the matters have now been brought out into the open. The preparers and the larger accounting firms appear to be lined up against the accounting and auditing standard-setting bodies. Where government stands is not yet clear. However, in any system where standards have the support of law, government intervention is always possible. The users of financial reports and the general public do not appear to be high on the list of concerns of the preparers or the accounting profession.

The importance of the debate for conceptual framework development is that it demonstrates an example of SAC 4 being used as a focus for underlying dissent within the whole field of standard setting and accounting regulation. This is possibly the first time that a conceptual framework has had this effect.

The Australian *Conceptual Framework* SACs have been considered at some length because this is the most organised and detailed of recent attempts to structure the process of financial reporting. Elements of previous work in this area, such as the SFAC project and the Corporate Report, may be discerned, together with important new initiatives, such as the recognition of executory contracts as assets and liabilities requiring disclosure. A further important reason to consider the AARF programme at some length is the likely influence which it may have upon Australian and New Zealand developments.

The AARF programme is, of course, incomplete and subject to the modifying influences of tradition and vested interests, which may affect the final form. It is, however, one of the most exciting approaches to the development of a conceptual framework for external financial reporting for many years.

International Accounting Standards Committee

The IASC has issued a statement entitled *Framework for the Preparation and Presentation of Financial Statements*. The purpose of the statement is mainly to assist with standard setting and the evaluation of existing standards, although nothing in the standard should override any specific international accounting standard. In the event of conflict, existing standards should prevail over the statement, but conflicts are expected to diminish over time.

The framework is concerned with general purpose financial statements (para. 6) which include a balance sheet, a profit and loss account and a statement of changes in financial position, as well as notes and other statements and explanatory material that are integral to the financial statements. The added materials which may be included, such as reports by directors, are not regarded as part of the financial statements (para. 7).

The framework applies to financial statements produced by reporting enterprises in both the private and public sectors. Reporting enterprises are those: 'for which it is reasonable to expect the existence of users who rely on the financial statements as their major source of financial information about the enterprise' (para. 8).

The objectives of financial statements are covered in paragraphs 9–11, and are given as providing information about the financial position, performance and changes in financial position of the enterprise to assist users in making economic decisions.

Users are referred to as investors, employees, lenders, suppliers and other trade creditors, government and their agencies and the public. However, the information is referred to as being for economic decision-making purposes. Unlike the Corporate Report, there is no reference to any group having a right to information.

In paragraphs 14–22, financial position, performance and change in financial position are discussed. The arguments put forward are in favour of the continued use of traditional accounting statements.

A significant part of the framework (paras 23–45) deals with the qualitative characteristics of financial statements which must be understandable to users who must be assumed to have a reasonable knowledge. Usefulness is determined primarily by relevance and reliability. Comparability interacts with both of these. The true and fair view will be achieved by relevance and reliability applied together with appropriate accounting standards. In addition, there are two constraints which must be applied to relevance and reliability. These are timeliness and cost/benefit considerations.

The IASC statement discusses the elements of financial statements in paragraphs 46–79. The treatment is fairly standard, covering assets, liabilities and equities, and in the area of performance, income and expenses. The recognition of the elements of financial statements is covered by paragraphs 80–96. This section includes the probability of future economic benefit, the reliability of measurement and the recognition of assets, liabilities, income and expenses. The recognition issue is summed up by paragraph 81:

> An item that meets the definition of an element should be recognised if:
> a. it is probable that any future economic benefit associated with the item will flow to or from the enterprise; and
> b. the item has an attribute which can be measured with reliability.

The statement concludes with sections on the measurement of the elements of financial statements and on concepts of capital and capital maintenance. Measurement is the process of determining amounts and selecting the attribute to be measured. Attributes discussed include historical cost, current cost, realisable (settlement) value and present value. It is noted that the attribute selected is usually historical cost.

The final section discusses financial and physical capital maintenance. The final paragraph (108) notes that:

> Different accounting systems exhibit different degrees of relevance and reliability and, as in other areas, preparers must seek a balance between relevance and reliability . . . At the present time, it is not the intention of the Board of IASC to prescribe a particular measurement model other than in exceptional circumstances . . .

The IASC conceptual framework contains elements drawn from both the narrow SFAC concept of financial reporting and the wider view of the Corporate Report. It would be applicable to IASC member countries without conceptual frameworks of their own.

New Zealand

There has been discussion for some time about the need to develop a conceptual framework for financial reporting in New Zealand, especially since the AARF began to do so for Australia. The response by the ARSB was to recognise the limited resources available for such a project, and instead to widen the scope of the revised Explanatory Foreword to Statements of Standard Accounting Practice. This was carried out during 1990–1992 and the ARSB issued simultaneously seven exposure drafts; together they comprised a proposed framework for financial reporting in New Zealand consisting of:

*   Explanatory Foreword (ED 59)
*   Statement of Concepts (ED 60)
*   Interpreting the Statement of Concepts for Public Sector Entities (ED 61)
*   Framework for Differential Reporting to Existing SSAPs (ED 63)
*   FRS 1: Disclosure of Accounting Policies (ED 64)
*   FRS 2: Presentation of Financial Reports (ED 65).

The key aspects of the proposed framework were given as follows.

1
It is proposed that both public and private

sector financial reporting requirements henceforth be dealt with through one series of accounting standards.

2
A new Explanatory Foreword to general purpose External Financial Reporting will replace the existing public and private sector explanatory forewords.

3
A new Statement of Concepts for General Purpose External Financial Reporting will be a fundamental aspect of the framework.

4
A guide to Interpreting the Statement of Concepts for Public Sector Entities will in due course replace the existing Statement of Public Sector Accounting Concepts issued in 1987.

5
A new accounting standard on Disclosure of Accounting Policies will replace the existing public and private sector standards on the topic.

6
A new accounting standard will deal with the Presentation of Financial Reports, replacing parts of the existing SSAP 9: Information to be Disclosed in Company Balance Sheets and Profit and Loss Accounts.

7
The new standard on the Presentation of Financial Reports introduces discussion about a new Statement of Changes in Financial Wealth. The purpose of this statement is to give greater prominence to changes in values and other movements in reserves.

8
A framework for differential reporting in New Zealand is proposed.

9
Proposals concerning the application of

differential reporting to existing SSAPs are published.

Statement of Concepts for General Purpose Financial Reporting

The 1993 Statement of Concepts for General Purpose Financial Reporting is structured in the normal manner for such pronouncements. It includes: an introduction; principal components/definitions of the reporting entity; objectives of general purpose financial reports; qualitative characteristics; assumptions underlying the preparation of these statements; and definitions of financial and non-financial elements and measurement bases.

The introduction states that the purpose of the statement, which covers all general purpose financial reports from 1 January 1995, is to:

(a) assist users to interpret the information contained in financial reports prepared in conformity with generally accepted accounting practice;

(b) assist preparers of financial reports to apply financial reporting standards and to deal with topics that are not the subject of a financial reporting standard;

(c) assist auditors to form an opinion as to whether financial reports provide a fair presentation of an entity's financial and service performance, financial position and cash flows; and

(d) assist the Financial Reporting Standards Board (the Board) to develop future financial reporting standards and to review existing financial reporting standards.

Paragraph 1.5 states that these reports are intended:

to provide information to meet the needs of external users who are unable to require, or contract for, the preparation of special reports to meet their specific information needs. As the transactions being reported may have both financial and non-financial effects, general purpose financial reports may contain both financial and non-financial information.

The reporting entity is defined in the following terms:

2.1 A reporting entity exists where it is reasonable to expect the existence of users dependent on general purpose financial reports for information which will be useful to them in terms of the objectives stated in paragraph 3.1.

Examples of users include the providers of resources and representatives of groups and analysts. Employees and members of the general public are not referred to.

The objectives of general purpose financial reporting are given in paragraph 3.1 as:

to provide information to assist users in:
(a) assessing the reporting entity's financial and service performance, financial position and cash flows;
(b) assessing the reporting entity's compliance with legislation, regulations, common law and contractual arrangements, as these relate to the assessment of the reporting entity's financial and service performance, financial position and cash flows; and
(c) making decisions about providing resources to, or doing business with, the reporting entity.

These objectives would normally be achieved by means of financial reports containing the financial position, financial and service performance and cash flows. The qualitative characteristics are considered on page 105.

The New Zealand conceptual framework provides a section on the assumptions underlying the preparation of general purpose financial reports. These are: going

concern; periodic reporting; accrual basis; and a section entitled the influences of qualitative characteristics, which refers to the balance between qualitative characteristics, including benefit and cost, materiality, and prudence. The role of judgement in these matters is noted also.

One of the most important sections of any conceptual framework deals with the definition and recognition of the financial elements of general purpose financial reports. The financial elements relating to the financial position are assets, liabilities and equity, financial performance, revenues and expenses. The format employed to explain these defines the element, provides a list of essential characteristics drawn from the definition, and then details the criteria to be employed in recognising the particular element. Although the presentation is clear, the content does not break any new ground and is firmly grounded in historical views of performance. For example, the definition of liabilities does not provide any opportunities to include executory contracts. The definitions and criteria for recognition of the main elements are given below.

7.7
Assets are service potential or future economic benefits controlled by the entity as a result of past transactions or other past events.

7.9
An asset shall be recognised in the statement of financial position when and only when:
(a) it is probable that the service potential or future economic benefits embodied in the asset will eventuate; and
(b) the asset possesses a cost or other value that can be measured with reliability.

7.10
Liabilities are the future sacrifices of service potential or of future economic benefits that the entity is presently

obliged to make to other entities as a result of past transactions and other past events.

7.14
A liability shall be recognised in the statement of financial position when and only when:

(a) it is probable that the future sacrifice of service potential or future economic benefits will be required; and

(b) the amount of the liability can be measured with reliability.

7.15
Equity is the residual interest in the assets of the equity after the deduction of its liabilities.

7.18
Since equity is a residual interest in the assets of an entity and the amount assigned to equity will always correspond to the difference between the amounts assigned to the entity's assets and the amounts assigned to the entity's liabilities, the criteria for the recognition of assets and liabilities provide the criteria for the recognition of equity.

7.19
Revenues are inflows or other enhancements, or savings in outflows, of service potential or future economic benefits in the form of increases in assets or reductions in liabilities of the equity, other than those relating to contributions by owners, that result in an increase in equity during the reporting period.

7.21
Revenues shall be recognised in the determination of the result for the reporting period, when and only when:

(a) it is probable that the inflow or other enhancement or savings in outflows of service potential or future economic benefits have occurred; and

(b) the inflow or other enhancement or savings in outflows of service

potential or future economic benefits can be measured with reliability.

7.22
Expenses are consumptions or losses of service potential or future economic benefits in the form of reductions in assets or increases in liabilities of the entity, other than those relating to distributions to owners, that result in a decrease in equity during the reporting period.

7.24
Expenses shall be recognised in the determination of the result for the reporting period, when and only when:

(a) it is probable that the consumption or loss of service potential or future economic benefits resulting in a reduction in assets and/or an increase in liabilities has occurred; and

(b) the consumption or loss of service potential or future economic benefits can be measured with reliability.

Definition and recognition criteria are also provided for the non-financial elements of general purpose financial reports.

8.2
Inputs are the resources used to produce the goods and services which are the outputs of the reporting entity.

8.3
Outputs are the goods and services produced by the reporting entity.

8.4
Outcomes are the impacts on, or consequences for, the community resulting from the existence and operations of the reporting entity.

8.5
A non-financial element should be included if:

(a) the item has an appropriate basis of measurement; and

(b) it can be reliably measured.

Measurement bases discussed in the framework include historical cost, current cost, real (settlement) value and present value. The statement notes after lengthy discussion:

9.9
The combination of the historical cost system with the practice of remeasuring certain non-current assets to current value is known as the 'modified historical cost system'. This system is adopted by many entities in New Zealand. Subject to the considerations described in paragraph 9.4 above (the reference is to qualitative characteristics), the Board believes that the modified historical cost system meets the objectives of general purpose financial reporting better than the historical cost system.

Framework for differential reporting

The framework, which became effective on 1 February 1994, has two purposes: to indicate the criteria which may enable entities to take advantage of differential reporting exemptions; and to guide standard setters in providing those exemptions.

The framework is intended to make allowance for the costs and benefits in compliance with financial reporting standards and is based on the following assumptions.

3.3
(a) compliance with reporting standards creates costs (usually for the reporting entity) and benefits (usually for the users of the financial reports);
(b) compliance should be required only when the benefits of compliance exceed the costs;
(c) financial reporting standards will be more accepted if they apply only where benefits are generally agreed to exceed costs.

The development of a benefit cost criterion leads to three considerations: public accountability, separation of owners and

governing body and size. Where there is no public accountability, the owners are all members of the governing body of the entity, and it is below the size criteria (total revenue $2.5 million, total assets $1.5 million, twenty employees) the entity may claim exemption from certain specified provisions of specific reporting standards, as provided for in the appendix to the framework statement.

This is an interesting departure from the normal approach which is to apply all standards to all entities at all times. The framework clearly recognises the small business nature of much of the economic activity in New Zealand.

Explanatory foreword to General Purpose Financial Reporting 1993

This foreword has been issued:

(a) to explain the relationship between general purpose financial reports, the statement of concepts and financial reporting standards; and
(b) to advise members of their responsibilities in relation to the statement of concepts and financial reporting standards.

The relationships are established through a series of definitions and explanations, culminating in a statement of the responsibilities of members to observe the results of the conceptual framework and the standard-setting process.

2.1
General purpose financial reports are financial reports which are intended to provide information to meet the needs of external users who are unable to require, or contract for, the preparation of special reports to meet their specific information needs.

3.2
The statement of concepts defines the nature, subject, purpose and broad content of general purpose financial reports. It sets out the concepts upon

which the preparation and presentation of such reports should be based.

3.4

Financial reporting standards are rules which establish requirements for recognising, measuring and disclosing transactions and other events in general purpose financial reports.

4.1

Generally accepted accounting practice is the term used to describe the basis on which financial reports are normally prepared. The term encompasses:

(a) specific rules, practices and procedures relating to particular circumstances; and

(b) broad concepts and principles of general application, including those outlined in the statement of concepts.

Members are required to prepare financial reports and to report on financial statements produced by others according to generally accepted accounting practice, so far as they are able to do so. Unspecified action by the NZSA is stated to be the outcome of not conforming with these expectations. In complying with the NZSA reporting standards, members will normally ensure that they also comply with Australian and international standards.

Common conceptual frameworks: Australia and New Zealand

In a paper presented by Perera and Rahman (1994) the main features of financial reporting frameworks in Australia and New Zealand have been identified and the authors considered whether there is an underlying commonality of purpose. They located areas which are described as identical as well as those which need further attention. Areas which were found to be similar are the functions of general purpose financial reports, the qualitative characteristics and the definitions and recognition

criteria of the elements of financial reports. Areas where there are still differences and problems to be addressed include the issue of measurement in financial reporting and the need for mandatory compliance with concept statements. Perera and Rahman state that there is evidence of commitment at governmental and professional levels to accounting harmonisation under CER and a commonality of purpose between the two countries in the area of financial reporting.

Clearly, the Framework for Financial Reporting in New Zealand is a relatively modest effort, compared with the AARF Conceptual Framework (which might be seen as a local comparison). There is no deep discussion and analysis of, for example, the nature of assets and liabilities, and the need to report on contracts which are equally proportionately unperformed (AARF, SAC 4, 1992). There is not the same emphasis placed on accountability as in the AARF framework.

Nevertheless, the efforts of the NZSA must be commended compared with the work of the ASB in the UK, which has been content to adopt the IASC approach without modification.

Qualitative characteristics of accounting information

It is necessary for the preparers of conceptual frameworks to attempt to set out a series of definitions for the qualitative characteristics which are considered to be important. These characteristics often appear to be the same or at least very similar; for example both the IASC and AARF exposure drafts are similar in that relevance and reliability are of prime importance. However, the problems that arise when acquiring commonly agreed upon definitions should not be underestimated (Howard, 1994, p.1). The IASC approach is summarised as follows.

Relevance is involved in the process of

influencing economic decisions and the prediction of the future activities of an organisation, including the expected cash flows.
Relevance is influenced by materiality
which provides a threshold or cutoff point,
but is not a primary qualitative characteristic which information must have if it is to
be useful (para. 30).

Reliability is present when information
is free from material error and bias and
provides a faithful representation of that
which is purported or expected to be provided. Reliability is aided by neutrality but
hindered by the exercise of prudence and
conservatism to the extent that values are
distorted and secret reserves are created.

Usefulness of information will be assisted
by an appropriate balance between relevance
and reliability in order to satisfy the economic decision-making needs of users.

Comparability is another important
quality of financial statements, permitting
the identification of trends in the results of
a given organisation over several time
periods, or between several organisations at
the one time. In order for comparability to
be fully exercised, details of accounting
policies must be provided and any changes
to the established policies must be given
appropriate publicity.

There are two constraints on relevance
and reliability. These are timeliness and
cost/benefit. Information must be reported
on a timely basis, otherwise it will lose the
quality of relevance. The cost/benefit problem is described by the statement as a per-
vasive constraint rather than a qualitative
characteristic. The benefits derived should
exceed the cost of provision, but it is very
difficult to determine the position in any
specific case.

The qualitative characteristics referred to
in SAC 3 (AARF, 1990) are comparability,
materiality, relevance, reliability and understandability. The definitions employed are:

a Comparability . . . users are able to
   discern and evaluate similarities in,

and differences between, the nature
and effects of transactions and events,
at one time and over time, either
when assessing aspects of a single
reporting entity or a number of
reporting entities.

b Materiality . . . used to assess the
   extent to which relevant and reliable
   information may be omitted, mis-
   stated or not disclosed separately
   without having the potential to
   adversely affect the decisions of an
   economic nature made by users of a
   particular set of financial statements
   or of the rendering of accountability
   by preparers.

c Relevance . . . quality of financial
   information which exists when that
   information influences decisions of an
   economic nature by users by:
   i helping them form predictions
     about the outcomes of past,
     present, or future events and/or,
   ii confirming or correcting their past
      evaluations, and which enables
      users to assess the rendering of
      accountability by preparers.

d Reliability . . . that quality of financial information which exists when
   that information can be depended
   upon to represent faithfully, and
   without bias or undue error, the
   transactions or events that either it
   purports to represent or could reasonably be expected to represent.

e Understandability . . . that quality
   of financial information which
   exists when users of that information are able to comprehend its
   meaning.

The SAC 3 discusses two constraints on
relevant and reliable financial information,
namely timeliness and cost versus benefit.
Under the latter topic, paragraph 45 considers the extent to which reporting
requirements should be the same for all
entities. No conclusion is reached,

excepting that these issues should be the subject of a separate SAC dealing with what should constitute a reporting entity for the purposes of general purpose financial statements.

The SAC concludes with the proposed SAC in paragraphs 48–49.

Para. 48—
General purpose financial reports shall include all financial information which satisfies the concepts of relevance and reliability, and which passes the test of materiality.

Para. 49—
General purpose financial reports shall be presented on a timely basis and in a manner which satisfies the concepts of comparability and understandability.

The Statement of Concepts for General Purpose Financial Reporting, issued in a revised form by the NZSA in August 1994, lists four primary qualitative characteristics: relevance, understandability, reliability and comparability (NZSA, 1994, para. 4.1). *Relevance* applies to information where it has feedback or predictive value, or both, depending on how it is used. In both instances information must be timely to be of use to readers (NZSA, 1994, paras 4.2–4.4). *Understandability* exists where users, with a reasonable knowledge of the entity and its environment and who are prepared to study the information with rea-sonable diligence, will comprehend its meaning (NZSA, 1994, paras 4.5–4.8). *Reliability* is dependent on the characteris-tics of representational faithfulness (infor-

Table 6.1
A comparison of qualitative characteristics included in conceptual frameworks

	Relevance	Materiality	Reliability	Freedom from bias/neutrality	Comparability/consistency	Understandability	Recognition of substance over form	Decision usefulness	Cost/benefit	Predictive value	Feedback value	Timeliness	Verifiability	Representational faithfulness	Completeness	Objectivity	Accuracy	Uniformity
AICPA (1973)	*	*	*	*	*	*	*											
FASB (1980)	*	*	*	*	*	*		*	*	*	*	*	*	*				
ASSC (1975)	*		*		*	*						*				*	*	
HMSO (1977)												*						*
CICA (1980)	*	*		*	*				*							*	*	
ASAC (1987)	*	*	*	*	*	*		*		*	*	*	*	*	*	*		
AARF (1990)	*	*	*		*	*						*						
IASC (1988)	*	*	*		*				*			*						
NZSA (1994)	*		*	*	*	*				*	*	*	*	*				

mation corresponds with actual underlying transactions and events), verifiability (where independent observers agree that a basis of measurement is correctly applied) and neutrality (data has not been selected to produce a predetermined result; NZSA, 1994, paras. 4.9–4.12). *Comparability* enables users to identify similarities and differences between items of information in different reports. These may be from the same organisation at different times, or different organisations at the same time. Comparability is affected by the disclosure of accounting policies. Information for different periods should show variations resulting from changes in policies (NZSA, 1994, paras 4.13–4.16).

The qualitative characteristics referred to in the various conceptual frameworks are set out in Table 6.1. Although there are difficulties in making a comparison such as this, it is fairly clear that relevance, materiality, reliability, comparability, understandability and timeliness are the most frequently stated characteristics. It must be noted that these characteristics are stated *a priori*, and little empirical study has been made of their usefulness in practice.

Conceptual frameworks reconsidered

The largely socially constructed nature of accounting leads to a number of varied but similar conceptual frameworks for accounting throughout the Anglo-American accounting world. This may be seen from the relatively detailed account of these projects on pages 109–111. Given the difficulties associated with the production of a conceptual framework or a series of objectives of accounting, why should the accounting profession persist with these expensive and time consuming activities?

The response to this question appears to be that the world of commerce has become too complicated for accountants to rely upon historical answers or responses based

upon generally accepted accounting principles when encountering new problems. Accounting standards are required, or in the absence of these standards a conceptual framework, which will 'provide answers' is required. One accepted view is contained in SFAC 2 where the function of the conceptual framework is stated as:

> to serve the public interest by providing structure and direction to financial accounting and reporting to facilitate the provision of even handed financial and related information that is useful in assisting capital and other markets to function efficiently in allocating scarce resources in the economy. (SFAC 2, 1980, p.1)

However, this approach would not satisfy all parties or resolve the conflict inherent in the provision of information. Conflict is likely between the demands of different user groups and the objectives (or functions) of financial statements are divided between stewardship, decision making (decision usefulness) and in demonstrating accountability.

The benefits of a conceptual framework

Chye (1984) has identified a conceptual framework for financial accounting as a necessary foundation for the development of a set of generally accepted accounting standards. The standard-setting bodies can work within the framework to produce standards that are consistent and form a coherent pattern. The benefits to be obtained from having a conceptual framework for financial accounting, in addition to providing guidance to standard-setting bodies, include resolving accounting problems, determining bounds for judgement, increasing the understanding of and confidence in financial statements and in enhancing comparability. In the absence of a specific standard, the conceptual framework provides a frame of reference through which accountants can address specific issues.

The bounds for judgement by both individuals and bodies may be set by an appropriate conceptual framework. A balance must be achieved between a structure which is too detailed, and does not leave sufficient room for judgement to be exercised, and one which is too broad and therefore ineffective in providing guidance.

A conceptual framework may also increase the understanding of and confidence in financial statements through the use of a common set of objectives and terminology. In particular, agreement on definitions and qualitative characteristics is important.

It has been argued that comparability between accounting statements may be assisted by the development of a conceptual framework which will act to limit the alternatives available to reporting bodies. There is no guarantee that there will be a reduction in alternatives, unless the development of a conceptual framework results in an increase in the production of standards having a coherent basis.

The limitations of a conceptual framework

The limitations of a conceptual framework include: the time and cost of preparation; any rigidity which it might give to accounting and standard setting; the conflict which appears to exist between established standards and the framework; and the possibility that a conceptual framework may benefit only some of the groups identified as users.

Conceptual framework projects are time consuming and expensive to set up and operate, and countries with smaller or less developed economies may not be able to afford them. The production of the IASC framework is an attempt to overcome this problem. However, a uniform conceptual framework may be difficult to achieve (Staunton, 1984).

It may be argued that the conceptual framework provides too much guidance to accounting and standard setting and encourages rigidity by making it difficult to introduce new ideas. However, there is little evidence of this having occurred to date.

There may be some conflict between a conceptual framework and accounting standards which were prepared prior to the development of the conceptual framework. This situation is covered in the short term by statements, such as those used by the IASC and the AARF, to the effect that the standard must prevail until rewritten to bring it into line with the framework. Clearly, if this rewriting does not take place the integrity of the conceptual framework will be affected.

If the conceptual framework is poorly designed or allowed to get out of date it may benefit only some of the potential user groups which exist in society. For example, the Trueblood and SFAC 1 Reports give inadequate recognition to the needs of user groups other than investors and creditors. Later approaches such as those of the IASC and AARF attempt to accommodate other user groups. More recently, conflict has arisen where part of a conceptual framework (SAC 4) is thought to move disclosure too far ahead of extant practice (Steel, 1993; Wedlick, 1993).

The future of conceptual framework projects

Conceptual framework projects are intimately associated with the standard-setting processes which are now recognised as being both technical and political in nature. There are a number of theorists who argue that standard setting is entirely political but must conform to a related need to use a public interest rhetoric:

> Why then has so much time and effort been devoted to conceptual framework projects? We conjecture that the answer to this question lies in the political arena in which the standard setting game is

played. We argue that accounting standards are a means by which private sector organisations can redistribute wealth — a role in pluralistic societies typically assigned to government and its regulatory agencies. The exercise of such power must, of necessity, be cloaked in the public interest rhetoric — both to protect the private sector organisation wielding the power and the government that has implicitly delegated the responsibility for exercising that power. In a sense, conceptual framework projects are a means of increasing the rule-making legitimacy of private sector regulations and hence are a mechanism by which political costs might be reduced. (Whittred and Zimmer, 1988, p.15)

Given this at least partial rejection of traditionally accepted reasons for developing conceptual frameworks, is there a future for such activities? The answer would seem to be that professional accounting organisations, which are usually the motivating forces behind drives to develop conceptual frameworks to assist with standard setting, periodically need to re-establish the status and direction of their discipline (Hines, 1989). This conjecture would appear to be borne out by the three conceptual frameworks which are currently under development.

The ASAC project in Canada appears to be part of a drive for a higher profile by the Certified General Accountants of Canada, which is the body behind the ASAC. The standard-setting process in that country is under the control of the Canadian Institute of Chartered Accountants and is done without the benefit of a universally accepted conceptual framework. Consequently, any attempt to establish the ASAC as an alternative standard-setting body would be assisted by the acceptance of a conceptual framework.

The need to be noticed may also be part of the motivation for the highly elaborate structure being developed by the AARF. The involvement of the Australian

Commonwealth Government in standard setting through the ASRB since 1984 has clearly changed the balance of power in the standard-setting arena. The two accounting bodies which propose accounting standards through the AARF are required to provide a considerable amount of detail as background and support. The conceptual framework provides much of that added material. Recent controversies in Australia would suggest that the AASB is perceived by industry and commerce as becoming too influential. The SACs have been taken seriously in developing more stringent accounting standards.

The IASC programme of standard development is committed to narrowing the differences between financial statements produced in different parts of the world by seeking to harmonise accounting standards. This policy has been challenged in recent years by an emphasis on the cultural differences which underlie social, economic and legal differences between countries. The development of a conceptual framework may be seen either as an attempt to provide the standard-setting process with increased status, or as a necessary step towards re-establishing the authority of the drive towards harmonisation which is such an important part of the IASC mission.

Therefore, it would seem likely that where the professional bodies and accounting discipline appear to be in need of support *vis-à vis* other institutions in society, there will be pressure for the establishment or continuation of conceptual framework projects. The Australian project will continue for some time if the resources are available. It has some features in common with that of the IASC, and may provide the NZSA with a model should that body require one. Consequently, there would seem to be a future for conceptual framework projects in the short and perhaps medium term, unless the European tendency for standards to be set by government extends further into Anglo-American accounting.

Chapter summary

This chapter has been concerned with the development of conceptual frameworks for financial accounting and reporting. It began with a brief consideration of conflicts of interest which exist in the provision of information. Three objectives (more strictly functions) of financial statements were identified. These are: to demonstrate stewardship, to provide information to aid in decision making (sometimes referred to as decision usefulness) and to demonstrate accountability.

The chapter then considered in turn the conceptual framework projects which have been developed in the USA, the UK, Canada, Australia, the IASC and New Zealand. This was followed by a review of the qualitative characteristics which are contained in many of the conceptual frameworks. Finally, the benefits, limitations and likely future of conceptual framework projects were discussed.

Essay and examination questions

6.1   Compare and contrast the US and UK approaches to developing conceptual frameworks for accounting.

6.2   In what manner do the recently developed conceptual frameworks differ from those developed prior to 1980?

6.3   Compare and contrast SFAC 1 and the Trueblood Report.

6.4   Compare and contrast the IASC exposure draft with SFAC 1.

6.5   The Corporate Report and the 1980 CICA *Corporate Reporting: its Future Evolution* have similar backgrounds. To what extent do their recommendations agree?

6.6   There are many similarities between the ASAC conceptual framework and the SFAC project. Comment on the differences between them.

6.7   Comment on the similarities between the IASC and AARF SACs.

6.8   Comment on the differences between the IASC and the AARF conceptual frameworks.

6.9   To what extent does the Statement of Accounting Concepts for General Purpose Financial Reporting offer a conceptual framework for New Zealand accounting? What would be needed to complete the task?

6.10   The whole notion of a conceptual framework is a normative superfluity in a world explained by agency theory. Discuss.

6.11   Comment on the need for careful consideration of the qualitative characteristics of financial reports as an integral part of a conceptual framework project.

6.12   The problems associated with SAC 4 demonstrate that the political dimension of standard setting is now being extended to conceptual frameworks. Discuss.

6.13   Perera and Rahman (1994) have suggested that there is an increasing commonality between Australian and New Zealand financial accounting. Discuss.

6.14   The New Zealand approach to a conceptual framework includes a reference to 'differential reporting' which does not exist elsewhere. Explain the purpose and mode of operation of this process.

6.15 The New Zealand approach to a conceptual framework includes reference to the assumptions underlying the preparation of General Purpose Financial Reports. Comment.

References and additional reading

Accounting Research and Standards Board (1991). ED 59: *Explanatory Foreword to General Purpose External Financial Reporting.* Wellington: NZSA.

Accounting Research and Standards Board (1991). ED 60: *Concepts for General Purpose External Financial Reporting.* Wellington: NZSA.

Accounting Research and Standards Board (1991). ED 61: *Interpreting 'Concepts for General Purpose External Financial Reporting', for Public Sector Entities.* Wellington: NZSA.

Accounting Research and Standards Board (1991). ED 62: *Framework for Differential Reporting.* Wellington: NZSA.

Accounting Research and Standards Board (1991). ED 63: *Application of Differential Reporting to Statements of Standard Accounting Practice 3 to 28.* Wellington: NZSA.

Accounting Research and Standards Board (1991). ED 64: FRS 1: *Disclosure of Accounting Policies.* Wellington: NZSA.

Accounting Research and Standards Board (1991). ED 65: FRS 2: *Presentation of Financial Reports.* Wellington: NZSA.

Accounting Standards Board (1991). *Exposure Draft Statement of Principles: The Objective of Financial Statements and the Qualitative Characteristics of Financial Information.* London: ASB.

Accounting Standards Review Board (1994). *Release 1: Accounting policies that have authoritative support within the accounting profession in New Zealand.* Wellington: ASRB.

Accounting Standards Review Board (1994). *Release 2: Australia–New Zealand harmonisation policy on accounting standards.* Wellington: ASRB.

Accounting Standards Steering Committee (1975). *The Corporate Report.* A Discussion Paper: London: ICAEW.

American Accounting Association (1966). Committee to prepare a statement on basic accounting theory. *A Statement of Basic Accounting Theory.* AAA.

American Accounting Association (1977). Committee on concepts and standards for external financial reports. *Statement of Accounting Theory and Theory Acceptance.* Sarasota: AAA.

American Institute of Certified Public Accountants (1973). *Objectives of Financial Statements* (The Trueblood Report). New York: AICPA.

Australian Accounting Research Foundation (1987). *Objective of Financial Reporting.* Exposure Draft No. 42A. Melbourne: AARF.

Australian Accounting Research Foundation (1987). *Qualitative Characteristics of Financial Information.* Exposure Draft No. 42B. Melbourne: AARF.

Australian Accounting Research Foundation (1987). *Definition and Recognition of Assets.* Exposure Draft No. 42C. Melbourne: AARF.

Australian Accounting Research Foundation (1987). *Definition and Recognition of Liabilities.* Exposure Draft No. 42D. Melbourne: AARF.

Australian Accounting Research Foundation (1988). *Definition of the Reporting Entity.* Exposure Draft No. 46A. Melbourne: AARF.

Australian Accounting Research Foundation (1988). *Definition and Recognition of Expenses.* Exposure Draft No. 46B. Melbourne: AARF.

Australian Accounting Research Foundation: (1990). *Qualitative Characteristics of Financial Information.* SAC 3. Caulfield: AARF.

Australian Accounting Research Foundation (1992). *Definition and Recognition of the Elements of Financial Statements.* SAC 4. Caulfield: AARF.

Canadian Institute of Chartered Accountants (1980). *Corporate Reporting: Its Future Evolution.* Toronto: CICA.

Chye, M.H.F. (1984). The FASB's conceptual framework for financial accounting and reporting, in M.R. Mathews (Ed.), *Readings in the Development of Accounting.* Palmerston North: Dunmore Press.

Davey, H.B. (1984). Epistemology in accounting, in M.R. Mathews (Ed.), *Readings in the Development of Accounting.* Palmerston North: Dunmore Press.

Financial Accounting Standards Board (1976). *Scope and Implications of the Conceptual Framework Project.* Connecticut: FASB, 2.

Financial Accounting Standards Board (1978). *Objectives of Financial Reporting by Business Enterprises.* Statement of Financial Accounting Concepts No. 1. Stamford: FASB.

Financial Accounting Standards Board (1980). *Qualitative Characteristics of Accounting Information.* SFAC 2. Stamford: FASB.

Financial Forum **2**(4), May 1993, 1, 3, 5.

Financial Forum **2**(5), June 1993, 1, 4–5.

Financial Forum **2**(7), August 1993, 1.

Financial Forum **2**(8), September 1993, 7.

Financial Forum **2**(9), October 1993, 3.

Financial Forum **2**(9), November 1993, 8.

Financial Forum **2**(10), December 1993, 5.

Financial Forum **3**(1), February 1994, 3.

Financial Forum **3**(5), June 1994, 3.

Financial Forum **3**(7), August 1994, 1, 3.

Financial Forum **3**(8), September 1994, 1, 3.

Henderson, S. and Peirson, G. (1988). The conceptual framework and the objectives of financial reporting, in *Issues in Financial Accounting.* 4th edn. Melbourne: Longman Cheshire, 2–39.

Hines, R.D. (1989). Financial accounting knowledge, conceptual framework projects and the social construction of the accounting profession. *Accounting, Auditing and Accountability Journal,* **2**(2), 72–92.

Howard, P. (1994). Heated debate at standards seminar. *Financial Forum* **3**(8), 1, 3.

International Accounting Standards Committee (1988). *Framework for the Preparation and Presentation of Financial Statements.* London: IASC.

Kerkin, D.J. (1984). Objectives of accounting: Current trends and influences, in M.R. Mathews (Ed.), *Readings in the Development of Accounting.* Palmerston North: Dunmore Press.

Moonitz, M. (1961). *The Basic Postulates of Accounting.* Accounting Research Study No. 1. New York: AICPA.

New Zealand Society of Accountants (1994). *Explanatory Foreword to General Purpose Financial Reporting*. Wellington: NZSA.

New Zealand Society of Accountants (1994). *Framework for Differential Reporting*. Wellington: NZSA.

New Zealand Society of Accountants (1994). *Statement of Concepts for General Purpose Financial Reporting*. Wellington: NZSA.

Page, M. (1992). The ASB's proposed objective of financial statements: Marching in step backwards? A review essay. *British Accounting Review,* **24**(1), 77–85.

Perera, M.H.B. and Rahman, A.R. (1994). Conceptual Foundation of Accounting and Financial Reporting: Emerging Commonality of Purpose Between Australia and New Zealand. A Paper presented at the American Accounting Association Annual Convention, New York, August 1994.

Secretary of State for Trade (1977). *The Future of Company Reports. A Consultative Document*. London: HMSO Cmnd 6888.

Sprouse, R.T. and Moonitz, M. (1962). *A Tentative Set of Broad Accounting Principles for Business Enterprises*. Accounting Research Study No. 3. New York: AICPA.

Staunton, J. (1984). Why a 'Conceptual Framework for Accounting'? *Accounting Forum,* **7**(2), 85–92.

Steel, G. (1993). SAC 4 and against. *Financial Forum,* **2**(4), 5.

Wedlick, S. (1993). Group of 100 seeks greater influence. *Financial Forum,* **2**(9), 8.

Whittred, G. and Zimmer, I. (1988). *Financial Accounting: Incentive Effects and Economic Consequences*. Marrickville, NSW: Harcourt Brace Jovanovich (Australia).

Zeff, S.A. (1977). Forging accounting principles in New Zealand: an analysis and criticism. *Accountants Journal*, **56**(5), 169–173.

Chapter 7
Setting accounting standards
in Anglo-American countries:
issues and prospects

Learning objectives

After studying this chapter the reader will be able to:
- explain the accounting standard-setting process in New Zealand
- compare the institutional arrangements for accounting standard setting in Anglo-American countries
- describe the factors that influence the accounting standards and practices of a country
- identify the recent trends in the area of accounting standards at global, regional and local levels
- examine the main issues involved in assessing the effectiveness of accounting standards
- consider the various approaches to accounting standard setting.

Introduction

Accounting standards are no longer considered to be exclusively the concern of accountants. In many countries, even though professional accounting bodies generally have to take the initiative, non-accountants are increasingly becoming involved in the process of setting accounting standards. Tweedie (1985) holds that accounting standards result from the interaction of five major factors, namely, economic events, self-interest, the spread of ideas, accidents of history and international influences. According to Nobes and Parker (1988, p.63), political, social and cultural factors have a dominant influence on the type of accounting regulation found in a country. It is clear that accounting standard setting is not a purely technical matter any more. The issues are extremely complex and are often resolved in the political arena through the interaction between different interest groups. Furthermore, with the growing competition in international business and rapidly advancing technology in transport and communication, no standard setter can afford to ignore what is happening overseas. As a result, the setting of accounting standards has become an international process. There is also a ten-dency for many countries to closely examine the standards issued by the IASC which assumes a major role in coordinating the efforts of national standard setters (see Chapter 17 for details). The extent and the varied nature of the factors affecting accounting standards are evident from the different institutional arrangements set in place in different countries for developing such standards. This chapter proposes to examine the issues involved in setting accounting standards in Anglo-American countries with a discussion of current trends and future prospects.

Generally accepted accounting principles

Financial statements are expected to be prepared in accordance with generally accepted accounting principles. The nature of these principles will determine the quality of the information contained in financial statements. However, the meaning of the phrase 'generally accepted accounting principle' has never been made clear. Grady (1965) indicates a wide variety of methods of accounting for almost every major item found in published accounts. A good indication of the sources of currently 'accepted

principles' is provided in AICPA (1975).
They include:

- Statements and interpretation issued by the FASB
- APB statements and opinions
- American Institute accounting research bulletins
- American Institute accounting interpretations and statements of position
- American Institute industry audit guides and accounting guides
- industry accounting practices
- pronouncements of other professional associations
- statements of regulatory agencies such as the SEC
- accounting text books and articles
- common business usage.

This list of sources is so open-ended that almost anything can be considered a 'generally accepted accounting principle'. This situation is common to all Anglo-American countries.

The usual audit report in the British tradition expresses the opinion that the balance sheet, the statement of income and retained earnings, and the cash flow statement to which it relates present a 'true and fair view' of the state of affairs of the entity and the results of its operations, 'in conformity with generally accepted accounting principles' applied on a basis consistent with that of the preceding year. Questions may be raised about the conjunction of 'present a true and fair view' and 'in conformity with generally accepted accounting principles' because it can be any one of the following:

- the financial statements present a true and fair view *per se* and are in accordance with generally accepted principles, or
- the financial statements present a true and fair view because they are in accordance with generally accepted principles, or
- the financial statements present a true and fair view of the facts whatever generally accepted principles may have been used.

It seems that the required statement of opinion by the auditor relates to the manner in which the financial statements are drawn up, rather than to the contents of the end product.

An opinion published by the English Institute in 1965 for the guidance of members stated: 'The purpose for which annual accounts are normally prepared is not to enable individual shareholders to take investment decisions'. This may be contrasted with the conceptual frameworks dating from the 1970s and later. As Chambers, Ramanathan and Rappaport (1978, p.38) point out, it appears that a balance sheet prepared according to professionally endorsed principles could not be taken as giving an indication of up-to-date realisable values of assets, nor an indication of net worth; and that the results (profits) are not a measure of increase or decrease in wealth in terms of purchasing power, and are not necessarily serviceable in price-fixing, wage negotiation or taxation. It appears that the accounts were considered to be useless for most of the purposes for which accounts are, in fact, used.

The professional accounting organisations of different countries have been concerned with establishing some degree of uniformity between diverse accounting practices adopted by entities. For example, the Institute of Chartered Accountants in England and Wales started to publish 'recommendations' in 1946. The Australian Institute (Zeff, 1973) and the New Zealand Society (Zeff, 1979) followed the same course. In general, the subjects of professional pronouncements were determined by what appeared from time to time to be particular matters causing some confusion in practice. This has since been termed a fire fighting approach to standard setting.

Furthermore, the standards seem to presume that users of the standards and the financial statements will understand the terms employed, such as 'state of affairs', 'profit' and 'true and fair view'. But there are no explicit definitions of such terms and they can be interpreted and understood in a variety of different ways. Consequently, there is no safeguard against inconsistent treatment of the subject matter under a particular standard.

The politics of standard setting

Most accounting issues are politically sensitive because (a) the need for standards arises where there is controversy, and (b) accounting partitions wealth between different groups. As a result, different groups interested in a particular accounting issue can be expected to attempt to lobby for the standard most beneficial to them, or to prevent the establishment of a proposed standard which they think would be less favourable than the status quo. The various proposals put forward to address accounting issues caused by inflation are a classic example. Each method would affect companies differently. For example, CPP (general price-level adjusted historical cost accounting) tends to make utilities with heavy debt capital look better off. Replacement cost accounting and CCA tend to make companies with a large investment in depreciable assets, such as steel companies, look relatively less profitable. Continuously contemporary accounting, which uses exit values, makes firms with assets that are not readily saleable look bad. It is clear that the political implications of inflation accounting proposals have been largely responsible for the difficulty in reaching agreement in this area.

The relationship between the political sensitivity of accounting issues and the formulation of standards on such issues has often been the subject of discussion and debate. Compromise is an essential ingredient, particularly in any decision involving political considerations. A standard-setting body should be clear about the extent to which a compromise can be made without losing the actual thrust of a proposed standard. Referring to the FASB, Horngren

(1973) describes this situation as a dilemma faced by the board: although its decisions should rest — and be seen to rest — chiefly on accounting considerations, it must also study — and be seen to study — the possible adverse economic and social consequences of its proposed actions. He summarises the situation as follows:

> The job, then, of the FASB is a twofold one of production and marketing: (1) to develop the best possible accounting standards and (2) to see that such standards are accepted. The latter task is more formidable than the former. (p.65)

The fact that accounting is an area of knowledge which has a political significance does not necessarily mean that the processes by which accounting knowledge is advanced, or by which new applications are found for old knowledge, are themselves political processes. The following statement by the American Financial Accounting Foundation (FAF) indicates its awareness of this situation:

> The process of setting accounting standards can be described as democratic because, like all rule-making bodies, the Board's right to make rules depends ultimately on the consent of the ruled. But because standard setting requires some perspective, it would not be appropriate to establish a standard based solely on a canvass of the constituents. Similarly, the process can be described as legislative because it must be deliberative and because all views must be heard. But the standard setters are expected to represent the entire constituency as a whole and not be representatives of a specific constituent group. The process can be described as political because there is an educational effort involved in getting a new standard accepted. But it is not political in the sense that an accommodation is required to get a statement issued. (FAF, 1977, p.15)

The importance of neutrality as a necessary quality of accounting information has also been emphasised by various researchers and conceptual frameworks. The argument is that unless accounting information which influences human behaviour seeks to be neutral as between different modes of behaviour, it is difficult to see how it can be relied on to guide behaviour (Chambers, 1966, p.326; Solomons, 1978, p.70).

Approaches to standard setting

The issue of what approach should be taken in setting accounting standards has been the subject of extensive research and debate in recent years. The need for accounting standards seems to be a matter of controversy. For example, some researchers argue that within the market mechanism there are already means that provide for an efficient generation of quality financial information for users and, therefore, standards do not serve a useful purpose in improving the quality of financial reporting. There are others who argue that the market mechanism fails to provide the information needed by users of financial statements in a manner that is equitable and efficient and, therefore, accounting standards are necessary to regulate the provision of information through financial reports (Rahman, Perera and Tower, 1992). The advocates of the former view take a free-market approach while those of the latter view take a regulatory approach to setting accounting standards.

Free-market approach

The basic assumption of the free-market approach is that accounting information is an economic good similar to other goods or services. As such, it is subject to the forces of demand and supply: demand by interested users, and supply by entities in the form of financial statements. Through the interaction between these market forces, an equilibrium is reached where an optimal amount of information is disclosed at an optimal price. Whenever a given piece of information is demanded, the market will generate the information if the price offered is right. The market is thus presented as the ideal mechanism for determining the types of information to be disclosed, the recipients of the information and the accounting standards to govern the production of such information (Kam, 1990, pp.549–550). The proponents of this view also argue that mandatory standards are undesirable because they tend to overproduce standards in view of the fact that the cost of production of information is not borne by users.

Regulatory approach

Advocates of a regulatory approach to accounting seem to believe that market failures or anomalies and perceived asymmetry in regard to the quantity and quality of financial information available to various interested parties, which lead to a decline in investor confidence, can be rectified through regulation. Furthermore, researchers have indicated that regulation, particularly through accounting standards, may be useful to preparers, auditors and regulatory agencies as it provides clear guidelines for reporting, verification and overseeing purposes, respectively (Rahman, Perera and Tower, 1992).

Regulation theory

In view of the inadequacies of the free-market approach to setting accounting standards, attention has been drawn to alternative approaches. It has been argued that perceived crises initiate accounting regulatory policies or standards. Accordingly, as the demand for such policies or standards is stimulated by perceived crises, the regulators (standard setters) respond by supplying the policies. The interaction between the demand and supply factors leads to an equilibrium. In a dynamic regulatory mechanism there is a continuous process of adjustment of the policies or standards to changing demand and supply patterns.

As Belkaoui (1985, p.48) explains, regulation is generally assumed to be designed and operated for the benefit of a given industry. There are two major categories of regulation theory: public-interest theories; and interest-group or capture theories (Stigler, 1971; Posner, 1974). The public-interest theories maintain that regulation is supplied in response to the demand of the public for the correction of inefficient or inequitable market practices. They are instituted primarily for the protection and benefit of the general public. Regulation, according to the interest-group capture theories, is supplied in response to the demands of special-interest groups in order to maximise the income of their members. There are two main versions of this theory: the political ruling-elite theory of regulation (Posner, 1974) and the economic theory of regulation (Peltzman, 1976). The political ruling-elite theory uses political power to gain regulatory control; the economic theory relies on economic power.

Regulation theory, or the theory of what constitutes maximising behaviour in an accounting regulatory agency, is in its infancy. The fundamental issues of why regulate at all, and whether regulation is efficient and desirable are still being discussed. The subject of regulation for competition has become increasingly important in recent years. Among the relevant issues here are: What constitutes an efficient allocation of resources? How does this relate to the question of distribution of income? What is the cost of competition law? What is the definition of the market? What is the definition of public benefit? (For a summary of papers presented at two conferences held in Auckland, New Zealand and Sydney, Australia, in March 1988 on Regulating for Competition in a Changing Economic Environment, see *Australian Accountant*, June 1988, pp.96–101.) As many of the crucial issues of regulation have not been resolved

yet, obviously more research is needed to develop a theory of regulation of accounting standards.

Approaches to regulation of accounting standards

The question of who should set accounting standards has been the subject of detailed discussion and debate in recent years. While the advocates of private sector regulation of accounting standards argue that public interest is best served if standard setting is left to the private sector, the arguments for public sector regulation have also gained a high degree of legitimacy in recent years. Some of the arguments put forward by the proponents of these two viewpoints are given below.

Arguments in favour of private sector regulation

1
Private sector regulation would mean close association with the accounting profession. This would automatically ensure involvement by knowledgeable and experienced people in the standard-setting process.

2
A board in the private sector commands more prestige and acceptability among the business community, because a board in the public sector would be seen to be subjected to pressures to help accomplish the socio-economic objectives of the government (Kam, 1990, p.553).

3
Since a government body staffed with bureaucrats is likely to be insensitive to the cost effectiveness of additional disclosure requirements, the cost of compliance with government regulation would be substantially higher than with private sector regulation.

4
There is the danger that political appointees to the board may feel that witch hunts are

necessary to protect the public interest or may want to take certain actions at the expense of accounting standards and the accounting profession.

5

The legislative process and government authority could be as susceptible to political lobbying and pressures as private bodies.

6

Government standards would be drawn up with an overriding concern for enforce-ability and thus would tend to be more rigid, leaving less room for judgement than standards developed in the private sector. The procedures to be followed in formulat-ing standards would make them less adap-tive to changing circumstances than standards generated by the private sector.

Arguments in favour of public sector regulation

1

A public sector regulatory body has greater legitimacy through its explicit statutory authority. Added to that is a greater enforcement power than a private agency. Standards set by a non-public body are difficult to enforce.

2

A governmental board would be less sub-ject to the influence of corporate manage-ment and large professional accounting firms and would work for better disclosure for investors (Kam, 1990, p.553).

3

A governmental body can be the catalyst for change. The private sector and market forces do not provide the leadership neces-sary to effect such change.

4

Public sector regulation of accounting stan-dards is motivated by the need to protect the public interest. It provides mechanisms to offset the preparer bias that institution-ally exists in the standard-setting process as

well as to offset the economic limitations of investors seeking adequate information. (Burton, 1982).

5

The private sector has to be watched and controlled, given that its objectives may sometimes contradict the public interest. A minimum of government intervention may be necessary to avoid extreme and negative behaviours.

6

Accounting standards have the effect of law and should therefore be established in accordance with the general rules and pro-cedures for making laws. As the public interest is at stake, it would be wrong to leave the setting of standards to non-public bodies which could be affected by conflicts of interest.

The impact of accounting standards

It appears that among the proponents of a regulatory approach there are different views about the purpose of financial reports. Some emphasise that the main pur-pose is to provide information for economic decision making. Others argue that the pur-pose is to satisfy the requirements of public accountability. While these two purposes are not mutually exclusive, they can lead to the provision of different types of informa-tion. For example, from the point of view of decision usefulness, emphasis would be on the efficient production of information, whereas from the point of view of account-ability, emphasis would be on producing information both efficiently and equitably (Tower, 1991).

Within the regulatory approach, accounting standards play a significant role in achieving the objectives of financial state-ments, whether they are based on decision usefulness or accountability. The success or otherwise of accounting standards is re-flected in the level of compliance achieved among the preparers of financial statements. In the absence of compliance, standard setting is a futile exercise.

Compliance

In recent years attempts have been made in Anglo-American countries to raise the level of compliance with accounting standards. The level of compliance achieved in regard to a particular accounting standard is determined by the extent to which it is accepted by the parties concerned and also by the mechanism set in place for its enforcement. The determinants of the level of compliance with standards are shown in Figure 7.1.

Figure 7.1
Determinants of the level of compliance

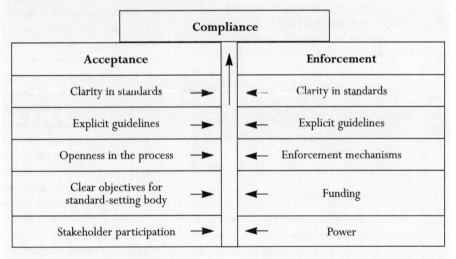

The acceptability of a standard will depend on factors such as: the clarity of the standard; explicit guidelines on its implementation; openness in the standard-setting process; clear objectives for the standard-setting body; and stakeholder participation. Deficiencies in any of these factors will lead to problems of acceptance. For example, broad representation of the stakeholder groups on the standard-setting body would provide a strong constituent base for its activities and this would help enhance the level of acceptability accorded to the standards by those groups. As Horngren, commenting on the FASB, stated, 'the key to a successful enterprise is to generate a product that is acceptable to customers' (1973, p.62).

Zeff (1988) says that openness has been instrumental in enhancing the credibility of the FASB standard-setting process. Among the Anglo-American countries, the USA has the most transparent system with its due process procedures which include open discussions. New Zealand certainly has a long way to go in this regard. For example, proposals on new accounting issues are made public only at the exposure draft stage (Porter, 1990). As a result, some of the options may never be available to the outsiders for consideration. It is also not clear to an outsider how the issues are chosen in the first place.

Similarly, enforcement depends largely on the enforcement mechanism and the amount of power and resources given to organisations entrusted with the task of enforcing accounting standards. For example, the *New Zealand Financial Reporting Act* 1993 recommended that accounting standards be granted legal backing. Both the

Wheat Committee in the USA (AICPA, 1975) and Dearing Committee in the UK (CCAB, 1988) sought to ensure that adequate funding was available for the standard-setting body when they made recommendations to establish the FASB and the ASB, respectively.

Institutional arrangements for setting accounting standards

In accounting, what is an acceptable practice or standard is highly influenced by authoritative bodies involved in setting those standards. Within each country, an organisation is given the authority to set the accounting standards. Such an organisation can be a part of the private sector or public sector. The institutional arrangements for setting accounting standards in the UK, Australia, New Zealand, the USA and Canada are considered in this section.

United Kingdom

The UK has no unitary professional institute equivalent to the NZSA in New Zealand or AICPA in the USA. In fact there are six accounting bodies:
• Institute of Chartered Accountants in England and Wales
• Institute of Chartered Accountants in Scotland
• Institute of Chartered Accountants in Ireland
• Chartered Association of Certified Accountants
• Chartered Institute of Management Accountants
• Chartered Institute of Public Finance and Accountancy.
Although only the members of the first four accounting bodies are recognised as auditors by the UK Government's Department of Trade, all six have formed a joint committee to present the views of the accounting profession. This committee, known as the Consultative Committee of Accountancy Bodies (CCAB), was established in May 1974.

In November 1987 the CCAB set up a committee under the former Post Office head Sir Ron Dearing as chair to review the standard-setting process in the UK. This was in response to the criticisms with regard to the lack of an effective means of monitoring compliance, the lack of sufficient staff support and the quality of the SSAPs under the ASC. The ASC (which was originally called the ASSC) was established by the ICAEW in 1970. The role of the ASC was confined to developing statements of standard accounting practice. The adoption and enforcement of accounting standards remained the responsibility of the six professional bodies, every one of which had an effective power of veto. The report of the Dearing Committee, titled *The Making of Accounting Standards*, was published in November 1988 (CCAB, 1988). It made significant recommendations to restructure the standard-setting process. They included the following:
• The ASC should be dismantled and its functions assigned to a new body, the Accounting Standards Board.
• The funding for the ASB should be increased from £440 000 to £1.5 million.
• The process of standard setting should be under the policy control of a newly created Financial Reporting Council (FRC) which should have around twenty members, drawn equally from the accounting profession and from representatives of the users and preparers of accounts.
• The chairperson of the FRC should be appointed jointly by the Secretary of State for Trade and Industry and the Governor of the Bank of England.
• The Council of the FRC should provide from among its number the chairperson of the proposed ASB.
• The ASB should consist of no more than nine members and be able to issue standards on its own authority with a two-thirds majority.
• At least the chairperson and technical director of the ASB should be full-time executives.

- In order to oversee compliance, a review panel should be created.

The recommendations of the Dearing Committee were implemented in August 1990 with the establishment of the ASB, a government mandated, quasi-independent body under the authority of the FRC. The institutional arrangements under the new structure are shown in Figure 7.2.

Figure 7.2
Institutional arrangements for setting accounting standards in the UK

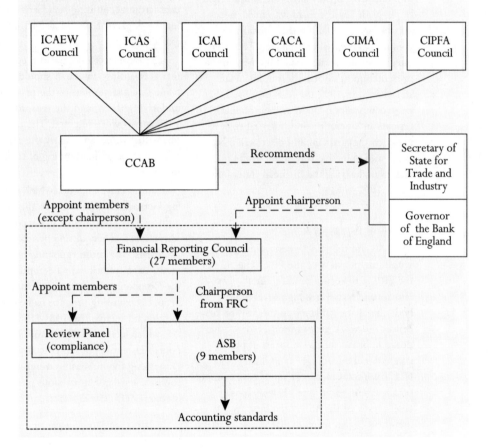

Accounting Standards Board

Under the 1990 arrangements, the Secretary of State designated the ASB as the source of accounting standards. The ASB relates to the FRC, although the ASC was answerable to the CCAB. The ASB is also able to issue standards on its own authority, unlike the ASC which had to work through the six institutes forming the CCAB. Further, the ASB has nine members compared with twenty-one in the ASC, and is able to issue a standard with a two-thirds majority, compared with the ASC requirement of unanimity. Like the FASB, the ASB is institutionally separated from the accounting bodies, and is funded by a number of sources in addition to the accounting bodies. The chairperson and technical director of the ASB are fulltime appointments. The Urgent Issues Taskforce, an offshoot of the ASB, addresses urgent matters not covered by the ASB.

Review panel

The review panel, chaired by a Queen's Counsel, has been delegated authority to bring suits in accordance with company legislation. In doing so, the review panel examines financial statements to determine whether they have complied with accounting standards; if they have not, it undertakes to persuade the companies to make necessary changes, or, failing that, institutes a civil suit to compel compliance. The main purpose of the review panel is to ensure fair presentation of information in financial statements. In 1992 the ASB proposed that large companies include in their annual reports an 'operating and financial review', in which they explain and discuss in a balanced and objective way some of the main factors underlying the financial statements (Zeff, 1992, p.6)

Financial Reporting Council

The ASB and the review panel function within the purview of the FRC. The role of the FRC is to secure funding for the two entities and to act as a high-level policy body that gives guidance to the ASB on priorities and work programmes, advises the Board in broad terms on issues of public concern and encourages compliance. The FRC has a total membership of twenty-nine (chairperson, three vice-chairpersons, chairperson of the ASB, secretary, twenty members drawn from a wide range of activities, and three observers; see *Public Finance and Accountancy*, 1990, p.3). The FRC is linked to the State and the profession. Its link with the State is through the appointment of a deputy secretary at the Department of Trade and Industry as a member and the presence of other civil servants and a representative of the Bank of England as observers. Its link with the profession is established by making the president of the ICAEW and the chairperson of the CCAB *ex officio* members (Willmott *et al.* 1992).

The Dearing Report did not wish to see accounting standards incorporated into law because of the reduction in flexibility that could result. However, the report recommended that the government introduce legislation to require the directors of large companies specifically to draw attention in their annual accounts to any material departures from accounting standards. Reasons for the departure would also have to be explained.

The Dearing Report also recommended that accounting standards should be accompanied by a statement of the principles underlying them, and the reasons why alternatives were rejected. The intention of this is that those who apply the standards have a better understanding of their meaning.

Additionally, a feature which is becoming increasingly important in the UK is the influence of a number of EU accounting 'directives' on accounting practices and standards. Minimum reporting requirements have traditionally been prescribed in the Companies Acts, leaving matters of proper accounting practice to be decided in the private sector. The 1981 UK *Companies Act*, which adapted UK law to the EU's Fourth Directive, broke with that tradition. Describing the increasing trend in the UK towards legislative provisions in accounting matters, Zeff (1992) states:

> In late 1989, the *Companies Act* 1989 was approved, referring for the first time in legislation to 'accounting standards' and authorizing the Secretary of State for Trade and Industry to designate the source of accounting standards. The Act also required the directors of large companies to state in the notes to their financial statements whether or not they had been prepared in accordance with 'applicable accounting standards', drawing attention to material departures and explaining the reasons for such departures. The Act authorized the Secretary

of State to apply to the courts for an order requiring the revision of accounts that do not give a true and fair view. The burden of proof falls on companies whose financial statements reflect a material departure from applicable accounting standards to demonstrate that the statements nonetheless give a true and fair view. (p.6)

Australia

In Australia there are two professional accounting bodies: the ICAA and the ASCPA. The Australian standard-setting process has evolved through several distinct phases of development. Before 1964 the structure of accounting standards in Australia was not coordinated. The next phase witnessed the creation of the AARF in 1964. The creation of the ASRB in 1984 represents another phase. The merger of the AARF and ASRB in 1989 signified the next phase with major reform. The current system of accounting regulation in Australia is governed by the terms of an agreement reached in June 1990 between the Australian Commonwealth and the states (Baxt, 1990, p.124).

Standard setting in Australia: before 1990

The two professional bodies in Australia have tried to merge from time to time but have never succeeded. To save them from issuing independent and competing standards, they joined forces to the extent of establishing the AARF in 1964 and they jointly funded the research foundation with the intention that it would produce appropriate standards to guide the profession.

The AARF has been active in developing exposure drafts, in soliciting public comment and in amending the drafts and eventually approving them as professional standards. It has followed something like the FASB approach. Corsi and Staunton (1994, p.18) state that the Australian profession moved from a reliance on English

practice and thought in the 1950s to imitations of American practice in the 1970s. In the early 1980s however, it became apparent that the enforcement mechanisms within the profession were not sufficient to cause the companies to comply — nor indeed to cause auditors to comply — with the requirement that they would disclose significant departures from the standards. Surveys showed considerable deviation from the standards in some areas.

The profession's response to this situation was to turn to the government and request legislation to make accounting standards law. The government agreed, but wanted to see that the public interest was fully taken into account before turning the standards into law. Consequently, the ASRB was established in 1984 to perform a review function. (For a comprehensive analysis of the circumstances that led to the establishment of the ASRB, see Rahman, 1992).

With the establishment of the ASRB, Australia entered a phase of dual regulation of accounting standards: professional and legal. Australia showed a preference for a legalistic approach to drafting accounting standards, for example the word 'shall' is used instead of 'should'. The ASRB consisted of seven members, all of whom were part-time. The members of the ASRB were supposed to represent a range of interest groups, namely preparers, users, academics and public accounting firms. The rationale was that the legally enforceable standards as established by the ASRB should be determined by a mix of persons reflecting a wide range of community experience and interests. It is interesting that, although the then Big Eight influence was not strong, all the members were fully qualified accountants. They were appointed by the Ministerial Council from panels of names submitted by a number of interested organisations, including the ICAA, ASCPA and AARF.

Before issuing an accounting standard, the AARF was required to submit it to the

ASRB for its review and approval. The ASRB engaged in its own exposure period to get responses from a wider audience. However, usually those who responded to the ASRB were the same people who responded to the AARF. Approval of a standard required an affirmative vote by five members of the Board.

The relationship between the AARF and the ASRB was not always cordial. Walker (1987), one of the founding members of the ASRB, states:

> With the benefit of hindsight, it is difficult to avoid the conclusion that representatives of the accountancy bodies and AARF ensured that the ASRB was unproductive. The Board was hampered by the tardiness of those bodies in formally communicating their demands about copyright, by delays in the submission of redrafted versions of two relatively uncontentious standards, and by the failure of AARF to redraft and submit the three standards which the Board considered should have priority. (pp. 280–281)

As described by Morley and Martin (1987), the problems that arose between the ASRB and AARF particularly during the first two years included the following:

> First, there was a battle over copyrights. It was resolved, that the copyright will vest in the board and legislature but it will be assigned to the research foundation. Second, there had been considerable problems with drafting. Accounting standards were not written in the usual legal form — 'thou shalt do this'. And so there was a question as to how one might turn a standard produced by the profession into something that was enforceable as law. There was a fear that the board might end up approving standards that could not be enforced in a court of law. Third, a problem of sourcing of standards also arose. The legis-

lature allowed for the possibility that, in addition to the AARF, other bodies might submit standards as well. Any other body or any other person was, in fact, free to make up a standard and submit it for approval. But, later the board decided that it should not accept any standard for review without referring back to AARF for its own consideration.

Fourth, the conceptual framework caused problems for the board. The board was supposed to review standards against some criteria, but it had none. So the board over a weekend created its own conceptual framework consisting of ten accounting assumptions, similar to FASB's SFACs. This caused a certain amount of friction with AARF, which thought it was its job to get on with the conceptual framework.

Fifth, the independence question was also interesting. The ASRB was in a difficult position in that, on the one hand, [its members] were criticised for being the captive of the accounting bodies because the standards ultimately approved by them looked very much like those submitted by the research foundation; on the other hand, if they approved standards that were not similar to those submitted by AARF, then they would be criticised for having created their own standards, when they were indeed set up to perform a review function. (p. 41)

The two bodies merged in 1989. The new entity was known as AARF (ASRB), with the standard-setting power to be controlled by a nine-member board appointed by the government (four seats of which were reserved for the accountancy bodies). There was no separate review function and the ICAA and ASCPA would not have veto power.

Walker (1987) suggested that the ASRB was a classic case of 'regulatory capture', arguing that the special-interest groups (notably the ICAA, ASCPA and AARF) had captured the ASRB. The 1989 merger of the AARF and the ASRB seems to strengthen Walker's argument. However, the merger also resulted in a loss of the veto power enjoyed by the profession. It is interesting to note that the structure of the new AARF (ASRB) resembled some of the changes proposed by the Dearing Committee in the UK.

Standard setting in Australia: after 1990

The key features of the Australian accounting regulatory system currently in place are governed by the terms of an agreement reached in June 1990 between the Australian Commonwealth and the States. Under this agreement the Australian Corporations Law is to apply to all States and territories with specific applications of legislation promulgated by individual States. As discussed in Rahman, Perera and Tower (1994), the ASRB was reorganised as the AASB in 1990, making it the main standard-setting body in Australia. The standards formulated by the AARF have to be submitted to the AASB for approval. The AASB approved accounting standards receive statutory recognition and are applicable to companies operating under the *Australian Corporations Law* 1991 and its constituents. Under this arrangement the ASCPA and ICAA would participate in the standards approval process through their membership on the AASB. The AASB is funded by the government and is composed of nine part-time members representing various sectors interested in accounting standard setting (see McGregor, 1989a, b; O'leary, 1989. Its members are appointed by the Australian Commonwealth Attorney-General from panels of names submitted by the ASCPA, ICAA and other organisations, in the following manner:

- the Chairperson
- two members are selected from a panel of names submitted by the ASCPA
- two members are selected from a panel

of names submitted by the ICAA
- four members are selected from panels of names submitted by other organisations and bodies.

The functions of the AASB as set out in the *Australian Securities Commission Act*, Section 226(1), are to:

a develop a conceptual framework, not having the force of an accounting standard, for the purpose of evaluating proposed accounting standards

b review proposed accounting standards

c sponsor or undertake the development of possible accounting standards

d engage in such public consultation as may be necessary to decide whether or not it should make changes to proposed accounting standards

e make changes to the form and context of a proposed accounting standard.

Commonwealth Parliament has the right to veto accounting standards issued by the AASB. Legislative support for the enforcement of accounting standards on all private and public sector entities is provided by the Commonwealth and the States through the coordinating mechanism of the Ministerial Council for Companies and Securities. The Ministerial Council (comprising the relevant law Ministers of the Commonwealth, States and Territories), created under the previous cooperative scheme for companies and securities, has a consultative role only. In regard to matters concerning company law, the Commonwealth has a weighted vote compared to the States (Baxt, 1990, p.124).

The administration of the new legislation (total companies and securities regulation scheme) is within the sole province of the Australian Securities Commission (ASC). Accordingly, the standards approved by the AASB are enforced by the ASC. The rulings of the ASC (which replaced the National Companies and Securities Commission (NCSC)) with respect to the adequacy or otherwise of disclosure will have the force of law. The ASC will be able

Figure 7.3
Institutional arrangement for setting accounting standards in Australia.

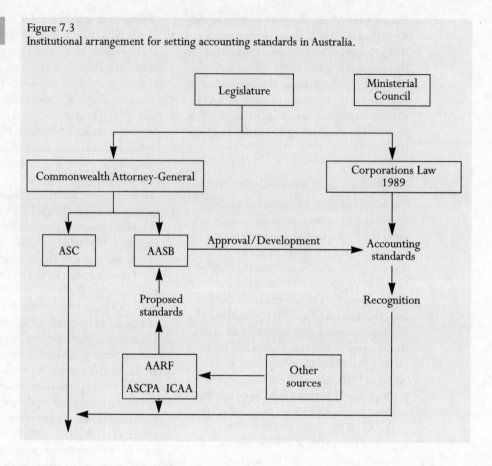

to prosecute non-compliers immediately. No such enforcement power was available under the NCSC. Furthermore, the ASC has adequate resources to enable it to function effectively (English, 1992, pp. 20–25). This structure is illustrated in Figure 7.3.

Peirson Report on further reforms

In August 1990 a report prepared by Professor C.G. Peirson on institutional arrangements for accounting standard setting in Australia was issued by the AARF's Board of Management for public comment. The Peirson Report proposed three major reforms. They are:

- The formation by 1992 of two broadly constituted consultative groups, one for

the private sector and one for the public sector.
- The establishment by 1995 of a foundation to be called the Australian Accounting Standards Foundation (AASF) which will be independent of the accounting profession, business and government, and whose funding will be broadly based.
- The establishment by 1995 of one national accounting standard-setting board within the AASF to be called the ASB. This Board would result from a merger of the AASB and the PSASB of the AARF.

The proposed structure under Peirson recommendations was presented in AARF's 'Invitation to Comment', and is shown in Figure 7.4.

Figure 7.4
Proposed institutional arrangements for accounting standard setting in
Australia (Peirson Report)

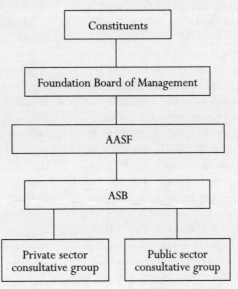

- *Constituents*: In addition to professional bodies, the term constituents would include users, preparers and government departments acting as watch dogs.
- *ASB*: The AASB would be replaced by the ASB with nine part-time members and a full-time chairperson. It would have a wider role in standard setting. It would prepare, approve and issue accounting standards for all private and public sector entities in Australia.
- *AASF*: The AASF is expected to play a role similar to the current AARF. It would assist the ASB in preparing accounting standards by providing administrative and technical support. The AASF Board of Management would comprise ten members generally representing the constituents. The Board would appoint members of the ASB and the consultative groups, arrange funding and approve the budget of the ASB and the consultative groups.
- *Consultative groups:* Two consultative groups for the private and public sectors would

be established. They would each comprise about twenty members broadly representing the constituents. Their task would be to provide advice to the ASB on major technical issues, work programmes, project priorities, adequacy of due process and other relevant matters.

In 1991, based on Peirson's recommendations, the AARF introduced a new independent standard-setting structure (AARF, 1991). This involved the establishment of:
- a foundation to be called the Australian Accounting Standards Foundation (AASF) which will be independent of the accounting profession, business and government and whose funding will be broadly based
- one national accounting standard-setting board within the Foundation to be called the Accounting Standards Board (ASB); formed from a merger of the AASB and the public sector ASB.

In September 1992 the AARF issued ED 57, 'Present Procedures for the Development of Statements of Accounting

Concepts and Statements of Accounting Standards'. The submissions received in response to this ED indicated, among other things, strong support for the merger of the AASB and PSASB (Day, McPhee and Keys, 1993).

Recently, the AASB has been concerned about international comparability of accounting standards. It has issued a policy discussion paper, entitled *Towards International Comparability of Financial Reporting*, which explains its views on the subject (AASB, 1994). The discussion paper considers why differences exist between accounting standards throughout the world, examines the arguments for and against comparability and discusses how best to achieve improved comparability without sacrificing the quality of financial reporting within the country. It also reviews each existing AASB accounting standard and compares them with those of the other major standard-setting bodies, including the IASC.

New Zealand

New Zealand has one national professional accounting body, the NZSA, which was established by an Act of Parliament in 1958. The NZSA has been empowered to control and regulate the practice of accountancy in New Zealand. Due to historical reasons, the NZSA has been strongly influenced by the British tradition of self-regulation. However, the changes that were introduced in 1993 marked the beginning of a new era of accounting regulation in New Zealand.

Standard setting in New Zealand: before 1993

The arrangements for setting accounting standards in New Zealand have undergone significant changes over the years. During the period 1958–1965, the NZSA followed the English Institute's recommendations almost verbatim. The next eight years saw the evolution of New Zealand-based standards. These standards still reflected over-

seas promulgations, particularly the British and the American, and were not mandatory. The NZSA started issuing mandatory standards in 1974.

Until 1993 the standard-setting function remained wholly in the private sector. Following the old British-style self-regulation of standard setting, the promulgation and enforcement of accounting standards were functions performed by the professional accounting body wherein only the NZSA was expected to discipline its members. Enforcement of standards by the NZSA relied on persuasion and the requirement to disclose departures from standards with possible sanctions against members who failed in respect of such required disclosures. (For a detailed discussion on various aspects of accounting regulation in New Zealand, see Tower, 1991).

Accounting Research and Standards Board

Prior to November 1992, the Accounting Research and Standards Board (ARSB) of the NZSA was responsible for developing the accounting standards. The Board appointed functional committees on an annual basis; in turn these committees appointed project teams to conduct studies on particular issues. There were no public hearings or meetings of the Board open to the public. The different stages in the production of accounting standards in New Zealand are explained in Porter (1990). The ARSB had also issued a series of research bulletins on financial accounting, auditing and farm accounting. The ARSB's terms of reference were to

- formulate and direct national policy with regard to accounting and research
- keep under review accounting and auditing standards
- propose to the Council definitive statements, SSAPs, statements of auditing practice and recommendations on auditing practice
- publish interpretations of definitive

statements, Board opinions and consultative documents with the object of maintaining and advancing accounting standards
- consult as appropriate with representatives of finance, commerce, industry and government and other persons concerned with financial reporting
- meet the obligations imposed on the Board as a member of the IFAC and the IASC
- establish, set guidelines for, and if necessary, subsequently to amend, the structure of functional committees to which responsibility for the conduct of research or other work might be delegated.

The Board was composed of twelve members of the NZSA appointed by its Council. There were five functional committees of the Board: accounting research, auditing, farm accounting, financial accounting and public sector accounting. The Council, in appointing members, was required to give regard to the need for:
a adequate cooperation with the functional committees of the Board
b adequate liaison with NZ universities
c the Board's being seen —
- as reasonably representative of preparers, users and auditors of accounts
- as having an overall stature and operational effectiveness consistent with the importance of the advancement of accounting and auditing standards.

Financial Reporting Standards Board

In November 1992 the ARSB of the NZSA was dissolved and replaced with two new boards: the FRSB and the Professional Practices Board (PPB). The FRSB is responsible for preparing financial reporting standards, publishing interpretations to financial reporting standards, conducting research into financial reporting and consulting with others concerned with financial reporting.

The terms and reference of the FRSB are as follows:
a to formulate and direct national policy with regard to accounting and research;
b to keep under review accounting standards
c to propose to the Council definitive statements, i.e. Financial Reporting Standards
d to publish interpretations of definitive statements, Board opinions and consultative documents with the objective of maintaining and advancing accounting standards
e to meet the obligations imposed on the Society as a member of the International Federation of Accountants and the International Accounting Standards Committee
d to establish, set guidelines for, and if necessary, subsequently to amend, the structure of functional committees, to which responsibility for the conduct of research or other work might be delegated.

The FRSB consists of twelve members appointed by the Council of the NZSA. The guidelines developed by the NZSA for determining the composition of the FRSB includes that not less than three members of the Board shall be persons not directly involved in the preparation and auditing of financial statements. These persons need not be members of the NZSA. Its work is structured under four committees: two FRCs, the Primary Sector Accounting Committee and the Research PhD Scholarship Selection Committee. One of the FRCs has the responsibility for transforming all existing SSAPs into new FRSs. The other FRC is responsible for reviewing submissions on the Financial Reporting Framework and finalising documents contained in the Framework package. The PPB is responsible for issuing professional engagement standards and guidelines (*Accountants' Journal*, February, 1993, pp.57–58).

Standard setting in New Zealand: after 1993

With the enactment of the *Financial Reporting Act* and a new *Companies Act* in 1993, accounting in New Zealand entered a new era of co-regulation with a joint government–profession standard-setting mechanism. This was the result of a series of events that took place during the preceding five years.

The future direction of accounting regulation has been widely discussed in New Zealand (Tower, Perera and Rahman, 1992). Three ministerial reviews examined different aspects of the reporting of financial information: a Ministerial Committee of inquiry headed by the former Reserve Bank Governor, Russell Spencer, was appointed in October 1988 to review share market law and practices and to recommend changes needed to ensure a fair and efficient market. They submitted two reports (1989a, b): the New Zealand Law Commission (1987; 1989; 1990) offered an update to company law; and the Securities Commission (1990) prepared a brief on financial reporting.

The Russell Committee criticised the quality of financial reporting and the level of non-compliance with accounting standards in New Zealand. They recommended that:

- the Eighth Schedule to the *Companies Act* be updated
- legal backing be awarded to accounting standards
- an Accounting Standards Review Board (ASRB) be established to approve accounting standards
- the Securities Commission be revamped as overseer to the equity market
- stock exchange listing requirements be given the force of law
- funding for the Securities Commission be increased from $1.9 million to $3.9 million
- sanctions be put in place for non-compliance with standards

- certain regulatory agencies or any security holder or creditor of an issuer be allowed to appeal to the statutory authority for remedy of a qualified set of financial statements.

The Securities Commission (1990) supported the Russell Committee's position and recommended the establishment of the ASRB to approve standards. The report further envisaged that the ASRB would:

- have the power to amend standards
- be located outside the accounting profession's domain
- limit the Society's representation to a large minority
- use accountants' technical expertise
- receive submissions from the NZSA and others
- monitor qualified audit reports.

The Securities Commission Report also called for a statutory provision for the revision of defective accounts.

The Law Commission took a free market approach and preferred to leave enforcement of accounting standards in the hands of shareholder suits. They offered an update to company law and kept the overriding provision of true and fair view.

In May 1991 the NZSA, the New Zealand Stock Exchange and the Securities Commission made a joint submission to the Minister of Justice recommending, among other things, the establishment of an independent Accounting Standards Board. In August 1991 a Ministerial Working Group on Securities Law Reform emphasised the need for a link between the true and fair view criterion and accounting principles within a self-regulatory framework. In February 1992 the NZSA issued a proposed framework for financial reporting in New Zealand which included seven exposure drafts. At the end of 1991 a Financial Reporting Bill incorporating many of the earlier recommendations was presented to the New Zealand Parliament.

The *Financial Reporting Act* 1993 granted the accounting standards legislative support.

It requires issuers of securities to the public to file financial statements that comply with generally accepted accounting practice and also give a true and fair view of their affairs. As a result, these standards are now mandatory for all public issuers of securities and all companies except those specifically exempted by the Act or any regulations enacted under the Act. The explanatory note to the Act says that it is an Act which:

a requires issuers of securities to the public to file financial statements that comply with generally accepted accounting practice and give a true and fair view of their affairs

b prescribes requirements for financial reporting by other entities

c establishes an ASRB and defines its functions and powers

d gives legal force to accounting standards approved by the Board

e provides for related matters.

Part three of the *Financial Reporting Act* explains, among other things, membership, functions and powers of the proposed ASRB. Accordingly, the Board consists of not less than four and not more than seven members appointed by the Governor-General on the recommendation of the Minister of Justice. The functions of the Board include the following.

a Review and, if it thinks fit, approve financial reporting standards submitted to it for approval for the purpose of this Act or for the purposes of the *Public Finance Act* 1989.

b Review, and if it thinks fit, approve amendments to any approved financial reporting standards.

c Make recommendations in relation to the submission for approval of financial reporting standards or amendments to approved financial reporting standards.

d Give directions as to the accounting policies that have authoritative support within the accounting profession in New Zealand.

e Encourage the development of financial reporting standards, including financial reporting standards for different classes of entity.

f Liaise with the ASRB established by the *Australian Securities Commission Act* 1989 with a view to harmonising New Zealand and Australian reporting standards.

Accounting standards or amendments to accounting standards may be submitted to the Board by the NZSA and any other organisation or person for approval. The current institutional arrangements for setting accounting standards in New Zealand are illustrated in Figure 7.5.

Under the new standard-setting arrangements in New Zealand that came into effect in 1993, the Minister of Justice holds the responsibility for the formulation and enforcement of corporate law. The Minister appoints the Registrar of Companies and the members of the Securities Commission and the ASRB. The Minister of Justice, in respect of corporate law, is the counterpart of the Commonwealth Attorney-General in Australia (Rahman, Perera and Tower, 1994).

The role of the ASRB in New Zealand is similar to that of the pre-1988 Australian ASRB. Unlike the AASB, which establishes and monitors financial disclosure standards, the ASRB only reviews and approves standards for the purposes of the *Financial Reporting Act* 1993.

The Financial Reporting Standards Board is responsible for the preparation of accounting standards to be submitted to the ASRB for approval. Although other bodies can submit standards for approval, the *Financial Reporting Act* 1993 explicitly identifies the NZSA as a frequent source of standards (para. 24). Financial reporting standards approved by the ASRB have full legislative backing. The approved standards will be applied with the overriding concept of true and fair view. Monitoring of compliance with accounting standards is undertaken by the Registrar of Companies and the Securities Commission.

Figure 7.5
Institutional arrangements for accounting standard setting in New Zealand

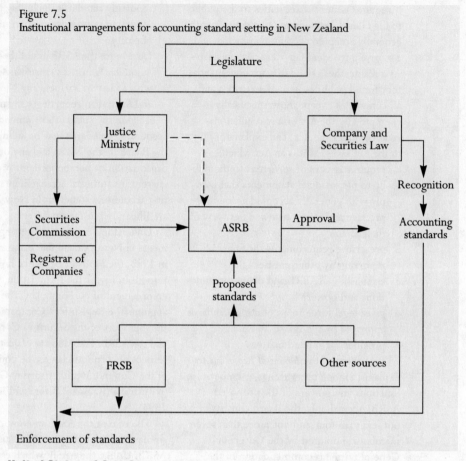

United States of America

Each of the fifty states of the USA has its own legislative body with extensive powers to control business activity within its own boundaries, including the conferment of the right to practise as a public accountant. Membership of the AICPA, the national body, is not required as a condition for exercising the right to practise and many practitioners elect not to become members. The responsibility for setting accounting standards in the USA is in the private sector. Figure 7.6 shows the associated institutional arrangements.

Financial Accounting Standards Board
The FASB was created in 1973 by recommendation of the AICPA-sponsored Study Group on Establishment of Accounting Principles (called the Wheat Committee after its chairperson) because of dissatisfaction with the existing arrangements. Unlike its two predecessors, the Committee on Accounting Procedures (CAP) and the APB, the FASB is not an arm of the AICPA. It is also independent of any organisation or enterprise that may be affected by its actions. One of the allegations against the APB was that clients of its members influenced those members' opinions. The members of the FASB serve full time, are adequately compensated and are required to have severed all economic relationships with former employers or firms. Members generally are appointed for a five-year term and are eligible for reappointment for one additional five-year term.

Figure 7.6
Institutional arrangements for setting accounting standards in the USA

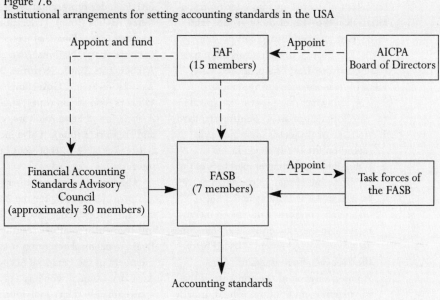

They are required to maintain up-to-date information about their personal investments in corporate securities, which is available for inspection by anyone who has a legitimate interest. These precautions have been taken with the intention of freeing board members from external influence. With the establishment of the FASB, for the first time standard setting was removed from the organised accounting profession.

The FASB consists of seven full-time members. Typically they represent academia (one), government (one), private industry (one), financial analysts (one), and public accounting (three). With this new set-up, for the first time non-CPAs were invited to serve on the standard-setting body.

The SEC and the AICPA officially recognise the FASB's standards as authoritative. Upon the establishment of the FASB in 1973, the AICPA council amended its code of professional ethics, and designated the FASB as the body to establish accounting principles. In 1973 the SEC issued Accounting Series Release No. 150 which gave FASB's pronouncements its authoritative support.

The FASB's Research and Technical Activities Division is headed by a director whose status is equivalent to that of a board member. The division consists of about thirty to forty professionals who provide substantial staff support for the Board's activities. In addition, outside researchers are often commissioned, particularly to conduct types of research for which the FASB staff do not have the necessary qualifications. The activities of this division include conducting research, participating in public hearings, analysing oral and written comments received from the public and preparing recommendations and drafts of documents for consideration by the Board.

The FASB's primary research document is a discussion memorandum in which the issues involved with a particular accounting problem and alternative solutions are set forth in a neutral fashion. Discussion memoranda are widely distributed free of charge for comment. A public hearing is also held to allow interested parties to communicate directly with board members on particular issues. Subsequent to the public hearing, the Board deliberates the issues in a series of meetings which are open to public observation. The FASB was established with the intent of providing a broader representation than the APB of those groups interested in or affected by accounting standards. The Board's deliberations culminate in an exposure draft of a proposed statement of financial accounting standard.

The following 'due process' is typical in the development of an accounting standard.
1 An issue or project is identified and placed on the FASB's agenda.
2 A task force consisting of members of the FASB's technical staff, in consultation with experts in the accounting and business community, prepares a discussion memorandum on the issue or project. Sometimes an invitation to comment is issued before the discussion memorandum.
3 A public hearing of the contents of the discussion memorandum is held, usually after at least sixty days have passed since its release.
4 An exposure draft of the proposed standard is prepared by the FASB, after considering the oral and written responses.
5 A second public hearing is sometimes held after a minimum thirty-day period of 'exposure' of the ED.
6 The proposed standard may be revised after the Board considers the responses.
7 The Board votes on the final draft of the proposal; if a majority favours it, a standard is issued.

The FASB's mission statement commits the Board to be objective in its decision making; to weigh carefully the views of constituents in developing concepts and standards; to issue standards only when the expected benefits exceed the perceived costs; to bring about needed changes in ways that minimise disruption to the continuity of reporting practice; and to review the effects of past decisions.

Financial Accounting Foundation

The FAF is responsible for the structure and process by which accounting standards are established. The Board of Trustees of the FAF includes representatives from the AAA (one), AICPA (four), Federation of Financial Analysts (one), Financial Executives Institute (two), National Association of Accountants (one), Securities Industry Association (one), Government Finance Officers Association (one), and National Association of State Auditors, Controllers, and Treasurers (one). It also includes three trustees at large to represent other interests.

The FAF appoints members of the FASB and provides funding for the Board's activities. It is precluded, however, from any involvement in matters relating to the Board's technical activities. It also appoints members of the Financial Accounting Advisory Council which is a group of approximately thirty individuals representing even broader backgrounds and interests than those of the trustees. For example, its membership regularly includes lawyers, Federal Government officials, heads of small businesses and executives from non-profit organisations. In October 1989 the FAF Board of Trustees set up an oversight committee to evaluate whether the FASB's standard-setting activities are consistent with its mission statement. In May 1990 the FAF Board of Trustees voted 11–5 to change the majority for approving FASB standards from 4–3 to 5–2.

Securities Exchange Commission

The accounting profession clearly prefers to have the authority for setting standards located in the private sector. However, the SEC, a public agency, has the potential legislative power to issue accounting standards. The SEC is not cited in Figure 7.6. because it does not normally exercise that power and relies on the accounting profession for accounting standards. The relationship between the FASB and the SEC, with respect to the establishment of accounting standards, has been described as 'top management' and 'lower management' (Horngren, 1972, p.38).

In 1938 the SEC delegated its power to establish accounting standards (as per the *Securities and Exchange Act* (1934)) to the private sector of the accounting profession. However, the SEC still monitors this area in the private sector and maintains an influence through its Financial Reporting Releases (formerly Accounting Series Releases), by which it explains certain accounting procedures for reports filed with it. Regulation S-X is the authoritative document that relates to the form and content of the financial statements required in the registration and periodic financial reports filed with the SEC. Until the 1970s the SEC had an aversion to departures from historical cost accounting (HCA). However, during the period of high inflation in the 1970s it favoured CCA. Currently, although the rate of inflation is low in many countries including the USA, there seems to be a renewed interest in accounting methods based on current values.

The SEC consists of five members appointed by the President of the United States of America with the approval of the Senate. No more than three can be from the same political party. The members serve a five-year term.

Canada

In Canada the accounting profession has responsibility for authoritative statements of acceptable accounting practices. At the Commonwealth level, the main organisation is the CICA. However, each of the ten provinces has its own institute of chartered accountants and membership in the provincial institutes constitutes membership in the CICA.

For many years the main sanction against failure to follow accounting recommendations was qualification of the audit report. However, additional legal backing for those

recommendations was introduced with the passing of the *Canada Business Corporations Act 1975*. As a result, companies that are incorporated under this Act are required to follow the CICA Handbook which acts as legal authority. Therefore, Canada has a standard-setting framework influenced by a combination of legal and professional interests (Bloom and Naciri, 1989, p.73).

A number of different stages can be identified in the evolution of accounting standard setting in Canada: the establishment of the Accounting Research Committee (ARC) and the Auditing Standards Committee (ASC) in 1973; the replacement of the ARC with the ASC in 1982; and the restructuring of the ASC as the ASB in 1991 (Gorelik, 1994, p.107).

Accounting Standards Committee

The ASC was established by the CICA in 1973 as a replacement for the ARC. The ASC was a standing committee of the CICA. A recommendation could be issued only if it had the support of a two-thirds majority of the Committee's twenty-one members and only after the committee had followed a due process by publishing an exposure draft for public comment. The ASC, which was divided into four geographic sections, comprised twenty-one part-time, unpaid members including accountants in public practice, commerce, finance and education, as well as a minority of non-accountants.

The Accounting Research Advisory Board (ARAB), with a membership of between ten and fifteen, provided a forum for debating the issues related to the proposed recommendations. The membership of this board consisted mainly of non-accountants.

The ASC held no open meetings or public hearings. The Canadian public was not appraised of the ASC's position on any accounting issue until late in the standard-setting process: the exposure draft stage.

In the late 1980s the ASC ran into problems. Gorelik (1994) explains:

> The *ad hoc* approach to standard-setting, preference for general standards rather than specific rules, excessive reliance on individual judgments of the Committee members in the development of standards and of auditors in their application, emergence of a challenger, and increasing inability of the AcSC to cope effectively with new reporting issues, emerged as some of the major threats to its long-run viability. (p.115)

The Accounting Standards Authority of Canada (ASAC) was incorporated in 1981 under the *Canada Business Corporations Act*, and was sponsored by the Certified General Accountants Association of Canada. In 1987 the ASAC issued a conceptual framework for accounting. The ASAC emerged as a challenger to the ASC, offering an alternative mechanism to standard setting. (The ASC also suffered from inadequate funding.)

Accounting Standards Board

The ASC was restructured in October 1991 as the ASB. The ASB consists of fifteen members (thirteen volunteer voting members and two staff non-voting members). However, the CICA continues to influence the activities of the ASB. For example, eight of the thirteen volunteer members are appointed by the CICA. The other five places are for individuals representing each of the five professional bodies: Canadian Council of Financial Analysts, Financial Executives Institute of Canada, Society of Management Accountants of Canada, Certified General Accountants Association of Canada, and Canadian Academic Accountants Association.

The granting of a semi-legislative authority to a private sector body (such as

Figure 7.7
Institutional arrangements for setting accounting standards in Canada

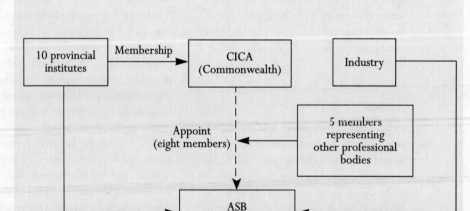

the ASB) to set accounting standards is unique to Canada.

Various provincial securities commissions require companies that trade in those provinces to comply with CICA requirements. Furthermore, like the ASC, the ASB has received support from Commonwealth and provincial government bodies and from Canadian industry. This has also helped in establishing pronouncements that have authority. The institutional arrangements for setting accounting standards (recommendations) in Canada are shown in Figure 7.7.

extreme is liberalism, whereby regulation is provided exclusively by market forces. At the other extreme is legalism, which relies upon legislation for regulation. Associationism and corporatism lie between these extremes and combine liberalism and legalism, respectively, with a small measure of community influence. (See also Nobes and Parker, 1988, pp.64–79.)

On the basis of this framework, elements of legalism and associationism can be found in the accounting regulatory arrangements in the USA, Australia, Canada and

Figure 7.8
Modes of accounting regulation

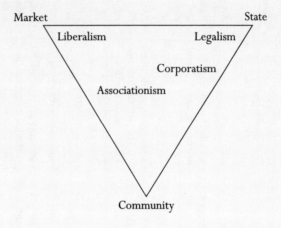

A framework

Figure 7.8 presents a framework to explain different modes of accounting regulation. This has been developed by Puxty, Willmott, Cooper and Lowe (1987). They have identified three ideal cases: regulation through the market, the state and the community. Within these three extremes, four different modes of regulation have been described: liberalism; legalism; corporatism; and associationism.

As displayed in Figure 7.8, market and state have the dominant influence. At one

New Zealand. Although the UK can be described as principally associationist, its position appears to be changing under the influence of the EU. For example, as Rutherford (1989) points out, one consequence of the EU Fourth Directive has been that accounting standards and the law are intertwined to a degree hitherto unknown in the UK. This is evident from the specific provisions contained in the UK *Companies Act* 1985.

A comparative analysis of the structures for setting accounting standards in the UK, USA, Australia, New Zealand and Canada is provided in Table 7.1.

Table 7.1
Accounting standard-setting frameworks in the USA, Canada, the UK, Australia and New Zealand

USA	Canada	UK	Australia	New Zealand
		Nature of the standard-setting body		
1 FASB	ASB	ASB	AASB	FRSB
2 7 full-time, independent, well-paid members.	13 volunteer voting members, 2 staff non-voting members.	9 members. Full-time Chairperson and Technical Director.	9 part-time members, and a full-time chairperson.	12 part-time members.
3 SEC oversees FASB's work.	Nothing comparable to SEC. Standards issued by ASB have legal backing.	Nothing comparable to the SEC. The British Companies Acts constitute the basic legal framework and incorporate EU directives on financial reporting.	ASC functions somewhat like the American SEC. It enforces accounting standards issued by ASB.	Nothing comparable to SEC. Standards approved by ASRB have legal backing.
		Process of standard setting		
4 An external task force is used for each project	External task forces are used to a limited extent.	A working party, much like an external task force, is used.	External parties are often requested by the AARF to prepare a discussion paper or theory monograph.	Functional committees appoint project teams.
5 Openness and due process are emphasised, all FASB meetings are open to the public.	Secrecy is emphasised. No ASB meetings are open to the public.	A set of procedures to be followed, which call for public hearings and consultation with financial reports users and the press, is emphasised.	Meetings of the AARF and ASB are not open to the public.	Meetings are not open to the public.

Table 7.1
Accounting standard-setting frameworks in the USA, Canada, the UK, Australia and New Zealand (continued)

	USA	Canada	UK	Australia	New Zealand
			Process of standard setting		
6	Research to a significant extent (e.g. the economic consequences of standards) is conducted internally or funded externally.	Research of other standard-setting bodies is relied upon, ASB sponsors research studies which may serve as backgrounds for subsequent standards.	Research studies are carried out by ASB.	Research studies are generally carried out by AARF.	Reliance is largely placed on research of standard-setting bodies in other countries.
7	A conceptual framework is used for guidance.	A conceptual framework is used.	IASC conceptual framework is used as the basis.	A conceptual framework is used. AARF has developed four SACs.	A conceptual framework is used.
8	Discussion memoranda and exposure drafts are circulated to the public.	Only exposure drafts are circulated to the public.	Discussion papers, statements of intent and exposure drafts are circulated to the public.	Exposure drafts are widely circulated by AASB to invite feedback. Due process is emphasised.	Exposure drafts are widely circulated to the public. Comments are solicited from interested parties.
9	Public hearings on discussion memoranda are held.	Public hearings are not held.	Public hearings are held in accordance with the consultation plan of the working party.	Forums may be held to solicit the views of users, preparers, auditors and other interested parties.	Public hearings are not held.
10	5–2 vote of FASB members to pass a standard.	Two-thirds vote of ASB members to pass a standard.	Two-thirds majority of ASB members to pass a standard.	Majority vote of AASB members to pass a standard.	Majority vote of FRSB members to pass a standard.

Adapted from Bloom and Naciri (1989)

Trends in accounting standard setting

Based on the recent developments in the setting of accounting standards in the Anglo-American accounting world, it can be expected that the current trends will continue at least in the foreseeable future. Zeff (1992), in his speech at a plenary session of the Annual Conference of the Accounting Association of Australia and New Zealand held in Palmerston North, New Zealand, identified several such trends. First, there is intensive lobbying by preparers of financial statements, such as companies and banks. This is particularly noticeable in the USA and UK. Zeff predicted that with greater enforcement of accounting standards, Australia and New Zealand could also expect to share this trend in the near future. Second, there is a common trend to expand the number and range of interested parties who are involved in the standard-setting process. As a consequence of the inclusion of non-accountants on the standard-setting bodies, he noted an increased sympathy for current value accounting. Third, there is strengthening of enforced compliance with standards, for example in the UK, New Zealand and Australia. Fourth, there is an introduction of narrative explanations in order to provide a context for the figures in the financial statements. This has happened in the USA and Canada. Proposals have been made to introduce the same in the UK and Ireland. Fifth, there has been increased emphasis on eliminating 'free options' under the IASC's international harmonisation movement. Since July 1991 the IASC has issued nine exposure drafts to implement its comparability project. There is also an increasing trend towards regional harmonisation of accounting standards through free trade agreements among neighbouring countries, for example the North American Free Trade Agreement between the USA, Canada and Mexico, and the Closer Economic Relations

(CER) Agreement between New Zealand and Australia (Perera and Tower, 1989; Rahman, Perera and Tower, 1994).

Finally, there is explicit reference to accounting standards in addition to 'true and fair view'. For example, the *Companies Act* 1989 in the UK recognised accounting standards for the first time. It is interesting that, in view of the recent amendments to the Corporations Law in Australia, the continued use of the concept 'true and fair view' has been questioned. McGregor (1992), for example, advances the view that the time is right for the entire removal of the concept of 'true and fair' from the Corporations Law. He concludes:

> while the concept of 'true and fair' may have been justified in an environment lacking an explicit framework of accounting standards and statements of accounting concepts, in today's environment it is an accounting anachronism. (p.71)

As Tweedie (1991) explains, accounting standard setting will continue to be under great pressure to respond to changing circumstances. For example, there will be pressure on the regulator arising from the increased use of creative accounting by managers; there will be pressure on the auditor to safeguard the interests of shareholders and society at large; there will be pressure coming from the trend towards global capital markets and international harmonisation of accounting standards; and there will be pressure on the standard setter and the accountant to address the measurement issues in accounting.

Chapter summary

There is a need for quality standards in accounting and financial reporting, but the establishment and enforcement of accounting standards are becoming increasingly complex. In the past accounting standards have been developed on an *ad hoc* basis, dominated first by management and then by the profession. Now standard setting has become a truly political exercise. Different countries have different approaches to, and adopted different institutional arrangements for, setting accounting standards. There are arguments for and against each of those approaches and arrangements. The best choice for a particular country at a particular point in time will depend upon its environmental circumstances prevalent at that time. As Tweedie (1985) says:

Many of our current practices arose in different economic climates and in the institutional settings of the past — they should not be allowed to imprison our thinking as we face the varied challenges of the 1990s. (p.35)

Accounting is becoming too important to be left in the hands of the accountants alone. Judging from the recent developments in the setting of accounting standards in Anglo-American countries, it is clear that the emphasis is on developing a mechanism that combines the profession and the government, assisted by other interested parties.

Essay and examination questions

7.1   The concept of 'true and fair view' as the primary quality standard in financial reporting is currently under challenge. Explain and discuss.

7.2   Explain what is meant by 'politicisation of accounting standard setting'.

7.3   Discuss the salient features of the post-1989 developments relating to accounting regulation in New Zealand, with consideration of the likely future direction.

7.4   Evaluate the impact of the ASRB on accounting and financial reporting in Australia.

7.5   Discuss the institutional arrangements for setting accounting standards in the UK, Australia and New Zealand.

7.6   Outline the arguments for and against government involvement in designing, approving and enforcing accounting standards.

7.7   Discuss the institutional arrangements for setting accounting standards in the USA, Canada and New Zealand.

7.8   Identify the major international trends in the setting of accounting standards, with particular reference to Anglo-American countries.

References and additional reading

American Institute of Certified Public Accountants (1972). *Establishing Financial Accounting Standards: Report of the Study on Establishment of Accounting Standards.* New York: AICPA.

American Institute of Certified Public Accountants (1975). *Statement on Auditing Standards, No. 5.* New York: AICPA.

Australian Accounting Research Foundation (1991). *Proposed Reform of the Institutional Arrangements for Accounting Standard Setting in Australia.* Melbourne: AARF.

Australian Accounting Standards Board (1994). *Towards International Comparability of Financial Reporting.* Policy Discussion Paper No.1, Caulfield: AARF.

Baxt, R. (1990). Competition and Securities Law on institutional arrangements and issues, in K.M. Vautier, J. Farmer, and R. Baxt (Eds), *CER and Business Competition — Australia and New Zealand in a Global Economy.* Wellington: CCH New Zealand Ltd.

Belkaoui, A. (1985). *Accounting Theory.* New York: Harcourt Brace Jovanovich.

Bloom, R. and Naciri, M.A. (1989). Accounting standard setting and culture: A comparative analysis of the United States, Canada, England, West Germany, Australia, New Zealand, Sweden, Japan, and Switzerland. *The International Journal of Accounting,* **24**, 70–97.

Burton, J.C. (1973). Some general and specific thoughts on the accounting environment. *Journal of Accountancy,* October.

Burton, J.C. (1982). The SEC and financial reporting: The sand in the oyster, in *Journal of Accountancy.* June, 34, 36, 38, 40, 42, 44, 46, 48.

Chambers, R.J., (1966). Accounting, Evaluation and Economic Behaviour, Englewood Cliffs, New Jersey: Prentice Hall.

Chambers, R.J., Ramanathan, T.S. and Rappaport, H.H. (1978). *Company Accounting Standards,* Report of the Accounting Standards Review Committee. Ultimo, New South Wales: Government Printer.

Consultative Committee of Accountancy Bodies (1988). *The Making of Accounting Standards: Report of the Review Committee.* London: ICAEW.

Corsi, R.A. and Staunton, J.J. (1994). Australian Accounting Standard Setting and the Conceptual Framework Project. *Advances in International Accounting,* **6**, 15–41.

Day, P. McPhee, I. and Keys, R. (1993). The development of SACs and accounting standards. *The Australian Accountant,* 46–48.

English, L. (1992). Regulating corporate Australia. *Australian Accountant,* February 20–25.

Financial Accounting Foundation (1977). *The Structure of Establishing Financial Accounting Standards.* Stamford, Ct: FAF.

Gorelik, G. (1994). The Setting of Accounting Standards: Canada, The United Kingdom, and the United States. *International Journal of Accounting,* **29**, 95–122.

Grady, P. (1965). *Inventory of Generally Accepted Accounting Principles for Business Enterprises.* Accounting Research Study No. 7, AICPA.

Horngren, C. (1972). Accounting principles: private or public sector? *Journal of Accountancy,* May.

Horngren, C. (1973). The marketing of accounting standards. *Journal of Accountancy,* October, 61–66.

Kam, V. (1990). *Accounting Theory.* New York: Wiley.

McGregor, W. (1989a). New accounting standard-setting Arrangements. *Australian Accountant.* September, 87–89.

McGregor, W. (1989b). The new standard bearer. *The Chartered Accountant in Australia.* September, 48–49.

McGregor, W. (1992). True and fair view: An accounting anachronism. *Australian Accountant,* February, 68–71.

Morley, B. and Martin, C.A. (1987). Institutional arrangements for setting standards: Australia, in *Standard Setting for Financial Reporting.* Proceedings of an International Conference sponsored by the American Accounting Association with Klynveld Main Goerdeler, pp. 38–42.

New Zealand Law Commission (1987). *Company Law: A Discussion Paper.* Preliminary Paper No. 5. Wellington: Government Printing Office.

New Zealand Law Commission (1989). *Company Law: Reforms and restatements.* Wellington: Government Printing Office.

New Zealand Law Commission (1990). *Company Law Reform: Transition and revision.* Wellington: Government Printing Office.

Nobes, C.W. and Parker, R.H. (1988). *Issues in Multinational Accounting.* Oxford: Philip Allan.

O'Leary, C. (1989). 'According to Deasing', *The Chartered Accountant in Australia,* **40**, 42–43.

Peirson, C.G. (1990). *A Report on Institutional Arrangements for Accounting Standard Setting in Australia.* Melbourne: AARF.

Peltzman, S. (1976). Toward a more general theory of regulation. *The Journal of Law and Economics,* August, 211–40.

Perera, M.H.B. and Tower, G. (1989). *Closer Economic Relations (CER) Agreement Between New Zealand and Australia: A Catalyst for a New International Accounting Force.* Paper presented at the Annual Conference on the Accounting Association of Australia and New Zealand, Melbourne, July, 1989.

Porter, B.A. (1990). A standard is born. *Accountants' Journal,* October 25–31.

Posner, R.A. (1974). Theories of economic regulation. *Bell Journal of Economics,* Autumn, 335–58.

Public Finance and Accountancy (1990). Dearing picks team to set standards agenda. 18 May, 3.

Puxty, A.G., Willmott, H.C., Cooper, D.J. and Lowe, T. (1987). Modes of regulation in advanced capitalism: Locating accounting in four countries. *Accounting, Organisations and Society,* **12**(3), 273–291.

Rahman, A.R. (1992). *The Australian Accounting Standards Review Board: The Establishment of its Participative Review Process.* New York: Garland Publishing Inc.

Rahman, A.R., Perera, M.H.B. and Tower, G.D. (1992). Reforming the institutional arrangements for accounting standard setting in Australia. Unpublished paper, Division of Accountancy, Massey University, Palmerston North.

Rahman, A.R., Perera, M.H.B. and Tower, G.D. (1994). Accounting harmonisation between Australia and New Zealand: Towards a regulatory union. *International Journal of Accounting,* **29**(3), 171–192.

Report of Ministerial Committee of Inquiry into the Sharemarket. Russell Committee Report (1989a). Wellington: Government Printing Office.

Report of the Ministerial Working Group on Securities Law Reform (1991). Wellington: Department of Justice.

Report of the Sharemarket Inquiry Establishment Unit. Russell Committee Report (1989b). Wellington: Tribunal Division, Department of Justice.

Rutherford, B. (1989). No escaping the long arm of the law. *Accountancy,* April, 33.

Securities Commission (1990). *Capital Structure and Financial Reporting in New Zealand.* Wellington: Government Printing Office.

Simpkins, K. (1992). Financial Reporting Bill unmasked. *Accountants' Journal,* March, 20–21.

Solomons, D. (1978). The politicisation of accounting. *Journal of Accountancy,* November, 65–72.

Sterling, R.R. (1990). Positive accounting: An assessment. *Abacus,* **26**(2), 97–135.

Stigler, G.J. (1971). The theory of economic regulation. *Bell Journal of Economics,* Spring, 3–21.

Tower, G.D. (1991). Accounting Regulation as an Instrument of Public Accountability: A Case Study of New Zealand. Unpublished Ph.D. thesis, Massey University, Palmerston North, New Zealand.

Tower, G.D., Perera, M.H.B. and Rahman, A.R. (1992). Accounting regulatory design: A New Zealand perspective. *Advances in International Accounting.* Jai Press Inc. Vol. 5, 115–142.

Tweedie, D.P. (1985). *The Accountant: A Crusader or a Prisoner of the Past? Financial Accounting in the late 1980s.* 75th Anniversary Invitation Research Lecture, New Zealand Society of Accountants. Wellington: NZSA.

Tweedie, D.P. (1991). *The Law and Financial Reporting Reform: The Challenge Facing Business and the Profession.* Paper presented at the Technical Session of the New Zealand Society of Accountants 1991 Convention, Auckland, 24–27 March.

Walker, R.G. (1987). Australia's ASRB. A Case Study of political activity and regulatory 'capture'. *Journal of Accounting and Business Research,* 269–286.

Willmott, H.C., Puxty, A.G., Robson, K., Cooper, D.J. and Lowe, E.A. (1992). Regulation of accountancy and accountants: A comparative analysis of accounting for research and development in four advanced capitalist countries. *Accounting, Auditing and Accountability Journal,* **5**(2), 32–56.

Zeff, S.A. (1973). *Forging Accounting Principles in Australia.* Melbourne: ASA.

Zeff, S.A. (1979). *Forging Accounting Principles in New Zealand.* Wellington: Victoria University Press.

Zeff, S.A. (1988). Setting accounting standards — some lessons from the US experience. *The Accountants' Magazine,* 20–22.

Zeff, S.A. (1992). Accounting Standards Programmes Worldwide: The Pressures Mount in the US, UK, and at the IASC. Paper presented at a Plenary Session of the Annual Conference of the Accounting Association of Australia and New Zealand, Palmerston North, 5–8 July.

Section 4

Issues in conventional financial accounting and reporting

Learning objectives

After studying this chapter the reader will be able to:

- distinguish between assets and non-assets for accounting purposes
- discuss whether a particular item which comes under the definition of asset should be included in financial statements
- consider the issues of measurement in regard to assets
- explain the main features of community assets
- comment on the wisdom of classifying assets into fixed and current categories
- examine some of the theoretical issues concerning the concept of depreciation in accounting.

Introduction

The next two chapters discuss the balance sheet elements of assets and liabilities. This chapter includes a discussion of various aspects of the treatment of assets in accounting. The issues dealt with are those related to definition, recognition, measurement and disclosure. Definition is important because it identifies the characteristics that an item must have if it is to be considered as an asset. In other words, it provides guidance for distinguishing assets from non-assets. Recognition is important because it provides a set of criteria to be applied in deciding whether a particular item, which comes under the definition of an asset, is appropriate for inclusion in the financial statements. Measurement is important because accounting reports are expected to provide quantitative information about, *inter alia*, the various elements of the financial position of an entity at a particular time, including its assets. The way the information is disclosed is also important because improper disclosure can lead to distortion, misinformation and confusion. This chapter also includes a brief discussion on the accounting issues associated with executory contracts. Furthermore, the application of some of the ideas concerning asset definition, recognition, measurement and disclosure in the context of public sector entities is dealt with

in a separate section. Finally, some conceptual issues regarding accounting depreciation are raised as they are considered to be pertinent in the treatment of assets in financial statements.

Definition of assets

Attempts have been made from time to time, at least since the turn of the century, to provide a satisfactory definition of assets for accounting purposes. The asset definitions put forward by various authors range from 'something represented by a debit balance' to 'future service potentials'. For example, the AIA (1953) defines assets as:

> Something represented by a debit balance that is or would be properly carried forward upon a closing of books of account according to the rules or principles of accounting (provided such debit balance is not in effect a negative balance applicable to a liability), on the basis that it represents either a property right or value acquired, or an expenditure made which has created a property or is properly applicable to the future . . .
> (para. 26)

A notable feature in this definition is that it defines assets in terms of accounting rules or principles. The AICPA (1970) also adopts a similar approach:

economic resources of an enterprise that are recognized and measured in conformity with generally accepted accounting principles. Assets also include certain deferred charges that are not resources but that are recognized and measured in conformity with generally accepted accounting principles. (para. 132)

The AICPA (1970) definition says very little about the characteristics of an asset, but it emphasises the fact that assets cannot be defined in isolation from other accounting principles.

Attempts have also been made to define assets in terms of their inherent properties. Accordingly, the notion that assets are a storage of services or future service potentials has been frequently used in defining assets. Examples are:

- 'storage of services to be received' (Sprague, 1907, p.46)
- 'any future service' (Canning, 1929, p.22)
- 'they are aggregates of service-potentials' (AAA, 1957, p.3)
- 'any economic resource that is capable of providing services to the entity' (Staubus, 1977, p.126)
- 'assets are probable future economic benefits' (FASB, 1980, para. 19, and FASB, 1985, para. 25)
- 'measurable probable future economic benefits' (Arthur Andersen and Co., 1974, p.29)
- 'assets are future economic benefits' (Miller and Islam, 1988, para. 3.03).

However, while defining assets as future service potentials, different authors have placed emphasis on additional features such as the convertibility into, or measurability in terms of, money and the right to future services and so on. For example, Canning (1929, p.22) says assets are any future service in money or convertible into money. Staubus (1977, p.126) also includes measurability in terms of money as part of his definition of assets. Some authors have

emphasised legal ownership rights to future services, while others have emphasised property use rights as a key characteristic. For example, Lall (1968) says 'assets must necessarily have the protection of law in the sense that the enterprise to which they belong should have a legal claim to their enjoyment' (p.244). Canning (1929), however, does not insist on legal ownership rights. According to him the right to future services could be either legally or equitably secured (p.22).

Many authors have included in their definitions of assets a feature which requires that rights to future economic benefits be acquired as a result of a past transaction or event. Sprouse and Moonitz (1962) emphasise that rights to future economic benefits should be acquired as a result of some current or past transaction. They have excluded from assets future economic benefits acquired as a result of past events. However, all the recent conceptual framework statements define assets as future economic benefits acquired through either transactions or events. On the other hand, Miller and Islam (1988, para. 3.03) drop the word transactions from their definition, and merely use events, in that they have treated transactions also as events.

Recent definitions of assets have identified three essential characteristics, that is, future economic benefits, control of others' access to such benefits and resulting from past transactions or events (e.g. FASB, 1985, para 26; AARF, 1992, para. 12; NZSA, 1993, para. 7.7). A distinct feature here is the emphasis placed on control rather than ownership of future economic benefits by a particular entity. The FASB (1985, para. 25) defines assets as 'probable future economic benefits obtained or controlled by a particular entity as a result of past transactions or events'; the AARF (1992, SAC 4, para. 12) as 'service potential or future economic benefits controlled by the entity as a result of past transactions or other past events'; the ASB (1992,

Chapter 3, para. 7) as 'rights or other access to future economic benefits controlled by an entity as a result of past transactions or events'; and the NZSA (1993, para. 7.7) as 'economic resources or service potential controlled by an entity as a result of past transactions or events from which future economic benefits are expected to be obtained'.

Chambers (1966) defines assets as any severable means in the possession of an entity (p.103). What he means by severable means is 'any means which, at any given time of action, may be converted to other means by exchange or the processes of production, or which may be alienated' (pp.103–104). The measurability emphasised by Canning (1929), Staubus (1977) and Arthur Andersen and Co. (1974) requires assets to be separately identifiable. Therefore, it is similar to the notion of severability in Chambers's definition of assets. Chambers (1966) also explains the notion of possession in terms of control, when he says: 'It is convenient to describe all such means under the control of any entity as its assets' (p.103).

However, it was Ijiri who pointed out for the first time that control was an essential characteristic of an asset. He said 'accounting is not concerned with economic resources in general, but only those which are under the control of a given entity' (Ijiri, 1967, p.69). In the context of identifying an asset, control entails the ability of a particular entity to procure the benefits from a resource.

The ASB (1992) explains the concept of control as follows:

The definition of an asset requires that the access to the future economic benefits is controlled by the entity, 'control' in this context means the ability to obtain the economic benefits and to restrict the access of others, for example to those who pay. Where access to economic benefits is equally open to all parties – as, for example, in the case of public infra-structure which all may enjoy equally – none of these parties has an asset by virtue of such access. (Chapter 3, para. 14)

The AARF (1992) also takes a similar view about the concept of control in the context of defining an asset. It says:

Control relates to the capacity of the entity to benefit from the asset in the pursuit of its objectives and to deny or regulate the access of others to that benefit. The entity controlling an asset is the one that can, depending on the nature of the asset, exchange it, use it to settle liabilities, hold it, or perhaps distribute it to owners. (SAC 4, para. 22)

The question of whether legal ownership rights to the title of the asset are essential for control purposes is relevant here. Kam (1990, p.105) points out an entity's right to use or control an asset can never be absolute. This is so even where there is legal ownership. The right to use and control an asset by a particular entity is subject to the general rights of the state and the particular statutory limitations (Paton, 1962, p.56). This is especially true of the resources in the context of public sector entities, an issue discussed separately later in the chapter. Furthermore, legal definitions and concepts may not be helpful in formulating accounting definitions of assets (FASB, 1976, para. 122) because for accounting purposes the commercial substance of the transaction should take precedence over its legal form (ICAEW, 1976, para. 4). As Canning (1929) argued, 'the fundamental test for determining whether a thing is or is not an asset is economic rather than legal' (p.19). In any case, in law 'there is no clear asset concept, and the terms property, property rights, ownership, title, and possession have similar but distinctly different meanings' (Wolk, Francis and Tearney, 1989, p.302). Therefore, while legal ownership may be used as one of the criteria for determining the existence of control, it is not essential. As Ijiri (1980) argues, 'control may be based on legal ownership, economic control, or organizational responsibility' (p.76).

Finally, the inclusion in the definition of assets of a control test rather than a legal enforceability test means that the definition is less rigid and more reliable in assessing the capacity of an entity to secure the service potential or future economic benefits (AARF, 1992, para. 26).

The FRSB (1993b) does not explain the meaning of the three characteristics of an asset, whereas AARF (1992) provides definitions for them as follows:

> 'Service potential' or 'future economic benefits' is the essence of assets. This characteristic, which can be described as the scarce capacity to provide services or benefits to the entities that use them, is common to all assets irrespective of their physical or other form . . . (SAC 4, para. 16)
>
> 'Control of an asset' means the capacity of the entity to benefit from the asset in the pursuit of the entity's objectives and to deny or regulate the access of others to that benefit. (SAC 4, para. 8)
>
> Most assets are obtained by an entity from cash, credit or barter transactions. The transactions may be exchange transactions whereby assets are acquired in exchange for existing assets of the entity, or by undertaking an obligation to transfer assets in the future. Alternatively, the transactions may be non-reciprocal transfers, for example, donations, grants, appropriations and contributions by owners or members. Assets may also result from events such as accretion and discovery. (SAC 4, para. 27)

The AARF (1992) also identifies four other characteristics which are indicative but not essential in defining an asset, that is, acquisition at a cost, tangibility, exchangeability and legal enforceability (SAC 4, paras 30–35).

Recognition of assets

As mentioned at the beginning of this chapter, the resolution of the issue of recognition of assets is important because it provides a set of criteria to be applied in deciding whether a particular item which comes under the definition of assets is appropriate for inclusion in the financial statements. In other words, an item which satisfies the definitional requirements may not satisfy the recognition criteria, for example human resources. Also, reference to an item in notes to the financial statements does not constitute recognition (AARF, 1992, para. 9; ASB, 1992, Chapter 4, para. 1). Recognition rules have been developed because of the desire of accountants for evidence in an environment of uncertainty.

The AICPA (1970, para. 145) describes recognition also in terms of control and emphasises that recognition occurs when the transaction transferring control takes place. Other authors have described recognition in terms of a variety of other features and suggested different sets of criteria to be adopted in recognising assets. For example, Kam (1990, pp.109–111) mentions four criteria: (a) reliance on the law; (b) use of the conservatism principle; (c) determination of the economic substance of the transaction or event; and (d) ability to measure the value of the asset. Sterling (1985, pp.56–64) suggests six tests: (a) there must be detection of the existence of a thing that may be a candidate for recognition; (b) the thing must be an economic resource, which means that it must be scarce and desirable commanding a price; (c) the entity must control the resource (the entity association test); (d) the thing must have a non-zero magnitude; (e) the previous tests must all be satisfied at balance sheet date (the 'temporal association' test); and (f) there must be adequate empirical evidence to permit independent, qualified observers to reach a consensus that all of the previous tests are satisfied (the 'verifiability' test). The AARF

(1992, para. 36) provides that an asset shall be recognised in the financial statements when, and only when: (a) it is *probable* that the service potential or future economic benefits embodied in the asset will eventuate; and (b) it possesses a cost or other value that can be measured *reliably*. The NZSA (1993) has exactly the same requirement. The AARF goes on to explain that where the chance of the service potential or future economic benefit arising is more likely than less likely, then its occurrence is probable (para. 38).

The FASB (1984, para. 63) provides four criteria for recognising any financial statement element: (a) Definition — the item meets the definition of an element of financial statements; (b) Measurability — it has a relevant attribute measurable with sufficient reliability; (c) Relevance — the information about it is capable of making a difference in user decisions; and (d) Reliability — the information is representationally faithful, verifiable and neutral.

It is clear that there is much more to the recording of assets in financial statements than simply defining what they are. A common feature in all the above sets of criteria is the requirement that an item possess a relevant attribute that can be measured with an acceptable degree of accuracy before it is recognised as an asset in the financial statements. In other words, when it is not possible to measure the relevant attribute of an asset with sufficient reliability, the asset does not qualify for recognition, for example a mineral deposit of unknown quantity. Also under the current accounting standards, where an acceptable basis for measuring the consumption or loss of benefit cannot be determined, the item is not recognised as an asset.

Measurement of assets

Measurability of assets is important because accounting reports are expected, *inter alia*, to provide quantitative information about the financial position of an entity at a particular time, and the amount of assets is a determining factor here. In the recent conceptual framework statements of the UK, USA, Australia and New Zealand, asset recognition is linked to measurability in that measurability is regarded as a precondition for the recognition of assets. Also, it was mentioned earlier that some authors have included measurability in their definitions of assets (for instance Canning, 1929; Arthur Andersen and Co., 1974; Staubus, 1977). It can be argued, therefore, that measurability is an essential characteristic of assets. Consequently, it can also be argued that to be measurable, assets should be capable of being separately identified, for the simple reason that measurement cannot be performed if the object or event to be measured is not separately identifiable. This is similar to the severability test suggested by Chambers (1966, pp. 103–104).

However, on the issue of separability the ASB (1992) states that 'separability is not included in the recognition criteria and a lack of separability does not disqualify an item from being recognised' (Chapter 4, para. 4).

Measurement is 'the assignment of numerals to objects or events according to rules' (Stevens, 1946, p.677). The measurement process consists of three components, that is: (a) an object or an event, (b) a property (quality, attribute or a characteristic) to quantify and (c) a scale or a set of units which can be used to quantify the property. Any object or event has several properties that could be measured. The selection of the property to be measured depends on the purpose for which the measurement is carried out. Similarly, the scale of measurement depends on the property to be measured. For example, if the object is a table, its height and weight are two different properties that can be measured and, if the height is the chosen property to be measured, then the scale can be either feet or metres.

In accounting, as Henderson and Peirson (1988, p.98) point out, the appropriate attribute to be measured will depend upon the model of accounting being applied. The AARF (1992) also recognises this (para. 43). Different accounting models are based on different behavioural assumptions. For example, the CCA model has the assumption that business entities strive to continue with the present mode of operation as its basis, while the CoCoA model assumes adaptive behaviour of business entities, that is they continuously strive to adapt to the changing business environment in order to get the best advantage, and in doing so they may not want to continue with the present mode of operation. Under the former model, replacement of existing assets or maintenance of the physical capacity becomes the crucial issue; therefore, the appropriate property to be measured is the current cost or the replacement cost of assets. On the other hand, the latter model has the capacity to adapt as the crucial issue; therefore, the appropriate property to be measured is the current cash equivalent of the assets.

It is clear that there is disagreement among accounting researchers about the type of property that should be measured in reporting various accounting elements, including assets. However, aggregation is an essential function of accounting information. Therefore, the properties and scales selected must be capable of aggregation. For example, in the case of assets, aggregation is not meaningful if either different properties are measured (such as acquisition cost and the market selling price) or different scales are used (such as dollars of 1975 and dollars of 1995) in respect of different assets. This can be more clearly explained by referring to the earlier example: if the measurement of the height of the table is added to that of its weight, then the resulting total is meaningless; similarly, if the weight of one table is measured in terms of pounds and that of another is measured in terms of kilograms,

then those two amounts cannot be added together to get a meaningful total representing the total weight of the two tables, because pounds and kilograms are two different scales. However, the conceptual frameworks, in general, have avoided the measurement issues in accounting. It is interesting to note that there seems to be a renewed interest in this area at the present time, particularly in the USA and the UK.

The ASB has taken the initiative in addressing the issue of measurement in financial reports (Perera and Rahman, 1994). Through its discussion draft on Measurement in Financial Statements (ASB, 1993a) and the discussion paper on the Role of Valuation in Financial Reporting (ASB, 1993b), the ASB has clearly expressed its commitment to move towards using current values on a more comprehensive basis (Lennard, 1993). By taking an evolutionary approach, the ASB attempts initially to address some of the important anomalies that exist within the current accounting practice (which is based on historical cost). The ASB (1993a) supports the concept of 'value to the business' in valuing assets. The adoption of this concept results in most assets being stated at replacement cost. The arguments are similar to those put forward by the Sandilands Committee which recommended CCA in 1974. Recently, the FASB has shown some renewed interest in this area by issuing two discussion memorandums on 'Present Value-Based Measurements in Accounting' and 'New Basis of Accounting' (see Weygandt, 1994b, pp 114–122).

Disclosure of assets

As mentioned earlier, the way the information about the assets of an entity is disclosed is important because improper disclosure can lead to misinformation. This section addresses some conceptual issues concerning asset classification; in financial statements the classification of assets is directly related to both asset measurement and disclosure. To simplify the discussion, the terms 'asset valuation' and 'asset measurement' are used synonymously, although theoretically they can have quite different meanings.

Asset classification

Asset valuation under conventional accounting is based on an initial consideration of asset classification (Walker, 1974). Different categories of assets should be valued differently. For financial reporting purposes, assets are classified, accordingly, into 'fixed' and 'current' assets and the valuation method for each category is selected from a large number of available, conventionally acceptable alternatives. As any firm may make its own choice of the alternative rules, the amount of reported income is determined in part by the method of asset classification used. For example, for an item of machinery classified as a fixed asset, the valuation method adopted would be cost less depreciation, whereas for an item of machinery classified as a current asset, the valuation method would be lower of cost and market. The amount used to represent a particular item therefore depends on the valuation method adopted. But the valuation method is selected according to the manner in which an item has been classified.

It is intended here to discuss the validity of the distinction between fixed and current assets, and the usefulness of such a distinction for financial reporting purposes.

An import from economics via the courts

The distinction between 'fixed' and 'circulating' assets was imported into accounting practice from economics via the courts, late in the nineteenth or early in the twentieth century. There is no mention of such a distinction in the English *Companies Acts* 1867 and 1877. These terms appear to have first found their way into the law reports in the case of *Lee vs Neuchatel Asphalte Co* (41 CDI,

1889) from the contemporary economic literature (see Palmer, 1895, p.436). Later some court cases also touched upon the methods of valuing 'fixed' and 'circulating' assets. For example, in the case of *Verner vs General and Commercial Investment Trusts* (Chapter 2, p.239, 1894), it was held in the appeal court that, 'Fixed capital may be sunk and lost, and yet . . . the excess of current receipts over current payments may be divided, but . . . floating or circulating capital must be kept up'. This has been interpreted as an approval by the courts of valuing fixed assets at historical costs and floating assets at some current amount (see Warner, 1899, p.251).

What economists and the courts described as 'capital', accountants described in their own terms as 'assets'. As Walker (1974) says:

> the suggestion that assets should be classified may have been prompted by an attempt to translate economists' notions of 'fixed' and 'floating' capital into an accounting context . . . The language of the courts appears to have influenced accounting terminology. (pp.288–289)

It is also important to note that since the early twentieth century, 'managers' intentions' have been frequently adopted as the criterion for asset classification in accounting (Cropper, 1911, pp.121, 128–129). One of the main advantages of classifying assets into 'fixed' and 'current' categories is said to be that it provides an indication of an entity's liquidity. For example, the Cohen Committee Report says: 'The section shall define "fixed assets" as assets not held for sale or for conversion into cash, and "current assets" as cash and assets held for conversion into cash' (HMSO, 1945, p.58). While placing emphasis on intention as the basis of classification, by relating that to convertibility into cash, the committee also attempts to stress the importance of providing an indication of liquidity of an entity in its balance sheet.

However, the propriety of using managers' intentions as the criterion of representing liquidity is questionable because assets which managers intend to realise may not be all 'readily realisable'. For example, assets which are regarded as 'fixed', such as motor vehicles, may be more easily converted into cash than some of the so-called 'current' assets, such as commodity stock or debtors. Further, the distinction between 'fixed' and 'current' assets is merely one of degree, often arbitrary and often difficult to draw. If managers' intentions are to be taken as the criterion, an asset which was bought for use in business, but which is now made available for sale, would be a fixed as well as a current asset. Similarly, goods which were bought for the purpose of resale, but subsequently retained for some other purpose, for example speculatively, for taking advantage from an expected price rise, would be fixed as well as current assets.

It would not be incorrect to say that, although the terms were imported from economics, accounting definitions have not kept pace with the developing concepts of economics. By the early twentieth century economists were already expressing doubts as to the validity of the distinction. For example, Palgrave (1925) said: 'It is interesting to trace how little of what is ordinarily termed "fixed capital" is really permanent' (p.223).

Even in accounting there has been some concern about the arbitrariness of the distinction between 'fixed' and 'current' assets. For example, Norris (1949) says that inventories are more nearly akin to 'fixed' assets than to such 'current' assets as cash and book debts (p.616). Further, as Schedule 8 (para. 4(2)) of the UK Companies Act 1948 as amended by the Companies Act 1967 states, there may be assets which are neither fixed nor current. Furthermore, the notion of the link between asset classification and asset valuation has started to lose ground and company legislation has recognised the importance of current values, at least in respect of some so-called fixed assets. For example, there is the requirement to state in the directors' report which accompanies the annual accounts any significant change in fixed assets and, if the market value of land differs substantially from the figure in the balance sheet, to indicate the difference with such degree or precision as is possible (see section 16 of the Companies Act 1967).

The ability to meet financial obligations when they fall due in the ordinary course of business is important to any business entity, be it in the private sector or in the public sector, if it is expected to be financially viable. This ability is reflected in the liquidity position of an entity. Liquidity can be described as the ready convertibility of an asset into other assets by exchange. Since money is the most readily convertible asset, the liquidity of other assets is expressed by their convertibility to money. But the classification of assets into 'fixed' and 'current' categories would not provide the basis for assessing a firm's liquidity, unless all the assets were measured by their current money equivalents (Wells, 1973, p.17). Initial costs, replacement price or any other fabricated amounts are not capable of reflecting liquidity, for they are not indicative of the amount of money that may be obtained in exchange for the assets. Therefore, one could argue that the liquidity position of an entity would be reflected better if the 'fixed–current' classification were abandoned and assets were arranged in accordance with the ease with which they could be converted to money.

Executory contracts

The notion that assets are a result of past transactions and events can be interpreted differently (Kam, 1990, pp. 106–107). For example, it can be argued that the signing of an executory contract amounts to an event and, therefore, the rights arising from such contracts qualify as assets. It can also be argued that under a lease contract, control over a resource owned by a lessor is transferred to a lessee. Executory contracts may exist in a variety of different forms, such as leases, purchase orders for inventory or capital items, forward exchange contracts, hedge contracts, commodity futures contracts, certain types of employment contracts and so on (Miller and Islam, 1988, para. 5.04).

In general a contract is an enforceable, but as yet unperformed, promise given to or by an external party to transfer assets and/or liabilities in the future (ASB, 1992, Chapter 4, para. 13).

However, the traditional view of accounting does not support the above arguments, although the future benefits arising from certain types of lease agreements (that is finance leases) are recognised as assets under existing standards. The traditional view is that no recognition of benefits arising from executory contracts is necessary because the binding exchange has yet to occur. For example, Canning (1929) explicitly excludes such items from his definition of assets:

> An asset is any future service in money or any future service convertible into money (except those services arising from contracts the two sides of which are proportionately unperformed) the beneficial interest in which is legally or equitably secured to some person or set of persons. (p.22)

The AICPA (1970) also takes the same view:

> An exchange of promises between the contracting parties is an exchange of something of value, but the usual view in accounting is that the promises are offsetting and nothing need be recorded until one or both parties at least perform(s) under the contract. (para. 181)

Ijiri (1980) approaches the issue differently from the traditional view and points

out that 'wholly executory contracts' seem to meet the first test for recognition as assets in financial statements (p.8). However, he qualifies the above statement by saying that after meeting the definition of an asset (the first test), a contractual right should then meet certain 'recognition criteria' before it is recorded, such as usefulness and firmness of the contract (pp.65–67). He also explains what is meant by firmness:

> A commitment is said to be 'firm' if it is unlikely that its performance can be avoided without a severe penalty. A penalty is considered to be 'severe' if in the normal course of business an enterprise would perform what is required under the commitment rather than incur the penalty. (p.63)

Miller and Islam (1988) also point out that the exchange of promises included in an executory contract is a past event; most contracts give rise to probable future economic benefits and control of a contractual right exists when the contract becomes a firm commitment. Contrary to existing accounting standards, they conclude that, in the case of leases, the rights under both finance leases and non-cancellable operating leases meet the asset definition and recognition criteria (para. 5.15).

The ASB (1992) has included contracts as one of the past events that may result in an asset (or a liability) when it says 'there are three classes of past events that may involve a measurable change in assets or liabilities and hence that may trigger recognition–transactions, contracts for future performance ("contracts"), and other events' (Chapter 4, para. 11). The AARF (1992) takes the view that the same criteria should be applied in recognising assets arising from all events, including executory contracts. In guidances on the application of SAC 4 (item 5) it says that:

assets that arise from agreements equally proportionately unperformed would need to be recognised where: (a) it is probable that, in respect of the assets, the service potential or future economic benefits arising from the agreement will eventuate; and (b) the amounts of those assets can be measured reliably.

Unlike in the past, executory contracts are being extensively used as an instrument of transferring resources between modern business entities. Therefore, it is important that accounting is capable of addressing the issues related to this relatively new development in order to be able to perform its function as a source of information. The criteria to be adopted in determining the accounting treatment of executory contracts are still in the process of being evolved. It is clear that clarification of the issues related to asset definition and recognition is a significant factor contributing to this evolutionary process.

Assets in the public sector

The issues about the accounting treatment of assets have been discussed in the literature almost exclusively in the context of private sector profit oriented entities with no explicit consideration for public sector entities or not-for-profit entities in the private sector. However, the ASB and the PSASB of the AARF initiated a project for developing a conceptual framework for financial reporting applicable to both the private and public sectors. The New Zealand Financial Reporting Framework seems to have taken a similar approach.

Public sector entities are also responsible for resources which provide future economic benefits. Skinner (1987) attempts to apply the notion of future economic benefit to non-business entities. He says: 'In a non-business organization, that future economic benefit often consists of the capacity to render service in furtherance of the entity's

programmes without requiring a further expenditure of economic resources' (p.633). As mentioned earlier, control signifies the ability of a particular entity to procure the benefits from a resource, and that right to use and control an asset can never be absolute, as it is subject to various statutory and other limitations. This is particularly true in the context of public sector entities where there are assets which have peculiar characteristics, labelled 'community assets'. As Pallot (1987) describes them:

> These are fixed assets of long life acquired for the benefit of the community at large and controlled by public sector entities for use in carrying out their functions. They are frequently large and not capable of subdivision for ready disposal, have no readily determinable economic life . . . (p.41)

The examples of community assets include roads, railway tracks, bridges, dams, parks, power lines, reservoirs, drainage networks, embankments, museums, memorials, signalling networks and so on. These resources provide benefits, but the entities responsible for them may have limited control over them in respect of their utilisation, hire or sale to other entities, their use in settling liabilities and of being able to deny access to them by others. For example, sale of these resources may not be at the discretion of the entity responsible for them but require legislative approval (Pallot, 1987, p.41; Sutcliffe, 1985, p.30). The *Statement of Public Sector Accounting Concepts* (NZSA, 1987) provides a very similar description of these resources:

> The fixed assets held by a public sector entity are many and varied. Some are held for service oriented purposes, some for commercially oriented purposes and some for both. (para. 4.14)

Some of the assets are infrastructural assets which have no determinable useful life and provide a social service rather than a commercial service. These assets are referred to as community assets. They are frequently large, not capable of subdivision for ready disposal, usually have no readily determinable market value and there may be constraints on the capacity of the reporting entity to dispose of such assets. (para. 4.15)

The NZSA (1987) goes on to explain how to determine whether a particular asset is a community asset, and says regard should be had to the following factors:
- the period of use of the asset
- the degree to which there is a market in which the asset could be sold
- whether or not it is within the capacity of the reporting entity to dispose of the asset
- the purpose for which the asset is used (para. 4.16).

The peculiar nature of community assets raises the question of how to decide if there is sufficient control for a resource to be considered as an asset. It is quite clear that community assets do provide future benefits to the entities responsible for them. Furthermore, if they are destroyed reconstruction would probably require a substantial amount of resources. Therefore, it can be argued that in the context of a public sector entity, community assets are a significant part of its resource base and that information about such assets is often relevant to any interested party in making decisions with regard to its performance, results and current position. However, one of the distinct features of community assets is the limitation on control. As a result, they do not seem to satisfy the criteria for asset definition and recognition, which means they cannot be included in the financial statements. Therefore, it has been pointed out that these assets should be treated differently from other assets. For example, the NZSA (1987) says 'they should be identified and reported in a statement of resources in non-financial terms, or in physical terms where feasible some estimate of the value to the community shown' (para. 4.19).

Attmore, Miller and Fountain (1989) point out that research on the user's needs for information about capital assets has indicated strong interest in information about:
- budget versus actual expenditures including estimated total costs of capital projects
- the replacement cycle and aging schedule of capital assets
- capital project plans
- expenditures for maintenance
- deferred maintenance
- assessment of condition
- anticipated infrastructure needs (p.14).

It has been pointed out that it is inappropriate to charge depreciation on community assets (NZSA, 1987, para. 4.17). In the USA depreciation has been called the most controversial single issue in accounting for non-business organisations (Anthony, 1978, p.135). In the UK it has been argued that in the case of infrastructure assets like dams, railway tunnels, power lines, highways, reservoirs, embankments, railway tracks, distribution pipelines, signalling networks and so on, renewals accounting may be more appropriate than depreciation accounting methods (Currie, 1987, p.8). This argument is based on the grounds that:

> some of these assets have very little alternative use and their lives are very long and almost impossible to quantify. In others, elements are renewed, but the whole block of assets is unlikely to be replaced at any one foreseeable time. (Currie, 1987, p.8)

The recent conceptual frameworks make no distinction in defining assets in the public sector, as they are expected to be commonly applicable to entities in both private and public sectors (e.g. AARF, 1992; NZSA, 1993).

Accounting depreciation

It appears that depreciation is a major issue in the context of public sector assets (e.g. Fremgen, 1986). However, a closer examination reveals that it has been a highly controversial accounting issue in general. This section discusses some of these controversies. The accounting practice of providing for depreciation probably has a longer history than the double entry principle itself (Hatfield, 1936). It appears however, that there is some confusion of thought about what the accountant is *actually* doing and what it is generally *assumed* that he or she is doing in this regard. As a result, the terms 'depreciation' and 'depreciation provision' have become misleading to readers of financial statements as well as to accountants.

Depreciation and appreciation

It would not be inappropriate to say that most problems of depreciation under conventional accounting are caused by the attempt to identify assets in their physical form. As a result, there is a tendency to presume that durable assets generally depreciate. Since accounting is primarily concerned with the monetary properties of assets rather than their physical form, this presumption may not be true in certain cases. The monetary equivalents of assets may have in fact increased during a period of time. In such a case, there is an appreciation instead of depreciation from an accounting point of view.

Some conventional ideas about depreciation

In line with the presumption that all durable assets depreciate, funds invested in such assets are regarded in conventional accounting as prepayments for the services they are expected to provide over a series of future accounting periods. Accordingly, depreciation is often approached as a problem of allocation or distribution of original cost or some other calculated figure to different accounting periods to be matched against revenues. For example, the ICAEW (1945) states:

> Depreciation represents that part of the cost of a fixed asset to its owner which is not recoverable when the asset is finally put out of use by him. Provision against this loss of capital is an integral cost of conducting the business during the effective commercial life of the asset and is not dependent upon the amount of profit earned . . .

The basic notion underlying this attitude is very similar to that of Lamden, Gerboth and McRae (1975, p.xi), namely, that an amount representing the original outlay less the recovery on retirement is to be apportioned over the useful life of the asset. The attitude of the accounting profession in general has not changed much since then. For example, the NZSA (1985) holds the same view in its standard on accounting for depreciation (paras 3.1 and 3.2). Closely related to the above is the notion that the cost of an asset should be recovered from the selling price of its products. The cost of an asset, however, is incurred usually in one accounting period, whereas the services rendered extend over a number of subsequent periods. Therefore, if the cost of such services is calculated on the basis of the original cost of the asset, when there is a continuous change in price past costs are then mistakenly identified with actual cost of production. This is exactly what happens under the accrual principle of HCA — 'matching' yesterday's costs with today's revenue.

The main reason for the confusion about this long-standing accounting practice appears to be the lack of agreement among accountants on what the word 'depreciation' really means in accounting (e.g. Goldberg, 1962, p.236). The basic meaning of the word 'depreciation' is a decline in price of any kind of asset. It is derived from

Latin *de* meaning from, and *pretium* meaning price. Even in conventional accounting, in respect of depreciable assets, depreciation means reducing the purchasing price to the ultimate selling price at the point of disposal. In doing so, however, reference is made to the market only at the beginning and at the end of the lifetime of an asset. At the end of every accounting period during the lifetime of an asset, the amount to be charged as depreciation is determined by some arbitrary method and the difference between that amount and the opening balance of the asset is used to represent the asset at the end of the period. Therefore, there seems to be a logical inconsistency in the application of the concept.

Accounting depreciation has been interpreted in a variety of different ways. First, it has been described to mean the physical deterioration of an asset (Bonbright, 1937, p.183). But the fact that the effect of most of the causes leading to physical retirement of an asset may be counteracted or prevented by adequate maintenance has led some to look at depreciation in the sense of deferred maintenance. For example, the United States Supreme Court (*Lindheimer vs Illinois Bell Telephone Co.*, 292, US 151, 1934) once defined depreciation as the loss not restored by current maintenance, which is due to all factors causing the ultimate retirement of the property. In any case, if the depreciation is to be taken as a physical event or a series of physical events, it may not be suitable for accounting purposes; accountants are concerned with its financial counterpart which may have no direct relation to physical factors. As Wells (1968) says: 'Physical attributes are an engineering not an accounting problem, and depreciation has a special meaning in engineering which is difficult to reconcile with the conventional concept used in accounting' (p.374).

The situation is further complicated by the fact that physical assets are composed of parts which can be replaced when worn out

or needing repairs, sometimes to such an extent that over a period of time practically no part of the original asset is functioning any more. In such a case, it is hardly possible to determine what physical deterioration really means. It is also practically impossible to get a measure of periodical deterioration of most assets.

Second, depreciation is seen as the loss in usefulness due to causes external to the asset in its physical aspect, such as technical obsolescence through time and inadequacy or lack of the capacity to supply what is required or demanded. Again, there are no durable assets for which a measure of technical obsolescence or inadequacy is possible. They are a function of such factors as the general advancement of the industrial technology and economic conditions, which cannot be measured in short intervals.

The loss in usefulness of an asset due to technical obsolescence and inadequacy is certainly a cause for change in the economic significance of the asset, which is generally reflected in the monetary equivalent of that asset. But neither technical obsolescence nor inadequacy is capable of providing a measure of such change for accounting purposes. For example, it is quite possible that a durable asset which has suffered technical obsolescence during a period may still have an increased or decreased monetary equivalent at the end of the period, depending upon the changes in market conditions.

Third, depreciation has also been interpreted as the diminution in value. Matheson (1884, p.1) said that depreciation was originally applied as a convenient form of expression for the phrase 'diminution of value by reason of wear and tear'. Even today it is not uncommon to find attempts to identify depreciation as that part of diminution in value suffered by assets due to their being used in the production of goods. But physical deterioration of assets may be caused not only by using them in production but also by other factors such as decay, rust, corrosion and so on. In that case, according to the above description, a question will arise as to whether it should be separately identified from the wear and tear caused by production operations.

Further, in economics there are a number of different concepts of value, namely cost value or cost of production or acquisition; exchange value or rate of exchange or purchasing power or exchange equivalent; use value or usefulness or utility; and esteem value or relative (subjective) importance. Therefore, one is faced with considerable difficulty in understanding a definition such as the above, unless it is specified which concept of value is relevant to the measurement of depreciation.

Fourth, depreciation has further been described as a provision for replacement of durable assets when they are worn out. The notion of physical replacement of assets has been greatly supported in discussions of economic principles. For example, Taussig (1925) says:

> The manufacturer knows that his machinery wears out, and that if his capital is to remain unimpaired, he must set aside something annually to replace it . . . If he is to secure a permanent profit, he must reckon their amounts as part of his expense. (p. 77)

It should be noted first that machinery and capital are not the same thing. However, asset replacement is a rather vague proposition. There are a number of alternative replacement possibilities. Edwards (1961, p. 58), for example, distinguishes four such possibilities, namely, the replacement or maintenance of subjective value; the replacement of original cost; the physical replacement of the machine when its economic life has been exhausted — ultimate replacement; and the replacement or maintenance of some form of market value. Therefore, to describe depreciation simply as a provision for replacement is not

sufficient to provide a clear idea of what it really means.

In any case, since the demand for goods and services and, of course, industrial technology does not remain unchanged over time, the exact replacement of physical assets or their productive capacities is not likely. In practice, every investment decision is always considered under the circumstances at the particular time it is to be made. Moreover, the decision to replace any asset in any form at some time in the distant future has no relationship at all to the treatment of depreciation in periodic accounting calculations, and setting aside an amount equal to the original cost of an asset is unlikely to have any connection with the replacement price, however defined, particularly in periods of price fluctuations.

It is observable that there is considerable confusion about the nature and significance of the concept of depreciation in current accounting thought. The concept of depreciation has been described variously as a loss suffered by physical deterioration, a loss in usefulness due to causes external to the asset in its physical aspect, a diminution in value, a process of cost allocation, a provision for replacement of assets and so on. Surely it cannot be all these things. For that matter it was shown that none of the above mentioned traditional concepts is able to provide a satisfactory interpretation of what the accountant is trying to do in recording depreciation.

Depreciation as a financial concept

The methods of calculation based on historical cost are not likely to be amenable to any logical explanation of accounting for durable assets. Probably the trouble lies, as Baxter (1970, p. 120) says, 'partly in the bastard mixture of a past cost with estimates of future life and scrap proceeds'. The propriety of conventional methods depends on certain assumptions. First, that the original money cost is the appropriate depreciable base, and that the maintenance of that amount will ensure that capital is maintained intact; second, that the expectations of the entrepreneur as to the life span of the asset, the scrap value of the asset at the end of its effective life, etc. are fully realised; third, that no change in the prices occurs between the acquisition and the retirement of the asset and, therefore, the identical amounts of money received or paid in different times have the same significance. But there is no evidence to support any of these assumptions.

In accounting depreciation is essentially a financial notion. It is related to the financial significance of an asset. The financial significance of any asset at a particular point in time is represented by the money equivalent or the selling price of that asset at that time. For accounting purposes, therefore, depreciation should be defined strictly as a decrease in price. The Discussion Paper, entitled *Making Corporate Reports Valuable*, published by the ICAS (1988) also supports this view.

It cannot be generalised that the money equivalent of an asset always decreases. Prices may decrease or increase depending upon the forces interacting in the market. In the case of any increase, there will be an appreciation instead of depreciation. Therefore, one could argue that the presumption in conventional accounting that all durable assets depreciate is not acceptable.

Chapter summary

The importance of assets to financial reporting cannot be overemphasised, because assets are an integral part of both the results of operations of an entity during a given period of time, and the position of an entity at a particular time. Some conceptual issues concerning various aspects of asset accounting have been discussed in this chapter. It is clear that there are many problems yet to be resolved. Some of the problems are the result of the changing business environment, for example many of those related to executory contracts, while others are deeply rooted in conventional wisdom, for example many of those related to asset classification and depreciation. Regardless of the source of the problems, clarification of ideas at the conceptual level is essential in any sensible attempt at resolving them. However, it should also be mentioned that this approach is likely to lead to conclusions which may not be exactly in line with the conventional wisdom in accounting. For examples, refer to the conclusions reached in the sections dealing with executory contracts, asset classification and depreciation. This is the challenge accounting has to face as a profession at the present time.

Essay and examination questions

8.1   What are the essential characteristics of an asset for accounting purposes?

8.2   'Control' is more important than 'legal ownership'. Explain and discuss in the context of asset recognition in accounting.

8.3   Describe the nature and significance of measurement in accounting.

8.4   Examine the meaning of 'severability' as described by Chambers in his definition of assets.

8.5   Classification of assets into 'fixed' and 'current' categories is not necessary and it may well be misleading. Do you agree? Why?

8.6   No recognition of benefits arising from executory contracts is necessary because the binding exchange has yet to occur. Discuss.

8.7   Critically examine the recognition criteria stated in the conceptual frameworks of Australia and New Zealand.

8.8   What are the traditional concepts of depreciation? Why are they unable to provide a satisfactory interpretation of depreciation?

8.9   Depreciation in accounting is strictly a financial concept. Explain and discuss.

8.10 Accounting reports without provision for depreciation would violate both accounting principles and common sense. Discuss.

References and additional reading

Accounting Standards Board (1992). *Discussion Draft on Statement of Principles.* London: ASB.

Accounting Standards Board (1993a). *Measurement in Financial Statements, Statement of Principles* — Chapter 5, London: ASB.

Accounting Standards Board (1993b). *The Role of Valuation in Financial Reporting,* Discussion Document, London: ASB.

American Accounting Association (1957). *Accounting and Reporting Standards for Corporate Financial Statements.*

American Institute of Accountants (1953). Committee on Terminology, *Accounting Terminology.* Bulletin No. 1: Review of Resumé, AIA.

American Institute of Certified Public Accountants (1970). *Basic Concepts and Accounting Principles.* APB Statement No. 4. October, AICPA.

Anthony, R.N. (1978). *Financial Accounting in Non-business Organizations.* Stamford, Connecticut: FASB.

Arthur Andersen and Co. (1974). *Accounting Standards for Business Enterprises throughout the World.* Arthur Andersen & Co.

Attmore, R.H., Miller, J.R. and Fountain, J.R. (1989). Government capital assets: The challenge to report decision-useful information. *Government Finance Review,* August, 13–17.

Australian Accounting Research Foundation (1992). *Statement of Accounting Concepts No. 4: Definition and Recognition of the Elements of Financial Statements.* Melbourne: AARF.

Baxter, W.T. (1970). Depreciating assets: The forward looking approach to value. *Abacus,* 19 December.

Bonbright, J.C. (1937). *The Valuation of Property.* New York: McGraw-Hill.

Canning, J. (1929). *The Economics of Accountancy.* New York: Ronald.

Chambers, R.J. (1965). Edwards and Bell on business income. *The Accounting Review.* Reprinted in R.J. Chambers, *Accounting, Finance and Management.* Butterworths, 426–438.

Chambers, R.J. (1966). *Accounting, Evaluation and Economic Behaviour.* Englewood Cliffs, New Jersey: Prentice Hall.

Committee on Terminology (1953). *Review and Résumé.* Accounting Terminology Bulletin, No. 1, AICPA.

Cropper, L.C. (1911). *Bookkeeping and Accounts.* London: Macdonald and Evans.

Currie, B. (1987). Accounting for infrastructure assets, *Public Finance and Accounting,* **34**, 7–10.

Edwards, E.O. (1961). Depreciation and the maintenance of real capital, in Meij, J.L. (Ed.), *Depreciation and Replacement Policy.* Amsterdam.

Financial Accounting Standards Board (1976). *FASB Discussion Memorandum: An Analysis of Issues Related to Conceptual Framework for Financial Reporting: Elements of Financial Statements and their Measurement* (FASB).

Financial Accounting Standards Board (1980). *Elements of Financial Statements of Business Enterprises*. December, SFAC 3.

Financial Accounting Standards Board (1984). *Recognition and Measurement in Financial Statements of Business Enterprises*. SFAC 5.

Financial Accounting Standards Board (1985). *Elements of Financial Statements*. SFAC 6.

Fremgen, J.M. (1986). On the role of depreciation in governmental accounting. *The Government Accountants Journal,* 10–12.

Goldberg, L. (1962). Concept of depreciation, in W.T. Baxter and S. Davidson (Eds), *Studies in Accounting Theory*. London: Sweet and Maxwell.

Hatfield, H.R. (March 1936). What they say about depreciation. *The Accounting Review,* 18–26.

Henderson, S. and Peirson, G. (1988). *Issues in Financial Accounting* (4th edn). Melbourne: Longman Cheshire.

Her Majesty's Stationery Office (1945). *Report of the Committee on Company Law Amendment*. London: HMSO.

Hylton, D.P. (1965). On matching revenue with expenses. *The Accounting Review,* October.

Ijiri, Y. (1967). *The Foundation of Accounting Measurement*. Englewood Cliffs, New Jersey: Prentice Hall.

Ijiri, Y. (1980). *Recognition of Contractual Rights and Obligations*. FASB.

Institute of Chartered Accountants in England and Wales (1945). *Recommendations on Accounting Principles. No. 9: Depreciation of Financial Assets*. London: ICAEW.

Institute of Chartered Accountants in England and Wales (1976). *Accounting Recommendations: Accounting for Goods Sold Subject to Reservation of Title*. London: ICAEW.

Institute of Chartered Accountants in Scotland (1988). *Making Corporate Reports Valuable*. Kogan Page.

Kam, V. (1990). *Accounting Theory*. John Wiley.

Lall, R.M. (1968). An inquiry into the nature of assets. *New York Certified Public Accountant,* November.

Lamden, C.W., Gerboth, D.L. and McRae, T.W. (1975). *Accounting for Depreciable Assets*. Accounting Research Monograph I, AICPA.

Lemke, K.W. (1966). Asset valuation and income theory. *The Accounting Review,* January.

Lennard, A. (1993). The death knell for historical cost? *Accountancy,* May, 91.

Matheson, E. (1884). *Depreciation of Factories, Mines and Industrial Undertakings and Their Valuation*. London: Spon.

May, G.O. (1948). Postulates of income accounting. *The Journal of Accountancy,* August.

Miller, M.C. and Islam, M.A. (1988). *The Definition and Recognition of Assets*. Accounting Theory Monograph — 7, Caulfield: AARF.

New Zealand Society of Accountants (1985). *Accounting for Depreciation*. SSAP 3, Wellington: NZSA.

New Zealand Society of Accountants (1987). *Statement of Public Sector Accounting Concepts*. Wellington: NZSA.

New Zealand Society of Accountants (1993). *Statement of Concepts for General Purpose Financial Reporting.* Wellington: NZSA.

Norris, H. (1949). Fixed assets and current assets — illogicalities of classification. *The Accountant*, December.

Palgrave, R. H. I. (1925). *Dictionary of Political Economy.* London: MacMillian.

Pallot, J. (1987). Are public sector assets different? Report of a survey on the concept of community assets. *Accountants' Journal*, May 41–45.

Palmer (1895). *Company Precedents* (Sixth edition).

Paton, W.A. (1962). *Accounting Theory.* Scholars Book Company (originally published in 1922).

Paton, W.A. and Littleton, A.C. (1940). *An Introduction to Corporate Accounting Standards,* AAA.

Perera, M.H.B. and Rahman, A.R. (1994). *Conceptual Foundation of Accounting and Financial Reporting: Emerging Commonality of Purpose between Australia and New Zealand.* Paper presented at the Annual Conference of the Accounting Association of Australia and New Zealand, Wollongong, July.

Skinner, R.M. (1987). *Accounting Standards in Evolution.* Holt, Rinehart and Winston of Canada Ltd.

Sorter, G.H. and Ingberman, M. (1987). The implicit criteria for the recognition, quantification, and reporting of accounting events. *Journal of Accounting, Auditing and Finance,* Spring.

Sprague, C. (1907). *The Philosophy of Accounts.* New York.

Sprouse, R.T. and Moonitz, M. (1962). *A Tentative Set of Broad Accounting Principles for Business Enterprises.* ARS No. 3, AICPA.

Staubus, G.J. (1977). *Making Accounting Decisions.* Scholars Book Co.

Staunton, J.J. (1973). Realisation: A misapplied concept in accounting. *Abacus,* December.

Sterling, R.R. (1985). *An Essay on Recognition,* Sydney: University of Sydney, Accounting Research Centre.

Sterling, R.R. and Flaherty, R.E. (1971). The role of liquidity in exchange valuation. *The Accounting Review*, July.

Stevens, S.S. (1946). On the theory of scales of measurement. *Science,* January–June, 677–680.

Storey, R.K. (1959). Revenue realisation, going concern and measurement of income. *The Accounting Review,* April.

Sutcliffe, P. (1985). *Financial Reporting in the Public Sector — A Framework for Analysis and Identification of Issues.* Accounting Theory Monograph No. 5, AARF.

Taussig, F.W. (1925). *Principles of Economics,* 2nd edn.

Van Daniker, R.P. and Kwiatkowski, V. (1986). *Infrastructure Assets: An Assessment of User Needs and Recommendations for Financial Reporting.* Research Report, Government Accounting Standards Board.

Vatter, W. (1947). *The Fund Theory of Accounting and its Implications for Financial Reporting.* Chicago: University of Chicago.

Walker, R.G. (1974). Asset classification and asset valuation. *Accounting and Business Research,* Autumn.

Warner, R. (1899). 'Fixed' and 'circulating' assets. Correspondence. *Accountant,* 4 March.

Wells, M.C. (1968). A note on the amortisation of fixed assets. *The Accounting Review,* April.

Wells, M.C. (1973). Costing for Activities or Products — Which should it be? *Proceedings*, the 21st Advanced Accountancy Seminar on Management Accounting in a Changing Environment, Wellington, June. Victoria: University of Wellington, Department of Accountancy.

Weygandt, J. J., Barth, M. E., Collins, W. A., Crooch, G. M., Frecka, T. J. Imhoff, E. A., McDonald, C. L., Revsine, L. and Searfross, D. G. (1994a). Comment letter to the FASB Discussion Memorandum 'New Basis of Accounting', *Accounting Horizons*, **8**(1), 119–121.

Weygandt, J. J., Barth, M. E., Collins, W. A., Crooch, G. M., Frecka, T. J., Imhoff, E. A., McDonald, C. L., Revsine, L. and Searfross, D. G. (1994b). Response to the FASB Discussion Memorandum 'Present Value-Based Measurements in Accounting', *Accounting Horizons*, **8**(1), 114–122.

Wolk, H.I., Francis, J.R. and Tearney, M.G. (1989). *Accounting Theory — A Conceptual and Institutional Approach,* Second edition. Boston: PWS Kent.

Learning objectives

After studying this chapter the reader will be able to:
- define liabilities
- explain how liabilities have been treated in various conceptual frameworks within Anglo-American countries
- discuss the problems of accounting for liabilities caused by executory contracts
- examine the accounting issues of contingent liabilities
- explain the circumstances under which deferred taxes might, or might not, be considered a legitimate liability
- describe the anomalies between the current treatments of contingent liabilities and executory contracts.

Introduction

The theoretical principles underlying the identification, measurement and disclosure of liabilities are not well developed and for a long time liabilities were regarded as simply the 'other side' of asset determination. Recent developments, for example in the disclosure of the liabilities resulting from financial leases, have reversed this order and it is the assets which have tended to follow from the measurement of liabilities.

This chapter begins by considering a number of traditionally employed definitions of liabilities before examining the views put forward by Ma and Miller (1978) and the AARF (1992). The Ma and Miller definition leads logically to the recognition of additional liabilities such as executory contracts and is reflected in the conceptual framework, issued by the AARF and reviewed in Chapter 6 (AARF, 1992).

Specific attention is given to the problems of accounting for executory contracts, contingent liabilities and tax credits.

Defining liabilities

Henderson and Peirson (1983, p.100) and Ma and Miller (1978, p.259) use a number of definitions to illustrate the lack of a logical relationship between the way in which liabilities are defined in the literature and disclosed in practice. For example, the CICA (1962, p.41) employed a rather circular form of definition: 'In general, a debt owed. In accounting, the money cost of discharging an enforceable obligation and represented by a credit balance that may properly be included in a balance sheet in accordance with accepted accounting principles'. Kohler (1957, p.291) stated that a liability is: 'An amount owing by one person (a debtor) to another (a creditor), payable in money, or in goods and services, the consequences of an asset or service received or a loss incurred; particularly any debt'. Henderson and Peirson (1983, p.100) observe that these definitions appear to be simplistic because:

> There are some items which are apparently enforceable obligations which are not shown as liabilities and there are other items which do appear to be enforceable obligations or debts which are listed among the liabilities. Either the quoted definitions are inadequate or practice is at fault.

Ma and Miller (1978, pp.258–259) note that the problem of defining liabilities logically precedes the valuation issue. Furthermore, they observe that the definition of liabilities has been a neglected area, possibly because of a belief that liabilities always follow assets and that no independent theory of liability recognition and measurement is needed. This is a view which the authors seek to change.

Ma and Miller consider four definitions drawn from the established literature. These are stated below, beginning with Canning (1929, pp.55–56):

> A liability is a service, valuable in money, which a proprietor is under an existing legal (or equitable) duty to render to a second person (or set of persons) and which is not unconditionally a set off to its full value against specific services of equal or greater money value from this second person to the proprietor.

Moonitz (1960, pp.41–46) gives four characteristics of a liability:

> i   A liability involves a future outlay of money, or an equivalent acceptable to the recipient.
> ii A liability is the result of a transaction of the past, not the future . . .
> iii The amount of the liability must be the subject of calculation or close estimation.
> iv Double entry is taken for granted.

Sprouse and Moonitz (1962, p.37) provide another definition:

> The liabilities of a business enterprise are its obligations to convey assets or perform services, obligations resulting from past or current transactions and requiring settlement in the future. The term 'obligation' connotes a claim or series of claims against the business enterprise, each of which has a known or reasonably determinable maturity date and an independent value which is known or reasonably measurable.

All of these definitions are concerned with the value of an anticipated future outflow. In contrast, the tautological products of the AICPA are represented by the definition given in APB 4:

> Liabilities [are] economic obligations of an enterprise that are recognised and measured in conformity with generally accepted accounting principles, liabilities also include certain deferred credits that are not obligations but that are recognised and measured in conformity with generally accepted accounting principles. (AICPA, 1970, para. 132)

Ma and Miller (1978, pp.259–260) produce a definition which they suggest may be distilled from a study of accounting practice:

> A liability is an anticipated cash or other resource outflow, or its present value measured at the internal rate of return, where the activities that give rise to the outflow lie in a past period and where there is no substantial uncertainty concerning the future occurrence or amount of the outflow. Commitments under executory contracts are excluded. Deferred credits, some of which are not associated with an anticipated outflow, are effectively treated as liabilities.

Ma and Miller (1978) go on to propose a definition which conceptualises the liability instead of describing current practice. It is a normative deductive approach based upon what a liability should disclose, rather than an empirical examination of what are currently included as liabilities:

> A liability is a negative present value of an anticipated actual or constructive cash flow, other than distributions to owners, where any discretion with respect to the flow is restricted by legal or other compelling sanctions and where the activity that gives rise to the flow is completed or otherwise has progressed to a determinative stage. (p.260)

The general approach taken by Ma and Miller has appeared in the AARF SAC 4 (AARF, 1992):

> 'Liabilities' are the future sacrifices of service potential or future economic benefits that the entity is presently obliged to make to other entities as a result of past transactions or other past events. (para. 46)
>
> A liability shall be recognised in the statement of financial position when and only when:
> (a) it is probable that the future sacrifice of service potential or future economic benefits will be required; and
> (b) the amount of the liability can be measured reliably. (para. 60)

Almost identical definitions and recognition criteria are given in the New Zealand Statement of Concepts for General Purpose Financial Reporting in paragraphs 7.10 and 7.14. It may be argued, therefore, that in Australasia the definition and recognition criteria issues have been standardised.

Applications of the definition of a liability

The test of a definition is its usefulness when applied to a particular problem requiring solution. The various solutions to the problems of how to account for executory contracts, contingent liabilities and tax credits will be discussed in this section. In particular, the approaches offered by Henderson and Peirson (1983), Ma and Miller (1978) and AARF (1992) will be employed.

Executory contracts

Henderson and Peirson (1983) state that: 'A contract can be described as executory when both parties are yet to perform their obligations under the contract' (p.93).

After quoting from Canning (1929) on the exclusion from both assets and liabilities of identities arising from 'contracts the two sides of which are proportionately unperformed', Henderson and Peirson (1983, p.101) note that:

> An obligation under such a contract is sometimes referred to as a 'future liability'. There is agreement throughout the Anglo-American accounting world, however that future liabilities should not be included among the liabilities on the balance sheet.

This 'agreement' has certainly become a problem insofar as new developments in industry and commerce have encouraged forward planning and contractual arrangements for the supply of goods and services. In come cases, forward contracts are employed to ensure that proposed new developments will be commercially viable. However, in many cases these contracts would not be reported or give rise to disclosed assets or liabilities, either because of the circular definitions, which only accept as liabilities those items which are already accepted under GAAP, or because of the use of traditional definitions based upon Canning (1929). Neither position will satisfy the growing need for fuller disclosure which must recognise changing economic practices.

A considerable volume of academic writing has attempted to extend the debate about the disclosure of financial leases to encompass executory contracts. Many of the contributions in favour of the inclusion of executory contracts are discussed in Mathews (1984, pp.197–214) together with the arguments against any liberalisation of current practices. There are, of course, many shades of opinion in relation to the degree of certainty and measurability which is needed before executory contracts can be recognised as liabilities (and assets) and disclosed in the balance sheet.

Some of the views expressed by Burns, Jaedicke and Sangster (1963), Birnberg

(1965), Wojdak (1969), Hughes (1978) and Ijiri (1975; 1980), may have been influential in leading towards a gradual recognition that there is a problem to be addressed. Ma and Miller (1978) have addressed the issue directly through their revised definition of a liability. In addressing the concept of the liability, they acknowledge that:

> No broad concept can be expected to offer instant solutions to complex problems, but it should provide a frame of reference in which real world problems can be analysed. Our concept captures the fundamental characteristics common to all liabilities, and provides a logical and internally consistent framework for liability recognition in specific problem areas. (p.263)

Ma and Miller (1978) apply this principle to commitments and executory contracts. Their definition of a liability may be applied and will produce a disclosable executory contract if:

> there is a genuine restriction on management discretion over the future outflow under the contract. But commitments that may be reversed readily by penalty free cancellations are fundamentally different from noncancellable contracts and it is for this reason that our liability concept does not cover flexible commitments. (pp.263–264)

A similar position is taken by AARF (1992) in the appendix to SAC 4:

> In applying the definitions of assets and liabilities to agreements that are equally proportionately unperformed, the critical considerations are, respectively, whether the entity has control over the service potential or future economic benefits in completing its acts of performance under the agreements. (para. 4)

It is clear from an examination of the definitions of liabilities from the past thirty years that a considerable change has taken place. We have moved from the use of descriptive statements of extant practice to a conceptualisation of what should be disclosed. The more recent definitions of liabilities concentrate upon expected future outflows of economic resources which are measurable with reasonable certainty, and which have a high probability of occurrence. These conditions allow for the recognition and disclosure of those contracts which are non-cancellable without penalty, but which would not have been disclosed under the older definitions.

However, as discussed in Chapter 6, attempts to recognise executory contracts through SAC 4 have resulted in tremendous opposition from parties which would be required to report such contracts. Since the issue of the original ED, the position on executory contracts has become confused, along with their relegation to an appendix and an extended period for application, to the subsequent withdrawal of the mandatory standing of SAC 4 and the probable removal of the section altogether. The cynic might observe that, clearly, there would be a considerable amount of additional information forthcoming from the disclosure of executory contracts, otherwise there would not be such a battle to prevent the disclosure becoming mandatory! In the long term, executory contracts may have to be disclosed, but that time would appear to now be quite distant.

Contingent liabilities

As noted by Henderson and Peirson (1983, pp. 102–103), contingent liabilities are possible liabilities which may be uncertain in amount or occurrence or both. Examples are claims under warranty or long service leave, sick leave and superannuation provisions. These items are frequently disclosed on the balance sheet because it is argued that the amount can be predicted with reasonable accuracy and there is a high probability that an obligation will arise. Other contingent liabilities with lower levels of predictability and measurability are often disclosed as footnotes.

Henderson and Peirson (1983, p.104) highlight one of the anomalies of present accounting practices as follows:

> Future liabilities are obligations which, given the usual accounting assumption of continuity, will occur in the future. Their amount is known exactly but conventional accounting leaves them off the balance sheet. Contingent or possible liabilities, on the other hand, may arise in the future and their amount is unknown, but conventional accounting frequently includes them on the balance sheet.

It is to be hoped that revised definitions of liabilities will assist in overcoming anomalies of this type.

Ma and Miller (1978) do not address the issue of contingent liabilities at any length but indicate that their concept of a liability would include any item which meets the assurance and estimation criteria. Other contingent liabilities would be disclosed by means of notes.

Paragraphs 18 and 19 of the appendix to SAC 4 (AARF, 1992) deal with contingencies. It is argued that, by adopting the definition and recognition criteria in SAC 4, the need to classify items separately as contingent liabilities would be avoided. If a future definition of economic benefits was needed to satisfy the contingency and this could be measured reliably, then recognition in the financial statements would follow. Other items which did not meet these criteria could be included as notes to the accounts. The provision for the recognition of contingencies among assets and liabilities was one of the features of SAC 4 which was attacked by representatives of preparers in Australia.

There is a clear trend running through the recent literature. Major items under contingent liabilities are not regarded as different from other liabilities, provided that the basic criteria have been met. Lesser items which do not meet these criteria may be shown as notes, presumably if they reach certain minimum levels of materiality to be stated in this way.

One major source of contingent liabilities in recent years has been the discovery of chemical dumps and contaminated land (especially in the USA) which will eventually have to be cleaned up at considerable expense by the current operators and owners of the sites. The magnitude of the problem is such that after payment for site restoration the financial statements over many years will have been distorted, first by ignoring many of the costs of production . . . and then by retrospective recognition in the form of mandatory clean up costs. Because the final cost of this operation is not known, the liability is regarded as contingent.

The anomalous treatment of executory contracts and contingent liabilities highlighted by Henderson and Peirson could be addressed by a revised approach to the recognition and disclosure of liabilities. However, as discussed in Chapter 6 and in this chapter, there are forces that are against many of the proposed changes and the position is perhaps less clear than previously thought.

Deferred credits

Henderson and Peirson (1983, pp. 104–105) state that the term 'deferred credit' 'describes items classified among liabilities on the balance sheet which are neither enforceable obligations (actual liabilities) nor contingent liabilities'.

The category appears to include so many different items, including deferred taxes, that Henderson and Peirson state that all 'liabilities' which are neither enforceable debts nor contingent liabilities are possible deferred credits. Henderson and Peirson (1983) go on to argue that because deferred credits are not obligations but simply 'credit leftovers', it would be better if they could be shown separately on the balance sheet. Their definition of a liability would exclude both deferred credits and executory contracts from the liability section of the balance sheet.

Ma and Miller (1978) consider the issue of deferred taxes and not the whole range of deferred credit items. The use of their definition of a liability means that: 'the correct criterion for recognising a liability is the anticipation of future compulsory tax payments resulting from current (or past) operations' (Ma and Miller, 1978, p.264).

There are considerations of growth and contraction of organisations which will affect the actual payment of taxes. Ma and Miller note that: 'It could be that continuing growth is an unreasonable expectation. If circumstances change and revised anticipations indicate a cash outflow on account of deferred tax will be payable, a liability arises and should be recognised' (p.264). When these latter circumstances are satisfied there will be a cash outflow and then a liability arises which should be recognised in the accounts.

The position of deferred credits is not as clear as it is with executory contracts or contingent liabilities, because there are a large number of potential entries under this heading. However, if the definition used for liabilities and the recognition criteria employed are clearly understood, they may be applied to each potential deferred credit and an appropriate decision made in each case.

Chapter summary

This chapter has addressed the definition and recognition of liabilities. A number of definitions have been identified, ranging from the circular or tautological statements that liabilities are those items recognised as liabilities by generally accepted accounting principles, to the more advanced normative–deductive definitions provided by Ma and Miller (1978) and SAC 4 (AARF, 1992).

The older descriptions of practice are deficient in that they do not permit the disclosure of contractual obligations which are certain to occur (executory contracts) but do allow the disclosure of contingent liabilities and deferred credits. These anomalies would be eliminated to a considerable degree by more recent definitions which evaluate all potential liability disclosures using one set of criteria, namely the degree of certainty and measurability which can be applied to the outflow of economic resources from the entity.

Use of the more recent definitions and recognition criteria to evaluate the executory contract, contingent liability and deferred liability issues would result in the following changes. Executory contracts would be disclosed under appropriate circumstances; there would probably be little change to the position of contingent liabilities; but many if not all of the deferred credit items would disappear from the balance sheet.

It should be noted that most accounting standards and applications of generally accepted accounting principles do not yet operate on the latest definitions and criteria for recognition set out herein. However, it may be only a matter of time before changes are effected to give a more logical and consistent treatment to the disclosure of liabilities.

Essay and examination questions

9.1   Explain the circular nature of many of the older practice-based definitions of liabilities. What problems might arise from the employment of these definitions?

9.2   Ma and Miller (1978) have developed a definition of a liability. Explain the rationale behind the various parts of this definition.

9.3   Compare and contrast the various definitions of liabilities to be found in conceptual frameworks within Anglo-American accounting.

9.4   Henderson and Peirson (1983) have highlighted anomalies between the current treatment of contingent liabilities and executory contracts. Explain the inconsistencies observed.

9.5   Argue the case for the disclosure of executory contracts in financial statements.

9.6   Argue the case against the disclosure of executory contracts in financial statements.

9.7   If we disclose financial leases in the balance sheet we must do the same for executory contracts. Discuss.

9.8   Contingent liabilities may or may not be sufficiently important for inclusion on the balance sheet. Where they are important they are not contingent anyway. Explain.

9.9   Explain the circumstances under which deferred taxes might be considered a legitimate liability (and where they would not be).

9.10   Consider the Henderson and Peirson (1983) definition of a liability (p.106) and their reference to anomalies in the treatment of liabilities. In your opinion would their definition assist in overcoming the perceived anomalies?

9.11   Outline the argument which might be used against the recognition of executory contracts in financial statements. To what extent are these arguments generic to any discussion of reform?

9.12   Contingent liabilities may obscure rather than illuminate an issue. Discuss.

9.13   The non-inclusion of waste disposal costs in previous periods could result in the distortion of financial statements over many years. Explain with reference to government-mandated clean up costs.

9.14   Explain the case for including executory contracts and contingent liabilities in financial statements, grounding your arguments in the discussion of conceptual frameworks in Chapter 6.

9.15   How can accounting reports be 'true and fair' if large amounts of data are excluded? Discuss.

References and additional reading

American Institute of Certified Public Accountants, Accounting Principles Board (1970). *Statement No. 4: Basic Concepts and Accounting Principles Underlying Financial Statements of Business Enterprises.* New York: AICPA.

Australian Accounting Research Foundation (1992). *Definition and Recognition of the Elements of Financial Statements. SAC 4.* Melbourne: AARF.

Birnberg, J.G. (1965). The reporting of executory contracts. *Accounting Review*, 814–820.

Burns, T.S., Jaedicke, R.K. and Sangster, T.M. (1963). Financial reporting of purchase contracts used to guarantee large investments. *Accounting Review*, 1–3.

Canadian Institute of Chartered Accountants (1962). *Terminology for Accountants*. Toronto: CICA.

Canning, J.B. (1929). *The Economics of Accountancy*. New York: Ronald Press.

Durden, C.H. (1988). *A Reconsideration of the Accounting Treatments of Executory Contracts and Contingent Liabilities*. Discussion Paper No. 66. Palmerston North: Massey University, Department of Accountancy.

Henderson, S. and Peirson, C.G. (1983). *Financial Accounting Theory: Its Nature and Development*. Melbourne: Longman Cheshire.

Hughes, J.S. (1978). Toward a contract basis of valuation in accounting. *Accounting Review*, 882–894.

Ijiri, Y. (1975). *Theory of Accounting Measurement*. AAA.

Ijiri, Y. (1980). *Recognition of Contractual Rights and Obligations: An Exploratory Study of Conceptual Issues*. Stamford: FASB.

Kohler, E. (1957). *Dictionary for Accountants*. Englewood Cliffs, New Jersey: Prentice Hall.

Ma, R. and Miller, M.C. (1978). Conceptualising the liability. *Accounting and Business Research*, Autumn 258–265.

Mathews, M.R. (1979). Should executory contracts be disclosed in company accounts? *Australian Accountant*, 81–84.

Mathews, M.R. (1984). *Readings in the Development of Accounting*. Palmerston North: Dunmore.

Moonitz, M. (1960). The changing concept of liabilities. *Journal of Accountancy*.

New Zealand Society of Accountants (1994). *Statement of Concepts for General Purpose Financial Reporting*. Wellington: NZSA.

Sprouse, R.T. and Moonitz, M. (1962). *Accounting Research Study No. 3: A Tentative Statement of Broad Accounting Principles for Business Enterprises*. New York: AICPA.

Wojdak, J.F. (1969). A theoretical foundation for leases and other executory contracts. *Accounting Review*, 362–370.

Chapter 10
Accounting and income determination

Learning objectives

After studying this chapter the reader will be able to:
• define the concept of income
• identify the major differences between the traditional and modern approaches to accounting income
• consider accounting and economic concepts of income
• comment on the realisation and matching concepts and their impact on the measurement of business income
• discuss cost allocation in accounting
• examine the ritual nature of income determination in accounting.

Introduction

A major function of accounting is to provide information about the performance of an entity during a given period of time. This information is generally reflected in income (profit) or loss as reported through the income statement. The AARF (1992) states that:

> SAC 2 defines performance as the proficiency of a reporting entity in acquiring resources economically and using those resources efficiently and effectively in achieving specified objectives. The primary financial measures of an entity's performance are reported in the operating statement the elements of which are revenues and expenses. (SAC 4, para. 93)

Income determination is an integral part of the accounting process. Accounting income is often used as the basis for taxation on income, an indication of the result of operation of an entity, a criterion for the determination of dividend payments, a determining factor in wage fixing, management compensation and so on. The concept of income is widely used also in economics. This is only natural as both economics and accounting deal with the same subject matter. As Whittington (1977) says:

Accounting is concerned with the provision of data relating to economic activity. Economic analysis should therefore clarify the questions which the accountant is trying to answer. Furthermore, the accountant's answers to these questions should provide important data for the economist who is concerned to test his theories against events in the real world. Accounting and economics are therefore complementary disciplines. (p.192)

In spite of the closeness of the subject matter, there appears to be a lack of agreement between accounting and economics regarding the timing and measurement of income. This is mainly due to the fact that the two disciplines have taken different paths in their development. Accounting arose out of a practical need to report the results of economic activity, whereas economics arose out of a desire to understand the workings of the economy (Whittington, 1977, p.193). The gap between accounting and economic concepts became so wide that Boulding (1962) called the two disciplines 'uncongenial twins'. However, now there is evidence to suggest that attempts are being made, particularly in accounting, to narrow this gap, if not to close it. The recent conceptual framework projects for accounting in the USA, UK, Australia and New Zealand are good examples. The trend in accounting towards using concepts similar to those developed in economics is highlighted in this chapter.

Revenues and expenses are the key elements in the income determination process. There are certain rules and principles of traditional accounting, which govern the recognition and measurement of revenues, expenses and income. However, the relevance or adequacy of these rules and principles has been questioned on many occasions as most of them were introduced to accounting at different points in time in the past to serve various practical purposes. This chapter proposes to examine critically some of these rules and principles in the context of a modern accounting environment.

Concepts of accounting income

Economists generally define income in terms of well-offness, that is, the extent to which an entity has become better off during a given period of time. This view is clearly reflected in Hicks (1946):

> The purpose of income calculation in practical affairs is to give people an indication of the amount which they can consume without impoverishing themselves. Following out this idea it would seem that we ought to define a man's income as the maximum value which he can consume during a week, and still expect to be as well off at the end of the week as he was at the beginning. (p.172)

Although this definition is concerned with individual income, the concept of income as an increment of well-offness is generally applicable to any entity.

Traditionally, accountants have taken a different view of income, for example:

> Income and profit . . . refer to amounts resulting from the deduction from revenues, or from operating revenues, of cost of goods sold, other expenses, and

losses . . . (AIA, 1955, para. 8), and Net income (net loss) — the excess (deficit) of revenue over expenses for an accounting period . . . (AICPA, 1970, para. 134)

These two definitions clearly represent the narrow, revenue–expense or operating income approach.

However, attempts have been made to widen the scope of the accounting concept of income, for example by arguing that income should include all gains and losses in assets or liabilities held by an entity during a particular period (e.g. Edwards and Bell, 1961; Sprouse and Moonitz, 1962). Edwards and Bell (1961) identify four types of income:

- *current operating profit* — the excess of sales revenues over the current cost of inputs used in production and output sold
- *realisable cost savings* — the increases in the prices of assets held during the period
- *realised cost savings* — the difference between historical costs and the current purchase price of goods sold
- *realised capital gains* — the excess of sales proceeds over historical costs on the disposal of long-term assets.

They argue that the information about these four types of income would be a better indication of 'well-offness' and would allow users more information in analysing enterprise results (p.111). This is a more comprehensive view of income and it represents a major change from the traditional view as it advocates the reporting of holding gains and losses during a period, on the ground that such reporting would increase the information content of financial statements.

The US conceptual framework project formally recognises the importance of adopting a comprehensive approach to income in accounting. The FASB (1980), later superseded by the FASB (1985), attempts to widen the scope of the measurement of the business enterprise operations by using an asset–liability approach instead of the traditional revenue–expense approach. The FASB (1985) defined comprehensive income as follows:

> Comprehensive income is the change in equity (net assets) of an entity during a period from transactions and events and circumstances from non-owner sources. It includes *all changes in equity* during a period except those resulting from investments by owners and distributions to owners. (para .70, emphasis added)

The NZSA (1993) and the AARF (1992) take a similar view.

It can be argued that this approach represents an attempt to bring the traditional accounting concept of income and the economic concept of income as an increment of well-offness closer together.

Revenues and expenses

Under any income concept, revenues and expenses are the key elements in the determination of its amount in accounting. Therefore, it is important to examine what these terms mean for accounting purposes. The next two sections include a discussion of the main characteristics of revenues and expenses and the criteria used in recognising them for inclusion in the financial statements.

Revenues

The general trend towards a comprehensive income concept in accounting, mentioned earlier, can be seen in the way revenues and expenses have been defined by various authors over the years. In its definition of revenues, the AIA (1955) says 'revenue results from the sale of goods and rendering of services and is measured by the charge made to customers, clients, or tenants for goods and services furnished to them'

(para. 5). This reflects a current operating income approach and the AICPA (1970) also provides a similar definition based on generally accepted accounting principles. It equates revenues to 'gross increases in assets and gross decreases in liabilities measured in conformity with generally accepted accounting principles that result from those types of profit-directed activities' (para. 134). However, the AICPA attempts to define revenues in terms of changes in assets and liabilities.

The FASB (1985) provides a definition of revenues based on an all-inclusive income concept. It says:

> Revenues are the inflows or other enhancements of assets of an entity or settlements of its liabilities (or a combination of both) during a period from delivering or producing goods, rendering services, or other activities that constitute the entity's ongoing major or central operations. (para. 78)

The AARF (1992) has a similar definition but it does not emphasise 'activities that constitute the entity's ongoing major or central operations' as the origin of revenues (SAC 4, para. 95). The NZSA (1993) defines revenues in exactly the same way (para. 7.19).

The AICPA (1970) and the FASB (1985) make a distinction between revenues and gains. For example, the AICPA (1970) identifies gains as revenues from other than sales of products, merchandise or services (para. 198), while the FASB (1985) describes gains as increases in equity (net assets) from peripheral or incidental transactions (para. 82). However, whereas the FASB (1985) includes all revenues and gains, regardless of source, in its concept of income, since the AICPA (1970) adopts a current operating income concept, it does not include gains as part of income on the ground that they do not represent recurring income from the entity's main area of income producing activities.

The ASB (1992) takes a different approach in that it uses the word 'gains' to include all increases in equity, other than those relating to contributions from owners (Chapter 3, para. 52). It explains the concepts of gains (and losses) as follows:

> Various kinds of gains and losses may be distinguished, amongst the most fundamental of which are revenue gains and revenue losses, which are those gains and losses which are generally included in the profit and loss account of the entity. Another type of gains and losses is the effect on the assets and liabilities of the entity of changes in market values (to the extent such changes are recognised in accounts). (para. 54)

The definition of revenue suggests that it is either an addition to assets or a reduction in liabilities. The measurement of revenue, therefore, depends upon the properties of assets and liabilities which are measured.

Expenses

Although it is not uncommon to find in the literature that the terms 'expense' and 'cost' have been used synonymously, they have different meanings for accounting purposes. The term 'cost' covers all uses of resources, including those used by an entity to acquire assets, whereas the term 'expense' covers only those resource uses which are matched against revenues in the process of determining income for an entity within a given period of time. For example, the AIA (1953) makes this distinction as follows:

> Cost — The amount given in consideration of goods received or to be received. Costs can be classified as unexpired (assets), which are applicable to the production of future revenues, and expired, those not applicable to the production of future revenues and thus deducted from revenues or retained earnings in the current period.

The present discussion is concerned with expenses. As in the case of revenues, the definitions of expenses also indicate a clear trend towards a comprehensive view of income. The AIA (1957) definition, 'expenses in the broadest sense include all expired costs which are deductible from revenues' (para. 3), represents the traditional revenue–expense orientation. The AICPA (1970) defines expenses as 'gross decreases in assets or gross increases in liabilities recognized and measured in conformity with generally accepted accounting principles that result from those types of profit-directed activities of an enterprise' (para. 134). Although this definition attempts to establish a relationship between expenses and net assets, measurement is still based on generally accepted accounting principles.

The FASB (1985) defines expenses with a strong asset–liability approach; it says expenses are:

> outflows or other using up of assets or incurrences of liabilities (or a combination of both) from delivering or producing goods, rendering services or carrying out other activities that constitute the entity's ongoing major or central operations. (para. 80)

The FASB makes a distinction between expenses and losses when it defines losses as 'decreases in equity (net assets) from peripheral or incidental transactions of an entity and from all other transactions and other events and circumstances affecting the entity during a period except those that result from expenses or distributions to owners' (FASB, 1980, para. 68). But both expenses and losses are included in the calculation of income.

It is interesting to note that the AARF (1992) goes even further in its definition of expenses. It defines expenses as:

> consumptions or losses of economic benefits or service potential in the form of reductions in assets or increases in

liabilities of the reporting entity, other than those relating to distributions to owners, that result in a decrease in equity during the accounting period. (SAC 4, para. 101)

The NZSA (1993, para. 7.22) offers a definition of expenses which is identical to the AARF's definition. The AARF (1992) and the NZSA (1993) take a comprehensive approach to expenses and do not consider losses as a separate element of financial statements, and therefore, do not distinguish between expenses and losses. Accordingly, the concept of expenses encompasses items that have typically been reported in the financial statements as 'losses'.

Allocation of costs

Cost allocation under conventional accounting is a major issue which has caused many problems for accountants. If any business enterprise is to survive in the long run, its revenues must cover the costs of all factors of production, including an adequate return on investment. An enterprise that is capable of doing so is regarded as financially viable. This is often mentioned as an essential requirement for both private and public sector entities. In practice, however, this basic proposition has been extended by accountants and managers to mean that the price of every individual item of an entity's products must recoup and every division or department of the production process must be responsible for its share of the costs of production on an all-inclusive basis. This in turn requires that, in addition to the direct (or attributable) costs, the amount of indirect costs applicable in each case must be ascertained. As a result, the allocation of indirect costs among individual products and divisions has become an important part of conventional accounting. However, after extensive study of the cost allocation problem in accounting, Thomas (1969) concludes that selection of a particular

allocation method over alternative methods is meaningless because the superiority of one allocation method over another can be neither verified nor refuted.

Under conventional accounting it is necessary to ascertain the cost of inventories as a basis for valuation for income determination and balance sheet purposes. This in turn requires the collection of production costs at various stages of production. But if the balance sheet is to represent the financial position of an entity on a particular date, and if income for a period is the difference between the residual equities at the beginning and end of that period (after making adjustment for any change in the purchasing power of money), all assets including inventories must be stated in current dollar terms, which may be their market selling prices. Stating inventories at current market prices does not involve any calculation of either production or acquisition cost. Therefore, it can be argued that it is possible to develop an allocation free system of accounting by changing the basis from historic cost to current market prices.

Realisation

'Realisation' is one of the rules of conventional accounting which dominates the determination of income or profit. According to May (1948): 'Among the standard postulates of accounting . . . is one that income is "realised" gains and that, therefore, income emerges when the revenue from which it is derived is realised' (p.108). The word 'realisation' may be defined briefly as converted into money or a claim to money. The point of realisation is often described as the point of sale. For example, the AIA (1953) said, 'profit (revenue) is deemed to be realized when a sale in the ordinary course of a business is effected, unless the circumstances are such that collection of the sales price is not reasonably assured' (Chapter 1, para. 1); the AAA (1965) recommended that the concept of realisation could be improved if the following criteria were applied, namely: (a) revenue must be capable of measurement; (b) the measurement must be verified by an external market transaction; and (c) the crucial event must have occurred (p. 318). The AICPA (1966) also expressed the same view, when it said, 'revenues should ordinarily be accounted for at the time a (sale) transaction is completed, with appropriate provision for uncollectible accounts' (p.149).

Realisation often refers to the formal recognition of revenue in the computation of income. As mentioned earlier, the use of the realisation test usually results in revenue being recognised at the point of sale. However, there are variations in the timing of revenue realisation and recognition, depending on the circumstances. In otherwords, revenue realisation and recognition can occur simultaneously or at different points in time. For example, of the different methods of earning revenue available to an entity, under the completion-of-production method and the percentage-of-completion method, revenue is recognised prior to realisation; under the instalment method, recognition is delayed even after revenue is realised. The percentage-of-completion method provides for the earliest point of revenue recognition while the instalment method provides for the latest. (For a discussion of the relationship between recognition and realisation, see Coombes and Martin, 1982, pp.12–14; Thomas, 1966.)

Conventionally, income is regarded as the difference between sales revenue or selling prices of the products sold and the historical cost of earning that revenue. On this basis, all unrealised or unsold assets are deferred costs yet to be matched with future revenues and should be valued at cost. As the realisation and matching rules provide a theoretical justification for valuation of inventories at cost, they have gained important positions in conventional accounting (Storey, 1959, pp.237–238).

Misuse of the meaning of realisation

It is evident from the accounting literature that there is some confusion about the concepts of 'revenue' and 'income' in relation to realisation. Although revenues are contributory to profit, profit is a different concept from revenue. Canning (1929, p.100) tried to explain the point, and said: 'It [the gross income] is the summation of the amount of gross operating income plus the amount of gross financial income'. Revenues are receipts of money or claims to money by an entity. In ordinary business practice, revenues are recognised in the accounts at the time when the rights, measurable in money, are established, that is at the point of realisation. But the concept of income or profit has a broader meaning. As mentioned earlier, currently there seems to be a trend in accounting towards a more comprehensive or all inclusive approach to income, instead of the traditional revenue–expense approach. It includes, in addition to revenues, net gain accrued from external events such as changes in specific prices and the general level of prices. The realisation rule cannot be used in determining net gain accrued from such events. It has been argued that the use of the realisation rule in connection with income is a misapplication of the realisation idea (Staunton, 1973). As Chambers (1965) says:

> the notion of realisation should be applied more strictly — to revenues only. Income is the result of a calculation, an inference; it seems hardly correct to apply the term realised or realisable to it. In commercial usage generally, to realise means to convert into monetary assets; 'realisation' has a definite usefulness as describing this event, which it loses if it is also used in relation to income or profit. (p.437)

Realised revenue and income

If the price of an asset continues to rise over a number of accounting periods, under the realisation rule there will be a large amount of profit at the time of sale. But obviously the full amount is not solely due to the events of that period. If the purpose is to discover the extent to which the financial position of a firm in relation to the rest of the environment has changed from one accounting period to another, dependence on the realisation test is likely to obscure the discovery. Sterling and Flaherty (1971, p.455) argue that some of the logical inconsistencies in the rules underlying historical cost valuation methods are related to this concept.

The main difference between the income concepts of accounting and economics lies in the accountant's reliance on realisation as the primary test for recognising income because the realisation test does not allow for the fact that revenue is earned continuously over time. Zeff and Keller (1985) describe this as follows:

> The guidelines that are followed in the establishment of accounting principles are that the allocation methods should be 'reasonable' and 'systematic'. The results should be conservative in that recognition should be delayed until realization is near certain. The general guidelines are that the earning process is complete when the product is in condition for sale and the sales price has been established by contract with a buyer from whom the receivable is reasonably certain of being collected. In most cases, these guidelines delay the recognition of revenue to the period in which a sales transaction takes place. In short, the revenue earned during manufacture is arbitrarily shifted to the period in which sales take place. (p.319)

It is interesting to note that the realisation principle was not always a part of standard accounting practice. For example, May (1950) says:

> A review of accounting, legal and economic writing suggests that the realization postulate was not accepted prior to the First World War. In 1913 leading authorities in all these fields in England and America seemed to agree on the 'increase in net worth' concept of income . . . (p.316)

However, there have been a number of contributory factors to the establishment of the realisation principle in accounting in later years. First, the early income tax laws in the UK and USA, which considered revenue to be cash receipts, had a significant influence on how accountants calculated business income. Second, the Great Depression of the 1930s also played a role in establishing the realisation principle in accounting. Chatfield (1977) points out that:

> The abuse arising from appraisal valuations in the 1920s contributed in part to the disastrous economic events leading to the Great Depression of the 1930s. The accounting profession was criticized for allowing companies to value assets over-optimistically. In the face of these criticisms, accountants adopted a conservative attitude, and the recognition (realization) principle was an outcome of this defensive posture. The first authoritative use of the word 'realization' in the USA occurred in 1932, in correspondence between a special committee of the American Institute and the New York Stock Exchange. (p.260)

Third, the legal opinion on the subject also favoured a realisation concept. For example, in the *Eisner vs Macomber* case in 1920, Charles Evans Hughes, in his brief to the court, said:

> It is of the essence of income that it should be realized . . . Income necessarily implies separation and realization . . .

The increase in the value of lands due to growth and prosperity of the community is not income until it is realized. (*Eisner vs Macomber, 25 USA 188, 195, 1920*)

It has been argued that the above development is due to the influence of conservatism on all aspects of accounting. Sterling (1970, p.256) called conservatism the most influential principle of valuation in accounting. However, in recent years the pressures for more up-to-date and relevant information have reduced the influence of this concept. It can be argued that conservative financial statements are usually unfair to present shareholders and biased in favour of prospective shareholders because of the tendency to underestimate assets and overestimate liabilities, resulting in a relatively lower value for existing shares.

Matching

In addition to the realisation principle, the matching principle also plays a key role in the process of determining periodic accounting income. Paton and Littleton (1940) describe the matching concept as the association of effort and accomplishment (p.15). The AAA (1965) recommends that costs should be related to revenues realised within a specific period on the basis of some correlation of these costs with the recognised revenues. (AAA, 1965 provides an excellent review of the matching concept literature.)

It is important to have some rules for matching financial gains and losses during a period, for otherwise it would be impossible to prepare an income statement. But it is also important to note that there are limitations to the applicability of the notion of matching in accounting. Take, for example, the cost of oil explorations. If, after the expenditure of large sums of money, it turned out that there were no oil reserves at a particular site, there would be no products against which the cost of exploration

could be matched. In such cases, the notion of matching cannot be applied at all. Further, as indicated earlier, the matching process normally entails first identifying revenues of a given period and then matching certain costs against them to obtain net income or profit. But the percentage-of-completion method completely reverses this procedure by identifying the costs incurred in a given period first and then matching future revenue to them.

The application of the term 'matching' in conventional accounting is not consistent with the meaning of the term as commonly understood. For example, matching has been described as assigning revenue earned and expenses incurred to the accounting period in which these events occur (Hylton, 1965, p.828). But in conventional accounting the notion of matching is used in the sense of matching particular events and their financial magnitudes or numbers representing monetary amounts regardless of the time at which they occur, or of the significance of the underlying financial facts. For example, depreciation based on historical costs may reflect cost levels which prevailed years ago when dollars had a vastly different purchasing power; depending on the inventory method in use, cost of goods sold may represent a figure which is quite current or it may not. In such cases, the current revenue dollars may be matched against expenses which are far from current.

Furthermore, matching might just as well be interpreted as identifying events with their periods. This implies that all the events which have a bearing on the financial position of an entity within each period should be identified and accounted for. But in conventional accounting the matching process does not take into account all the gains and losses of an entity during a period. There is a tendency to recognise losses but not gains. For example, according to the lower of cost and market rule, when the market price of short-term inventories falls below cost, the difference is recognised as a loss but, when the price rises above cost, the difference is not recognised as a gain.

The consistent application of the matching notion requires that all gains made during a period, whether realised or not, should be brought into account and matched with all the losses incurred during the period. This is in line with the all-inclusive approach to income. As early as 1936, the AAA supported this view. For example, the AAA (1936) says, 'the income statement for any given period should reflect all revenues properly given accounting recognition and all costs written off during the period, regardless of whether or not they are the result of operations in that period . . .' (section 8). Accordingly, it can be argued that, first, gains and losses should be taken to include those resulting from the dealing in both short-term and durable inventories; and second, any change in the general level of prices during the period should also be brought into account.

Capital maintenance

Capital maintenance is a long-standing concept in accounting. The basic rationale for this concept has been that the capital of the entity should be maintained intact before distributing dividends to the owners in order to safeguard the interests of creditors. Capital maintenance is concerned with identifying the capital to be maintained when determining the results for the reporting entity. Different accounting models use different bases for this purpose. For the historical cost model the capital to be maintained is the nominal capital; for the CPP model and the CoCoA model, it is the purchasing power of the initial capital; for the CCA model, it is the physical capital (see also Chapter 11). The NZSA (1993) and the AARF (1992) emphasise the importance of capital maintenance although they do not specify the capital to be maintained.

They define capital maintenance adjustments as 'adjustments made under certain accounting models to the entity's capital to take account of the effects of price changes on the entity's assets and liabilities' (NZSA, 1993, para. 7.30; AARF, 1992, para. 132).

The Companies Act 1993 of New Zealand, which took effect from July 1994, however, replaces the concept of capital maintenance with a solvency test (Perera and Rahman, 1994). According to this Act, the directors of a company have complete discretion to distribute company's resources to shareholders, provided the company satisfies the solvency test immediately after making the distribution (section 52). The two-pronged solvency test includes: '(a) The company is able to pay its debts as they become due in the normal course of business; and (b) The value of the company's assets is greater than the value of its liabilities, including contingent liabilities' (section 4(1)). In determining the value of a contingent liability, the likelihood of the contingency occurring may be taken into account, as well as any claim the company is entitled to make and can reasonably expect to be met to reduce or extinguish the contingent liability (section 4(4)). The directors who vote in favour of a distribution are required to sign a certificate stating that in their opinion the company will, immediately after the distribution, satisfy the solvency test and the grounds for that opinion (section 52(2)). Any director who fails to comply with this commits an offence and is liable on conviction to a penalty of $5000 (sections 52(5) and 373(1)).

This is a situation where company legislation in New Zealand has taken the lead in changing a long-standing accounting concept which has been built into conceptual frameworks for accounting and financial reporting.

Chapter summary

Income determination is a major function of accounting. Income is a concept widely used in accounting and economics.

Although there have been differences in the concepts of income as used in these two disciplines, currently there is evidence to suggest that attempts are being made to reduce or eliminate such differences. In conventional accounting the computation of income for financial reporting purposes is governed by a number of accounting rules and principles such as realisation, cost allocation and matching. A close examination clearly points to the need for reconsideration of their relevance and adequacy in the context of modern business.

Essay and examination questions

10.1 Accounting and economics are complementary disciplines as they both deal with the same subject matter. Explain and discuss.

10.2 Do you have any evidence to suggest that currently there is a trend in accounting towards a comprehensive approach to the concept of income (profit)?

10.3 Revenues and expenses are the key elements under any approach to the computation of accounting income. Discuss.

10.4 Explain the meaning of the realisation test.

10.5 'Realisation' is a misapplied concept in conventional accounting. Do you agree? Why?

10.6 What is meant by the matching principle?

10.7 Critically examine the application of the matching principle in determining the period income of an entity.

10.8 Discuss the impact of the conservatism principle upon the calculation of accounting income.

References and additional reading

Accounting Standards Board (1992). *Discussion Draft on Statement of Principles*. London: ASB.

American Accounting Association (1936). *A Tentative Statement of Accounting Principles Underlying Corporate Financial Statements*. AAA.

American Accounting Association (1965). The matching concept. AAA 1964 Concepts and Standards Research Study Committee: The Matching Concept. *The Accounting Review*, 4, 368–372.

American Institute of Accountants (1953). *Review and Resumé* (of the eight original terminology bulletins). Accounting Terminology Bulletin No. 1. Committee on Terminology. AIA.

American Institute of Accountants (1955). *Proceeds, Revenue, Income, Profit and Earnings*. Accounting Terminology Bulletin No. 2. Committee on Terminology. AIA.

American Institute of Accountants (1957). *Cost, Expense and Loss*. Accounting Terminology Bulletin No. 4. Committee on Terminology. AIA.

American Institute of Certified Public Accountants (1966). APB Opinion. No.10: Omnibus Opinion. New York: AICPA.

American Institute of Certified Public Accountants (1970). *Basic Concepts and Accounting Principles*. APB Statement No. 4. AICPA.

Australian Accounting Research Foundation (1987). *Definition and Recognition of Expenses*. ED 46b. Caulfield: AARF.

Australian Accounting Research Foundation (1992). *Statement of Accounting Concepts No. 4: Definition and Recognition of the Elements of Financial Statements.* Melbourne: AARF.

Boulding, K.E. (1962). Economics and Accounting: The uncongenial twins, in W.T. Baxter and S. Davidson (Eds). *Studies in Accounting Theory.* Irwin, 44–55.

Canning, J. (1929). *The Economics of Accountancy.* New York: Ronald.

Chambers, R.J. (October 1965). Edwards and Bell on business income. *The Accounting Review.*

Chatfield, M. (1977). *A History of Accounting Thought.* Krieger.

Coombes, R.J. and Martin, C.A. (1982). *The Definition and Recognition of Revenue.* Accounting Theory Monograph No. 3. Melbourne: AARF.

Edwards, E.O. and Bell, P.W. (1961). *Theory and Measurement of Business Income.* Berkeley and Los Angeles: University of California Press.

Financial Accounting Standards Board (1980). *Elements of Financial Statements of Business Enterprises.* SFAC 3. FASB.

Financial Accounting Standards Board (1985). *Elements of Financial Statements.* SFAC 6. FASB.

Hicks, J.R. (1946). *Value and Capital.* Oxford: Clarendon Press.

Hylton, D.P. (1965). On matching revenue and expenses. *The Accounting Review,* October.

May, G.O. (1948). Postulates of income accounting. *The Journal of Accountancy.*

May, G.O. (1950). Business income. *The Accountant,* September.

New Zealand Society of Accountants (1993). *A Proposed Framework for Financial Reporting in New Zealand.* Wellington: NZSA.

Paton, W.A. and Littleton, A.C. (1940). *An Introduction to Corporate Accounting Standards.* AAA Monograph No. 3, AAA.

Perera, M.H.B. and Rahman, A.R. (1994). *Conceptual Foundation of Accounting and Financial Reporting: Emerging Commonality of Purpose between Australia and New Zealand.* Paper presented at the Annual Meeting of the Accounting Association of Australia and New Zealand. Wollongong, July.

Sprouse, R.T. and Moonitz, M. (1962). *A Tentative Set of Broad Accounting Principles for Business Enterprises.* ARS No. 3. New York: AICPA.

Staunton, J.J. (1973). Realization: A misapplied concept in accounting. *Abacus,* December.

Sterling, R.R. (1970). *Theory and the Measurement of Enterprise Income.* Lawrence: University of Kansas Press.

Sterling, R.R. and Flaherty, R.E. (1971). The role of liquidity in exchange valuation. *The Accounting Review,* July.

Storey, R.K. (1959). Revenue realization, going concern and measurement of income. *The Accounting Review,* April.

Thomas, A.L. (1966). *Revenue Recognition.* Ann Arbor: University of Michigan, Bureau of Business Research, Graduate School of Business Administration.

Thomas, A.L. (1969). *Allocation Problems in Financial Accounting Theory.* Studies in Accounting Research 3. AAA.

Whittington, G. (1977). Accounting and economics, in B. Carsberg and T. Hope, (Eds). *Current Issues in Accounting.* Oxford: Philip Allan, 192–212.

Zeff, S.A. and Keller, T.F. (1985). *Financial Accounting Theory — Issues and Controversies* (Third edition). New York: McGraw-Hill.

Learning objectives

After studying this chapter the reader will be able to:

- identify the main characteristics of money and prices
- explain the nature of income and wealth
- consider the impact of price changes on the measurement of income and wealth
- discuss the concept of capital maintenance
- examine the alternative approaches available to address the accounting problems caused by price changes
- describe the experiences in Anglo-American countries in the area of price variation accounting.

Introduction

The importance of reliable information about the financial relationship between an enterprise and the rest of the environment at a specified date is two-fold. On the one hand, it enables the ascertainment of any change in the financial position of an enterprise between two particular points in time. On the other hand, it provides the basis for calculating the expected consequences of causes of future actions that are financially feasible. The financial relationship of an enterprise with the rest of the environment is affected by changes resulting from transactions, transformations and external events such as changes in prices of specific goods, and in the general level of prices. Unless all such changes are accounted for, analysis and judgement will be misdirected.

This chapter proposes to consider the effects of price movements on the financial result and position of an enterprise, to explain the features of some alternative accounting methods proposed or adopted in taking account of such effects and to examine the approaches taken in this area in different countries, namely the UK, Australia, New Zealand, the USA and Canada.

Money and prices

Money has its own characteristics. While as the medium of exchange it is used to measure the prices of all other goods and services, the general purchasing power of the monetary unit is measured by its capacity to command other goods and services.

A period of inflation is characterised by two accompanying features: (a) a rise in the general level of prices; and (b) a change in the structure of prices or shifts in specific prices. These two features take place concurrently and are interdependent. However, although the rise in the general level of prices reflects the combined effect of the changes in all prices, it is not necessarily indicative of the rate or even the direction of change of any particular price, for that is determined by the demand and supply conditions of the particular product. In a period of inflation the price of a specific asset may increase at a lower or higher rate than the general price level, it may remain unchanged, or it may even change in the opposite direction. Alternatively, there may be a change in the price structure without any change in the general level of prices if the rises and falls in prices offset each other. This is illustrated in Figure 11.1.

Figure 11.1
General price level and specific price changes

With general price level change

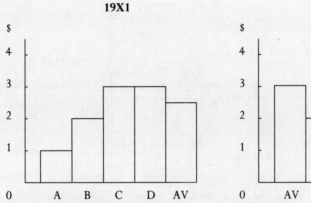

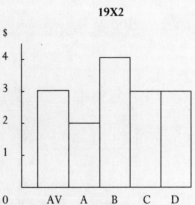

With no general price level change

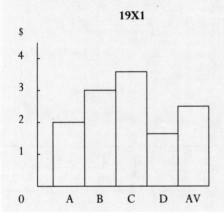

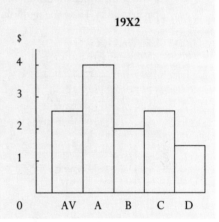

It is clear from Figure 11.1 that there can be specific price changes when there is no change in the general level of prices. These specific price changes are important, therefore, in ascertaining wealth irrespective of general price level changes.

Wealth, income and capital maintenance

A change in the purchasing power possessed by an individual represents a change in his or her capacity to engage in transactions. This is true also of business entities. The stock of purchasing power possessed by an entity is commonly referred to as wealth. The wealth of an entity in this sense depends on two factors: (a) the general level of prices and (b) the amount of money or money equivalent at its command. Firms usually do not keep their financial resources in cash, rather they invest them in other assets. If the market prices of such assets change, the capacity to command other goods and services will change also. Furthermore, if the value of money as expressed by the general level of prices decreases over a period, the amount of money or its equivalent at the end of the period will have less purchasing power than at the beginning. Therefore, it is important that, in financial reporting, any change in these two factors should be identified and accounted for.

Income in a real sense is the change in purchasing power possessed by an entity between two points in time. This is illustrated in Figure 11.2.

Figure 11.2
The nature of income and wealth

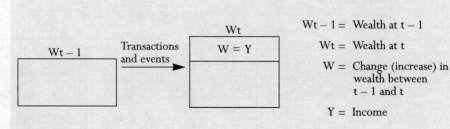

$Wt - 1 =$ Wealth at $t - 1$

$Wt =$ Wealth at t

$W =$ Change (increase) in wealth between $t - 1$ and t

$Y =$ Income

Accounting income provides indications of the earning power and future cash flows of a company, which determine its dividend paying ability. The expected value of its shares will depend largely on its dividend paying ability. These relationships are shown in Figure 11.3.

Figure 11.3
Why measure income?

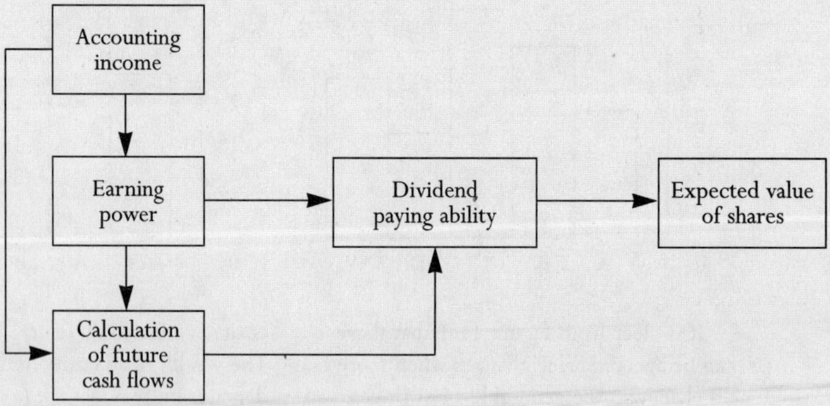

```
┌──────────────┐
│  Accounting  │
│    income    │
└──────────────┘
        │
        ▼
┌──────────────┐     ┌──────────────┐     ┌──────────────┐
│   Earning    │ ──▶ │   Dividend   │ ──▶ │ Expected value│
│    power     │     │ paying ability│     │   of shares   │
└──────────────┘     └──────────────┘     └──────────────┘
        │                    ▲
        ▼                    │
┌──────────────┐             │
│ Calculation  │ ────────────┘
│  of future   │
│  cash flows  │
└──────────────┘
```

In addition to being useful to managers, accounting income is also important for stewardship purposes, wage and price fixing and dealing with governments (tax authorities).

The conventional style of accounting does not make any provision for the changes in purchasing power. The conventional accounting model based on historical costs was designed for use in a situation where prices are stable or where prices change slowly. Although it may appear that a reasonably informed reader of conventional accounting reports can make his or her own judgements and allow for the effects of price movements, such effects are likely to be different in different cases, depending upon the composition of assets, method of financing and sources of income. Therefore, accounting reports should contain such information. As Slimmings (1974) says:

Guessing, however shrewd, about the possible interaction of such important factors as these is not an adequate substitute for having the information supplied by the company itself. If you accept that a set of published accounts is a communication designed to give the reader as true and fair a view as possible of the results and the financial position of the undertaking concerned, . . . information about the effect of inflation is a necessary ingredient of that communication. (p.212)

The financial relationship of a firm with the rest of the environment at any time is determined by its present assets and liabilities. The stock of assets in excess of those committed to the settlement of outside liabilities of a firm is described as its capital. Income or profit can arise only if there has been a genuine increment in the amount of capital over a period. This is implied in any company law which provides that dividends should not be paid out of capital. The definition given to capital is important in measuring accounting profit because, being an increment, the amount upon which it is an increment must be known. Capital is essentially a financial notion which has reference only to the available finance or the actual money sum employed at the risk of busi-

ness. In this sense, capital is represented by the money equivalent to the net assets at the beginning of an accounting period. Since money is wanted for its general purchasing power, and a certain amount of money or its equivalent represents the capacity of the holder to engage in transactions, it is only logical to say that at least this capacity must be maintained before there can be any surplus or improvement in position.

The effect of borrowing

Apart from asset composition, the effects of price movements on a firm will also depend on its financing arrangements. For example, a firm may 'hedge' against inflation by borrowing. This is because, under any loan agreement, the borrower is required to pay only the contractual amount of the loan in current monetary units, irrespective of the time of repayment. For example, if a firm borrows $1000 and keeps that amount in cash throughout a five year period which experienced a constant rate of annual inflation of 10 per cent, it would sustain no loss, although the lender would. The gain which the firm makes at the expense of the creditor exactly offsets the loss sustained by it through the holding of cash. The position would be as shown in Table 11.1.

Table 11.1
Effect of borrowing as a 'hedge' against inflation

1 End of year	2 Dollars ($)	3 Loan	4 Gain at the expense of creditor	5 Loss in purchasing power by holding cash	6 Cash
1	1	1000	100	100	1000
2	2	1000	110	110	1000
3	3	1000	121	121	1000
4	4	1000	133	133	1000
5	5	1000	146	146	1000

Whether the borrower gains or not will depend on a number of other factors. First, since money can be either left idle or invested, the gain or loss will depend on what the borrower does with the borrowed money. Second, there is an expense or interest associated with borrowings and, therefore, interest payments also have to be taken into account in determining net gain or loss. Third, if the interest on loans is an allowable deduction for tax purposes, tax rates will also affect the net gain or loss. Although borrowing is a 'hedge' against inflation, it does not necessarily mean that the borrower will gain. Whether the borrower gains or loses will be determined by the combined effect of all the factors mentioned above.

Alternative approaches to price variation problems

Two fundamentally different approaches have been taken in different countries at different times to reflect the effect of inflation in financial statements. One can be characterised as comprehensive, the other as piecemeal. Under a comprehensive approach, all or at least the main elements of the financial statements affected by inflationary price movements are modified from their original amounts. Examples are CPP, RPA, CCA and CoCoA. Under a piecemeal approach only selected elements will be modified. Examples are the procedure of provision for the increased cost of asset replacement, revaluation of assets, last-in-first-out (LIFO) inventory method and accelerated depreciation method. Details of these approaches are complex. Only their main features are discussed in this section.

Piecemeal approaches

Provision for increased cost of asset replacement

Under this method a provision is made for the increased cost of asset replacement due to inflation by transferring a proportion of reported surplus to a reserve specially created for the purpose. This method was popular in the UK in the early 1950s.

One of the major defects of this procedure is that it says nothing about the effects of inflation on balance sheet figures; it is solely concerned with making increased provisions for asset replacement.

Revaluation of assets

The object of this method is to bring the book values of individual assets up to date by periodic revaluations so that they approximate changes in market values of those assets. In countries such as the UK, Australia and New Zealand, revaluation is not specifically required by company legislation, but the flexibility of the law permits its adoption; whereas in some other countries such as Argentina, Brazil and Chile, recent legislation has made revaluation compulsory in respect of certain types of assets.

Accelerated depreciation and LIFO

Accelerated depreciation methods and LIFO inventory methods can also be mentioned under piecemeal approaches to inflation accounting. These two methods have almost the same effects on financial calculations. Although both methods result in more current costs being matched against current revenues, they do not cause any change towards current amounts in the balance sheet. In a period of rising prices, these practices will have the effect of creating secret reserves to the extent of the difference between the past costs and the current costs as at the date of the statement. In the case of LIFO, it tends to understate the closing figure for stocks, and hence to give a lower current ratio than if the prices used were contemporary prices. Similarly, when prices are falling, it tends to give an artificially high current ratio. Neither of these methods make any concession to the diminishing purchasing power of the monetary unit.

Finally, adjustment of one or two elements of expense such as depreciation and cost of goods sold, while leaving others unadjusted, is not sufficient to represent the impact of price changes on a firm's finances.

Comprehensive approaches

Current purchasing power accounting

Under CPP accounting, non-monetary assets are adjusted by an index of changes in the general level of prices; all items in the income statement are adjusted by using the same index; gains and losses in monetary items, that is cash, receivables and payables which result from changes in the purchasing power of money are recorded additionally to the other conventional items in the income statement. According to the Provisional Statement of Standard Accounting Practice 7 (PSSAP 7), the method is justified on the grounds that, 'It is important that managements and other users of financial accounts should be in a position to appreciate the effects of inflation on the business with which they are concerned' (para. 3).

The degree of objectivity under CPP accounting is virtually the same as for HCA, apart from the selection of the index. Ease of verification is also similar. The effect of this method is to maintain purchasing power capital instead of financial or nominal capital. The income figure becomes a somewhat better guide to economic performance than that yielded by the historical cost model because CPP accounting attempts to measure income in such a fashion that it represents the maximum amount of resources that could be distributed during a given period, while maintaining the firm's purchasing power at the end of the period as it was at the beginning. However, the adjusted cost figure for particular assets may not be a good indicator of their current value, although it is usually better in times of inflation than the unadjusted cost figure.

However, CPP accounting fails to reflect the full effects of the price changes occurring in a period of inflation because it covers only one of the two effects of inflationary price changes mentioned above. Under CPP accounting it is assumed that no change in purchasing power arises from the investment in non-monetary assets. Accordingly, it quantifies only the purchasing power losses and gains arising from net monetary assets. For example, the PSSAP 7 says: 'holders of non-monetary assets are assumed neither to gain nor to lose purchasing power by reason only of inflation as changes in the price of these assets will tend to compensate for any changes in the purchasing power of the pound' (para. 7). But it is improper to make a general assumption such as the above because it is true only if the prices of the assets of any firms tend to move in the same direction and at the same rate as the general price level index. It is also false to assume that firms having the same monetary items are affected equally by the events of an inflationary period when the composition of their non-monetary items is different.

If the aim is to discover how the purchasing power of an original investment has changed over a period, adjustments to original costs by using a price level index are not going to help make that discovery because it does not give any information about the purchasing power of the net assets at the balancing date, though this is essential for the purpose. To provide that information it is first necessary to find the amount of money or money equivalent of assets possessed independently of the book figures, but CPP accounting does not require such a thing.

The events of recent years have demonstrated the most serious faults of historical cost accounting and inadequacies of the CPP approach. For example, if the price of an asset has been moving in the opposite direction to the general price level, such an adjustment does not make any sense at all. Electronic products provide a classic example in this respect. In spite of inflation, the prices of these products have declined dramatically in recent years. If, for example, the price of a particular model has decreased today to $600 from $1000 last year, no sensible decision can be made by adjusting the last year's price by a general price index, just because there has been an increase in the general level of prices.

Under CPP accounting there is no change in the principles on which the financial statements are conventionally prepared and they will continue to be based on historical costs. Therefore, many of the existing defects of conventional accounting reports are likely to continue, in spite of the process of conversion.

Replacement price accounting

Accounting systems designed to account for current values or changes in specific prices are collectively called current value accounting. These include RPA, CCA and CoCoA.

Much of the discussion on current value accounting has been centred on different versions of RPA, the object of which has variously been interpreted as 'to replace physical assets', 'to replace physical productive capacity', 'to replace operating capability' and so on. The RPA model is aimed at charging the current replacement costs of factors of production, particularly inventories and plant services, to gross revenue. Under this system any holding gains arising from the restatement of assets at replacement prices are not included in income calculations, but are treated as reserves not available for distribution.

Unlike HCA, which ignores specific price changes, and CPP accounting, which supposes that the specific prices of all nonmonetary assets change at the same rate, RPA takes changes in the prices of particular assets into account. But as a method of representing the full consequences of inflationary price changes, RPA does not escape the criticism of being partial. It is partial because it tends to disregard the effects of inflation on the significance of the monetary unit in which all financial statement items are represented, and to deal only with the rising purchase costs to a firm of engaging in future transactions.

If the aim is to discover the financial result from events which have occurred up to a particular point of time, it is necessary to find out the financial position at that time. Financial position is the position of a firm in respect of its present assets and equities. However, one could argue that the RPA balance sheet does not represent the current financial position because, in any form of RPA accounting, the figures given for assets are not representative of money equivalents of assets currently held. Asset amounts under RPA are the prices that a firm would have to pay if it did not already have those assets. Such amounts are dependent upon the present intentions of the managers, for example assets are valued at replacement price if replacement is intended, and at net realisable value if replacement is not thought to be necessary to the continuance of operations. The intentions of managers do not determine the present state of a firm. It is the relationship that exists between the firm and the rest of the environment, quite independent of the managers' intentions, which determines the present state of a firm. The relevance of the figures arrived at on the basis of managers' intentions to discover the consequences of what has happened in the past could also be questioned. As Gray and Wells (1973) state:

> Replacement cost is irrelevant to any ex-post measure of a firm's present financial position in respect of assets actually currently possessed. If income is a measure of the change in a firm's position between two points of time (that is, an increase in its wealth) then replacement cost is also irrelevant to that measure. (pp. 166–167)

Current cost accounting

The more widely used and discussed version of current value accounting is known as CCA, which is a variation of RPA. In 1975 the British Government's Inflation Accounting Committee (Sandilands) recommended a fundamental change from historical cost convention to 'value to the business' in financial statement preparation. Subsequently, in a number of countries the accounting profession has issued pronouncements dealing with the supplemental disclosure of current cost accounting information. In the following discussion, reference is frequently made to the Sandilands Report.

The CCA model is aimed at (a) eliminating from operating profit those gains arising on stock appreciation and (b) charging by way of depreciation an amount based on the 'value to the business' of the asset consumed during the accounting period. Figure 11.4 shows how the value to the business of an asset is arrived at under CCA.

Figure 11.4
Calculation of value to the business

Value to the business	When valuations are			Value to the business
Lower of — RP, Higher of — PV, NRV	NRV > PV > RP			RP
	NRV > RP > PV			RP
	PV > RP > NRV			RP
	PV > NRV > RP			RP
	RP > PV > NRV			PV
	RP > NRV > PV			NRV

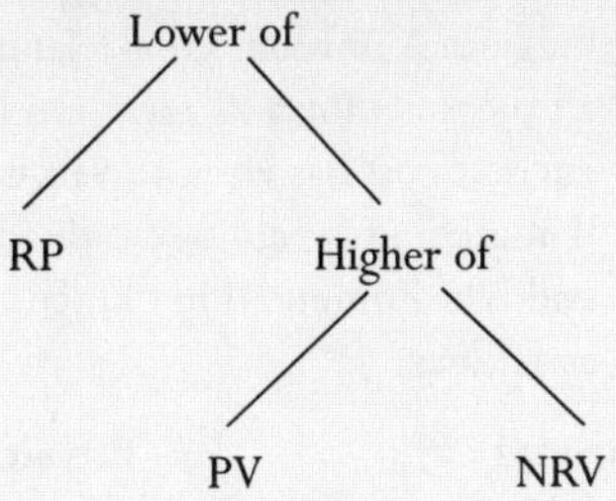

Value to the business is calculated by reference to replacement price, either by reference to specific market prices or by expert direct valuation. In some cases appropriate price indices specific to some particular class of asset may be used, particularly for less significant items. In those instances where a company would not logically replace an asset, for example where replacement cost exceeds the higher of net realisable value or the present value, or the present value of future cash flows expected to accrue from the asset, a different method could be adopted. However, as shown in Figure 11.4, current cost will be equal to the replacement price of the asset in the majority of cases.

The CCA model views income as the amount of resources that could be distributed during a given period, while maintaining a company's productive capacity or physical capital. One way to achieve this is to adjust a firm's original net assets position to reflect the current cost at the end of the period.

The CCA model generally uses the nominal dollar as the unit of measurement in the same way as the HCA model without adjustment for changes in its purchasing power. The routine recording of transactions is also the same as in the HCA model. Differences arise from the capital maintenance concept used under CCA, which is aimed at maintaining productive capacity or operating capability. This leads to periodic adjustments for changes in the replacement cost of inventories and fixed assets. Cost of goods sold is arrived at by adjusting opening inventories to reflect the current (replacement) cost at the end of the period. In times of rising prices this results in a holding gain and also a lower operating profit. In this model the holding gain is treated not as income but as a necessary direct addition to owners' equity. Similarly, fixed assets are restated each period at their current (replacement) cost. Depreciation expense is based on the current cost, while increases in replacement cost, period by period, are treated as direct additions to owners' equity. There is divided opinion as to whether this model should recognise gains or losses on holding monetary resources or having financial obligations measured in financial terms during periods in which changes have occurred in the purchasing power of the dollar.

Edwards and Bell (1961) provide the rationale for RPA and CCA. It is based on the premise that current cost is a measure of the cost of the services embodied in the actual asset owned by the company. They assume that the present production process will not change but continue. The un-realised holding gains represent actual economic phenomena occurring in the current period, and therefore something which

should be recognised. There is sufficient objective evidence to support the price changes. They also argue that operating profit based on current cost is an indication that the firm is making a positive long run contribution to the economy, and that the production process in use by the firm is effective (pp.98–99).

The main difference between the financial capital concept under HCA and the physical capital concept under CCA is whether or not holding gains (losses) should be included in income. This problem is explained in the following example.

Example

A begins operations with $5000 cash on 1 January and immediately purchases 500 units for $10 each. On 31 January she sells all the units for $18 each. On this date the current cost has risen to $15 a unit. Assume that income is paid out as dividends at the end. The computation of income would be as follows:

	Financial capital view	Physical capital view
Sales revenue (500 × $18)	9000	9000
Cost of sales (500 × $15)	7500	7500
Current operating profit	1500	1500
Holding gain (500 × $5)	2500	–
Payable as dividends	4000	1500

The firm had 500 units at the beginning and, according to the physical capital maintenance concept under CCA, it must be able to purchase 500 units at the end of the period at $15 each if capital is to be maintained. For this purpose the firm needs $2500 more at the end of the period to maintain its beginning position of capital. If $4000 were paid as dividends the company would have only $5000 at the end and could purchase only 333 units in February. Therefore, the $2500 is not a holding gain, but a capital maintenance adjustment.

Under the CCA model certain

adjustments are required to be made in the preparation of financial statements. They include the following:

1 *Depreciation adjustment* — This will be the difference between historical cost depreciation and current cost depreciation for the accounting period.
2 *Cost of sales adjustment* — This is meant to represent the differences between the value to the business of the stock consumed in the period and the historical cost of the same stock.
3 *Monetary working capital adjustment* — This is an adjustment to debtors and creditors calculated in the same way as

the COS adjustment. (Cash is excluded from the calculation.)

4   *Gearing adjustment* — Capital gearing is the relationship between debt and equity. The adjustment has the effect of reducing the MWC, COS and depreciation adjustments if a proportion of the net operating assets is financed by net borrowings.

However, since CCA is a variant of RPA, it is subjected to most of the criticism applied to RPA. One of the fundamental defects of CCA as proposed in the Sandilands Report is that, although the committee which produced the report was described as the 'Inflation Accounting Committee' and the report itself claims that it constitutes a comprehensive system of accounting for inflation (para. 535), it does not deal with the most distinctive feature of inflation, namely the rise in the general level of prices and the corresponding fall in the general purchasing power of money. The report makes its stand clear in this respect when it argues that the computation of profit should take no account of losses or gains on monetary items.

Furthermore, under CCA the calculations in respect of the financial result and position of a firm are made on the basis of unrealistic assumptions regarding the value of money. According to the Sandilands Report, 'the value (or purchasing power) of money as a medium of exchange changes in inverse proportion to the changes in price of the items on which it is spent' (para. 40). But this is contrary to the common usage of the notion. The value or purchasing power of money expressed in terms of a general index of prices does not refer to any specific goods or persons. It refers only to the quality of money as the medium of exchange. The report further assumes that a general index of prices is of little practical use to any particular individual or entity (para. 42). This is not acceptable either for, contrary to what the report assumes, changes in the value of money affect every

monetary unit or its equivalent spent, received or held by all individuals and entities, in the same way.

In the Sandilands Report capital is regarded as the capitalised value of future net cash inflows and profit is defined as 'the discounted net present value of all future net cash flows at the end of the year, less the discounted net present value of the future net cash flows at the beginning of the year, plus the net cash flow arising within the year after making adjustments for the introduction of new capital during the year' (para. 100). But, since the figures resulting from the processes of the above calculations are the products of the personal expectations about future inflows and outflows and the choice by somebody of a discount rate, they cannot be regarded as reflecting the consequences of the price movements on a firm's past performance or its current position.

Sterling and Lemke (1982) criticise the physical capital concept under CCA. They argue that income under this concept is meaningful only if the following conditions are met: (a) the firm continues to replace identical units; (b) it faces continuously increasing costs; (c) it buys and sells in different markets; and (d) it is fully invested in the physical units. If any one of these conditions is not met, serious measurement problems are encountered (see Kam, 1990, pp.422–426).

Because the concept of physical capital maintenance cannot be defined operationally in simple terms, the output of this model is less easily explained than that of the HCA model. Another issue is the allocation problem described by Thomas (1974). Allocation continues to be an issue under CCA as it is under HCA. Instead of allocating historical cost, the allocation here is of current cost.

Chambers (1976) maintains that the notion of value to the business overlooks a number of other reasons for value. Assets are valuable to a business for:

- the use that can be made of them
- the borrowing that can be based on them
- the cash they may bring in and
- the potential hedge against inflation in the case of non-monetary assets.

There are different variations of CCA, for example 'real' CCA and 'geared' CCA. Under real CCA, an attempt is made to combine specific price changes to maintain purchasing power of share-holders (for example, FAS 33 in the USA has this kind of approach). It is assumed that under geared CCA loans will be forthcoming when replacement is to be made, and that only the assets financed by equity are to be maintained (for example, SSAP 16 in the UK has this kind of approach).

Continuously contemporary accounting

The CoCoA model is based on the adaptive behaviour of business entities, which implies a continual attempt by them to adjust to the changing environmental cir-cumstances. The rationale for CoCoA is fully explained in Chambers (1966). MacNeal (1939) and Sterling (1970) undertook different approaches in their analysis of accounting and arrived at the same conclusion: exit prices of assets should be used in financial statements. MacNeal took an historical perspective and Sterling examined the type of decisions users of financial statements are likely to make by using a very simple example of a wheat trader.

The rationale for CoCoA can be sum-marised as follows. Adaptive behaviour is essential for the attainment and mainten-ance of given levels of satisfaction of the expectations of the interested parties asso-ciated with the entity. In the last analysis survival of the entity depends on the amount of cash it can command. To con-tinue in business a firm must have the capability to act in the market or to engage in transactions. This capability is represented by its financial position, which is the relationship between the money amounts of its assets, liabilities and owners' equity. In a market economy the money amounts of assets and liabilities can be determined objectively by reference to market prices. But the only way to find current cash equivalents of assets and, hence, the capability to act in the market, is through market selling prices of those assets. Adaptive behaviour, therefore, calls for knowledge of the cash and cash equiva-lents of the entity's net assets. According to Chambers (1966), 'the single financial property which is uniformly relevant at a point of time for all possible future actions in markets is the market selling price or realizable price of any or all goods held' (p.92).

The CoCoA model requires the revi-sion of asset values to their current cash equivalents (defined as their market resale price if disposed of in the ordinary course of business) at the end of each period. The *price variation adjustments* arising from asset revaluations are combined with the trad-ing results in arriving at the periodic income. In addition, an adjustment is also made for the effects of general price level change, called the *capital maintenance adjustment*, which also forms part of the income determination process. The capital maintenance adjustment is arrived at by multiplying the opening total of net assets by the proportionate change in the gen-eral price index during the period. For example, if opening net assets were $100 000 and the index moved from 100 to 110 during the period, the adjustment would be 100 000 × 10/100 = 10 000. This would be debited to capital main-tenance adjustment and credited to *capital maintenance reserve*. Income is the sum of the total net sales revenue, price variation adjustment and capital maintenance adjustment. The process of income deter-mination under CoCoA is shown in Figure 11.5.

Figure 11.5
Income (profit) determination under CoCoA

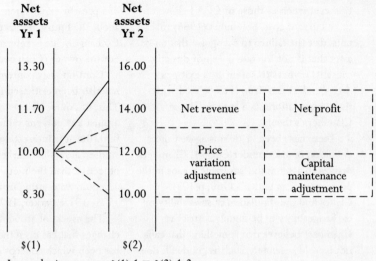

In purchasing power, $(1) 1 = $(2) 1.2

Source: Chambers (1975) (cover illustration). See also Chambers (1976, p.162)

Since each set of financial statements is expressed in the current or dated dollars applicable at the end of the period, CoCoA is more logically consistent than any of the other accounting models. While it attempts to eliminate the distortions caused by general price level changes, it also reflects the changes in specific prices.

Chambers considers the question of additivity to be a key factor in support of CoCoA. A prominent feature of this system is its demand that only a single characteristic, the CCE of assets and liabilities, be measured. It is argued that the purchase price of an asset cannot be added to an amount of cash if the total is to be meaningful. The total must pertain to the firm's ability to enter and engage in transactions to be able to buy and sell.

Another feature is that, under CoCoA, the financial statements are allocation free (Thomas, 1974, pp.112–114). The income statement is not a report of changes in allocated amounts, but of asset inflows and changes in the exit values of a firm's assets and liabilities in a given period. Net income displays the amount of change in purchasing power of the net assets, excluding additional investments by and distributions to owners.

However, most accountants seem to think that CoCoA is too radical. It has been criticised for using exit prices for assets on the grounds that there may be disputes where assets are unique, not readily sold or subject to major price variation depending upon the quantity sold or the combination in which assets are sold. It has also been criticised for what is described as divergence from reality in a situation where large and potentially fruitful assets are treated as having zero value because they do not have a selling price. Edwards (1975, p.240) claims that using exit prices leads to anomalous revaluations on acquisition because of transportation costs, installation and removal charges and imperfect access to markets. Immediately after the purchase of a new machine, its value usually falls so that it is less than acquisition cost.

Mattesich (1971) accuses Sterling of 'chopping off so much of reality until a narrow pattern emerges satisfying a particular view'.

Another criticism directed against the

CoCoA model is that it ignores the concept of value in use. The advocates of HCA believe such value is represented by acquisition cost whereas those of CCA believe it to be current cost. Solomons (1966) maintains that the failure to recognise that an asset that is not for sale does not directly cause its owners to suffer if its exit price drops, unless this drop is associated with their expectations, is a serious flaw in Chambers's theory.

There have been criticisms against the definition of assets under CoCoA. Chambers defines an asset as the 'severable means in the possession of an entity' (1966, p.103). Critics find the stipulation of severability or exchangeability to be unduly restrictive. Chambers believes that something that cannot be sold separately, such as goodwill, does not help the firm assess its capability to adapt to a changing environment. Critics claim that exchangeability emphasises only one way to ascertain value. A firm can consider an asset to have value because of its use in the business rather than its sale. The general meaning of economic value has to do with an object's scarcity and utility, not its exchangeability. (For a criticism of the exit price system see Larson and Schattke, 1966; Iselin, 1968 Friedman; 1978). In defence, Chambers argues that, although in principle every asset has a value in exchange and a value in use, exchange or market value represents the firm's capability to act in the market, to buy things, to pay debts at a given date and so on. Value in use is basically a calculated amount of a present expectation. It represents beliefs about the future, not facts of the present. Exchange value is determined by the market, not the owner (Chambers, 1975, p.21).

Continuously contemporary accounting has also been criticised for being subjective. This, of course, is a common criticism against any current value accounting system. But it is interesting that research studies show that market prices are more objective than the methods under generally accepted accounting principles (McKeown, 1971; 1973; Parker, 1975).

The aspect of accounting for price changes that has been the most controversial has been which concept of capital maintenance to use and the related treatment of monetary items. The concept underlying the systems of historical cost/constant dollar accounting is financial capital measured in units of constant purchasing power. The concept of capital maintenance underlying the current cost accounting systems is physical capital or operating capacity. However, considerable variations exist among countries on how this concept is applied. Under CoCoA the concept of capital maintenance relates to real purchasing power. The concepts of capital maintenance under different accounting models are illustrated in Table 11.2.

Table 11.2
Asset valuation and capital maintenance

Capital maintenance Asset valuation	Money/ nominal capital	Physical/ operating capability capital	Real/ purchasing power capital	Geared physical capital	Economic value capital
Historical cost	X				
Price-level adjusted historical cost		X			
Replacement or current cost		X	X	X	
Selling price			X		
Economic value					X

The price variation accounting calculations involved under various accounting models are illustrated in the following examples.

Example 1
New Zealand Wine Company **(Historical cost accounting)**
Profit and loss Account for T2

	$
Sales	1500
Less Historical cost of goods sold	1000
Profit	500

Facts:
Purchases = 100 bottles at $10.00
Sales   = 100 bottles at $15.00

Balance sheet at beginning of T1

	$		$
Cash	1000	Proprietor's capital	500
		Bank	500
	1000		1000

Assumptions:
Interest not payable on bank loan
Purchases of stocks at beginning of T1
Sales at end of T1

At end of T1

	$		$
Cash	1500	Proprietor's capital	500
		Plus Profit	500
		Total capital	1000
		Bank loan	500
	1500		1500

(General purchasing power accounting)
Profit and loss Account for T1

	$
Sales	1500
Less Historical cost of goods sold in current $	1100
Operating profit	400
Add Gain on borrowing	50
Total 'real' profit	450

Facts:
Inflation = 10%

Balance sheet at end of T1

Cash	$ 1500	Proprietor's capital	$ 500
		Plus Capital maintenance reserve	50
		Plus Profit	450
		Total capital	1000
		Bank loan	500
	1500		1500

(Current cost accounting)
Profit and loss Account for T1

	$
Sales	1500
Less Current cost of goods sold	1250
Profit	250

Facts:
Current replacement cost = $12.50 per bottle

Balance sheet at end of T1

Cash	$ 1500	Proprietor's capital	$ 500
		Plus Capital maintenance reserve	250
		Plus Profit	250
		Total capital	1000
		Bank loan	500
	1500		1500

('Real' current cost accounting)
Profit and loss Account for T1

	$	$
Sales		1500
Less Current cost of goods sold		1250
Operating profit		250
Add Real holding gain on stock (1250 − 1100)	150	
Gain on borrowing	50	
		200
Total 'real' profit		450

Note:
Inflation = 10%

Balance sheet at end of T1

	$		$
Cash	1500	Proprietor's capital	500
		Plus Capital maintenance reserve	50
		Plus Profit	450
		Total capital	1000
		Bank loan	500
	1500		1500

('Geared' current cost accounting)
Profit and loss Account for T1

	$
Sales	1500
Less Current cost of goods sold	1250
Operating profit	250
Add Gearing adjustment	125(a)
Geared profit	375

Notes:
Gearing = Proportion of loan finance
Gearing adjustment = Proportion of holding gains financed by loan
Inflation 10%

(a) Shareholders' proportion of realised gains $250 \times \frac{1}{2} = 125$

Balance sheet at end of T1

	$		$
Cash	1500	Proprietor's capital	500
		Plus Capital maintenance reserve	125
		Plus Profit	375
		Total capital	1000
		Bank loan	500
	1500		1500

('Real' selling price accounting)
Profit and loss Account for T1

	$
Historical cost profit	500
Asset price adjustments	–
Profit	500
Less Capital maintenance adjustment	50
Total 'real' profit	450

Note:
Capital maintenance adjustment = Proprietor's capital adjusted for inflation

Balance sheet at end of T1

	$		$
Cash	1500	Proprietor's capital	500
		Plus Capital maintenance reserve	50
		Plus Profit	450
			1000
		Bank loan	500
	1500		1500

Example 2
New Zealand Wine Company **(Historical cost accounting)**
Profit and loss Account for T1

	$
Sales	1500
Less Historical cost of goods sold	1000
Trading profit	500
Less Depreciation	100
Profit	400

Facts:
Purchases = 120 bottles at $10.00
Sales   = 100 bottles at $15.00
Purchase of machine at $500
Proprietor's capital increased to $1500

Assumptions:
Purchase of stocks and machine at beginning of T1
Sales at end of T1
FIFO inventory flow
The machine is to be depreciated over a period of 5 years, using the straight line method

Balance sheet at beginning of T1

	$		$
Cash	2000	Proprietor's capital	1500
		Bank loan	500
	2000		2000

Assumption:
Interest not payable on bank loan

Balance sheet at end of T1

	$			$
Cash		1800	Proprietor's capital	1500
Stock		200	*Plus* Profit	400
Machine	500			
Less Depreciation	100			1900
		400	Bank loan	500
		2400		2400

(General purchasing power accounting)
Profit and loss Account for T1

	$
Sales	1500
Less Historical cost of goods sold in current $	1100
	400
Less Historical cost depreciation in current $	110
	290
Add Gain on net monetary items	20(a)
Total 'real' profit	310

Facts:
Inflation = 10%
Note:
Gain on net monetary items = loss on cash at beginning of $30 + gain on borrowings of $50.

(a) Loss on cash $(2000 - 500 = 300 \times {}^{10}\!/_{100})$ = (30)
     Gain on borrowing $(500 \times {}^{10}\!/_{100})$ = 50
     = 20

Balance sheet at end of T1

	$	$		$
Cash		1800	Proprietor's capital	1500
Stock		220	*Plus* Capital maintenance reserve	150
Machine	550			
Less Depreciation	110		*Plus* Profit	310
		440		1960
			Bank loan	500
		2460		2460

(Current cost accounting)
Profit and loss Account for T1

	$
Sales	1500
Less Current cost of goods sold	1250
Profit	250
Less Current cost depreciation	120
Operating profit	130

Facts:
Current replacement costs:
  Stock   = $12.50 per bottle
  Machine = $600
Assumption:
  The machine is to be depreciated over a period of 5 years, using the straight line method

---

Balance sheet at end of T1

		$			$
Cash		1800	Proprietor's capital		1500
Stock		250	*Plus* Capital maintenance		
Machine	600		Stock	300(a)	
Less Depreciation	120		Machine	100(b)	
		480		——	400
			Plus Profit		130
			Total capital		2030
			Bank loan		500
		2530			2530

(a) 250 (realised) + 50 (unrealised) = 300
(b) 20 (realised) + 80 (unrealised) = 100

('Real' current cost accounting)
Profit and loss Account for T1

	$	$
Sales		1500
Less Current cost of goods sold		1250
Less Current cost depreciation		250
		120(a)
Add Real holding gains		130
Stock	180(b)	
Machine	50(c)	
Net gain on borrowing	20(d)	
		250
Total 'real' profit		380

Facts:
Inflation 10%

Balance sheet at end of T1

	$		$
Cash	1800	Proprietor's capital	1500
Stock	250	*Plus* Capital maintenance reserve	150(e)
Machine	600		
Less Depreciation	120	*Plus* Profit	380
	480		2030
		Bank loan	500
	2530		2530

(a) $600 \times \frac{1}{5} = 120$
(b) $(120 \times 12.50) - (120 \times 11) = 180$
(c) $600 - 550 = 50$
(d) Loss on cash = $300 \times \frac{10}{100}$ = (30)
   Gain on borrowing $(500 \times \frac{10}{100})$ = $\underline{50}$
   $ \underline{20}$

(e) Machine   100
    Stock $\underline{50}$
            $\underline{150}$

('Geared' current cost accounting: the UK model)
Profit and loss Account for T1

	$
Sales	1500
Less Current cost of goods sold	1250
	250
Less Current cost depreciation	120
	130
Less Monetary working capital adjustment	375(a)
Operating loss	(245)
Add Gearing adjustment	161(b)
Geared loss	84

Note: Monetary working capital = Debtors *less* Creditors
(a) $1500 \times \frac{1}{4} = 375$
(b) $[250 \text{ (COGS)} + 20 \text{ (Dep.)} + 375 \text{ (MWC)}] \times \frac{1}{4} = 161$
Assumption:
All sales were on credit

Balance sheet at end of T1

	$			$
Cash	300			
Debtors	1500	Proprietor's capital		1500
Stock	250	*Plus* Capital maintenance reserve		
Machine	600			
Less Depreciation	120	480	Stock	300
			Machine	100
			MWCA	375
			Gearing	(161)	614
			Less Loss		(84)
			Total capital		2030
			Bank loan		500
	2530				2530

('Real' selling price accounting)
Profit and loss Account for T1

	$	$
Trading profit		500
Less Asset price adjustments		
Stock	+ 100	
Machine	− 150	
		50
		450
Less Capital maintenance adjustment		150
Total 'real' profit		300

Facts:
Selling prices
Stock   = $15.00
Machine = $350
Inflation = 10%

Balance sheet at end of T1

	$		$
Cash	1800	Proprietor's capital	1500
Stock	300	*Plus* Capital maintenance reserve	150
Machine	500	*Plus* Profit	300
Less Price adjustment	150		
	350		1950
		Bank loan	500
	2450		2450

(Adapted from Gray, 1983)

Price variation accounting: different experiences

Literature on price variation accounting has been available in English-speaking countries for more than fifty years (e.g. Sweeney, 1936), although it was not until the 1970s that this subject became of widespread interest. In the 1970s there was a dramatic increase in the rate of inflation in most countries and this produced renewed interest in the effects of price changes on accounting. During this period several countries engaged in different experiments to address the associated issues. It appears that, as the inflation rates of many countries began to fall in the mid-1980s, the interest in price variation accounting has faded away. The experiences of different countries in this area are briefly discussed in this section.

The United Kingdom

Some professional pronouncements on inflation accounting were issued in the UK in the period following the end of World War II. However, they had virtually no effect on practice. In the 1950s and early 1960s, since the rate of inflation dropped to a low level of about 4 per cent per annum, there was no great interest in inflation accounting during that period. In the late 1960s and early 1970s, particularly after the world energy crisis, the situation changed again. As a result, the ASC produced three documents on inflation accounting (ASC 1971; 1973; 1974). All were concerned about changes in the general purchasing power of money.

The PSSAP 7 (ASC, 1974) showed only a small number of changes from the 1971 and 1973 documents. The major recommendations contained in it were:

a   Companies will continue to keep their records and present their basic annual accounts in historical pounds, i.e. in terms of the value of the pound at the time of each transaction and revaluation.

b   In addition, all listed companies should present to their shareholders a supplementary statement in terms of the value of the pound at the end of the period to which the accounts relate.

c   The conversion of the figures in the basic accounts into the figures in the supplementary statement should be by means of a general index of the purchasing power of the pound.

d   The standard requires the directors to provide in a note to the supplementary statement an explanation of the basis on which it has been prepared and it is desirable that directors should comment on the significance of the figures. (para. 12)

The Sandilands Report recommended that as soon as practicable all companies should adopt an accounting system to be known as CCA, the main features of which were:

a   Money is the unit of measurement.

b   Assets and liabilities are shown in the balance sheet at a valuation.

c   Operating profit is struck after charging the value to the business of assets consumed during the period, thus excluding holding gains from profit and showing them separately. (para. 519)

On the basis of these recommendations, the ASC published an exposure draft (ED 18) in November 1976. However, the members of the profession (particularly ICAEW) did not like the idea of making CCA statements compulsory on the grounds that the proposals were extremely complicated and subjective. As a result of the objections the ASC issued a new set of proposals in November 1977 under the title *Inflation Accounting — an Interim Recommendation*. These proposals, which became known as the *Hyde Committee Guidelines*, were extremely brief (only twelve pages compared with the ninety-four page ED 18) and were concerned only with the provision of supplementary profit statements for companies listed on the stock exchange.

Three adjustments were suggested. The cost of sales and depreciation adjustments were (as in ED 18) based on the difference between historical and CCA figures. In many companies these two adjustments had already been shown to reduce profits by a substantial amount. The third adjustment, the gearing adjustment, was based on the proposition that the effects of inflation accounting on profits will vary according to the capital gearing structure of the organisation.

The introduction of a gearing adjustment, which had not been included in the profit statement under the Sandilands Report and the ED 18 recommendations, was an acceptance by the ASC that monetary adjustments could not be completely ignored in an inflation accounting system. The suggested calculation in the case of an industrial company produced an 'add-back' to profit.

In April 1979 the ASC issued an exposure draft (ED 24), *Current Cost Accounting*. The recommendations contained in ED 24 were similar to those contained in the *Hyde Guidelines*. In March 1980 SSAP 16 was issued to apply to accounting periods starting on or after 1 January 1980. As in ED 24, the major recommendation was for the publication of a CCA profit statement and balance sheet.

The SSAP 16 required companies to publish CCA financial statements either as supplementary statements or as the main accounts, with the proviso that historical cost must also be provided. Most of the companies which complied with this recommendation have provided CCA data in supplementary form.

With the fall in the rate of inflation in the early and mid-1980s, the enthusiasm for SSAP 16 began to fade away and an increasing number of listed companies decided to stop publishing CCA data.

In July 1984 ED 35, *Accounting for the Effects of Changing Prices*, was issued. Its recommendations were similar to SSAP 16, although there were some changes of emphasis. However, because of the opposition which the new ED produced, it was abandoned. In 1985 SSAP 16 was removed from mandatory status and in 1988 withdrawn completely.

Table 11.3
The UK experience

	Historical cost adjusted for changes in the general price level (CPP)	Current value accounting
Theoretical roots	— Sweeney (1936) — ICAEW published *Accounting for Stewardship in Periods of Inflation* (1968)	— Bonbright (1937) — Edwards and Bell (1961) (distinction between holding and operating gains)
Implementation	— ED 8 (January 1973) — PSSAP 7 (May 1974) — Stop	— Sandilands (January 1974) — Sandilands Report (September 1975) — ED 18 (November 1976) — Compulsory CCA rejected by ICAEW members (July 1977) — Hyde Guidelines (November 1977) — ED 24 (April 1979) — SSAP 16 (March 1980) — SSAP 16 removed from mandatory list (1985) — SSAP 16 withdrawn (1988)

The USA

Most of the AICPA publications on inflation accounting have been concerned with general purchasing power (GPP or CPP) accounting. For example, in 1963 a detailed research study was produced entitled *Reporting the Financial Effects of Price Level Changes*. This created very little interest among business organisations, mainly due to the fact that the inflation rate at the time was below 3 per cent per annum.

Similar to many other countries, there was a renewed interest in the subject in the mid-1970s. In 1974 the FASB issued an exposure draft entitled *Financial Reporting in Units of General Purchasing Power*, suggesting that supplementary GPP financial statements should be provided, but the business community did not consider it to be cost effective. In addition, the SEC made it clear that it would prefer a reporting system based on replacement costs.

In 1976 the inflation accounting debate in the USA entered a new stage when the SEC published Accounting Series Release (ASR) No.190 which required the disclosure of replacement cost information by major listed companies in the return submitted to the SEC at the end of each financial year. The objective of this requirement was to provide information for investors to assist them in obtaining an understanding of the current costs of the business. There was no requirement that this information should be published in the annual reports for shareholders.

The SEC regulation did not get much support from the business sector, mainly because of the amount of time involved in preparing the replacement cost data and the doubtful value of such figures.

Following the publication of SFAC 1, which recommended that 'financial reporting should provide information that is useful to present and potential investors and creditors and other users in making rational investment, credit and similar decisions', the FASB decided to address the subject of inflation accounting. In December 1978 a new ED was published entitled *Financial Reporting and Changing Prices*. This document recommended that the major American companies should publish supplementary financial statements based on either general purchasing power or current cost principles.

In October 1979 the FASB issued FAS 33, *Financial Reporting and Changing Prices*. The major change from the 1978 ED was that both general purchasing power and current cost statements had to be published. The required GPP information was:

- income from continuing operations adjusted for the effects of general inflation
- the purchasing power gain or loss on net monetary items.

In addition, the following current cost information had to be disclosed:

- income from continuing operations on a current cost basis
- the current cost amounts of inventory and property, plant and equipment at the end of the fiscal year
- increases or decreases in current cost amounts of inventory and property, plant and equipment net of inflation.

In December 1984 a new ED was issued. This was similar to FAS 33, although the requirement for the publication of GPP data within the income statement was withdrawn. The new accounting standard, *Financial Reporting and Changing Prices: Elimination of Certain Disclosures* (FAS 82), was issued in November 1984 as an amendment of FAS 33. In December 1986 another standard, *Financial Reporting and Changing Prices* (FAS 89), was issued to supersede FAS 33. This standard makes voluntary the supplementary disclosure of current cost/constant purchasing power information.

Canada

In Canada accounting has been influenced by American and British ideas. Although the CICA made proposals in 1975 and in 1976 for supplementary GPP financial statements and current value accounting respectively, there was not enough support for these proposals to be implemented.

In December 1979 an ED entitled *Current Cost Accounting* was issued and this was followed by an accounting standard, *Reporting the Effects of Changing Prices,* in October 1982. The standard requires companies to publish supplementary inflation accounting data of CCA nature. This standard evoked very little response from the business community.

Australia

In 1975 the Mathews Committee which examined the Australian taxation system (*Report of the Committee of Inquiry into Inflation and Taxation*, 1975) recommended that the business taxation system should be adjusted for specific price changes. But the proposal did not get government support.

In December 1974 the AASC issued a preliminary ED, *A Method of Accounting for Changes in the Purchasing Power of Money*. A further preliminary ED, *A Method of Current Value Accounting,* was issued in June 1975.

In October 1976 a provisional statement entitled *Current Cost Accounting* (DPS 1.1) was issued as it appeared that the majority of Australian accountants preferred the current value accounting proposals. In August 1978 an amended provisional statement was issued. This was concerned only with the disclosure in supplementary form of CCA information about fixed assets, depreciation, inventories and the cost of goods sold.

In July 1978 a separate ED, *The Recognition of Gains and Losses on Holding Monetary Resources in the Context of Current Cost Accounting,* containing the recommendations concerning monetary items was issued. A revised exposure draft was issued in August 1979.

At the end of 1983 it was decided that an accounting standard would not be issued, primarily because of strong opposition in the business sector. However, a statement of accounting practice, *Current Cost Accounting* (SAP 1), was issued later to provide guidance for those companies producing CCA statements. In Australia SAPs do not have the same power as standards.

New Zealand

In December 1974 the NZSA issued an ED, *Accounting for Changes in the Purchasing Power of Money*, suggesting a CPP approach, but it did not generate much support. In August 1976 a new ED, *Accounting in Terms of Current Cost and Values* (ED 14), was issued.

Meanwhile, the government set up a special committee (the Richardson Committee) to look at all aspects of inflation accounting. The report of this committee was published in December 1976 entitled the *Report of the Committee of Inquiry into Inflation Accounting.*

The committee had the benefit of two major government-sponsored reports — the Sandilands Report in the UK and the Mathews Report in Australia. The recommendations of the Richardson Committee were in many respects similar to those contained in the two reports mentioned above. For example, it was recommended that revised cost of sales and depreciation figures should normally be based on current replacement costs. The approach on monetary items was, however, very different. It was suggested that an additional charge should be made against profits for the maintenance of the purchasing power of circulating monetary assets. Monetary liabilities were not to be included in this calculation. The revised profit figure after these adjustments was to be described as CCA operating profit. Further adjustments were then to be made to arrive at the profit attributable to the owners.

In 1978 the NZSA issued a guideline document (GU 1). An ED, *Current Cost Accounting* (ED 25), was issued in 1981. These documents were followed by an accounting standard, *Information Reflecting* the *Effects of Changing Prices* (CCA 1), in April 1982.

The standard required all companies which had securities listed on the New Zealand Stock Exchange to publish supplementary CCA statements for financial periods commencing on or after 1 April 1982. In the supplemental balance sheet all non-monetary assets are to be stated at their value to the business. The supplemental profit and loss account is to present two measures of profitability: the 'current cost operating profit of the enterprise' and the 'profit attributable to the owners'.

The recommendations contained in the New Zealand standard are similar to those contained in the UK standard (SSAP 16), although there are slightly different calculations of the monetary working capital and gearing adjustments.

The rate of compliance by New Zealand companies with this standard was very low. There was little response by government to this standard. As a result, in March 1986 CCA 1 was reduced to the status of a recommendation, Current Cost Accounting Recommendation 1.

Chapter summary

If accounting reports are to provide a true and fair view of the state of affairs of a business entity, the effects of price changes must be identified and accounted for in preparing such reports.

Different models have been developed to address the issues of price variation accounting. Since different accounting models are based on different behavioural assumptions, it is important that they should be evaluated in terms of those assumptions. For example, in the case of the RPA or CCA models, the assumption is that businesses will continue to do the same thing in the future, whereas in the case of the CoCoA model, adaptive behaviour of business entities is assumed. Business entities may or may not want to go in the same direction in the future as they have in the past if following the CoCoA model.

In the early 1970s there was a worldwide trend towards supplementary price level adjusted financial statements. In the late 1970s and early 1980s there was strong support for CCA statements. As the rates of inflation started to fall and reached low levels of less than 5 per cent per annum in the mid-1980s the interest in inflation accounting also faded away. It is likely that high rates of inflation will re-emerge in the 1990s. But have the accountants learnt from their past experience? It will be interesting to see how they respond next time around.

Essay and examination questions

11.1 Explain what is meant by price variation?

11.2 Why should accountants be concerned about price variations?

11.3 Evaluate the suitability of the conventional historical cost accounting model during periods of changing prices.

11.4 What are the salient features of each of the alternative accounting models that have been proposed to overcome the shortcomings of the historical cost model?

11.5 Among the alternative accounting models discussed in this chapter, what is the best model for dealing with the effects of price variations?

11.6 'Borrowing is a "hedge" against the adverse effects of inflation'. Explain and discuss.

11.7 New Zealand Wine Company
Facts for T2:
Purchases = 110 bottles at $12.50
Sales = 100 bottles at $18.00
Replacement costs:
Stock = $15.00
Machine = $800
Selling prices:
Stock = $18.00
Machine = $200
Inflation rate = 15%
Required: Prepare profit and loss accounts for T2 and balance sheets at end of T2 in accordance with the following accounting systems:
(a) Historical cost
(b) Current cost
(c) General purchasing power
(d) Real selling price.

References and additional reading

Accounting Standards Committee (1971). *Inflation and Accounts*. A discussion document and facts sheet. London: ASC.

Accounting Standards Committee (1973). *Accounting for Changes in the Purchasing Power of Money*. Exposure Draft No.8. London: ASC.

Accounting Standards Committee (1974). *Accounting for Changes in the Purchasing Power of Money*. A Provisional Statement of Standard Accounting Practice (PSSAP 7). London: ASC.

Accounting Standards Committee (1976). *Current Cost Accounting*. Exposure Draft No.18. London: ASC.

Bell, P. (1971). On current replacement costs and business income, in Sterling, R. (Ed.). *Asset Valuation and Income Determination*. Kansas: Scholars Book Co.

Bonbright, J.C. (1937). *The Valuation of Property*. (Reprint.) The Michie Company, 1965.

Chambers, R.J. (1966). *Accounting, Evaluation and Economic Behavior*. Englewood Cliffs, New Jersey: Prentice Hall.

Chambers, R.J. (1975). *Accounting for Inflation — Methods and Problems*. Sydney: University of Sydney.

Chambers, R.J. (1976). Accounting for inflation — Part or whole. *Accountants' Magazine,* March.

Edwards, E. (1975). The state of current value accounting. *The Accounting Review,* April.

Edwards, E.O. and Bell, P.W. (1961). *The Theory and Measurement of Business Income*. Berkeley and Los Angeles: University of California Press.

Friedman, L. (1978). Exit-Price Liabilities: An analysis of the alternatives. *The Accounting Review,* October.

Gray, S.J. (1983). *Invitation lecture on Inflation Accounting*. Belgium: Katholik University of Leuven. Belgium, November.

Gray, S.J. and Wells, M.C. (1973). Asset values and ex-post income. *Accounting and Business Research,* Summer.

Inflation Accounting Committee (Sandilands) (1975). *Report.* London: HMSO, Cmnd 6225.

Institute of Chartered Accountants in England and Wales (1968). *Accounting for Stewardship in Periods of Inflation.* London: ICAEW.

Institute of Chartered Accountants in England and Wales (1973). *Accounting for Changes in the Purchasing Power of Money,* ED 8. London: ICAEW.

Institute of Chartered Accountants in England and Wales (1974). *Accounting for Changes in Purchasing Power of Money,* PSSAP 7. London: ICAEW.

Institute of Chartered Accountants in England and Wales (1976). *Current Cost Accounting,* ED 18. London: ICAEW.

Institute of Chartered Accountants in England and Wales (1977). *Inflation Accounting — an Interim Recommendation* (Hyde Guidelines). London: ICAEW.

Institute of Chartered Accountants in England and Wales (1979). *Current Cost Accounting,* ED 24. London: ICAEW.

Iselin, E. (1968). Chambers on accounting theory. *The Accounting Review,* April.

Kam, V. (1990). *Accounting Theory.* John Wiley.

Larson, K. and Schattke, R. (1966). Current cash equivalent, additivity, and financial action. *The Accounting Review,* October.

McKeown, J. (1971). An empirical test of a model proposed by Chambers. *The Accounting Review,* January.

McKeown, J. (1973). Comparative application of market and cost based accounting models. *Journal of Accounting Research,* Spring.

MacNeal, K. (1939). *Truth in Accounting.* (Reprint.) Kansas: Scholars Books.

Mattesich, R. (1971). The market value method according to Sterling: A review article. *Abacus,* **7**(2).

Parker, J. (1975). Testing comparability and objectivity of Exit Value Accounting. *The Accounting Review,* July.

Slimmings, W. (1974). Inflation accounting. The text of an address given at a conference. *Accountants' Magazine,* June.

Solomons, D. (1966). Review Article. *Abacus,* December.

Sterling, R. (1970). *Theory of the Measurement of Enterprise Income.* Lawrence: University of Kansas Press.

Sterling, R. and Lemke, K. (Eds) (1982). *Maintenance of Capital: Financial Vs. Physical.* Kansas: Scholars Books.

Sweeney, H.W. (1936). *Stabilized Accounting.* (Reprint.) Holt, Rinehart and Winston, 1964.

Thomas, A. (1974). *The Allocation Problem.* Studies in Accounting Research No. 9, AAA.

Weston, F. (1971). Response to evidence for a Market Selling Price Accounting system, in R. Sterling (Ed.). *Asset Valuation and Income Determination.* Kansas: Scholars Books.

Chapter 12
Incremental financial disclosures

Learning objectives

After studying this chapter the reader will be able to:
- explain what is meant by incremental financial disclosures
- define debt defeasance and discuss the associated disclosure issues
- define segmental reporting and discuss the associated disclosure issues
- define employee reporting and discuss the associated disclosure issues
- define leases and executory contracts and discuss the associated disclosure issues
- define value added and discuss the associated disclosure issues
- define statements of future prospects and discuss the associated disclosure issues
- define brand valuation and discuss the associated disclosure issues
- consider the recent developments in New Zealand and overseas of incremental disclosure in financial statements.

Introduction

With the growth and expansion of business activities it has become necessary for financial statements to reflect the effects of those changes. However, since accounting is almost always reactive rather than proactive, it is only natural that at any given point in time there are issues of financial disclosure that are yet to be resolved. Furthermore, there can be other issues which have already been addressed in some countries but not in others. This chapter proposes to discuss some of those issues. The title 'Incremental financial disclosures' means that all the topics discussed involve incremental disclosures to conventional financial statements. The chapter is organised into seven sections: debt defeasance; segmental reporting; employee reports; leases and executory contracts; statements of value added; statements of future prospects; and accounting for brands. Human resource accounting is discussed in detail in Chapter 13.

Debt defeasance

Accounting for the varied kinds of debt instruments available to a business is challenging, but never more so than at the present time in the area of debt defeasance. Debt defeasance has gained the attention of

practitioners, standard-setting bodies and theorists in recent years because of the number of controversial issues surrounding its use. Proponents of debt defeasance view it as a new and important financial planning tool for management. However, others see debt defeasance as 'nothing more than balance-sheet cosmetics for hiding poor operating performance' (Chaney, 1985, p.54).

Given the importance of this emerging issue, this section will define and discuss the main forms of debt defeasance. It will evaluate the benefits and risks associated with the use of debt defeasance and briefly overview New Zealand's SSAP 26, *Accounting for Defeasance of Debt*. It will conclude by discussing some of the major conceptual issues involved.

Definition and types of debt defeasance

Before defining debt defeasance, the related term of 'extinguishment of debt' must be clarified. In general, extinguishment means to 'wipe out of existence' (*The Macquarie Dictionary*, 1991). Debts can be extinguished or removed from an entity's books in a number of ways.

(a) A debt can be paid off. This completes a loan transaction and relieves a debtor of any further obligations with respect to the debt.

(b) A debt can be extinguished by replacing it with another debt. However, as with (a) above, it completes the first debt transaction and the debtor is no longer obliged to make any further payments on the first debt.

(c) A debt can be legally extinguished or defeased. This relieves a debtor from the primary obligation of the debt such that it is unlikely that the debtor will be called upon to make future payments on the debt. Legal extinguishment has the implied consent of the creditor in question and may include forgiveness, assumption of the debt by a third party or through a legal judgement.

These three forms of extinguishing debt are legal and no controversy exists in the removal of the debt in question from the books. The controversy arises in the new way of removing debts from the books of the entity through in-substance debt defeasances.

Generally, defeasance means to nullify or make void. Accordingly, defeasance has been defined as the release of a debtor from the primary obligation for a debt and in-substance debt defeasance as a defeasance other than a legal defeasance (SSAP 26). In-substance debt defeasance differs from debt extinguishment in two important respects. First, there is no legal satisfaction of the debt and, second, the consent of the creditor is not necessary. However, for accounting purposes, the effect of an in-substance defeasance is similar to a legal defeasance in that the debt is permitted to be removed from the books of the debtor company as if it had been legally extinguished.

In-substance debt defeasance

In-substance debt defeasance attempts to achieve the same effects as a legal defeasance by effectively releasing a debtor from the primary obligation for a debt. In the 'trust' method the debtor is relieved from the

primary obligation for the debt when assets are irrevocably placed in a trust set up for the sole purpose of servicing and repaying the debt. The assets placed in the trust must be adequate to meet the servicing and repayment requirements of the debt. In the 'assumption' method, the debtor is relieved of the responsibility for the debt when a risk-free entity is nominated to assume the debt responsibilities (SSAP 26, para. 4.10).

Historically, in-substance defeasance (the 'trust' method) was first undertaken in the USA by the Exxon Corporation in 1982 when it retired US$515 million of debt by depositing US$312 million of government securities in a trust. The transaction generated sufficient funds to cover the repayment of both the interest and principal sum of the debt and added US$130 million to the earnings of Exxon (Walton, 1985).

The 'assumption' method of in-substance defeasance was used by Kellogg Co. shortly after the Exxon case to defease US$75 million worth of debt. Kellogg paid a total of US$65.6 million to several unnamed companies to assume the US$75 million debt. The presumption here is that the companies will invest the funds at a return sufficient to cover the interest and repayment of the Kellogg debt (Chaney, 1985).

Instantaneous in-substance defeasance

In instantaneous in-substance defeasance, debt is defeased at the same time that it is incurred. In other words, the debt is incurred for the purpose of reinvesting in higher yielding assets. To take advantage of interest rate differentials, this form usually makes it possible for a company to incur debt in one country and 'retire' it with higher yielding risk-free securities bought in another country, resulting in an instantaneous profit for the company.

An example of an instantaneous in-substance defeasance was performed by Pepsi Co. in 1984 when it issued debt denominated in deutschmarks on the

American bond market and simultaneously purchased higher interest yielding West German government securities to defease that debt. This resulted in an instant gain to the company without affecting its balance sheet (Deegan, 1985). The debt and asset never appeared in the balance sheet; only the instant gain made appeared in the income statement.

Debt defeasance as a financial planning tool

There are many alleged benefits of debt defeasance. Increasingly, debt defeasance is viewed as an important financial planning tool for management in that it provides an alternative means of retiring debt. For example, when the prevailing interest rate is high, defeasing a lower interest rate debt by placing funds in a riskless, but higher yielding, asset is more attractive than paying off the debt in cash. The company is able to retain the benefits of the lower interest rate of the debt.

Defeasance can also retire an entire debt in one transaction without the complications and costs associated with repurchasing the debt in the open market. In repurchasing in the open market, the company may not be able to redeem the entire debt and the debt's price may rise if the company attempts to repurchase a significant portion of its own debt (Bradbury, 1987). Defeasance also overcomes the possibility of violating the loan agreement covenants, especially where the company has no option of early redemption of the debt. Being a unilateral transaction on the part of the company, in defeasing its debt, the company avoids having to obtain the consent (implied or explicit) of its creditors.

By eliminating the debt from the balance sheet, defeasance lowers gearing ratios and this may relax the limits set on the ratios by debt covenants. In this way, the company may be able to invest in ventures previously restricted by its high gearing ratios. For example, in New Zealand, Carter Holt

Harvey, in its 1988 accounts, defeased NZ$860 million of its term liabilities for a profit of NZ$174 000. With the defeasance, the company's ratio of equity to total assets rose from 30.5 per cent to 39.0 per cent (Fry, 1989).

As compared with retiring debt by issuing shares in its place, defeasance is also beneficial from the investor's point of view in that no additional shares are issued to dilute earnings per share (Bradbury, 1987).

By placing riskless assets in trust, the company is effectively setting aside funds to ensure the timely servicing and repayment of its debt. This reduces the risk of penalties on late payment and ensures that cash flows from its trust are always matched with the servicing requirements of its debt. Most importantly, by taking advantage of the lower interest rates implicit in the debt, the company is able to post an instant profit from that interest rate differential in the year of the defeasance. This is invaluable in boosting flagging profits or changing a loss into a profit making situation. For example, assume that Debtor Ltd issued a debt of $5000 with an interest rate of 10 per cent per annum. The debt will mature in five years. The current interest rate on government bonds is 12 per cent per annum. To defease the debt of $5000, Debtor Ltd will need to place only $4639.55 in government bonds today to generate sufficient funds to service and repay the loan in five years' time. By defeasing the debt, Debtor Ltd has made a profit of $360.45, being the result of settling a debt with a face value of $5000 at a cost of only $4639.55.

Risks of debt defeasance

One of the most important risks of debt defeasance is that management must believe that the current interest rate has reached its peak or that there are no alternative higher yielding investments available to the company. The danger exists because if interest rates continue to rise or if alternative investments are available, placing funds in an irrevocable trust for defeasing debt may be a costly means of retiring debt (Walton, 1985). Similarly, if the company has to borrow in order to purchase risk-free assets to defease debt, the benefits of debt defeasance are reduced. The company, in this instance, is just replacing debts with lower interest rates with higher interest rate debts.

Debt defeasance may reflect poorly on management because a company with surplus funds should be able to reinvest in higher yielding investments (Brunner, 1989). The need to place funds in risk-free assets for defeasing debt means that lower returns are obtained from the lower risks. The opportunity costs may be high because the company may be forgoing returns on higher yielding investments. If management is unable to invest in securities with a higher return than risk-free assets, then there is a case to be made for a return of this capital to investors who may undertake the investments themselves.

Moreover, while the instant profits made in defeasing debt may increase income and, therefore, share prices in the short run, in the longer term, finance theory dictates that debt defeasance may reduce share prices (Roden, 1987). This is because debt defeasance decreases the amount of future cash flows, decreases the company's liquidity, redistributes wealth from common stock holders to bond holders and decreases the company's debt–equity ratio.

According to Roden (1987), only the last of these may result in an increase in share price. Under finance theory, the first three influences are likely to reduce share prices in the long run.

Finally, in a debt defeasance, other than a legal defeasance, the creditor is not legally satisfied. Thus there is the risk that the debtor company may be called upon at a later date to make further payments on the debt. There is also the related question of whether the trust is protected in the event of the failure or bankruptcy of the debtor company, since a liquidator has the power to revoke all trusts.

Debt defeasance and creative accounting

Besides the actual risks involved, permitting companies to defease debt may result in increased avenues and instances of creative accounting. First, debt defeasance promotes off-balance-sheet financing. By removing debts from the balance sheet, debt ratios will improve. This is aggravated by permitting instantaneous in-substance defeasance under SSAP 26. Instantaneous in-substance defeasance encourages companies to keep borrowing without the debts ever appearing on the books to be incorporated in the calculation of the company's gearing ratios. Similarly, return on assets ratios will appear better as the denominator is lowered with the omission of the corresponding asset.

A second creative element is the profit to be derived from defeasing debt. While the debt and its corresponding asset under debt defeasance need not be reflected in the books, the profit derived from defeasing the debt can be recognised in the profit and loss account in the year of the defeasance. This inflates the profits of the company by that element of unrealised profit from defeasing debt. Again, allowing instantaneous in-substance debt defeasance means that the profit of a company can be inflated by merely taking out a debt and defeasing it instantly.

Third, the ability to defease debt and recognise the profit will encourage companies to smooth income streams. It will be more advantageous for companies to defease debt and recognise profits in loss making years. Yet, logically, it is in the profitable periods when excess funds are available that the company may wish to retire debts. In loss making years, funds will need to be better invested in higher yielding investments, not in lower yielding risk-free assets for defeasing debts.

Allowing the use of debt defeasance, in effect, makes it possible for companies to indulge in off-balance-sheet financing and income smoothing. This has the effect of reversing the trend of eliminating creative accounting in company accounts.

New Zealand: SSAP 26

In October 1990 the NZSA issued *Accounting for Defeasance of Debt* (SSAP 26).

One of the purposes of SSAP 26 was to set down strict conditions for when debt can be treated as having been extinguished by defeasance. SSAP 26 permits both in-substance and instantaneous in-substance debt defeasances as long as risk-free assets are lodged with an independent trust or with risk-free entities for the servicing and repayment of the debt (para. 4.6). The assets transferred to the trust must provide cash flows (from interest and maturity of these assets) that coincide in timing and in amount (approximately) to the servicing requirements of the debt that is being extinguished and must be denominated in the same currency as the debt being de-feased (paras 5.2(b) and 5.2(c)). For debt defeasance to take place it must be virtually certain that the debtor will not be required to assume the primary obligation for the servicing and repayment of the debt or to satisfy any guarantees, indemnities or the like relating to such requirements (para. 5.3).

Where gains and losses on defeasance are concerned, SSAP 26 permits the recognition of the gain or loss in the income statement in the year that the defeasance takes place (para. 5.8). However, in determining the appropriate classification, 'it would need to be decided whether a gain or loss on defeasance of a debt was attributable to the ordinary operations of the business' (para. 4.22).

As debt defeasance effectively removes the debt liability and its corresponding asset from the balance sheet, all that SSAP 26

requires by way of disclosure is a note or otherwise to the financial statements that debt defeasance has taken place. In the period of the defeasance, it is required to disclose:

* the aggregate carrying amount of assets given up for defeasance
* the aggregate carrying amount of debt extinguished by defeasance
* the net gain or loss on defeasance in the income statement or its equivalent (para. 5.10(a)).

Disclosure is also required of details of any amounts defeased which are outstanding, together with their maturity dates, and of any outstanding guarantees, indemnities, borrowing covenants, or the like given by the debtor or on behalf of the debtor (para. 5.10(b)).

The ED 47A differs from the American standard, Statement of Financial Accounting Standards (SFAS) 76, *Extinguishment of Debt*, in two ways. First, SFAS 76 does not permit instantaneous in-substance debt defeasance whereas the SSAP 26 does. Second, SFAS 76 does not allow the 'assumption' method of defeasing debt. SFAS 76 allows only the 'trust' method of defeasance. The SSAP 26, though, permits the debtor company to nominate a 'suitable' risk-free entity to assume the responsibility for servicing and repaying the debt.

In September 1993 the NZSA issued ED 71, *Accounting for Defeasance of Debt* and reissued SSAP 26. The exposure draft proposes changes to the format and wording of SSAP 26. It also proposes to define certain terms in SSAP 26, for example 'risk-free assets', 'risk-free entity' and 'risk-free securities'. The ED has not been issued as an accounting standard at this stage.

Issues of concern

There are three major conceptual issues of contention in debt defeasance. These include the way the terms asset and liability are defined, whether debt defeasance takes the 'substance over form' argument too far and the issue of whether financial statements show a true and fair view when debts and their corresponding assets may never ever be reflected on a balance sheet under an instantaneous in-substance defeasance.

Definition of asset and liability

Central to the debt defeasance controversy is the issue of how assets and liabilities are defined. For its purpose in SSAP 26 only, a liability is defined as a 'future disposition of economic benefits that a reporting entity is presently obliged to make to another entity as a result of a past transaction or other past event' (para. 41). Since the issue of SSAP 26, the NZSA has issued the Statement of Concepts for General Purpose Financial Reporting (1993). This statement defines 'liabilities' as 'the future sacrifices of service potential or of future economic benefits that the entity is presently obliged to make to other entities as a result of past transactions or other past events' (para. 7.10).

Using the definition in SSAP 26, it therefore follows that once sufficient funds and assets are set aside to meet the servicing and repayment requirements of the liability, a 'disposition of economic benefits' has effectively occurred. Since no further future disposition is required on the part of the debtor, the liability effectively also ceases to exist and, therefore, could be removed from the books of the debtor company.

However, arguments have been put forward in the USA by members of the FASB that:

> the setting aside of assets in trust does not, in itself, constitute either the disposition of assets with the potential gain or loss recognition or the satisfaction of a liability with potential gain or loss recognition. Though dedicated to a single purpose, assets in trust continue to be assets (that is, probable future economic benefits) of the debtor until applied to

payment of the debt. Likewise, the liability continues to be a liability of the original debtor until satisfied by payment or by agreement of the creditor that the debtor is no longer the primary obliger. Dedicating the assets might ensure that debt is serviced in a timely fashion, but that event alone just matches up cash flows; it does not satisfy, eliminate, or extinguish the obligation. For a debt to be satisfied, the creditor must be satisfied. (SFAS 76, p.5)

As Gaumnitz and Thompson (1987) rightly criticise, in an effort to cover a wide variety of circumstances, the broad definitions of asset and liability can be interpreted as support for conflicting views, thus rendering them useless in deciding how to account for in-substance defeasances.

Substance over form

Following on from the argument over the definitions of asset and liability is the issue of economic substance over legal form. The question here is whether this criterion has been taken too far by the standard setters and proponents of debt defeasance. In New Zealand, SSAP 1, *Determination and Disclosure of Accounting Policies* lists 'substance over form' as one of four important criteria that should be considered in selecting the appropriate accounting policy from the range of alternatives: 'Transactions and other events should be accounted for and presented in accordance with their substance, that is their financial and economic reality, and not necessarily in accordance with their legal form' (para. 4.8).

This statement alone can provide support for defeasing debt since, in substance, a debt has been extinguished if sufficient assets are set aside for its servicing and repayment. It must be argued, however, that this criterion should not be interpreted so rigidly that its own substance is lost. The criterion should be interpreted with the overall objective of financial statements in mind, that is, collectively to provide a true and fair view of the state of affairs and profit and loss for the period under review (Explanatory Foreword, para. 1.1).

Traditionally, the substance over form criterion has been used to ensure that companies do not avoid disclosure and, hence, present a less than true and fair view of their performance and state of affairs. According to Shearer (1986), the application of substance over form, which 'attempts to represent what has actually happened in commercial terms, claims to shed light where before there was dark, and so present a more truthful picture' (p.10). Hence, for the substance over form argument to work in favour of debt defeasance, proponents must be able to show that removing the debt and its corresponding asset presents a more truthful picture of the performance and state of affairs of a company.

In the debt defeasance issue, it can be argued that the economic reality is that the company still owns the asset and its liability is not extinguished until the creditor is legally satisfied. Thus, it would seem that reporting the legal form of the debt and its corresponding asset would present a more truthful picture and better reflect the economic reality of the state of affairs of the company.

True and fair view

Under Sections 11 (1 and 2) and 14 (1 and 2) of the *Financial Reporting Act* 1993, financial statements and group financial statements of reporting entities must now comply with GAAP. If, in complying with GAAP, the financial statements do not give a true and fair view of the matters to which they relate, the directors of reporting entities must add such information and explanations as will give a true and fair view of those matters. While widely used in existing accounting and professional literature, there is no formal definition of what constitutes a 'true and fair' view.

The Macquarie Dictionary (1991) defines 'true' as something being in accordance with the actual state of things; conforming to fact; not false. 'Fair' is defined as free from bias, dishonesty, or injustice; that is legitimately sought.

The NZSA Explanatory Foreword to its SSAPs uses only parts of the dictionary meanings of true and fair. To the profession, providing a true and fair view requires 'disclosure and appropriate classification and grouping of all material items and consistent application of acceptable accounting principles' (para. 1.2). Based on this prescription, defeasing debt under the conditions set out in SSAP 26 will still result in financial statements showing a true and fair view because the defeasance is accounted for and presented in conformity with set rules and standards.

However, using 'true and fair' in the sense of the financial statements being in accordance with the actual state of things conforming to fact, it is difficult to see how the omission of debts and their corresponding assets from financial statements (which have no legal right of set-off) can be said to present a true and fair view of the performance and state of affairs of the company. First, the performance of the company may not be factual or free from discrimination to the extent that its profit figure may be inflated with that element of profit from defeasing its debt which has not been realised. This profit becomes distributable even though it may never be realised, for example when the company goes into liquidation.

Second, the state of affairs of the company may not conform with reality in that the company actually owns more income generating assets and has a greater liability than is presented in its financial statements. The host of accounting ratios calculated based on the company's profit, assets and liabilities will accordingly be distorted. Hence, it is debatable whether the financial statements of a company which defeases debt actually present a true and fair view of the performance and state of affairs of the company.

Section summary

Debt defeasance is an emerging issue in financial accounting in Australia and New Zealand. While SSAP 26 has been issued to deal with this modern practice, it cannot correctly be classified as an issue of incremental disclosure. The reason is that permitting its use actually decreases the disclosure of the actual amount and level of debt and financial resources in published accounts.

Debt defeasance has been recognised by many as having advantages over other forms of retiring debt but there are risks associated with its use. It is being seen by many as 'those arrangements whereby debts are turned into accounting profits' (Wise and Wise, 1988, p.40). The reason is that its use is of assistance to creative accounting. Instead of presenting a true and fair view, debt defeasance is likely to encourage off-balance-sheet financing, thereby reversing the trend of eliminating such creative techniques.

Segmental reporting

Introduction

In recent years, a salient feature of the business environment in many countries has been the significant increase in the diversification of businesses into new product lines, markets and industries. Internal growth, expansion and the increasing number of mergers and takeovers at national and multinational levels have been two contributory factors. The increased diversification of business activities has given rise to a concern over corporate accountability and disclosure, which is reflected in the regulations on segmental reporting in the USA, Canada, the UK, Australia and New Zealand, as well as in some international organisations such as the United Nations (UN) and the Organisation for Economic Cooperation and Development (OECD). Segmental reporting is a response to the call for more specific reporting on the activities of identifiable and reportable segments of the firms rather than disclosing a high level of aggregated information.

There are a number of ways to identify segments. These include legal entities, organisation structure, product and services, classes of customers and geographical areas. However, because of the unique nature of each organisation and its activities, it is very difficult to provide a universal definition of reportable industry segments. As a result, the existing standards and regulations offer only general guidelines. The identification of industry segment, in particular, is largely left to the discretion of management.

This section will examine briefly the need for segmental disclosure, trace the development of segmental reporting in a number of countries and discuss the inherent problems and future prospects associated with such incremental disclosures.

The need for segmental disclosure

As firms become more diversified, there emerges the problem of aggregated information. This is more acute with large conglomerate firms that obtain their diversification through mergers or the acquisition of a wide variety of unrelated businesses. Reporting the operating results in the form of a consolidated statement usually provides little information to a shareholder or creditor about a firm's business by product group and geographical area. There is a loss of information to the investor community and to the general public with every combination, especially when the standard external reporting requirements are maintained (Hendriksen, 1982). Rates of profitability,

opportunities for growth, future
prospects and risks to investments may
vary greatly among industry and geographical segments. As a result, bankers,
financial analysts, investors and other
potential users, such as creditors, management and even host governments, all
demand additional financial information
to facilitate their analysis of these increasingly complex organisations.

It is hoped that by disseminating segmental information, more relevant economic information is provided. With this
information, users are expected to be able
to make a more informed evaluation of the
reporting entity's past performance, future
prospects, risk exposure and management's
diversification strategy. As a result, it will
assist them in making better investment
and credit decisions. Consequently, segmental reporting aids the stewardship and
decision usefulness aspects of accounting
reports.

In the intervening years since the call
for segmental reporting, numerous empirical studies have been conducted to
examine the possible benefits of segmental
data. Early survey research (Mautz, 1968)
attempted to assess the attitudes of users
and preparers towards the public dissemi-
nation of disaggregated data. Studies on
predictive ability have shown that industry
and geographical segmental data for the
prediction of earnings are more useful
than consolidated data (Kinney, 1971;
Balakrishnan, Harris and Sen, 1990;
Swaminathan, 1991; Aitken, Czernkowski
and Hooper, 1994). Studies on the relationship between segmental disclosure
and securities returns have provided
inconclusive results (Horwitz and
Kolodny, 1977; Ajinkya, 1980), while
stock market research relating to systems
risks reveals that segmental disclosure
results in a decrease in risk-taking by
companies as perceived by investors
(Dhaliwal, 1978; Collins and Simonds,
1979).

The development of segmental reporting

Realising that disaggregated information
about the various segments of an organisation will assist the users in making more
relevant economic decisions, professional
bodies in many countries have issued
accounting standards and regulations to
provide a framework for disclosure. It is
against such a background that this section
will examine the development of segmental
reporting guidelines and standards in various organisations and countries.

The Organisation for Economic Cooperation and Development

In 1976 the Organisation for Economic
Cooperation and Development (OECD)
issued a *Code of Conduct for Multinational
Companies* (revised in 1979), providing
guidelines on segmental disclosure for
national accounting bodies to follow in setting down their requirements. Its recommendations include: the disclosure of the
geographical areas and principal activities in
each area; operating results and sales by
geographical and industry segments; capital
investment by geographical and, where
applicable, industry segments; and the average number of employees by geographical
segment (Arpan and Radebaugh, 1985).
However, these guidelines are persuasive
rather than legally enforceable. Compliance
by companies is voluntary.

The United Nations

The UN (1977) proposals, entitled
*International Standard of Accounting and
Reporting for Transnational Corporations,* are
similar to the OECD guidelines. They place
special emphasis on the disclosure of disaggregation by geographical area and line of
business in terms of sales, transfers, operating profit, assets, new investment, employees, accounting polices used for transfers and exposure to exceptional risks of

operating in foreign countries. Caution is taken not to require disclosure of sensitive data that would damage the company's competitive position.

The United States of America

In the mid-1960s there was a demand in the USA for organisations to identify the exact line-of-business (LOB). In 1969, 1970 and 1974 the SEC issued requirements for the reporting of LOB information in registration statements, annual 10K (for those companies wanting to trade on the major exchanges) and annual reports. The Federal Trade Commission (1974) also required large manufacturing companies to comply with the LOB requirement.

In December 1976 the FASB issued Statement 14 (FAS 14), *Financial Reporting for Segments of a Business Enterprise*, requiring disclosure of information on four segments: industry, foreign operations, export sales and major customers. This is applicable to companies of all sizes.

Firms are called upon to identify separate reporting purposes, segments with revenues, profits or losses, or assets which are 10 per cent of the combined revenue, profits or losses, or assets of the identifiable segments of the firm. In addition, the total of all reportable segment revenues (excluding inter-segment sales) should comprise at least 75 per cent of the combined revenues from sales to unaffiliated customers of all industry segments. Once the industry segments are identified, information on revenue, profit or losses and identifiable assets are disclosed. Three disclosure options are available: (a) in the body of financial statements; (b) all in footnotes; and (c) as a separate schedule.

The 10 per cent test also applies to the disclosure of sales to major customers. That is, if 10 per cent or more of total revenue is derived from sales to a single customer, that amount of sales must be disclosed. Likewise, the 10 per cent materiality rule

applies to foreign operations and export sales.

In the light of changing circumstances, some provisions of FAS 14 have been amended by the later standards: FAS 18, FAS 21, FAS 24 and FAS 30.

Canada

The requirements of the CICA, *CICA Section 1700 (1979): Segmental Information,* closely follow the FASB standards. Firms are required to disclose segmental information by industry and by geographical area. The CICA also adopted similar requirements for determining those segments which are significant and thus reportable.

The United Kingdom

Compared with the USA and Canada, regulations are relatively general and flexible in the UK (Arpan and Radebaugh, 1985, p.179). In 1965 the London Stock Exchange was the first institution to require the disclosure of international segmental information. For domestic companies, section 17 of the *Companies Act* 1967 (UK) provided some requirements for directors to disclose information regarding the profitability of the separate operations of diversified firms. These were later found to be inadequate.

However, the concept of disaggregation was approved by the Corporate Report 1975 (ASSC, 1975). Despite the difficulties in this type of disclosure, the Corporate Report 1975 suggested improvements on the provisions of the *Companies Act* 1967 offering some guidelines on the type of information to be provided (paras 6.48–6.53).

Segmental reporting was further supported by the Government Green Paper (1977, paras 39–44), which expressed dissatisfaction with the *Companies Act* 1967 for allowing too much discretion to the directors. By acknowledging the OECD guidelines and the provisions in the draft Fourth

Directive of the EU, it proposed some specific guidelines on industry segment-ation, analysis by geographical area and the test of significance. The *Companies Act* 1981 later incorporated some segmental disclo-sure requirements when the provisions of the EU Fourth Directive were adopted (later consolidated into the *Companies Act* 1985).

In 1987 the ASC produced a consultative paper on segmental disclosure, followed by ED 45 in November 1988. Comments on the documents were collated and consid-ered. After a prolonged gestation period, *Segmental Reporting* (SSAP 25) was issued in June 1990. It extended the existing legal and stock exchange requirements. It also adopted the 10 per cent materiality rule (but not the 75 per cent test) tantamount to American standards.

The International Accounting Standards Committee

The IAS 14, *Reporting Financial Information by Segment,* was issued by the IASC in August 1981. It is as comprehensive as FAS 14 in terms of information requirement per segment. It is different from FAS 14 in that it requires data only on industry and geographical segments and not on export revenues and revenues from significant customers. It also allows more leeway for management to determine what 'signifi-cant' business and geographical segments are. In addition, this standard applies only to enterprises whose securities are publicly traded and other economically significant entities. (This standard is currently under review.)

Australia

Australia enjoys a 'dual accounting standard system' (Gavens and Carnegie, 1988). The AAS 16, *Financial Reporting by Segments,* issued by the AARF in 1984 and ASRB 1005 (now AASB 1005), *Financial Reporting by Segments,* issued by the ASRB in 1986, are

the two concurrent standards prescribing the disclosure requirements of segment reports.

Both standards follow very closely the provisions of IAS 14. Segmentation of reporting entity is by industry and geo-graphical location. The 10 per cent guide-lines are employed to determine the significance of the segments. The informa-tion to be disclosed is: (a) segment revenue; (b) segment result; (c) the carrying amount of segment assets; and (d) the basis of inter-segment pricing. The standards also specify (as does FAS 14) that, where a reporting entity operates predominantly in one indus-try, it should be disclosed together with a general description of the products and ser-vices from which revenue is derived.

There are two main differences between these two standards. First, they have different application criteria. The AAS 16 applies to *all* companies whereas ASRB 1005 applies to all 'relevant companies'. (A relevant company is defined as a listed company or a company which is the subsidiary of a foreign listed company.) In 1992 the application was extended to all reporting entities. Second, ASRB 1005 has more 'teeth' in enforcing compliance because of its 'government back-ing'. A survey conducted in June 1986 showed a widespread non-compliance rate with AAS 16 of about 48.9 per cent, whereas a similar survey in 1988 found increased compliance since ASRB 1005 became effective (Gavens and Carnegie, 1988).

New Zealand

In 1985 Devonport and McNally were commissioned by the NZSA to conduct a study on segmental reporting. The re-searchers carried out a detailed examin-ation of the overseas pronouncements and analysed the New Zealand economic environment to identify any needs for dis-closure. The outcome of that project was the publication of a research bulletin, *The Reporting of Segmental Information* (R115).

In August 1988 ED 44, *Financial Reporting for Segments,* was issued for comment from interested parties. In July 1989 SSAP 23 was published. The ultimate aim of this new standard is to provide a true and fair view of the relationship between a holding company and its subsidiary companies in view of the increasingly complex corporate structure. The purpose is to prescribe disclosures to inform users of the results of the diverse operations of a reporting entity. Closely following the overseas pronouncements and adapting to the local context, SSAP 23 provides general guidelines on the basis of segmentation and the items to be disclosed.

Similar to its overseas counterparts, SSAP 23 requires segmentation by industry and geographical location. The information to be disclosed resembles that of Australia except that besides segment revenue, segment result, the carrying amount of segment assets and the basis of intersegment pricing, New Zealand adds another requirement: abnormal items.

The new standard requires companies to disclose earnings for each industry and geographical segment of their operations. Like IAS 14, it does not define how detailed the breakdown should be, but states broadly that the 'significance' of any segment can be measured by its contribution to revenue, profit and assets. The 10 per cent criterion is to be applied in the absence of other factors. Likewise, there is no requirement on disclosing revenues from export sales and major customers.

Problems and prospects

There is a growing body of standards and regulations relating to segmental information not only at the national level but also internationally. It is a reflection of the trend of developments in business, especially in view of the growing number of multinational corporations. However, segmental reporting is but 'an innovation in information disclosure which has yet to be fully developed' (Gray, McSweeney and Shaw, 1984, p.84).

Experience in many countries indicates that firms are reluctant to provide segmental information for various reasons. Questions are raised about the logical breakdown of segments, the allocation of join costs, the treatment of transfer pricing and the measurement of segment assets (Hendriksen, 1982; Gray, McSweeney and Shaw, 1984). There are also arguments about the reliability, objectivity and verifiability of specific financial information disclosed for segments especially when such segments are identified on a haphazard basis. The financial data provided will be meaningless as conscious manipulation or inadvertent discrimination may play a part in the selection of segments (Emmanuel and Gray, 1977, p.50). Thus critics have called for more specific and effective criteria for the identification of line of business and geographical segments as well as the related areas. Potential constraints on segmental disclosure also include the cost of compiling, processing and disseminating information and more importantly, the cost of competitive disadvantage (Emmanuel and Garrod, 1992; Radebaugh and Gray, 1993).

Gray, McSweeny and Shaw (1984) note that the development of segmental reporting so far has been limited to the disclosure and presentation of analyses of summary information such as sales, income or earnings, assets, new investment and so on. What they are suggesting is that there is a potential for segmental reporting to explore some new avenues, such as providing disaggregated information by country, so as to benefit governments and trade unions who not only wish to evaluate the multinational corporations as a whole and in segments, but also require more comprehensive information at country level (p.85).

Section summary

The objective of general purpose external reporting is to communicate relevant information about a firm to interested parties to enhance their decision-making process. This is what segmental reporting aims to achieve. By providing disaggregated information, users will be better informed about the financial performance, risk and prospects of the individual segments. It will, therefore, enable them to analyse the organisation in a more efficient way.

Disaggregation of information is a new type of disclosure created by the increasingly complex business environment and user demand for fuller disclosure. It is a new and difficult challenge requiring the development of new measurement and reporting techniques. There is also the possible expansion of the boundaries of the audit function.

Already, like all other reporting issues, segmental reporting has 'generated a debate about its implementation, the nature of accounting standards, its impact on users and the market and its potential predictive ability' (Belkaoui, 1986, p.103). To date, there is no conclusive evidence to show the benefits of segmental reporting. However, since it is widely regarded as being capable of providing useful information about the risk, return and profitability of different activities of a business, further research is necessary to clarify the issues which have not yet been resolved. A cost–benefit analysis is also deemed to be necessary. Furthermore, a careful consideration of company structure, the identification issue and the differing emphases on disclosure have to be examined.

Employee reports

Introduction

Since the 1960s a new social consciousness has emerged in many countries. As a result, business enterprises are charged with the wider responsibility of providing standard financial information as well as information about the social impacts of their operations. This concept of a much broader societal responsibility has thus prompted accountants to respond with suggestions of more comprehensive and varied financial reports and supporting schedules.

There are many users who are dependent on financial information. Traditionally and legally, it is the needs of shareholders, investors and creditors that are to be catered for. However, the growing trend is for businesses to communicate their operating results as well as social activities to other users who have a 'right to information' (Hussey and Craig, 1980; Haggie, 1984).

Employees have a vested interest in the organisations they work for. They also have certain information needs and expectations from their workplace. One way of fostering a healthy relationship between employer and employee is for organisations to communicate the results of business operations to their employees by means of employee reports. It is an effective method of building employee commitment and participation.

This section is concerned with the development of employee reports in Continental Europe, the UK, Australia and New Zealand. It will also briefly discuss the purpose of employee reports, their potential benefits, attendant problems and future prospects.

What is an employee report?

Shareholders often measure their returns by financial and capital appreciation of their investment. Employees, who have invested their human resources in the organisations they serve, seek security, improvements in pay, status, and job satisfaction (Alexander, 1973). As a result, they have certain information needs relating to job security, working conditions, achievement and performance indicators, and equity and fairness in the distribution of economic rewards

(Forley and Maunders, 1977). The information employees require will assist them in making decisions in regard to participation and effort (Maunders, 1981). The success of an organisation depends on how effectively its management develops and harnesses the capabilities of its employees. It is therefore in the interests of the organisation and its employees that the information needs of the employees be satisfied.

Employee reports are the end product of a number of wider social changes: (a) the general pressure for greater company disclosure; (b) the practice and problems associated with industrial relations; (c) the emergence of industrial democracy; and (d) an awareness of information provision in other countries (Purdy, 1981).

An employee report is a recognition by management of the employees' right to information about the organisation where their human resources are invested. It is, according to Hussey (1980, p.149): 'a statement produced at least annually, in written form, specifically for all employees and which provides information relevant to a financial period of the undertaking'.

The aim is to present corporate financial performance information to employees in the context of information about a broad spectrum of company activities, both financial and non-financial, qualitative and quantitative. It is hoped that such reporting is capable of satisfying the additional information needs of employees and that it is an integral part of the total communication process between central management and employees (Taylor, Webb and McGinley, 1979).

Benefits of providing employee reports

Who is likely to benefit from financial reports to employees? Parker (1976) observed that there would be positive benefits accrued to: (a) management; (b) employees; and (c) the organisation as a whole.

Taylor, Webb and McGinley (1979) attempted to analyse these benefits further. First, by imparting information through the employee report, management can build a favourable image among the employees. This can also reduce the resistance of employees to changes initiated by management. In addition, it can provide a useful response to union pressure for more corporate financial information.

Second, the personal benefits that might accrue to employees through wider information are perceived as: (a) having a basis to decide whether to continue employment with the company; (b) having a basis to assess the relative position of the employees within the organisational structure; and (c) understanding the corporate image of the company and ultimately deciding whether to identify personally with that image.

Third, having accrued some benefits on the management and the employee levels, the company as a whole can gain through the improved climate of management–employee relations. It is the fundamental intention of issuing such reports to achieve 'improved employee understanding, openness, trust and acceptance of the broader and higher level corporate issues which directly or indirectly affect them personally' (Taylor, Webb and McGinley, 1979, p.37). To this end, organisational profitability and stability can be enhanced through improved employee productivity, retention of skilled workers and more realistic wage demands (Taylor, Webb and McGinley 1979; Reynolds, 1992).

Development of employee reports

To understand the development of employee reports, it is important to take into account the social and cultural factors existing in different environments (refer also to Chapter 17). The different dominant social concerns in the USA, for instance on the impacts of consumerism, equal rights and the ecological movement, are the reasons why US practice has tended to be directed towards the interests of the general public and consumers rather than those of employees and the impact of the trade unions as in the case of European countries (Gray, Owen and Maunders, 1987, p.23).

Continental Europe

Continental Europe has a tradition of state intervention and anti-individualism (Perera and Mathews, 1987, p.21). Government support of this societal attitude has led to the establishment and regulation of accounting procedures and practices. For a number of years, the prevalent belief in these countries has been that employees have a right to know what is happening in complex national and multinational corporations. The EU has wanted disclosure procedures to be mandatory and objective. In accordance with the recommendations of the Sudreau Report in 1977, the EU adopted a law requiring a firm with 750 or more employees (extended to 300 or more employees in 1982) must have disclosure procedures.

The EU Fifth Directive and the Vredeling Directive (1980, revised 1983 as reported in Hussey, 1984) are the most recent attempts to date to introduce an international, legally binding instrument. They require companies to communicate with their employees as follows:

   i provide them systematically with information;
  ii consult them on a regular basis;
 iii encourage their involvement in the company's performance; and
  iv make them aware of the financial and economic factors affecting the performance of the company. (Haggie, 1984, p.67)

France is far ahead of most other countries in this area. The large socialist movement in France has made increased demands on the government to require

firms to make more employee related disclosures. Since 1977 France has adopted a law requiring all French firms with 300 or more employees to prepare annual social balance sheets (Bilan Social), which are based on indicators of their social situation and working conditions as well as relationships between the workforces (Hilton, 1978). A similar approach to reporting has also been experimented with by other European countries, such as Germany and the Scandinavian countries (Webb and Taylor, 1980, p.32; Gray et al., 1987).

The United Kingdom

Prior to World War II there was little information in the UK on the provision of financial information to employees. It was the 'war effort' that gave impetus to practical employee communications (Hussey, 1981). Since 1945 management and workers have learned much about the use and development of management information and the development of 'consultative' or 'participative' styles of management (Hussey and Marsh, 1983). During the 1950s there was increasing pressure for better employee communications policies. In 1957 the British Institute of Management published a booklet advocating the methods and reasons for giving information to employees.

The trend of the 1960s and early 1970s was manifested by trade union movements pressing for legislation in the direction of greater disclosure. Section 57 of the (Conservatives') Industrial Relations Act 1971 made it obligatory for companies employing more than 350 persons to disclose financial information to employees. Although this Act did not become effective, the basic requirement of reporting to employees via an annual printed document was effectively made.

Subsequent legislation, the Employment Protection Act 1975, is considered the real turning point which made an impact on reporting to employees. It laid down the most stringent conditions for more formalised disclosure between the boards of companies and the unions (Hilton, 1978, p.5).

After joining the EU in 1973, the UK underwent some changes in its accounting practices in order to harmonise with EU company law. One such change is to increase employees' access to company information. The influence of the EU was first reflected in the Corporate Report 1975, which recognised that the 'reporting entity has a responsibility for the future livelihood and prospects of its employees' (ASSC, 1975, para. 2.15). The Corporate Report is significant in the sense that it formally established that an employee had a 'right', at least a 'moral' right, to receive information from the organisation he or she serves.

The Government Green Paper (1977) was also supportive of this cause; so was the Bullock Report (1977), which was in favour of changes to the traditional management structure of corporations and advocated giving employees greater decision making rights and powers. At present, there are no statutes or accounting standards requiring companies to give employees information about their financial results. Employee reporting is a voluntary exercise in the UK. In the absence of any specific statutory requirements or accounting standards, companies are left to decide for themselves whether to disclose and, if so, what is the most appropriate format for disclosure (Hussey and Craig, 1980, p.46).

However, as observed by Burchell, Clubb and Hopwood (1985, pp.405–406), this type of reporting is subject to the political climate of the day. The incumbent Conservative government is less interested in the discussion of industrial democracy, participation and the enhancement of worker rights. Despite such a government attitude, *Accountancy Age* and the Industrial Society have been sponsoring an annual award for the best employee report since 1977. (It is now called the Simplified

Reporting Award). Employee reporting was immensely popular in the late 1970s and early 1980s with voluminous literature on the subject. Since then interest has seemed to wane. More recently, though, a growing number of multinationals domiciled in the UK, such as Hewlett Packard, IBM, P&O European Ferries, BP, Digital and Wellcome Pharmaceutical, have been employing various communicating techniques to keep their employees across Europe informed so as to imbue a common sense of purpose among their workforce (Reynolds, 1992; Marks, 1993).

Australia

Being closely associated with the UK, Australian companies have been 'exposed to the various recommendations on improving employee communications in general and disclosing corporate financial information in particular' (Craig and Hussey, 1982, p.5).

Although there had been individual company experiments like Ampol in 1955 and Comalco in 1962, the majority of Australian companies showed little interest in formally disclosing financial information to employees until about 1975, when various pressures within Australia and on the international scene caused a sudden surge of activity. The production of corporate financial reports to employees grew as a result of voluntary adoption by corporate managements.

The Australian trade union movement, in pursuing industrial democracy, was in favour of the concept of employee reporting (Craig and Hussey, 1982, p.6). The Confederation of Australian Industry also stressed the need for its members to communicate information to employees, in a booklet entitled *Involving Employees in the Enterprise: A Guide to Employers*. Likewise, the Australian Quality Council (formerly Enterprise Australia), a non-party political organisation set up to promote the free enterprise ideology and to improve the private sector's public image, has been particularly active in encouraging managers to become involved in employee reporting (Craig and Hussey, 1982, p.7). A booklet called *A Guide to Employee Annual Reports* was issued in 1977, explaining to company managers the 'why' and 'how' about reporting to employees through a special annual report. It also offered a series of employee report award competitions (Parker, 1980; Craig and Hussey, 1982).

However, at the government level, there is no specific legislation comparable to that of the UK, concerning the range and quality of financial information disclosure to employees. There is also no official pronouncement on the matter by the professional accounting bodies. Interest in this development was demonstrated by the volume of articles appearing in professional and administrative journals and the surveys that were carried out in the 1970s and early 1980s.

New Zealand

Being connected with the UK culturally and socially in the same way as Australia has been, undoubtedly New Zealand has been exposed to the repercussions of the Corporate Report 1975 and the occurrences of employee reporting. However, New Zealand is by far the least developed in this area in terms of the number of reports published, the issuing of guidelines and even empirical studies.

In his book on practical guidelines and suggestions on employee involvement, Meldum identified 'Presentation of Financial Reports to Staff' as one means of informing employees in New Zealand (Chye, 1984, p.223). This was well demonstrated by the New Zealand Chamber of Commerce's annual award for the best report to staff. This organisation had also published a booklet on *How and Why to Report Business Results to Employees*, in addition to the periodic seminars it held for employees through its various branches.

A study of employee reporting undertaken by Firth and Smith in 1984 under the sponsorship of the Cost and Management Accounting Division of the NZSA is the major contribution to the area in this country. Prior to that there was no formal research into this area in New Zealand. The researchers found that employers and employees in New Zealand had a favourable view of employee reporting. One major area of concern, however, was the content of current employee reports. It appears that even though employers are not unaware of the information needs of their employees, somehow they are not actually providing such information in the current employee reports. This is something the researchers recommend that the employers should pay attention to in the future.

In summary, the UK has obviously shown an interest in employee reporting, especially in the late 1970s. However, in setting a social and industrial climate in which worker participation can be fostered, it lags behind its Western European counterparts. The Australian experience is conducted in an 'unstandardised' manner and on a scale that is relatively small. This is in great contrast with the wide scale of adoption in the UK, where employee reporting is encouraged by non-specific parliamentary recommendations. It also contrasts sharply with the consistency of disclosure in the Western European countries where legislation clearly prescribes the type of information that must be conveyed to employees (Webb and Taylor, 1980, p.34). In comparison, employee reporting in New Zealand is the least developed, and can learn in every respect from the UK and Australia.

While interest in employee reporting has diminished in the UK, Australia and New Zealand, the South African Institute of Chartered Accountants finds that employee reporting offers an opportunity to break away from conventional accounting practices and provides considerable scope for imagination in finding a new and effective means of communication. Together with Anglo Alpha Limited, the institute established an annual award for the organisation producing the best employee report in 1991 (Everingham, 1991 and 1994).

Presentation styles: form and content

The overwhelming characteristic of employee reporting is the incredible variation in concept, content, format and length. The European countries have placed great emphasis on standardised and comparable approaches. In the UK and Australasia employee reports are not bound by convention or statute, as shareholders' reports are.

On the whole, the majority of employee reports are fairly brief. The length ranges from a two page broadsheet to booklets of about ten to twelve A4 pages. The format tends to be glossy colour with considerable use of photographs. Almost all employee reports use diagrams, especially bar charts, pie charts, graphs, illustrations and even cartoons to present simplified versions of financial statements. The aim is to 'capture interest and enhance understanding of monetary information' (Craig and Hussey, 1982, p.27). Parker (1980) commented that employee reports are a 'mixed bag' in terms of quality of content, styles of presentation and management motives.

Various other media have been used to convey information to employees: notices, in-house newsletters and newspapers, annual shareholders' reports, audio-visual presentations, posters and wall charts, work group briefs, and general meetings. (Craig and Hussey, 1982; Hussey and March, 1983; Parker, Ferris and Otley, 1989). With the advancement of technology, videos and even electronic mail (Reynolds, 1992) are being experimented with as an alternative medium to written reports. All these, no matter in what medium, are designed specially for general employee readership and comprehension.

Attendant problems

Given that there are so many potential benefits in employee reporting, it is pertinent to ask why some organisations are hesitant to produce such reports. A perusal of the relevant literature reveals that criticisms of employee reporting abound.

There are concerns that a written report would not provide a full picture of company policy. Employee reports are mainly simplified and they contain only a brief sketch of the company's activities. They are termed 'cryptic reports' because of their lack of explanation and detail, and their superficiality (Mitchell, Sams and White, 1986, p.31).

Employee reports are also criticised for using 'patronising vernacular'. They are perceived to be cluttered with a plethora of pie charts, coloured building blocks, piles of coins and cartoon presentations. These, together with the chairperson's address, tend to lapse into patronising language and do not find favour with some employees.

Some companies consider disclosure to employees to be a breach of confidential information which will blunt the competitive edge. They are reluctant to impart any more information than that disclosed in statutorily required annual accounts.

Mostly, employee reports will contain only what management wishes to disclose. Some managers take for granted that employees are not interested and, as a result, management's perception of employee communication needs may not match employee views (Parker, 1980, p.21). Incongruity of views tends to make employee reports a 'monologue', if they are ever produced at all.

Finally, there is also a tendency for the disclosed information to be misinterpreted by employees and by trade unionists. Unless worded carefully and succinctly, there is always a possibility that management's motives of industrial relations and public relations are perceived by the intended audience as propaganda and as a means of warding off union claims in collective bargaining (Taylor, Webb and McGinley, 1979). The size of the company and associated costs have also been cited as reasons for not issuing employee reports.

Future prospects

Reflecting on the recent development of employee reporting in the UK, Australia and New Zealand, does the waning of interest signify that employee reporting is a 'phenomenon of the past' as Burchell, Clubb and Hopwood (1985) have commented on the fate of value added statements?

Indeed, interest in employee reporting has declined. Its likely future depends on beliefs about whether employees have the right to information. With the increasing importance attached to fuller disclosure and with the growing level of worker literacy, it may reasonably be predicted that employee reporting will be more widespread in the future.

Employee reports are but one type of social reporting that is still in its experimental phase. The future importance of employee reporting lies in the areas of industrial relations, internal communication and also public relations. Questions will be raised about establishing standards or statutory requirements for employee reports in the future, provided there is widespread adaptation. In the meantime, emphasis should be placed on the cultivation of a two way communication process and information sharing. Further research is required to explore the identity of the user groups, their information needs, the content and format of the report and the behavioural and market impact that may follow such disclosure (Belkaoui, 1986).

Section summary

Employee reporting is a relatively recent phenomenon, one that has developed out of the increasing importance of corporate social accounting. In Continental Europe, this practice has been well established because those countries are more collectivistically concerned and consequently are more inclined to promote the welfare of workers. In the UK, Australia and New Zealand, employee reporting experienced rapid growth in the late 1970s but this was not sustained, partly due to the existing political climate and partly due to the attitude of management.

Even though it has declined in popularity in these English-speaking countries, it is apparent that employee reporting has not been totally discarded. Given the rising status of employees as a major user group of published information and the increasing demand for fuller disclosure, it can be envisaged that employee reports will be accepted favourably, not only at the conceptual level, but also at the operational level. Their increasing importance will be further strengthened if those organisations producing or intending to produce employee reports realise that employee reporting is not a panacea for the improvement of the employer–employee relationship but a two way communication process, with both parties continually learning and adapting to the needs of the other.

Leases and executory contracts

Provisions now exist in most Anglo-American accounting countries for the valuation and disclosure of financial leases. This development took many years and much argument to achieve. Reformers argued that it was necessary to disclose financial leases because of their use to finance long term assets which would not otherwise be disclosed in the accounts (sometimes called off-balance-sheet financing).

The disclosure of leases necessitated the formulation of a theory of liabilities, as distinct from regarding liabilities primarily as the result of recognising and valuing an asset. To value a financial lease it is necessary to calculate the outflow associated with the lease contract and discount this figure to determine the present value, using either the rate implicit in the lease contract or the long term borrowing rate paid by the entity and placing the resulting figures on the balance sheet as both an asset and a liability. These balances would then be amortised and expensed. This arrangement was applied to financial leases which are regarded by some as executory contracts, leading to arguments about the need to recognise other forms or examples of the executory contract principle.

The major technical problems involved in the disclosure of leases were solved many years ago — for example FAS 13 in the USA was issued in 1976 — and yet wider implementation has only been achieved comparatively recently. The reason for this delay is that the political strength and lobbying power of those opposed to the disclosure of information about financial leases has been extreme and standards in the UK, Australia and New Zealand were held up for a long time. Now that standards are available, the next issue will be to ensure that they are implemented and not circumvented.

The reformers are now free to address the next issue arising out of this debate: what should be done to account for executory contracts in general?

An executory contract is a contract for future execution between two or more parties. The contract will lead to action and it is binding on the parties concerned, but because it is only part performed (and not necessarily equal parts between the different parties) it is not recognised by Anglo-American accounting practices (Henderson and Peirson, 1983, p.101). In the case of a financial lease, the lessor supplies the asset (this is full performance) but full performance by the lessee is only achieved at the end of the contract, during which a series

of lease payments are made by the lessee to the lessor.

The resolution of the lease recognition and disclosure issue means that attention must be given to the wider problem of how to deal with other executory contracts connected with the receipts and delivery of power supplies, raw materials or other goods or services. Contracts of a long-term nature give rise to assets and liabilities which, it may be argued, should be recognised, valued and disclosed in external accounting reports.

In order to include executory contracts as liabilities (and assets) on the balance sheet, Anglo-American accounting would have to have a broader definition of a liability than that in current use. The current definition may be traced to Canning (1929) and is very limited compared to that of Ma and Miller (1978, pp.259–260):

> A liability is a negative present value of an anticipated actual or constructive cash flow, other than distributions to owners, where any discretion with respect to the flow is restricted by legal or other compelling sanctions and where the activity that gives rise to the flow is completed or otherwise has progressed to a determinative stage.

This type of definition is also put forward in SAC 4 (1993). This definition would enable the present value of contractual obligations to be included on the balance sheet, together with the assets which represent future service potentials arising out of the contracts, provided that two conditions can be met. These are that management cannot unilaterally amend the contracts and that the activity of the contract has progressed to a deterministic (that is measurable) stage.

Although the definitional and technical issues would suggest few problems in formulating a system (or standard) for the valuation and disclosure of executory contracts in financial statements, it is likely that this refinement is some distance away. The reason is quite simple: the implementation is a political decision, not a technical decision, and further consideration will be needed within the substance versus form debate in the context of accounting reports.

Value added statements

The concept of value added has existed since at least the nineteenth century, but accounting interests have been concerned since the Corporate Report (ASSC, 1975) publicly advocated the use of the value added statement in enhanced corporate disclosures. The subsequent expansion and contraction of value added statement usage has been recorded by Burchell, Clubb and Hopwood (1985). Valued added statements are complex matters having both a 'technical' and a 'social' dimension. We shall first deal with the technical dimension.

Valued added has been defined as sales (or turnover) less the cost of bought-in materials or services (HMSO, 1977, p.7). In practice, turnover includes sales revenue, interest earned and minority interests. Value added may be gross or net. The difference results from the location of the depreciation charge. If depreciation is not included with the bought-in goods and services in calculating value added, then this is a measure of gross value added. Net value added would result from the inclusion of depreciation as a part of bought-in goods and services. In the case of gross value added, the depreciation charge is included with retained earnings as set down in the *pro forma* examples in Table 12.1. The calculation of value added makes up the first part of the statement.

The second part of the value added statement is the distribution of value added between the 'team members' involved in producing it — capital, labour and government — and that remaining in the business. Capital receives interest and dividends, labour gets wages, salaries and bonuses. Taxes and duties paid form the government's share of value added, while retained earnings and depreciation (if gross value added is being used) form a fourth category.

Table 12.1
Value added statement

	Net basis		Gross basis
	Sales		Sales
Less	Bought in goods and services	Less	Bought in goods and services
Less	Depreciation		
Equals	Value added, to be distributed between:	Equals	Value added, to be distributed between:
Labour	Wages, salaries, bonuses	Labour	Wages, salaries, bonuses
Capital	Dividends, interest	Capital	Dividends, interest
Government	Taxes and duties	Government	Taxes and duties
Balance	Retentions	Balance	Retentions and depreciation

As with most accounting statements and reports, there are a number of definitional matters to be decided. For example, when determining the proportion of value added going to labour, do we try to determine all of the benefits received, for example purchases at a discount arising through specific employment, or simply calculate the most obvious — salaries, wages and bonuses? How does one deal with subsidised pension schemes? When determining the proportion of value added going to government, how far do we go in trying to trace all the payments? Are local rates bought-in services or are they payments made to a branch of government? Do we charge excise duty on petrol used in company vehicles separately from bought-in goods?

When considering returns to capital it is usual to separate these between debt holders (interest) and shareholders (dividends). However, returns to capital are not shown as including retained earnings, which are shown as retained for the future development of the entity. This approach is following an entity rather than a proprietary viewpoint. It could also be said to be misleading because it reduces the proportion of value added going to capital compared to that going to labour.

Because value added statements deal with returns to different groups they have a social dimension, since the notion of differential rewards is, by definition, a social matter.

The initial popularity of value added statements was associated with the concept of participatory management, but the amount of value added going to employees has also been used as an industrial bargaining factor. Value added has been suggested as a new form of intercompany comparison (for example value added per $1000 of capital invested) and for the calculation of productivity bonuses (value added per employee).

The recent development of value added may be traced to the Corporate Report

(ASSC, 1975) and the UK Government Green Paper on the reform of company disclosures (HMSO, 1977) which were a product of the social and economic conditions of the period. The increase and decrease in interest in value added statements in the UK have been documented by Burchell, Clubb and Hopwood (1985). They provide data to suggest that the use of the value added statement peaked in 1980 and may not be a major issue in the future. However, the conditions which gave rise to the use of the value added statement in the UK can occur in New Zealand. These include a perceived need to demonstrate teamwork (hence the use of value added and not profit) and the large share of value added going to labour compared to capital (wages, salaries and bonuses compared to dividends and interest).

Value added statements are employed in New Zealand company reports but not to the same extent that they have been used in the UK. In a recent survey of 100 annual reports, various forms of value added statements were provided by only four companies (Ryan, 1989, p.15). This may be compared with an earlier study which showed thirteen such statements (Ryan, 1987, p.9).

It is difficult to predict the future employment of value added statements in New Zealand (or elsewhere). However, under the appropriate social and economic conditions they may become important in presenting additional or reorganised information about an enterprise to a wider audience. These statements have a place in the employee reports which are covered on pages 226–232.

Statements of future prospects

Traditional accounting reports are conservative (prudent) and concerned with past events (historical perspective). Although these conditions are likely to pertain in the future, there have been a number of developments which may lead to the involvement of accountants in the preparation and validation of statements of future prospects. In other words, the accountants of the future may be required to attest to the probable validity of projections, estimates and planned operating forecasts.

The development of a statement of future prospects was discussed in the Corporate Report (ASSC, 1975, pp.55–56). The authors accepted the inherent difficulties in the production of statements of future prospects including: the misunderstanding by users of the nature of forecasts (which are inherently uncertain); a possible strategy by management of lowering their targets to form easily attainable forecasts; and the situation where the provision of forecasts by organisations suffering financial problems might precipitate the difficulties which management are seeking to avoid. Despite their concerns, the authors of the Corporate Report (ASSC, 1975, para. 6.37) recommended that, as a minimum position, corporate reports should include a statement of future prospects for the year following the balance sheet date. The statement should include information about future profit levels, future employment levels and prospects and future investment levels. Also suggested was a note of the major assumptions underlying the statement.

The UK Government Green Paper also referred to the usefulness of having a statement of future prospects. It was noted that the planned development of a corporation was the subject of a disclosure requirement in the EU Fourth Directive on company accounts. However, the Green Paper concluded that the time was not yet right (1977) for future prospects to be the subject of a regular statement. Instead, *ad hoc* disclosures were suggested, including orders in hand, information about major new investment projects including an indication of the likely effect on employment,

and any currently known facts likely to affect materially the future of the company (HMSO, 1977, para. 50).

The reporting and validating of forecasts as well as of past events will eventually become part of the accountant's work. The difficulties should not be overlooked or minimised because it is likely that forecasts will be misunderstood by users and this could be the cause of a loss of confidence in a company already under threat. On the other hand, statements of future prospects will provide an improved data base for both investors and the general public, especially with regard to investment and employment prospects.

Accounting for brands

Introduction

Accounting for brands has become an important topic for accountants, chief financial officers (CFOs) and marketers in the UK and Australia. Although accountants and CFOs in Canada and the USA have not paid much attention to this issue to date, marketers in these countries have become very interested in overseas developments. The valuation of brands is, therefore, an issue to be considered by academic and professional accountants.

The United Kingdom

Until 1990 SSAP 22 required the instant write-off of goodwill against reserves. This approach could result in the consolidated cash flow showing negative equity when purchased goodwill was greater than the acquiring company's reserves. In order to restore the balance sheet to what was believed to be a more sensible position, several UK companies began separating brands from goodwill and including them as assets on the balance sheet at current market value. Some companies went further and also included self-generated brand names on the balance sheet.

In an attempt to make financial statements more consistent, the ASC issued TR 738 in 1989, stating that companies could include purchased brands on the balance sheet, but strongly discouraged the inclusion of self-generated brands as assets. After TR 738 was issued, few companies included self-generated brands on the balance sheet, but many continued to separate purchased brands from goodwill, stating that a market transaction had taken place, and that the value of brands could be determined separately from goodwill.

In 1990 the ASC issued *Accounting for Intangible Fixed Assets* (TR 780) and ED 52 which dealt with intangible fixed assets. The ASC proposed that brands should be included in goodwill and accounted for accordingly. In particular, brands acquired through business combinations were to be treated as purchased goodwill and amortised over a period of not more than twenty years.

Accounting for Intangible Fixed Assets (TR 780) stated that:

> an intangible fixed asset should be recognized in the balance sheet as a fixed asset in its own right if and only if: either the historical costs incurred in creating it are known or it can be clearly demonstrated that they are readily ascertainable; and its characteristics can be clearly distinguished from those of goodwill and other assets; and its cost can be measured independently of goodwill, of other assets and of the earnings of the relevant business or business segment. (ASC, 1990, p.153)

Based on these criteria, it appeared as though the ASC would allow brands to be separately stated on the balance sheet. However, ED 52 stated shortly after that brands should be included within goodwill.

Prior to TR 780 and ED 52, many UK companies chose not to amortise brands included on the balance sheet because, in the opinion of most accountants, the lives were not finite and residual value often exceeded cost. In addressing this issue the ASC concluded that companies were unable to state with reasonable certainty that economic benefits would continue to flow indefinitely from an intangible fixed asset in its existing form.

One issue which remains unresolved in the UK is the fact that tangible assets are accounted for based on their value, whereas intangibles, including goodwill and brands, are not. Sherer (1991, p.179) noted that the brands issue is part of a larger debate which might be assisted by a conceptual framework for accounting.

Are brands separable from goodwill?

Stobart has argued that brands and goodwill are separate issues and should be treated as such. A brand has a separate and independent legal status including any associated goodwill and has only been included as part of goodwill because accountants do not accept the methods of valuing brands, and because of their 'fundamental misunderstanding of the marketing, financial and legal characteristics of a brand' (Stobart, 1989, p.27).

The ASC, in *Accounting for Intangible Fixed Assets* (TR 780) stated that brands:

> may be of considerable value to the business but it is seldom meaningful to recognise them individually for accounting purposes since the benefits from them are derived when they are used in conjunction with the assets and characteristics which go to make up the business. (ASC, 1990, p.153)

According to the ASC, brands are a form of goodwill and should be accounted as such.

Market valuation

Unless brands are included on the balance sheet, there is a danger of the business being undervalued in the market place (Cooper and Carey, 1989, p.28). According to John Murphy, Chairperson of Interbrand (the British company that has conducted numerous brand valuation assignments for companies in the USA, Canada, Europe, Asia, and Australia), the demand for brand valuations was brought about by the increase in mergers and acquisitions. According to Murphy, 'People are paying massive premiums to get their hands on brands and they want to crystallize values' (Eisenhart, 1989, p.36).

As well as being an aid to merger calculations, brand valuation provides Interbrand's clients with a basis for: more critical management; establishing values for licensing purposes (both internal and external); tracking marketing performance; and for understanding in detail the strengths and profitability of brands when buying or selling brands or brand-rich companies.

Cooper and Carey (1989), in a report published by the London Business School (LBS), indicated that the use of unaudited brand valuations might be acceptable in management accounts because the valuations' subjectivity and lack of verifiability are outweighed by their relevance to various management decisions.

Arguments against market valuation

The Institute Research Board (UK) commissioned a team from the LBS to survey existing brand valuation practices and analyse valuation methods, the nature and separability of brands and the impact of relevant accounting practices on financial markets. The research team sought the views of brand valuers, preparers, finance directors and analysts. They concluded that brands should not be accounted for separately from goodwill and the rest of the business.

In response to those who believe that separating brands from goodwill and reflecting those brands at market value on the balance sheet allows the capital market to correctly value the business, the LBS research team stated that: 'market analysts

reveal very clearly that they have not been, and are never likely to be, impressed by balance sheet branding as presently practised'. Furthermore, 'such exercises disclose remarkably little new information about brands, and only the most naive analyst could be influenced by the impact of such soft information'. Analysts and bankers were more interested in cash flow, interest coverage and underlying asset values 'and their treatment of these is unlikely to be coloured by the sudden appearance of an unexplained asset on the balance sheet' (Cooper and Carey, 1989, p.28).

With regard to valuation methods, the survey revealed that there is no generally accepted method of calculation and the valuations currently used do not meet the requirement that an asset's magnitude be measurable and verifiable with reasonable certainty. The LBS research team stated that it was impossible to identify a valid and objective way of separating a brand's incremental cash flow from the rest of the business. They also thought that the issues of verifiability and separability would pose severe problems for auditors: auditors would be able to audit only the process and not book values because of the difficulty of separation of the brands.

When the LBS report was issued in the UK, goodwill was written off against reserves. It did not affect net income, neither did it appear as an asset on the balance sheet. The LBS research team revealed that a major goal of brand valuation by UK companies had been to:

> repair or pre-empt equity depletion caused by SSAP 22, *Accounting for Goodwill*, and suggested that if goodwill were to be carried in the balance sheet with parallel treatment of intangibles, much of the immediate pressure for brand accounting would evaporate. (Cooper and Carey, 1989, p.28)

Another concern of the LBS research team was that 'a dangerous circularity may

arise when accounts try to measure the economic value of the business rather than provide information for outsiders to do so'
(Cooper and Carey, 1989, p.28).

As Greener (1989) has observed, British
companies that included the market value
of their brand names in the balance sheet
must be able to demonstrate their ability to
earn adequate returns on those assets. He
reminded managers that although including
current brand values among fixed assets
would bring the net asset value more in line
with the company's market value, it could
have a dramatic effect on the apparent
return on capital employed.

Methods of brand valuation

Interbrand have claimed that their technique could help companies place an
accurate value on their brand names.
Interbrand:

> establishes a brand's profitability and
> then analyses its strengths and weak-
> nesses according to seven factors: lead-
> ership, stability, international presence,
> investment support, trademark protec-
> tion, long-term trends, and stability of
> the brand's market. Interbrand then
> develops a multiple it applies to the
> brand's profit to determine the brand's
> asset value. (Eisenhart, 1989, p.36)

Interbrand's executives consider their
techniques to be more accurate than others
which are based exclusively on market
value, the cost of a brand's research and
development, or marketing and advertising, because it includes other factors such
as financial, accounting and marketing
practices (Eisenhart, 1989, p.36).
P. Stobart (1989), Managing Director of
Interbrand, admitted that subjectivity is
involved in valuing brands, but did not
think there was any difference between
seeking help on brand valuation and the
valuation of property (p. 27).

Australia

The Australian ASRB issued *Accounting for
Goodwill* (ASRB 1013) in April 1988.
Goodwill in the Australian standard was
defined as 'the future benefits from uniden-
tified assets'. When acquired, goodwill is
included as an asset on the balance sheet
and is amortised over a maximum period of
twenty years. Self-generated goodwill is not
included on the balance sheet.

The AARF published *Accounting for
Identifiable Intangible Assets* (ED 49) in
August 1989. Brands are accounted for
differently in that acquired, as well as
internally-developed, brands are included
on the balance sheet and are amortised
over the period of time during which benefits are expected to arise. The amortisation period is not set at any maximum
number of years. However, ED 49 requires
detailed disclosures when the period
exceeds twenty years.

Australia, which used a modified HCA
system, requires revaluation of assets,
including goodwill and brands, when their
market values differ from initially-recorded
costs of acquisition. Exposure draft 49
requires brands to be 'recorded at the lowest cost at which the assets could currently
be obtained in the normal course of business' (Rutteman, 1990, p.26).

Because of the different methods of
accounting for goodwill and brands, many
Australian companies are now separating
brand names from goodwill and including
them on the balance sheet. An Australian
survey by Ernst & Young found that thirty
out of Australia's top 150 companies
included an amount for brand values, news-
paper mastheads or other intellectual property in their accounts. Rutteman is critical
of the Australian position because it prescribes different accounting treatment for
similar assets. One important difference
between the Australian and UK positions is
the support given by the conceptual framework in Australia.

New Zealand

The position in New Zealand is less advanced than in Australia. There is no standard covering the disclosure of goodwill, either purchased or internally generated, although the treatment of goodwill is covered as a small entry in *Accounting for Business Combinations* (SSAP 8). In this standard goodwill acquired through the purchase of a going concern must be disclosed and then written off over no more than ten years. There are several large New Zealand corporations which disclose the valuations placed upon the brands owned or controlled. However, the closest that the New Zealand accounting profession has come to a standard dealing with intangible assets and internally generated goodwill (including brands) was ED 43 which has been withdrawn. The issues encompassed by both purchased and internally generated goodwill in general and brand valuation and disclosure in particular are not likely to disappear and New Zealand accounting standard setters will be required to address them again in the near future.

The United States of America and Canada

Collins (1991) reported that the CFO of sixty-eight large North American corporations responded to a questionnaire regarding their interest in including brand values on the balance sheet and, contrary to expectations, they were 'opposed to brand valuation in almost every instance and in almost any form — even for the purpose of internal use'.

When exploring reasons for the different attitudes of countries which hold the same basic philosophy of accounting (USA and Canada versus the UK), Collins pointed to the existence of the SEC and the FASB in the USA. These bodies, 'whose legal positions are much more deeply entrenched than that of regulators in the UK', have set explicit rulings on the procedures for the write-off of intangible assets (Collins, 1991,

p. 2). Related to this is the fact that the USA and Canada prohibit the revaluation of fixed assets.

Collins offered other reasons for the negative attitude found among North American CFOs. Reasons included a possible lack of information regarding the development of brand valuation practices and differing philosophies of brand management and control between the USA and Canada and other countries. Although Collins found that North American CFOs were not interested in reporting brand values on their balance sheets, other American managers have spoken up with regard to the issue. Marketing and financial managers are criticising CFOs for using traditional measures only such as cash flow, sales and profits to value companies. These managers have pointed to the importance of attempting to value brands, especially with regard to mergers and acquisitions.

Allan Baldinger, Director of Marketing Research for the ARF, believes there are four major trends from outside the traditional world of marketing research propelling the interest in brand equity measurement. These are: brand dominance; the new products to brand extension shift; new learning on the advertising and promotion mix; and the merging of financial and marketing needs and principles (Baldinger, 1990, p. 3). Baldinger has stated that strong profits come from brand dominance and consequently, building and maintaining strong brands is very important. With regard to the shift from new products to brand extension, there is a move away from building brands from scratch. In addition, marketers have discovered important trends in advertising and promotion with regard to brands. Baldinger argued that product quality perceptions fostered by brands are becoming more important than price. In discussing the merging of financial thinking with marketing, Baldinger suggests that a firm's financial decisions will be increasingly dependent upon marketing decisions in the

1990s. Whereas marketing spending was thought of as merely an expense in the 1970s and 1980s, these expenditures will be considered as increasing the value of companies' franchises in the 1990s. To understand the importance of brands more clearly, the ARF has established a Brand Equity Committee. The Committee found that the concept of brand equity is difficult to define and measure.

American and Canadian accountants, managerial and financial, will undoubtedly become more involved in brand valuation decisions as companies become more aware of valuation techniques being developed abroad as well as by domestic marketers. Although including the market value of brands on the balance sheet is not possible under the present historical cost convention, valuation is certainly possible and increasingly necessary for internal purposes. Unless the accounting profession develops methods of brand valuation and supplies this information to management, marketing and financial managers will develop their own calculations which may or may not be based on sound accounting practices. With regard to financial accounting, brand valuation points to many of the same questions and arguments raised by American and Canadian accountants in respect of other issues. Some of these questions are discussed briefly below.

(a) Should the costs of internally developed brands be considered assets or should they be expensed immediately?

(b) Do financial statements based on historical cost provide investors, creditors, and other stakeholders with relevant information?

(c) Would financial statements be more relevant to users if current value information were included as supplementary information?

(d) Could current values be considered neutral and could they be verified?

(e) Would the cost of establishing and verifying current values outweigh the benefits derived from the information?

Should the costs of internally-developed brands be considered assets, or should they be expensed immediately?

Assets are defined by the FASB SFAC 3 as:

> probable future economic benefits obtained or controlled by a particular entity as a result of past transactions or events. The three basic characteristics are: (1) probable future economic benefits, (2) control by the entity and (3) the result of a past transaction or event. (Hendriksen, 1982, p.251)

Based on this definition and these characteristics, brands would be considered an asset. The entire purpose of establishing strong brand names is to incur future economic benefits through increased sales to loyal customers, or through an increased sales price of the brand or the business that owns the brand. Future values are difficult to measure, but according to Hendriksen (1982, p.251):

> the fact that the future value of a right or service potential may be uncertain does not remove it from the definition of assets. The uncertainty affects the valuation, but it changes the nature of the item only if the uncertainty is so great that the expected future benefit is zero or negative.

Companies with valuable brands register those names and are legally entitled to sole ownership and use of them (and there is no question of control over them). Finally, brands are created through marketing efforts over time; they are the result of several past transactions and events:

> Expenses are the using or consuming of goods and services in the process of obtaining revenues. They are the expirations of factor services related either directly or indirectly to the producing and selling of the product of the enterprise. The values of these factor services expire when they leave the enterprise by

final consumption or by the transfer of the product to customers. (Hendriksen, 1982, p.187)

Since the value of brands does not leave the enterprise in the same period as marketing expenditures are incurred, most of these expenditures should not be considered expenses in the period incurred. In addition, to properly match expenses with revenues, marketing expenditures which create brand value should not be treated as expenses until period revenue is realised.

In the USA all marketing expenditures are expensed as they are incurred. No asset is established for the future benefits of those expenditures and no calculations are made regarding the value of brands. This is inconsistent with the way other organisational resources are accounted for, leaving brand managers at a disadvantage when competing for finite organisational resources. Treating expenditures for investments in brands as expenses rather than as assets results in a distorted measure of an organisation's return on investment and therefore creates problems for investors who attempt to value an organisation. Since return on investment is the ratio of net income to total assets, the ratio is distorted when brands are all accounted for in the denominator. Consequently, investors must attempt to adjust for brand investments if they wish to base decisions on an organisation's return on investment.

Another result of including all brand costs as expenses in the income statement is the unintended emphasis on short term results. This could motivate management to disregard the long-term interests of the organisation and emphasise short-term results because managers are concerned with the 'bottom line', and under current accounting practice, brand expenditures directly decrease net income.

Are financial statements relevant and reliable when they are based only on historical cost information?

Statement of Financial Accounting Concept 2 defines the primary qualitative characteristics of accounting as 'relevance' and 'reliability'. The relevance of accounting information is determined by its timeliness, feedback value and predictive value. Reliability of information involves verifiability, neutrality and representational faithfulness. The FASB argues that the principal concern of existing investors and creditors is to evaluate prior expectations about cash flows that occurred in the current period and with the inclusion of the statement of cash flows, these users should be able to make that evaluation. Historical cost provides relevant information to them.

However, the principal concern of potential investors and creditors and a related concern of existing providers of funds is the prospect for favourable cash flows in the future. Balance sheet and income statement information, including the related disclosures, should be presented in a manner that facilitates evaluation of the prospect for future cash flows. Recording assets at fair value seems to give financial statement users more relevant information for predictive purposes than assets based on historical cost. Because of this, assets such as inventories and financial instruments must now be reported at their fair value if that value is less than original cost.

In the USA materiality is sometimes used as a proxy for relevance. Auditors traditionally have treated materiality quantitatively, calculating a threshold dollar amount of assets, liabilities, revenues and expenses which supposedly depicts financial statement users' boundary of relevance. As accountants become increasingly concerned with supplying information to identified users (after determining those users' needs) materiality has become much more qualitative. Materiality is no longer a set of numbers, but is a determination of what items users need to make informed decisions and which of those items users are most sensitive to.

As the concept of materiality evolves, the demand for more relevant information will increase. Accountants will search for new and better ways to supply financial statement users with the information they require to make informed investment decisions. Issues, such as reporting assets at fair value, will become increasingly debated. This will probably eventually lead to a widespread interest in determining and disclosing the value of non-traditional assets such as brands. Examples of these concerns can already be found.

In the USA historical cost information might not provide the most relevant information, but it continues to be the most reliable. Historical cost is verifiable and neutral and it represents what it purports to represent. Measuring the fair value of assets presents problems with reliability. The FASB is currently wrestling with the issue of whether market value or present value of future expected cash flows is a better approximation of fair value.

Section summary

Financial and marketing managers and investors in Anglo-American accounting countries have become increasingly interested in determining the value of brands. Because of a lack of support from the accounting profession, these financial statement users are developing their own methods for calculating brand values. If standard-setting bodies recognise that the valuations are necessary, consistent methods of valuation can be devised by the accounting profession.

As long as the balance sheet continues to be presented on the historical cost basis, brand valuations are presented as supplementary information to the financial statements, satisfying the needs of managers and investors alike.

The current positions in Australia, the UK and North America have been found to be different. These differences are probably related to other developments such as conceptual framework projects, valuations other than strictly historical cost and the manner in which accounting standards are determined. These issues point to the need for further research, to examine the necessity for and methods of valuing brands and also the general need for more relevant and consistent information. If financial accountants are going to continue to do what they purport to do — to provide information useful to financial statement readers — then they must remain aware of what information the users need and want.

Essay and examination questions

Debt defeasance

12.1   Debt defeasance: financial tool or window dressing? Discuss.

12.2   The controversy surrounding debt defeasance highlights the need for a conceptual framework in standard setting. Discuss.

12.3   Should debt defeasance be allowed? Why?

Segmental reporting

12.4   Discuss some of the problems you consider to be inherent in any attempt by accountants to engage in segmental reporting.

12.5   Segmental reporting has had a mixed reception among preparers of financial statements. Suggest why this should be so. (Make recommendations where appropriate.)

12.6   Examine segmental reporting. Relate its developments in the USA, the UK, Australia and New Zealand. Comment on the similarities and differences.

12.7   Examine a recent set of financial accounts and identify the manner in which the segmental information has been organised. To what extent do you perceive the segmental information to be beneficial?

12.8   Examine at least two accounting standards for segmental reporting. To what extent are they the same? What differences are there?

Employee reporting

12.9   Employee reports are part of the communication process. Discuss.

12.10 What is an employee report? Discuss its origin, development, current status and likely future importance.

12.11 Why should special reports be used to give information to employees? How does this relate to the pluralistic, extended view of corporate accountability expounded by the Corporate Report (ASSC, 1975).

12.12 Employee reports are used by a relatively small proportion of corporations, and yet the management of these same organisations would regard themselves as good communicators. Discuss.

12.13 Do employees have rights to information about the organisations for which they work? Explain your position?

Leases and executory contracts

12.14 Executory contracts are a logical extension of reporting on lease contracts. Discuss.

12.15 Argue the case for and against the inclusion of executory contracts in company reports.

12.16 Explain the illogicality of presently established disclosure practices in respect of executory contracts and contingent liabilities.

12.17 To what extent has the controversy over SAC 4 affected the disclosure of leases in financial statements?

12.18 To what extent has the controversy over SAC 4 affected the disclosure of executory contracts in financial statements?

Statements of value added

12.19 The inclusion of value added statements in company accounts is an example of recognising the needs of a wider audience. Discuss.

12.20 Value added statements are simply a reorganisation of existing information and contribute little to added understanding. Discuss.

12.21 Argue the case for and against the inclusion of value added statements in company reports.

12.22 To what extent does the AARF conceptual framework assist in arguing the case for the disclosure of value added in financial statements?

12.23 The rise and fall of value added as a frequently used disclosure device was a product of particular circumstances. Discuss.

Statements of future prospects

12.24 To include statements of future prospects in annual reports of corporations is to invite legal action from dissatisfied investors. Evaluate this statement.

12.25 Accountants are known for their ability to record the past and analyse the present; they should leave the future to take care of itself. Discuss.

12.26 Consider the likely result of the use of statements of future prospects; would the future be changed as much as some observers suggest?

Accounting for brands

12.27 The recognition, valuation and disclosure of brands creates as many problems as it solves. Discuss.

12.28 Distinguish between accounting for purchased goodwill, internally generated goodwill and the valuation of brands. How can financial statements be consistent in the treatment accorded to these identities?

12.29 If we account for purchased goodwill in a particular manner, then we should account for internally generated goodwill in the same way. Discuss.

12.30 Examine the disclosure of brands from the perspective of the AARF conceptual framework.

12.31 Review the arguments both for and against the valuation and disclosure of brand values in financial statements in the light of traditional accounting positions on objectivity, transactions and prudence.

References and additional reading

Accounting Standards Committee Report (1990). Brands: A Valuable Part of Goodwill. *Accountancy,* **105**, 153.

Accounting Standards Review Board (1986). *ASRB 1005: Financial Reporting by Segments.* Australia.

Accounting Standards Steering Committee (1975). *The Corporate Report: A Discussion Paper.* London: ICAEW.

Aitken, M.J., Czernkowski, R.M. and Hooper, C.G. (1994). The information content of segment disclosures: Australian evidence: *Abacus,* **30**(1), 65–77.

Ajinkya, B. (1980). An empirical evaluation of line-of-business reporting. *Journal of Accounting Research,* **18**, 343–361.

Alexander, M.O. (1973). Social accounting if you please. *CA Magazine,* **102**, 23–33.

Arpan, J.S. and Radebaugh, L.H. (1985). *International Accounting and Multinational Enterprises* (2nd edn). New York: John Wiley & Sons.

Australian Accounting Research Foundation (1988). *Set-off and Extinguishment of Debt.* Statement of Accounting Standards AAS 23. Melbourne: AARF.

Australian Accounting Research Foundation (1993). *Definition and Recognition of Liabilities SAC 4.* Melbourne: AARF.

Australian Society of Accountants and the Institute of Chartered Accountants in Australia (1984, reissued 1987). *AAS 16: Statement of Accounting Standards — 'Financial Reporting by Segments'.*

Backer, M. and McFarland, W. (1968). *External Reporting for Segments of a Business.* New York: National Association of Accountants.

Balakrishnan, R., Harris, T.S. and Sen, P.K. (1990). The predictive ability of geographic segment disclosures. *Journal of Accounting Research,* **28**, 305–325.

Baldinger, A. (1990). Defining and Applying the Brand Equity Concept: Why the Research Should Care. *Journal of Advertising,* **30**, 2–5.

Belkaoui, A. (1986). *The New Environment in International Accounting.* Westport: Quorum.

Bradbury, M. (1987). Debt defeasance: Financial tool or window dressing? *Accountants' Journal,* **66**, 30–31.

Brunner, P. (1989). Set-off and extinguishment of debt. *Accountants' Journal,* **68**, 39–42.

Bullock, A. (1977). *Report of the Committee of Inquiry on Industrial Democracy.* London.

Burchell, S., Clubb, C. and Hopwood, A.G. (1985). Accounting in its social context: Towards a history of value-added in the United Kingdom. *Accounting, Organizations and Society,* **10**(4), 381–413.

Canning, J.B. (1929). *The Economics of Accountancy.* New York: Roland Press.

Chaney, P.K. (1985). Defeasance: Financial tool or window dressing? *Management Accounting,* **67**, 52–55.

Chye, M.H.F. (1984). Employee reports: Another channel of communication, in M.R. Mathews (Ed.), *Readings in the Development of Accounting.* Palmerston North: Dunmore Press, 217–257.

Collins, D. and Simonds, R. (1979). SEC line-of-business disclosure and market risk adjustments. *Journal of Accounting Research,* **17**, 352–383.

Collins, R. (1991). Brand Valuations and Executive Opinion: Issues Raised by the Results of a Survey of Chief Financial Officers in the US and Canada, Concerning Their Reaction to the Placing of Brand Valuations in the Financial Statements of Corporations. *3rd Asian-Pacific Conference on International Accounting Issues,* Honolulu, 277–280.

Cooper, M. and Carey, A. (1989). Brand Valuation in the Balance. *Accountancy,* **104**, 28.

Craig, R. and Hussey, R. (1981). Employee reports: What employees want: *The Chartered Accountant in Australia,* **52**(4), 29–34.

Craig, R. and Hussey, R. (1982). *Keeping Employees Informed.* Melbourne: Butterworths.

Deegan, C. (1985). In-substance debt defeasance — time for guidance? *The Chartered Accountant in Australia,* **56**, 54–57.

Delbridge, A. *et al.* (Eds) (1991). *The Macquarie Dictionary.* Sydney: The Macquarie Library.

Devonport, F. and McNally, G. M. (1985). *RII5: The Reporting of Segmental Information.* Wellington: NZSA.

Dhaliwal, D. (1978). The impact of disclosure regulations on the cost of capital. *Economic Consequences of Financial Accounting Standards: Selected Papers.* Stamford: FASB.

Eisenhart, T. (1989). Marketers Eye Technique to Find Brand Value. *Business Marketing,* **74**, 36.

Emmanuel, C. and Garrod, N. (1992). *Segment Reporting: International issues and evidence.* Hertfordshire: ICAEW–Prentice Hall.

Emmanuel, C.R. and Gray, S.J. (1977). Segmental disclosures and the segment identification problem. *Accounting and Business Research.* Winter. 37–50.

Emmanuel, C.R. and Gray, S.J. (1978). Segmental disclosures by multibusiness multinational companies: A proposal. *Accounting and Business Research.* Summer. 169–177.

Everingham, G. (1991). Financial reporting to employees. *Accountancy SA,* **8**(8), 216–17, 220.

Everingham, G. (1994). Employee report award. *Accountancy SA*, May, 30–31.

Financial Accounting Standards Board (1976). *Accounting for Leases FAS 13*. New York: FASB.

Financial Accounting Standards Board (1976). *SFAS No. 14: Financial Reporting for Segments of a Business Enterprise*. Stamford.

Financial Accounting Standards Board (1983). *Extinguishment of Debt*. Statement of Financial Accounting Standards No. 76. Stamford: FASB.

Firth, M. and Smith, A. (1984). Reporting to employees. *Cost and Management Accounting Bulletin, No. 26*. Wellington: NZSA.

Forley, B.J. and Maunders, K.T. (1977). *Accounting Information Disclosure and Collective Bargaining*. London: Macmillan.

Fry, E. (1989). The art of masking life's realities. *Sunday Star,* 2 April, D1.

Gaumnitz, B.R. and Thompson, J.E. (1987). In-substance defeasance: Costs, yes; benefits, no. *Journal of Accountancy,* March, 102–105.

Gavens, J. and Carnegie, G. (1988). Segment reporting. *The Australian Accountant,* **58**(3), 29–34.

Gray, R., Owen, D. and Maunders, K. (1987). *Corporate Social Reporting: Accounting and Accountability*. London: Prentice Hall.

Gray, S.J. (1978). Segment reporting and the EEC multinationals. *Journal of Accounting Research,* **16**(2), 242–253.

Gray, S.J., McSweeney, L.B. and Shaw, J.C. (1984). *Information Disclosure and the Multinational Corporation*. Chichester: John Wiley.

Gray, S.J. and Radebaugh L.H. (1984). International segment disclosures by US and UK multinational enterprises: A descriptive study. *Journal of Accounting Research,* **22**(1), 351–360.

Greener, M. (1989). The Bomb in the Balance Sheet. *Accountancy,* **104**, 74–75.

Haggie, D. (1984). The annual report as an aid to communication. *Accountancy,* 66–69.

Henderson, S. and Peirson, C.G. (1983). *Financial Accounting Theory: Its Nature and Development*. Melbourne: Longman Cheshire.

Hendriksen, E. S. (1982). *Accounting Theory*. Homewood, Ill.: Irwin.

Hendriksen, E.S. (1982). *Accounting Theory* (Fourth edition). Homewood, Ill: Irwin.

Hilton, A. (1978). *Employee Reports: How to Communicate Financial Information to Employees*. Cambridge: Woodhead-Faulkner.

HMSO (1977). *The Future of Company Reports: A Consultative Document*. London.

Horwitz, B. and Kolodny, R. (1977). Line of business reporting and security prices: An analysis of an SEC disclosure rule. *Bell Journal of Economics*, **8**, 234–249.

Hussey, R. (1980). Communicating financial information to employees: An evaluation. *Certified Accountant,* 149–151, 153–154, 214.

Hussey, R. (1981). Reporting to employees. *Accountancy,* 122–126.

Hussey, R. (1984). Vredeling ready to spring trap on the unwary. *Accountancy,* 75–76.

Hussey, R. and Craig, R.J. (1979). Employee reports: What employees think. *The Chartered Accountant in Australia,* **50**(4), 39–44.

Hussey, R. and Craig, R.J. (1980). Why some companies do not issue employee reports: UK and Australian perspectives. *The Chartered Accountant in Australia,* **51**(2), 45–49.

Hussey, R. and Marsh, A. (1983). *Disclosure of Information and Employee Reporting.* Aldershot: Gower.

International Accounting Standards Committee (1981). *IAS 14: Reporting Financial Information by Segment.* London.

Kinney, W. (1971). Predicting earnings: Entity vs. subentity data. *Journal of Accounting Research,* **9**, 127–136.

Ma, R. and Miller, M.C. (1978). Conceptualising the liability. *Accounting and Business Research.* Autumn, 258–265.

Marks, R. (1993). Insider reporting. *Accountancy Age,* March, 21–22.

Maunders, K.T. (1981). Employee reporting, in T.A. Lee (Ed.), *Development in Financial Reporting.* Oxford: Philip Allan, 171–194.

Mautz, R. (1968). *Financial Reporting by Diversified Companies.* New York: Financial Executives Research Foundation.

Mitchell, F., Sams, K.I. and White, P.J. (1981). Financial disclosure to employees: A managerial view. *The Accountants' Magazine,* 110–112.

Mitchell, F., Sams, K.I. and White, P.J. (1986). Directors' reports on employee involvement. *The Accountants' Magazine,* 30–31.

New Zealand Society of Accountants (1979). *Explanatory Foreword to Statements of Standard Accounting Practice.* Wellington: NZSA.

New Zealand Society of Accountants (1983). *Determination and Disclosure of Accounting Policies.* Statement of Standard Accounting Practice SSAP 1. Wellington: NZSA.

New Zealand Society of Accountants (1988). *ED 44: Financial Reporting for Segments.* Wellington: NZSA.

New Zealand Society of Accountants (1989). *Set-off and Extinguishment of Debt.* Exposure Draft ED 47. Wellington: NZSA.

New Zealand Society of Accountants (1989). *SSAP 23: Financial Reporting for Segments.* Wellington: NZSA.

New Zealand Society of Accountants (1990). *Accounting for Defeasance of Debt.* Exposure Draft ED 47A. Wellington: NZSA.

Organization for Economic Cooperation and Development (1979). *International Investment and Multinational Enterprises, Review of the 1976 Declaration Decisions.* Paris: OECD.

Owen, D. (1981). Why accountants can't afford to turn their backs on social accounting. *Accountancy* 44–45.

Parker, L.D. (1976), Social accounting: Don't wait for it. *The Accountants' Magazine,* 50–52.

Parker, L.D. (1977). Financial reporting to corporate employees: A growing practice in Australia. *The Chartered Accountant in Australia,* **48**(2), 5–9.

Parker, L.D. (1980). Reflections on corporate financial reporting to employees in Australia. *The Chartered Accountant in Australia,* **51**(10), 21–22.

Parker, L.D. (Ed.) (1988). *Financial Reporting to Employees: From Past to Present.* New York: Garland.

Parker, L.D., Ferris, K.R. and Otley, D.J. (1989). *Accounting for the Human Factor.* Sydney: Prentice Hall.

Perera, M.H.B. and Mathews, M.R. (1987). *The Interrelationship of Culture and Accounting with Particular Reference to Social Accounting.* Discussion Paper No. 59. Palmerston North: Massey University, Department of Accountancy.

Preston, L.E. (1981). Research on corporate social reporting: Directions for development. *Accounting, Organizations and Society,* **6**(3), 255–262.

Purdy, D. (1981). The provision of financial information to employees: A study of the reporting practices of some large public companies in the United Kingdom. *Accounting, Organizations and Society,* **6**(4), 327–338.

Radebaugh, L.H. and Gray, S.J. (1993). *International Accounting and Multinational Enterprises* (3rd Ed.). New York: John Wiley.

Reynolds, R. (1992). Team talk. *Accountancy Age,* January, pp.30–32.

Roden, P.F. (1987). The financial implications of in-substance defeasance. *Journal of Accounting, Auditing and Finance,* **2**, 79–89.

Rutteman, P. (1990). Boosting the Profits of the Brands Industry. *Accountancy,* **105**, 26–27.

Ryan, J.B. (Ed.) (1987). *New Zealand Company Financial Reporting: 1987.* Wollongong: University of Wollongong Press.

Ryan, J.B. (Ed.) (1989). *New Zealand Company Financial Reporting: 1989.* Auckland: AIT. Wollongong: University of Wollongong Press.

Ryan, J.B., Heazlewood, C.T., Wong, J. and Chye, M.H.F. (1984). *New Zealand Company Financial Reporting: 1984.* Wollongong: University of Wollongong Press.

Schreuder, H. (1979). Employees and the corporate social report: The Dutch case: *The Accounting Review,* 294–308.

Shearer, B. (1986). Substance over form: Fine but not as a concept. *The Accountant,* **194**, 10.

Sherer, M.J. (1991). Accounting for Brands: A Review Essay. *British Accounting Review,* **23**, 179–182.

Smith, A. and Firth, M. (1986). Employee reporting in New Zealand: What employees think. *Accountants' Journal,* **65**(10), 24–26.

Smith, A. and Firth, M. (1987). Employee reporting in New Zealand: What employers think. *Accountants' Journal,* **66**(11), 55–57.

Stobart, P. (1989). Brand Valuation: A True and Fair View. *Accountancy,* **104**, 27–28.

Swaminathan, S. (1991). The impact of SEC mandated segment data on price variability and divergence of beliefs. *The Accounting Review,* **66**(1), 23–41.

Taylor, D., Webb, L. and McGinley, L. (1979). Annual reports to employees: The challenge to the corporate accountant. *The Chartered Accountant in Australia,* **50**(2), 33–39.

United Nations (1977). *International Standards of Accounting and Reporting for Transnational Corporations.* New York: UN.

Unruh, A.R. and Mathews, M.R. (1993). Should Anything be Done about the Valuation and Disclosure of Brands? *Indian Journal of Accounting.* Vol. XXIV, 7–15.

Walton, P. (1985). Extinguishment by in-substance defeasance. *The Accountant,* **192**, 14–15.

Webb, L. and Taylor, D. (1980). Employee reporting: Don't wait for it. *The Australian Accountant,* 30–34.

Wise, T. and Wise, V. (1988). Debt defeasance. *The Chartered Accountant in Australia,* **59**, 40–41.

Learning objectives

After studying this chapter the reader will be able to:
* define human resource accounting
* explain the functions of human resource accounting
* consider the recent developments in human resource accounting
* describe models and methods that have been developed for the measurement of human resource costs and values
* discuss the associated disclosure issues relevant to human resource accounting
* present a possible procedure for the development and implementation of a human resource accounting system.

Introduction

For thirty years some accountants have been attempting to place a value on human resources, although not a lot of interest has surrounded this issue since the late 1970s. However, with the development of a more technically competent and highly educated workforce, and as there are more mergers and acquisitions, a small number of managers and accountants are once again investigating the importance of valuing human resources.

This chapter will explore the definitions and functions of human resource accounting (HRA), highlight the criticisms associated with recording human resources as assets and describe some models and methods developed for the measurement of human resource costs and values. It will also examine applications of HRA and present one possible procedure for the development and implementation of an HRA system.

Definitions of human resource accounting

In 1973 the AAA's Committee on Human Resource Accounting defined HRA as 'the process of identifying and measuring data about human resources and communicating this information to interested parties' (AAA, 1973, p.169). According to the Work Institute in America (WIA, 1978) HRA is:

the development of a theoretical perspective explaining the nature and determinants of the value of people to formal organizations; the development of valid and reliable methods for measuring the cost and value of people to organizations; and the design of operational systems to implement the proposed measurement methods. (p.2)

The WIA (1978) stated that the functional objectives of HRA are:

1. To furnish cost-value information for making management decisions about acquiring, allocating, developing, and maintaining human resources in order to attain cost-effective organisational objectives
2. To allow managerial personnel to effectively monitor the use of human resources
3. To provide for a determination of asset control, i.e., whether assets are conserved, depleted, or appreciated
4. To aid in the development of management principles by clarifying the financial consequences of various practices. (p.2)

Functions of human resource accounting

Since the early 1960s, a number of research studies have found that management, investors and the public in general can all benefit from the use of HRA information.

Human resource accounting was considered to be a valuable management tool. Flamholtz (1975) identified three major functions of HRA as a management tool: an information function; a paradigm function; and a catalyst function. He argued that HRA provided information to managers about the cost and value of personnel to an organisation and that the specific type of information provided was determined by the specific needs of a given organisation. According to Flamholtz (1974), HRA provided managers with a way of thinking about the management of people as valuable organisational resources.

In organisations without HRA systems, all human resource expenditures are expensed as incurred, without any future benefits resulting from those expenditures and no calculations are made regarding the value of human resources. Because this is inconsistent with the way other organisational resources are accounted for, personnel managers are at a disadvantage when competing for finite organisational resources. For example, plant asset managers can present a case using both costs and benefits. Personnel managers, however, are more likely to present a case using costs only. When competing for dollars, plant asset managers may have a more convincing case and a better basis for evaluation. Dawson (1988, p.32) has suggested that HRA has provided a framework to make the personnel manager's investment argument compatible and consistent with that of other managers.

Gall (1988, p.8) pointed out that accounting for costs and effectiveness are the only two methods human resource professionals have to evaluate their performance. He argued that management is seeking more ways to relate the performance of human resources to the accomplishment of business objectives and strategies (1988, p.22).

In addition to providing managers with important evaluative information, HRA also helps investors obtain information about an organisation's human assets. Research studies have indicated that investors change their minds about investment decisions when human resource information is disclosed (Rogow and Edmonds, 1988, p.169). Current financial accounting practice for most companies treats all expenditures for investment in human resources as expenses rather than as assets, resulting in a distorted measure of return on investment (Flamholtz, 1974, p.21). Since return on investment equals the ratio of net income to total assets, the ratio is distorted when human resources are accounted for in the denominator. Consequently, investors must attempt to adjust for investments in human assets if they wish to base decisions on an organisation's return on investment. Another result of including all human resource costs as expenses in the income statement is the unintended emphasis on short-term results. According to Flamholtz (1974, p.20), this accounting convention motivates management to emphasise short-term results because managers are concerned with the bottom line and under current accounting practice human resource expenditures directly decrease net income.

Another group affected by the use of HRA is society. Increasingly, business organisations are expected to meet defined standards of corporate responsibility with regard to issues such as minority employment, women's rights and employee satisfaction. Human resource accounting can provide valuable information, facilitate corporate social accountability for employees and control the liquidation and depletion of the economy's human capital (Flamholtz, 1974, p.306).

Recording human resources as assets

Flamholtz (1974) identified three main criteria for recognising an asset: future service potential; measurable in monetary terms; and subject to the ownership or 'control' of the accounting entity. Advocates see the recording of human resources as assets as an essential element of HRA. However, there are problems associated with this accounting treatment and the debate is far from complete, particularly because of the difficulty of measuring the attributes used to recognise an asset.

The Work Institute in America (1978) has indicated that the arguments used by those who are opposed to disclosing human resources as assets include the legalistic definition of ownership of assets (Newell, 1972; Jauch and Skigen, 1974; Nicholls, 1975). Jauch and Skigen (1974) and Nicholls (1975) have also noted the inability of the accounting profession to develop a system of human resource valuation. Nicholls indicated that there would be difficulties with depreciation and the renewal of human assets. These arguments resemble those used to oppose the capitalisation of leases and executory contracts over many years. The responses from advocates of HRA are also familiar. Brummet (1970) refers to the legalistic bias that accountants have frequently adopted; Flamholtz (1974) counters with an emphasis on 'asset control' similar to that of a lessee; and WIA (1978) cited Robinson (1975), agreeing that human assets are not capable of personal ownership, but nevertheless there is often a high degree of permanence in the relationship from year to year (WIA, 1978, p.3)

The main arguments used by the advocates of HRA to refute the criticism that there is no assurance of future benefits came from Gilbert (1970), Flamholtz (1974), Robinson (1975) and Jaggi (1976). Their positions may be summarised based on the service potential of employees. The potential for providing economic benefits for the firm indicates that human resources should be treated as assets (WIA, 1978, p.3). However, there are objections to the process of valuing human beings.

Measuring human resource cost

There are problems associated with measurement of the human asset: what costs are involved, how can these costs be amortised and how is the write-off to be accomplished? Flamholtz (1974, p.33) has defined cost in terms of sacrifices that need to be made to be able to acquire tangible or intangible benefits. At least three different concepts may be employed in measuring human resource costs: (a) original or historical cost; (b) replacement cost; and (c) opportunity cost (WIA, 1978, p.8).

Original or historical cost is calculated by capitalising all the costs incurred to recruit, hire, and train an employee. These are treated as assets and then amortised. A model for measuring human resource costs developed by Flamholtz (1974) contains two basic components: acquisition costs and learning costs.

The original cost system has advantages and disadvantages. The advantages include objectivity and consistency with the conventional use of cost as a measure of value. Disadvantages, as noted by Baker (1974), include 'traditional weaknesses of this basis of asset valuation, notably of the stable dollar assumption' and the narrowness and rigidity of considering cost to be a full measure of value (WIA, 1978, p.10).

An alternative method of determining human resource costs involves measuring the cost to an organisation of replacing that employee with another of equal ability. Flamholtz (1974) described two types of replacement costs: positional, where the best substitute would fill a vacancy; and personnel, which required the employment of a substitute who is similar in ability (WIA, 1978, p.10). Flamholtz's (1974) model for measuring human resource replacement costs added a third main component — separation costs — to the acquisition and learning costs contained in the original cost model. Separation costs are costs incurred with the departure of a particular employee. As with the original cost method, there are advantages and disadvantages to the replacement cost method. One advantage noted by Jaggi (1974) was that replacement cost has the potential to consider the performance of an individual within the organisation, rather than only the position the individual holds. Flamholtz (1974) noted two additional advantages of the replacement cost method: human resource planning and control processes, and potential uses in developing surrogate measures of the value of people to organisations.

Disadvantages of the replacement cost method included the problem of sub-jectivity in applying the replacement cost technique. A study conducted by Likert and Bowers (1969) reported that managers' estimates of the cost of completely replacing their personnel ranged from two to ten times their annual payroll cost.

Another method of measuring human resource costs is the concept of opportunity cost proposed by Hekimian and Jones (1967). Under the opportunity cost approach, assets are thought to have value only when there is an alternative use for them. According to Hekimian and Jones (1967), human resource value is determined by the amount they could earn if employed in alternative functions, therefore providing for a more optimal allocation of personnel. Jaggi (1974) suggested that one advantage of this method was that it provided greater flexibility, taking into account the fact that different individuals have different values. According to Baker (1974), the opportunity cost approach is limited in that it depends upon the information, judgement and impartiality of the divisions bidding for particular employees. Jauch and Skigen (1974) also criticised the opportunity cost method because it excluded recruitment from the outside and treated employees who are not in short supply as having little or no value.

Measuring human resource value

According to Flamholtz (1974, p.114) the value of the human resource is derived from the future services to be rendered to the organisation. In principle, the value of people can be defined as the present worth of their expected future services in the same way as for other resources. Flamholtz (1974) developed a model that identified the determinants of an individual's value to an organisation and explained the determinants' interrelationships.

An individual's expected realisable value was described as the amount an organisation expects to derive from an individual's services, taking into account the individual's likelihood of turnover. The Flamholtz model considered not only an individual's maximum potential value to a firm, but also their likelihood of staying with the firm. Flamholtz also described an individual's expected realisable value as an important tool for determining the opportunity costs of turnover. However, many management theorists argue that studies should focus on groups rather than individuals. A model presented by Likert and Bowers (1973) identified the variables which affect a group's value to an organisation. These variables included causal variables such as management behaviour and organisational structure, and intervening variables such as group processes, leadership and organisational climate.

Examples of measurement of human resource value

Hermanson (1964) proposed two monetary human resource valuation techniques: the *unpurchased goodwill method* and the *adjusted present value method*. The unpurchased goodwill method was based on the belief that if a firm earned a higher than normal rate of income, that was evidence of the existence of superior operational assets (including human resources). Earnings above normal expected earnings, when compared to firms within the same industry, were allocated to human resource valuation. Goodwill was argued to be the result of managerial ability, social and personal attributes, special skills or knowledge, established clientele and staff and favourable trade developments which lead to a good reputation.

The adjusted present value method produced a surrogate human resource valuation measure by using a weighted average of the last five years' performance and then modifying the present value of the expected wage payments over the next five years. The modified present value of future earnings is adjusted by a performance efficiency ratio factor (WIA, 1978, p.13). Flamholtz (1974) and Baker (1974) have pointed out that the disadvantages of the unpurchased goodwill and adjusted present value methods are their subjectivity and imprecision of calculation.

Another approach to determining the value of human resources originated in the UK. According to Farmer (1975) and Robinson (1975), the UK approach was based on the assumption that the costs incurred in relation to an individual bears no direct relationship to their value to the organisation at any particular time. The UK method separated human resources into four categories: (a) senior management; (b) middle management; (c) supervisors; and (d) clerical, personnel and operative grades. Using these four groups, a valuation method called the *multiplier method* was used to allocate a total human resource value between all employees according to their perceived value (WIA, 1978, p.8). Problems with the multiplier method include the degree of subjectivity in determining the multiplier weights and asset value distribution.

Several other methods of measuring human resources in monetary terms have been presented, including Lev and Schwartz's (1971) *monetary human resource valuation model*, where employee salaries are

surrogates for economic value. Another is Flamholtz's *stochastic rewards valuation model* which determines the value of employees based upon the expected service they perform in each 'service state'. Each model presents the issue of human resource valuation from a different angle and each was subject to criticism. To date, no method of valuing human resources has been developed which is widely accepted or used by a number of firms.

Important information pertaining to human resource value includes not only monetary measures, but also non-monetary measures. Several concepts and techniques can be used as non-monetary measures of human resource value. Measurements are commonly used in personnel research and personnel management and include skills inventories, performance evaluation methods, potential assessments and attitude measurements (Flamholtz, 1974, p.151). The concept of subjective expected utility, which combines the concepts of utility and subjective probability, may also be used for the non-monetary measurement of human resource value. Flamholtz described utility as a user's perceived value of a resource and subjective probability as the subjective estimation of an event's likelihood.

Development and implementation of human resource accounting systems

According to Flamholtz (1974, p.271) some firms required a rudimentary system of HRA while other companies needed an HRA system with the most advanced capability. Likewise, as companies move from one stage of development to another, the HRA system must also be adapted. Flamholtz (1974) illustrated five different types of HRA systems. System I was called the *Prerequisite Personnel System*; System II the *Basic HRA System*; System III the *Intermediate HRA System*; System IV the *Advanced HRA System*; and System V was called the *Total*

HRA System. These five systems were evaluated using five criteria: human resource planning; human resource decision making, budgetary and policy; human resources conservation, after-the-fact and before-the-fact; human resource evaluation; and human resource management efficiency control.

When determining the degree of HRA capability required by a company, Flamholtz (1974, p.275) suggested evaluating four major factors: type of organisation; size and structure of organisation; existing HRA capability; and availability of data for developing HRA. Larger decentralised organisations had a greater need for HRA. In addition, existing HRA capability and the availability of data pertaining to HRA influence the choice of an HRA system because companies with inadequate personnel systems or insufficient data will be unable to develop sophisticated HRA systems.

Flamholtz (1974, p.277) suggested five phases that a company should go through in the development of an HRA system: identify HRA objectives; develop HRA measurements; develop a data base for the system; pilot test the system and revise it if necessary; and implement the system in the organisation.

Applications of human resource accounting systems

One example of the application of HRA was that of R.G. Barry Corporation, a small light manufacturing company, which set up an HRA programme in 1969–1971 to account for its human asset investments:

The historical (original) outlay cost approach implemented at Barry utilized seven capital accounts for assessing human resource value: recruiting outlay costs, acquisition costs, formal training and familiarization costs, informal training costs, familiarization costs, investment building experience costs, and development costs. Quarterly

information on human resource status was reported to the operating management. For the years 1969 and 1971 Barry developed pro forma balance sheets and income statements, reflecting the impact of human resource accounting information on the conventionally generated figures. In both instances large income increases were reported. (WIA, 1978, p.15)

Woodruff, the Vice-President of R.G. Barry Corporation, stated that the results of the study indicated that, aside from providing managers with more accurate profitability statements and increasing managerial awareness of the importance of human resources, an HRA system can help to answer these questions, among others:

1. How should an organization allocate resources among various competing opportunities?
2. What are the real costs to the company of the replacement turnover of personnel?
3. What will be the real cost of moving a plant to a new location?
4. What development investments are required to have present people available for new responsibility or new technology? (WIA, 1978, p.15)

Alexander (1971) studied another HRA system developed to account for human asset investments in an office of Touche Ross and Company. Touche Ross and Company calculated the investment in each employee, in terms of outlay (out-of-pocket expense) and opportunity costs and generated four human resource reports: 'The Cost of Time Analysis Report', 'A Summary of Human Resource Investments Report', 'A Statement of Human Resource Flows Report' and 'Contribution Report'. After obtaining the information from the HRA system, Touche Ross and Company reassessed its traditional approach to staff mix and resource allocation. The firm found that profit contributions per individual for various experience levels were somewhat different from those expected.

In another application of HRA, Flamholtz and Lundy (1975) successfully developed an accounting system for human resource value at a CPA firm, Lester Witte and Company. The system used Flamholtz's stochastic process model.

HRA systems may also be applied to problem situations. At AT & T an HRA system was designed to increase managerial effectiveness in the development and re-training of employees. A second example was a *Force-Loss Cost Analysis* designed to measure the costs of employing and developing toll directory and assistance operators (McRae, 1974). An historical cost approach was used to measure four separate cost components: employment costs; training costs; efficiency recovery costs; and extra supervision costs.

Virtually no research regarding new methods or models or HRA has been conducted since the late 1970s. Flamholtz and Coff (1989) addressed the issue of using HRA for tax-saving purposes when buying service companies. The authors pointed out three reasons why acquirers of knowledge-based businesses should understand the value of human assets:

1
'Initially, both buyer and seller must gain a perspective on the value of the people to agree on a purchase price' (p.40). They use the example of General Motors Corporation, which acquired Hughes Aircraft Co. for $5.2 billion in 1985. In the purchase, $4.4 billion was assigned to goodwill, but a substantial portion of that actually represented payment for the expertise of Hughes' people.

2
'The acquirer will want to conserve its

human assets when the business revolves around them. Acquisition often leads to high personnel turnover, and in a service business loss of key people can be disastrous' (p.40). The authors believe that the acquirer will be encouraged to offer incentives that encourage key people to stay when they view turnover as a liquidation of valuable assets.

3
The third concern mentioned was the tax treatment of acquired human assets. By applying a valuation approach to its acquired human resources, an acquirer of a service company could achieve considerable tax savings.

Chapter summary

Human resource accounting remains potentially as important today as it was two decades ago when research studies and experimental applications were undertaken. It may be argued that managers, investors and society in general would benefit from further research in HRA. In particular, many of the models and methods presented need to be validated. As Western economies move away from manufacturing into the service sector, and as technology continues to become more complex, we could gain from measuring the costs and values of human resources, an asset that is important to organisations.

There have been many changes in accounting thought since the original HRA research was undertaken. It is possible that the accounting community, academic and professional, would view HRA differently now than it did two decades ago. New conceptual frameworks, such as that put forward by the AARF, may be more encouraging to proponents of HRA. Has the time arrived to review HRA?

Essay and examination questions

13.1 Including the value of human resources employed by an organisation would increase the meaningfulness of financial statements to a marked degree. Discuss.

13.2 Consider the various methods by which the value of the human resource may be determined. Discuss the characteristics, strengths and weaknesses of each.

13.3 The transient allegiance of employees to an organisation gives rise to problems which render HRA largely meaningless. Discuss.

References and additional reading

Alexander, M.O. (1971). Investments in people. *Canadian Chartered Accountant*, **99**, 38 45.

Baker, G. M.N. (1974). The feasibility and utility of human resource accounting. *California Management Review*, **16**, 17–23.

Brummet, R.L. (1970). Accounting for human resources. *The New York Certified Public Accountant*, **40**, 547–555.

Committee on Human Resource Accounting. (1973). Report of the Committee on Human Resource Accounting. *The Accounting Review*, **48**, Supplement.

Dawson, C. (1988). The accounting approach to employee resourcing. *Management Decision*, **26**(5), 31–36.

Farmer, R. (1975). Progress in human resource accounting: A review. *Certified Accountant*, 549–554.

Flamholtz, E.G. (1974). *Human Resource Accounting*. Encino, California: Dickenson Publishing Co.

Flamholtz, E.G. (1975). The metaphysics of human resource accounting and its implications for managerial accounting. *Accounting Forum*, 51–61.

Flamholtz, E.G. and Coff, R. (1989). Valuing human resources in buying service companies. *Mergers and Acquisitions*, **23**, 40–44.

Flamholtz, E.G. and Lundy, T. S. (1975). Human resource accounting for CPA firms. *Certified Public Accountant Journal*, **45**, 45–51.

Gall, A.L. (1988). What should human resource accounting systems count? *Training and Development*, **42**, 20–26.

Gilbert, M.H. (1970). The asset value of the human organization. *Management Accounting*, **52**, 25–28.

Hekimian, J.S. and Jones, C.H. (1967). Put people on your balance sheet. *Harvard Business Review*, **45**, 105–113.

Hermanson, R.H. (1964). Accounting for Human Assets. *Occasional Paper No. 14*. East Lansing, Michigan: Bureau of Business and Economic Research, Michigan State University.

Jaggi, B.L. (1974). The valuation of human resources in a firm. *Chartered Accountant* (India), **22**, 467–470.

Jaggi, B.L. (1976). Human resources are assets. *Management Accounting*, **57**, 41–42.

Jauch, R. and Skigen, M. (1974). Is human resource accounting really practical? *Management Review*, **63**, 40–42.

Lev, B. and Schwartz, A. (1971). On the use of the economic concept of human capital in financial statements. *Accounting Review*, **46**, 103–112.

Likert, R. and Bowers, D.G. (1969). Organizational theory and human resource accounting. *American Psychologist*, **24**, 585–592.

Likert, R. and Bowers, D.G. (1973). Improving the accuracy of P/L reports by estimating the change in dollar value of the human organization. *Michigan Business Review*, 15–24.

Maslow, A.H. (1965). *Eupsychian Management*. Homewood, Illinois: Richard D. Irwin, Inc., and the Dorsey Press, 1.

McRae, T.W. (1974). Human resource accounting as a management tool. *Journal of Accountancy*, **138**, 32–38.

Newell, G.E. (1972). Should humans be reported as assets? *Management Accounting*, **54**, 13–16.

Nicholls, F.A. (1975). Human asset accounting. *Certified Accountant* (England), 323–324.

Robinson, D. (1975). Two approaches to human asset accounting. *Accountancy* (England), **86**, 46–48.

Rogow, R.B. and Edmonds, C.P. (1988). Tallying employees as assets. *Personnel Administrator*, **33**, 168–170.

Unruh, A.R. and Mathews, M.R. (1992). Human resource accounting: An important topic revisited. *Accounting Forum*, **16**(3), 47–63.

Work Institute in America, Inc. (1978). Studies in Productivity. Scarsdale, New York.

Section 5

Emerging issues in financial accounting and reporting

Learning objectives

After studying this chapter the reader will be able to:

- define creative accounting
- discuss the determining factors leading to creative accounting
- describe some of the obvious and more subtle forms of creative accounting
- critically examine the ethical overtones of creative accounting
- evaluate the measures put in place to control creative accounting
- consider the implications of creative accounting for accountants and auditors.

Introduction

Creative accounting is not a new phenomenon. Elements of creative accounting can be found as early as the nineteenth century, initially in the form of income smoothing and, later, through the creation of secret reserves. The practice of accounting creatively gained momentum as the joint stock company with its separation of ownership and management became the common form of business organisation. The absence of accounting standards and legislation in the early days meant that creativity was necessary in the development of accounting as new business methods and structures emerged. However, there is often a fine line between creativity for the development of accounting practice and outright fraud.

Today, accounting standards and legislation exist to protect investors and owners of businesses in many ways. However, as more sophisticated business methods evolve, and in spite of extensive legislation and numerous accounting rules and guidelines, creative accounting still abounds. The prevalence of creative accounting methods has prompted writers like Griffiths (1986) to comment that 'every company in the country is fiddling its profits . . . Any accountant worth his or her salt will confirm that this is no wild assertion' (p.1).

This chapter will attempt to define creative accounting and enumerate some

reasons why management indulges in creative accounting. It will also describe some of the obvious and subtle forms and examples of creative accounting and conclude with some implications for accountants.

Creative accounting defined

There is no generally accepted definition of creative accounting. While creative, in connection with accounting, is often thought of as a 'dirty word' with negative connotations, from a creativity point of view it may have positive effects if it enhances the development of accounting practice. Creative accounting is negative when it is used by unscrupulous management to mislead and defraud investors, creditors, bankers and other users of financial statements. In these cases, terms like 'fiddling the books', 'cooking the books', 'cosmetic reporting' and 'window-dressing the accounts' are often used to describe creative accounting.

Creative accounting is positive when used appropriately, in an innovative manner, to reflect the underlying trends in the value of the business and to show a true and fair state of the affairs of the company. This is especially so when no other methods exist to account for a new business transaction.

Owing to the double sided nature of creative accounting, the term can be defined in two ways. At its best, it is any accounting method that does not conform to generally accepted practice or prescribed standards and guidelines. At its worst, creative accounting is the process of adjusting the accounts of a business so that they present the most acceptable and favourable view of its operations to shareholders, investors and other interested parties. It is any accounting method that presents a desired rather than a factual state of the affairs of the company.

Factors giving rise to creative accounting

Creative accounting and agency relationships

While many factors may give rise to creative accounting, the need to indulge in it arises only when the performance of the business is being evaluated in some way by parties outside the business, especially where an agency relationship exists between the owner(s) and the manager(s) of the firm. Once management and owners are separated, there is pressure on management to report positive or flattering results to those who have an interest or potential interest in the business. For instance, a sole proprietor who runs and manages his or her own business is unlikely to account creatively to himself or herself on the state of affairs of the business.

The use of creative accounting methods can be explained using the agency theory originally set out by Alchian and Demsetz (1972) and extended by Jensen and Meckling (1976). Under agency theory, individuals are seen to be rational, maximising beings who seek to promote self-interest above all else. Firms necessarily exist as a means of controlling the 'destructive opportunism' (also known as shirking or perquisite consumption) of individuals, especially those acting in the capacities of agents (Thornton, 1984). Accounting numbers, which reflect the performance and state of affairs of a firm, become important because the numbers form an observable

basis for wealth distribution contracts between different interest groups within a business (Thornton, 1984). As evaluative indicators of both the manager or agent and of the firm itself, creative accounting is attractive if one interest group (for example the manager or agent) is in a better position to decide on which accounting number to present to the rest of the interest groups.

Under agency theory, cost not ethics provides the only restraint on the self-interest behaviour of an agent. Lenders and investors take into account the 'destructive opportunism' and self-interest behaviour of the agent in their decisions to lend to or invest in the firm by requiring higher rates of return on their loans or investments. Hence, without some monitoring device, the manager or agent faces higher costs of debt and equity. As such, agency theory places great importance on generally accepted accounting practices and standards because compliance with the standards and audits of accounting numbers, whether voluntary or statutory, provides a mechanism for reducing the costs of debt and equity to be borne by the agent. However, loopholes still exist for the promotion of self-interest because of interpretive differences in current generally accepted practices and standards.

Besides this inherent, self-preservation factor on the part of those who manage the business, three other major factors also encourage the use of creative accounting: vagueness of accounting rules; advancement of technology and business methods; and the stewardship versus allocation conflict.

Vagueness of accounting rules

Legislation and accounting rules or guidelines that are set to legitimise or guide accounting practice are often framed in vague and flexible terms. Legislation and standards that are set to govern how financial statements should be prepared and presented aim only at narrowing down the available options. They require consistent use but do not purport to standardise all accounting methods. Legislation and standards leave the impression of uniformity but actually endorse a wide variety of accounting treatment for any particular accounting issue.

The vagueness and flexibility of legislation and standards governing accounting are aggravated by tenuous and undefined concepts like 'true and fair' and 'materiality'. These concepts leave a lot of room for subjective judgement and manoeuvre in practice. For instance, the use of the materiality concept in auditing means that all published financial statements automatically assume a 5–10 per cent margin of error.

Current accounting concepts and standards in themselves also allow for some 'acceptable' level of creative accounting. For instance, the practice of stating inventory at the lower cost or market and the conservatism principle of deferring the recognition of income but recognising possible losses immediately are no different from the use of secret reserves in the early days.

Advancement of technology and business methods

Technology and business methods are advancing faster than legislation and prescribed accounting rules or guidelines. Accounting, as a socially constructed discipline, tends to lag behind rapidly advancing business methods. With the lack of up-to-date accounting prescriptions, practitioners have no alternative but to use innovative methods to account for new accounting issues that arise.

Stewardship versus resource allocation conflict

In competing for the economy's scarce resources, there is pressure on companies to report flattering results. Financial statements are no longer just a record of a com-

pany's performance and state of affairs. In a competitive market, financial statements must keep present and prospective investors satisfied by presenting smooth income flows and growth.

The conflict arises when the actual performance of the company is unstable or unflattering, or both. On the one hand, a smooth growth is required to keep present and, especially, potential investors satisfied so that the company can obtain a share of the economy's scarce resources. On the other hand, stewardship reporting requires companies to report on the actual performance of the company regardless of how unstable or unflattering the results may be.

Modes of creative accounting

Normally, the true state of affairs and profitability of a business cannot be determined until the whole venture is terminated. For the period between the incorporation and termination of a business, estimates are required to determine its profitability and state of affairs. The concepts of periodicity and matching of expenses and revenues necessarily mean that financial statements are just estimates and therefore cannot reflect, unless by coincidence, the true state of affairs of a business. Estimates require judgement and experience and it is because so many estimates are required in drawing up a set of periodic financial statements that numerous ways exist to account creatively. The following material outlines only a few examples of creative accounting to inflate or smooth income flows. A host of creative methods also exist to reduce or defer taxes.

Income smoothing

Income smoothing is the process of deflating the reported profits of a business in good periods and deferring them to loss making periods in an effort to portray a 'stable' income stream over the years. This is possible because of the flexibility of the matching concept and because breaking down the results of a business venture into financial periods is not always appropriate.

There are many reasons for income smoothing. First, investors prefer a smoothed income flow because it supposedly reflects stability, strength and growth within a company. It is perceived to be a better indicator of stewardship, risk and the ability of management. Since this pleases the investors, it is reflected in a higher share price.

Second, in a company with profit sharing schemes between the owners and management, the manager can obtain the maximum benefit if income is smoothed over the periods. This maximises the manager's utility since additional income in good years attracts higher personal taxes such that the net benefits to be derived from a profit sharing scheme can be achieved only through smoothed income flows for all the relevant years.

Income smoothing can be separated into 'real' and 'artificial' smoothing (Dascher and Malcom, 1970). In real income smoothing, the smoothing is achieved by a decision either to incur or not to incur a particular expense. One example is to defer the spending of advertising money to the following year and inflate income for the current year.

Under artificial smoothing, different policies are used to shift income between the different financial periods. Changes in the method of depreciating assets are a means of achieving 'artificial' income smoothing.

Window-dressing and secret reserves

Window-dressing is the process of adjusting the financial statements of a company to achieve the maximum effect on its financial position at a particular date, for instance at balance date or the date of taking out a loan. As mentioned, practically any item on the balance sheet and profit and loss account can be adjusted to portray a desired

picture. For instance, adjustments can be made to the allocation of expenses between different periods. Revenue can be recognised at an earlier or later period, and current assets and liabilities like debtors and creditors can be stated either as gross figures or net of discounts. A company intending to take out a loan may inflate its sales figures by selling to its related companies. Similarly, readers' attention may be drawn away from low profit margins by healthy cash balances, giving the impression that cash is equal to profits.

Besides the outright creation of bizarre reserves and funds, as in the earlier years of creative accounting, secret reserves in the present day may take the more mundane form of increasing or decreasing provisions for items such as warranties and bad debts. The effect of providing for such contingencies is that the actual impact on the profit figure is reduced when the need to, say, write off a bad debt actually occurs.

Off-balance-sheet financing

In off-balance-sheet financing, the total debt of a company increases but the increased borrowing is not reflected in the financial statements of the company. This enables the company to show better gearing ratios, obtain additional borrowing and allows the company access to additional funds while still maintaining its gearing limits with its lenders.

Off-balance-sheet financing can take many forms but, in all instances, it distorts the actual loan commitment of a company. In some cases, disclosure is required only in footnotes, for instance executory contracts and, hence, the gearing ratio calculated from its financial statements remains low.

In more sophisticated methods, subsidiaries or other related companies with low gearings may be utilised to borrow on behalf of a highly geared parent company. On consolidation, the intercompany debts are eliminated. The parent company's gearing remains the same although it has the use of additional borrowed funds.

In a similar way, subsidiaries and related companies may be used to borrow and distribute additional borrowings around a group. But, as the focus is usually on the parent company, the higher gearing of a subsidiary or related company is not highlighted.

The classic case of off-balance-sheet financing is the financial lease. In New Zealand, financial leases are now required to be capitalised under *Accounting for Leases and Hire Purchase Contracts* (SSAP 18).

Off-balance-sheet financing can, at best, be seen to be a stopgap measure only. This is because the loan still has to be repaid eventually and the company still has to obtain sufficient funds to pay off the 'hidden' loan to the ultimate lender which, in most cases, is an outsider to the group.

Pooling versus purchase methods

Abuses also exist in accounting for takeovers and mergers, mainly in the recording of the cost of the acquisitions. The problems centre around the pooling versus purchase methods of accounting for acquisitions.

Pooling is a method of accounting for the merger of two or more companies. It is attractive because no goodwill is created in the combined companies' books. This increases future income streams because no amortisation of goodwill is necessary. Moreover, under pooling, all pre- and post-acquisition reserves and earnings of the combined companies are distributable to the combined companies' shareholders. Owing to these perceived advantages, pooling became a useful tool to the creative accountant to account for all kinds of takeovers other than mergers of companies.

The purchase method of accounting for takeovers was seen to be unattractive because goodwill may be created at the date of acquisition. The amortisation of goodwill will decrease profits in future years. Moreover, under the purchase method, only post-acquisition profits are distributable to the shareholders of the combined companies.

Australia banned the pooling method under *Accounting for the Acquisition of Assets* (ASRB 1015) from 31 December 1988. In New Zealand *Accounting for Business Combinations* (SSAP 8) now specifies that certain conditions must exist before the pooling method can be used.

However, under the purchase method problems still exist. For instance, the use of 'fair market values' in valuing the assets taken over is subjective and can be manipulated to undervalue assets. This decreases future depreciation charges and increases future income streams, thereby increasing the 'benefits' of the purchase.

Other methods

Determination and Disclosure of Accounting Policies (SSAP 1) requires that appropriate accounting policies be adopted and disclosed in financial statements for the purpose of giving a true and fair view. It also requires companies to disclose changes in accounting policies where such changes are made in the reporting period.

However, the reported profit figure and financial position of a company can become the result of the accounting policies adopted rather than of its trading. For example, in Harcourt Corporation Limited's 1988 accounts, three changes in accounting policies were made and appropriately disclosed according to SSAP 1. The three changes made relate to the way the company accounts for its associates, asset revaluations and goodwill.

1   In 1987, the Group's share of associated company results was included in the consolidated financial statements on an equity accounting basis. In 1988 equity earnings were not included, except for dividends received

in cash. The effect of the change is disclosed in note 5.

2   In 1987, certain asset revaluations were recognised in the profit statement. In 1988 they were taken directly to reserves as disclosed in note 11.

3   In 1987, amortised goodwill was charged against profits. In 1988 it was charged against reserves, as disclosed in note 16. (Annual Report 1988, p.18)

In each of these situations, the new accounting treatment adopted is a departure from generally accepted accounting practice. More importantly, these changes and their effects on the operations and state of affairs of the company are not obvious from the financial statements. A reader would need to read the changes in accounting policies and the notes to the accounts to determine the changes that have been made. The overall net effect on profits and financial position of the company as a result of the changes is left to the interpretation of the reader.

A whole host of psychological methods can also be used to influence market behaviour. Some examples include delaying the release of bad news and speeding up the release of good news, selective reporting of news and items and the voluntary disclosure of qualitative disclosures to boost market confidence.

Empirical research in creative accounting

Theoretically, there are numerous ways and motives to account creatively. Articles on creative accounting often list anecdotes of how and where creative accounting exists. However, empirical research to test the presence of creative accounting is inconclusive. This is because the effects of creative accounting are often subtle, interrelated and may span more than one financial period. At its best, empirical research on

creative accounting can only guess at the possible creative accounting variable(s) used by the company to smooth its income flow. Since the actual variables having potential manipulation characteristics are numerous, any study of creative accounting does not and cannot measure every potential effect of manipulating any or all of the variables. For example, creative accounting through 'real smoothing' and control exercised over a subsidiary or associate with regard to the level of dividends to declare can never be analysed because they are not overt, publicly known activities.

The studies that have been carried out have ranged from income smoothing tendencies between management-controlled and owner-controlled firms (Kamin and Ronen, 1978) to whether failed companies are more prone to creative accounting (Rosser and Stevenson, 1984). In general, the following conclusions have emerged from some of the studies.

Kamin and Ronen's (1978) study provides support for agency theory and the possibility of self-interest promotion by managers. Their study concluded that a majority of firms behave as if they were income smoothers. In particular, management-controlled firms appeared to smooth income more than owner-controlled firms.

Rosser and Stevenson's (1984) Australian study found that, compared to a control group, failed or failing companies tended to exhibit higher non-compliance with statutes and professional standards. This is consistent with Schwartz's (1982) study which found that distressed firms were four times more likely to make discretionary accounting changes which had a material effect on net income as compared to healthy firms. These studies indicate that failing firms are more likely to indulge in creative accounting in an effort to show more favourable balance sheet and income statement ratios.

However, under EMH, it is maintained that investors are able to discern relevant information from irrelevant, cosmetic reporting changes and will not be fooled by creative accounting techniques. As such, there is now a host of empirical research dealing with the impact, if any, of non-mandatory accounting changes on share prices. While these are more directly related to the body of research in EMH, the results of some of the studies are relevant here. For example, Archibald (1972) found that firms which switched from an accelerated method of depreciating assets to a straight line method for financial reporting purposes had, on the whole, below normal stock market performances in the last two years before the switch. The switch in depreciation methods had the effect of increasing reported incomes. However, the 'switch-back announcement and resultant profit improvement apparently had no immediate substantial effect on stock market performance' (p. 30).

In a 1978 study on pooling versus the purchase methods of accounting for business combinations, Hong, Kaplan and Mandelker found that companies reported higher earnings using pooling rather than the purchase method of accounting for combinations. However, there was no evidence to support the hypothesis that the stock prices of the acquiring company were raised as a result of the method of accounting used.

Whether the market is efficient or not, at its best, any creative accounting technique can be only a temporary measure. In the long term, creative accounting in itself cannot reverse a loss making situation or prevent the impending failure of a company.

Attitudes towards creative accounting
Ethical or professional

The issue of creative accounting is directly linked to the issue of professional ethics. This is because accounting as a discipline

that is socially constructed has no immutable laws and truths (Tilley, 1972). Accounting numbers are assigned meanings by their preparers and users. Ideally, an accounting number should mean the same thing to both preparer and user, that is there should be no 'interpretive gap' between the preparer of the accounting numbers and how they are perceived by their user. In practice, perceptions vary between different people. As such, legislation and accounting rules or guidelines which are framed in broad terms are subject to different interpretations by users and preparers. Even among each of these two groups there will be differences in interpreting a particular rule or guideline.

From the start, a variety of methods of adhering to an accounting rule is possible. When the concept of self-preservation by the managers of businesses is included, it is easy to see how accounting rules can be given even wider interpretations to suit each manager or preparer of financial statements.

From the accountant's point of view, attempting to eliminate all the differences in interpretations by users and preparers is not realistic. Passing legislation and accounting rules or guidelines framed in rigid terms may mean requiring endless rules for each specific situation. More importantly, it reduces the accounting function to a rule-following exercise and removes the professional judgement aspect which is so important in a profession. Given legislation and accounting rules or guidelines which are framed in broad terms, it is the professional duty and moral obligation of the accountant to present accounting numbers in a way that reflects a 'true and fair' state of affairs of a company, to the extent of reflecting substance over the legal form of a transaction. In this way, the amount and level of negative creative accounting existing at any one time are directly dependent on the ethical attitude of the accountant.

Legal and professional moves to control creative accounting

Accounting by nature, being socially constructed, is creative. However, when the ownership of the business becomes separated from management and as organisations grow, some form of protection must be accorded to investors and potential investors. From the accounting discipline's point of view, principles, concepts and doctrines are necessary for some form of coherence and uniformity to exist. To ensure adherence to the generally accepted principles or concepts or doctrines, some form of professional or legal guidelines or rules are required.

In New Zealand, the legal moves to control creative accounting were set out basically in the *Companies Act* 1955 which laid down the rules for disclosure in financial statements and, where appropriate, the audit of the statements. The *Financial Reporting Act* 1993 now explicitly requires all financial and group financial statements of reporting entities to comply with GAAP. If, in complying with GAAP, the financial statements do not give a true and fair view of the matters to which they relate, the directors of the reporting entity must add such information and explanations as will give a true and fair view (sections 11(1), 11(2), 14(1) and 14(2)). This legislation effectively gives legal backing to accounting standards that have been approved by the ASRB. Where no approved standard exists, entities are required to adopt policies which are appropriate in the circumstances and which have authoritative support within the accounting profession in New Zealand (section 3). The provisions of the *Financial Reporting Act* place greater responsibility on the accountant or auditor to ensure that creative accounting practices are minimised and the true and fair view is emphasised in financial statements.

Another piece of legislation that may be important in curbing creative accounting is the *Fair Trading Act* 1986. Commenting on it, Christiansen (1988) writes:

> In fact legal opinion now suggests that the *Fair Trading Act* can be applied to any misleading or deceptive information in accounts for sales of businesses, forecasts or annual accounts. There have been some cases recently in Australia testing these areas under equivalent law in that country. (p.41)

Problems like the cost and length of litigation and the need to prove beyond reasonable doubt that creative accounting was involved may deter stakeholders from bringing a charge against the creative accountant.

Australia has legislative and professional deterrents to creative accounting which are similar to those found in New Zealand. First, the Companies Code contains provisions for financial reporting to shareholders and debenture holders.

Second, the Companies Regulations, Schedule 7, lists the items which must be disclosed in accounting reports but does not specify the form and classification of presentation.

Third, accounting standards are set out by the ASRB. The equivalent of the ASRB in New Zealand is the *Financial Reporting Act* 1993 and GAAP. The *Financial Reporting Act* also established the ASRB. One of the main functions of the Board is to review, approve and amend financial reporting standards.

As in New Zealand, Australian companies are also bound by the provisions of the relevant stock exchanges. Australia's *Trade Practices Act* is similar to New Zealand's *Fair Trading Act*.

Implications of creative accounting

Creative accounting increases the risk faced by auditors and accountants. For example in Singapore, Price Waterhouse sued Coopers and Lybrand for S$105 million for not picking up all the window-dressing in the collapsed Pan-Electric's accounts. Coopers adjusted Pan-Electric's 1983 accounts by only S$15.9 million when the actual window-dressing was for S$44.07 million (*World Accounting Report*, July 1988, p.14).

Creative accounting increases the scope and skill needed to prepare and audit a set of accounts. This is because not all creative accounting is bad and not all of the effects of negative creative accounting are obvious. For example, off-balance-sheet financing is difficult to detect without inside information and documentation on the loan.

Creative accounting also increases the need to redefine tenuous concepts like 'true and fair' and 'materiality' with respect to published financial statements. There is a need for the acceptance of a conceptual framework of accounting to guide practitioners. From a standard-setting point of view, creative accounting can best be reduced by the acceptance of a conceptual framework of accounting. In the past, the absence of a conceptual framework in New Zealand has often resulted in one or more of the following.

First, standards tend to lag behind business methods and practices. As evidenced from the past, accounting is socially constructed and will necessarily follow business needs.

Second, standards are fire-fighting, loophole-plugging statements which have no real punitive power over offenders. For example, the 1985 *Accounting for Investment Properties by Property Investment Companies* (SSAP 17) had to be withdrawn in June 1988 because of lack of adherence. Changes were made to the standard by the NZSA even though the original standard had been hailed as sound and far reaching. 'With the introduction of SSAP 17, the New Zealand profession has undoubtedly taken the lead in accounting for investment properties' (Tweedie, 1985, p.20).

However, the NZSA has no power to penalise companies which fail to comply. The situation should improve now that the

Financial Reporting Act 1993 has given legal backing to approved financial reporting standards and sets out penalties for non-compliance with such standards.

Third, standards are often conflicting for similar transactions (the lease versus executory contracts issue) and are too specific for general application. However, the Statement of Concepts recently issued by the NZSA should go some way towards reducing such conflicts.

Fourth, standards can be used to legitimise methods used by the most powerful organisations within a country. This is because the NZSA's Research Board comprises preparers and auditors of some of the biggest business enterprises in New Zealand. There is thus a very fine line between obtaining input from practitioners and maintaining independence in the setting of the standards.

While a conceptual framework may not eliminate all creative accounting, it may reduce the instances of creative accounting because it provides a general framework against which new accounting or business problems can be evaluated. At the very least, a conceptual framework which specifies and defines what constitutes the accounting elements of assets, liabilities, revenues and expenses will narrow down the manner in which an item can be classified in the accounts.

Chapter summary

This chapter has attempted to define creative accounting, list the types of creative accounting methods and provide some examples of how accounts can be 'fiddled'.

On the theoretical level, creative accounting is linked to concepts like 'true and fair' and professional ethics. Eliminating all creative accounting is not realistic as it calls for rigid rule making for each specific situation, resulting in the restriction of professional judgement. A long-term professional approach is the only way of curbing creative accounting. Accountants should be given a grounding in professionalism and ethics. The acceptance of a conceptual framework of accounting constitutes a necessary second step towards reducing ways of creative accounting as they help in defining and classifying accounting elements, thus narrowing down different interpretations and treatments.

On the empirical level, numerous studies have been conducted in the area with inconclusive results. Still, attempts to curb creative accounting are necessary because its implications for accountants and auditors are many. Increasingly, accountants and auditors are facing lawsuits brought against them for not detecting creative accounting practices in the course of an audit. The challenges facing the accounting profession are likely to increase with the rapid advances in technology and business methods and the often lagging accounting standards and guidelines.

Essay and examination questions

14.1   Accountants need the flexibility of 'creative accounting' techniques in some instances to show the 'true and fair' state of affairs of a company. Discuss.

14.2   Creative accounting is inevitable in a modern and progressive business environment. Discuss.

14.3   What are some of the factors that give rise to creative accounting? Discuss, giving examples.

14.4   Current accounting concepts and standards allow for some 'acceptable' level of creative accounting. Discuss.

14.5   It is postulated under the efficient market hypothesis that investors will not be fooled by creative accounting. Why then do you think accountants indulge in creative accounting?

14.6   The same rules and standards that exist to protect investors can also be used by the creative accountant to 'fiddle the books'. How is this possible?

14.7   What are some of the implications of creative accounting?

14.8   What is creative accounting? In your opinion, how does creative accounting affect the quality of the financial statements that are produced?

References and additional reading

Accounting Standards Review Board (1988). *Accounting for the Acquisition of Assets*. Approved Accounting Standard ASRB 1015.

Alchian, A.A. and Demsetz, H. (1972). Production, information costs, and economic organisations. *American Economic Review,* **62**, 777–795.

Annual Report 1988, Carter Holt Harvey Limited.

Annual Report 1988, Fletcher Challenge Limited.

Annual Report 1988, Harcourt Corporation Limited.

Archibald, T.R. (1972). Stock market reaction to the depreciation switch-back. *The Accounting Review*, **47**, 22–30.

Australian Accounting Research Foundation (1988). *Set-off and Extinguishment of Debt*. Australian Accounting Standard No. 23.

Christiansen, D.V. (1988). *Corporate Reporting Update*. Continuing Education Course Paper No. 302.

Commerce Clearing House (New Zealand) (1985). *Companies and Securities Legislation*. 1985 edn. Glenfield, Auckland: Tax and Business Law Publishers.

Dascher, P.E. and Malcom, R.E. (1970). A note on income smoothing in the chemical industry. *Journal of Accounting Research*, **8**, 253–259.

Financial Accounting Standards Board (1983). *Extinguishment of Debt*. Statement of Financial Accounting Standards No. 76.

Fry, E. (2 April 1989). The art of masking life's realities. *Sunday Star*, D1, D3.

Griffiths, I. (1986). *Creative Accounting*. London: Sidgwick and Jackson Limited.

Hong, H., Kaplan, R.S. and Mandelker, G. (1978). Pooling vs. purchase: The effects of accounting for mergers on stock prices. *The Accounting Review*, **53**, 31–47.

Jensen, M.C. and Meckling, W.M. (1976). Theory of the firm: Managerial behaviour, agency costs, and ownership structure. *Journal of Financial Economics*, **3**, 305–360.

Kamin, J.Y. and Ronen, J. (1978). The smoothing of income numbers: Some empirical evidence on systematic differences among management-controlled and owner-controlled firms. *Accounting, Organizations and Society*, **3**, 141–157.

New Zealand Society of Accountants (1987). *Accounting for Business Combinations*. Statement of Standard Accounting Practice. No. 8.

New Zealand Society of Accountants (1988). *Accounting for the Effects of Changes in Foreign Currency Exchange Rates*. Statement of Accounting Practice No. 21.

New Zealand Society of Accountants (1988). *Accounting for Intangibles*. Exposure Draft No. 43.

New Zealand Society of Accountants (1988). Volume G-9. Wellington: NZSA.

New Zealand Society of Accountants (1989). *Accounting for Defeasance of Debt*. Exposure Draft No. 47A.

PW sues Coopers over Pan-El audit (July 1988). *World Accounting Report*, 14.

Rosser, B. and Stevenson, M. (1984). Differential accounting behaviour of failed Australian listed companies. Paper presented at AAANZ Conference, Tasmania.

Schwartz, K.B. (1982). Accounting changes by corporations facing possible insolvency. *Journal of Accounting, Auditing and Finance*, 32–43.

Thornton, D.B. (1984). A look at agency theory for the novice — Part 1. *CA Magazine*, 90–96.

Tilley, I. (1972). Accounting as a scientific endeavour: Some questions the American theorists tend to leave unanswered. *Accounting and Business Research*, **2**, 287–297.

Tweedie, D. (1985). All Blacks (SSAP 17) 4   Lions (SSAP 19) 0. *The Accountants Journal*, **64**, 20–22.

Learning objectives

After studying this chapter the reader will be able to:
* define insider trading
* explain the effects of insider trading on the securities market
* discuss the ethical overtones of insider trading
* consider the extent of insider trading in New Zealand
* comment on the legal issues concerning insider trading
* critically examine the various attempts to restrict or outlaw insider trading.

Introduction

The issue of insider trading has been contentious in the securities market for some time and usually commands widespread attention where cases are exposed. In the USA, the UK and Australia, legislation exists to 'control' the activities of 'insiders'. In New Zealand, insider trading is a topical issue with the passing of the *Securities Amendment Act* 1988 to prohibit insider trading.

Given the emphasis on this emerging issue in New Zealand, it is the aim of this chapter to explore the wider aspects of insider trading using the literature, legislation and empirical research that currently exist in countries like the USA, the UK and Australia. It will attempt to define 'insider' trading, discuss its relationship with aspects such as profitability, EMH and the leading indicator effect. The chapter will also discuss the major provisions of the *Securities Amendment Act* 1988 which prohibit insider trading. It will conclude with some practical problems associated with regulation.

Insider trading defined

In lay terms, insider trading refers to the dealing in a particular company's stocks by individuals (insiders) using specific unpublicised information for their own financial benefit. Implicit in the definition of insider trading is the belief that such unpublicised information, when made available to the public, will affect the share prices of the company in some manner, the benefit of which will be reaped in the first instance by the insiders.

Technically, legislation in the various countries that have outlawed insider trading develops the definition of the term 'insider'. For example, in the USA, insiders are defined as corporate officers, directors and large stockholders under the *Securities Exchange Act* 1934. 'Large' shareholders are deemed to be holders of 10 per cent or more of any equity class of securities (section 16(a) of the Act).

In the UK, however, the definition of insiders under the *Company Securities (Insider Dealing) Act* 1985 covers a wider range of people. Basically, it is divided into primary and secondary insiders. Primary insiders include executive and non-executive directors, officers and employees of both the company in question and its related companies.

More interesting is the inclusion as primary insiders of all those who have a professional and/or business relationship with the company and its related companies (section 1(2)(d)). Under this wide umbrella, primary insiders are possibly the auditors, accountants, company secretaries, solicitors, commercial and merchant bankers and trade union officers of the company and its related companies. However, the position of shareholders as insiders is not dealt with in the regulation. They also could possibly be deemed as insiders (Kennen, 1986, p.113). Secondary insiders under the UK Act include 'tippees', that is persons who have been counselled or procured to act on inside information by the primary insiders.

In Australia, insiders are defined as persons who are connected with a company and/or its related companies under the Chapter 7 of the *Corporations Law*. The term 'persons connected with a company' is not specifically defined in the Act. However, in the *Corporations Law*, a person is said to be 'connected to a company' if the person is a director, secretary, employee or a special manager appointed to the company or its related companies. A substantial shareholder with more than 10 per cent of the voting shares of the company is also classified as being connected to a company and so is considered an insider. The term 'person' is also extended to include companies or bodies corporate and any other person whose position may reasonably be expected to give him or her access to price sensitive information (Baxt *et al.*, 1982, p.253). The scope of the Australian definition of an insider appears to be similar to the definition adopted in the UK, where persons having business relationships with a company and

its related companies are precluded from dealing in any inside information. As in the UK, tippees are also precluded from trading in any information received from an insider.

In New Zealand, under the *Securities Amendment Act* 1988, an insider is defined as the public issuer, its 'immediate' insiders (principal officer, employee, company secretary or substantial shareholder of the public issuer) and tippees of the public issuer or 'immediate' insider who have price sensitive inside information about the public issuer or about another public issuer. Under this definition, insiders in New Zealand comprise three tiers, as illustrated in Figure 15.1.

As Figure 15.1 shows, under the Law insiders may be the public issuer, 'immediate' insiders of the public issuer itself (first tier), tippees, 'immediate' insiders of the tippees (second tier), those who have been tipped by the tippees or the 'immediate' insiders of this second group of tippees (third tier).

In addition, inside information in New Zealand may be indirect in that unpublicised price sensitive information gained in one company with respect to another company can be considered as inside information. One example is the situation where a company director sells short on a

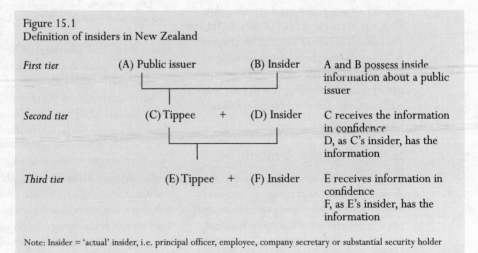

Figure 15.1
Definition of insiders in New Zealand

First tier	(A) Public issuer	(B) Insider	A and B possess inside information about a public issuer
Second tier	(C) Tippee +	(D) Insider	C receives the information in confidence D, as C's insider, has the information
Third tier	(E) Tippee +	(F) Insider	E receives information in confidence F, as E's insider, has the information

Note: Insider = 'actual' insider, i.e. principal officer, employee, company secretary or substantial security holder

competitor's stocks after receiving information that his or her own company has won a contract over the competitor's firm.

In New Zealand, 'substantial' shareholders are also classified as insiders. However, 'substantial' shareholder appears to have been more strictly defined than the American and Australian 'large' shareholders. In New Zealand, shareholdings of 5 per cent or more of a company's shares are deemed to be substantial and the holder is, therefore, prohibited from dealing in inside information. However, the shareholders need to have only a potential beneficial holding of 5 per cent or more of the securities to fall within the substantial shareholder category of an insider.

In the countries considered (including New Zealand), for purposes of legislation, an insider is deemed to be an insider with regard to that specific piece of price sensitive information for up to six months after termination of his or her office or employment. The six months' period is arbitrarily set but it is believed that any price sensitivity should have disappeared in that period.

In short, an insider can basically be any person or company that has privileged price sensitive information to a company, its related companies and/or another company with which the insider has a business or professional relationship. From this, insider trading can then be defined as the dealing in stocks of a company by insiders based on the unpublicised price sensitive information for the insiders' own financial benefits.

Legal moves to restrict or outlaw insider trading

As has been mentioned, a number of countries have passed regulations to restrict or outlaw insider trading. Therefore, an overview of the various pieces of legislation is appropriate.

The United States of America

The USA is probably one of the first countries to have outlawed insider trading. Its insider trading rules and regulations are administered by that very powerful quasi-judicial body, the SEC under the *Securities Exchange Act* 1934. The regulations are phrased in very broad terms and are based on standards of fair trading and disclosure of information to the market participants. The following is an overview of each relevant section of the Act as applied to insider trading.

Section 10(a) and 10(b)

This is the basic control over insiders and prohibits manipulative and deceptive practices. It also prohibits the short sale and use of stop–loss orders in the sale and purchase of any security. This section has been applied increasingly over the years in civil actions.

Section 16(a)

Every shareholder of more than 10 per cent of any class of security, director and officer of a company must disclose and report to the exchange and to the SEC:
- the amount of all securities held
- any changes to these holdings within ten days after the close of the month in which the changes occurred.

Section 16(b)

This section prevents any short-term transactions by any insiders and explicitly holds the insider liable for any dealings in securities held for less than six months. This applies even if it was the insider's intention to sell within six months at the time of purchase.

More importantly, this section allows the company concerned to recover all profits made by the insider on the short-term transaction and empowers any shareholder to bring a suit against the insider on behalf of the company to recover such 'short swing' profits.

Section 32(a)

This section provides criminal penalties for violating the anti-fraud provisions of section 10(b). Penalties for a criminal act are a fine of up to $100 000 and/or imprisonment of up to five years. A fine of up to $500 000 can be imposed on the stock exchange that is involved.

Rule 10B-5

In 1982 the SEC issued Rule 10B-5 to elaborate on the intent of section 10(b). Baxt *et al.* (1982) comment:

> This new doctrine rests on a theory of civil liability arising from penal legislation broadly similar to the English theory of tortious liability for breach of statutory duty, but the American doctrine has been developed with a boldness having no counterpart in contemporary English law. (pp.245–246)

The reasons for this boldness are:
- for civil actions under this section, contractual privity between the plaintiff and the defendant is not required
- the scope of the section is wide enough to cover those who obtain inside information from the insiders (Baxt *et al.*, 1982, p.246).

It can be seen that the SEC's rules and regulations cover practically anyone who, directly or indirectly, contravenes the rules and regulations of the SEC with respect to the purchase or sale of any security in a deceptive or manipulative manner. The rules and regulations pertain to listed and unlisted securities. The various sections provide protection to buyers and sellers of securities who have been induced by the fraudulent means of the insiders to transact. Baxt *et al.* (1982, p.245) further comment that the above legislation, combined with an active financial press, has been successful. The courts also apply the statute rigorously in every event to ensure a fair and honest securities market which reflects all pertinent data and information necessary for trading on an equal basis by all market participants concerned.

The United Kingdom

In the UK, the *Company Securities (Insider Dealing) Act* 1985 outlaws insider trading in the securities market. The technical term used is 'unpublished price-sensitive' information and refers to major pieces of specific information which are likely to cause sharp price movements in the securities concerned. Where primary insiders are concerned under section 2 of this legislation, insider trading is deemed to have been committed when the primary insider:
- deals in the inside information
- counsels or procures someone else to deal
- communicates the inside information to someone else.

Where a secondary insider or a tippee is concerned, no liability is attached if he or she deals in the information or passes it on. A tippee will be liable only if he or she knows or has reasonable cause to believe that it would not be proper for the insider to disclose the information except as part of his or her function, that is that the disclosure is a breach of confidentiality (Kennen, 1986, p.114). In all events, the primary insider faces criminal penalties whether or not the tippee deals in the information under section 8. The maximum penalty is an unlimited fine and/or imprisonment for up to seven years.

Under the Act several exceptions can be used as defences to a charge of insider trading. For example, in a takeover situation, an individual cannot deal in the shares of the company being taken over except for the purpose of gaining a controlling stake in the company.

Moreover, 'special agents' like liquidators, receivers, trustees in bankruptcy, trustees or personal representatives and jobbers are not likely to be liable when dealing in unpublished price sensitive information if they can prove that they were acting in good faith in the normal course of their professional capacities. Their defence is especially strong if they fall into the tippee group of insiders.

Australia

Insider trading regulations have been promulgated in Australia since the mid-1970s. Major changes to insider trading legislation were introduced in August 1991 under the Australian *Corporations Law* 1989. For example, Section 1002(G) of the *Corporations Law* (Div. 2A of Pt 7.11) deals with insider trading.

Section 1002(G)

Section 1002(G)(1) defines an insider as a person who possesses price sensitive information that is not generally available. The assumption is that if the information were generally available, a reasonable person would expect it to have a material effect on the price or value of securities of a body corporate and the person knows, or ought reasonably to know, that the information is not generally available; and if it were generally available, it might have a material effect on the price or value of those securities.

Section 1002(G) also prohibits an insider from the following activities which include tipping:

a subscribe for, purchase or sell, or enter into an agreement to subscribe for, purchase or sell, any such securities: or procure another person to subscribe for, purchase or sell, or to enter into an agreement to subscribe for, purchase or sell, any such securities. (section 1002(G)(2))

c where trading in the securities referred to in subsection (1) is permitted on the stock market of a securities exchange, the insider must not, directly or indirectly, communicate the information, or cause the information to be communicated, to another person if the insider knows, or ought reasonably to know, that the other person would or would be likely to engage in (a) above. (section 1002(G)(3))

Definition of an insider

The definition of an insider under the new legislation in Australia includes any person who possesses price sensitive information which is not generally available in relation to securities of a company. Under this definition an insider may not have anything to do with the company and the information may have been obtained from some other source. As Bostock (1992) explains, 'one does not have to be an insider to be an "insider"' (p.169). The Australian legislation has taken a much broader view in defining an insider, compared to similar legislation in many other countries, for example the UK, USA and New Zealand.

Section 1005(1 and 2)

Section 1005(1 and 2) provides that a person who suffers loss or damage caused by insider trading may recover the amount of the loss or damage by taking legal action at any time within six years after the day on which the event took place.

Despite the broader view of 'insider' taken in the Australian legislation, only a small number of persons have been prosecuted for insider trading. The lack of prosecution has been attributed to: difficulty in detecting crime; the complexity of the legislation; the high standard of proof required; the attitude of the courts; low penalties; and lack of resources and enthusiasm (Ziegelaar, 1994, p.698).

It has been suggested that in order for insider traders to be successfully prosecuted, the prosecuting authorities should make the enforcement of the insider trading provisions a priority, and the existing legislative provisions may have to be amended in acknowledgement of the fact that insider trading is not an ordinary offence to which the ordinary rules of law can be applied. These amendments may require the introduction of legislation covering such matters as rewards for whistleblowers, penalties to suit the crime, reversals of the onus of proof, and confiscation of short-swing profits (Ziegelaar, 1994, p.702).

Overview of legal restrictions on insider trading

From the very brief examination of the regulations in the USA, the UK and Australia, a number of common factors can be seen. First, insider trading is seen as being undesirable in any securities market. Insider trading introduces an unfair element to the securities market, with the insider who possesses the privileged price sensitive information reaping a profit (or reducing a loss) at the expense of the uninformed outsider. As such, legislation and control must be exercised to restrict and outlaw such practices in an effort to protect the ordinary investor and ensure that the securities market is a 'fair game' for all participants.

Second, insider trading is increasingly being seen not only as a criminal, but also as a civil offence. Only the UK does not provide civil remedies for those disadvantaged by insider trading. In the USA, the far reaching consequences of Rule 10B-5 require no contractual privity to sue the insider for damages in an insider trading case. Those found guilty of the offence face severe penalties in terms of unlimited fines and/or imprisonment up to seven years as in the UK.

Third, in all situations, the term 'insider' is being seen to encompass not just the actual insider to a company (the primary insider), but all those connected to the company in terms of having either business or professional relationships with the company. The legislations also extend to those who, not being insiders nor having any business or professional relationships with the company in question, have reasonable grounds to believe that the information

received either directly or indirectly from the insider is inside information. Hence, the nets that have been cast by the various pieces of legislation are very wide.

Even with such far reaching legislation, insider trading, with its huge potential profits, is still rife in all the three countries mentioned. In Australia and the USA, proposals have been made to tighten insider trading laws. In Australia, the criminal penalties imposed are not seen as credible deterrents to insider trading. It has been proposed that the minimum fine be increased to A$100 000 for each offence. In the USA, it is proposed that the maximum fine be increased to US$1 million.

Insider trading in New Zealand

Position before 1988

Up until December 1988, no legislation existed specifically to deal with insider trading in New Zealand. Instead, reliance was placed on peer pressure and on the very minimal legislation and guidelines in the hope of keeping the insiders in line. First, in the past, section 195 of the *Companies Act* 1955 required every company to keep a register of the holdings of its directors' shares and debentures in the company and its related companies. Where the holdings ceased to be recorded in the register, the date, price or other consideration for the holdings must be recorded in its place. The public availability of the register supposedly discourages improper dealings in the company's shares.

Second, common law prohibits any person in a fiduciary position from making profits out of this position. If a director does take a secret benefit out of the position, he or she is liable to account to the company. The liability of persons in fiduciary positions under common law are based on equitable principles.

Third, the New Zealand Stock Exchange puts forward suggested guidelines for securities transactions by directors of listed companies. However, such jurisdiction is limited only to its own exchange members, not to all stock exchange participants.

All the above legal and suggested 'controls' do not appear to be sufficient to curb insider trading. The reasons are that they are limited in scope and jurisdiction. For example, the *Companies Act* 1955 was an attempt mainly to keep directors in line. Other individuals such as managers and employees of the company are excluded, as are persons counselled or procured by the directors to act on inside information. In other words, the flow on effect on individuals who could strictly be classified as insiders is missing.

The problem of insider trading was compounded in New Zealand by the fact that a business person will usually sit on the board and be involved in the activities of a number of companies. In this way, access to inside information of multiple companies becomes possible. It is difficult for insider trading not to take place under these circumstances.

The Securities Commission's proposals

The New Zealand Securities Commission's report on insider trading released on 27 December 1987 was introduced into Parliament in July 1988. The main aim of the proposals was to try to clean up the New Zealand securities market and rid it of its reputation of being 'the last frontier for those who wish to manipulate the price of securities for their own gain' (Palmer, 1988, p.2).

The Commission proposed the enactment of legislation in the civil arena via the *Crimes Act* 1961 to deal with the problem of insider trading, although the report focussed on prevention rather than on punishment. Civil remedies proposed included the following:

• the company whose securities have been traded is entitled to recover from the

insiders any gain made or loss avoided on the sale of the securities
• shareholders in the said companies should have the right to recover such sums
• third parties who have bought or sold securities on the basis of the information should also have the right to recover the loss.

These remedies basically allowed all those concerned in the transaction(s) to undo the wrongs done to them through the insiders' actions.

The Commission also proposed that stricter criminal penalties via the *Crimes Act* 1961 be enacted to deal with those involved in dealing with the inside information, including giving the courts jurisdiction to disqualify an insider from holding office in a company.

Reasons for legislation

The New Zealand Securities Commission recognised that there are problems with trying to measure the impact of insider trading on the securities market. In proposing legislation, the Commission believed that no cost or benefit analysis on insider trading is possible because such an analysis requires data and such 'data is not available, and is never likely to become available' (1987, p.28). Nevertheless, the Commission gave its opinion on a series of questions on the impact of insider trading in the securities market. Briefly, these included the following.

(a) Insider trading is not seen as an efficient means of rewarding insiders for their services since insiders' profits are outsiders' losses on a dollar for dollar basis.

(b) Within a company, insider trading interferes with and delays corporate decision making based just on the merits of the issue at hand.

(c) Insider trading affects the timely disclosure of corporate information to the market since insiders who trade tend to postpone favourable and unfavourable news.

(d) Insider trading creates incentives for insiders to manipulate the market prices of securities issued by the company and by other companies.

(e) Insider trading increases the risk taken by all outsiders by exposing them to an informed insider on an unequal footing.

(f) Uncertainty about the frankness and timeliness of the disclosures increases the cost of capital for all companies.

(g) Insider trading affects the choices of outsiders between investment companies and other forms of investment as it creates uncertainty.

(h) While no data is available in monetary terms to measure the costs or benefits of insider trading to insiders, other investors in the company, to companies in general or to the New Zealand economy, the New Zealand Securities Commission believes that insiders do make abnormal profits in New Zealand based on the results of overseas studies on the same issue.

(i) The costs to the economy of insider trading exceed the benefits, although it is impossible to quantify costs and benefits over any period of time.

(j) No data is available to measure the cost or benefit of attempting to prevent insider trading by company self-regulation, market participant self-regulation, licensing market participants, by legal civil procedures, by criminal procedures or by government agencies.

(k) Insider trading is not an efficient substitute for public announcements based on the negative impacts.

Overall, the New Zealand Securities Commission was still of the opinion that the economic benefits of attempting to prevent insider trading exceeded the costs, although it could not quantify them and did not believe that anyone else could (pp. 28–33). The New Zealand Securities Commission concluded that legislation to prohibit insider trading was supported (p. 33). Moreover, the New Zealand Securities Commission admitted that:

> We gave careful consideration to the question of commissioning empirical research on these questions, but concluded that the results would probably be inconclusive. We prefer to rely on the judgements of people with experience in the market, but these are not unanimous. (p. 31)

It appeared that after evaluating various overseas legislation, in proposing controls for New Zealand, the actual cost or benefit of curbing insider trading is still not measurable. The main basis for calling for legislation still rested on the tenuous concepts of fairness and morality, especially on the part of those with a fiduciary duty to fulfil.

The Securities Amendment Act 1988

The proposals of the New Zealand Securities Commission are incorporated in the *Securities Amendment Act* 1988 passed on 21 December 1988. The Act is divided into two parts. Part I, which comprises the insider trading legislation, came into force on 21 December 1988. Part II, which deals mainly with disclosure rules for publicly listed companies, became effective on 1 July 1989.

Part I of the Act

Definitions

Insider trading legislation in New Zealand applies only to public issuers, that is a person who is a party to a listing agreement with a stock exchange or was previously a party to a listing agreement with a stock exchange. In relation to a public issuer, section 2 of the Act defined 'inside information' as information which '(a) Is not publicly available; and (b) Would, or would be likely to, affect materially the price of the securities of the public issuer if it was publicly available'. However, price sensitivity is not defined in the Act.

As mentioned, insiders in the Act under section 3 are defined in a three tier manner and cover not just insiders of the public issuer but tippees who receive information in confidence, the insiders of the tippees, the tippees of this first group of tippees and their respective insiders. This range of companies and individuals extends to information received about another public issuer. (Hereafter, the term 'insiders' will refer to both insiders and tippees unless otherwise specified.)

Like its overseas counterparts, the definition of an insider is also very wide. In addition, the New Zealand 'substantial security holder' is more strictly defined than in the overseas legislation.

Restrictions on insiders

Under the Act, an insider is precluded from:
* trading in the shares of the company
* tipping (that is, encouraging or advising) third parties to trade
* communicating to third parties knowing that they will trade, advising or encouraging others to trade
* all of the above actions on the insider information of another public issuer (sections 7, 9 and 11).

In this respect, the insider trading legislation in New Zealand is very similar to that in the UK and Australia.

Liabilities of the insiders

An insider who breaches the insider trading legislation is liable to two main groups under the Act. The insider is liable to the third parties who buy or sell to the insider or tippee. The amount liable is equivalent to the loss incurred by the third party buyer or seller as a result of the transaction.

The insider is also liable to the public issuer whose shares were transacted. The liability to the public issuer comprises:
* the gain (loss) made (avoided) by the insider
* a pecuniary penalty to be imposed by the court

* any consideration or benefit received by the insider from a tippee (sections 7 and 9)

The pecuniary penalty to be imposed can be up to the greater of the actual consideration paid for the shares or three times the gain made (loss avoided) by the insider (section 9(4)).

The New Zealand legislation is different from overseas insider trading legislation in that insider trading under the *Securities Amendment Act* 1988 is not a criminal offence. The Act provides only for civil remedies to those who have lost to the insider.

Limitation of liability

An insider is not liable under the Act under certain circumstances. These include:
* if procedures for the insiders to trade had been laid down by the company and had been complied with by the insider
* if arrangements are in place to ensure that insiders who trade have no access to inside information (Chinese walls)
* where the public issuer consents to the transaction of the insider (sections 10,12 and 14).

Part II of the Act

Part II of the Act, which came into force on 1 July 1989, deals with disclosures by substantial shareholders and public issuers.

Disclosure by substantial shareholders

Within fourteen days of the commencement of the Act, every existing substantial shareholder must give notice of the fact to the public issuer in which he or she is a substantial shareholder and to the stock exchange on which the security is listed. Thereafter, every person who becomes a substantial shareholder has to give notice of the fact to the public issuer and the stock exchange as soon as the person knows or ought to know that he or she is a substantial shareholder (section 20).

Where there is a change in the total holdings of a substantial shareholder of 1 per cent or more in a particular public issuer, this fact needs also to be disclosed to the public issuer and the relevant stock exchange as soon as possible. The same information is necessary when the substantial shareholder ceases to be a substantial shareholder (section 21).

Section 22 also requires the substantial shareholder to notify the public issuer and the relevant stock exchange of changes in the nature of relevant interests in the public issuer.

Disclosures by public issuers

On receipt of the information from its substantial shareholders under this Act, the public issuer is required to maintain files of the information for public inspection. The file is to be kept in New Zealand at:

- the registered office of the public issuer, or
- the office of the public issuer's share register, or
- the principal place of business of the public issuer.

Failure to comply is an offence subjecting every person involved to a fine not exceeding $10 000 (section 25).

Besides displaying the information, the public issuer is also required to publish the information about the substantial security holders. Under section 26(1), every public issuer that is a New Zealand company has to publish, as at that date, the names of the substantial holders, the number of shares held and the total number of issued shares of the company. This information has to be published as a note accompanying the balance sheet to be laid before the public issuer's annual general meeting.

All other public issuers are required to publish and send the same information to each holder of their voting securities in New Zealand at a date not later than 30 June of each year.

Failure to comply with this section is an offence, making the public issuer liable to a fine not exceeding $10 000.

The public issuer and holders of a total of not less than 5 per cent of the voting securities of the public issuer may request, through the public issuer, that persons who are registered as the holder of voting securities in the public issuer disclose:

- the name and address of every person who holds a relevant interest in those voting securities and the nature of the interest
- any other information to assist in identifying the person and the nature of the interest, where the information above is not possible (section 28).

Section 28 effectively allows the public issuer and other voting security holders to require nominee holders to expose the identities of the security holders behind the nominees.

Section 29 extends this right of the public issuer and other security holders in the public issuer (holding an aggregate of not less than 5 per cent shares) to require disclosure from those whom the public issuer or other security holders believe have or may have a relevant interest in the voting securities of the public issuer.

Where there are reasonable grounds to suspect that a substantial security holder has not complied with the Act, section 31 allows the Commissioner, the public issuer, security holders in the public issuer, persons who sold or purchased shares when the non-compliance took place, persons making takeover offers when the non-compliance took place and any other person, by leave of the court, to apply to the court to make orders on the substantial security holder. These orders are wide ranging and include requiring compliance with the necessary disclosure sections to forfeiting the voting securities of the public issuer (sections 30, 31 and 32).

The provisions set out in these sections effectively require greater disclosures of the identities and interests of security holders in a public issuer. In contrast to Part I of the Act, non-compliance with Part II of the Act is a criminal offence.

Liability of the substantial security holder

Where the substantial security holder fails to comply with the disclosure provisions set out in the Act, he or she is liable to the seller or purchaser of the shares. Under the Act, the amount liable is the difference between the 'value of the security' and the price payable.

Section 34(4) defines the 'value of securities' as the higher of:

- the value of the consideration offered, or
- the value the securities would have had at the time of the sale or purchase if the notice had been given or the information that would have been included in the notice had become publicly available on that date.

Under the *Companies Act* 1993, a director of a company registered under the Act in accordance with the *Companies Reregistration Act* 1993 who has a relevant interest in any shares issued by the company must, after the reregistration of the company, disclose to the board of the company the number and class of shares in which the relevant interest is held and the nature of the relevant interest. In addition, the director must ensure that the particulars disclosed to the board are entered in the interests register. When the director acquires or disposes of a relevant interest in the shares issued by the company, the following information must be disclosed to the board and entered in the interests register:

- the number and class of shares in which the relevant interest has been acquired or disposed of
- the nature of the relevant interest
- the consideration paid or received
- the date of the acquisition or disposition (sections 148(1) and 148(2)).

Under section 211(1e), every annual report of a company must disclose the entries in the interests register made during the accounting period. Where the board of a company fails to prepare an annual report, or where it fails to send a copy of the annual report to every shareholder of the company not less than twenty working days before the date fixed for holding the annual meeting of shareholders, each director commits an offence and is liable on conviction to a fine not exceeding $10 000 for each offence. Section 149 of the Act also places certain restrictions on share dealing by directors.

Insider trading and the market for securities

After the overview of the legislation that exists in various selected countries and the *Securities Amendment Act* 1988 in New Zealand, it is now appropriate to review the actual effects (if any) of insider trading on the securities market.

It cannot be denied that insiders possess inside information on a routine basis by virtue of their being insiders in an organisation, that is they are more 'informed' than outsiders. However, it must be stressed that insider trading legislation is based on the assumption that insiders in possession of specific, inside, privileged, price sensitive information act upon it and obtain an illegal advantage or profit from trading in the information. Implicit in the assumption is that the information is unavailable to the public at large and will affect the security price in a material way once it is made available. This assumption is reasonable since, in the absence of disclosure rules, not all information pertaining to a company will be available to an outsider to the same extent as it would be to an insider. Even with disclosure rules, the information may not be timely enough for outsiders to make decisions based on the information.

Profitability of insider trading

Considerable empirical research has been conducted in the area of insider trading. The studies undertaken all implicitly assume that insider trading exists. What is less clearcut is whether such activities are profitable to the insiders. As such, most insider trading studies focus mainly on the profitability of the insiders' activities. However, the results of these studies are not conclusive. For example, Jaffe (1974) summarised the results of various previous studies on the profitability of insider trading as follows:

> In summary, the evidence with respect to the profitability of insider trading is not clear-cut. On the one hand, Rogoff, Glass, and Lorie–Niederhoffer find evidence that insiders can predict price movements in their own securities as much as 6 months in the future. On the other hand, Scholes's results suggest that residuals drop on the day of the secondary distribution with no further systematic changes. Both Wu and Driscoll find no evidence of successful forecasting by insiders. (p.411)

Jaffe lists some reasons for the contradictory results. These include outdated studies, small sample sizes, the relative risks of different securities, general market conditions and the disregard of transaction costs in some studies (1974, p.411). Of the reasons put forward, the most important practical deficiency unrelated to the samples under study is the issue of transaction costs. The few studies which do incorporate transaction costs were able to show that returns to insiders after taking into account a minimum transaction cost of 2 per cent dramatically and significantly reduce the insiders' profitability on the activities.

Jaffe's (1974) study shows that while insiders do possess special information, only the intensively trading insiders with eight months holding periods were earning statistically large returns of the order of 2.5 per cent after taking into account the 2 per cent minimum transaction cost. Jaffe, however, concludes that these results indicate that 'trading on inside information is wide-

spread [and] suggest that insiders do violate security regulations' (p.428).

Similarly, the Rozeff and Zaman study (1988) shows that, after imposing a 2 per cent transaction cost, the abnormal return to insider trading averages about 3–3.5 per cent per year. However, they concluded that:

> This is a magnitude that is approaching the point of economic insignificance and might even be considered essentially nil if transaction costs are higher than 2 per cent and/or if abnormal returns are measured net of opportunity costs of time. (p.43)

In interpreting the above results, the following factors must be considered. First, all the studies mentioned were conducted in the USA where legislation has long existed to outlaw insider trading. In New Zealand, prior to the *Securities Amendment Act* 1988, Jaffe's conclusion that insiders possess special information and do trade on this information for personal benefit would take on a special significance. The reason is that, even if New Zealand insiders then did not trade on the special information themselves, there was no legislation to prevent them from procuring others to trade on their behalf. However, under the *Securities Amendment Act* 1988, insiders in New Zealand are now prohibited from trading and tipping on the inside information of public issuers.

Second, while these studies indicate that the abnormal returns to insiders trading on special information appear to be insignificant, it must be emphasised that these studies relate only to insiders trading in their own company's securities. It is possible that insiders may be earning substantial profits from information indirectly related to other companies based on information received in their own company. This was especially relevant in New Zealand where directors sit on multiple boards of companies and were, thus, granted access to special information not only in their own but also in a number of other related companies. The *Securities Amendment Act* 1988 now prohibits insiders from trading not just in the inside information of the public issuer with which they are associated, but also in the inside information of other public issuers.

Third, the US legislation on insider trading requires the prompt disclosure of the insiders' transactions with the SEC. Similar requirements for disclosure exist in New Zealand under the *Securities Amendment Act* 1988 Part II and the *Companies Act* 1993. However, the *Securities Amendment Act* 1988 requirements apply only when a particular security holder is, becomes or ceases to hold 5 per cent or more of the public issuer's securities or if there is a more than 1 per cent change in holdings. The New Zealand legislation does not require publication of every transaction entered into by the substantial security holder such that, while American insiders may reap a profit from special information, the prompt disclosure of this information dissipates any further profits for the insider. In New Zealand there is a possibility that an insider will be able to make multiple transactions on a piece of special information before the public obtains the information. This is plausible given that, even with the prompt reporting required in the USA, studies have shown that outsiders do make profits from an analysis of the insiders' transactions as published belatedly in the *Official Summary* (Lorie and Niederhoffer, 1968).

Fourth, the American *Securities Exchange Act* 1934 precludes an insider from selling or buying securities within six months of their purchase or sale. Even with this ruling, Jaffe's (1974) study revealed that intensively trading insiders are able to profit from their activities. No such prohibitions are contained in the insider trading legislation in New Zealand. From this it can be envisaged that New Zealand insiders, in the absence of such a ruling, should be able to make even greater profits from their activities.

Insider trading and the efficient market hypothesis

Besides the studies on the profitability of insider trading *per se* (Lorie and Niederhoffer, 1968; Jaffe, 1974), a number of studies have been done in conjunction with EMH studies. This is because an important concern of the researchers of insider trading and of the ability of the insiders to make abnormal returns in the market is that it contradicts the strong form of the EMH which states that security prices reflect all publicly available and insider information. However, numerous studies in the EMH area have shown that the strong form of EMH does not exist (Scholes, 1972; Finnerty, 1976). This is reasonable in that the studies have been carried out in countries with insider trading legislation. By definition, the strong form of market efficiency cannot exist if inside information is prohibited by legislation from being disseminated through trading by insiders.

Market efficiency, to the extent that it exists, is usually in the semi-strong form where security prices reflect all publicly available information. However, research in the insider trading arena has shown that the semi-strong form of EMH may also be threatened. This is because, in the USA, investors who act on the information gleaned from the insiders' activities which are published in the SEC's monthly *Official Summary* can also earn abnormal returns, even though the time lapse between trading and publication of the *Official Summary* can be up to five weeks. In other words, the *Official Summary* still has information content even after a lapse of five weeks. This is a serious contradiction of the semi-strong form of EMH. For example, in their 1968 study using the *Official Summary* of stock transactions, Lorie and Niederhoffer concluded that 'prompt and proper analysis of data on insider trading can be profitable . . .' (p.52).

Moreover, reviews of accounting research into market efficiency have led writers to believe that even after twenty years, 'a definitive conclusion on the efficiency of the NYSE [New York Stock Exchange] cannot be drawn' (Dyckman and Morse, 1986, p.85).

The EMH issue is important in the study of insider trading because, first, in showing that the strong form of EMH does not exist, the implication of the researcher is that insider trading is possible and exists. The reason for this is that security prices at any one time reflect only publicly available information, not insider information. Insiders in possession of special insider information thus have the opportunity to use this unpublicised information if so desired.

Second, if the semi-strong form of the EMH is threatened, the insiders are placed in a more advantageous position. This is because, even when the inside information becomes available for the first time, the relatively inefficient market means that there is a delay before this information is reflected in the security prices and is such that the insider is able to profit more than once before the information is reflected in the security prices and the profits eliminated by the market.

Just as Kirk (1988, p.12) believes that 'if empirical research showed that markets were inefficient or that serious doubts about the efficiency existed, I saw the potential inefficiency as a way to substantiate the need for standards', a similar argument can be put forward for insider trading legislation. In the absence of conclusive evidence that market efficiency of any form exists in New Zealand, the *Securities Amendment Act* 1988 is a necessary means of deterring insider trading.

An alternative view: the leading indicator hypothesis

According to the EMH, within an efficient market, information is reflected instantly in share prices. Investors are believed to be sufficiently sophisticated and competent to discern relevant from irrelevant information. However, as the studies mentioned have shown, the ability of outsiders to earn abnormal returns from an analysis of the insider's trades after a time lag means that the assumptions made under the EMH may be erroneous, that is information may not be impounded instantly in the market.

While studies have been conducted to determine if insiders earn abnormal profits from their trades, few researchers have attempted to separate abnormal returns earned from illegal use of specific inside information from abnormal returns earned by the insiders from *bona fide* trading. One exception is a study by Givoly and Palmon (1985). The study covered a sample of sixty-eight randomly selected companies over the three years between 1973 and 1975 with the following two criteria:
- the companies have year ends on 31 December
- the companies were listed on the American Stock Exchange.

The study concluded that:

> The results from our sample indicated that a major part of the observed abnormal performance of insiders is likely to be due to price changes arising from the information revealed through the trades themselves. The findings also suggest that there is a low incidence of insider trading in anticipation of an impending new disclosure. (Givoly and Palmon, 1985, p.69)

The study brings out some important points about the effects of trading by insiders on the securities market. First, the mere occurrence of trading by insiders will cause a reaction in the securities market. This is irrespective of whether the trades were based on specific privileged inside information or not. One reason is that all trades by insiders are watched closely by outsiders, for example financial analysts, investors and financial reporters. These people, in turn, trigger off a reaction in the rest of the market, normally in the same direction as the trade by the insider. Givoly and Palmon (1985) name this the 'leading indicator effect' whereby investors have a tendency to follow in the footsteps of the insiders because they believe and accept the superior knowledge of the insiders (p.86).

Second, if the insider's superior performance is due to better assessment of their firm's affairs and economic and industrial trends (informed trading) rather than because of specific undisclosed information (insider trading), and in view of the possible inefficiency of security markets, a case can be presented for the non-legislation of insider trading. This is because insiders have a role to play in security markets in that they disseminate information to outsiders in the quickest and most inexpensive manner through their trades. One example that is often quoted is the market for futures where a quasi-Delphi system exists to incorporate each futures trader's 'expert' opinion on the demand and supply of a commodity at some future date such that an equilibrium futures price is agreed upon. The existence of multiple informed traders also makes the market more liquid than it otherwise would be (Grossman, 1986).

It should be noted that in their proposals, the New Zealand Securities Commission rejected the argument that trading by insiders is an efficient and inexpensive way of disseminating information. The rejection was based on moral, fair and economic grounds (1987, pp.12–33).

Third, it is very difficult to separate beneficial informed trading from the less desirable insider trading: controlling insider trading will automatically curb informed trading. This will impact negatively in the securities market as a whole in that it will reduce liquidity by limiting the number of shares available for transfer. That is, as the definition of insiders widens, the total number of shares effectively held by insiders

will increase. This, in turn, will result in more shares being restricted in their marketability thus reducing the liquidity of the securities market.

It will also affect the duties and responsibilities of insiders in that it no longer benefits them to hold shares in their own companies with the resultant loss in initiative and loyalty. This issue is also directly addressed by the New Zealand Securities Commission in their proposals for insider trading legislation:

> We have proposed stringent rules that may deter insiders from taking up securities in their companies. That would be unfortunate, in our opinion, because we think it is desirable that those who are involved with companies should not be discouraged from holding securities in them. (New Zealand Securities Commission, 1987, p.56).

To solve the problem, the New Zealand Securities Commission recommends the existing practice whereby directors, officers and employees of a company must obtain the written consent of the Chairperson before buying or selling securities in the company (p.56). Under the *Securities Amendment Act* 1988, these proposals are incorporated to an extent in the exceptions to liability (sections 8, 10, 12 and 14).

The impact of insider trading on the securities market cannot be easily determined or accurately measured because, by its very nature, insider trading is not an overt activity. Intuitively, in the absence of legislation to control and prohibit insider trading, it is assumed to exist. Results from empirical studies overseas in the profitability of insider trades and market efficiency have not been conclusive.

The practical problems of legislation

While the New Zealand legislation to control insider trading has been adopted without empirical evidence to show that insider trading is harmful, overseas evidence is available which indicates that practical problems abound in attempting to outlaw insider trading. Three of these problems include who is responsible for policing, the cost of legal action and how to differentiate informed trading from insider trading.

The first problem of who is responsible for policing any legislation to curb insider trading is a pertinent one because, as has been mentioned, insider trading is not an overt activity. For example, in Australia, while insider trading legislation has been in force since the mid-1970s, there has not been a single successful prosecution for the past fifteen years (Ricketson, 1988, p.40). In Britain, only seven convictions have been obtained and no one has gone to jail yet (Seig, 1988, p.21).

In the opinion of the New Zealand Securities Commission, the best method of preventing insider trading is to equip companies and shareholders with legal rights and powers to detect and deal with insider trading. The New Zealand Securities Commission proposed that laws be introduced to enable companies and shareholders to expose the transactions and obtain remedies where appropriate (1987, p.74). As such, under the *Securities Amendment Act* 1988, a charge of insider trading can be brought by the public issuer, existing shareholders, ex-shareholders and/or those who traded with the insider (section 18).

However, the problem is the difficulty of detection and proof of insider trading (Gill, 1988, p.9). This is especially so in cases where tippees are procured to trade on the insider's behalf and where an insider trades on information obtained about another company in the course of his or her duties. These cases will escape detection unless a constant and knowing surveillance mechanism is available to monitor all unusual price movements. As in the USA, an alert financial press has a very important role in detecting violations of insider trading regu-

lations. However, while the press may play watchdog in the absence of regulation, the question is whether it is still appropriate to rely on it to police such acts carried out in the face of regulation.

Associated with the problem of detection is the task (and cost) of proving that a person is engaged in insider trading. The New Zealand Securities Commission in its proposals admits that from knowledge of the US proceedings against two famous insider traders, Dennis Levine and Ivan Boesky, it is very much doubted whether the large recoveries from prosecution could have covered the enormous direct costs incurred (1987, p.32). This cost, coupled with the lengthy process of legal action which can take up to ten years for white-collar crime, makes the benefit worth very much less than the cost of prosecution. For example, Hall (1988), in citing various white-collar crime prosecutions in New Zealand, comments:

> It appears that massive costs can be run up quickly in investigating white-collar crime — and that police believe that penalties never match the effort. Police resources are seriously stretched in dealing with such complex matters: and likely defendants, often with huge resources at their disposal, can delay court actions for years. (p. 13)

The final practical problem is differentiating informed trading from insider trading. Insider trading legislation outlaws an insider from trading in specific pieces of unpublicised information which may impact on the security prices. The problem here is twofold.

(a) The market may react to the insider's mere act of trading, which may be unrelated to any specific piece of inside information (the leading indicator effect). An insider who is aware of this may manipulate the market to his or her advantage with the defence that the act was unrelated to any specific piece of information. In New Zealand, the *Securities Amendment Act* 1988, unlike its US counterpart, does not provide for share manipulation by insiders.

(b) As per the New Zealand Securities Commission's comments, insider trading legislation is not aimed at discouraging those involved with companies from holding and trading in the securities of the companies (1987, p.56). Hence, a *bona fide* 'insider' should not be penalised for trading because he or she is better informed generally about the firm and industrial and economy-wide factors, that is informed trading versus insider trading.

In theory legislation is not aimed at curbing general informed trading — in practice it may be difficult to isolate specific information from general information about the firm. To overcome the problem will require a constant watch over all information that is released into the market place and ultimately comes back to the initial problem of who is to be responsible for policing such activities.

While theoretically insider trading legislation is necessary based on fiduciary, fair and moral grounds, the practical problems associated with implementing and policing the regulation will need to be resolved.

Chapter summary

The recent deregulation of the New Zealand economy has widespread repercussions for every aspect of the economy.

The deregulation will mean a greater number of outside investors coming into New Zealand. However, this will be limited if the New Zealand market is not perceived to be a 'fair' market. As it is, New Zealand is about fifty-five years behind the US market where insider trading controls are concerned. The deregulation together with the stock market crash in October 1987 highlighted this problem and the issue has just recently been remedied.

This chapter has very briefly reviewed existing insider legislation in the USA, the UK, Australia and New Zealand. While legislation cannot guarantee that all insider trading activities will be removed, it will at least prevent the most blatant cases. With legislation, insiders who violate the regulations will not be able to enjoy the profits that they have made as freely as they used to do.

On the theoretical level, insider trading and its impact on the securities market were discussed. Based on existing overseas literature, the relationships between insider trading, profitability, the efficient market hypothesis and the leading indicator effects were examined. The chapter concluded with some practical problems associated with legislation.

However, while these problems will need to be resolved, based just on fiduciary, fair and moral grounds, legislation is still necessary to control, if not totally eliminate, the actions of insiders who, by virtue of their positions, benefit at the expense of the rest of the uninformed market.

Essay and examination questions

15.1 What is insider trading? Why should it be outlawed?
15.2 What is the leading indicator hypothesis? How does it affect the case for legislating against insider traders?
15.3 Evaluate the existing controls over insider trading in New Zealand.
15.4 'Insider trading does not need to be widespread to be a matter of concern', (Tomasic and Pentony, 1988). Discuss.

15.5 From the legislation in place in the USA, UK, Australia and New Zealand, who are insiders? What criteria would you use to distinguish an insider from a mere investor?

15.6 Insider trading is seen to erode market confidence. How and why?

15.7 Discuss the advantages and disadvantages of insider trading.

15.8 There are no beneficial effects from insider trading. Discuss.

References and additional reading

Australians face insider deal charges (1988). *The Dominion*, 8 June, 16.

Baxt, R., Ford, H.A.J., Samuels, G.J. and Maxwell, C.M. (1982). *An Introduction to the Securities Industry Codes* (Second edition). Sydney: Butterworths.

Born, J.A. (1988). Insider ownership and signals. *Financial Management*, **17**, 38–45.

Bostock, T.E. (1992). Australia's new insider trading laws. *Company and Securities Law Journal*, **10**(3), 165–181.

Buckley, J.W., Buckley, M.H. and Plank, T.M. (1980). *SEC Accounting*. New York: John Wiley.

Commerce Clearing House (1988). *Companies Amendment Act 1988*. Wellington: Commerce Clearing House New Zealand Limited.

Commerce Clearing House (New Zealand) (1984). *Guidebook to New Zealand Companies and Securities Law*. Auckland: Tax and Business Law Publishers.

Company Securities (Insider Dealing) Act 1985.

Cunningham, A. (1988). *National Business Review*, 5 January, 5.

Downes, D., and Dyckman, T.R. (1973). A critical look at the efficient market empirical research literature as it relates to accounting information. *The Accounting Review*, **48**, 300–317.

Dyckman, T.R. and Morse, D. (1986). *Efficient Capital Markets and Accounting: A Critical Analysis*. Englewood Cliffs, New Jersey: Prentice Hall.

Fama, E.F. (1970). Efficient capital markets: A review of theory and empirical work. *The Journal of Finance*, **25**, 383–417.

Finnerty, J.E. (1976). Insiders and market efficiency. *The Journal of Finance*, **31**, 1141–1148.

Gill, P. (1988). Business council urges clampdown on insider trading. *National Business Review*, 22 June, 9.

Givoly, D. and Palmon, D. (1985). Insider trading and the exploitation of inside information: Some empirical evidence. *Journal of Business*, **58**, 69–87.

Gonedes, N.J. (1976). The capital market, the market for information, and external accounting. *The Journal of Finance*, **31**, 611–630.

Grossman, S.J. (1986). An analysis of the role of 'insider trading' on futures markets. *Journal of Business*, **59**, S129–S146.

Hall, T. (1988). Crash brings out the dirty washing. *The Dominion*, 16 May, p.13.

Insiders on the way out (1988). *Accountants' Journal*, **67**, 30–32.

Jaffe, J.F. (1974). Special information and insider trading. *Journal of Business*, **47**, 410–428.

Keane, S.M. (1988). Share tipsters and fair advertising. *Accounting and Business Research*, **18**, 141–147.

Kennen, D. (1986). PSI and insider trading. *Accountancy*, **97**, 113–114.

Kirk, D.J. (1988). Looking back on fourteen years at the FASB: The education of a standard setter. *Accounting Horizons*, March, 8–17.

Lorie, J.H. and Niederhoffer, V. (1968). Predictive and statistical properties of insider trading. *Journal of Law and Economics*, **11**, 35–53.

McMillan, N. (1988). Early action to combat insider trading. *NZ Financial Review*, 31 February.

New Zealand Securities Commission (1987). *Insider Trading*. (Volumes 1 and 2.) Wellington.

Osborne, R. (1988). More attention is required by law firms. *NZ Financial Review*, 30 February.

Palmer, Rt Hon. G. (1988). Fair markets. Press release, 23 March.

Ricketson, M. (1988). Wall Street — a film review. *Australian Accountant*, **58**, 39–40.

Rozeff, M.S. and Zaman, M.A. (1988). Market efficiency and insider trading: New evidence. *Journal of Business*, **61**, 25–44.

Scholes, M.S. (1972). The market for securities: Substitution versus price pressure and the effects of information on share prices. *Journal of Business*, 179–211.

Securities Amendment Act 1988. Wellington: Commerce Clearing House New Zealand Limited.

Securities Exchange Act 1934.

Seig, L. (1988). Anti-insider trade laws queried. *The Dominion*, 14 September, 21.

Seyhun, H.N. (1988). The information content of aggregate insider trading. *Journal of Business*, **61**, 1–24.

Skousen, K.F. (1980). *An Introduction to the SEC* (Second edition). Cincinnati, Ohio: South-Western Publishing Co.

South Africa slow to tackle insider traders. (25 May 1988). *The Dominion*, 21.

Tomasic, R. and Pentony, B. (1988). *Insider Trading in Australia (Parts I–IV)*. Canberra College of Advanced Education.

Wall St man charged with insider trade (29 June 1988). *The Evening Post*, 18.

Ziegelaar, M. (1994). Insider-trading Law in Australia, in Walker, G. and Fisse, B. (Eds.) (1994). *Securities Regulation in Australia and New Zealand*, Auckland: Oxford University Press, 677–12.

Chapter 16
Professional ethics

Learning objectives

After studying this chapter the reader will be able to:
- define what a profession is and discuss its basic attributes
- differentiate between a profession and an occupation
- consider the concept of professionalism in the modern world
- critically examine the various ethical issues facing the accounting profession
- comment on the significance of professional ethics in the accounting profession
- discuss the role of education in making people behave ethically.

Introduction

Professions are an integral part of society. Their contributions have been regarded as indispensable. For generations, people have aspired to be professionals, whether in the field of medicine, law, engineering, architecture or accounting, to name but a few. The logic of this aspiration is the higher social status, the respect of the general public and the greater wealth which membership of a profession carries with it. In short, the professions are generally recognised as the 'elites' of society.

However, rapid social changes have eroded this image. With increased literacy and higher levels of education, not only are the numbers of 'professions' on the increase, but the public are becoming sceptical of 'them'. We now live in the age of mass denigration of the professions.

One of the prime factors why professions are under close scrutiny is the decline of professional ethics, which have always been considered the basis of public confidence. The subject of ethics is not new, but the attention given to it by the legislators and especially the media has raised the awareness of the public about ethical transgressions, particularly among the respected professions. It is indeed a serious matter in terms of professional survival. If society perceives no public benefit in the service performed by the professions, then it will withdraw its trust

and confidence in them and, in the end, there will be no profession.

To keep abreast with the pace of social change, the professions must carry out continual evaluation aiming to serve the ever changing environment. Professional ethics — the guiding force of the professions — will have to be adjusted to provide more relevance to the existing circumstances.

The accounting profession is a critical and indispensable element in any economy that depends on private capital. The intention of this chapter is to explore the issues pertaining to professional ethics in the accounting profession. First, a definition of profession will be sought; basic attributes of the professions will be identified; and a differentiation made about what makes an occupation grouping a profession. Second, the subject of ethics will be pursued by examining the development of professional ethics and the need for them in the accounting profession. Recent developments in the Anglo-American accounting scene will also be traced.

What is a profession?

In this complex, status-conscious society, all of a sudden there is an increase in the number of 'professions'. Any occupation group can call itself a profession. Thus, there is the profession of hairdressers, the profession of welders and fitters and even the profession of undertakers. Some jobs that used to be in

the very low job strata are promoting themselves to professional status!

Consequently, it is necessary to dwell on
the definition of profession. Emmet (1966,
p.159) describes a profession as follows:

> A profession . . . carries with it the
> notion of a standard of performance, it
> is not only a way of making a living, but
> one in which the practitioners have a
> fiduciary trust to maintain certain stan-
> dards. These are partly standards of com-
> petence, or technical ability in carrying
> out functions valued in the society. But
> not only so: professional competence
> has to be joined with professional
> integrity . . . A professional [sic] man
> carries out his functions in relation to
> people who also stand in a particular
> role relation to him. The relationship
> carries specific obligations, to be distin-
> guished from those of purely personal
> morality, or from general obligations to
> human beings as such.

A profession is different from other occupations in the sense that 'enhancing profit' is
not the goal of professional activities. The
concern is with service and quality in work
undertaken. The more professional a job, the
greater the responsibilities that go with it. A
modern professional is no longer constrained
by the traditional view that he or she is self-
employed, fee-earning and independent.
Circumstances have changed to such an
extent that there is a more liberalised conno-
tation of the term 'professional'.

Basic attributes

A sociological view of a profession is:

> an organisation group which is constantly
> interacting with the society that forms its
> matrix, which performs its social func-
> tions through a network of formal and
> informal relationships, and which creates
> its own subculture requiring adjustments
> to it as a prerequisite for career success.
> (Greenwood, 1957, p.45)

A careful canvass of the sociological literature
on occupations enabled Greenwood to draw
the conclusion that all professions seem to
possess five common attributes: (a) systematic theory, (b) authority, (c) community
sanction, (d) ethical codes and (e) a culture. A
brief examination of these will follow.

Systematic body of theory

At present, the element of superior skill is
no longer regarded as the major difference
between a professional and a non-
professional occupation. To be recognised as
a profession, this skill must be supported by
a body of theory, the mastery of which is
prerequisite to the acquisition of the skill.
The function of the theory is a groundwork
for practice. It serves as 'a base in terms of
which the professional rationalises his [sic]
operations in concrete situations'
(Greenwood, 1957, p.46). Preparation for a
profession is therefore considered both an
intellectual and a practical experience.
Formal education in an academic institution
is deemed necessary to provide the desirable foundation for practice and for entry
into the profession.

Professional authority

An extensive education in the systematic
theory related to the profession will provide
the professional with 'a type of knowledge
that highlights the layman's comparative
ignorance' (Greenwood, 1957, p.47). As
such, the client will rely on the professional's expertise and judgement by
bestowing on the latter the authority which
embodies 'a monopoly of judgement'. The
source of this authority is thus two-fold:
from within the profession itself (its body of
knowledge, its disciplinary sanctions and the
calibre of its members) and from without
(the recognition by the clients and users).

Sanction of the community

To maintain professional authority, community sanctions are necessary. In some cases,

legal jurisdiction is granted to enhance or reinforce this authority. Among the powers bestowed is the profession's control over its training centres by means of an accreditation process: 'the right to set conditions for entry, examine and admit members, set standards of conduct, police these standards, and enjoy an economic monopoly within the designated area of jurisdiction' (Buckley, 1978, p.67). Among the privileges are confidentiality towards clients and a relative immunity from community judgement on technical matters. In short, the profession is granted autonomy as well as self-regulation.

Regulative code of ethics

Since the profession is granted so many powers and privileges, there is always the threat that 'a monopoly can be abused; powers and privileges can be used to protect vested interests against the public weal' (Greenwood, 1957, pp.49–50). To maintain social control, every profession has a built-in regulative code which compels ethical behaviour on the part of its members, regulating client–professional, colleague–colleague and professional–society relations. There is also a disciplinary aspect exercised by the professional associations 'to criticise or to censure, and in extreme cases to bar recalcitrants' (Greenwood, 1957, p.51). This, in fact, is a potent force towards conformity — to uphold the professional image.

Professional culture

The professional image can be enhanced greatly by the culture and subcultures existing within the profession. Every profession operates through a network of formal and informal groups. Through the interactions of these groups, where the social values, the behavioural norms and the symbols of the groups are internalised, a professional culture is generated. The values are the basic and fundamental beliefs upon which the

existence of the profession rests. The norms, based on the values, are the guides to behaviour in social situations. The symbols, like insignias and emblems, are meaning-laden items unique to the profession. All of these features will enhance the sense of professional identification. Also essential is the implicit career concept in which the members treat their career as a calling and, as such, are dedicated to their work and their long-term career aspirations. Such a dedication, ideally, is to put unselfish service to clients and the public ahead of income considerations (Olson, 1978, p.79).

This sociological basket of professional attributes is similar to the ones often espoused in accounting literature (Benson, 1981; O'Leary and Boland, 1987), namely, a body of specialised knowledge supported by a recognised educational process; specific professional qualifications governing entry and post-entry development; high ethical standards of conduct and performance; an avowed commitment to the public interest; and a governing body regulating the above.

The difference: profession and non-profession

Burns and Haga (1977) find that there are two major fallacies inherent in the sociologists' 'shopping list of professional attributes'. First, most of the attributes fit most of the recognised professions as well as the pretenders or non-professional groups. Second, the list is an inadequate guide to convert an occupation into a profession or to enhance the status of an established profession. Greenwood (1957) also recognises this problem and admits that there are no clearcut classes of professions having all these pertinent attributes. Both the professional and non-professional occupations possess them, with the latter possessing them to a lesser degree. Therefore, it is more constructive to consider all occupations in a society as distributed along an occupational continuum. At one end of the continuum are the well recognised and respected professions such as law and medicine and at the other end are the least skilled and least attractive occupations such as night guards and labour hands. The rest are scattered along the continuum.

It must be noted that possessing all these attributes does not make a person a true professional. What makes a true professional is the 'spirit' in which the job is carried out. It must be borne in mind that professionalism is:

> an attitude of mind. Whenever outrunning the desire for personal profit, (one finds) joy in work, eagerness for service, and a readiness for cooperative process, then trade has been left behind and a profession entered. (Mitchell, 1965, p.34)

Professionalism is indicative of high purpose. It denotes a genuine regard for excellence, interwoven with other qualities like integrity, wisdom, maturity, knowledge, understanding and expertise. As such, it can be generalised that the traditional view of professionalism is outmoded in the sense that there is no guarantee that an 'elite' professional will provide work of high quality and a so-called non-professional does not necessarily produce low quality work. It is up to the individual and is mainly determined by his or her attitude towards work.

Professional ethics

As observed by Greenwood (1957), Burns and Haga (1977) and many other sociologists, every profession has a built-in code of ethics to compel ethical behaviour on its members. The rationale for this is obvious. Individuals from time to time have to face ethical dilemmas and the problem of 'weakness of will'. Accountants are no different. In their working life they encounter numerous situations where they are tempted to do something morally wrong. That is why a feature of accountancy's claim to pro-

fessionalism is its commitment to ethical actions (Puxty, Sikka and Willmott, 1994). This involves an assurance that the accountancy bodies and their members will not pursue their material self-interests in ways that conflict with their duties to the public interest. Ethics, the matter of the conscience, have traditionally been regarded as a 'lubricant' of social and economic systems and are highly regarded by the professions. There are basically two strategies for overcoming weakness of will (Bowie, 1982, p.89). One relies on internal mechanisms of self-control and the other on external constraints. Internal mechanisms for self-control include the codes of ethics, whereas the chief external constraint is government regulation. It is the former that this chapter is concerned about.

General ethics are about moral rules, comprising a code of principles (written and unwritten) about what is right and what is wrong. Historically, religion has played an important role in enforcing ethical behaviour by invoking an omniscient being with the power to reward and punish behaviour (Noreen, 1988, p.368). Family and culture have also played a significant part in conditioning moral behaviour. It is the imposition of the law on oneself without any pressures from the outside. The ultimate purpose is for group cooperation or harmony.

For centuries, ethics have been a philosophical study of morality. Ethics investigate the fundamental principles and basic concepts that concern how all persons should live and behave. Various notions of ethics have been advanced at different times. One common theme among them is that they all tend to work for the good or welfare of all humankind. For instance, Socrates used knowledge as a rational basis for right conduct; Aristotle expounded the virtues, such as courage and justice, to be qualities that would bring about the overall state of well-being for the individual and for society; Locke believed that ethical conduct and moral principles were acquired through perception and conception and as such were subject to the 'law'; Hume explained ethics in terms of empirically verifiable observations and relationships — what is done rather than what ought to be done; Kant believed in self-imposed action conforming with one's sense of duty as the supreme sense of morality; while Mill held the view that right conduct was what maximised the good (Mautz and Sharaf, 1961; Marsh, 1980; Scribner and Dillaway, 1989). However, none of these ethical considerations offers a universally acceptable way of resolving ethical issues. A combination of them often forms the philosophical bases of existing political, economic and cultural institutions.

With the development of professions, a new branch of ethics has developed — 'professional ethics'. Professional ethics are also concerned about moral behaviour, but are more restrictive in a sense that they encompass the expected ethical pattern unique to a certain profession. This accepted behaviour will, however, be adjusted according to the changing circumstances of professional practice, with the purpose of a profession unchanged and acting as a 'normative filter'. Ethics are normative in nature because their purpose is to guide action in making moral choices (towards human welfare). They can also be regarded as applied ethics because their focus is on the tools, concepts and concerns of normative ethics to arrive at concrete moral judgements in specific circumstances (Powers and Vogel, 1980).

Professional ethics have a dual role. They have philosophical and social implications (Loeb, 1978; Abbott, 1983). The philosophical aspect involves questions of morality — what is right and what is wrong — whereas the sociological perspective is concerned with the question of professional self-regulation and control. The former deals with moral action, encompassing a 'sense of duty' to society. The latter is needed because society grants a profession the exclusive right to perform certain tasks within the bounds of the profession. Concomitant with such a right are some privileges, one of which is self-regulation.

To maintain social control, a profession has to devise rules to govern its members. Generally, these rules are encoded in a code of ethics which is a guide to members of a professional community in performing their professional roles. It is a moral code unique to the specific professional community comprising, essentially, 'a set of rules and precepts designed to induce an attitude and a kind of behaviour on the practitioners of the profession concerned, which will encourage public confidence' (Carey, 1978, p.86). As such, each professional community tends to have its own restrictive prescriptions suited to the needs or welfare of the community. However, there always exists the threat that society can rescind the privilege of self-regulation if the profession concerned is not perceived to be behaving in a way acceptable to society. Therefore, a profession has to be seen to be enforcing its code of ethics and committed to ethical actions, otherwise its autonomy will be in jeopardy.

Advantages of a code of professional ethics

Setting ethical standards will not spontaneously instil morality in professional members. Nonetheless, it can help the honest members base their decisions and actions on the dictates of their conscience. It will also discourage those who use unethical practices because it will be easier to detect such practices. The advantages of a formal written code of ethics are summarised well by Boulanger and Wayland (1985, p.51) and are as follows.

- Professional members will be more aware of the moral aspects of their work.
- An easily accessible reference tool will prompt managers to keep ethical concerns in mind.

- Abstract ideas will be translated into concrete terms applicable to every situation.
- Members, as a whole, will act in a more standardised fashion throughout the profession.
- There will be a known standard for assessing members' conduct and the profession's policies.
- Members will be better able to assess their own performance.
- The profession will be able to make their members and the public at large fully aware of their ethical policies.
- Members can justify their conduct if it is criticised.

A code of ethics has to be supported by concrete actions. The governing bodies of the profession will look after this function by monitoring the members' practices, ruling on cases submitted for arbitration and imposing penalties for infractions (Boulanger and Wayland, 1985, p.53).

Development of professional ethics in the accounting profession

Professional ethics in the accounting profession have been developed over time by means of an evolutionary process (Brown, 1975; Carey and Doherty, 1966). They have a practical purpose and this practicality is vividly shown in the way these rules are developed (Carey, 1978, p.89).

With the enactment of the first *Joint Stock Companies Act* 1844 in the UK, the workload of accountants gradually increased, not only in the financial accounting area, but also in the handling of audits and bankruptcies. Public confidence in accountants promoted the growth of the profession. Well into the twentieth century, the support displayed by the financial sector also consolidated the professional status of accountants. However, the credibility of the accounting profession can be maintained only if accountants themselves are perceived to be independent and competent

and the quality of their work is adequate. Thus, over a period of sixty years or more, the code of professional ethics evolved as the product of thousands of minds which were guided by the experience of decades. A number of rules were adopted as the result of specific events urging the need for additional standards to accommodate changing circumstances (Carey and Doherty, 1966, p.7).

When devising the specific rules of conduct, accountants have always borne in mind three important factors: the public, their clients and other accountants. A priority list has been established in case of conflicts. The public, being the larger group, generally have priority. The specific professional rules of conduct are the direct result of the accountants pooling their wisdom to identify the most acceptable behavioural patterns among professionals in accordance with the set priority. At times, certain rules are formed as a result of particular events, as the governing bodies of the accounting societies fear that public confidence would be further impaired if future repetition were not prevented. The code of ethics thus evolved; the rules were modified and expanded as circumstances within the environment changed over time. A more recent example is the abolition of the rule against advertising within the accounting profession. There were sufficient societal and economic demands that the US accounting profession deregulated the solicitation and advertising rules in 1978, followed by the UK and Australia in 1984. New Zealand did not follow until 1986. These demands reflect the accounting profession's 'responses to the expectations and challenges created by itself, the business community, regulation and other users of financial statements who rely on members' independence, integrity, objectivity and adherence to professional standards' (Mintz, 1992, p.1).

At present, the accounting profession in some countries is divided into a number of segments, each of which has its own code of ethics. The main one is the group of public accountants; the others include internal auditors, management accountants and financial executives. Accountants can hold membership of one or more associations. Lately, there has been talk that a code of ethics will be produced to regulate the non-public accountants and academic account-ants (Loeb 1984; 1990).

The need for professional ethics in the accounting profession

In the past few decades, the structure of society has changed as a result of the redis-tribution of wealth, the levelling of income, the availability of higher education, comput-erisation and the expansion of social ser-vices. All these have impacted on the organisation and attitudes of society, with significant consequences for the professions. The tremors of various monetary and polit-ical crises are felt worldwide and even the accounting profession is not left untouched. Many questions have been raised about the ethical conduct of individual accountants as well as the profession as a whole. As the loss of public confidence will have dire con-sequences for the accounting profession, it is necessary for accountants to take steps to improve their performance and at the same time redefine their societal roles as circum-stances require.

Changes in the accounting profession

As mentioned earlier, the accounting pro-fession has experienced considerable changes. More services are offered, more qualified people are admitted into the pro-fession and some accounting firms have expanded into corporate conglomerates (Olson, 1978; 1979). The accounting pro-fession has diversified its services into many 'information-based' services such as consul-tancy work, marketing services, executive

search, strategic planning, tax planning and other financial services (Reed, 1985). Undoubtedly, this is a far cry from the days when the profession was mainly concerned with bookkeeping, auditing and bankrupt-cies. Some observant people have even called this phenomenon the 'accounting industry' (Olson, 1978; Zeff, 1987). However, despite the growth in size and expertise, the profession is not without problems. It exists in an increasingly mate-rialistic, sceptical or cynical society where ethical values are treated 'at a discount'. In addition, it is subject to increasing scrutiny by wide sections of society who see their interests affected by what accountants do because of their effect on public policy. Changes in the nature and extent of compe-tition in the profession have highlighted the following conflicts between professional attitudes and current commercial reality.

Professionalism versus commercialism

Capital markets depend very much on reli-able, relevant, understandable and compara-ble financial information in allocating scarce resources. As such, financial statements are the primary source of such financial infor-mation. Financial accountants as well as independent auditors have to recognise the significance of professionalism in perform-ing their respective roles. They should be committed to upholding technical standards and ethical standards of conduct. Financial accountants are expected to be dedicated to serving the public, not for pecuniary gain, but for the sake of service and job satisfaction.

However, since the 1970s, the account-ing profession has also been affected by the general competitiveness in the business environment. Such an increase in competi-tion has raised doubts about the indepen-dence of accountants and heightened the issue of professionalism versus commercial-ism (Reed, 1985, p.18; Sack, 1985). The accounting profession, especially the big accounting firms, are perceived to be obsessed with growth. Through the process of merger, they have expanded not only nationally but also internationally, establishing affiliations on a worldwide basis. While trying to retain existing clients, they are also keen to expand their client base. The sheer size and structure of such accounting firms are indications that 'they are engaged in an activity which may sometimes be more of a business than a profession in its character' (Editorial, *The Accountant's Magazine*, May 1985, p.197).

Public interest versus private interest

Closely related to the issue of professionalism and commercialism is the conflict of public interest and private interest. The professional status of any profession rests on social consent and, in return for its rights and privileges, the profession accepts social responsibility and the subordination of self-interest. All members of the profession are expected to exercise an altruistic quality by putting service ahead of income considerations.

However, in recent years the accounting profession has been found to be retreating from this ideal (Parker, 1994; Puxty, Sikka and Willmott, 1994). There is a general 'restiveness' with traditionally accepted attitudes; the emphasis is on 'commercial', 'efficient', 'business-like' and 'realistic' (Editorial, *The Accountant's Magazine*, May 1985, p.197). Accountants are perceived to be guided by their own system of materialistic values. It is obvious that there is a divergence between accountants' objectives and those of society. This tends to lead them into paradoxical situations. Many of them behave in an opportunistic manner for self-interest or short-run gains. As a result, the image and credibility of public accountants have been eroded.

Profession under threat

George D. Anderson, a past Chairman of the Board of the AICPA and Chairman of the Institute's special committee on standards of professional conduct for CPAs, made the following remarks to the Institute's Council in May 1985:

> There has been an erosion of self-restraint, conservatism, and adherence to basic professional values at a pace and to an extent that is unprecedented in the profession's history. [We believe] . . . the profession is on the brink of a crisis of confidence in its ability to serve the public interest.

Indeed, this is a critical time in the history of the accounting profession. Investors and depositors are losing faith in the ability of the profession to perform the job that has historically been its unique function: assuring the integrity of the financial information on which our capitalistic society depends (Wood, 1985, p.142). The 'restiveness', instigated by fundamental changes occurring in the accounting profession, is 'threaten[ing] its cohesion and sense of purpose' (Zeff, 1987, p.22). The perverse self-interest that has surfaced and the 'competitive edge' in professional practice have become sharper than ever before.

Coupled with the deregulation of the advertising restraint and the growth of a better educated and more inquisitive public, the accounting profession is seen to be burdened with increased litigation. There are charges of diluted independence, substandard work, deceptive advertising, growing commercialism, opinion shopping, predatory pricing, insider trading, conflicts of interest, a lax attitude towards management fraud and even a decline in intra-professional courtesy (Olson, 1978; Anderson and Ellyson, 1986; Gandz, 1988). The list is by no means exhaustive. It is highly unlikely that the majority of accountants are performing in such an unacceptable manner; however, a few 'black sheep' in the flock will put the good name of the profession on the line!

Ethical issues in the accounting profession

In a pluralistic society where there are many expectations to be met, ethical conflicts are inevitable. These are times when an individual interacts with other people and finds that his or her duties towards one group are inconsistent with his or her duties towards other groups. The attempt to resolve these opposing obligations will, according to the current standards, determine whether his or her behaviour is ethical or not (Finn, Chonko and Hunt, 1988). This happens in practically every segment of accounting. To illustrate the problem, some examples of ethical conflicts are provided and are also listed in Table 16.1.

- A public accountant may feel a conflict between his or her wish to invest in securities and the profession's standards relating to independence.
- Practising accountants may find the existing professional standards not appropriate in a particular circumstance.
- When preparing income tax returns, accountants encounter difficulties when clients specifically request some form of tax evasion or when they attempt to fraudulently misstate their tax information.
- For a small town accountant who has a limited client base, conflicts of interest will surface when he or she is asked to offer advice to clients who, for example, happen to be the parties engaged in a 'buy and sell' situation.
- Other cases include:
  — too much wining and dining at the insistence of clients
  — client proposals to alter outcomes from prepared financial statements for investor and creditor purposes
  — pressures from colleagues and superiors to produce misleading accounts
  — use of budget to maximise the department's share of resources
  — moving offshore because of cheaper production costs and lax rules.

Certainly, these examples are not exhaustive. They merely demonstrate that ethical and unethical actions are contingent upon a number of determining factors: one's personal values; the organisational culture; top management attitudes; peer pressure; and the opportunity to do so.

A survey by Finn et al. (1988) has confirmed that there are ethical problems in accounting. The result of the survey is reproduced in Table 16.1.

Professional ethics for disciplinary purposes

Ethical issues are being talked about more openly than they have been in the past. In addition, the business and lay press are interested in highlighting unethical practices. Therefore, the activities of the

Table 16.1
Ethical issues in the accounting profession

Rank	Issue	Frequency	(%)
1	Client proposals of tax alteration and tax fraud	98	(47)
2	Conflicts of interests and independence	35	(16)
3	Client proposals of alteration of financial statements	26	(12)
4	Fee problems (billing, collection, contingent fee problems, competitor bids)	22	(10)
5	Other issues	32	(15)
		213	(100)

Source: Finn, Chonko and Hunt, 1988, p.609

accounting profession are under continual public scrutiny. As such, it is unrealistic to rely solely on the initial qualification requirements and the code of ethics to protect the public from malpractice and to protect the professional image from being tarnished.

The threat of withdrawal of licence or deregistration must be present for wrongdoing. Suspensions, revocations of rights to practise and even civil and criminal liability for serious cases will form part of the total system of public protection. Human nature is such that compliance has to be enforced. Thus the disciplinary measures will act as a control mechanism to add teeth to the existing code of ethics.

The purpose of the combined forces of disciplinary measures is threefold: (a) to enhance the quality of practice and the stature of the profession in the eyes of the public; (b) to ensure that practitioners adhere to the high ideals of a professional; and (c) to maintain self-regulation.

Professional ethics for survival

It must be realised that no profession will have everlasting tenure. To survive, it must follow a course of reorientation, redefining its roles in the light of changing circumstances. As new concepts and standards of behaviour are evolving in society and in the profession, moral and ethical norms are shifting. Hence professional ethics will have to be adjusted.

By adjusting the code of professional ethics to current societal needs, roles of professional members will be redefined and, as a result, public acceptability will be enhanced. By enforcing compliance with the code of professional ethics by means of a disciplinary mechanism, it is expected that professional status will be maintained.

Parker (1994) has remarked that this is but a 'private interest model' of professional ethics and associated disciplinary process, initiated by the 'self-interest' of the profession. For him, such a model of professional ethics comprises five inter-related roles.

a   The insulation of the profession from observation and evaluation by external parties.
b   The avoidance or minimisation of interference in the profession's domain.
c   The exercising of self-control over its work and activities by the profession.
d   The general maintenance of professional autonomy and authority.
e   The safeguarding of profession members' socio-economic status.
(pp.510–514)

Apparently, Parker regards the protection of the profession as a political process: 'The public interest is readily declared but the private interest remains submerged yet powerful' (1994, p.508). The role of ethics is therefore an important element of the accounting profession's ongoing commitment to ensuring its own survival.

What has been done to improve the state of affairs?

There is now an increased awareness of ethical issues and the potential damage which non-observance will bring about. Accounting educators, researchers, and professional bodies in Anglo-American countries have responded to criticisms of their profession. The following sections will examine the various courses of action taken by them — individually or jointly — to react dynamically to the changing values and expectations of society.

The United States of America

Comparatively, the USA seems to have given more attention to resolving this issue. The Anderson Committee (1986) spent three years working on a final report, *Restructuring Professional Standards to Achieve Professional Excellence in a Changing*

Environment, a visible, meaningful response to the challenge of balancing the needs of the public and the profession. The report recommends a constructive way to restructure the code of ethics, to provide guidance to accountants on the scope of services and adherence to professionalism, to develop a programme for monitoring compliance with professional standards and to establish educational requirements for new entrants and existing members. These recommendations were adopted in February 1988.

The National Commission on Fraudulent Financial Reporting (the Treadway Commission, 1987) has also made recommendations on restructuring professional education, in harmony with the Anderson Committee's suggestions. One of the suggestions is for more coverage of ethics in accounting and business education. Firms are encouraged to adopt, publicise and enforce written codes of conduct and colleges and examinations (for example the IIA and CPA) are to increase their emphasis on controlling fraud.

In 1986 the AAA Committee on the 'Future Structure, Content, and Scope of Accounting Education' (the Bedford Committee) recommended a programme of general professional education to develop the technical skills and to instil the ethical standards and commitment of professional accountants. In a similar vein, the position paper issued by the chief executives of the then Big Eight accounting firms in 1989 (Arthur Andersen *et al.*, 1989) and the first position statement of the Accounting Education Change Commission (AECC, 1990) also advocated that the accounting curriculum changes should take into account the nurturing of the professional's ability to understand the ethics of the profession and to apply value-based judgements in addressing ethical issues.

In addition to the growing volume of literature on business and accounting ethics, there are other parties that have made significant contributions to assist and encourage the ethical consciousness of accountants and accounting students. For instance, workshops and seminars run by the AAA and Arthur Andersen and Co.; case studies by the AAA, Windal (1991) and Mintz (1992); video vignettes by the Institute of Management Accountants (IMA) and Arthur Andersen & Co.; and regular ethics columns in accounting journals such as *Management Accounting* and the *Journal of Accountancy*. The IMA has also offered a toll-free ethics hotline to provide members with advice on ethical issues.

The United Kingdom

The UK is markedly less advanced and organised in the areas of ethics reform. Literature on ethics in accountancy is scarce (Jack, 1994). However, there is a general perception that it is a field that requires more serious consideration. Progress has been made. The accounting professional bodies are involved in ethical issues within their constituencies through the joint ethics committee of the UK and Ireland institutes.

In 1992 a new *Guide to Professional Ethics* was approved by three UK and Irish institutes of chartered accountants to provide overall guidance to members. This reflects the institutes' determination to ensure that members' behaviour is ethically correct. The substantially revised and updated guidelines are not strict, legalistic, ethical rules; they flow from fundamental principles supported by a series of statements. Members are to follow them in spirit rather than to the letter. More specific guidelines are underway on topics such as opinion shopping, low balling (predatory pricing) and the rotation of audit partners. As another means to assist members in resolving ethical conflicts, the ICAEW, since 1981, has offered an ethical advisory service, Industrial Members' Ethical Advisory Committee (IMEAC), for accountants in business who require advice to rectify ethically questionable pressures from colleagues and superiors.

Australia

Parker, in a paper entitled 'An historical analysis of ethical pronouncements and debate in the Australian accounting profession' (1987), has traced ethical development in the Australian accounting profession. He relates the fact that in the period between 1978 and 1983, a new series of ethical pronouncements were produced by the Joint Standing Committee of the ASCPA and the ICAA. The Australian Ethical Rulings/Australian Ethical Pronouncements (AER/AEP) codes provided basic statements of ethical rules with supporting discussion, explanation and examples. The topics discussed included general ethical approaches and housekeeping rules such as confidentiality of client records, conflict of duty to clients, inconsistent business, competence, independence and, above all, advertising.

A new *Code of Professional Conduct* was published on 1 July 1988, replacing the ethical pronouncements. It is said to be more relevant to today's business environment and professional expectations (*The Australian Accountant*, March 1988, p.42).

The teaching of business and accounting ethics has also become prevalent in Australia with the establishment of ethics centres in the major cities and the incorporation of ethics into tertiary curricula (English, 1990a, b). The ICAA has run lectures and seminars on ethics in conjunction with Australian educational institutes. Since 1992 it has established an Academic Ethics Network to promote information exchange among academics interested in business ethics education. Acknowledging that ethics education can play a role in enhancing the existing environment, the ASCPA has also committed itself to a series of practical initiatives to improve the ethical understanding of members and business students. Cases on ethics are compiled as educational aids on the subject.

New Zealand

Although no commissions or reforms of a similar nature have been set up in New Zealand, this does not mean that the accounting profession in this country is indifferent to the ethical issues and happenings elsewhere. The accounting profession in New Zealand is also concerned about the public interest and is intent on making use of the disciplinary mechanism to enforce compliance.

The NZSA's new revised code of ethics came into effect on 1 January 1992 with public interest as the main thrust (NZSA, 1991). The code consists of seven 'goal-oriented and aspirational' fundamental principles (integrity, objectivity, professional competence, due care and timeliness, technical standards, professional behaviour, confidentiality and independence), forming the basis of seventy ethical provisions.

The NZSA is keen to promote the ethical consciousness of its members. Ethics has been an integral component of the Society's existing Final Qualifying Examination (FQE) for accountants intending to join the profession. The Society's official journal, the *Chartered Accountants Journal of New Zealand* (formerly *Accountants' Journal*) publishes from time to time an ethics awareness column. The teaching of accounting ethics, however, is not as widespread as its counterparts in the USA and Australia, with only minimal coverage in existing accounting courses.

Ethics in the accounting curriculum

It can be seen that the accounting profession has to bridge the gap between public expectations and the level of performance responsive to present ethical norms (Anderson, 1985). Codes of ethics are upgraded, professional standards are improved and ethics are proposed for inclusion in educational programmes. It is high time to seek expert advice and input from ethicists and moral philosophers if the profession is to combat increasingly tricky ethical issues.

Briloff (1986, pp.40–41), a long time critic of the accounting profession, attacked the profession for failing in moral education:

> We are especially competent in the teaching of techniques and skills; we are sorely *deficient* in transmitting to students the critical understanding of the interface between business and society and of the leaders of business and the business professionals to comprehend that they have been vested with enormous resources and power to be exercised for their own advancement of course — but beyond that by far for the transcendent objectives of society. [Emphasis added.]

Briloff argued that the teaching of moral values — the real meaning of professionalism — is far from satisfactory. As a result, he urged accounting educators to instil an 'ethical compass' in their students and start off the 'reprofessionalisation' of accountancy to 'recapture its soul' and proceed to the fulfilment of the responsibilities vested in it by society. He reminded the accounting profession of the words of Professor Barzun:

> The message for the professionals today is that their one hope of survival with anything like their present freedoms is the recovery of mental and moral force. No profession can live and flourish on just one of the two . . . What all the professions need today is critics from inside, men [*sic*] who know what the conditions are, and also the arguments and excuses, and in a full sweep over the field can offer their fellow practitioners a new vision of the profession as an institution. (p.42)

Even though Briloff's target was the auditing segment of accounting, the basic concept of reprofessionalisation is also applicable 'across the board'. It is vital that the profession respond effectively to the challenge, recognising the role it can play in corporate governance and accountability and the progress of its 'capitalistic democracy' (Briloff, 1986, p.45).

The question is: can the teaching of professional ethics be effective in improving ethical behaviour? This has generated considerable debate. Some critics are of the opinion that it is too late to start ethics education at university because moral values are said to be set at an early age. Proponents of ethics education, however, assert that human beings are not born with an innate desire to be ethical or to be concerned with the welfare of others. An important tenet of developmental psychology is that individuals 'progress' from lower stages to higher stages provided they have the appropriate environment (Armstrong, 1987). Research conducted by Rest (1988) confirmed that formal schooling is a powerful catalyst to ethical development and that moral behaviour can be developed from a thorough understanding of the ethical concepts and be reinforced by reference to ethical considerations.

The belief that ethical behaviour can be taught is also supported by individual writers such as Armstrong (1987 and 1993), Carey (1978), Gandz (1988), Loeb (1988), Noreen (1988) and Smith (1988), and groups like the Anderson Committee (1986), the Bedford Committee (1986), the Treadway Committee (1987), the Big Eight Position Paper (Arthur Andersen *et al*, 1989) and the AECC (1990). A recent research conducted by the Harvard Business School on MBA students (Piper, Gentile and Parks, 1993) also provides support in line with the argument that appropriate ethics education can help budding professionals mature ethically and assume a sense of responsibility to society, themselves and the profession.

Chapter summary

The future opportunities of the accounting profession depend very much on the maintenance of public confidence. The profession has reached a critical period and is under constant public scrutiny. This critical atmosphere should be understood by the accountants who must adjust their organisation and attitude to it if their worthwhile contribution to society is to be maintained and strengthened.

It is not only the organisation itself but also the members who should be responsible for upholding the reputation and wellbeing of the profession. Upgrading the codes of ethics is but one way to attain such a goal. All accountants must bear in mind that:

> Professions are neither 'made by law' nor 'just born'. Careful thought, planning, and toil are required of many individuals to develop self-concepts, techniques, and procedures; perform research; and disseminate appropriate information about the ideals and work of the would-be professional group. In a real sense, a profession can only evolve out of the individual efforts of a large number of persons, each of whom is dedicated to ideals and standards of service which are only dimly seen during the formative stages of a profession. Perhaps the most outstanding attribute of the professional should be the spirit in which he/she does the job. (Dierks and Davis, 1980, p.46)

Accounting may not be able to completely 'reshape' the ethical thinking of the age. However, by emphasising the importance of ethics in the curriculum, at least it can make some contributions to society. It can help raise the sense of responsibility for the effects of one's actions on others. If ethics education does not motivate 'altruistic' behaviour, hopefully it will induce utilitarian ethical behaviour with the person 'making a contribution to a practice or institution in the knowledge that it benefits him [sic] and is dependent for survival on contributions from people like him' (Noreen, 1988, p.367).

Essay and examination questions

16.1 What is meant by professional ethics? What are the implications of professional ethics in accounting?

16.2 Why does a professional accountant have responsibilities beyond those of a business executive?

16.3 What are the attributes of a profession? Do you agree with the view that a profession possesses a list of identifiable characteristics? Comment.

16.4 Explain how a code of ethics can be in part formal and in part informal.

16.5 Ethical codes may also play a role in safeguarding the socio-economic position of the members of a profession. Discuss.

16.6 What has happened to our value system? Is accounting professionalism dead?

16.7 Discuss the impact of ethics education upon the restructuring of the standards of the accounting profession.

16.8 What do you understand by the concept of professionalism?

References and additional reading

Abbott, A. (1983). Professional ethics. *American Journal of Sociology*, **88**(5), 855–885.

Accounting Education Change Commission (1990). *Position Paper No. 1 — Objectives of Education for Accountants*. AAA.

American Accounting Association, Committee on the Future Structure, Content, and Scope of Accounting Education (The Bedford Committee) (1986). Future accounting education: Preparing for the expanding profession. *Issues in Accounting Education*, **1**(1), 168–195.

American Institute of Certified Public Accountants, Committee on Standards of Professional Conduct (The Anderson Committee) (1986). *Restructuring Professional Standards to Achieve Professional Excellence in a Changing Environment*. New York.

Anderson, G.D. (1985). A fresh look at standards of professional conduct. *The Journal of Accountancy*, **160**, 91–92, 95–96, 98, 102, 104–106.

Anderson, G.D. and Ellyson, R.C. (1986). Restructuring professional standards: The Anderson Report. *The Journal of Accountancy*, **163**(1), 92–104.

Armstrong, M.B. (1987). Moral development and accounting education. *Journal of Accounting Education*, **5**, 27–43.

Armstrong, M.B. (1993). Ethics and professionalism in accounting education: A sample course. *Journal of Accounting Education*, **11**(1), 77–92.

Arthur Andersen & Co., Arthur Young, Coopers & Lybrand, Deloitte Haskins & Sells, Ernst & Whinney, Peat Marwick Main & Co., Price Waterhouse, and Touche Ross (1989). *Perspective on Education: Capabilities for Success in the Accounting Profession*.

Bedford, N.M. and Schenkir, W.G. (1987). Reorienting accounting education. *The Journal of Accountancy*, **164**, 84, 86, 88, 90–91.

Benson, H. (1981). The professions and the community. *The Australian Accountant*, **51**(4), 239–244.

Bollom, W.J. (1988). Ethics and self-regulation for CPAs in the USA. *Journal of Business Ethics*, **7**(1/2), 55–61.

Boulanger, R. and Wayland, D. (1985). Ethical management: A growing corporate responsibility — Part 2. *CA Magazine*, April, 50–53.

Bowie, N. (1982). *Business Ethics*. Englewood Cliffs, New Jersey: Prentice Hall.

Briloff, A.J. (1986). Accountancy in the public interest/The broken covenant. An address before the Accounting Research and Education Centre, McMaster University, Canada.

Brown, H.J. (1975). Professional Ethics in Required Auditing Courses in the Education of Public Accountants. Unpublished doctoral dissertation, New York University, New York.

Buckley, J.W. (1978). An exploration of professional identity, in S.E. Loeb (Ed.), *Ethics in the Accounting Profession*. Santa Barbara: John Wiley, 63–84.

Burns, D.C. and Haga, W.J. (1977). Much ado about professionalism: A second look at accounting. *The Accounting Review*, **52**(3), 705–715.

Carey, J.L. (1978). The realities of professional ethics, in S.E. Loeb (Ed.), *Ethics in the Accounting Profession*. Santa Barbara: John Wiley, 85–92.

Carey, J.L. and Doherty, W.O. (1966). *Ethical Standards of the Accounting Profession*. New York: American Institute of Certified Public Accountants.

Cottell, P.G. Jr. and Perlin, T.M. (1990). *Accounting Ethics: A Practical Guide for Professionals*. New York: Quorum.

Dierks, P.A. and Davis, E.A. (1980). The cruciality and mystique of internal auditing: Last prerequisites for professionalism? *The Internal Auditor*, **37**(2), 36–46.

Editorial (1985). Professionalism on the line? *The Accountant's Magazine*, May, 197.

Emmet, D. (1966). *Rules, Roles, and Relations*. Boston: Beacon Press.

English, L. (1990a). Business and professional ethics. *The Australian Accountant*, **60**(1), 18, 20–21.

English, L. (1990b). The teaching of ethics. *The Australian Accountant*, **60**(1), 22–25.

Finn, D.W., Chonko, L.B. and Hunt, S.D. (1988). Ethical problems in public accounting: The view from the top. *Journal of Business Ethics*, **7**(8), 605–615.

Gandz, J. (1988). Ethics come out of the closet. *Business Quarterly*, **53**(2), 61–63.

Graber, D.E. (1979). Ethics enforcement — How effective? *The CPA Journal*, **49**(9), 11–14, 16–17.

Greenwood, E. (1957). Attributes of a profession. *Social Work*, **2**(3), 45–54.

Institute of Chartered Accountants in England and Wales (1987). Circular Letter to Members, November.

Jack, A. (1994). Accountancy and ethics, in J. Drummond and B. Bain (Eds). *Managing Business Ethics*. Oxford: Butterworth Heinemann, 186–193.

Larson, R.E. (1987). For the members, by the members. *The Journal of Accountancy*, **164**, 116, 117–118, 120, 122.

Loeb, S.E. (Ed.) (1978). *Ethics in the Accounting Profession*. Santa Barbara: John Wiley.

Loeb, S.E. (1984). Codes of ethics and self-regulation for non-public accountants: A public policy perspective. *Journal of Accounting and Public Policy*, **3**(1), 1–8.

Loeb, S.E. (1988). Teaching students accounting ethics: Some crucial issues. *Accounting Education*, **3**(2), 316–329.

Loeb, S.E. (1990). A code of ethics for academic accountants? *Journal of Accounting Education*, **5**(1), 123–128.

Marsh, P.D.V. (1980). *Business Ethics*. London: Associated Business Press.

Mathews, M.R. (1984a). Continuing education: The new defence of professionalism, in M.R. Mathews (Ed.), *Readings in the Development of Accounting*. Palmerston North: Dunmore Press, 305–311.

Mathews, M.R. (1984b). Professional ethics and continuing education, in M.R. Mathews (Ed.), *Readings in the Development of Accounting*. Palmerston North: Dunmore Press, 312–320.

Mautz, R.K. and Sharaf, H.A. (1961). *The Philosophy of Auditing*. Sarasota: AAA.

Mintz, S.M. (1992). *Cases in Accounting Ethics and Professionalism* (Second edition). New York: McGraw-Hill.

Mitchell, C.L. (1965). The criteria of a profession. *The Internal Auditor*, **34**, 30–34.

National Commission on Fraudulent Financial Reporting (the Treadway Commission) (1987). *Report of the National Commission on Fraudulent Financial Reporting*. Washington DC.

New code of professional conduct (1988). *The Australian Accountant*, **58**(2), 42.

New Zealand Society of Accountants (1984). *Horizon 2000 — And beyond*. Wellington: NZSA.

New Zealand Society of Accountants (1991). *Code of Ethics*. Wellington: NZSA.

Noreen, E. (1988). The economics of ethics: A new perspective on agency theory. *Accounting, Organizations and Society*, **13**(4), 359–369.

O'Leary, T. and Boland, R.J. Jr. (1987). Self regulation, public interest and the accounting profession. *Research in Accounting Regulation*, **1**, 103–121.

Olson, W.E. (1978). Is professionalism dead? *The Journal of Accountancy*, **146**, 78–82.

Olson, W.E. (1979). The accounting profession in the 1980s. *The Journal of Accountancy*, **148**, 54–55, 58–60.

Parker, L.D. (1987). An historical analysis of ethical pronouncements and debate in the Australian accounting profession. *Abacus*, **23**(2), 122–140.

Parker, L.D. (1994). Professional accounting body ethics: In search of the private interest. *Accounting, Organizations and Society*, **19**(6), 507–525.

Piper, T.R., Gentile, M.C. and Parks, S.D. (1993). *Can Ethics be Taught?* Boston: Harvard Business School.

Powers, C.W. and Vogel, D. (1980). *Ethics in the Education of Business Managers*. Hastings-on-the-Hudson, NY: The Hastings Center.

Puxty, A., Sikka, P. and Willmott, H. (1994). (Re)forming the circle: Education, ethics and accountancy practices. *Accounting Education*, **3**(1), 77–92.

Reed, R.O. (1985). An American accounting dilemma: Professionalism vs commercialism. *The Chartered Accountant in Australia*, 18–20.

Rest, J.R. (1988). Can ethics be taught in professional schools? The psychological research. *Easier Said Than Done*, pp. 103–107.

Sack, R.J. (1985). Commercialism in the profession: A threat to be managed. *Journal of Accountancy*, **160**(4), 125–134.

Scribner, E. and Dillaway, M.P. (1989). Strengthening the ethics content of accounting courses. *Journal of Accounting Education*, **7**(1), 41–55.

Smith, K.J. (1988). Ethics in crisis. *The Internal Auditor*, **45**(5), 31–35.

Stewart, I.C. (1986). Ethics and financial reporting in the United States. *Journal of Business Ethics*, **5**(5), 401–408.

Windal, F.W. (1991). *Ethics and the Accountant: Text and Cases*. Englewood Cliffs: Prentice Hall.

Windal, F.W. and Corby, R.N. (1980). *The Accounting Professional: Ethics, Responsibility and Liability*. Englewood Cliffs, New Jersey: Prentice Hall.

Wood, A.M. (1985). What must be done: A report from the POB. *The Journal of Accountancy*, **160**, 142, 144–146, 148.

Zeff, S.A. (1987). Does the CPA belong to a profession? *The Accountant's Magazine*, 22, 24.

Learning objectives

After studying this chapter the reader will be able to:

• define comparative accounting
• describe the international diversity in accounting practices and the problems caused by such diversity
• discuss some of the important international accounting issues, including the classification of accounting systems
• consider the environmental factors that influence the accounting system of a country
• discuss the various attempts at harmonising accounting standards at global and regional levels
• explain the importance of incorporating an international dimension in the accounting curriculum.

Introduction

There are a number of reasons why the study of comparative accounting is important. It can be argued that accounting has always been international because of its concern with international trade and of the spread of ideas across countries since its emergence. Therefore, the history of accounting is an international history. A number of countries have made important contributions to the development and expansion of accounting. For example, double entry bookkeeping, often thought of as the genesis of today's accounting, emanated from the Italian city states of the fourteenth and fifteenth centuries. This method extended first to the rest of Europe and eventually round the whole world. In the sixteenth century, Italian bookkeeping migrated to Germany, France and the Netherlands. It then extended to Britain whose dominant world economic position during the seventeenth and eighteenth centuries facilitated its spread to other parts of the world, such as North America and the then member countries of the British Empire. Similarly, Dutch accounting was carried to Indonesia and South Africa, French accounting to some countries in

Africa and Polynesia and the German system of accounting to Japan, Sweden and Czarist Russia. As the economic influence of the USA grew during the first half of the twentieth century, US accounting thought and practices were transmitted to many countries, including Germany, Japan, Brazil, Israel, Mexico and the Philippines. Many of the concepts and practices of management accounting throughout the industrialised world originated in the USA.

Observation of accounting development in other countries may be useful in determining how to address accounting issues in a particular country. It may also help us understand the reasons for the differences in accounting practice between countries. As Nobes and Parker (1986) explain:

> In the UK and USA, for instance, there have at times been calls for greater uniformity in the layout of financial statements and in valuation principles; for a closer connection between accounting profit and taxable income, and for the establishment of an accounting court. American accountants have on occasion argued for stronger company legislation; and some British accountants have recommended the establishment of a

governmental regulatory body with power over accounting matters.

All these proposals have already been adopted in one country or another. France and West Germany provide good examples of uniformity, in one case by means of a national accounting plan, in the other through statute law. The same two countries also provide examples of a very close connection between the rules of financial accounting and the rules for corporate taxation. Dutch financial reporting has neither of these characteristics, but the Netherlands is the only country which operates an accounting court.

American accountants who wish to study the role of company legislation in financial reporting can look not only at the British and German experience, both of long standing, but also at the Netherlands where company legislation has grown from a minor to major influence since 1970. British accountants in search of a regulatory body have the obvious precedent of the American Securities and Exchange Commission (SEC), but it is possible that a study of the French Commission des Opérations de Bourse (COB) might prove just as relevant. (p.3)

A clear understanding of the environmental factors which determine the nature of the accounting standards in individual countries is essential in any sensible attempt at harmonisation. There may be good reasons for the country differences in accounting practices and standards, and unless these reasons are properly understood there is little chance of success in harmonisation. The comparative analysis of accounting systems and practices leads to an identification of patterns of accounting development. This in turn results in an enhanced awareness of the influences of national differences in terms of history, culture and economic development. The identification of patterns of accounting

development should also be useful in permitting a better understanding of the potential for change, given any change in environmental factors. Policy makers may also be better able to predict problems that a country may be likely to face and solutions that may be feasible, given the experience of countries with similar development patterns.

There has been an increasing interest in comparative accounting over the last three decades due to the unprecedented growth in international business during that period. Much of international business is carried out by multinational corporations (MNCs). An MNC is a business firm which has its home in one country but is resident and operates under the laws and customs of other countries as well. However, they can also be defined in terms of the scale of foreign operations, worldwide distribution of assets, nationality of owners, suppliers of capital, employees and sources of profit. For example, from a performance perspective, a company is multinational if it does business in more than one country in such a volume that its wellbeing and growth rest in more than one country. The multinational nature of today's world economy can be easily understood by considering some of the well known products. For example, Volkswagen, Mitsubishi and Ford cars are found around the globe; Japanese televisions and cameras are commonplace worldwide; Boeing and Macdonald Douglas airplanes deliver passengers to every major airport in the world; Italian shoes, Swiss watches and American Coca-Cola can be bought in most countries. The collective strength of the multinationals is likely to increase in the future. The UN has recognised the existence and power of these business organisations by establishing the Commission on Transnational Corporations, which is in the process of developing a body of research in this area. As a result of the activities of MNCs, not only have many new international problems emerged, such as the translation of foreign currencies in the preparation of consolidated financial statements, but a number of problems already familiar in the domestic context, such as transfer pricing, have acquired an international dimension. To be able to understand the financial statements prepared by MNCs in accordance with the requirements of their home countries, investors and lenders need to become knowledgeable in the financial reporting systems of more than one country

    This chapter is organised into five sections. In the first section, the environmental factors affecting accounting practices and standards are discussed. The second section deals with an international classification of accounting systems. Some aspects of the accounting systems of non-Anglo-American countries, e.g. France, Germany, Japan, the People's Republic of China and Eastern European countries are considered in the third section. The fourth section introduces some specific comparative accounting issues, that is consolidation accounting and foreign currency translation. Finally, the last section addresses the issue of international harmonisation of accounting standards with a brief discussion on the efforts of harmonising accounting standards and practices between Australia and New Zealand under the CER Agreement between the two countries.

Environmental influences

There is a wide variety of differences between the accounting practices adopted in different countries, and no two accounting systems are exactly alike (for example, see Appendix 17.5). The underlying reasons for these differences are essentially environmental because accounting is a product of its environment. The accounting environment in one country can differ from that of another in terms of a variety of factors such as:
* stage of economic development
* nature of business enterprises
* extent of government involvement in business affairs

* sophistication of the users and preparers of financial information
* nature of the accounting profession
* presence of specific accounting regulations
* rate of inflation
* cultural attitudes
* legal system
* political system
* education system
* academic influence
* international influences such as colonial history
* extent of foreign investment in the country.

For an analysis of the various environmental factors as identified by different researchers, see Appendix 17.1.

    The environment in a given country will affect many aspects of accounting in that country, for example:
* need for accounting information by decision makers
* type and extent of accounting information required
* basic approach to the setting of accounting standards
* level of sophistication in the accounting standards
* status of accounting and accountants in society
* importance of the accounting profession within society
* specific accounting principles and procedures that are followed.

    In a number of countries, such as the UK and the USA, financial accounting information is directed towards the needs of investors and creditors, and the overriding criteria for judging its quality are decision usefulness and the true and fair view. In some other countries, such as most South American countries, financial accounting is designed primarily to ensure that the proper amount of income tax is collected by the government. There are also countries, for example France, where financial accounting is designed to help accomplish macro-economic policies, such as achieving a predetermined rate of growth in the nation's economy. Further, if most companies in a country are small family businesses, as in France, the need for a strong accounting profession and detailed comparable published accounts is less. If most of the shares in public companies are owned or controlled by banks, as in Germany, it is again the case that the need for 'true and fair' comparative information for private shareholders is reduced. If, on the other hand, there are many public listed companies whose ownership is widely spread, published accounting information which has been prepared and audited for shareholders in an Anglo-American way becomes useful and necessary.

The lack of a substantial body of private shareholders of public companies in some EU countries reduces the need for auditors in those countries.

The influence of taxation on accounting practice can also be considerable. In many EU countries, including France, Germany, Italy and Belgium, if expenses are claimed for tax purposes they must usually be charged in the financial statements as well. The most obvious example of this is the necessity to show accelerated depreciation, as allowed for tax purposes, in the financial statements. This affects the profit figure because the company must charge not the depreciation it considers appropriate, but the larger amount claimed for tax purposes.

As an illustration, the different orientations between Anglo-American and French accounting can be explained in terms of environmental factors. The growth of economic activity in the UK took place in an atmosphere of classical liberalism with a strong influence from classical economists, and a broadly laissez-faire approach by government. This was also true of the economic growth that began to gain momentum in the USA in the mid-nineteenth century. In such highly individualistic societies, the promotion of investment by trying to interest

people with uncommitted funds in various investment projects became an important activity. Once prospective investors began to assess investment opportunities on the basis of their expected earnings, financial statements that included some kind of earnings figure became a necessity for the functioning of the entire system of channelling resources to productive uses. This was the background for the development of capital market activity which is the main source of funds for investment in both countries. The activities of these markets have resulted in continuous pressure being exerted for the provision of financial information for investors, making investors the most important recipients of external accounting reports by companies. The pressures for disclosure have had a significant effect on the development of accounting principles and practices in these countries and the requirements of the capital markets became a major influencing factor in their disclosure patterns. In this atmosphere, it was assumed that the development of accounting should take place through professional self-regulation, with minimum government involvement.

The position in France and in much of Continental Europe, is quite different from that outlined above. In France there has been a tradition of state intervention in economic affairs. The influence of the classical economists was minimal in Continental Europe. Instead, there has been a succession of economic theories with a common thread of anti-individualism. Financial accounting in France is generally influenced by legislation, due mainly to the determination of the French government to obtain data for macro-accounting purposes. The French General Accounting Plan, which has been adopted by virtually all enterprises in the country since 1947, contains a detailed chart of accounts and series of model financial and statistical reports which are designed to serve micro- and macro-accounting purposes (see Appendix 17.2). The French General Accounting Plan makes it clear that among its objectives in seeking data on an enterprise are: (a) the promotion of more reliable national economic policies; (b) the minimisation of social misunderstandings; (c) ensuring the availability of data for government studies of market trends; and (d) assistance to the government authorities in exercising control over the economy. Furthermore, French companies have traditionally relied much less upon an active new issue market as a source of long term funds than have UK and US companies. This has resulted in a lower emphasis being given to the provision of investor oriented corporate financial information and to the audit function as a safeguard for investors. The primary influence upon the development of accounting principles and practices in France has been the General Accounting Plan, rather than the pronouncements of the accounting profession.

Classification of accounting systems

There are a number of advantages to having an international classification of accounting systems. They include the following:
- as an efficient way of describing and comparing different systems
- by facilitating accounting development, for example in understanding the logic of and the difficulties facing harmonisation
- by assisting in the training and educating of accountants and auditors who operate internationally
- by enabling a country to consider the appropriate options available in addressing a particular accounting problem or in predicting the problems that are likely to arise, through observation of the developments in other countries in its group or in other relevant groups (Nobes and Parker, 1986, pp.2–4).

As the differences in accounting practices between countries became increasingly evident, attempts were made to classify countries on that basis. The methods adopted by accounting researchers can be described as subjective (Mueller, 1967; 1968), judgemental (Nobes, 1983; 1984), sphere of influence (Previts, 1975) and statistical (AAA, 1977; Da Costa, Bourgeois and Lawson, 1978; Frank, 1979; Nair and Frank, 1980).

Mueller (1967) represents the first systematic classification of accounting systems. He identifies four categories of accounting systems in Western capitalist countries. They are:
- accounting in a macro-framework, where enterprise accounting is closely linked with national economic policies
- accounting based upon micro-economic factors, where accounting is regarded as part of business economics
- accounting as an independent discipline, where accounting is regarded as a separate service function in business practice
- uniform accounting, where accounting is viewed as a regulatory device.

Previts (1975) bases his classifications upon perceived 'sphere of influence of mother countries' and categorises accounting systems into three models under:
- British
- American and
- Continental European.

The AAA (1977) identifies five zones of influence in accounting systems. They are:
- British
- French–Spanish–Portuguese
- German–Dutch
- American and
- Communistic.

Da Costa et al. (1978) classify accounting systems into groups by using cluster analysis on the accounting practices reported in the Price Waterhouse surveys (1973; 1975; 1979). The two groups are (a) UK and former colonies and (b) others. By analysing the same data, Frank (1979) identifies four groups of countries, namely:
- British Commonwealth
- Latin American

- Continental Europe and
- American.

The same data have been used by Nair and Frank (1980) in an attempt to classify accounting systems separately based on measurement and disclosure. Having carried out a statistical analysis, they classify accounting systems into eight groups on the basis of disclosure practices, and four groups on the basis of measurement practices.

By adopting Mueller's analysis as the basis, Nobes (1984) classifies the accounting systems of Western capitalist countries into two broad categories under:

- micro-based and
- macro-uniform.

Mueller then continues to classify these categories into a number of subgroups. This is illustrated in Figure 17.1. For a detailed review of this topic, see Nobes (1984) and Choi and Mueller (1992; Chapter 2).

Mueller, Gernon and Meek (1994, p.9) identify four major accounting models. They are:

- British–American
- Continental
- South American and
- Mixed Economy (which includes Eastern European countries and member states of the former USSR).

Comparative accounting: a general overview

Various aspects of the Anglo-American style of accounting were discussed in earlier chapters. By way of providing a broader perspective of comparative accounting, this section introduces some aspects of accounting in a non-Anglo-American context. The discussion includes France, Germany, Japan, the People's Republic of China and Eastern European countries, with a brief comment on developing countries. For age and size of public accountancy bodies of different countries, and for company law directives relevant

to corporate accounting within the EU, see Appendixes 17.3 and 17.4, respectively.

France

Some of the features of French accounting which are different from the Anglo-American model are as follows.

- French financial statements are prepared in a much more standardised manner.
- The capital market (Paris Bourse) is relatively small. Many large companies are still dominated by family holdings. Loan capital is more important than in Anglo-American countries.
- Financial reporting is much influenced by the government, especially through the tax system, company legislation and the national accounting plan administered by a National Accounting Council. In the absences of a strong capital market, taxation has been a major reason for the preparation and publication of financial statements.
- There is relatively little emphasis on disclosure of information to equity shareholders.
- Auditing is not dominated by the international accounting firms.
- The terms used in audit reports are that the annual accounts are 'regular' and 'sincere'. (After the Fourth Directive this also includes the term 'true and fair view'.)

The National Accounting Plan (Plan Comptable Général)

The National Accounting Plan is a detailed accounting guide which includes the definition of accounting terms, measurement rules and model financial statements. An example of the chart of accounts as given in the French National Accounting Plan is given in Appendix 17.2. This is also used for national and local government accounting and for the production of detailed national statistics. The first plan was produced in

Figure 17.1
Nobe's classification of accounting systems by practices

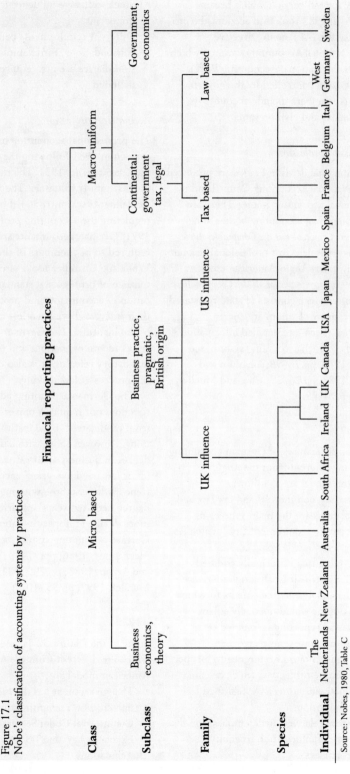

Financial reporting practices

Source: Nobes, 1980, Table C

1947. A revised version which became effective in 1982 took into account the provisions of the EU Fourth Directive.

The National Accounting Council which controls the National Accounting Plan is organised and controlled by the government. Its members include accountants, industrialists and civil servants.

Accounting profession

Accounting standards in France are produced by the National Accounting Council and the professional accounting bodies. There are two professional accounting bodies, the *Ordre des Experts Comptables et des Comptables Agrées* which is equivalent to a professional accounting body in any Anglo-American country, and the *Compagnie Nationale des Commissaires aux Comptes* which consists of state registered auditors, many of whom are *experts comptables*. (For more detailed information about the French accounting system, see Parker, 1986, pp.75–96; Alhashim and Arpan, 1988, pp.26–29; Choi and Mueller, 1992, pp.90–95.)

Germany

Some of the features of German accounting which are different from the Anglo-American model are as follows.
* Company, commercial and tax law and regulations are the main sources of accounting requirements, or 'principles of orderly bookkeeping'.
* There is a lack of formally codified auditing standards, although there are professional pronouncements to which the auditor would normally adhere.
* Financial reporting is founded on a 'true–accurate–complete' basis.
* There is an overall reference to 'proper accounting principles' which are not codified but indirectly established by court decisions.
* There is relatively little emphasis on disclosure of information to equity shareholders.

* Stock exchange influence is less important.
* Different requirements concerning consolidations, for example foreign subsidiaries are not required to be included.

Accounting profession

The professional accounting institute was formed in 1931 following the provisions of the *Companies Act* 1931. The membership of the institute is voluntary. The Chamber of Accountants was introduced by the law regulating the accounting profession in 1971. German accountants are legally required to be members of the Chamber. While the Chamber looks after the maintenance of professional standards, the education of accountants and protection of their interests have been left in the hands of the Institute. The German Institute issues recommendations and non-mandatory releases. It is also consulted in the process of law making.

The German accounting education system does not require a university degree from candidates for the Institute's examinations. However, those with a university degree in business administration, economics or law need five years' accounting experience, whereas those without a university degree need ten years' experience. (For more detailed information about the German accounting system, see Macharzina, 1986, pp.97–131; Alhashim and Arpan, 1988, pp.299–331; Choi and Mueller, 1992, pp.95–100.)

Japan

Some of the features of Japanese accounting which are different from the Anglo-American model are:
* The government has the most significant influence on accounting through the Commercial Code, Securities and Exchange Law and Tax Laws and Regulations.

- The Japanese accounting profession has little influence on the preparers of financial information.
- The stock exchanges are all government-regulated rather than self-regulated.
- Japanese companies normally rely heavily on debt rather than equity as their main source of finance.
- Banks are the main providers of finance.
- Banks have exerted relatively little influence on external financial reporting.
- The Japanese Institute of Certified Public Accountants (JICPA) has a relatively weak influence on the standard-setting process.

Sources of government influence

The Commercial Code, which is applied to all public companies, is administered by the Ministry of Justice. The Securities and Exchange Law, which is applied to listed public companies, is administered by the Ministry of Finance. This law was enacted shortly after World War II and was largely influenced by the US *Securities Act* 1933 and the *Securities and Exchange Act* 1934.

The Ministry of Finance has a widely represented advisory body, the Business Accounting Deliberations Council (BADC) which prepares accounting standards and business accounting principles which are issued by the Ministry. Tax laws and regulations have a significant impact on financial reporting in Japan.

Accounting profession

The JICPA was established by the *Certified Public Accountants Law* 1948. Its membership is relatively small (see Appendix 17.2). The JICPA issues recommendations on minor accounting matters. The main financial accounting issues are addressed by the Ministry of Finance in its business accounting principles. (For more detailed information about the accounting system in Japan, see Campbell, 1986, pp.152–173; Alhashim and Arpan, 1988, pp.31–33; Choi and Mueller, 1992, pp.100–107.)

An entrant into the Japanese accounting profession must pass three levels of CPA examinations (JICPA, 1982). Exemption from the preliminary CPA examination is granted to university and college graduates. After passing the intermediate examination, one is referred to as 'Junior CPA' or 'Assistant CPA'. A Junior CPA is required to undergo a three-year apprenticeship before sitting the final examination, which is a test of technical competence. (For more detailed information about the accounting systems in Japan, see Campbell, 1986, pp.152–173; Alhashim and Arpan, 1988, pp.31–33; Choi and Mueller, 1992, pp.100–107.)

Eastern Europe

As mentioned earlier, Mueller, Gernon and Meek (1994, p.9) classify accounting systems in different countries into four models. One of them is the Mixed Economy model which includes Eastern European countries and members of the former USSR. The collapse of communism in Eastern Europe in the late 1980s, followed by a 'dash for democracy and capitalism', led by the former USSR, held out the prospect of reintegration of Eastern Europe into the global economy after nearly fifty years of economic isolation. Healy (1994) describes the situation that existed in Eastern Europe prior to 1989 as follows:

> Since 1945, the region has been a commercial "black hole". The economies were centrally planned and most enterprises were almost wholly state-owned. Investment by Western companies was stifled by bureaucratic regulation and official disapproval. Trade was effectively restricted to other (Communist) members of the COMECON bloc. A raft of import restrictions and capital controls kept goods and business out, while outdated technology made most Eastern European products (with the notable exception of arms) uncompetitive in overseas markets (p.63).

The productivity levels were significantly lower in Eastern European countries compared with those of the countries in Western Europe. For example, Deutche Bank estimated that at the time of German reunification, overall productivity levels in East Germany were only 47 per cent of those in West Germany (Healy, 1994, p.68).

Eastern Europe is not a homogeneous group of countries. Currently there are about thirty independent states, each with its own particular culture, history and industrial and social structure. Their efforts aimed at transition to capitalism have proved more painful than anticipated. Soaring inflation, unemployment and ethnic tension have all become part of the post-1989 experience in most of these former communist states. They all aspire to join the EU at some stage. However, before they can do that they must adopt the rules of the *acquis communautaire* (the EU's body of laws and regulations). By the end of June 1995, the EU is expected to prepare a White Paper defining the main elements of the *acquis communautaire* (*Economist*, 10 December, 1994, p. 44).

Eastern Europe enjoys a highly skilled workforce. The percentage of workers who have received vocational training is among the highest in the world (Healy, 1994). From the point of view of attracting foreign investments, the positive aspects include skilled low cost labour, a supportive political environment, a potentially large market, comprising some 400 million consumers, and consumer awareness of Western products through exposure to Western satellite television and advertising.

These countries need to develop their export industries and modernise their existing enterprises in order to become internationally competitive. This will require large amounts of new capital investments. As the prospects for raising adequate capital through loans from international lending institutions are not encouraging, they will have to rely heavily on foreign

direct investments. They will also have to create a domestic economic environment which is conducive to inward investment by foreign companies. Many Eastern European governments have chosen privatisation and joint ventures as a way of attracting foreign investments. Gray and Roberts (1991) explain the growth of joint ventures in these countries as follows:

> In Eastern Europe, including the Soviet Union, there has been a dramatic growth in joint ventures especially since 1988. Indeed, registrations have soared from 43 in 1980 to over 3500 by the end of 1989. The Soviet Union, Hungary and Poland have been the main locations with foreign partners primarily from Western Europe though the US and Japan are becoming increasingly involved. It has been estimated, for example, that more than 1000 joint ventures were registered in the Soviet Union by October 1989 compared to only 23 at the beginning of 1988. In Hungary, more than 600 joint ventures were registered compared to 102 and in Poland, the relevant figures were more than 400 compared to just 13. (p.44)

The adoption of a free-market economy has created pressure for change in accounting practices as the existing accounting systems are inappropriate. Hungary, Poland and the Czech Republic gave priority to establishing a stock exchange. Hungary reopened its Stock Exchange in 1990, Poland in 1991 and the Czech Republic in 1993 (*IASC Insight*, June, 1994, p.10). The Hungarian Government contracted with Price Waterhouse to help modernise the country's accounting system in 1990. Attempts have been made in some countries to develop a new chart of accounts based on the EU Fourth and Seventh Directives. In view of the enormity of the task ahead of these countries, the UN Centre for Transnational Corporations has taken an active role in supporting these countries (Mueller, Gernon and Meek, 1994, p.12).

Under a centrally planned economy, accounting reports are prepared for control purposes with an emphasis on uniformity. Accounting in that context is perceived as having primarily a record keeping function and is not decision-oriented or concerned with efficiency at the enterprise level. Rather, it is used as a means of centralised control (Bailey, 1988). Concepts of profitability and stockholder equity are not important. Instead, financial information is aimed at measuring performance against production goals. As Mueller, Gernon and Meek (1994) state: 'Indeed, financial accounting per se does not exist; what we refer to as *managerial accounting* comes closer to illustrating the overall accounting scene in communist regimes' (p. 13).

Because the accounting profession was weak or non-existent, the central regulatory institutions continued to have a strong influence, and progress towards introducing Western style accounting has been very slow. The accounting systems in Eastern European countries still lack a user emphasis.

One of the major problems facing these countries in the area of accounting and financial reporting is the difficulty in being able to coordinate different cultural and accounting traditions in a way that resolves issues relating to financial control, the measurement of profit and the valuation of joint venture investments. The specific issues include: (a) Are accounting differences being used, either deliberately or unconsciously, to the advantage of one or the other partner?; (b) To what extent can accounting differences be explained by reference to cultural and other environmental factor? and (c) How important are accounting differences as a source of disagreement between partners and how are such differences resolved in practice? (Gray and Roberts, 1991, p.46).

People's Republic of China

China accounts for 20 per cent of the world's population. Over the past few years it has continuously achieved annual economic growth rates of 8–12 per cent. This is much higher than the growth rates achieved by any Western industrial country. China has risen from thirty-one in the ranking of world traders in 1980 to eleven in 1993 (*Economist*, 14 May 1994, p.29). It has also expressed its interest in joining the World Trade Organisation (WTO) which replaced the General Agreement on Tariffs and Trade (GATT). If China is admitted to WTO, it will be one of the world's largest gainers from in the Uruguay round — China's export growth has centred on manufacturing, textiles in particular, and the Uruguay round liberalised trade in manufactured goods more significantly than trade in primary products.

To accelerate economic development, China has implemented a series of policies which have opened up its economy to the world. Although the new policies favour a market based economy, the total policy package for reform remains different from those implemented in many Eastern European countries. China has chosen to introduce economic reforms within the existing socialist political structure, whereas Eastern European countries have attempted to introduce both economic and political reforms at the same time. The characteristics of a centrally planned, communist regime are equally applicable to the situation in China.

Like Eastern European countries, China also needs to attract foreign investment in order to carry out its reform programme. Therefore, it becomes necessary for China to be able to create an environment within the country which is conducive to foreign investment. Provision of information about the performance and results of enterprise operations in a manner that is understandable to international investors is crucial in attracting foreign capital. In other words, the new economic policies have triggered the need to reform China's accounting systems in light of internationally acceptable practices.

The *IASC Insight* (June, 1994) explains the recent developments in China in the area of accounting regulation as follows:

> The reform of financial accounting systems has gone through three phases. In 1985 the Ministry of Finance promulgated 'Accounting Regulations for Sino-Foreign Joint Ventures' followed in 1992 by 'Accounting Regulation for Share Capital Enterprises' and in November 1993 by the 'Enterprise Accounting Standards'.
>
> The regulations for foreign joint ventures was the first pronouncement using international accounting practices as a reference, and introduced radical reforms in accounting measurement by departing from the fund based approach and introducing accounting elements such as assets, liabilities, capital, revenue and expenses. It also introduced the requirement for a balance sheet, income statement and statement of changes in financial position, and the principles of historical cost, matching and consistency. Further regulations and charts of accounts were introduced in 1992, enlarging the applicability of internationally based accounting practices to all enterprises with foreign investment.
>
> The 'Enterprise Accounting Standard' (EAS) is the first requirement to apply, with limited exceptions, to all enterprises, regardless of industry, type of ownership or operation. This is the first time in China's history that accounting systems for different industries have been unified. EAS is a basic accounting standard covering accounting assumptions, basic principles, accounting elements and accounting statements (p.9).

In addition to the accounting regulations in China, foreign investment enterprises are also subjected to several other laws, such as the PRC Sino-Foreign Equity Joint Venture Law (1979), the PRC Sino-Foreign Cooperative Joint Venture Law (1988), the PRC Wholly Foreign Owned Enterprises Law (1986), the PRC Income Tax Law for FIEs and Foreign Enterprises (1991; Coopers and Lybrand, 1993).

An examination of the accounting development patterns of most developing countries reveals that they had little chance to evolve accounting systems which would truly reflect the local needs and circumstances. Their existing systems are largely extensions of those developed in other countries, particularly the Western capitalist countries, such as the UK and the USA. These systems were either imposed through colonial influence or by powerful investors or multinational corporations (Wilkinson, 1965; Radebaugh, 1975; Perera, 1980; Chandler and Holzer, 1984). In addition, international accounting firms have also been an important vehicle for transferring Western-style accounting to developing countries (Briston, 1978, pp.110–111). Perhaps the international accounting standards promulgated by the IASC have been the most effective in this respect since its formation in 1973 (Perera, 1985, pp.12–15).

Comparative accounting issues

Every accounting issue which has an international dimension can be described as a comparative accounting issue. However, a full discussion of all such issues is beyond the scope of this chapter. Instead, it is proposed here to introduce two problem areas, consolidation and foreign currency translation, with a view to providing a general idea of the nature of such issues.

Foreign currency translation

International commerce, multinational business operations, foreign investments and international money capital market transactions all involve the use of foreign currencies. These transactions involve two or more national currencies and hence create a unique technical problem of foreign currency translation brought about by the internationalisation of accounting. Since exchange rates are subject to fluctuations, a major issue is concerned with which exchange rate is to be used to translate the financial statements and how to treat exchange differences.

To illustrate the issues involved, consider the following situation where a foreign currency borrowing takes place.

> X Ltd is a wholly owned subsidiary company of the New Zealand parent company, Y Ltd. Since interest rates on corporate borrowings are generally lower in Europe than in New Zealand, X Ltd borrowed 180 million Swiss francs during December 19X1 to be repaid in 19X8. At the time of borrowing, the exchange rate was $1.00 = SF1.20. Therefore, the consolidated financial statements of Y Ltd on 31 December 19X1 showed this indebtedness as $150 million.
>
> By 30 June 19X6, the dollar had risen against the SF to an exchange rate of $1.00 = SF1.80.

How should X Ltd's Swiss franc borrowing now appear in the consolidated financial statements of Y Ltd? Since the loan is not to be paid back until 19X8, should it be reported at its original equivalent of $150 million? If the current rate of exchange were to be used to translate the foreign currency debt involved, $100 million would be reported. Since there has been no change in the actual SF amount of the debt, is the $50 million difference a real economic gain or is it a paper amount only? For financial reporting purposes, foreign currency translation can be done in several different ways. They include the following.

- *The closing rate method.* This method uses the closing exchange rate for all assets and liabilities.

- *The current/non-current method.* This method uses the closing rate for current assets and current liabilities, and the historic rates for all other assets and liabilities.
- *The monetary/non-monetary method.* This method uses the closing rate for monetary items and the historic rate for non-monetary items.
- *Temporal method.* This was proposed by Lorensen (1972) and introduced as a Statement of Financial Accounting Standard in the USA (SFAS 8). Under HCA this turns out to mean something similar to the monetary/non-monetary method. The temporal method translates a balance sheet at the exchange rate ruling at the date that the valuation basis was established.

In 1981, the US statement FAS 52 required US companies to use the closing rate method. The same line was followed by other Anglo-American countries, including New Zealand. In France there is no uniform method of foreign currency translation. However, the closing rate method appears to be the most commonly used, with average rates used in the income statement.

The Japanese statement, *Accounting Standard for Foreign Currency Translation* requires a group to use a modified temporal method to translate the financial statements of foreign subsidiaries for consolidation purposes. Under this method, historical rates are used for assets held at historic costs and the closing rates for most assets and liabilities measured at current values. Either the closing rate or historical rate may be used to translate current monetary items, but historic rates should be used for non-current monetary items. This is different from the normal practice in Anglo-American countries where the closing rate is used to translate all items in a foreign subsidiary balance sheet.

The other related issue is how the translation gains or losses should be treated in the accounts, to be included in income or reported as an element of equity. SFAS 52 recommends the latter.

In France translation differences are also dealt with in various ways.

In Japan the BADC statements require that translation gains and losses should be described as 'foreign currency translation adjustments' and disclosed as an asset or liability in the balance sheet. This again is different from practices in Anglo-American countries.

Consolidation of the financial statements of foreign subsidiaries

In the UK and Continental Europe consolidated statements were a later development than in the USA, which started the use of such statements as a result of the wave of mergers at the turn of the twentieth century. As recently as the late 1960s consolidated statements were almost unknown in France (Nobes and Parker, 1986, p.89). They are still rare in countries such as Italy, Greece and Luxembourg.

Although consolidation techniques present financial reporting difficulties even in the domestic context, they pose even more difficult problems in the international context. To give an example of the accounting challenge that is often involved, consider the fairly simple case of a New Zealand company with a subsidiary in Brazil. Under Brazilian law the official accounting records of the Brazilian operation must be denominated in real, must be written in Portuguese and must be prepared and maintained according to Brazilian accounting procedures. In addition, the Brazilian subsidiary must report to the Brazilian government and shareholders in a method, format and frequency dictated by Brazilian accounting law. At the same time, the New Zealand parent is required by New Zealand tax laws to prepare a consolidated tax return for the New Zealand Inland Revenue Department. The company must also prepare a consolidated financial report to its

New Zealand shareholders. And if the company's shares are traded on the New Zealand Stock Exchange, it has to satisfy its listing requirements. The New Zealand reports must be in dollars, in English and according to New Zealand tax regulations and FRSs. Obviously the accounts and numbers of the Brazilian subsidiary's books cannot be simply added to the parent firm's books without several conversions being made in currency, language, format and accounting procedures.

The Brazilian government and shareholders may also require some information about the parent company's operations. This information must also be converted, in this case in the opposite direction.

There are grounds for serious doubts about the benefits of consolidated financial statements in an international context owing to confusion about their purpose and the significant aggregation problems involved. There is a wide variety of fundamentally different concepts and practices adopted by different countries in the field of consolidated accounting. For example, according to the Continental European approach, a group is defined in terms of the existence of effective management control, whereas according to the Anglo-American approach, it is defined in terms of the legal power to control another company.

There are country differences in the concept of a group. First, in the UK and USA it has traditionally been the 'parent company' concept which emphasises the fact that group accounts are prepared for the shareholders of the parent company. This concept is based on legal control. While it ignores the interests of minority shareholders, it also does not allow for the possibility of equal participation of two or more companies in the group. This type of situation can be accommodated under the 'entity concept' of a group, which emphasises the economic unity of all participant companies whether majority or minority. However, none of these concepts is adequate to cope with a situation where there is neither legal dominance nor economic unit, for example companies which belong to more than one group.

The 'proprietary concept' which emphasises ownership, allowing the possibility of exercising 'significant influence' over decision making, covers the above situation. Under this concept a proportionate share of the profit or loss for the year and a proportionate share of the assets and liabilities are brought into the consolidated statements, either item by item ('proportional consolidation') or on a 'one-line' basis (the 'equity method').

Although the UK and US practices are based mainly on the parent company concept, practices based on other concepts are also commonly found, for example the equity method (based on the 'proprietary concept') in the UK and pooling of interest (based on the 'entity concept') in the USA.

In contrast to the UK and the USA, German practices are based mainly on the entity concept, where a group exists as a legal entity. The law precludes the use of practices based on the proprietary concept, such as the equity method and proportional consolidation. Also in Germany, the inclusion of overseas subsidiaries is optional. In France these practices are allowed. The French law and practice are based on the parent company and proprietary concepts. However, the Seventh Directive of the EU is expected to bring about harmonisation in this regard within the EU. There will be more use of equity accounting and, in general, more disclosure of information on a consolidated basis, similar to the UK practices. It also requires that consolidated statements include foreign as well as domestic subsidiaries.

In Japan the Commercial Code does not require consolidated financial statements. The Securities and Exchange Law requires them only as supplementary information.

Since 1983 Japanese groups must use the equity method to account for investments in associated companies, as in the UK and the USA.

Harmonisation of accounting standards

Global harmonisation

The differences in accounting practices have been highlighted in various research studies over the past two decades. For example, Choi and Bavishi (1982) provide an interesting synthesis of world diversity of accounting practices (see Appendix 17.5). As a result of the increased awareness of such diversity, attention was drawn to the need for international harmonisation of accounting practices. As Rahman, Perera and Tower (1994) point out, the benefits of international harmonisation of accounting standards and practices have been described by various authors to include: (a) improving international comparability in financial statements; (b) enhancing international capital flows; (c) raising the general level of accounting practice; (d) reducing the costs of preparing financial reports for multinational corporations (Carey, 1990); (e) facilitating social control over the global corporation; and (f) improving the resource allocation decisions of international portfolio managers (Moulin and Solomon, 1989) (see also Turner, 1983; Choi and Bavishi, 1982; Choi and Mueller, 1992, pp. 258–259). However, the word *harmonisation* appears to mean different things to different people. Some see harmonisation as the same as unification or complete standardisation, while others view it as the process of increasing the compatibility of accounting practices by setting boundaries to variations (Nobes and Parker, 1985). Radebaugh and Gray (1993) distinguish between *harmonisation* and *standardisation* and state: 'harmonisation implies a more flexible approach compared to standardisation, which suggests a more strict approach resulting ultimately in a state of uniformity' (p.142). Most (1994) defines *uniformity, standardisation* and *harmonisation* as distinct, though related, concepts as follows.

Uniformity, the elimination of alternatives in accounting for economic transactions, other events, and circumstances.

Standardization, the reduction of alternatives while retaining a high degree of flexibility of accounting response.

Harmonization, the reconciliation of different accounting and financial reporting systems by fitting them into common broad classifications, so that form becomes more standard while content retains significant differences.

In this broader view, harmonisation is seen almost as the solution to universal comparability of financial data.

International Accounting Standards Committee

A number of organisations have attempted to respond to the perceived need for harmonisation of accounting standards. At the international professional level, the IASC attempts to achieve a degree of comparability between financial statements published by companies from different countries. The IASC was established by an agreement of the leading professional bodies in Australia, Canada, France, Germany, Japan, Mexico, the Netherlands, the UK, Ireland and the USA. The current membership of IASC consists of over 100 professional accounting organisations from about eighty countries, including the NZSA.

The basic objective of the IASC is to formulate international accounting standards to be observed in the preparation of financial statements. So far the IASC has issued over thirty definitive IASs (for a history of IASs and EDs see Appendix 17.6). Members of the Committee have committed themselves to introducing these standards in their respective countries. However, since the IASC has no powers of enforcement, adherence to these standards has been far from complete. Some accounting bodies do not have the power to enforce standards in their countries. Still others want to wait until they are sure that these standards are internationally accepted.

The IASC's most ambitious project to date has been its comparability project, announced in 1989 as E 32. This undertaking is aimed at eliminating most of the choices between various alternative accounting methods allowed under existing IASs. Recently, ten revised accounting standards were issued as a result of this project. The revised standards came into effect for accounting periods beginning on or after 1 January 1995.

The IASC cooperates with other standard-setting bodies, for example currently the IASC is involved in two joint projects with the FASB and the CICA. The IASC–FASB project is aimed at developing a standard on earnings per share. The purpose of the IASC–CICA project is to develop a common standard on financial instruments.

International accounting standards are developed through an international due process that involves accountants, financial analysts and other users of financial statements, the business community, regulators, stock exchanges, the OECD, UN, World Bank and other interested international organisations.

The IASC Board can consist of representatives of the accountancy bodies of thirteen countries and up to four other organisations (currently only one organisation has accepted a seat on the IASC Board) with an interest in financial reporting. The Board is responsible for approving all EDs and accounting standards. A two-thirds vote is necessary for approval of an exposure draft and a three-quarter majority for issue of an accounting standard. The FASB and the EU Commission are observers on the IASC Board (Sharpe, 1994).

The IASC Consultative Group includes

representatives of international organisations from the business community, financial groups, banking, legal firms, trade unions, valuers, stock exchanges, securities commissions, intergovernmental organisations, development agencies and standard-setting bodies.

The current work programme of the IASC falls into three main categories: (a) the Comparability–Improvements project which started with E 32; (b) the development of new standards, including financial instruments, earnings per share, intangible assets and the presentation of financial statements; and (c) the revision of other existing standards, including taxes on income and financial information by segment (Sharpe, 1994).

Whether worldwide standardisation is a feasible or even a desirable goal has been questioned on a number of grounds, including the danger of overriding national systems which have developed in response to local needs and priorities. A further aim underlying the existence of the IASC would seem to be to influence and, if possible, control the international standard-setting process, perhaps with a view to preserving the status of the accounting profession and perpetuating the Anglo-American philosophy of self-regulation.

International Organisation of Securities Commission

The International Organisation of Securities Commission (IOSC) represents the major securities regulators around the world. IOSC's aims have been expressed by a resolution of the member agencies as follows:

- to cooperate together to ensure a better regulation of the markets, on the domestic as well as on the international level in order to maintain just and efficient securities markets
- to exchange information on their respective experiences in order to pro-

mote the development of domestic markets
- to unite their efforts to establish standards and an effective surveillance of international securities transactions
- to provide mutual assistance to ensure the integrity of the markets by a rigorous application of the standards and by effective enforcement (Davidson, 1994, p.716). Radebaugh and Gray (1993) explain IOSC's mission as follows:

This is the leading organisation for securities regulators, which has as its mission the global coordination of stock exchange rules so as to encourage both multi-listing by corporations and international securities trading. The international standardisation of accounting regulations together with sufficiently detailed information disclosures is seen to be an important factor in achieving these objectives (p.163).

The IOSC has emphasised the need for mutually acceptable accounting and auditing standards for use in international offerings of securities. Since 1987, the IASC and the IOSC have been working together to create acceptable international accounting standards and disclosure for use in international securities offerings and other foreign listings. In particular, the IOSC was heavily involved in the IASC's comparability–improvements project. This means that the IOSC's views are reflected in the revised international accounting standards. The IOSC is also represented at meetings of the IASC Consultative Group and receives copies of all IASC Board papers.

In October 1993 the IOSC recommended to its members that IAS 7 'Cash Flow Statements' be endorsed for use in cross-border offerings and listings. The SEC, as a member of the IOSC, has accepted this recommendation. This is likely to be extended to other IASs. If that effort is successful, international companies will be able to offer their securities on world markets using one set of standards, that is IOSC endorsed IASs, and investors will need to understand only one set of standards to evaluate investment choices. This should lower the cost of raising capital and improve the efficiency of all capital markets.

International Federation of Accountants Committee

The International Federation of Accountants Committee, formed in 1977, is aimed at working toward establishing international standards of auditing, ethics, education and training, leaving the formulation of international accounting standards to the IASC. The IFAC has the following objectives:
*   enhance the standards and development of the profession by issuing technical and professional guidance and by promoting the adoption of IFAC and IASC pronouncements
*   promote the profession's role, responsibilities and achievements in advancing the interests of member bodies and in serving the public interest
*   foster a strong and cohesive profession by providing leadership on emerging issues, coordinating with regional organisations and member bodies and assisting them to achieve strategic objectives
*   assist with the formation and development of national and regional organisations that serve the interests of accountants in public practice, commerce, industry, public sector and education
*   liaise with international organisations to influence the development of efficient capital markets and international trade services.

United Nations

The UN, through its Commission on Transnational Corporations, has been actively involved in gathering information on multinational activities and is moving towards establishing international accounting policies for MNCs, with particular emphasis on increased disclosure in financial statements. The UN Intergovernmental Working Group of Experts on International Standards of Accounting and Reporting (ISAR) was established in 1982. The objectives of the group are to serve as an international body for the consideration of issues of accounting and reporting by transnational corporations; make a positive contribution to national and regional standard setting; and take into account the interests of developing countries in the field of information disclosure. The group includes members from thirty-four countries and observers from various governmental and non-governmental bodies (including the IASC). The group is devoting an increasing amount of its resources to technical assistance in Africa and Russia, and to the development of the accounting profession (*IASC Insight*, March, 1994).

Organisation for Economic Cooperation and Development

The OECD is an intergovernmental entity of twenty-four countries, established in December 1960 to 'achieve the highest sustainable economic growth and employment and a rising standard of living in member countries while maintaining financial stability and, thus, to contribute to the world economy'. In 1976 the OECD proposed a code of conduct for multinational enterprises, dealing in part with accounting matters (that is, financial disclosure).

The OECD established a working group in 1979 to develop clarifications of the accounting terms used in the OECD Guidelines for multinational enterprises and promote efforts towards increased comparability of financial information and harmonisation of accounting standards. The OECD working group was influential in persuading the IASC to start its financial instruments project in 1988 (*IASC Insight*, March, 1994).

The creation of global accounting standards is not without its critics. Commentators see limitations to harmonisation, listing problems such as national tax policies and differences in levels of industrialisation and education (Arpan and Radebaugh, 1985). Some writers feel international standards are a useless, costly repetition of national standards; they question the need for promulgation of standards which are impossible to enforce (Fantl, 1971). Others feel the issuance of international standards by a separate body is yet another foolish component of the problem of standards overload (Kelley, 1982). Still other authors such as Meek (1984) have argued that the need for the IASC may be muted in the future due to financial markets: the market place will demand and receive the amount of financial information it desires, thereby lessening the necessity for an international accounting entity. Some even query the inherent need for having any accounting standards, arguing that standards are costly, stilted and difficult to implement.

However, the strongest arguments against international accounting standards rest with the advocates of the uniqueness of each society's environment. The basic tenet of this argument is that accounting is a product of its environment and, therefore, it is important for each country to have a set of accounting standards compatible with the environment in which it operates (Perera, 1985). Choi (1981, p.29) spoke of the dilemma of global accounting standards: 'Of course, the thesis of environmentally stimulated and justified differences in accounting runs directly counter to efforts at the worldwide harmonization of accounting. Hence, the dilemma.'

Regional harmonisation

It has been suggested that the most useful route towards harmonisation could rest

with the concept of regionalisation, wherein like-countries band together to form economic subgroups. Choi (1979), in discussing the Association of Southeast Asian Nations (ASEAN) group, states:

> Pacific nations today are acutely aware that in an interdependent world, no nation can hope to solve all of its development problems alone. At the same time, none appears ready to embrace the concept of economic globalism. Regionalism is, therefore, preferred as a logical compromise between purely nationalistic and global philosophies. Accordingly a number of regional economic groupings has been formed. (p.54)

Copeland and Butcher (1979) argue that regional groups have a greater political viability, possessing a greater chance of lessening trade barriers. Choi and Mueller (1984) suggest that, within the realm of accounting, the regional groups' efforts have complemented the IASC's. Three distinct roles for regional groups in respect of global harmonisation of accounting standards are mentioned by Choi (1981). The first role is a leadership position within the accounting cluster, another role is to tailor international accounting standards to the regional environment and the third role is to educate the IASC and other international groups to specific regional needs.

Choi (1981) further discusses the fact that accounting principles and practices of countries tend to cluster and are not as diverse as is usually assumed. He then states: 'A direct implication of this clustering thesis is that harmonization efforts within clusters may be a more fruitful and feasible development strategy than attempts to harmonize accounting standards on a worldwide basis' (p.29).

There are many regional organisations dealing with accounting matters, such as the following:

- Union Européenes des Experts Comptables Economiques et Financiers, or 'Union of European Accountants' (UEC), which was replaced as of 1 January 1987 by the Fédération des Experts Comptables Européenes (FEE)

- EU
- Inter-American Accounting Association (IAA)
- Confederation of Asian and Pacific Accountants (CAPA)
- ASEAN Federation of Accountants (AFA)
- Gulf Cooperation Council (GCC)
- South Asian Federation of Accountants (SAFA)
- African Accounting Council (AAC)
- Nordic Federation of Accountants (NFA)
- Association of Accountancy Bodies in West Africa (AABWA)
- North American Free Trade Association (NAFTA)

The above organisations have succeeded in generating some interest in the establishment of international accounting standards. As a pioneer regional organisation, the EU was established by the Treaty of Rome on 25 March 1957 to promote full freedom in the movement of goods and labour between member countries. The EU currently consists of Belgium, Denmark, France, Greece, Ireland, Italy, Luxembourg, the Netherlands, Portugal, Spain, the UK and Germany. One of the objectives of the EU has been the creation of a unified business environment, involving the harmonisation of company laws and taxation, and the creation of a community capital market. As a byproduct of this cooperation, the EU has issued Directives for the harmonisation of accounting standards for its members.

The EU has progressed far further than any other regional group within the realm of accounting issues. The EU is a combination of governments grouping together with the hope of strengthening trade links. The major difference between the EU and the other trade agreements, such as NAFTA, is that the EU Directives possess the force of law, giving the EU a rare advantage from an implementation and enforcement point of view (Choi and Mueller, 1992, pp.274–275). The EU experience provides useful insights into the mechanics of accounting harmonisation within a given cluster of countries. The Fourth and Seventh Directives issued by the EU set common requirements for financial statements within the Union which possess a legal enforcement mechanism.

Copeland and Butcher (1979) discuss the similar traits possessed by all the EU countries: all are industrially based, wealthy with comparable standards of living, high trade links and good transport links, with similar political goals though having quite different domestic policy objectives.

Closer Economic Relations Agreement between Australia and New Zealand

In 1983 the Governments of New Zealand and Australia entered into a CER Agreement with a view to freeing up trade and investment between the two countries. In 1988 CER became the first major international trade agreement to cover services. The 1992 review has opened some significant new areas for cooperation, for example business law (see *The Harmonisation of Australian and New Zealand Business Law — Closer Economic Relations Trade Agreement*, Report to Governments by Steering Committee Officials, July 1992). The accounting standard-setting bodies in Australia and New Zealand are now required by law to consult each other in an attempt to harmonise accounting standards between the two countries (Rahman, Perera and Tower, 1994).

The environmental conditions affecting accounting in New Zealand and Australia are so similar that the two countries could be classified as an accounting subgroup or a cluster within the British model.

Substantial similarities exist between New Zealand and Australia in the area of accounting:

- the two countries have taken almost identical approaches to developing their conceptual frameworks for accounting and financial reporting (Perera and Rahman, 1994)
- the concept of presenting a true and fair view in financial reports seems to prevail in the statutory requirements of both countries
- for detailed accounting prescriptions, both countries seem to favour delegated legislation
- the *Australian Corporations Law* 1991, similar to the *New Zealand Financial Reporting Act* 1993, relies on the accounting standard-setting system for the provision of detailed disclosure and accounting requirements
- accounting standards in New Zealand and Australia, for the most part, cover similar issues and have comparable accounting requirements (Rahman, Perera and Tower, 1994)
- there are many similarities between various categories of disclosure and measurement rules between the two countries (Rahman, Perera and Ganeshanandam, 1994)
- the elements within the recently adopted New Zealand scheme have a close one-to-one correspondence with the major elements of the Australian scheme.

The important elements of the standard-setting schemes in the two countries are shown in Table 17.1.

In view of the spirit of the CER Agreement, the similarities in many aspects of accounting regulation and practice in the two countries and the recent developments in both countries in this area, Rahman, Perera and Tower (1994) suggest that the accounting regulatory mechanisms of New Zealand and Australia be merged. They also suggest a

Table 17.1
Elements of accounting regulation: a comparison of Australia and New Zealand

Elements of regulation	Australia	New Zealand
Structure		
Policy making	Ministerial Council Government Minister (Federal Attorney-General)	Parliament Government Minister (Minister of Justice)
Standard setting	Government created independent body (AASB)	Government created independent body (ASRB)
Standard formulation	Profession backed research body (AARF)	Profession backed research body (FRSB)
Enforcement	Government body (ASC)	Government bodies (Registrar of Companies and Securities Commission)
Regulated	Companies and public sector entities	Companies, public issuers and public sector entities
Beneficiaries	Users of financial reports	Users of financial reports
Concept of reporting	True and fair	True and fair
Mode of regulation	Accounting standards	Accounting standards
Mode of enforcement	Legislative backing for standards	Legislative backing for standards

Source: Rahman, Perera and Tower (1994)

mechanism for such a merger which consists of the following:

a. To achieve company law harmonisation, New Zealand joins Australia in a co-operative scheme similar to the Australian Co-operative scheme for companies and securities.

b. The Justice Minister of New Zealand and the Australian Federal Attorney-General form a Ministerial Council to oversee the legislative activities in the two countries.

c. New Zealand seeks participatory rights in the Australian Scheme for establishing of accounting standards.

d. The New Zealand FRSB be merged with the Australian AARF or the proposed AASF.

Chapter summary

Comparative accounting is an essential part of accounting education in the modern world where accountants are increasingly becoming involved in transactions and events which have an international dimension. To be successful in dealing with specific accounting issues at that level, it is necessary not only to know the accounting practices adopted in different countries, but also to understand why sometimes different countries adopt different approaches to similar situations. This is becoming increasingly important, particularly in view of the growing tendency for Western business organisations to establish joint ventures with firms in Eastern Europe and China. In general, these differences can be explained in terms of the environmental needs and circumstances prevailing in those countries. Such an understanding is also necessary if the harmonisation efforts, either at the global level or at the regional level, are to make any progress towards achieving the given objectives.

Essay and examination questions

17.1 Explain why the study of comparative accounting is important.

17.2 The national differences in accounting practices can be explained in terms of environmental factors. Do you agree? Explain.

17.3 What are the advantages of an international classification of accounting systems?

17.4 Explain the basic differences between the accounting systems of Anglo-American and non-Anglo-American countries.

17.5 Discuss the nature and significance of foreign currency translation as a comparative accounting issue.

17.6 Examine the problems of the consolidation of financial statements in an international context.

17.7 The thesis of environmentally stimulated and justified differences in accounting runs directly counter to efforts at worldwide harmonisation of accounting. Comment.

17.8 Explain and discuss the cluster approach to harmonisation of accounting standards.

17.9 Discuss the main features of the 'Mixed Economy' model and the associated accounting issues.

17.10 Examine the prospects for accounting harmonisation between Australia and New Zealand in the context of global accounting harmonisation.

References and additional reading

Alhashim, D.D. and Arpan, J.S. (1988). *International Dimensions of Accounting,*
    Boston: PWS Kent.

American Accounting Association (1977). Report of the Committee on
    International Accounting Operations and Education, 1975–1976. *The
    Accounting Review* (Supplement).

Arpan, J.S. and Radebaugh, L.H. (1985). *International Accounting and Multinational
    Enterprises.* John Wiley.

Bailey, D.T. (Ed.) (1988). *Accounting in Socialist Countries.* London: Routledge.

Briston, R.J. (1978). The evolution of accounting in developing countries.
    International Journal of Accounting Education and Research, Fall.

Campbell, L. (1986). Financial Reporting in Japan, in C.W. Nobes and
    R.H. Parker (Eds), *Comparative International Accounting* (Second edition).
    Oxford: Philip Allan, 152–75.

Carey, A. (1990). Harmonization: Europe moves forward, *Accountancy*, March, 92–94.

Chandler, J.S. and Holzer, H.P. (Eds) (1984). *International Accounting.* New York:
    Harper and Row.

Choi, F.D.S. (1979). ASEAN Federation of Accountants: A new international
    accounting force. *International Journal of Accounting Education and Research,*
    Fall, 53–67.

Choi, F.D.S. (1981). A cluster approach to harmonization. *Management Accounting,*
    August, 27–31.

Choi, F.D.S. and Bavishi, V.B. (1982). Diversity in multinational accounting.
    Financial Executive, August, 46–49.

Choi, F.D.S. and Mueller, G.G. (1978). *An Introduction to Multinational Accounting.*
    Englewood Cliffs, New Jersey: Prentice Hall.

Choi, F.D.S. and Mueller, G.G. (1984). *International Accounting.* Englewood Cliffs,
    New Jersey: Prentice Hall.

Choi, F.D.S. and Mueller G.G. (1992). *International Accounting.* 2nd edn.
    Englewood Cliffs, New Jersey: Prentice Hall.

Coopers and Lybrand (1993). *International Accounting Summaries: A Guide for
    Interpretation and Comparison* (Second edition). New York: John Wiley.

Copeland, M.C. and Butcher, G.V. (1979). *Administrative Options for Closer Economic
    Relations between Australia and New Zealand.* Contract research paper,
    Wellington: New Zealand Institute of Economic Research.

Da Costa, R.C., Bourgeois, J.C. and Lawson, W.M. (1978). A classification of
    international financial accounting practices. *International Journal of Accounting
    Education and Research,* Spring.

Davidson, J.S. (1994). The International Organization of Securities Comissions, in
    G. Walker and B. Fisse (Eds), *Securities Regulation in Australia and New
    Zealand.* Auckland: Oxford University Press, pp. 715–729.

Fantl, I.L. (1971). The case against international uniformity. *Management
    Accounting,* May.

Frank, W.G. (1979). An empirical analysis of international accounting principles.
    Journal of Accounting Research, Autumn.

Gray, S.J. and Roberts, C.B. (1991). East–west accounting issues: A new agenda,
    Accounting Horizons, **5**(11), 42–50.

Healy, N.M. (1994). The transition economies of Central and Eastern Europe: A political, economic, social and technological analysis. *Columbia Journal of World Business,* Spring, 62–70.

International Accounting Standards Committee (1978). *Preface to International Accounting Standards.* London: IASC.

Japanese Institute of Certified Public Accountants (1982). *Corporate Disclosures in Japan.* Tokyo: JICPA.

Kelley, T.P. (1982). Accounting standards overload — Time for action. *CPA Journal,* May, 10–17.

Lorensen, L. (1972). *Accounting Research Study No. 12: Reporting Foreign Operations of US Companies in US Dollars.* New York: AICPA.

Macharzina, K. (1986). Financial Reporting in West Germany, in C.W. Nobes and R.H. Parker (Eds), *Comparative International Accounting,* 2nd edn. Oxford: Philip Allan, 97–131.

Meek, G. (1984). Competition spurs worldwide harmonization. *Management Accounting,* August, 47–49.

Most, K.S. (1994). Toward the international harmonization of accounting, *Advances in International Accounting,* **6,** 3–14.

Moulin, D.J. and Solomon, M.B. (1989). Practical means of promoting common international standards, *The CPA Journal,* December, 38–43.

Mueller, G.G. (1967). *International Accounting.* New York: Macmillan.

Mueller, G.G. (1968). Accounting principles generally accepted in the United States versus those generally accepted elsewhere. *International Journal of Accounting Education and Research,* Spring.

Mueller, G.G., Gernon, H. and Meek, G.K. (1994). *Accounting: An International Perspective,* Illinois: Irwin.

Nair, R.D. and Frank, W.G. (1980). The impact of disclosure and measurement practices on international accounting classification. *The Accounting Review,* July.

Nobes, C.W. (1983). A judgmental international classification of financial reporting practices. *Journal of Business Finance and Accounting,* Spring.

Nobes, C.W. (1984). *International Classification of Financial Reporting.* Croom Helm.

Nobes, C.W. (1985). Harmonisation of financial reporting, in C.W. Nobes and R.H. Parker (Eds), *Comparative International Accounting (Second edition).* Oxford: Philip Allan.

Nobes, C.W. (1994). *A Study of the International Accounting Standards Committee,* London: Coopers and Lybrand (International).

Nobes, C.W. and Parker, R.H. (Eds) (1985). *Comparative International Accounting.* Oxford: Philip Allan.

Parker, R.H. (1983). Some international aspects of accounting, in S.J. Gray, *International Accounting and Transnational Decisions.* Butterworths.

Parker, R.H. (1986). Financial Reporting in France, in C.W. Nobes and R.H. Parker (Eds), *Comparative International Accounting,* 2nd edn, Oxford: Philip Allan, 75–96.

Perera, M.H.B. (1980). *Accounting for State Industrial and Commercial Enterprises in a Developing Country: With Special Reference to Sri Lanka.* New York: Arno Press.

Perera, M.H.B. (1985). *International Accounting Standards and the Developing*

Countries. Research Report, School of Financial Studies: Glasgow University, UK.

Perera, M.H.B. (1989). Accounting in developing countries: A case for localised uniformity. *The British Accounting Review,* **21**(2), 41–57.

Perera, M.H.B. (1994). Culture and international accounting: Some thoughts on research issues and prospects, *Advances in International Accounting,* **7**, 265–283.

Perera, M.H.B. and Rahman, A.R. (1994). Conceptual foundation of accounting and financial reporting: Emerging commonality of purpose between Australia and New Zealand. Paper presented at the Annual Conference of the Accounting Association of Australia and New Zealand, Wollongong, July.

Previts, G.J. (1975). On the subject of methodology and models of international accounting. *International Journal of Accounting Education and Research,* Spring.

Price Waterhouse International (1973). *Accounting Principles and Reporting Practices: A Survey in 38 Countries.* London: ICAEW.

Price Waterhouse International (1975). *Accounting Principles and Reporting Practices: A Survey in 46 Countries.* London: ICAEW.

Price Waterhouse International (1979). *International Survey of Accounting Principles and Reporting Practices.* Ontario: Butterworths.

Radebaugh, L.H. (1975). Environmental factors influencing the development of accounting objectives, standards and practices in Peru. *International Journal of Accounting Education and Research,* Fall.

Radebaugh, L.H. and Gray, S.J. (1993). *International Accounting and Multinational Enterprises,* third edition, New York: John Wiley.

Rahman, A.R., Perera, M.H.B. and Ganeshanandam, S. (1994). Regional accounting harmonisation: A comparative study of the disclosure and measurement regulations of Australia and New Zealand. Paper presented at the Annual Conference of the Accounting Association of Australia and New Zealand, Wollongong, July.

Rahman, A.R., Perera, M.H.B. and Tower, G.D. (1994). Accounting harmonisation between Australia and New Zealand: Towards a regulatory union, *International Journal of Accounting,* **29**(3) 171–192.

Sharpe, M. (1994). International harmony of accounting standards. Paper presented at the Annual Meeting of the International Accounting Group of the Accounting Association of Australia and New Zealand, Wollongong, July.

Turner, J.N. (1983). International harmonization: A professional goal. *Journal of Accountancy,* January, 58–59.

Wilkinson, T.L. (1965). United States accounting as viewed by accountants of other countries. *International Journal of Accounting Education and Research,* Fall.

Appendixes

Appendix 17.1   Factors influencing the accounting system of a country

	LHR	AAA	GGM	GJP	CAM	NAF
1 Enterprise users:	x	x				
Management	x	x				
Employees	x	x				
Supervisory councils	x	x				
Board of directors	x	x				
2 Other external users:	x	x				
Creditors	x	x				
Institutional investors	x	x				
Non-institutional investors	x	x				
Securities exchanges	x	x				
3 Government:		x	x			
Users: tax, planners	x	x				
Regulators	x	x				
4 Accounting profession:	x					
Nature and extent of a profession	x	x		x		
Professional associations	x		x		x	
Education and training		x	x	x	x	
Enforcement of ethics and standards		x				
Auditing	x					
Objectives of financial reporting		x				
Presence of specific accounting legislation			x	x	x	
5 Nature of the enterprise:		x		x	x	x
Forms of business organisations	x		x	x	x	
Size and complexity of firms			x	x	x	
Operating characteristics	x					
Level of sophistication of business management			x	x	x	
Speed of business innovations			x	x	x	
6 Local environmental characteristics:	x					
Rate of economic growth	x		x	x	x	x
Per capita income						x
Private consumption						x
Gross capital formation						x
Balance of trade						x
Exchange rate changes						x
Stage of economic development		x	x		x	
Inflation	x		x	x	x	x
Public versus private ownership and control of the economy	x	x				
Cultural attitudes	x					

Appendix 17.1 *continued*

	LHR	AAA	GGM	GJP	CAM	NAF
Official language of the country						x
Social climate					x	
Political system		x			x	
Legal system					x	
Type of economy			x	x	x	x
Degree of legislative business interference			x	x	x	
General level of education			x	x	x	
Existence of a need for sophisticated financial reports				x		
7 Academic influence:	x					
Educational infrastructure	x					
Basic and applied research	x					
Academic associations	x					
8 International influences:	x					
Colonial history	x					
Foreign investors	x					
International committees	x					
Regional cooperation	x					
Regional capital markets	x					

Key
LHR — L.H. Radebaugh (1975)
AAA — American Accounting Association (1977)
GGM — G.G. Mueller (1968)
GJP — G.J. Previts (1975)
CAM — F.D.S. Choi and G.G. Mueller (1978)
NAF — R.D. Nair and W.G. Frank (1980)

Appendix 17.2   French plan comptable général: chart of accounts

	Financial accounting					Management accounts		Special accounts	Cost accounting
Balance sheet accounts									
Class 1 Capital accounts (capital, loans and similar creditors)	**Class 2** Fixed asset accounts	**Class 3** Stock and work-in-progress accounts	**Class 4** Personal accounts	**Class 5** Financial accounts	**Class 6** Expense accounts	**Class 7** Income accounts	**Class 8** Special accounts	**Class 9** Cost accounts
10 Capital and reserves	**20** Intangible assets	**30**	**40** Suppliers and related accounts	**50** Trade investments	**60** Purchases and stock movements (supplies and goods for resale)	**70** Sales of goods and services	**80** Contingent assets and liabilities	**90** Reciprocal accounts
11 Profit or loss brought forward	**21** Tangible assets	**31** Raw materials	**41** Trade debtors and related accounts	**51** Banks, financial and similar institutions	**61** Purchases from sub-contractors and external charges (related to investment)	**71** Movements in finished goods during the accounting period	**81***	**91** Cost reclassifications

Appendix 17.2: *continued*

	Financial accounting		Cost accounting
Balance sheet accounts	*Management accounts*	*Special accounts*	

Balance sheet accounts			Financial accounting		Management accounts		Special accounts	Cost accounting
Class 12 Profit or loss for the financial year	**Class 22** Fixed assets under concession	**Class 32** Other consumables	**Class 42** Employees and related accounts	**Class 52**	**Class 62** Other external charges (related to operations)	**Class 72** Work performed by the undertaking for its own purposes and capitalised	**Class 82***	**Class 92** Cost analysis centres
13 Investment grants	23 Fixed assets in course of construction	33 Work-in-progress (goods)	43 Social security and other public agencies	53 Cash in hand	63 Taxes, direct and indirect	73 Net income recognised on long term contracts	83*	93 Manufacturing costs
14 Provisions created for tax purposes	24	34 Work-in-progress (services)	44 The Government and other public bodies	54 Imprest accounts and credits	64 Staff costs	74 Operating subsidies	84*	94 Stocks
15 Provisions for liabilities and charges	25	35 Finished goods	45 Accounts current: group companies and proprietors	55	65 Other operating charges	75 Other operating income	85*	95 Cost of goods sold

Appendix 17.2: *continued*

Balance sheet accounts		Financial accounting			Management accounts		Special accounts	Cost accounting
16 Loans and similar creditors	**26** Participating interests and debts relating thereto	**36**	**46** Sundry debtors and creditors	**56**	**66** Financial costs	**76** Financial income	**86** Intra-company exchanges of goods and services (charges)	**96** Standard cost variances
17 Debts related to participating interests	**27** Other financial assets	**37** Goods for resale	**47** Suspense accounts	**57** Internal transfers	**67** Extraordinary	**77** Extraordinary	**87** Intra-company exchanges of goods and services (income)	**97** Difference in accounting treatments
18 Branch and inter-company accounts	**28** Provisions for depreciation of fixed assets	**38**	**48** Prepayments and accruals	**58**	**68** Depreciation, amortisation, transfers to provisions	**78** Depreciation and provisions written back	**88**	**98** Manufacturing profit and loss account
19	**29** Provisions for loss in value of fixed assets	**39** Provisions for loss in value of stocks and work-in-progress	**49** Provisions for loss in value on personal accounts	**59** Provisions for loss in value on financial accounts	**69** Profit sharing by employees, taxes on profits and similar items	**79** Charges transferred	**89**	**99** Internal transfers

* Accounts for possible use in connection with consolidated balance sheet and profit and loss account
Source: Nobes and Parker (1985), pp 78–79

Appendix 17.3   Age and size of public accountancy bodies

Country	Body	Founding date	Approximate number 1991–1992
Australia	Australian Society of Accountants	1952(1887)	62 000
	Institute of Chartered Accountants in Australia	1928(1886)	23 000
Canada	Canadian Institute of Chartered Accountants	1902(1880)	53 000
France	Ordre des Experts Comptables et des Comptables Agréés	1942	12 000
Germany	Institut der Wirtschaftsprüfer	1932	6 000
India	Institute of Chartered Accountants of India	1949	65 000
Japan	Japanese Institute of Certified Public Accountants	1948	10 000
Korea	Korea Institute of Certified Public Accountants	1954	3 000
Netherlands	Nederlands Instituut van Registeraccountants	1895	8 000
New Zealand	New Zealand Society of Accountants	1909(1894)	16 000
Spain	Instituto de Censures Jurados de Cuentas de España	1945	6 000
	Registro de Economistas Auditores	1982	4 000
United Kingdom	Institute of Chartered Accountants in England and Wales	1880(1870)	97 000
	Institute of Chartered Accountants of Scotland	1951(1854)	13 000
	Chartered Association of Certified Accountants	1939(1891)	38 000
	Institute of Chartered Accountants in Ireland	1888	8 000
United States	American Institute of Certified Public Accountants	1887	301 000

Note: Dates of earliest predecessor bodies in brackets

Appendix 17.4   Company law directives and regulations relevant to corporate accounting (mid 1985)

	Draft dates	Date approved	UK law	Purpose
Directives				
First	1964	1968	1972	*Ultra vires* rules, etc.
Second	1970, 1972	1976	1980	Separation of private from public companies, minimum capital, distributable income
Third	1970, 1973, 1975	1978		Mergers
Fourth	1971, 1974	1978	1981	Formats and rules of accounting
Fifth	1972, 1983			Structure, management and audit of public companies
Sixth	1975, 1978	1982		De-mergers
Seventh	1976, 1978	1983		Group accounting
Eighth	1978, 1979	1984		Qualifications and work of auditors
Ninth	—			Links between public company groups
Tenth	1985			International mergers of public companies
Vredeling	1980, 1983			Employee information and consultation
Regulations				
Societas Europea	1970, 1975			A European company subject to EU laws
European Economic Interest Grouping	1973, 1978	1985		A legal form for multinational joint ventures

Source: Nobes and Parker (1985), p.347

Appendix 17.5   Choi–Bavishi synthesis of world diversity in financial accounting practices

Accounting principles	Australia	Canada	France	Germany	Japan	Neth	Sweden	Switz	UK	USA
1 Marketable securities recorded at the lower cost or market?	Yes	Yes	Yes	Yes	Yes	Yes	Yes	Yes	Yes	Yes
2 Provision for uncollectible accounts made?	Yes	Yes	No	Yes	Yes	Yes	Yes	Yes	Yes	Yes
3 Inventory costed using FIFO?	Yes	Mixed	Mixed	Yes	Mixed	Mixed	Yes	Yes	Yes	Mixed
4 Manufacturing overhead allocated to year end inventory?	Yes	Yes	Yes	Yes	Yes	Yes	Yes	No	Yes	Yes
5 Inventory valued at the lower of cost or market?	Yes	Yes	Yes	Yes	Yes	Yes	Yes	Yes	Yes	Yes
6 Accounting for long term investments: less than 20% ownership: cost method?	Yes	Yes	Yes*	Yes	Yes	No(K)	Yes	Yes	Yes	Yes
7 Accounting for long term investments: 21–50% ownership: equity method?	No(G)	Yes	Yes*	No(B)	No(B)	Yes	No(B)	No(B)	Yes	Yes
8 Accounting for long term investments more than 50% ownership: full consolidation?	Yes	Yes	Yes*	Yes	Yes	Yes	Yes	Yes	Yes	Yes
9 Both domestic and foreign subsidiaries consolidated?	Yes	Yes	Yes	No**	Yes	Yes	Yes	Yes	Yes	Yes

Appendix 17.5 continued

Accounting principles	Australia	Canada	France	Germany	Japan	Neth	Sweden	Switz	UK	USA
10 Acquisitions accounted for under the pooling of interest method?	No(C)	No(C)	No(C)	No(C)	No(C)	No(C)	No(C)	No(C)	No(C)	Yes
11 Intangible assets: goodwill amortised?	Yes	Yes	Yes	No	Yes	Mixed	Yes	No**	No**	Yes
12 Intangible assets: other than goodwill amortised?	Yes	Yes	Yes	Yes	Yes	Yes	Yes	No**	No**	Yes
13 Long term debt includes maturities longer than one year?	Yes	Yes	Yes	No(D)	Yes	Yes	Yes	Yes	Yes	Yes
14 Discount/premium on long term debt amortised?	Yes	Yes	No	No	Yes	Yes	No	No	No	Yes
15 Deferred taxes recorded when accounting income is not equal to taxable income?	Yes	Yes	Yes	Yes	Yes	Yes	No	No	Yes	Yes
16 Financial leases (long term) capitalised?	No	Yes	No	No	No	No	No	No	Yes	Yes
17 Company pension fund contribution provided regularly?	Yes	Yes	Yes	Yes	Yes	Yes	Yes	Yes	Yes	Yes
18 Total pension fund assets and liabilities excluded from company's financial statement?	Yes	Yes	Yes	No	Yes	Yes	Yes	Yes	Yes	Yes

Appendix 17.5 *continued*

Accounting principles	Australia	Canada	France	Germany	Japan	Neth	Sweden	Switz	UK	USA
19 Research and development expensed?	Yes	Yes	Yes	Yes	Yes	Yes	Yes	Yes	Yes	Yes
20 Treasury stock deducted from owner's equity?	NF	Yes	Yes	No	Yes	Mixed	NF	NF	NF	Yes
21 Gains or losses on treasury stock taken to owner's equity?	NF	Yes	Yes	No	No**	Mixed	NF	NF	NF	Yes
22 No general purpose (purely discretionary) reserves allowed?	Yes	Yes	No	No	No	No	No	No	Yes	Yes
23 Dismissal indemnities accounted for on a pay-as-you-go basis?	Yes	Yes	Yes	Yes	Yes	NF	Yes	NF	Yes	Yes
24 Minority interest excluded from consolidated income?	Yes	Yes	Yes	No	Yes	Yes	Yes	Yes	Yes	Yes
25 Minority interest excluded from consolidated owner's equity?	Yes	Yes	Yes	No	Yes	Yes	Yes	Yes	Yes	Yes
26 Are intercompany sales/profits eliminated upon consolidation?	Yes	Yes	Yes	Yes	Yes	Yes	Yes	Yes	Yes	Yes
27 Basic financial statements reflect a historical cost valuation (no price level adjustment)?	No	Yes	No	Yes	Yes	No**	No	No	No	Yes

Appendix 17.5 *continued*

Accounting principles	Australia	Canada	France	Germany	Japan	Neth	Sweden	Switz	UK	USA
28 Supplementary inflation-adjusted financial statements provided?	No**	No**	No	No	No	No**	No	No**	Yes	Yes
29 Straight-line depreciation adhered to?	Yes	Yes	Mixed	Mixed	Mixed	Yes	Yes	Yes	Yes	Yes
30 No excess depreciation permitted?	No	Yes	No	Yes	Yes	No	No	No	No	Yes
31 Temporal method of foreign currency translation employed?	Mixed	Yes	No(E)	No(E)	Mixed	No(E)	No(L)	No(E)	No(E)	Yes
32 Currency translation gains or losses reflected in current income?	Mixed	Yes	Mixed	Mixed	Mixed	No(J)	Mixed	No(H)	No	Yes

Key

Yes — Predominant practice
Yes* — Minor modifications, but still predominant practice
No** — Minority practice
No — Accounting principle in question not adhered to
NF — Not found
Mixed — Alternative practices followed with no majority
B — Cost method is used
C — Purchase method is used
D — Long term debt includes maturities longer than four years
E — Current rate method of foreign currency translation
F — Weighted average is used
G — Cost or equity
H — Translation gains and losses are deferred
I — Market is used
J — Owner's equity
K — Equity
L — Monetary/non-monetary

Source: Choi and Bavishi (1982), pp.46–49

Appendix 17.6   The history of international accounting standards and exposure drafts

Exposure draft	International accounting standard	Effective date	Comments
ED 1 Disclosure of accounting policies (March 1974)	**IAS 1** Disclosure of accounting policies (January 1975)	1 January 1975	
ED 2 Valuation and presentation of inventories in the context of the historical cost system (September 1974)	**IAS 2** Valuation and presentation of inventories in the context of the historical cost system (October 1975)	1 January 1976	
ED 3 Consolidated financial statements and the equity method of accounting (December 1974)	**IAS 3** Consolidated financial statements (June 1976)	1 January 1977	Superseded by IAS 27 and IAS 28
ED 4 Depreciation accounting (June 1975)	**IAS 4** Depreciation accounting (October 1976)	1 January 1977	
ED 5 Information to be disclosed in financial statements (June 1975)	**IAS 5** Information to be disclosed in financial statements (October 1976)	1 January 1977	
ED 6 Accounting treatment of changing prices (January 1976)	**IAS 6** Accounting responses to changing prices (June 1977)	1 January 1978	Superseded by IAS 15
ED 7 Statement of source and application of funds (June 1976)	**IAS 7** Statement of changes in financial position (October 1977)	1 January 1979	Superseded by IAS 7, cash flow statements (revised 1992). Published December 1992 and effective January 1994
ED 8 The treatment in the income statement of unusual items and changes in accounting estimates and accounting policies (October 1976)	**IAS 8** Unusual and prior period items and changes in accounting policies (February 1978)	1 January 1979	

Appendix 17.6 *continued*

Exposure draft	International accounting standard	Effective date	Comments
ED 9 Accounting for research and development costs (February 1977)	**IAS 9** Accounting for research and development activities (July 1978)	1 January 1980	
ED 10 Contingencies and events occurring after the balance sheet date (July 1977)	**IAS 10** Contingencies and events occurring after the balance sheet date (October 1978)	1 January 1980	
ED 11 Accounting for foreign transactions and translation of foreign financial statements (December 1977)			Re-drafted and re-exposed as ED 23
ED 12 Accounting for construction contracts (December 1977)	**IAS 11** Accounting for construction contracts (March 1979)	1 January 1980	
ED 13 Accounting for taxes on income (April 1978)	**IAS 12** Accounting for taxes on income (July 1979)	1 January 1981	
ED 14 Current assets and current liabilities (July 1978)	**IAS 13** Presentation of current assets and current liabilities (November 1979)	1 January 1981	
ED 15 Reporting financial information by segment (March 1980)	**IAS 14** Reporting financial information by segment (August 1981)	1 January 1983	
ED 16 Accounting for retirement benefits in the financial statements of employers (April 1980)	**IAS 19** Accounting for retirement benefits in the financial statements of employers (January 1983)	1 January 1985	

Appendix 17.6 *continued*

Exposure draft	International accounting standard	Effective date	Comments
ED 17 Information reflecting the effects of changing prices (August 1990)	**IAS 15** Information reflecting the effects of changing prices (November 1981)	1 January 1983	In October 1989 the Board approved a statement to be added to IAS 15
ED 18 Accounting for property, plant and equipment in the context of the historical cost system (August 1980)	**IAS 16** Accounting for property, plant and equipment (March 1982)	1 January 1983	
ED 19 Accounting for leases (October 1980)	**IAS 17** Accounting for leases (September 1982)	1 January 1984	
ED 20 Revenue recognition (April 1981)	**IAS 18** Revenue recognition (December 1982)	1 January 1984	
ED 21 Accounting for government grants and disclosure of government assistance (September 1981)	**IAS 20** Accounting for government grants and disclosure of government assistance (April 1983)	1 January 1984	
ED 22 Accounting for business combinations (September 1981)	**IAS 22** Accounting for business combinations (November 1983)	1 January 1985	
ED 23 Accounting for the effects of changes in foreign exchange rates (March 1982)	**IAS 21** Accounting for the effects of changes in foreign exchange rates (July 1983)	1 January 1985	
ED 24 Capitalisation of borrowing costs (November 1982)	**IAS 23** Capitalisation of borrowing costs (March 1984)	1 January 1986	
ED 25 Disclosure of related party transactions (March 1983)	**IAS 24** Related party disclosures (July 1984)	1 January 1986	

Appendix 17.6 *continued*

Exposure draft	International accounting standard	Effective date	Comments
ED 26 Accounting for investments (October 1984)	**IAS 25** Accounting for investments (March 1986)	1 January 1987	
ED 27 Accounting and reporting by retirement benefit plans (July 1985)	**IAS 26** Accounting and reporting by retirement benefit plans (January 1987)	1 January 1988	
ED 28 Accounting for investments in associates and joint ventures (July 1986)	**IAS 28** Accounting for investments in associates (April 1989)	1 January 1990	
ED 29 Disclosures in the financial statements of banks (April 1987)			Re-exposed as ED 34
ED 30 Consolidated financial statements and accounting for investments in subsidiaries (September 1987)	**IAS 27** Consolidated financial statements and accounting for investments in subsidiaries (April 1989)	1 January 1990	
ED 31 Financial reporting in hyperinflationary economies (November 1987)	**IAS 29** Financial reporting in hyperinflationary economies (July 1989)	1 January 1990	
Framework for the preparation and presentation of financial statements (May 1988)	Framework for the preparation and presentation of financial statements (July 1989)		
ED 32 Comparability of financial statements (January 1989)	Statement of Intent– Comparability of financial statements (July 1990)		
ED 33 Accounting for taxes on income (January 1989)			

Appendix 17.6 *continued*

Exposure draft	International accounting standard	Effective date	Comments
ED 34 Disclosures in the financial statements of banks and similar financial institutions (July 1989)	**IAS 30** Disclosures in the financial statements of banks and similar financial institutions (August 1990)	1 January 1991	
ED 35 Financial reporting of interests in joint ventures (December 1989)	**IAS 31** Financial reporting of interests in joint ventures (December 1990)	1 January 1992	
ED 36 Cash flow statements (July 1991)	**IAS 7** (revised 1992) Cash flow statements (December 1992)	1 January 1994	IAS 7 revised, cash flow statements, superseded IAS 7 and statement of changes in financial position on 1 January 1994
ED 37 Research and development activities (August 1991)	**IAS 9** (revised 1993) Research and development costs (December 1993)	1 January 1995	Revised standard which formed part of the comparability/ improvements project
ED 38 Inventories (August 1991)	**IAS 2** (revised 1993) Inventories (December 1993)	1 January 1995	Revised standard which formed part of the comparability/ improvements project
ED 39 Capitalisation of borrowing costs (August 1991)	**IAS 23** (revised 1993) Borrowing costs (December 1993)	1 January 1995	Revised standard which formed part of the comparability/ improvements project
ED 40 Financial instruments (September 1991)			Re-exposed as ED 48, financial instruments, published 1 January 1994, comments due by 31 July 1994
ED 41 Revenue recognition (May 1992)	**IAS 18** (revised 1993) Revenue (December 1993)	1 January 1995	Revised standard which formed part of the comparability/ improvements project
ED 42 Construction contracts (May 1992)	**IAS 11** (revised 1993) Construction contracts (December 1993)	1 January 1995	Revised standard which formed part of the comparability/ improvements project

Appendix 17.6 *continued*

Exposure draft	International accounting standard	Effective date	Comments
ED 43 Property, plant and equipment (May 1992)	**IAS 16** (revised 1993) Property, plant and equipment (December 1993)	1 January 1995	Revised standard which formed part of the comparability/ improvements project
ED 44 The effects of changes in foreign exchange rates (May 1992)	**IAS 21** (revised 1993) The effects of changes in foreign exchange rates (December 1993)	1 January 1995	Revised standard which formed part of the comparability/ improvements project
ED 45 Business combinations (June 1992)	**IAS 22** (revised 1993) Business combinations (December 1993)	1 January 1995	Revised standard which formed part of the comparability/ improvements project
ED 46 Extraordinary items, fundamental errors and changes in accounting policies (July 1992)	**IAS 8** (revised 1993) Net profit or loss for the period, fundamental errors and changes in accounting policies (December 1993)	1 January 1995	Revised standard which formed part of the comparability/ improvements project
ED 47 Retirement benefit costs (December 1992)	**IAS 19** (revised 1993) Retirement benefit costs (December 1993)	1 January 1995	Revised standard which formed part of the comparability/ improvements project
ED 48 Financial instruments (January 1994)			(see also ED 40, financial instruments)

Source: *IASC 1994*

Learning objectives

After studying this chapter the reader will be able to:
*   define culture
*   identify the manifestations of culture at various levels in society
*   explain the cultural significance of accounting
*   discuss the possible interrelationship between societal values and accounting values, and hence accounting practices
*   describe the aspects of accounting which are most likely to be influenced by cultural factors
*   consider the possible implications of culture for international harmonisation of accounting standards and international transfer of accounting technology.

Introduction

One of the significant outcomes of research endeavours in the analysis of accounting in different countries has been an enhanced awareness of the importance of environmental factors in moulding a country's accounting system. This in turn has led to serious attempts at identifying both the relevant environmental factors and the mechanism by which such factors influence accounting. Here, culture is often considered to be one of the powerful environmental factors impacting upon the accounting system of a country. Accounting is a socio-technical activity. It involves dealing with human and non-human resources or techniques as well as with the interaction between the two. Therefore, it can be argued that, although the technical aspect of accounting is less culturally dependent than the human aspect, since the two interact, accounting cannot be culture free.

However, the impact of culture upon accounting has yet to be established. Most of what has been written on this subject consists of *ex cathedra* propositions without adequate analysis or of non-generalisable case studies. Obviously any exercise aimed at analysing the cultural influence on accounting should identify

(a) a set of specific societal values or cultural factors which are likely to be directly associated with accounting practices, and (b) the mechanism in which the association between societal values and accounting practices takes place, for it is only then that their impact can be examined through a logical process. This chapter proposes to address some of these issues. The study of culture and cultural structures by Hofstede will be reviewed, together with the application of these ideas to accounting. An attempt will also be made to develop a framework to analyse the impact of culture upon accounting. Finally, explanations within the literature on culture and accounting are sought for various differences in accounting practices in Anglo-American, Continental European and developing countries.

Aspects of culture

In most discussions of culture, reference is often made to the fact that members of a given culture tend to share common frameworks of meanings and social understandings. Culture is often regarded as an expression of norms, values and customs which reflect typical behavioural characteristics (Takatera and Yamamoto, 1987)

Hofstede defines culture as 'the collective programming of the mind which distinguishes the members of one human group from another' (1980, p.25).

Hofstede's definition emphasises three main points about culture.

(a) Culture is something collective and not a characteristic of individuals.

(b) Culture is in the mind, therefore invisible as such and only visible through people's behaviour.

(c) Culture is only interesting to the extent that it differentiates among categories of people, that is it is expressed in characteristics which some have and others have not.

Culture manifests itself in values, rituals, heroes and symbols within a society. Values may be defined as 'a broad tendency to prefer certain states of affairs over others' (Hofstede, 1984, p.18). Values are the primary determinants of human behaviour. They determine people's attitudes of 'good' and 'bad', 'right' and 'wrong', 'normal' and 'abnormal', 'rational' and 'irrational' and so on. In cultural systems values are expressed in rituals, and more superficially, in the choice of heroes and symbols (Hofstede, 1985). A ritual is any action that follows a set pattern and expresses meaning through the use of symbols. Rituals are often associated with myths. Heroes are people whom a culture takes as models for behaviour.

According to Hofstede's definition of culture, values at the collective level, for example organisational, professional and societal, as opposed to the individual level represent culture. Furthermore, the term 'culture' is usually reserved to represent values at the societal or national level, whereas the term 'subculture' is used to represent values at the levels of organisations, professions and other human groups within society (Gray, 1988, p.4).

Prior to 1970 most attempts to understand the determinants of human behaviour had a distinctly ethnocentric bias (Triandis, 1980). Recently, there has been an increased interest in cross-cultural research, primarily due to the desire to test the universality of Euro-American psychological theories (Berry, 1975). Research findings have resulted in the realisation that not all the key elements of contemporary psychological theories, such as motivation theory, may be universal. This has led to the present efforts to determine which aspects of psychological theorising are truly universal, which may be modified by cultural variables and which may be valid only in a particular culture.

Hofstede (1983c) observed how the cultural differences between nations, which often appear to share similar frameworks of meanings, values and symbols, manifest themselves in people's behaviour. For example, the British will form a neat queue whenever they have to wait but the French will not; the Dutch will, as a rule, greet strangers when they enter a small enclosed space (railway compartment, doctor's waiting room, lift, etc.) but the Belgians will not; Austrians will wait at a red pedestrian traffic light even where there is no traffic but the Dutch will not; the Swiss tend to become very angry when somebody, say a foreigner, makes a mistake in traffic, but the Swedes do not. Hofstede concluded that all these manifestations are part of an invisible set of mental programmes which constitute these countries' national cultures.

A major difficulty in cross-cultural research has centred on the contrast between emic and etic considerations. The emic concept is that cultures can only be understood in their own contexts. Individual features of different cultures have different 'cultural meanings' and hence they are not comparable. The etic concept considers behaviour across many cultures from a universal perspective. As such, etics present culture-free aspects that must operate in at least more than one culture. A potential pitfall is the tendency to use the emic concepts of one culture to explain characteristics of another (Perera and Mathews, 1990, p.222).

There are two generic interpretations of culture, that is as a variable and as a metaphor. The former emphasises culture as something a human group *has*. The latter emphasises culture as something a human group *is* (not a severable component). With regard to an organisation, the concept of culture as a variable would mean that it is something like strategy and systems which management can and should manipulate towards organisational ends. The ability to manage organisational culture is also part of being an effective manager. The concept of culture as a metaphor would mean that management is also part of organisation's culture. Through interaction, culture shapes management as management shapes culture (Dent and Green, 1985; Smircich, 1983).

It is clear that cross-cultural behavioural research in accounting is likely to provide some explanation about why there are differences in accounting techniques and practices between countries and to answer the question whether the findings of researchers in one culture can be transformed without modification for effective use in another culture. In this context, given the status of accounting research in this area, findings of similar research efforts in other related fields would be helpful. For example, in the field of management, Hofstede has sought to analyse differences in work-related values across cultures. His study was based upon data collected through an employee attitude survey in a multinational corporation. The survey took place twice between 1968 and 1973, involving different subsidiaries in sixty-four countries, and 116 000 questionnaires in twenty languages (Hofstede, 1983a). Accounting systems can be expected to vary along national cultural lines. As Hofstede (1987) argues, the less an activity is technically defined, the more it is ruled by values and thus influenced by cultural

differences. Accounting is a field in which the technical imperatives are weak (Cushing, 1987).

Culture has featured prominently in more recent discussions of the factors influencing the accounting development of a country (Bromwich and Hopwood, 1983; Gray, 1985; Nobes and Parker, 1985; Cushing, 1987; Gray, 1988; Choi and Mueller 1984; Radebaugh and Gray, 1993; Perera, 1989, 1994.) It has also been argued that the lack of consensus across different countries on what represents proper accounting methods is because their purpose is cultural, not technical. The content of reports depends on local history and convention (Hofstede, 1985). This is probably why the product of accounting, financial statements and reports, sometimes has a shareholder orientation, other times a creditor orientation and occasionally it serves the interest of national planners or public administrators (Mueller, 1985).

Accounting has been described as a ritual which provides a means of absorbing uncertainty, or acts as an 'answer machine' (Thomas, 1989, p.367). Rituals may also give the appearance of rationality and truth. Most accounting practices, such as capital budgeting and cost allocation, can be seen as uncertainty reducing rituals, fulfilling an emotional need for certainty, simplicity and truth in a confusing world. Accounting practice has a lot in common with religious practice which also serves to reduce uncertainty. Gambling (1984) goes further and argues that accounting performs the same function in modern society which witchcraft performed in a more primitive one. Accountants play an important role in identifying heroes in society by determining the level of success achieved by individuals and organisations. Finally, the study of culture is the study of humans as symbol users (Ansari and Bell, 1985). In accounting, various symbols such as assets, liabilities and monetary figures are used in preparing financial statements.

Culture-based societal value dimensions

In an attempt to develop a commonly acceptable, well defined and empirically-based terminology to describe cultures, Hofstede identified four distinct dimensions which he considered to reflect the cultural orientation of a country. These are:

- individualism versus collectivism
- large versus small power distance
- strong versus weak uncertainty avoidance, and
- masculinity versus femininity.

The main features of these dimensions and some of the issues associated with them are discussed below, followed by a consideration of their implications for accounting.

Individualism versus collectivism

This dimension relates to the degree of integration a society maintains among its members, or the relationship between an individual and his or her fellow individuals. Individualism stands for a preference for a loosely knit social framework in society, wherein individuals are supposed to take care of themselves and their immediate families only.

Collectivism stands for a preference for a tightly knit social framework in which individuals can expect their relatives or other in-group to look after them in exchange for unquestioning loyalty.

The identified characteristics of this dimension tend to raise some questions in regard to established theories which have a bearing on management thought in general, for example the general validity of economic theories based on self-interest and of psychological theories based on self-actualisation because, in a collectivist society, preference is given to collective interest and achievement. Hofstede concludes that the degree of individualism in a country is statistically related to that country's wealth (1983c, p.80). Accordingly, wealthy countries tend to be more individualistically oriented, whereas poor countries tend to be more collectivistically oriented. This would seem to indicate an aspect of clear difference in societal values that exist between countries (see Appendix).

Large versus small power distance

This dimension relates to the extent to which the members of a society accept that power in institutions and organisations is distributed unequally. For example, in large power distance societies, people tend to accept a hierarchical order in which everybody has a place which needs no further justification, whereas in small power distance societies people tend to strive for power equalisation and demand justification for those power inequalities that do exist. The identified characteristics of this dimension tend to draw attention to issues such as whether subordinate consultation is necessary or paternalistic management is accepted.

In a large power distance society subordinate consultation may not be as important as in a small power distance society because there is a tendency for its members to accept paternalistic management. The degree of inequality in a society is measured by the extent of power distance. The level of power distance is related to the degree of centralisation of authority and the degree of autocratic leadership. Societies in which power tends to be distributed unequally can remain so because this situation satisfies the psychological need for dependence of the people without power. In other words, the value systems of the two groups are complementary. Hofstede identifies a global relationship between power distance and collectivism (1983c, p.82). Collectivist countries always show large power distance, although individualist countries do not always show small power distance. It is interesting to note that all poor countries are collectivist with large power distance (see Appendix).

Strong versus weak uncertainty avoidance

This dimension relates to the degree to which the members of a society feel uncomfortable with uncertainty and ambiguity. The fundamental issue involved here is how society reacts to the fact that the future is unknown, that is whether it tries to control the future or to let it happen. In the weak uncertainty avoidance societies people have a natural tendency to feel relatively secure, whereas in strong uncertainty avoidance societies people tend to try and beat the future, because the future remains essentially unpredictable and there will be a higher level of anxiety. In such societies, there will also be institutions that try to create security and avoid risk. One important way of creating security is through the law and other formal rules and institutions, whereby protection is provided against the unpredictability of human behaviour.

The existence of a relatively high degree of planning of economic activities in strong uncertainty avoidance societies could also be explained in terms of this value dimension. Religion is another way of creating a feeling of security. All religions attempt to create in the minds of people an expectation of something which is certain. The identified characteristics of this dimension tend to draw attention, among other things, to the existence of an emotional need for formal and informal rules to guide behaviour, the degree of formalisation, standardisation and ritualisation of organisations, the extent of tolerance for deviant ideas and behaviour and the willingness to take risks. There are different patterns of relationship between the degree of uncertainty avoidance and power distance (see Appendix).

Masculinity versus femininity

This dimension relates to the division of the roles between the sexes in society. Masculinity stands for a societal preference for showing off, achievement, heroism, assertiveness, making money or enjoying material success, thinking big and so on.

Femininity stands for a preference for putting relationships with people before money, helping others and caring for the weaker, the quality of life, preservation of the environment, 'small is beautiful' and so on.

The characteristics identified by this dimension tend to draw attention to the existence within society of competitiveness as against solidarity, equity against equality and achievement motivation as against relationship motivation. Career expectations and the acceptability of macho manager behaviour are some of the issues raised by this dimension. On this dimension there is no identifiable pattern between countries (see Appendix).

Societal values and accounting values

In identifying a set of specific societal values which are likely to be directly associated with accounting practices, Arpan and Radebaugh (1985, pp.17–18) make a useful contribution. The societal values they have identified in this regard are conservatism, secrecy, attitudes towards business and attitude towards the accounting profession. They do not, however, provide any systematic analysis of the relationships between these factors and accounting practices.

Gray (1985) represents a significant attempt to develop a model by identifying the mechanism by which societal level values are related to the accounting subculture which directly influences accounting practices. Gray employs Hofstede's culture-based societal value dimensions as the foundation for his analysis. He also identifies four value dimensions of the accounting subculture which are also related to societal values.

- *Professionalism*. Where there is a preference for the exercise of individual professional judgement and the maintenance of professional self-regulation, as

354 Accounting theory and development

opposed to compliance with prescriptive legal requirements and statutory control.

- *Uniformity.* Where there is a preference for the maintenance of uniform accounting practices between companies and for the consistent use of such practices over time as opposed to flexibility in accordance with the perceived circumstances of individual companies.
- *Conservatism.* Where there is support for a prudent and cautious approach to measurement so as to cope with the uncertainty of future events.
- *Secrecy.* Where there is support for confidentiality and the restriction of information about the business to only those who are closely involved with its management and financing.

Furthermore, Gray classifies accounting systems on the basis of each of the four accounting values.

Using Gray's analysis it is possible to identify certain direct associations between the values of the accounting subculture and the societal dimensions of individualism and uncertainty avoidance (see Table 18.1).

Accounting values and accounting practice

Values of the accounting subculture are likely to influence certain aspects of accounting practice, namely (a) the authority for accounting systems, (b) their force of application; (c) the measurement practices used; and (d) the extent of the information disclosed (Gray, 1985). In particular, the degree of professionalism, preferred in an accounting subculture would influence the nature of authority for the accounting system. The higher the degree of professionalism the greater the degree of professional self-regulation and the lower the need for government intervention. The degree of uniformity preferred in an accounting subculture would have an effect on the manner in which the accounting system is applied. The higher the degree of uniformity, the lower the extent of professional judgement and the stronger the force applying accounting rules and procedures. The amount of conservatism preferred in an accounting subculture would influence the measurement practices used. The higher the degree of conservatism, the stronger the ties with traditional measurement practices. The degree of secrecy preferred in an accounting subculture would influence the extent of the information disclosed in accounting reports. The higher the degree of secrecy, the lower the extent of disclosure. These associations between culture-based societal values and accounting systems are set out in Figure 18.1.

Table 18.1		
Direct associations between societal and accounting values		
Values of accounting subculture	Relationship with societal values	
	Positive	**Negative**
Professionalism	Individualism	Uncertainty avoidance
Uniformity	Uncertainty avoidance	Individualism
Conservatism	Uncertainty avoidance	Individualism
Secrecy	Uncertainty avoidance	Individualism

Figure 18.1
Societal values and accounting practice

Societal values managerial/work related values →	Accounting values →	Accounting practice
Individualism v collectivism	Professionalism	Authority
Large v small power distance	Uniformity	Application
Strong v weak uncertainty avoidance	Conservatism	Measurement
Masculinity v femininity	Secrecy	Disclosure

Source: Adapted from Gray, 1985

However, any given aspect of accounting practice may be influenced by more than one accounting value. For example, the extent of disclosure is likely to be influenced not only by the degree of secrecy, but also by the degrees of conservatism, uniformity and professionalism preferred in an accounting subculture. The higher the degree of conservatism, the more prudence will be preferred to disclosure; the higher the degree of uniformity (or the lower the degree of professionalism), the more emphasis placed on compliance rather than disclosure. Therefore, the extent of disclosure in financial reports would seem to differ between countries in line with differences in the value orientations of the preparers of those reports.

Accounting and culture

On a broader perspective, societal values are affected by ecological influences through geographic, economic, demographic, historical, technological and urbanisation factors, which in turn are influenced by external factors, such as the forces of nature, trade, investment and conquest.

Alternatively, both ecological factors and societal values influence a society's institutional arrangements with regard to the legal and political systems, corporate ownership,

capital market, professional associations, education, religion and so on, which impact upon accounting values and accounting practices. These relationships are set out in Figure 18.2.

The foregoing analysis suggests some association between societal values and accounting values (hence accounting systems). Understandably, the associations are complex. Table 18.1 and Figures 18.1 and 18.2 indicate general relationships, based on a consideration of Hofstede's findings and an analysis of the activities of accountants. One could articulate some specific hypotheses on the basis of these relationships. The figures and table incorporate four variables concerning culture-based societal values, that is individualism versus collectivism, large versus small power distance, strong versus weak uncertainty avoidance, masculinity versus femininity; and four values of an accounting subculture, that is professionalism, uniformity, conservatism and secrecy.

Focusing on the relationship between societal values and the accounting subculture (and disregarding for the moment the link between the accounting subculture and accounting systems), Figure 18.2 could be restated as a series of specific hypotheses about those relationships, for instance:

1

The greater the individualism and the smaller the uncertainty avoidance within a society, *then* the greater the professionalism (or the smaller the uniformity) exhibited within an accounting subculture.

Corollary

2

The less the individualism and the greater the uncertainty avoidance within a society, *then* the less the professionalism (or the greater the uniformity) exhibited within an accounting subculture.

3

The greater the uncertainty avoidance and the less the individualism within a society, *then* the greater the conservatism exhibited within an accounting subculture.

Corollary

4

The smaller the uncertainty avoidance and greater the individualism within a society,

Figure 18.2
Accounting and culture

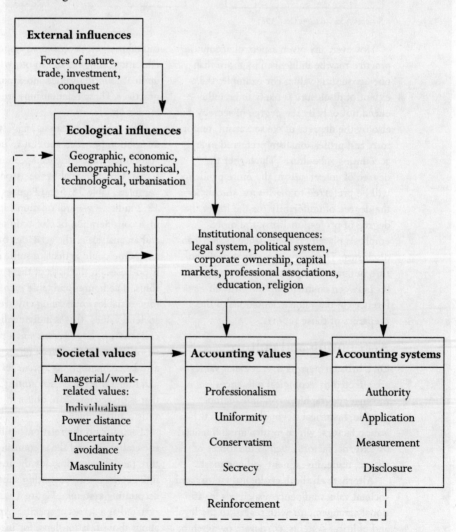

then the smaller the conservatism exhibited within an accounting system.

5

The greater the uncertainty avoidance and the less the individualism within a society, *then* the greater the secrecy exhibited within an accounting subculture.

Corollary

6

The smaller the uncertainty avoidance and greater the individualism within a society, *then* the smaller the secrecy exhibited within an accounting subculture.

As stated earlier, the above hypotheses were developed from Hofstede's observations and classification of circumstances in 1968–1973. Hofstede was concerned with management practices, and not with accounting values and practices or associations relevant to accounting values and practices. It would be possible to replicate the above analysis by remeasuring variables to see whether the relationships hypothesised from 1968–1973 data still hold in the 1990s.

The cultural relativity of accounting

Anglo-American and Continental European systems of accounting

As a result of many attempts at classifying countries according to their accounting systems, it has been suggested that significant differences exist between Anglo-American countries and Continental European countries in terms of their patterns of accounting development. The Anglo-American countries are grouped as micro-business practice-based systems whereas the European countries, with the exception of the Netherlands, are grouped together as macro-uniform systems (Mueller, 1967, Nobes, 1983; 1984).

The differences identified in the accounting systems between Anglo-

American and Continental European countries can be explained in terms of their cultural environments. The primary influence on the development of accounting principles and practices in France has been the General Accounting Plan, rather than the pronouncements of the accounting profession. Similarly, in Germany, as demand for industrial capital increased during the second half of the nineteenth century, strong banks, rather than individuals, organised by a promoter, emerged as suppliers of a significant portion of that capital.

Table 18.1 shows some direct associations between societal values and accounting values. Accordingly, where there is a high level of individualism in a society it will have a positive effect on the degree of professionalism and negative effects on the degrees of uniformity, conservatism and secrecy preferred in the accounting subculture. Where there is strong uncertainty avoidance in a society it will have a negative effect on the degree of professionalism and positive effects on the degrees of uniformity, conservatism and secrecy preferred in its accounting subculture. The former represents the situation in Anglo-American countries while the latter conditions apply in Continental European countries, particularly France and Germany.

These two countries are high on the uncertainty avoidance scale, whereas Anglo-American countries are relatively low on the same scale. The characteristics of the uncertainty avoidance dimension reveal that in cultures which are high on the scale, behaviour tends to be more rigidly prescribed, either by written rules or by unwritten social codes; the presence of these rules satisfies people's emotional needs for order and predictability in society, and people feel uncomfortable in situations where there are no rules. In cultures low on the scale, although there will be written and unwritten rules, people are able to live comfortably in situations where there are no rules. Therefore, in general one can expect more formalisation and institutionalisation of procedures in strong uncertainty avoidance societies than in weak uncertainty avoidance countries.

There is a preference for the exercise of individual professional judgement, the maintenance of professional self-regulation and flexibility in accordance with the perceived circumstances of individual companies in the accounting subcultures of Anglo-American countries, whereas there is a preference for compliance with prescriptive legal requirements and statutory control, the maintenance of uniform accounting practices between companies and the consistent application application of such practices over time in the accounting subcultures of Continental Europe. Also, there is more support in the latter group for a prudent and cautious approach to measurement to cope with the uncertainty of future events and the confidentiality of the information by restricting disclosures to only those involved with the management and financing of the organisation. These characteristics in turn tend to influence the degree of disclosure expected in the respective accounting systems or practices. For example, in France and Germany, where the level of professionalism is relatively low and the preference for conservatism and secrecy is relatively high, the combined effect on the degree of disclosure will be negative. In contrast, the collectivist or anti-individualist values of the society require business enterprises to be accountable to society by way of providing information. Therefore it becomes necessary for the government to intervene and lay down certain disclosure requirements, including those in regard to social accounting. For an analysis of the impact of culture upon social accounting disclosures, see Perera and Mathews (1990). Furthermore, this situation is not likely to be rejected by the accounting profession because, as discussed earlier, there is a preference for compliance with prescriptive legal regulation and statutory control in the

accounting subculture. By comparison, in the USA and UK, although the relatively high level of professionalism and the low level of preference for conservatism and secrecy tend to have a positive combined effect on the degree of disclosure in accounting practices, the individualistic values of the society are more concerned with the provision of information to shareholders or investors than with those issues involving accountability to society at large.

Accounting in developing countries

Hofstede's survey results clearly demonstrate that there are significant cultural differences between Anglo-American countries and many developing countries (see Appendix). These differences are most easily identifiable in the areas associated with the dimensions of individualism/collectivism and power distance. The identified characteristics of these dimensions raise some important issues in regard to accounting matters which involve the above two groups of countries, for example the transfer of accounting skills to developing countries. It may be that the skills so transferred from Anglo-American countries do not work because they are culturally irrelevant or dysfunctional in the receiving countries' context (Hofstede, 1983b). To the extent that accounting skills are culturally specific, these differences are certain to create gaps in virtually any such transfer which includes accounting standards and practices.

The developing countries in general are at the bottom end of the individualism versus collectivism scale. This indicates a relatively low degree of professionalism in the accounting subculture. As a result, there will be little regard for adequacy or accuracy of the published information. Therefore, an active role for governments in developing accounting principles and providing legal authority is likely to result in a higher reliability of published financial information, which may be essential for creating public confidence and trust in companies, and for creating an atmosphere where industrialisation can progress in these countries.

Most developing countries can be categorised as strong uncertainty avoidance societies, since the future remains essentially unpredictable and there is a high degree of anxiety among people. In such societies there is an emotional need for legal protection and government interference to safeguard the public interest. In addition, being large power distance societies, there is a high degree of centralisation of authority in developing countries and there tends to be a psychological need for dependence of the people without power. These factors would seem to indicate favourable conditions for legal and government control of accounting.

Furthermore, since developing countries in general are collectivist oriented, they tend to demonstrate a strong preference for maintenance of uniform practices between companies and consistency of practices over time. They are not likely to resist uniformity on the grounds of individualist values such as preference for flexibility in action. Also, to the extent that they are strong uncertainty avoidance societies, where there is an emotional need for formalisation to guide behaviour. This is supported by a tendency to regard deviant ideas as a threat and not to tolerate them. Finally, since all developing countries are large power distance societies, there is a significant emphasis on maintaining order, which is also a factor in favour of uniformity. Gray's (1985) classification of countries on the basis of accounting values clearly reflects these tendencies.

Internationalisation of accounting standards

It has been demonstrated that the standard-setting process of the IASC is strongly influenced by the Anglo-American accounting model (Perera, 1985). As a result, IASs tend to reflect the circumstances and the pattern of thinking in a particular group of countries. In view of the issues raised in this chapter, the IASs are likely to face additional problems of relevance in countries where different cultural environments exist from those found in Anglo-American countries.

Chapter summary

The impact of cultural factors upon accounting has been the subject of detailed discussion among researchers of international accounting in recent years. Clearly, there are many aspects of accounting theory and practice which are likely to be influenced by the value orientation of the preparers and users of accounting information. Some researchers have even attempted to classify the accounting systems of different countries on the basis of cultural factors.

In this chapter an attempt has been made to identify the mechanism by which the cultural factors are likely to influence the accounting system of a country and to explain some of the differences in accounting practices between countries in terms of cultural factors. However, the research results so far do not provide any conclusive evidence to support or to reject the view that accounting is culturally specific. Therefore, there is a need for further research in this important area of accounting.

Essay and examination questions

18.1 What is meant by the statement that accounting is culture bound?

18.2 Discuss the likely impact of the culture-based societal value dimension of individualism versus collectivism upon accounting.

18.3 Discuss the likely impact of the culture-based societal value dimension of large versus small power distance upon accounting.

18.4　Discuss the likely impact of the culture-based societal value dimension of strong versus weak uncertainty avoidance on accounting.

18.5　What are the aspects of accounting practice that are most likely to be affected by cultural factors?

18.6　Explain what is meant by accounting subculture. How does it relate to the national culture of a country?

18.7　How do you distinguish between the accounting subcultures of different countries?

18.8　Explain some of the accounting differences between Anglo-American and Continental European countries in terms of their cultural orientations.

18.9　What are the aspects of the transfer of accounting technology between countries which are likely to be affected by their cultural differences?

18.10　International accounting standards are likely to encounter additional problems of relevance in countries where different cultural environments from those found in Anglo-American countries exist. Explain and discuss.

References and additional reading

Abel, R. (1971). The impact of environment on accounting practices: Germany in the thirties. *International Journal of Accounting Education and Research*, Fall, 29–47.

American Institute of Certified Public Accountants (1973). *Objectives of Financial Statements*. New York: AICPA.

Ansari, S.L. and Bell, J. (1985). Implications of culture for the study of accounting and control systems. Paper presented at the EIASM Workshop on Accounting and Culture, Amsterdam, June.

Arpan, J.S. and Radebaugh, L.H. (1985). *International Accounting and Multinational Enterprises*. John Wiley.

Barrett, V.M. (1977). The extent of disclosure in annual reports of large companies in seven countries. *International Journal of Accounting Education and Research,* Spring, 1–25.

Berry, J. (1975). An ecological approach to cross-cultural psychology. *Netherlands Journal of Psychology,* **30**, 51–85.

Bromwich, M. and Hopwood, A.G. (1983). *Accounting Standard Setting: An International Perspective*. Pitman.

Choi, F.D.S. and Mueller, G.G. (1984). *International Accounting*. Prentice Hall.

Cushing, B.E. (Ed.) (1987). *Accounting and Culture*. Plenary session papers and discussants' comments from the 1986 Annual Meeting of the American Accounting Association, Sarasota: AAA.

Da Costa, R.C., Bourgeois, J.C. and Lawson, W.M. (1978). A classification of international financial accounting practices. *International Journal of Accounting Education and Research*, Spring, 1978.

Dent, J. and Green, S. (1985). Notes towards a framework for the cross cultural analysis of accounting practice, Paper presented at the EIASM Conference on Accounting and Culture, Amsterdam, June.

Financial Accounting Standards Board (1978). *Statement of Financial Accounting Concepts No. 1: Objectives of Financial Reporting by Business Enterprises,* Stamford: FASB.

Gambling, T. (1984). Accounting for rituals: Or the camel-drivers' guide to left-hand financing. Informal discussion paper, Department of Business Studies, England: Portsmouth Polytechnic.

Gray, S.J. (1985). Cultural influences and the international classification of accounting systems. Paper presented at Workshop on 'Accounting and Culture', European Institute for Advanced Studies in Management, Amsterdam, June.

Gray, S.J. (1988). Towards a theory of cultural influence on the development of accounting systems Internationally. *Abacus*, March, 1–36.

Hofstede, G. (1980). *Culture's Consequences*: Sage Publications.

Hofstede, G. (1983a). Dimensions of national cultures in fifty countries and three regions, in J.B. Deregowski, S. Dziurawiec and R.C. Annis (Ed.), *Expiscations in Cross-Cultural Psychology*. Swets and Zeitlinger, 335–355.

Hofstede, G. (1983b). *Culture and Management Development*. Geneva: International Labour Office.

Hofstede, G. (1983c). The cultural relativity of organizational practices and theories. *Journal of International Business Studies,* Fall.

Hofstede, G. (1984). National cultures revisited. *Asia and Pacific Journal of Management,* September.

Hofstede, G. (1985). The ritual nature of accounting systems. Paper presented at EIASM Workshop 'Accounting and Culture', Amsterdam, June.

Hofstede, G. (1985). The ritual nature of accounting systems. Paper presented at the EIASM Workshop on Accounting and Culture, Amsterdam, June.

Hofstede, G. (1987). The cultural context of accounting. In Cushing, B.E. (Ed.) (1987). *Accounting and culture*. Plenary session papers and discussants' comments from the 1986 Annual Meeting of the AAA, Sarasota, Florida: AAA.

Mueller, G.G. (1967). *International Accounting.* New York: Macmillan.

Mueller, G. (1985). Is accounting culturally determined? Paper presented at EIASM Workshop 'Accounting and Culture', Amsterdam (June).

Nobes, C.W. (1983). A judgemental international classification of financial reporting practices. *Journal of Business Finance and Accounting*, Spring, 1–19.

Nobes, C.W. (1984). *International Classification of Financial Reporting.* Croom Helm.

Nobes, C.W. and Parker, R.H. (1985). *Comparative International Accounting,* Oxford: Philip Allan.

Perera, M.H.B. (1985). *International Accounting Standards to Developing Countries,* Research Report, School of Financial Studies, University of Glasgow, UK.

Perera, M.H.B. (1989). Towards a framework to analyze the impact of culture on accounting. *International Journal of Accounting Education and Research,* **24**(1), 42–56.

Perera, M.H.B. (1994). Culture and international accounting: Some thoughts on research issues and prospects. *Advances in International Accounting,* **7**, 265–283.

Perera, M.H.B. and Mathews, M.R. (1990). The cultural relativity of accounting and international patterns of social accounting. *Advances in International Accounting.* **3**. New York: Jai Press Inc. 215–251.

Radebaugh, L.H. and Gray, S.J. (1993). *International Accounting and Multinational Enterprises*, third edition, New York: John Wiley.

Smircich, L. (1983). Concept of culture and organizational analysis. *Administrative Science Quarterly*, September.

Takatera, S. and Yamamoto, M. (December 1987). The cultural significance of accounting in Japan. Paper presented at Workshop on 'Accounting and Culture', European Institute for Advanced Studies in Management, Brussels.

Thomas, A.P. (1989). The effects of organisational culture on choices of accounting methods. *Accounting and Business Research*, **76**(19), 363–378.

Triandis, H. (1980). Reflections on trends in cross-cultural psychology. *Journal of Cross-Cultural Psychology,* March, 35–58.

Appendix

Country	Power distance		Uncertainty avoidance		Individualism		Masculinity	
	Index	Rank	Index	Rank	Index	Rank	Index	Rank
Argentina	49	18–19	86	36–41	46	28–29	56	30–31
Australia	36	13	51	17	90	49	61	35
Austria	11	1	70	26–27	55	33	79	49
Belgium ·	65	33	94	45–46	75	43	54	29
Brazil	69	39	76	29–30	38	25	49	25
Canada	39	15	48	12–13	80	46–47	52	28
Chile	63	29–30	86	36–41	23	15	28	8
Colombia	67	36	80	31	13	5	64	39–40
Costa Rica*	35	10–12	86	36–41	15	8	21	5–6
Denmark	18	3	23	3	74	42	16	4
Ecuador*	78	43–44	67	24	8	2	63	37–38
Finland	33	8	59	20–21	63	34	26	7
France	68	37–38	86	36–41	71	40–41	43	17–18
Germany (F.R.)	35	10–12	65	23	67	36	66	41–42
Great Britain	35	10–12	35	6–7	89	48	66	41–42
Greece	60	26–27	112	50	35	22	57	32–33
Guatemala*	95	48–49	101	48	6	1	37	11
Hong Kong	68	37–38	29	4–5	25	16	57	32–33
Indonesia*	78	43–44	48	12–13	14	6–7	46	22
India	77	42	40	9	48	30	56	30–31
Iran	58	24–25	59	20–21	41	27	43	17–18
Ireland	28	5	35	6–7	70	39	68	43–44
Israel	13	2	81	32	54	32	47	23
Italy	50	20	75	28	76	44	70	46–47
Jamaica*	45	17	13	2	39	26	68	43–44
Japan	54	21	92	44	46	28–29	95	50
Korea (S)*	60	26–27	85	34–35	18	11	39	13
Malaysia*	104	50	36	8	26	17	50	26–27
Mexico	81	45–46	82	33	30	20	69	45
Netherlands	38	14	53	18	80	46–47	14	3
Norway	31	6–7	50	16	69	38	8	2
New Zealand	22	4	49	14–15	79	45	58	34
Pakistan	55	22	70	26–27	14	6–7	50	26–27
Panama*	95	48–49	86	36–41	11	3	44	19
Peru	64	31–32	87	42	16	9	42	15–16
Philippines	94	47	44	10	32	21	64	39–40
Portugal	63	29–30	104	49	27	18–19	31	9
South Africa	49	18–19	49	14–15	65	35	63	37–38
Salvador*	66	34–35	94	45–46	19	12	40	14
Singapore	74	40	8	1	20	13–14	48	24
Spain	57	23	86	36–41	51	31	42	15–16
Sweden	31	6–7	29	4–5	71	40–41	5	1
Switzerland	34	9	58	19	68	37	70	46–47
Taiwan	58	24–25	69	25	17	10	45	20–21
Thailand	64	31–32	64	22	20	13–14	34	10
Turkey	66	34–35	85	34–35	37	24	45	20–21
Uruguay*	61	28	100	47	36	23	38	12
USA	40	16	46	11	91	50	62	36
Venezuela	81	45–46	76	29–30	12	4	73	48
Yugoslavia	76	41	88	43	27	18–19	21	5–6
Regions:								
East Africa*	64	(31–32)	52	(17–18)	27	(18–19)	41	(14–15)
West Africa*	77	(42)	54	(18–19)	20	(13–14)	46	(22)
Arab ctrs*	80	(44–45)	68	(24–25)	38	(25)	53	(28–29)

(*New data)

Learning objectives

After studying this chapter the reader will be able to:

- identify and explain reasons why managers might include non-traditional socially-oriented disclosures in annual reports
- explain the concept of the social contract between business and society
- discuss the concept of organisational legitimacy and the role it may have in motivating management to make non-traditional socially-oriented disclosures in annual reports
- consider the main arguments in favour of total impact accounting
- examine the main components in value for money auditing and explain its relationship to socio-economic accounting.

Introduction

Social accounting is a relatively new development of great potential for the accounting discipline. It might have widespread implications or conversely it might not develop at all. The reasons for suggesting these diverse outcomes will become apparent from the material covered in this chapter.

Social accounting means many things to many people; consequently definition and analysis are difficult tasks to accomplish. First, the subject area is relatively new; second, by its nature any attempt to account for the impact of organisations upon their social environment is bound to incorporate a political dimension. At the very least, social accounting means an extension of disclosure into non-traditional areas such as providing information about employees, products, community service and the prevention or reduction of pollution. However, the term 'social accounting' is also used to describe a comprehensive form of accounting which takes into account externalities (the costs imposed on the public by private sector organisations) as well as the more usual private costs. Public sector organisations may also be evaluated in this way, although most writers on the subject of social accounting appear to be concerned with private sector organisations.

Socially related non-traditional disclosures have been made in annual reports for some time. The type and extent of disclosures have been measured and recorded (Ernst and Ernst, 1972–78; Guthrie and Mathews, 1985; Brooks, 1986; Gray, Owen and Maunders, 1987). However, this type of measurement of social disclosures in annual reports is likely to suffer from subjectivity on the part of the analyst. What one observer believes to be meaningful, socially oriented information, another will see as public relations 'puff'; yet another will allege that the corporation is using these disclosures to create or maintain a dominant position in relation to its environment. Subjectivity is an ongoing problem, to which answers have been sought through the development of uniform content analysis (Guthrie and Mathews, 1985). Despite measurement and integration problems, the development of narrative and non-traditional reporting in the annual report has increased to such an extent that it cannot be ignored by modern accountants.

The chapter is divided into two parts: first, a discussion of the reasons why management may provide voluntary non-traditional disclosures in annual reports and, second, an examination of the different types of social accounting. The arguments put forward for the production of socially oriented information include: attempts to influence capital markets; recognition of the social contract between business and society; and acceptance of the concept of organisational legitimacy or, as some critical theorists would argue, an attempt to manipulate the environment in which the organisation operates. The framework used to examine social accounting covers the public and private sectors, long and short time periods and financial and non-financial measurement systems.

Arguments to justify additional disclosures

Managements of corporations are already required by law to make significant disclosures to shareholders (and indirectly to other parties) about the periodic performance and financial condition of the enterprise. The cumulative effects of Companies Acts, stock exchange listing requirements and the requirements of the accounting profession have led to significant disclosures being made about the organisation. It may

be argued that any further disclosures, financial or non-financial, must be justified in terms of the additional expenditure involved and the resulting benefits for the various user groups. This need for justification may be strongest where non-traditional disclosures of a social nature are involved, on the grounds that this additional information is untried and unproven, not requested by shareholders and of most use to non-shareholder groups. These are powerful objections and the issue of justification needs to be seriously addressed.

Attempts to influence capital markets

A number of empirical studies have attempted to demonstrate that a relationship exists between the disclosure of socially-oriented information and improved market performance as measured by share price or return on capital employed. Results have been conflicting, with some studies finding a positive relationship, while others do not indicate that any relationship exists. To the extent that managers believe that making socially-related disclosures will result in a favourable effect on the share market price of their company's stock, then they may be motivated to make these

Table 19.1
Choice of social responsibility measure

Method	Studies
1 Subjective ratings of corporation performance	Parket and Eilbirt (1975) Sturdivant and Ginter (1977)
2 Quasi-objective ratings based on annual report content or structural analysis	Bowman and Haire (1975) Vance (1975) Alexander and Bucholz (1978) Ingram (1978) Abbott and Monsen (1979)
3 Pollution measures as reported by companies themselves	Belkaoui (1976) Mahapatra (1984)
4 Pollution measures as reported by parties other than the companies	Fogler and Nutt (1975) Spicer (1978) Stevens (1982) Shane and Spicer (1983) Freedman and Stagliano (1984)

disclosures. Consequently, to them this would be a justification for non-traditional forms of accounting disclosure.

All the studies making up the market studies part of the social accounting literature attempt to relate some measure of social responsibility to measures of market performance. The choice of a measure of social responsibility varies widely as shown in Table 19.1.

Each of the four groups are reported separately as Tables 19.2 to 19.5 respectively. A reasonable amount of detail is provided, sufficient to identify the main features of each study and the results obtained. The format of these tables is taken from a survey by Arlow and Gannon (1982) but has been extended beyond the date of their article.

It can be seen that the outcome of these studies suggests a positive relationship between the subjective rating of the social responsibility performance of the corporation and the market measures. Table 19.3 repeats the same general approach but utilises measures of social responsibility performance which appear to be more objective, although still relying on judgement to a considerable extent.

Table 19.2
Studies using subjective ratings of corporate performance

Study	Sample	Indicator of social performance	Indicator of market performance	Outcome of study
1 Parket and Eilbirt (1975)	80 firms in 1971 Forbes Roster of Biggest Corporations	Author's judgement	NI NI as a per cent of sales NI as a per cent of shareholders equity EPS	Socially responsible firms (80) have greater median values on all dimensions compared to 1973 Fortune 500 list
2 Sturdivant and Ginter (1977)	28 corporations in 1975 Fortune 500	Moskowitz's ratings of best or worst, and authors' rating honourable mention	Growth in EPS relative to industry average 1967 to 1974	Best and honourable mention have significantly higher growth in EPS than worst

Table 19.3
Studies using quasi-objective ratings based upon annual reports or 'structural analysis'

Study	Sample	Indicator of social performance	Indicator of market performance	Outcome of study
1 Bowman and Haire (1975)	82 firms in food processing in 1973 Moody's *Industrial Manual*	Per cent of prose on social responsibility in annual report	Mean or median ROE 1968 to 1972 or 1969 to 1973	Both mean and median ROE higher for firms with some discussion than none. Medium mention firms have significantly greater median ROE than either high or low mention
2 Vance (1975)	45 and 50 major corporations	Ratings by students and executives in 1972 *Business and Society Review*	Per share stock price 1/1/75 as per cent 1/1/74 price	Average ratings of both groups negatively correlated with 1974 stock market performance
3 Alexander and Bucholz (1978)	41 firms from Vance (1975)	Same as Vance (1975)	Risk adjusted ROE 1970 to 1974 and 1971 to 1973	No significant relationships
4 Abbott and Monsen (1979)	450 corporations in 1975 Fortune 500. (Number of social action disclosures in annual reports)	Social involvement Disclosure scale	Total returns to investors 1964–1974	No meaningful difference in total returns to investors for high and low involvement firms
5 Ingram (1978)	287 Fortune 500 companies (1970 to 1976)	SRA disclosures Annual reports	Compustat Price dividends Earnings tape	Information content of firms' social responsibility disclosures conditional upon market segment rather than a general cross section of firms

Table 19.4
Pollution measures reported by companies

Study	Sample	Indicator of social performance	Indicator of market performance	Outcome of study
1 Belkaoui (1976)	Two groups of 50 US corporations from different industries	Pollution control expenses at least 1 per cent of sales plus control group	Monthly closing stock prices 12 months before and after disclosures Standard and Poor 500	Substantial but temporary positive effect on stock market prices for companies disclosing pollution expenditures
2 Mahapatra (1984)	67 firms from six industries 60 firms as control group (1967 to 1968)	Expenditure on pollution control	Compustat PDE tape	Pollution control expenditure and high profitability not positively associated Expenditures for pollution control do not automatically lead to higher market returns

Table 19.5
Pollution measures not reported by corporations: use of CEP Reports

Study	Sample	Indicator of social performance	Indicator of market performance	Outcome of study
1 Fogler and Nutt (1975)	Nine paper companies	Government pollution indices	P/E ratio. Mutual fund purchases (in dollars). Common stock price. (Data from selected quarters 1971)	No positive relationships
2 Spicer (1978)	18 firms in pulp and paper industry 1968 to 1973	CEP studies of pollution control developed into a pollution index, related to productive capacity and plant numbers	Profitability, size, total risk, systematic risk, price–earnings ratio	Companies with better pollution control records tend to have higher profitability, larger size, lower total risks, lower systematic risks and higher price–earnings ratios than companies with poorer pollution control records. Relatively short lived phenomena
3 Stevens (1982)	54 firms in four industries subject to CEP reports	CEP pollution reports	Effect of disclosure (through CEP reports of pollution status of corporation) on earnings per share	Cumulative average excess returns for portfolios of firms with 'high' estimated expenditures for pollution control are consistently below the returns for portfolios of firms with 'low' estimated expenditure
4 Shane and Spicer (1983)	72 firms in four industry areas	CEP pollution reports	Share prices over a six-day period before and after publication of CEP reports	Sample firms large negative abnormal returns on two days immediately prior to newspaper reports of release of CEP studies. Low rankings associated with more negative returns on publication
5 Freedman and Stagliano (1984)	27 weaving, finishing and knitting mills (1984)	OSHA dust disclosures through SEC 10 reports	Stock price movements	Disclosures on impact of new cotton dust emission standard significant information content for investors

The results set out in Table 19.3 show considerable variation, with Bowman and Haire (1975) showing a positive relationship especially for companies with a medium rate of social responsibility, and Ingram (1978) showing positive results when using a market segment approach. However, the other contributors found either no relationship or a negative relationship. It should be noted that a negative relationship still demonstrates information content to market participants. Table 19.4 shows the results of studies which have used pollution-related measures supplied by the companies themselves. Belkaoui (1976) found some short term increase in share prices as a result of disclosures:

> In general, this study refutes the suggestion that the worst offenders in the reporting of social costs will be rewarded more in the capital market. In fact, on the basis of these results, managers may be advised to allocate a proportion of their resources to pollution control and to report these expenditures to the stockholders. (p.30)

However, Mahapatra (1984) demonstrated that the 'ethical investor' was not active at the time his study was undertaken, since the results are consistent with the existence of a 'rational economic investor':

> The conclusion is that the investors view pollution control expenditures, legally or voluntary, as a drain on resources which could have been invested profitably, and do not 'reward' the companies for socially responsible behaviour. Thus an average investor is not an 'ethical investor' and industries and investors left to themselves do not have any incentive to spend for pollution control and manifest socially desirable behaviour. (p.37)

The studies in Table 19.5 are perhaps the most important in the series. They are generally more recent; they employ greater degrees of sophistication in the analysis; and they have a uniform basis, namely the reports on pollution activities of industries and companies supplied by outside parties.

Results may be described as mixed since, while Fogler and Nutt (1975) did not find any positive relationships, Spicer (1978) found that for a limited sample of pulp and paper companies the disclosures by an outside body (the Council on Economic Priorities) were associated with profitability, size of company, total risk, systematic risk and price–earnings. All associations were in the direction favouring disclosure. In other words, shareholders would benefit if companies worked towards better pollution control records. This study was criticised by Chen and Metcalf (1980) on a number of grounds. In his reply Spicer stressed the findings as *associations* between variables and not *caused relationships*.

In contrast to the positive findings of Spicer, the work of Stevens (1982), Shane and Spicer (1983) and Freedman and Stagliano (1984) show either a negative association between disclosures and share prices or no information content resulting from social responsibility accounting (SRA) disclosures. Stevens (1982) found that 'high' estimated expenditures for pollution control were associated with lower cumulative average excess returns, in comparison to 'low' estimated expenditures. The disclosures had information content, but present shareholders would suffer a loss of capital value as the information becomes available to the market. In the longer term, however, Stevens (1982, p.25) argued that shareholders should benefit from the increased supply of information:

> The data examined in this study represent a source of information which may have been previously unavailable to the market. As such, its publication could provide meaningful data for assessing the timing and magnitude of future cash flows.

Shane and Spicer (1983, p.353) demonstrated that the use of externally produced and publicised environmental information may have an effect on the share prices of polluting corporations when the disclosures are first made. In a similar manner to Stevens, this study demonstrates the information effect of the disclosures, although to the short term discomfort of the present shareholders. However, given the importance of the efficient market and the manner in which the marginal investor reacts, it is interesting to note that: 'The reported results also are consistent with investors using the information released by the CEP to discriminate between companies with different pollution-control performance records' (Shane and Spicer, 1983, p.353). In the longer term this should achieve environmental goals of lower pollution levels.

Freedman and Stagliano (1984) found no evidence of information content since there was no positive or negative association of share prices with the particular pollution disclosures under investigation. The authors offer a number of possible explanations, including an efficient market which had already impounded the information before it was disclosed or a submarket for particular firms that was not efficient at all.

Although the findings from a number of studies are conflicting it may be argued that the overall weight lies towards a view that the disclosure of non-traditional information does have utility for shareholders and the security market. However, there are other, perhaps stronger, arguments in favour of social accounting disclosures.

The association of social accounting disclosures with the concept of a social contract

The arguments in favour of forms of social accounting which may be used for shareholders will not necessarily be relevant to a wider audience. Sharemarket reaction to disclosures is less meaningful to non-equity holders, employees, customers and the general public. To interest these parties in social

accounting it is necessary to look at the basic functioning of industrial and commercial activities and to enter the moral debate surrounding the notions of a social contract.

Although it is not difficult to find references to the need for corporations to be accountable to a wider audience (Nader, 1973), the moral position of the corporation is much more difficult to establish. It is only after satisfactorily answering questions about the moral position of the corporation that the notion of a social contract can be considered.

The moral position of the corporation

Two very different positions may be examined: the moral person view and the structural restraint view. The more simplistic approach is the moral person view, which argues that corporations are moral persons and therefore are moral agents. Consequently, corporations are morally responsible for their actions. There are clearly difficulties in establishing this case, since corporations cannot act intentionally by themselves or exercise the normal functions of persons. The opposite view is that corporations cannot be moral agents of any kind, because their actions are controlled by their structures and, therefore, they often cannot exercise moral freedom. If taken to an extreme position, the structural restraint view would mean that the only way in which the actions of corporations could be controlled (in any moral sense) would be by extensive legislation. However, corporations vary considerably in size, type and public stance on many issues, and these differences allow the specification of certain conditions by which a corporation may qualify as a moral agent.

Donaldson (1982, p.30) outlines these conditions as follows:

> In order to qualify as a moral agent, a corporation would need to embody a process of moral decision-making. On the basis of our previous discussion, this

process seems to require, at a minimum:
1 The capacity to use moral reason in decision-making,
2 The capacity of the decision-making process to control not only overt corporate acts, but also the structure of policies and rules.

Corporations may qualify as moral agents (but not moral persons) if they subscribe to the conditions above. If not, there would seem to be support for a structural restraint view (which in turn may mean legislative control).

Donaldson suggests that one of the conditions for qualifying as a corporation would be that an organisation meets the conditions of moral agency. This view is reinforced by the rights and responsibilities which corporations possess and which point to conditions of moral agency being associated with conditions of corporate status (1982, pp.31–32). Corporate rights are granted in most developed industrial countries and include limited liability for the shareholders and unlimited life, the ability to sue and be sued and contractual rights as of a natural person for the corporation. In return, the responsibilities owed by corporations to the rest of society (including other corporations) include a number of direct and indirect moral obligations.

Direct obligations are specified explicitly and involve shareholders, employees, suppliers and customers. Indirect obligations are not specified formally and may involve parties with whom the corporation has no direct relationship. These may include competitors, local communities and the general public. Breaches of direct obligations are usually identifiable and may be settled through the legal system or by adverse publicity, if not through the specified terms of the contract. It is the indirect obligations that cause problems because they are not readily identifiable, may not be agreed between the parties to disputes, and frequently give rise to measurement and

valuation problems, even where their existence can be agreed. The indirect obligations give rise to the notion of a social contract of business with society.

The social contract of business with society

The notion of a social contract originated in political philosophy, which argues that society in general accepts an overriding control over individual freedoms in order to achieve collective goals. However, the social contract underlies the arrangement and a failure to generate the goal-satisfying outcomes may justify a revolt on the part of the general society:

> The political social contract provides a clue for understanding the contract for business. If the political contract serves as a justification for the existence of the state, then the business contract by parity of reasoning should serve as the justification for the existence of the corporation. (Donaldson, 1982, p.37)

The social contract exists between corporations and individual members of society. Society (as a collection of individuals) provides productive organisations with legal standing and attributes as well as the authority to own and use land and natural resources and to hire employees. It may be argued that the productive organisation has no inherent rights to these goods because it draws on community resources and outputs waste products to the general environment. In order to allow the productive organisation to exist, society must expect the benefits to exceed the costs (detriments) of so doing.

The operations of productive organisations will benefit consumers and employees (taking these categories in the widest sense). Consumers (and potential consumers) will benefit if productive organisations maximise the advantages of specialisation; have greater capacities for decision making than individuals do; have greater opportunities to aggregate capital and use it to obtain high-level technology; generate distribution channels; and are able to compensate individuals for faulty products (or services). Employees will benefit from these organisations if they earn more than they would working for themselves; have the strength of the organisation behind them (that is they are not exposed as individuals); and receive benefits in terms of long-term earnings and security that they would not otherwise have. However, productive organisations accumulate power as well as wealth. This power enables them to interact with governments in a manner which may be to the disadvantage of the ordinary consumer. The generation and enhancement of monopoly power may result from these interactions.

Employees may suffer disbenefits from working in organisations, including alienation and an inability (in the case of lower level employees) to control their working conditions. Furthermore, in some cases the design of the productive system may lead to monotony and the dehumanisation of workers; the production assembly line of motor vehicles is a classic example.

In addition to the maximisation of the benefits and the minimisation of the disbenefits outlined above, the social contract between productive organisations and the individual members of society would include an element of justice.

As Donaldson (1982) expresses the issue:

> the application of the concept of justice to productive organizations appears to imply *that productive organizations avoid deception or fraud, that they show respect for their workers as human beings, and that they avoid any practice that systematically worsens the situation of a given group in society.* (p.53, original emphasis)

Concluding comments on the social contract

The productive organisation, according to Donaldson (1982), exists to satisfy certain social interests:

> Productive organizations . . . are subject to moral evaluations which transcend the boundaries of the political systems that contain them. The underlying function of all such organizations from the standpoint of society is to enhance social welfare through satisfying consumer and worker interests, while at the same time remaining within the bounds of justice. When they fail to live up to these expectations they are deserving of moral criticism. (p.57)

Once this view is accepted it also follows that any techniques of data collection, analysis and disclosure that enable society to evaluate the performance of the organisation are not only legitimate but desirable. This brings into focus the development of social accounting through which specific performance is monitored.

The concept of organisational legitimacy

Lindblom (1983) examined the concept of organisational legitimacy which suggests that management can influence the perception the general public has of the organisation. There has been a change from 'not doing harm' to 'doing something positive' in terms of the expectations of society towards business. At the same time, changes in the organisational structure of developed societies are making responses to changing societal needs more difficult and time consuming.

Lindblom (1983, pp.15–16) goes on to argue that the social contract leads logically to the concept of organisational legitimacy, which has been defined in the following way by Dowling and Pfeffer, as quoted by Lindblom:

Organizations seek to establish congru-
ence between the social values associated
with or implied by their activities and
the norms of acceptable behaviour in the
larger social system of which they are a
part. Insofar as these two value systems
are congruent we can speak of organizational legitimacy. When an actual or
potential disparity exists between the
two value systems, there will exist a
threat to organizational legitimacy.

It is argued that neither value in
exchange nor the observation of legal
requirements will establish organisational
legitimacy. This quality can only come from
a reference to the norms and values of society. The notion of organisational legitimacy
is not an absolute or a constant, because
organisations differ considerably in their
visibility to society as a whole and some
depend more heavily than others upon
social and political support. Organisational
legitimacy is summarised by Lindblom
(1983) in the following terms:

1. Legitimacy is not synonymous with
   economic success or legality.
2. Legitimacy is determined to exist
   when the organisation goals, output,
   and methods of operation are in con-
   formance with societal norms and
   values.
3. Legitimacy challenges are related to
   the size of the organisation and to the
   amount of social and political support
   it receives with the more visible
   being most likely to be challenged.
4. Legitimacy challenges may involve
   legal, political or social sanctions.
   (pp.20–21)

The implications which the notion of
organisational legitimacy have for the management of the corporation include better
communication with society. This enlarged
accounting or accountability may be
essential for the continued existence of the
corporation in its present form.

The arguments put forward by Lindblom
(1983) connect the philosophical propositions of the social contract as put forward
by Donaldson (1982) with the need for corporate social disclosures, via the notion of
organisational legitimacy. Managers do not
have to accept the social contract position;
they may engage in social disclosure in
order to satisfy their perception of organisational legitimacy.

The position of the critical theorists

Those who support a radical approach are
critical of most aspects of current society and
seek to change it. They are unlikely to support social accounting as a result of the arguments put forward in the three previous
sections, although some of the concepts used
in developing the moral agency view of the
productive organisation may receive encour-
agement. A radical group will be persuaded
to take an interest in social accounting only
by means of arguments framed in terms of
the radical paradigmatic view of society. In
the last few years there have been an increasing number of contributors to this debate.

In general, the radical view concludes
that accounting has supported, and continues to support, a particular view of society.
This view is associated with capitalistic production and marginalist economics, does
not admit to problematic relationships
between organisations and society, and follows a positivist approach. The radical
theorists are critical of the socially related
arguments because that view envisages a
plurality of approach, the evolution of
accounting and organisational developments
and the acceptance of much of the
capitalist-based production and ownership
systems. The radical literature emphasises
different aspects of the radical approach,
however, a number of basic characteristics
may be distinguished.
(a) The market (as a device for allocating
    resources) must be de-emphasised or
    even abolished.

(b) Corporations are owned, organised and operated in a manner that is designed to exploit entrenched power relationships.

(c) The accounting profession as it is currently organised is engaged in wittingly or unwittingly maintaining the *status quo* by attaching itself to one party to social conflict (capital) to the exclusion of the other main party (labour).

(d) The accounting profession engages in mystifying processes in order to exercise power. Value positions held by accountants are based on marginal economics and are deficient because of (a) above.

(e) Accountants are ignorant of the extent to which the discipline is both socially constructed and socially constructing.

(f) Accounting as a discipline must be changed to take account of social relationships in a much wider manner, perhaps by incorporating a labour theory of value.

(g) Accountants, accounting educators and accounting students must appreciate that they have a choice in their social relationships; they must consciously take sides in social conflict.

(h) Social accounting as presently advocated by most of the literature is deficient because: it considers only additional disclosures and perhaps externalities; does not envisage a change in the ownership of capital resources; would regulate the market mechanism rather than dispose of the market altogether; is too close to the marginalist economic position; and is based on an extension of the *status quo* with some modification. Social accounting is evolutionary rather than revolutionary when viewed from a radical perspective and consequently is considered inadequate or even obstructionist.

Given this synthesis of the radical position, it is reasonable to ask what contribution the radical paradigm can make towards social accounting in the form advocated by the mainstream literature. The radical paradigm provides an alternative view of the place of corporations in society, together with the accounting discipline which supports and regulates these corporations. It is a necessary view which can stimulate researchers and students to question their value systems and that of the discipline within which they work.

The problem with the radical approach to social accounting is that the literature may interest only those readers already prepared to question the basis of societal organisation (in Western capitalist economies). In other words the radical literature tends to be an example of 'preaching to the converted' in some ways, and will be ineffective when attempting to convince most accountants and managers of the need for social accounting. Alternatively, it might provide a worst-case example of the future if corporations do not change some aspects of their organisation and embrace notions of a wider accountability.

The normal relationship of accounting to society and social change is that of a service activity which reacts to change, not that of a policy making system which is proactive and initiates change. Consequently, accounting as a discipline evolves and the social accounting area is evolving only slowly. If society indicates, through the political process, a desire for more rapid changes in disclosure practices, then the accounting discipline will respond.

A summary of the justifications for non-traditional disclosures

This part of the chapter has used four approaches to associate attributes of social accounting with the arguments put forward by different parties. It is suggested that the attributes of social accounting associated with a particular user group may lead to a strategy by which greater acceptance of non-traditional accounting and the attendant use of additional discretionary resources may be achieved.

The first section introduced the market-related arguments which may be used to justify social accounting disclosures via research into the information content of additional disclosures and the effects that these may have on corporate income and stock market values. Evidence of an association, or of information content, may be of interest to groups associated with traditional shareholder and management roles. The research associating additional social responsibility accounting disclosures with share prices and other market-related indices was reviewed. Although the evidence is conflicting there does appear to be information content present in these disclosures. It was concluded that shareholders and creditors may be interested in this information and that a justification based upon shareholder usefulness may be a partial strategy to obtain additional information in the form of social accounting disclosures.

The socially related arguments discussed in the second and third sections may be used to develop the notion of a social contract between productive organisations and other groups. The moral agency of the corporation may be established and, through the notion of a social contract with business, other groups such as employees, customers and the general public may expect additional disclosures. A strategy for achieving a greater demand for social accounting by those who are sympathetic to additional disclosures might be to stress the complementary rights and obligations of the corporation through moral agency and not by a radical attack upon the basic system. This approach leads logically to an emphasis on organisational legitimacy as the pragmatic expression of social permission theory. Managers who are unable to accept the moral imperative of the social contract arguments may be prepared to consider the amoral position of the organisational legitimacy approach.

The Corporate Report (ASSC, 1975)

referred to the information needs of a wider group of users, including employees and the general public — all those with 'reasonable rights' to the information. Despite the far reaching and apparently radical nature of the recommendations contained in the Corporate Report, there do not really appear to be any radical political or organisational considerations involved. The market-related and socially-related approaches are different means of looking at the world without envisaging radical changes in organisational structures. The strength of these approaches is that the world is similar to that as seen by most shareholders, creditors, managers, customers, employees and the general public. These groups may be socially conditioned, nevertheless, such that their reactions are predictable and in favour of evolution rather than revolution.

The radical approach is discussed in the last section. It offers a most interesting field for research. However, there is a considerable difference between developing an interesting field for research and communication between academics and achieving a degree of acceptance by management, accounting practitioners and the general public. The radical paradigm is offered as an alternative to the proponents of the social permission theory, the social contract and theories about organisational legitimacy. The economic nature of the corporation is seen as a part of the whole to be considered along with social, moral and quality of life factors which cannot be processed through the market place. The motives and interactions of individuals and collectives are seen as problematic. A particular problem is the extent to which organisations can manipulate the regulatory environment within which they operate, including the regulation exercised over disclosures in annual reports.

The radical literature is, by definition, unsympathetic to the shareholder–creditor group considered above, and impatient with the evolutionary nature of the reform and changes contained in the socially-related arguments. Perhaps the research efforts of the radical paradigm might be directed towards large scale public sector developments in the areas categorised by the author as socio-economic and social indicators accounting, but the majority of radical theorists are concerned with private sector organisations. However, a radical strategy is unlikely to generate the climate in which a majority of managers, investors and accountants will be inclined to favour the development of social accounting.

Classifying the various types of social accounting

References to social accounting may be found in company reports, press releases, the news media and occasionally political speeches. The frequency of these references would suggest that social accounting might become increasingly important in the future, as the discipline of accounting is extended to include a variety of items not disclosed at present. However, the development of alternative disclosures is particularly subject to social and economic conditions. Consequently, it cannot be claimed that development will be continuous or without periods of regression. As discussed in the first part of the chapter, a number of alternative approaches may be used to justify a concern with this form of reporting.

However, the argument for an increase in socially relevant accounting information cannot be made simply by justifying the basic notion; a closely argued case must be clearly established for the implementation of the disclosures. The case for an extension of social accounting measurements and disclosures is affected by confusion and problems with measurement and evaluation. The confusion arises partly because the term 'social accounting' is used in different ways by different groups of people and the mea-

surement difficulties are always present in any new area; they are what accounting is all about. The disagreements about how far accountants should go in their measurement and reporting activities are traceable to fundamental differences in philosophies about disclosure and reporting. Indeed, some of the issues are much more complex than simply disclosure and reporting and extend deeply into the social fabric of the host society. Deeply ingrained value positions affect the accountant and the resulting disclosures.

It is argued that a framework or classification is needed for social accounting. Such a classification would be of assistance in formulating empirical research, in analysing the existing literature and in developing teaching programmes.

Furthermore, the fit between current disclosure practices and desired disclosures may be examined. Those who conduct research in the area of social accounting often experience some difficulty in explaining their work to others. The use of 'social' in conjunction with 'accounting' does not seem to work as well as the addition of 'financial', 'management' or 'tax'. These words add a large measure of explanation and precision to 'accounting' which 'social' does not. Perhaps one difficulty, not encountered by the descriptors given above, is the range of total activity included under social accounting. In this chapter the term is used to cover the following activities which are summarised in Table 19.6.

Social responsibility accounting

Social responsibility accounting refers to disclosures of financial and non-financial, quantitative and qualitative information about the activities of an enterprise. This area also includes employee reports, HRA and accounting and industrial democracy. Alternative terms in common use are social responsibility disclosures and corporate social reporting. This is the most usual type of social disclosure but perhaps lacks the depth of philosophical concern which is present in other areas of social accounting. Examples include disclosures about employees, products, energy usage, pollution prevention and support for community activities.

Total impact accounting

Total impact accounting (TIA) is used here to refer to the aggregate effect of the organisation on the environment. To establish this effect it is necessary to measure both private and public costs; the public costs involve the valuation of externalities. This is the basis of the expanding area of environmental accounting.

Socio-economic accounting

Socio-economic accounting (SEA) is the process of evaluating publicly funded activities, using financial and non-financial quantification. The entire activity should be evaluated, with a view to making judgements about the value of the expenditure undertaken, in relation to the outcomes achieved.

Social indicators accounting

The term social indicators accounting (SIA) is used to describe the measurement of macro-social events, in terms of setting objectives and assessing the extent to which these are attained. The outcomes of this analysis should be of interest to national policy makers.

Societal accounting

Societal accounting (SA) is used by some writers in this area to suggest a form of accounting which integrates all other forms into an overarching or meta theory. The discussion of SA is conceptual since implementation at this level is not seen as desirable or practical.

Table 19.6 shows the basic divisions or components of the framework. The dimensions are based upon a division between the private and public sectors, the time scale involved and the types of measurement used. Thus, the area of SRA is predominantly a private sector short-term reporting system, using mainly non-financial quantitative and qualitative data. The second division concerns the difficult problem of the identification, measurement, valuation and disclosure of externalities. Together, SRA and TIA make up what most of the literature refers to as social accounting. In contrast, the third division, socio-economic accounting, is concerned with public sector activity, using qualitative and quantitative data (of financial and non-financial types) to evaluate programmes in the short and medium terms. Social indicators accounting is the macro-activity which complements socio-economic accounting activity. Taken together, these activities are intended to improve the performance and accountability of public sector activities. Societal accounting conceptualises all accounting as interrelated.

Measurement

The AAA, in the report of the Committee on Social Costs (1975), suggested that three levels of measurement may be involved in the development of social accounting.

- Level I, where the activity is identified and described. Examples might be the identification of polluting materials which are being discharged into the environment.
- Level II, where the activity is measured using non-monetary units. The polluting materials are measured in terms of rate of discharge, the timing of flows and compliance with existing standards formulated in physical terms.
- Level III, where attempts are made to value the effects of the discharge. The measurements are converted to financial estimates of costs and benefits applicable to all stakeholders, ranging from shareholders to the general public.

Table 19.6
The characteristics of the various component parts of social accounting

Division	Purpose	Area of main use	Time scale	Measurements used	Associated areas
1 Social responsibility accounting (SRA)	Disclosure of individual items having a social impact	Private sector	Short term*	Mainly non-financial and qualitative AAA Levels I, II	Employee reports, human resource accounting, industrial democracy
2 Total impact accounting (TIA)	Measures the total cost (public and private) of running an organisation	Private sector	Medium and long term	Financial AAA Level III	Strategic planning, cost-benefit analysis, environmental accounting
3 Socio-economic accounting (SEA)	Evaluation of publicly funded projects involving both financial and non-financial measures	Public sector	Short and medium term	Financial and non-financial AAA Levels II and III	Cost-benefit analysis, planned programmed budgeting systems, zero based budgeting, institutional performance indicators, value for money audit
4 Social indicators accounting (SIA)	Long term non-financial quantification of societal statistics	Public sector	Long term	Non-financial quantitative AAA Level II	National income accounts, census statistics
5 Societal accounting (SA)	Attempts to portray accounting in global terms — overarching theories	Both all embracing	All	Financial aggregates	Systems theory, mega-accountancy trends

*Normally short term to fit annual reporting patterns
Source: Adapted from Mathews, 1984

The three levels of measurement may be illustrated by reference to sulphur dioxide gas, a common cause of pollution. If sulphur dioxide is discharged into the atmosphere it will soon be detected by its odour, and elementary analysis will confirm that the odour is caused by sulphur dioxide. This is a Level I measurement. The discharge measured over a period of time in units such as parts per million (ppm), will provide a Level II measurement. A Level III measurement is made when we convert the effect of the discharge into financial terms by attempting to value the damage which results from emissions such as the effect of acid rain on buildings or rivers. Some recent environmental responses from EU/OECD countries are listed in Table 19.7.

Table 19.7
Some recent environmental responses from EU/OECD countries

Australia
- proposals for 'Polluter Pays Principle' laws.

Belgium
- proposals to tax waste water and solid waste.

Denmark
- has a CFC tax and a tax on rubbish
- refundable deposits on drink containers, planned for car batteries
- new legislation to triple rubbish charge and increase cost of raw materials in process.

Finland
- introduced a carbon tax
- removed sales tax from 'green products'
- increases in taxes on single-trip containers, waste oil and phosphate fertilisers.

France
- charges business for air and water pollution and uses the revenue to subsidise investments in pollution control by industry
- is considering redesigning water charges to discourage farmers from using nitrate fertilisers.

Germany
- introduced tax incentives on catalytic converters on cars, plans to tax cars on noise and emissions basis not engine size
- charges for industrial pollution emissions; reducing the charge in the early years of the installation of pollution control equipment
- has more environmental economic measures than any EU country (but less than Finland and Sweden).

Holland
- introducing a new environmental plan
- plans energy taxes and tax on carbon dioxide emissions
- recent call for environmental disclosure in financial statements.

Ireland
- has been giving a lot of (politically unpopular) attention to a coal tax

Italy
- introducing a range of taxes on non-biodegradable materials
- implementing new taxes on sulphur dioxide, particulates, plastic products, herbicides and non-biodegradable industrial waste
- taxes on airport noise pollution.

Norway
- raised tax on petrol and charges a toll in cities
- refundable deposit on oil and batteries
- tax on CFCs being introduced.

Sweden
- recently increased taxation of pesticides and fertilisers
- VAT on energy
- specific taxes on carbon dioxide, sulphur and nitrous oxide emissions
- carbon tax introduced
- car-usage taxation is rising and likely to rise much further.

Table 19.7
(continued)

USA
- an established Environmental Protection Agency
- required disclosure of compliance with federal emission levels and associated costs
- have experimented for many years with forms of 'pollution licences' which, if not used by the owning company, can be sold to another polluter.

Source: Gray, 1990b, pp.55–56

The last type of measurement is the most difficult, because it involves valuation and the assignment of costs to events which are external to the organisation. Examples might be damage to the paintwork of neighbouring housing areas, the destruction of parks and gardens, and the creation of health problems. These valuation problems may be difficult to overcome and the values assigned to the effects of pollution will be open to dispute. The discounting to present value of the cost of future events, such as repairs or replacements or the payment of damages, is obviously problematic. These measurements are made, however, in calculating compensation for injury, loss of earnings or death from accident, thus providing some experience to aid the computation of other effects such as externalities. Even if the local pollution measurement and valuation issues can be resolved, difficulties will arise where the damage is remote from the source in terms of time and distance. To continue the sulphur dioxide example, the effects of low levels of atmospheric sulphur dioxide over long periods of time may be more damaging to health than is currently recognised. This development (because it is currently unknown) cannot be allowed for in our valuation. Similarly, if sulphur dioxide discharged in one country leads to acid rainfall in another many miles away, this event cannot be measured and valued in any meaningful way at the present time. However, this position may change as the result of recent ecological disasters,

including the Chernobyl nuclear contamination and the discharge of chemicals into the river Rhine. There is a political dimension to the valuation of externalities because individual and group value positions are involved. Some possibilities for more environmentally sensitive external accounting and reporting systems are listed in Table 19.8.

The five categories of social accounting outlined in this part of the chapter are not exhaustive, and further subdivision and classification may result from the development of the subdiscipline of social accounting. Indeed, this may be predicted on the basis of past trends in the development of the accounting discipline. An example of a specific area of attention might be energy accounting, which would currently be regarded as a part of general social responsibility accounting disclosure, but which might become a separate concern in the event of another energy crisis. There is also an extensive literature devoted to employee-related accounting disclosures.

There seems to be relatively little attention paid to practical social accounting other than in the SRA area. This is probably due to SRA being short term and identifiable in the normal annual reporting procedure. Total impact accounting, being at the strategic level, is more likely to remain an internal document except in certain well publicised cases, often involving the policing of industrial activity by governmental agencies.

Table 19.8
Some possibilities for more environmentally sensitive external accounting and reporting systems

- Note that if one's own organisational reporting is not sufficient one may find oneself the subject of *external social audits*.

- There is a very wide range of previous experiments from which to learn and upon which to build further experiments.

- The current *United Nations initiative* offers a practicable and realistic policy option upon which *external environmental reporting* could be based. The initiative suggests that each organisation might include in its Annual Report:
  — the organisation's environmental policy
  — the capitalisation of environmental expenditures
  — specific identification of environmental contingent liabilities relating to (a) bringing the organisation into line with current regulations and (b) future potential liabilities such as site clean-up costs
  — disclosure of current period expenditure on environmental protection
  — disclosure of anticipated environmental expenditure in excess of that classified as contingent liabilities — both voluntary expenditure and that designed to satisfy current and future regulations
  — disclosure of organisational activity and performance.

- A more specific approach to the disclosure of activity and performance would be the production and disclosure of a systematic *compliance-with-standard report* where standards would consist of (a) legal standards; (b) anticipated legal standards plus EU directives not yet incorporated into UK law; (c) industry best practice standards; and (d) the organisation's own ethical code of conduct standards where these are in excess of (a), (b) and (c).

- If reporting is to reflect the extent of the environmental issues and to fully operationalise the Pearce Report, then it will be necessary to re-define the nature of assets and to disclose (a) man-made, natural and critical capital assets; (b) transfers between categories of assets; and (c) data on the maintenance of critical and other natural capital assets.

Source: Gray, 1990b, p.33

A general introduction to social responsibility accounting disclosures

In terms of current research and reporting, this area of non-traditional accounting disclosure has received the most attention. A suitable definition for social responsibility accounting might be: 'Voluntary disclosure of information, both qualitative and quantitative, made by organisations to inform or influence a range of audiences. The quantitative disclosures may be in financial or non-financial terms.'

Social responsibility accounting usually applies to private sector organisations and involves a wide variety of information, most of which is non-financial in nature and of interest to employees and the general public as well as shareholders and debt-holders. Although organisational management may have a target audience, it is usually unspecified; disclosure policy may be an implicit rather than an explicit aspect of the strategy. Reports of government-funded activities may contain elements of SRA. Other terms used to describe this area include 'social responsibility disclosures' and 'corporate social responsibility'. The pattern of development has been the inclusion of small amounts of data, in qualitative and non-monetary terms, as part of the annual report to shareholders. These disclosures are voluntary, unaudited and unregulated. Social responsibility accounting may be seen as an extension of the stewardship role and aimed at the maintenance or improvement of the corporate image.

Indeed these two aspects — stewardship and corporate image — may be in conflict where disclosures are voluntary and un-audited. In terms of justification, the organisational legitimacy arguments may be the strongest motivator for these disclosures. However, very little research has been carried out to determine the motivation of organisational management in authorising SRA disclosures.

American social responsibility accounting disclosures

The earliest documentary analysis of published SRA is usually credited to Ernst and Ernst (1972–1978), now Ernst and Whinney). This survey was started in 1972 using 1971 reports and continued until 1978 (1977 reports), using the published reports of the Fortune 500 corporations. Ernst and Ernst were aiming to inform their readership about what organisations were reporting and not to develop any theory, perform any detailed analysis or adopt a normative approach, although the categories adopted by the study may have influenced accountants about to develop a reporting system. No attempt was made to establish a connection between SRA disclosures and share price movements or to prescribe in a normative manner what should be disclosed. The reporting of certain social data has been criticised for a lack of accuracy and objectivity (Wiseman, 1982) but to date most attention has been devoted to observing and recording rather than to a critical analysis of what has been recorded. A number of writers have used the information provided by an independent body (in place of corporation sourced data) in attempts at relating disclosures and share price movements.

Australasian social responsibility accounting disclosures

Disclosures by New Zealand companies were examined by Robertson (1977), Davey (1985) and Ng (1985), while Australian company reports have been the subject of several studies: Trotman (1979), Kelly (1981), Trotman and Bradley (1981), Guthrie (1982) and Pang (1982).

British social responsibility accounting disclosures

General introductions to SRA disclosures in the UK may be found in the Corporate Report (ASSC, 1975), Lessem (1977), Gray and Perks (1982) and Gray, Owen and Maunders (1987). Specific references to value added statements may be found in Morley (1978), Renshall, Allan and Nicholson (1979), Gray and Maunders (1980), and to employment reports in Thompson and Knell (1979) and Maunders (1984). Employee reports are covered by Hussey (1979 and 1981) and Purdy (1981).

Canadian social responsibility accounting disclosures

There is an extensive Canadian literature dealing with this general area. References include Ross (1971), Chan (1975), Anderson (1976, 1977 and 1978), Anderson, Brooks and Davis (1978) , Burke (1980), Robinson (1980), Demers and Wayland (1982a and 1982b) and Brooks (1986).

The growing interest in general social responsibility accounting disclosures extends throughout the English-speaking accounting environment. The relationship between changes in market prices and SRA disclosures have been documented through a number of studies. In addition, investigations by Kelly (1981) and Trotman and Bradley (1981) on connections between the number of disclosures and the size and type of organisation included more sophisticated testing of statistical significance than had been used in other studies up to that time. Guthrie (1982) used content analysis in the measurement of disclosures by major companies and found that, in general, the larger organisations in terms of sales or market capitalisation were more inclined to make SRA disclosures than the smaller companies. Furthermore, Kelly (1981) found that primary and secondary industries disclosed information of a product or process nature, while tertiary industries emphasised community-related information. The overall impression provided by these studies is of a limited amount of information about employee and product matters, which is disclosed through mainly qualitative statements.

Although SRA appears to be becoming more acceptable to larger companies, it is necessary to maintain a sense of perspective. Guthrie (1982) reported an average disclosure of 0.2 pages per company report devoted to SRA, and this would appear to be a reasonable estimate, in line with the later of the Ernst and Ernst studies. However, there was no consideration given to the number of pages in the complete report and consequently no proportions could be calculated.

A number of surveys of accountants in Australia and New Zealand have shown some support for the basic principle of voluntarily disclosing social responsibility data in sections of the annual report (Anderson, 1980; Mathews and Heazlewood, 1983). This support does not extend to compulsory disclosure and most respondents would not want to be involved in an audit of this information at the present time. Similar surveys carried out among members of the AICPA (Benjamin, Stanga and Strawser, 1977; Stiner, 1978) and the National Accounting Association (Barnett and Caldwell, 1974) have shown some support for voluntary disclosures of social responsibility information. However, there is some evidence that lower levels of support accompany more difficult economic conditions (Mathews and Schafer, 1983).

Total impact accounting

The objective of this section is to introduce the second category of social accounting in the framework aimed towards a more socially relevant accounting. Total impact accounting is defined as follows:

> The term Total Impact Accounting (TIA) refers to attempts at measuring, in monetary terms, the total cost of running an organisation in its existing form. The total cost of running an organisation may be divided between private and public costs.

Unfortunately, confusion persists with the use of the term 'social accounting', because many writers refer to SRA material as 'social accounting' while economists use the term for what is here called TIA. The distinction between the two areas is made clearer in this chapter by the descriptions given in Table 19.6 on p.379.

The total cost of running an organisation may be divided between private and public costs. Private costs, also called internal costs, are already recorded and measured by the accounting system as the individual costs of material, labour and overheads. After accumulation, these costs are used in the preparation of intermediate and final accounts, many of which are published under statutory requirements and form the traditional disclosures to the shareholders. Internal costs are also used in the preparation of product costs and for the valuation of inventory. Public costs, also called external costs or externalities, occur as a result of the existence of an organisation and must be borne by the community as a whole. If the social benefits resulting from the existence of an organisation are greater than the public costs, then there is no net public cost and there may be a public gain. Net social benefits may result from the building of roads, railyards or harbour facilities as part of a new economic development. Many observers would also consider the production of goods and services and the employment generated by these activities to be positive features of corporate performance. The classic example of externalities leading to public costs are those of pollution by fumes, smell, noise and waste discharge. Others are plant-induced traffic congestion or excessive demands on medical or social services which result from the operation of a particular plant.

The difficulties faced by proponents of TIA are related to the identification, measurement and valuation of externalities prior to their possible disclosure in accounting reports. Although the identification of many potential social costs is not difficult, measurement and valuation will not be readily accomplished. It is possible to see smoke or dust pollution leaving factory premises and to smell gaseous contaminants polluting the atmosphere, but how can a value be attached to the *effects* of these phenomena? The process of valuation has the two aspects of occurrence and measurable effect, both of which are problematic.

The AAA Committee on Social Costs has suggested that three levels of measurement could be involved in any case of social accounting (see p. 378). Level III measurements require that non-financial quantification be converted into a financial estimate of costs and benefits. In the case of pollution, the cost of continued emissions above an acceptable limit may be internalised as a private cost, through fines or even closure, or through damage to buildings, increased maintenance costs and loss of amenities, or poor community health. Estimates of the public cost may serve as the basis for fines or damage awards.

Two measurement difficulties which have not been addressed by the Level I to III disclosure hierarchy are time and distance. How much time can be expected to elapse between the event (for example, the sulphur dioxide discharge) and the resulting effect (damage to something or someone)? Although a social cost undoubtedly exists, if discharges which were considered harmless are subsequently found to be cumulative and eventually harmful, it is difficult to see how the organisation could be made to bear the cost. However, once the knowledge is

made public, a different set of rules may be applied. Examples which come to mind are expectant mothers and thalidomide, miners and pneumoconiosis and the effects of asbestos on employees and members of the general public. In the area of cumulative pollution, we can refer to cadmium, lead and arsenic levels around plants processing these materials.

When considering the physical distance from effluent discharge and the resulting effects, what geographic limits should be placed on the measurement of social costs? It has been asserted that the improved local effects of passing sulphur dioxide into the atmosphere via tall chimneys in the UK has resulted in acid rainfall in Scandinavia, and the effects of atmospheric pollution from the USA are felt in parts of Canada. The fallout from the Chernobyl nuclear power plant is a prime example of the problems of time and distance which would apply if there was any intention to compensate losing parties.

How does TIA deal with time and distance problems? One approach would be to look at the costs and benefits of organisations over their entire life and get away from conventional accounting periods and short-term matching principles. It is difficult to do this with changing knowledge and technology. Moreover, there may still be costs which could not equitably be charged to an organisation, because of new developments and knowledge, although some form of insurance policy might be developed. In respect of distance, the matter is complicated by national boundaries. If an organisation discharges material inside one country, it does not matter whether the effect is felt next door or at the other end of the land, since only one jurisdiction is involved. However, where international pollution is involved the jurisdiction is likely to be more difficult to ascertain and enforce.

The consideration of pollution, its measurement and valuation are not new.

Estes (1973, p.253) has cited one of the oldest and most famous calculations of social cost, that of the estimate of smoke damage in Pittsburg. This 1913 study identified a cost, which in 1959 terms and if extended to the entire USA, would have been US$11 billion annually. The current cost would be much higher. Taylor (1975) has referred to the work of the Programmes Analysis Unit in Britain and describes some of the difficulties experienced in determining the social costs of pollution in that country, in particular who is responsible for the costs. Beams and Fertig (1971) have indicated that accountants need to take action to convert social costs into private costs in order to protect the environment.

One aspect of TIA which has been given considerable attention by a small group of academic accountants in recent years is that of the impact of business on the environment. Inevitably, environmental accounting has been called 'green' accounting (Gray, 1990b, 1991; Owen, 1992). The philosophical underpinnings include the need to protect the environment from irreversible damage, to distinguish between natural (including critical) capital and capital created by people, and to respect the intergenerational effects in order that the consumption of the present is not passed on to future generations as costs through environmental degradation.

A great deal of the work in this area has originated in the UK or Continental Europe, particularly through the economists Pearce et al. (1989) and the work of Gray (1990b, 1991, 1993) at the Centre for Social and Environmental Accounting Research at the University of Dundee. Several important concepts must be understood in order to appreciate the problems of the environment, in particular sustainable development and intergenerational effects.

There are many definitions of sustainable development (Pearce et al., 1989) but the general notion is one of economic activity which does not have a permanently deleterious effect on the environment: for example, harvesting timber only at the rate at which the resource is renewed, and not consuming critical natural capital, such as fishing a species to extinction.

Intergenerational effects occur where the present generation consumes resources in such a manner and at such a rate that future generations are left poorer in material and non-material terms. We need to avoid the position where future generations are unable to have the same standard of living (which involves both material and quality of life) that we enjoy.

The debate between environmental economists and environmental accountants may be summarised as follows. The environmental economists wish to assist the environment using the market mechanism wherever possible, avoiding the use of regulation, and in many cases continuing to endorse economic growth as an important economic policy tool. Their use of accounting techniques is essentially at the macro level.

The few environmental accountants who have written on the subject do not wish to use the market mechanism in finding a 'cure' for the problem, but tend towards disclosure requirements, the use of regulation, and audit of performance at the organisation level, to ensure that there are improvements in the way that the environment is treated. The accounting they envisage is at the micro level (Gray, 1990b, 1991, 1993; Owen, 1992).

Socio-economic accounting

Socio-economic accounting is concerned with a micro approach to the problems of project selection, operation, control and evaluation in the public sector. The term socio-economic accounting has been defined by Linowes (1968) as follows: 'Socio-Economic Accounting is intended here to mean the application of accounting in the field of social sciences. These include sociology, political science and economics' (p.37).

Although Linowes was using the term within the private sector the definition is more appropriate for use within the public sector and has been adopted for this purpose. The closest existing system of accounting to SEA is value for money (VFM) auditing and it is used here as an example. There is no existing system which routinely evaluates public sector activities in the manner envisaged by SEA.

Value for money auditing as a general practice has a relatively short history of some fifteen to twenty years, which corresponds to that of most of the developments reviewed in this chapter. Although there are variations in approach from one country to another, all are concerned with the review of publicly funded programmes from the perspective of the 'three Es'. These are economy, efficiency and effectiveness, defined in the following manner:

- *Economy*. The acquisition of resources in appropriate quantity and quality at the lowest cost.
- *Efficiency*. The relationship between the goods or services produced and the resources used to produce them.
- *Effectiveness*. The extent to which programmes or goods and services produced achieve their objectives.

The criticism levelled at VFM accounting is that, although the reviews of economy and efficiency are thorough, those of effectiveness are often inadequate.

Grimwood and Tomkins (1986) question whether VFM audits do address the issue of effectiveness. Sherer (1984) has drawn attention to conceptual and practical problems in respect of VFM audits of local authorities. The component parts of economy, efficiency and effectiveness are interrelated, with effectiveness the most important (in Sherer's view). Effectiveness is also the most difficult attribute to measure because of (a) the problem of finding suitable measures with which to evaluate the service under examination, and (b) the problem of commenting on the political decisions made

by members of elected bodies, for example local councils. Sherer (1984) has noted that in response to these difficulties auditors tend to adopt narrow definitions of effectiveness which appear to be capable of verification, and not broader definitions which impact on the final objectives of local authorities such as environmental health or the educational attainment of pupils: 'Indeed it may be thought that measures such as these can be interpreted as efficiency rather than effectiveness measures; at best they attempt only to quantify the intermediate outputs of a service' (p.8).

Sherer has also objected to auditing the other attributes of economy and efficiency because the processes of VFM audits are dominated by the ideology of profit: 'The use of accounting technologies, including VFM audits for local authorities, introduces a "bottom line" measure, equivalent to (and sometimes identical with) the net profit figure found in private sector financial accounts' (p.18).

This approach has an effect on employment policies and the willingness to provide public services despite the problematic nature of the profit determinations. McSweeney and Sherer (1985) have made similar observations:

> Many of the reports published thus far demonstrate an asymmetry in the recommendations of VFM auditors. A great deal of attention is given to possible cost savings that can be made achieving the same or lower levels of service quality, if best management practice is adopted. In contrast much less attention is given to an evaluation of the effectiveness of local authority activities . . . (p.3)

In the remainder of their paper, McSweeney and Sherer reiterate many of the arguments against VFM audits: the difficulty of setting standards, a tendency to concentrate on economy and efficiency and not effectiveness as though these were separable, and the fear that political and economic concerns are dominating technical concerns in the implementation of VFM.

Gray, Owen and Maunders (1987) have noted that the VFM audit is:

> unlikely to provide a significant improvement in public accountability. Its focus on spending — generally unrelated to performance measures — might improve the efficiency of services from local authorities etc., but appears to have little to do with the quality of service and virtually nothing to do with the broader social issues of the community, the labour force, and general accountability. (p.155)

The problems inherent in the term 'value for money' have been brought out by Jones and Pendlebury (1984): 'Strictly speaking it relates output (value) to input (money) and is therefore another way of saying efficiency' (p.10).

It is concluded that although the concept of VFM auditing is much closer to the concept of SEA than the other monitoring and controlling systems examined earlier in the chapter, the reality of implementation means that the distance between the two is quite wide. Socio-economic accounting is envisaged as a system which monitors inputs and outputs in financial and non-financial modes. The implementation of VFM, as reported in the literature, suggests that in practice a greater proportion of attention is given to financial measurements and that effectiveness is not given the same degree of attention as economy and efficiency.

The area of government-funded programmes is seen as a fertile ground for evaluation models, using financial and non-financial measurements and criteria, aimed at promoting efficiency and effectiveness. To a large extent all measurements result in partial indicators of performance. This applies to financial accounting reports as well as to less traditional forms of reporting. The socio-economic accounting discussed in this chapter is an attempt to convert unreported performance to a partial reporting of performance by publicly funded organisations. As such it would be a major advance in the overall usefulness of accounting to society, thus leading to a more socially relevant accounting.

Chapter summary

This chapter has provided an introduction to the topic of social accounting, a topic which is as yet undeveloped but which could provide accountants with a source of influence and employment in the future.

The first part of the chapter considered arguments which could be used to justify the expenditure of scarce resources on making voluntary disclosures of a non-traditional (socially-oriented) nature. These arguments may include attempting to influence capital markets by providing information useful to shareholders, demonstrating the relevance of social responsibility disclosures to the concept of the social contract between business and society, and recognising the need to legitimate the organisation with various audiences. The arguments of the radical theorist do not lend themselves to supporting additional disclosures, since they question the whole managerial and capitalistic structure of our society.

In the second part of the chapter, social accounting is classified into SRA, TIA, SEA, SIA and SA (Mathews, 1984). The first three categories are then discussed.

Social responsibility accounting is the main form of this type of disclosure and involves the inclusion in published annual reports of information about employment, energy, community relations, and environmental implications of the enterprise.

Total impact accounting is concerned with incorporating externalities into the cost structure of the corporation so that public and private costs enter the calculus. The philosophical issues surrounding this form of additional accounting have not been resolved and consequently this form of social accounting is really at a conceptual model building stage.

One of the models that has recently emerged has been environmental or green accounting, which attempts to develop information about the performance of the entity as it affects the environment. Environmentally inclined accountants have suggested that the impact on the environment may be reduced by setting standards of performance, monitoring these standards, requiring reports and auditing them. A number of suggested formats for these reports may be found in the literature cited.

Socio-economic accounting is represented by VFM auditing, which is probably the development closest to the form of social accounting envisaged by this category. The weakness of VFM is that at present it does not adequately take into account the non-monetary quantitative and qualitative factors. This category of social accounting is seen as particularly important in view of the desire to evaluate areas of the public sector such as health and education.

Essay and examination questions

19.1 Argue the case for and against the inclusion of socially-related disclosures in the annual reports of corporations.

19.2 Why should managers expend scarce resources on providing additional information? Answer by reference to the various justificatory arguments used in the chapter.

19.3 Consider the social contract. To what extent does this concept underlie the social relations in our society?

19.4 Organisational legitimacy is a powerful argument in directing the attention of managers towards additional disclosures in the annual report. Discuss.

19.5 Radical theorists would argue that social disclosures are made only to entrench the current relations between the organisation and its environment. Discuss.

19.6 What is meant by SRA? How widespread is this practice?

19.7 Examine the philosophical and pragmatic arguments about the place of externalities in any system of accounting. What do you conclude?

19.8 The public sector needs to be more accountable. Discuss this statement in the context of VFM auditing.

19.9 Social accounting is disruptive in that it diverts attention from the development of traditional accounting. Discuss.

19.10 Social accounting, through its constituent parts, is one of the features of the accounting discipline which will ensure the relevance of accounting and reporting in the future. Discuss.

19.11 Explain what accounting for the environment may involve as an aspect of non-traditional accounting.

19.12 Locate examples of environmental issues which have been reported in the media. How would environmental accounting address the specific problems you have identified?

19.13 The specific problem of payments for retrospective environmental clean up indicates that severe difficulties have occurred with past financial reports. Explain.

19.14 To what extent do contingent liabilities provide a solution to the problem of accounting for pollution?

19.15 Including the cost of preventing environmental degradation is necessary if the internal and external accounting systems are to function properly. Discuss.

References and additional reading

Abbott, W.F. and Monsen, R.J. (1979). On the measurement of corporate social responsibility: self reported disclosures as a method of measuring corporate social involvement. *Academy of Management Journal,* **22**.

Accounting Standards Steering Committee (1975). *The Corporate Report.* London: ICAEW.

Alexander, J.J. and Bucholz, R.A. (1978). Corporate social responsibility and stock market performance. *Academy of Management Journal,* **21**, 479–486.

American Accounting Association (1975). Report of the committee on the measurement of social costs, 98–113.

American Institute of Certified Public Accountants (1973). *Objectives of Financial Statements.* New York: AICPA.

Anderson, R.H. (1976). Social responsibility accounting: what to measure and how. *Cost and Management,* 34–38.

Anderson, R.H. (1977). Social responsibility accounting: evaluating its objectives, concepts and principles. *CA Magazine,* 32–35.

Anderson, R.H. (1978). Social responsibility accounting: how to get started. *CA Magazine,* 46–51.

Anderson, R.H. (1980). Attitudes of chartered accountants to social responsibility accounting in Australia. *The Chartered Accountant in Australia,* 12–14.

Anderson R.H., Brooks, L.J. and Davis, W.R. (1978). *The Why, When and How of Social Responsibility Accounting.* Toronto: CICA.

Arlow, P. and Gannon, M. (1982). Social responsiveness, corporate structure and economic performance. *Academy of Management Review,* **7**(2), 235–241.

Barnett, A.H. and Caldwell, J.C. (1974). Accounting for corporate social performance: a survey. *Management Accounting,* 23–26.

Beams, F.A. and Fertig, P.E. (1971). Pollution control through social cost conversion. *The Journal of Accountancy,* 37–42.

Belkaoui, A. (1976). The impact of the disclosure of the environmental effect of organizational behaviour on the market. *Financial Management,* Winter, 26–31.

Belkaoui, A. (1980). The impact of socio-economic accounting statements on the investment decision: an empirical study. *Accounting, Organizations and Society,* **5**(3), 263–283.

Benjamin, J.J., Stanga, K.G. and Strawser, R.K. (1977). Corporate social responsibility: the viewpoint of CPA's. *The National Public Accountant,* 18–22.

Bowman, E.G. and Haire, M. (1975). A strategic posture toward corporate social responsibility. *California Management Review,* **18**(1).

Bragdon, J.H. and Marlin, J.A.T. (1971). Is pollution profitable?, a paper given at the 1971 annual meeting of the Financial Management Association.

Brooks, L.J. (1986). *Canadian Corporate Social Performance.* Toronto: Society of Management Accountants of Canada.

Burke, R.C. (1980). The disclosure of social accounting information. *Cost and Management,* 21–24.

Chan, R.S. (1975). Social and financial stewardship. *The Accounting Review,* 533–543.

Chen, K.H. and Metcalf, R.H. (1980). The relationship between pollution control record and financial indicators revisited. *The Accounting Review,* **55**(1), January, 168–177.

Christophe, B. and Bebbington, J. (1992). The French Bilan Social — A pragmatic model for the development of accounting for the environment? A research note. *British Accounting Review,* **24**(3), 281–290.

Davey, H.B. (1985). *Corporate Social Responsibility Disclosure in New Zealand: An Empirical Investigation.* Occasional Paper No. 52. Palmerston North: Massey University, Faculty of Business Studies.

Demers, L. and Wayland, D.A. (1982a). Corporate social responsibility: is no news good news? *CA Magazine,* January, 42–46.

Demers, L. and Wayland, D.A. (1982b). Corporate social responsibility: is no news goods news? *CA Magazine,* February, 55–60.

Donaldson, T. (1982). *Corporations and Morality.* Englewood Cliffs, New Jersey: Prentice Hall.

Ernst and Ernst (1972–1978). *Social Responsibility Disclosure: Surveys of Fortune 500 Annual Reports.* Cleveland: Ernst and Ernst.

Estes, R.W. (1973). Accounting for social costs in Estes, R.W. (Ed.). *Accounting and Society.* Los Angeles: Melville.

Fogler, H.R. and Nutt, F. (1975). A note on social responsibility and stock valuation. *Academy of Management Journal,* March, 155–160.

Freedman, M. (1982). *Capitalism and Freedom.* Chicago: University of Chicago Press.

Freedman, M. and Stagliano, A.J. (1984). The market impact of social information: investigator reaction to public disclosure. *Proceedings,* AAA Mid Atlantic Regional Meeting.

Freedman, M. and Stagliano, A.J. (1991). Differences in social-cost disclosures: A market test of investor reactions. *Accounting Auditing and Accountability Journal,* **4**(1), 68–83.

Gray, R.H. (1990a). Accounting and Economics: The psychopathic siblings: A research essay. *British Accounting Review,* **22**(4), 373–388.

Gray, R.H. (1990b). The greening of accountancy: The profession after Pearce. *Certified Research Report 17.* London: The Chartered Association of Certified Accountants.

Gray, R.H. (1991). The accountancy profession and the environmental crisis. *Discussion Paper ACC/9102.* University of Dundee, Scotland.

Gray, R, Owen, D. and Maunders, K. (1987) *Corporate Social Reporting Accounting and Accountability.* London: Prentice Hall.

Gray, R.H., Owen, D.L. and Maunders, K.T. (1988). Corporate social reporting: Emerging trends in accountability and the social contract. *Accounting, Auditing and Accountability Journal,* **1**(1), 6–20.

Gray, R. and Perks, R. (1982). How desirable is social accounting? *Accountancy,* 101–102.

Gray, S.J. and Maunders, K.T. (1980). *Value Added Reporting: Uses and Measurement.* London.

Grimwood, M. and Tomkins, C. (1986). Value for money auditing — towards incorporating a naturalistic approach. *Financial Accountability and Management,* **2**(4), 251–272.

Guthrie, J.E. (1982). Social accounting in Australia: social responsibility disclosure in the top 150 listed Australian companies, 1980 annual reports. Dissertation. Perth: WAIT.

Guthrie, J.E. and Mathews, M.R. (1985). Corporate social accounting in Australasia. In L.E. Preston (Ed.), *Corporate Social Performance and Policy.* New York: JAI, 251–277.

Harte, G. and Owen, D.L. (1991). Environmental disclosure in the annual reports of British companies: A research note. *Accounting Auditing and Accountability Journal,* **4**(3), 51–61.

Henderson, H. (1991). New markets, new commons, new ethics: A guest essay. *Accounting Auditing and Accountability Journal,* **4**(3), 72–80.

Hines, H. (1991). On valuing nature. *Accounting Auditing and Accountability Journal,* **4**(3), 27–29.

Hussey, R. (1979). *Who reads Employee Reports?* Oxford: Touche Ross.

Hussey, R. (1981). Developments in employee reporting. *Managerial Finance,* **7**(2), 12–16.

Ingram, R.W. (1978). An investigation of the information content of (certain) social responsibility disclosures. *Journal of Accounting Research,* Autumn.

Jones, R. and Pendlebury, M. (1984). *Public Sector Accounting.* London: Pitman.

Kelly, G.J. (1981). Australian social responsibility disclosures: some insights into contemporary measurement. *Accounting and Finance,* **21**(2), 97–107.

Laughlin, R. and Varangu, L.K. (1991). Accounting for waste or garbage accounting: Some thoughts from non-accountants. *Accounting Auditing and Accountability Journal,* **4**(3), 43–50.

Lessem, R. (1977). Corporate social reporting in action: an evaluation of British, European and American practice. *Accounting, Organizations and Society,* **2**(4), 279–294.

Lewis, L., Humphrey, C. and Owen, D.L. (1992). Accounting and the social: A pedagogical perspective. *British Accounting Review,* **24**(3), 219–234.

Lindblom, C.K. (1983). The concept of organisational legitimacy and its implications for corporate social responsibility disclosures. *AAA Public Interest Section Working Paper No. 7.*

Linowes, D.F. (1968). Socio-economic accounting. *The Journal of Accountancy,* 37–42.

Luther, R.G., Matatko, J. and Corner, D.C. (1992). The investment performance of UK 'Ethical' unit trusts. *Accounting Auditing and Accountability Journal,* **5**(4), 57–70.

McSweeney, B. and Sherer, M.J. (1985). Value for money auditing: some observations on its origins and theory. A paper presented at the inter disciplinary perspectives on accounting conference, Manchester 1985.

Mahapatra, S. (1984). Investor reaction to a corporate social accounting. *Journal of Business Finance and Accounting,* **11**(1), 29–40.

Mathews, M.R. (1984). A suggested classification for social accounting research. *Journal of Accounting and Public Policy,* **3**(3), 199–221.

Mathews, M.R. (1991). A limited review of the green accounting literature. *Accounting Auditing and Accountability Journal,* **4**(3), 110–121.

Mathews, M.R. (1993). *Socially Responsible Accounting.* London: Chapman and Hall.

Mathews, M.R. and Heazlewood, C.T. (1983). *Accountants' Attitudes to New Developments in Accounting.* Occasional Paper No. 46. Palmerston North: Massey University, Faculty of Business Studies.

Mathews, M.R. and Schafer, E.L. (1983). *A Comparison of Accountants' Responses to New*

Ideas: Washington State CPA's and New Zealand ACA's. Discussion Paper No. 10. Palmerston North: Massey University, Department of Accounting and Finance.

Maunders, K.T. (1984). *Employment Reporting — An Investigation of User Needs Measurement and Reporting Issues and Practice.* London: ICAEW.

Maunders, K.T. and Burritt, R.L. (1991). Accounting and the ecological crisis. *Accounting Auditing and Accountability Journal,* **4**(3), 9–26.

Milne, M.J. (1991). Accounting, environmental resource values, and non-market valuation techniques for environmental resources: A review. *Accounting Auditing and Accountability Journal,* **4**(3), 81–109.

Morley, M.F. (1978). *The Value Added Statement.* London: Gee.

Nader, R. (1973). *The Consumer and Corporate Accountability.* New York: Harcourt Brace Jovanovich.

Ness, K.E. and Mirza, A.M. (1991). Corporate social disclosure: A note on a test of agency theory. *British Accounting Review,* **23**(3), 211–218.

Ng, L.W. (1985). *Social Responsibility Disclosures of Selected New Zealand Companies for 1981, 1982 and 1983.* Occasional Paper No. 54. Palmerston North: Massey University, Faculty of Business Studies.

Owen, D. (Ed.). (1992). *Green Reporting.* London: Chapman and Hall.

Owen, D.L. (1990). Towards a theory of social investment: A review essay. *Accounting, Organizations and Society,* **15**(3), 249–265.

Pang, Y.H. (1982). Disclosures of corporate social responsibility. *The Chartered Accountant in Australia,* 32–34.

Parket, I.R. and Eilbirt, H. (1975). Social responsibility: the underlying factors. *Business Horizons,* **18**(4), 5–10.

Patten, D.M. (1990). The market reaction to social responsibility disclosures: The case of the Sullivan Principles signings. *Accounting, Organizations and Society,* **15**(6), 575–587.

Pearce, D., Markandya, A. and Barbier, E.B. (1989). Blueprint for a Green Economy. London: Earthscan.

Perks, R.W., Rawlinson, D.H. and Ingram, L. (1992). *British Accounting Review,* **24**(1), 43–66.

Power, M. (1991). Auditing and environmental expertise: Between protest and professionalisation. *Accounting Auditing and Accountability Journal,* **4**(3), 30–42.

Purdy, D. (1981). The provision of financial information to employees: a study of the reporting practices of some large public companies in the United Kingdom. *Accounting, Organizations and Society,* **6**(4), 327–338.

Renshall, M., Allan, R. and Nicholson, K. (1979). *Added Value in External Financial Reporting.* London: ICAEW.

Roberts, C.B. (1991). Environmental disclosures: A note on reporting practices in mainland Europe. *Accounting Auditing and Accountability Journal,* **4**(3), 62–71.

Robertson, J. (1977). *Corporate Social Reporting by New Zealand Companies.* Occasional Paper No. 17. Palmerston North: Massey University, Faculty of Business Studies.

Robinson, C. (1980). Efficient markets and the social role of accounting. *CA Magazine,* 21–24.

Ross, G.H.B. (1971). Social accounting: measuring the unmeasurables. *Canadian Chartered Accountant,* 46–54.

Shane, P.B. and Spicer, B.H. (1983). Market response to environmental information produced outside the firm. *The Accounting Review,* July, 521–538.

Sherer, M.J. (1984). *The Ideology of Efficiency: A Critical Evaluation of Value for Money Auditing.* Discussion Paper Series No. 241. University of Essex, Department of Economics.

Spicer, B.H. (1978). Investors, corporate social performance and information disclosure: an empirical study. *The Accounting Review,* January, 94–111.

Spicer, B.H. (1980). The relationship between pollution control record and financial indicators revisited: further comment. *The Accounting Review,* January, 178–185.

Stevens, W.P. (1982). Market reaction to corporate environmental performance, a paper given at the 1982 AAA Convention.

Stiner, F.M., Jr. (1978). Accountants' attitudes towards social accounting. *Mid Atlantic Journal of Business,* **16**(2).

Sturdivant, F.D. and Ginter, J.L. (1977). Corporate social responsiveness: management attitudes and economic performance. *California Management Review,* **19**(3), 30–39.

Taylor, K. (1975). Social accounting — whose responsibility? *Management Accounting,* 361–364.

Thompson, E.R. and Knell, A. (1979). *The Employment Statement in Company Reports.* London: ICAEW.

Tinker, A.M., Neimark, M.D. and Lehman, C. (1991). Falling down the hole in the middle of the road: Political quietism in corporate social reporting. *Accounting Auditing and Accountability Journal,* **4**(2), 28–54.

Trotman, K.T. (1979). Social responsibility disclosures by Australian companies. *The Chartered Accountant in Australia,* 24–28.

Trotman, K.T. and Bradley, G.W. (1981). Association between social responsibility disclosure and characteristics of companies. *Accounting, Organizations and Society,* **6**(4), 355–362.

Vance, S.C. (1975). Are socially responsible corporations good investment risks? *Management Review,* **64**(8), 18–24.

Wiseman, J.W. (1982). An evaluation of environmental disclosures made in corporate annual reports. *Accounting, Organizations and Society,* **7**(1), 53–63.

Yamagami, T. and Kokubu, K. (1991). A note on corporate social disclosure in Japan. *Accounting Auditing and Accountability Journal,* **4**(4), 32–39.

Zeghal, D. and Ahmed, S.A. (1990). Comparison of social responsibility disclosure media used by Canadian firms. *Accounting Auditing and Accountability Journal,* **3**(1), 38–53.

Index